Lecture N 166

Commenced Publication in 1973
Founding and Former Series Editors:

Matthias Rauterberg (Ed.)

Entertainment Computing – ICEC 2004

Third International Conference
Eindhoven, The Netherlands, September 1-3, 2004
Proceedings

 Springer

Volume Editor

Matthias Rauterberg
Technical University Einhoven
Department of Industrial Design Den Dolech 2, 5612 AZ Eindhoven
The Netherlands
E-mail: g.w.m.rauterberg@tue.nl

Coventry University

Library of Congress Control Number: 2004110770

CR Subject Classification (1998): H.5, H.4, H.3.5, I.2.9-11, I.3, J.5, K.8, K.4, C.2

ISSN 0302-9743
ISBN 3-540-22947-7 Springer Berlin Heidelberg New York

Springer is a part of Springer Science+Business Media

springeronline.com

© IFIP International Federation for Information Processing, Hofstrasse 3, A-2361 Laxenburg, Austria 2004
Printed in Germany

Typesetting: Camera-ready by author, data conversion by PTP-Berlin, Protago-TeX-Production GmbH
Printed on acid-free paper   SPIN: 11312406   06/3142   5 4 3 2 1 0

Preface

The advancement of information and communication technologies (ICT) has enabled broad use of ICT and facilitated the use of ICT in the private and personal domain. ICT-related industries are directing their business targets to home applications. Among these applications, entertainment will differentiate ICT applications in the private and personal market from the office. Comprehensive research and development on ICT applications for entertainment will be different for the promotion of ICT use in the home and other places for leisure. So far engineering research and development on entertainment has never been really established in the academic communities. On the other hand entertainment-related industries such as the video and computer game industries have been growing rapidly in the last 10 years, and today the entertainment computing business outperforms the turnover of the movie industry. Entertainment robots are drawing the attention of young people. The event called RoboCup has been increasing the number of participants year by year. Entertainment technologies cover a broad range of products and services: movies, music, TV (including upcoming interactive TV), VCR, VoD (including music on demand), computer games, game consoles, video arcades, gambling machines, the Internet (e.g., chat rooms, board and card games, MUD), intelligent toys, edutainment, simulations, sport, theme parks, virtual reality, and upcoming service robots.

The field of entertainment computing focuses on users' growing use of entertainment technologies at work, in school and at home, and the impact of this technology on their behavior. Nearly every working and living place has computers, and over two-thirds of children in industrialized countries have computers in their homes as well. All of us would probably agree that adults and children need to become competent users to be prepared for life and work in the future. Especially children's increasing use of entertainment technologies brings with it both the risk of possible harm and the promise of enriched learning, well-being and positive development.

Between now and the near future, digital technologies will become more powerful and affordable for all users and at every level, in digital networks and in product offerings. An increasing number of people will be able to compile, program, edit, create and share content; as a result, they will gain more control and become more immersed in media experiences. But more than technical challenges, the social implications on human behavior will be of most importance. We need a media ecology movement to heighten consciousness to fight the waste and pollution that the media produces. It is indeed a question of the mental environment for our children and future generations. The questions we must ask ourselves are: Do we give them a world that is challenging, stimulating, inspiring, and really entertaining? Do we encourage their intelligence, creativity and curiosity?

To address and hopefully answer these questions and to advance this newly born area of entertainment technologies it is important to build a good relationship between academia and industry, and to set up a task force group. This was the main motivation that in August 2000 prompted the International Federation for Information Processing (IFIP) General Assembly to approve the setting up of the Entertainment Computing

Specialist Group (SG16) under the auspices of IFIP and the Committee for Cooperation with Industry (CCI).

First of all, the major efforts of SG16 activities were directed toward demonstrating that the subject could be mature enough to attract the broad interest of the ICT community. For this purpose a technical event, the 1st International Workshop on Entertainment Computing (IWEC), was planned, and IWEC Steering Committee members were appointed (Bruce Blumberg from MIT Media Lab, USA; Marc Cavazza from the University of Teesside, UK; Jaap van den Herik from the Universiteit Maastricht, Netherlands; Tak Kamae from Laboratories of Image Science and Technology, Japan; Donald Marinelli from Carnegie Mellon University, USA; Ryohei Nakatsu from ATR, Japan; Matthias Rauterberg from the Technische Universiteit Eindhoven, Netherlands; and Demetri Terzopoulos from the University of Toronto, Canada).

The first important opportunity came when IFIP TC13 on "Human-Computer Interaction" kindly offered a time slot for a first international panel on entertainment computing at the prestigious INTERACT 2001 conference in Tokyo (Japan) in July 2001. The IWEC Steering Committee decided to accept this kind offer to increase the presence of SG16 and IWEC. At the panel many participants showed interests in entertainment computing.

In the next year, 2002, the first international workshop on entertainment computing (IWEC) was launched. IWEC 2002 was successfully held at Makuhari (Japan) on May 14–17, 2002. IWEC 2002 attracted over 100 participants and over 60 papers were published in the proceedings by Kluwer (edited by Ryohei Nakatsu and Junichi Hoshino). At IWEC 2002 were many high-quality papers and several interesting technical demonstrations. In other words, evidence that entertainment computing was already an important technical area. At IWEC 2002 we had an extended SG16 meeting, and it was agreed unanimously that the formation of a new technical committee (TC) on entertainment computing should be proposed formally to IFIP at the General Assembly at Montreal in 2002.

Based on the success of IWEC 2002, SG16 organized the next International Conference on Entertainment Computing (ICEC 2003), that was held during May 8–10, 2003 at the Entertainment Technology Center at Carnegie Mellon University, Pittsburgh (USA). ICEC 2003 was also successful with more than 100 attendees, 20 highly select papers, several prestigious keynote talks, and invited panels. All the papers for ICEC 2003 were accepted by ACM for inclusion in their ACM online digital library.

To complete the first around-the-world cycle "Japan–USA–Europe", the 3rd International Conference on Entertainment (ICEC 2004) was held in Europe at the Technische Universiteit Eindhoven during September 1–3, 2004. This conference attracted 27 full papers. Around 150 attendees from academia and industry participated in this successful conference. In several parallel sessions full papers, short papers, posters, system demonstrations and exhibitions from industry were presented. The program included three well-received keynote talks, three specially invited topic talks, and an outstanding super-chess contest organized by Jaap van den Herik.

For more information about ICEC 2004 have a look at the homepage on the Internet: http://www.icec.id.tue.nl/

For making ICEC 2004 such an outstanding event, we have to thank the following people who volunteered in the organization: Jaap van den Herik and Anton Nijholt as co-chairs, Jacques Terken as review chair, Ben Salem as treasurer and chair of the organizing committee, as well as all members of the different committees, in particular the long list of distinguished experts from all over the world in the scientific and industrial program committee, the several sponsors, all cooperating societies, and last but not least all researchers who submitted and presented their outstanding research results at ICEC 2004, documented in this book. We gratefully acknowledge their contributions, effort and valuable input.

Eindhoven, June 28, 2004   Matthias Rauterberg

Committees

Chair

Matthias Rauterberg   (Technische Universiteit Eindhoven, The Netherlands)

Co-chairs

Jaap van den Herik   (Universiteit Maastricht, The Netherlands)
Anton Nijholt   (University of Twente, The Netherlands)

Review Chair

Jacques Terken   (Technische Universiteit Eindhoven, The Netherlands)

Program Committee

Espen Aarseth	(University of Copenhagen, Denmark)
Matt Adcock	(CSIRO ICT Centre, Australia)
Samir Akkouche	(Universite Claude Bernard Lyon 1, France)
Elisabeth André	(University of Augsburg, Germany)
Sebastiano Bagnara	(Politecnico di Milano, Italy)
Christoph Bartneck	(Technische Universiteit Eindhoven, The Netherlands)
Trevor Batten	(Media Art, The Netherlands)
Franck Bauchard	(Ministère de la Culture, France)
Maurice Benayoun	(Université Paris 1, France)
Aude Billard	(Swiss Federal Institute of Technology, Switzerland)
Mark Billinghurst	(University of Canterbury, New Zealand)
Mats Björkin	(Göteborg University, Sweden)
Edwin Blake	(University of Cape Town, South Africa)
Don Bouwhuis	(Technische Universiteit Eindhoven, The Netherlands)
Jonah Brucker-Cohen	(Trinity College Dublin, Ireland)
Brad Bushman	(University of Michigan, USA)
Marc Cavazza	(University of Teesside, United Kingdom)
Liming Chen	(Ecole Centrale de Lyon, France)
Adrian Cheok	(National University of Singapore, Singapore)
Jeffrey Cohn	(University of Pittsburgh, USA)
Roger Dannenberg	(Carnegie Mellon University, USA)
John Debenham	(University of Technology, Australia)
Jürgen Enge	(Zentrum für Kunst und Medientechnologie, Germany)
Loe Feijs	(Technische Universiteit Eindhoven, The Netherlands)

Sidney Fels	(University of British Columbia, Canada)
Franz Fischnaller	(University of Illinois at Chicago, USA)
Christian Freksa	(University of Bremen, Germany)
Masahiro Fujita	(SONY, Japan)
Catherine Garbay	(CNRS, France)
Bill Gaver	(Royal College of Art, United Kingdom)
Ian Gibson	(Academy of Interactive Entertainment, Australia)
Andrew Glassner	(Coyote Wind Studios, USA)
Martin Goebel	(fleXilution, Germany)
Tom Gross	(Bauhaus-University Weimar, Germany)
Reinder Haakma	(Philips Research, The Netherlands)
Sture Hägglund	(Linkoping University, Sweden)
Michael Haller	(Upper Austria University of Applied Sciences, Austria)
Dong-Han Ham	(ETRI, Korea)
Goffredo Haus	(State University of Milan, Italy)
Ernst A. Heinz	(International University, Germany)
Michael Herczeg	(University of Luebeck, Germany)
Jaap van den Herik	(University of Maastricht, The Netherlands)
Yibin Hou	(Beijing University of Technology, China)
Hiroyuki Iida	(University of Shizuoka, Japan)
Wijnand IJsselsteijn	(Technische Universiteit Eindhoven, The Netherlands)
Ebroul Izquierdo	(University of London, United Kingdom)
Anker Helms Jørgensen	(University of Copenhagen, Denmark)
Oussama Khatib	(Stanford University, USA)
Gudrun Klinker	(Technical University Munich, Germany)
Karl-Friedrich Kraiss	(RWTH Aachen, Germany)
Thomas Landspurg	(In-Fusio, France)
Fatima Lasay	(University of the Philippines, Philippines)
James Lester	(North Carolina State University, USA)
Peri Loucopoulos	(UMIST, United Kingdom)
Henry Lowood	(Stanford University, USA)
Michael Macedonia	(Georgia Tech, USA)
Don Marinelli	(Carnegie Mellon University, USA)
Jeroen van Mastrigt	(Hooghe School voor Kunst, The Netherlands)
Hitoshi Matsubara	(Future University-Hakodate, Japan)
Frans Mayra	(University of Tampere, Finland)
Gary McDarby	(MediaLab Europe, Ireland)
Ivica Mitrovic	(University of Split, Croatia)
Frank Nack	(CWI, The Netherlands)
Ryohei Nakatsu	(Kwansei Gakuin University, Japan)
Anton Nijholt	(University of Twente, The Netherlands)
Dietmar Offenhuber	(Ars Electronica Futurelab, Austria)
Michio Okada	(ATR Network Informatics Laboratories, Japan)
Kees Overbeeke	(Technische Universiteit Eindhoven, The Netherlands)
Mark Overmars	(Utrecht University, The Netherlands)
René Paré	(Grafico de Poost, The Netherlands)

Paolo Petta	(Medical University of Vienna, Austria)
Paul Plöger	(FH Bonn Rhein Sieg, Germany)
Andriana Prentza	(National Technical University of Athens, Greece)
Matthias Rauterberg	(Technische Universiteit Eindhoven, The Netherlands)
Theresa-Marie Rhyne	(North Carolina State University, USA)
Ben Salem	(Technische Universiteit Eindhoven, The Netherlands)
Jonathan Schaeffer	(University of Alberta, Canada)
Nikitas Sgouros	(University of Piraeus, Greece)
Takanori Shibata	(AIST, Japan)
Andy Sloane	(University of Wolverhampton, United Kingdom)
Otto Spaniol	(RWTH Aachen, Germany)
Pieter Spronck	(Universiteit Maastricht, The Netherlands)
Scott Stevens	(Carnegie Mellon University, USA)
Norbert Streitz	(Fraunhofer IPSI, Germany)
Kazuo Tanie	(AIST, Japan)
Naoko Tosa	(Entertainment Computing Labs., Japan)
Bodo Urban	(Fraunhofer Institute for Computer Graphics, Germany)
Frans Vogelaar	(Kunsthochschule für Medien Köln, Germany)
Magdalena Wesolkowska	(Concordia University, Canada)
Lars Wolf	(Technical University Braunschweig, Germany)
Jeremy Wyatt	(University of Birmingham, United Kingdom)
Ken Young	(University of Warwick, United Kingdom)

Organizing Committee

Chair

Ben Salem	(Technische Universiteit Eindhoven, The Netherlands)

Secretary

Helen Maas-Zaan	(Technische Universiteit Eindhoven, The Netherlands)
Martine Tiessen	(Universiteit Maastricht, The Netherlands)
Nora Tonnaer	(Technische Universiteit Eindhoven, The Netherlands)

Treasurer

Ben Salem	(Technische Universiteit Eindhoven, The Netherlands)

Web Design

Christoph Bartneck	(Technische Universiteit Eindhoven, The Netherlands)

Student Volunteers

Erik van Alphen, Willeke van de Linden, Serge Offermans, Joep van Poppel, Rik Runge, Dick Rutten, Linda Valk, Harry Vermeulen, Thomas Visser (Technische Universiteit Eindhoven, The Netherlands)

Sponsors

TU/e: Technical University of Eindhoven
TU/e-ID: Department of Industrial Design
TU/e-JFS: J.F. Schouten School for User-System Interaction Research
KNAW: Royal Netherlands Academy of Arts and Sciences
NWO: Netherlands Organisation for Scientific Research
ERCIM: European Research Consortium for Informatics and Mathematics
IOP-MMI: Innovation-Oriented Research Program Human-Machine Interaction

Cooperating Societies

Association for Computing Machinery: SIGCHI and SIGGRAPH
Association for Robotics & Automation
Associazione Italiana per l'Intelligenza Artificiale
Australian Computer Society
British Computer Society
Computer Professionals for Social Responsibility
Computer Society of India
Digital Games Research Association
Dutch Chapter of SIGCHI
Dutch Computer Society
Francophone Human-Computer Interaction Association
German Informatics Society: SIG Communication & Distributed Systems
Icelandic Society for Information Processing
Norwegian Computer Society
Philippine Computer Society
Royal Institution of Engineers in the Netherlands
Swiss Informatics Society
Usability Professionals' Association

IFIP SG16

A new Technical Committee (TC) on Entertainment Computing was proposed to IFIP (approval pending) in the following way:

TC Title

Entertainment Computing

Aims

To encourage computer applications for entertainment and to enhance computer utilization in the home, the technical committee will pursue the following aims:

- to enhance algorithmic research on board and card games
- to promote new types of entertainment using information technologies
- to encourage hardware technology research and development to facilitate implementing entertainment systems, and
- to encourage non-traditional human interface technologies for entertainment.

Scope

1. Algorithms and strategies for board and card games (algorithms of board and card games; strategy controls for board and card games; level setups for game and card games).
2. Novel entertainment using ICT (network-based entertainment; mobile entertainment; location-based entertainment; mixed reality entertainment).
3. Audio (music informatics for entertainment; 3D audio for entertainment; sound effects for entertainment).
4. Entertainment human interface technologies (haptic and non-traditional human interface technologies; mixed reality human interface technologies for entertainment).
5. Entertainment robots (ICT-based toys; pet robots; mental commit robots; emotion models and rendering technologies for robots).
6. Entertainment systems (design of entertainment systems; entertainment design toolkits; authoring systems).
7. Theoretical aspects of entertainment (sociology, psychology and physiology for entertainment; legal aspects of entertainment).
8. Video game and animation technologies (video game hardware and software technologies; video game design toolkits; motion capture and motion design; interactive story telling; digital actors and emotion models).
9. Interactive TV and movies (multiple-view synthesis; free viewpoint TV; authoring technologies).
10. Edutainment (entertainment technologies for children's education; open environment entertainment robots for education).

Members: As first members of this TC, Ryohei Nakatsu is named as chair (contact: nakatsu@ksc.kwansei.ac.jp), Matthias Rauterberg as vice-chair, and Claudio Pinhanez as secretary.

TC Activities: The 3rd International Conference on Entertainment Computing (ICEC) was organized. The next ICEC will be held in 2005 in Japan. SG16 became a sponsor of the international 10th Advances in Computer Games Conference (ACG-10), that was held in November 2003 at Graz, Austria. Two panel sessions were organized: (1) at the IFIP TC13 INTERACT conference in 2001 (Japan), and (2) at the IFIP World Computer Congress in 2002 (Canada). An additional Topical Day "Virtual Realities and New Entertainment" was held at the IFIP World Computer Congress in August 2004 (France).

TC Publications: Ryohei Nakatsu and Junichi Hoshino (2003, eds.). Entertainment Computing, Kluwer Academic Publishers. Matthias Rauterberg (2004, ed.). ICEC 2004, Entertainment Computing, Lecture Notes in Computing Science, Vol. 3166, Springer-Verlag.

Working Groups (WG) Under TC 'Entertainment Computing'

WG16.1 Digital Storytelling

Scope: Storytelling is one of the core technologies of entertainment. Especially with the advancement of information and communication technologies (ICT), new types of entertainment called video games have been developed where interactive story development is the key that makes those games really entertaining. At the same time, however, the difference between interactive storytelling and conventional storytelling has not been well studied. Also, as the development of interactive storytelling needs a lot of time and human power, it is crucial to develop technologies for automatic or semiautomatic story development. The objective of this working group is to study and discuss these issues.

Members: As a first member of this WG16.1, Marc Cavazza is named as chair (contact: m.o.cavazza@tees.ac.uk).

WG16.1 Activities: Already there are several conferences/workshops on digital storytelling. To establish a link between IFIP and these conferences/workshops is the first activity of WG16.1.

WG16.2 Entertainment Robots

Scope: Robots are becoming one of the most appealing forms of entertainment. New entertainment robots and/or pet robots are becoming popular. Also, from the theoretical point of view, compared with computer graphics based characters/animations, the robot is an interesting research object as it has a physical entity. Taking these issues into consideration, it was decided at the SG16 annual meeting that a new working group on entertainment robots is to be established.

Members: As a first member of WG16.2, Hitoshi Matsubara is named as chair (contact: matsubar@fun.ac.jp).

WG16.2 Activities: As a first activity of this working group, WG16.2 organized a national workshop on entertainment computing, Entertainment Computing 2003, held during Jan. 13–15 at Osaka (Japan). It attracted more than 120 attendees and 30 papers.

WG16.2 publications: The proceedings were published by IPSJ (Information Processing Society of Japan) as a special issue on "Entertainment Computing," IPSJ Symposium Series, No.1, 2003.

WG16.3 Theoretical Basis of Entertainment

Scope: Although there are huge entertainment industries already, such as video games, toys, robots, etc., little academic interest has been paid to such questions as what is the core of the entertainment, what are the technologies that could create new entertainment, and how can the core technologies of entertainment be applied to other areas such as education, learning and so on. The main objective of this WG is to study these issues.

Members: As a first member of WG16.3, Matthias Rauterberg is named as chair (contact: g.w.m.rauterberg@tue.nl).

Anyone who is qualified and interested in active participation in one of the working groups is kindly invited to contact one of the WG chairs.

Editor's Note

ICEC 2004 attracted 62 full-paper submissions, 40 short-paper submissions, 8 poster submissions and 4 demo submissions, in total 114 submissions.

Based on a thorough review and selection process done by 93 international experts from academia and industry as members of the program committee, a high-quality program was compiled. The international program committee consisted of experts from all over the world: 3 from Australia, 3 from Austria, 3 from Canada, 1 from China, 1 from Croatia, 2 from Denmark, 1 from Finland, 6 from France, 15 from Germany, 2 from Greece, 2 from Ireland, 2 from Italy, 8 from Japan, 1 from Korea, 16 from the Netherlands, 1 from New Zealand, 1 from the Philippines, 1 from Singapore, 1 from South Africa, 3 from Sweden, 1 from Switzerland, 7 from the United Kingdom, and 12 from the United States.

The final decision was made by review and conference chairs based on feedback from at least two reviewers available online via the conference management tool. As a result, 27 full papers were directly accepted as submitted, and for the acceptable remaining 21 submissions their status was changed: 9 were accepted as short papers, and 12 as posters; 14 full-paper submissions were definitively rejected; 19 short papers were directly accepted as submitted, and for 10 others their status was changed, to 8 posters and 2 demo papers, for final acceptance; 11 short-paper submissions were definitively rejected; 3 poster paper submissions were accepted and 5 rejected; 3 demo paper submissions were accepted and 1 rejected.

Finally 27 full papers, 27 short papers, 18 poster papers, 3 demo papers, and in addition 3 keynote papers plus 3 specially invited topic papers were compiled and are presented in this book. All these papers could be allocated to one of the following topics: (1) advanced interaction design; (2) art, design and media; (3) augmented, virtual and mixed reality; (4) computer games; (5) human factors of games; (6) intelligent games; (7) mobile entertainment; (8) sound and music; and (9) visual media engineering. Papers per topic are ordered as follows: full papers, short papers, demo papers, and poster papers.

Table of Contents

III Art, Design, and Media

IV   Augmented, Virtual, and Mixed Reality

V   Computer Games

VI   Human Factors of Games

VII   Intelligent Games

X   Visual Media Engineering

Invited Presentations

Ludic Engagement and Immersion as a Generic Paradigm for Human-Computer Interaction Design

Craig A. Lindley

Institution Technology, Art and New Media,
University of Gotland, Cramergatan 3, SE-621 57 Visby, Sweden
craig.lindley@hgo.se

Abstract. Ludic systems are interactive media productions typically generalised under the heading of computer games, but actually integrating elements of game play, simulation or modeling, and narrative. The success of ludic systems lies in their highly effective modes of player engagement and immersion. Game play, simulation and narrative have their own respective forms of engagement and immersion that have often been overlooked in the development of models for human-computer interaction. As game systems become more ubiquitous, technical platforms will evolve to support more game-like interaction in general. This will facilitate the development of many applications having ludic engagement and immersion modes that dissolve some of the distinctions between work and play, providing the potential for alleviating tedium in many computer-based work tasks.

1   Introduction

Computer games are the most successful commercial application of interactive media, perhaps with the exception of the world wide web as a complete system. Commercial computer games integrate elements of pure game play, simulation and narrative, resulting in very rich media experiences with different levels of meaning having complex interrelationships. Computer games did not evolve directly from any existing established media industry. Their origins lie in simulation systems and computer graphics, and while computer games have borrowed much from other media (including genre conventions and cinematic techniques), the computer game industry has evolved independently until more recent generations started to involve cross licensing arrangements between media forms (eg. computer games and cinema). This historical evolution of computer games has occurred within its own emerging subculture. The earliest games include projects developed as side interests or after hours work, and the culture of gamers has grown out of the subcultures of war gamers, table top role playing gamers and computer geeks. Gamer culture is closer to the culture of comic books than high art, or even television and film. Even with the current huge commercial success and popularity of computer games, the form is often dismissed as the lightest form of entertainment, more contemptible than television, poisoning the minds of children and wasting the time of adults.

Despite this bad press from those unable to relate to the medium, games are now gaining greater respectability. Game studies has emerged over the last few years as a

M. Rauterberg (Ed.): ICEC 2004, LNCS 3166, pp. 3–13, 2004.

new and serious field of academic enquiry. Research projects are addressing issues of technology and form in order to raise the perceived cultural quality of games, not just as an entertainment medium, but also as an art form. Games as a medium are gaining acceptance as a form with as much validity as any other expressive medium. In terms of engagement and immersion, games have been far more successful than most if not all other computer software applications. It is surprising from this perspective that games have nevertheless been so easily dismissed, rather than studied more intensively for what they achieve in human-computer interaction. Entertainment applications are surely valid in their own right, and there is much to be said for subjecting the dichotomy between "entertainment" and "serious" applications to intensive critique from the perspectives of the emotional loading of those terms, and from the perspectives of how games function from economic, sociological, psychological and existential perspectives. Beyond this, game form can be abstracted from its external functions as a general model of an engaging and immersive medium that can have effective applications in many areas. Klabbers [7] cites as potential areas of application of game systems including: business administration, public administration, educational institutions, environment, health care, human services, international relations, military, religion, technology, human settlements and imaginary worlds. This broad field of potential applications is not needed to justify taking games seriously; the huge market for games and their force of engagement and immersion is enough to justify a strong focus on game media. The broader application areas justify this interest from a much broader field than those interested only in entertainment or art: games provide a very strong paradigm for human-computer interaction across all possible application areas.

Since games are not simply games, they are perhaps more accurately referred to as *ludic* systems, systems that integrate game play with other formal systems of interaction and time structure. This paper discusses the different interaction forms involved from the perspective of how those forms structure the play experience. This discussion includes analysis of the forms of engagement and immersion involved, focusing in particular on how the different systems of temporal order involve different models of engagement and immersion.

2   Games, Models, and Narratives as Independent Formal Subsystems of Ludic Space

Ludic systems may involve three different kinds of formal system determining the temporal structure of the experience of players. Each of these types of formal system can be realized in ways that operate independently of the others, although any given ludic system may involve more than one of these forms to varying degrees and using different strategies of interrelationship or integration. The three types of formal system are: the formal system of games, the formal system of the model, and the formal systems of narratives. In Lindley [8] this trichotomy was expressed in terms of game, narrative and simulation, respectively. However, to be more accurate, simulation must be considered together with *fabrication* in the case of systems for which correspondence with an external system is of limited relevance, and the concept of the model captures this more effectively than that of simulation.

3   Games and Game Play

Computer games encompass a vast range of different kinds of interactive media productions. In the broadest possible sense we call all of these things games. However, it
is much more useful to adopt a narrower definition of game that can be associated
with different modes of engagement and immersion from those of other formal ludic
semiotic subsystems. Hence a game will be defined as follows:

A game *is a goal-directed and competitive activity conducted within a framework
of agreed rules.*

This can be referred to as the *ludic* or *ludological* definition of game, the kind of
definition at the heart of traditional game theory. This definition captures many features of the definitions considered by Juul [6], but omitting criteria based upon issues
of pragmatics or function that are highly subject to external accidents of history and
context.

In being *goal-directed*, a game involves activity aimed towards some final state. In
being *competitive*, that final state has some kind of payoff value or measure or progress associated with it that may be associated with win/lose criteria. The win/lose
criteria may involve absolute measures (first one to achieve a score of 9, or to complete level X) of relative measures (highest score after 10 minutes wins). Competition
may be between real players or some combination of real and simulated players (eg.
single player strategy games).

The definition does not require players to learn the rules; it only requires that activity obeys the rules, and that players implicitly or explicitly agree to those rules. For
games played without computational support, payers need to understand the rules.
However, as Juul [6] notes, one of the advantages of computer games is that the machine enforces the rules, relieving the player from the need to know all of the rules in
detail and supporting rule sets far too complex for manual operation.

The rules establish what as a player you can or cannot do, and what the consequences of actions may be within the game. Learning to play a game, making progress within a game and completing or winning a game are a matter of learning how
to interact within the game system and its rules in a way that supports progress. This
is a matter, not necessarily of learning the game rules, but of learning a *gameplay
gestalt*[1], understood as a pattern of interaction with the game system. Playing the
game is then a matter of performing the gestalt. It is what the player does, within the
system and as allowed by the rules of the game.

A gameplay gestalt can have many forms for a particular game, capturing different
playing styles, tactics and approaches to progressing through the game and (perhaps)
eventually winning. In general, it is a particular way of thinking about the game state
from the perspective of a player, together with a pattern of repetitive perceptual, cognitive, and motor operations. A particular gameplay gestalt could be unique to a person, a game, or even a playing occasion. Recurrent gameplay gestalts can also be
identified across games, game genres, and players. Some examples of gameplay gestalts in computer games include:

---

[1] A *gestalt* may be understood as a configuration or pattern of elements so unified as a whole
that it cannot be described merely as a sum of its parts.

- *Action games*: shoot while being hit, strafe to hiding spot, take health, repeat
- *RPGs*: send fast character to lure enemy from group, all characters kill enemy, take health, repeat.
- *Strategy Games*: order peasants, send to work, order soldiers, send to perimeters, repeat while slowly expanding the perimeters (up to the point of runaway win/lose); OR: move x archers to tower y every n minutes to head off the enemy camel musketeers from the east who arrive every n minutes.
- *In General*: confront barrier, save if successful, reload and retry if unsuccessful.

Patterns like these may or may not be explicitly designed for by the creators of a game. If designers do take them into account, it may be in supporting the development and emergence of these patterns in play, rarely by forcing them on the player. It may also be that a game has a single winning gestalt. This may not be a simple repetitive interaction pattern, but perhaps the performance of one very specific pattern (eg. in the case of puzzle games), or a generic pattern performed repetitively in variable instantiations.

The rules and ludic medium of a game imply and support a range of different types of valid actions performed by the player, typically with scope for variations in how those actions are performed, and how and when different actions are selected and sequenced. A *move* within a game is an abstraction over player action, mapping it to an abstracted action of significance within the rule set and independent of local, personal and idiosyncratic variations in performance; a move is a connotation of a physical action and its perceptual consequences, allowed and facilitated by the framing of the game (I can move a chess piece on the board at any time, but I only make *a move* in the game of chess when I'm playing the game). Hence a player performs actions having conventional connotations as moves within the formal system of the game. Those actions are likely to be highly stylized according to the game, and actions too dissimilar to the stylized set will be regarded as fouls or cheats if their performer intends them to have in-game significance, or as *extra-ludic* actions potentially frustrating other players if they are not intended to have in-game significance.

A gameplay gestalt, as described above, is a player's pattern of move performances. Douglas and Hargadon [4] discuss the function of *schemas* (or *schemata*) in conditioning affective responses to experiences of interactive media, with a particular focus upon narrative pattern schemas and how satisfaction of expectations embodies in a schema function to create immersion within an unfolding narrative, while disruption of expectations requires engagement with the unfamiliar narrative structure. Schemas are understood as cognitive frameworks determining what is known about the world, objects within it, tasks performed and what is perceived. Once a schema is associated with a situation, relevant scripts are called from it that shape perception, navigation and interaction within that scenario.

A gameplay gestalt may (once developed) be interpreted as constituting a kind of *schema* related to, but not identical with, those discussed by discussed by Douglas and Hargadon [4] When a gameplay gestalt functions as a reusable schema, the player will attempt to apply it within games that appear to resemble those within which the schema has previously been successful. Hence as players we may find ourselves repeating game play patterns without exploring new interaction possibilities provided with new games, as long as the established patterns support progress within the game. Douglas and Hargadon note that it is highly normative schemas that enable readers of texts to 'lose' themselves in the text in what they refer to as an *immersive affective experience*. Douglas and Hargadon contrast this with the *engaged affective experience* where contradictory schemas or elements defying conventional schemas tend to disrupt reader immersion in the text "obliging them to assume an extra-textual perspective on the text itself, as well as on the schemas that have shaped it and the scripts operating within it".

Applying these distinctions to games, a new kind of game in which previously established game play gestalts do not work might in these terms be said to require players to become involved in the engaged affective experience required for developing new gameplay gestalts (or indeed to initially determine which already available gestalts apply within a specific game). Once a successful gestalt is found or formed, the player shifts from engaged affective experience to immersed affective experience in the performance of the gestalt.

This process of player engagement and subsequence immersion within a game experience is strongly associated with the exploration, choice and performance of game moves. The potential for choosing moves results in a very loosely predefined time structure such that games are not strongly a priori time-structured in their design. A specific type of move is likely to have some time structure at least implicit within the rule-derived constraints bounding valid ways of performing it. But this is minimal, and the temporal structure of gameplay gestalts is an emergent structure developed during play by the player. Larger scale time structures specific to game form are reflected in the language of rounds, bouts, matches, tournaments, seasons and campaigns. The most primitive complete game experiences, at which a point of win or loss is reached, are bouts or rounds. Higher level game structures tend to be highly repetitive patterns of these simple game experiences, largely concerned with the organization of opponents and extension of the simple competitive situation of a game to include a broader field of opponents with a view to obtaining a global performance or game play ranking obtained by accumulation of the results of many bouts.

An interesting difference between textual forms and games forms is that while game genres manifest genre schemata within the fixed design of the game artifacts, the schemata involved in play, referred to here as gameplay gestalts, are inventions of the player. Hence the schemata connoting a first person shooter (involving features like: first-person point of view in a 3D world with player character mobility, armed facing antagonistic opponents, etc.) might invoke in the player a gameplay gestalt (a kind of performance schemata) of the form: shoot while being hit, strafe to hiding spot, take health, repeat. This may succeed across many games conforming to the appropriate set of first-person-shooter schemata for a given player, but different players may use very different game play gestalts. In this case, game schemata, that might characterise genres, rule sets, and game types, inform design processes and facilitate recognition of game types by players. But game *play* schemata, or gameplay gestalts, are a more personal and emergent phenomenon, cognitive adaptations by the player facilitating progress within a game of a particular type schema.

This means that it is the gameplay gestalt, or game play schema, that is the primary learning outcome of game play. It is the player's structuring or pattern development and selection activity that creates engagement with games, and the ongoing performance of an acquired or selected pattern that creates immersion in game play. As Douglas and Hargadon [4] suggest, and as previously observed by Turkle [9] game play often reaches states of timeless loss of self-consciousness, involving the state of consciousness that Csikszentmihalyi [2] calls *flow*, a state at the boundaries between engagement and immersion, of being totally absorbed in meeting a constantly unfolding challenge. Contrary to Douglas and Hargadon's view however, this need not have anything to do with narrative. For games it is a state of pure game play, in the present terms, a state of selecting and performing gameplay gestalts, an *immersion in performance*, in the internal world of a game, but not in the internal world of a narrative. The performance is itself a process requiring attention, and for successful flow the demands of performing an integrated cognitive and instrumental pattern must fall above thresholds of boredom and within the bounds of what is achievable and sustainable for the player in a flowing state of concentration. Csikszentmihalyi characterizes flow, an experience that is simultaneously challenging and rewarding, as one of the most enjoyable and valuable experiences that a person can have.

4 Narrative

The narrative structure of experience within ludic systems may be either pre-authored at the performance level, or an emergent pattern based upon combinatorial principles built into the generation level. Narrative in the strongest sense is perceived when a structure conforms to a very specific narrative pattern, the kind of narrative schema referred to by Douglas and Hardagon [4] An a example of such a pattern, commonly found both in commercial cinema in computer games, is the *three-act restorative structure* (see [3]). The three-act restorative structure has a beginning (the first act) in which a conflict is established, followed by the playing out of the implications of the conflict (the second act), and completed by the final resolution of the conflict (the third act). The three-act restorative model includes a central protagonist, a conflict involving a dilemma of normative morality, a second act propelled by the hero's false resolution of this dilemma, and a third act in which the dilemma is resolved once and for all by an act that reaffirms normative morality. Each act within the three-act structure culminates in a point of crisis, the resolution of which propels the plot into the following act, or to the final resolution. This structure is very common and highly immersive for audiences having strong anticipations of the structure's definitive elements.

In computer games incorporating a prespecified three act restorative structure within the player's experience, the central conflict form often manifests recursively (ie. the structure is repeated at different levels of temporal scale). For example, the overall restorative three-act model may be applied to the game experience as a whole, with the dramatic arch being completed when the user finishes the game. At this level the story is usually not interactive, since act one, key scenes within the story of act two (ie. primary plot points), and the playing out of the consequences of the final resolution in act three are typically achieved by cut scenes, sequences of non-interactive, pre-rendered video or non-interactive animation sequences. The next level down within the recursive structure is that of the game level. The game level is designed for the pursuit of a goal, that of the player reaching the end of the level, which progresses the player through the second act of the higher level three-act structure of the game narrative. There is rarely if ever a one-to-one correspondence between game levels and acts; more typically, the first act and the end of the third act are presented via cut scenes, with playable game levels summing to form a highly extended second act followed by the final resolution of the third act as the end of game play (eg. by overcoming the final and toughest enemy, usually a demonic character at the heart of the central conflict in the story). Although experience within a level typically has much of the structure of a match, a contest, a league or a tournament, the sense of level-specific narrative development can be enhanced by increasing difficulty through a level, or by an internal dramatic structure that emphasizes the point of completing the level, such as the defeat of a level boss, the big barrier creature at the end of the level. The false resolution that drives act two of the three-act restorative model at the highest structural level may be seen manifesting repetitively with each game level: when the game level is resolved (completed), the player finds themselves at the beginning of the next game level full of conflicts.

At the next level of the recursive decomposition of game structure, there is often a series of smaller scale conflicts and challenges within a game level, which may include monsters to be defeated or avoided, puzzles to be solved, or treasures, clues or keys that must be found in order to progress in the current or future game levels. Usually it is only this lowest level of the game plot that is highly interactive; these are actually the individual games played by the player (by the definition above). The linear and non-interactive cut scenes framing game play are revealed in a predefined order, and within a level all players usually start in the same place and must have completed the same set of tasks in order to complete the level. The low level and interactive parts of the game are played by performance of a gameplay gestalt, a repetitive pattern of moves by which the player progresses through the individual games of a level. Hence game play usually has little if any bearing on the story being told; the story is for the most part a structure imposed on top of, and different from, game play.

4.1 Narrative and Gameplay

The question of the relationship between gameplay and narrative is often regarded as problematic [1]. Considering the nature of engagement and immersion involved in each form, this should not be surprising. The apprehension of an experience as a narrative requires the cognitive construction of a *narrative schema* or *narrative gestalt*, a cognitive structure or pattern allowing the perception and understanding of an unfolding sequence of phenomena as a unified narrative. In playing a computer game, one must learn and then perform one or more gameplay gestalts in order to progress through the tasks of the game. To experience a ludic system as both a *game* and as a *narrative* requires the apprehension of a narrative gestalt unifying the flow of game experiences into a coherent narrative structure. But narrative gestalts and game play gestalts are not the same kind of patterns. Hence the tension between gameplay and narrative can be viewed as arising from competition between these respective gestalt formation and performance processes for perceptual, cognitive, and motor effort.

This can be a competition both for cognitive resources, and for formal influence in creating the apprehension of the experience. Within the range of effort required for immersion and engagement, and especially for the experience of flow, if gameplay consumes most of the player's available cognitive resources, there will be little scope left for perceiving complex narrative patterns (eg. we forget the motivation behind the character's battles, the names and relationships among the characters, etc.). Moreover, the narrative adds little to player immersion and engagement in game play (who cares, it's fun anyway!). On the contrary, cut scenes delivering plot points can be experienced as irritations when they interrupt the immersion and flow of game play, leading to forms of engagement that are uninteresting since the player can only wait to re-enter the play experience using the same patterns as before the cut scene interrupted it. Conversely, focusing on the development of the sense of narrative (eg. in the case of multipath movies or branching hypertexts) reduces the player's need for and interest in a highly engaging or immersive gameplay gestalt. In general, game play or the narrative are the sites of immersion. Transitions between game play and narrative cut scenes create engagement, signaling "now you should watch" or "now you should play". This can work well, but generally this requires engagement to be minimized by minimizing differences in the audiovisual style of the cut scenes and introducing them in a way in which their rhythm flows with that of game play performance.

An alternative strategy for overcoming this tension is to develop game play mechanics that are fundamentally dramatic, in that their consequences *do* affect the higher level narrative patterns of the game. While the three-act restorative structure is a useful heuristic for writers wishing to determine a high level story structure, it is too high level for effective integration with game play. For this, the basic game mechanics must constitute narrative action on the part of the player. This suggests a strategy for achieving narrative game play by moving away from high level predefined narrative schemata towards a more detailed integration of principles for narrative generation within the mechanics of player interaction. That is, narrative game play requires a more object-oriented approach (see [5]), in which game characters encapsulate narrative potential, and the specific narratives that emerge over time are a function of the players' history within a ludic world. Such a form of game play may *not* involve repetitive interaction patterns, just as most stories involve development rather than repetition. The primitive actions of a narrative are dramatically significant actions. A series of dramatically significant actions leads to a resolution (according to a specific narrative structure). For a player, the question driving play (for a truly interactive narrative) becomes: which move should I perform next, in this evolving dramatic situation? The game, if viewed as such, then has a closer resemblance to chess or a puzzle game. The series of choices made by the player will form a pattern of dramatic development, closer in nature to solving a puzzle than to winning a game. For a persistent world there will be no final solution state, and the game play experience will be a construction (fabrication) of the dramas and emotions of a life.

5 The Model

A simulation can be defined as: *a representation of the function, operation or features of one process or system through the use of another.* For game worlds, it must be possible for the simulation model to be a model of a system or world that is a fiction or *fabrication*. This makes *model* a preferable term, since it does not need to be a model of any aspect of reality, while a simulation is more typically understood as representing some aspect of a real system.

As noted above, all computer games involve a level of modeling at which the performance space of the game is fabricated. The experience of the game for the player as a game in the strict sense, as a narrative and/or as a simulation is then a matter of the degree to which the player experience is structured by the formal systems of a game or narrative. If there is little or no pre-structured game or narrative form shaping the play experience, the simulation system becomes the dominant structure informing the shape of the that experience. The presence of predefined game or narrative forms within the structure of the play experience tends to push the sense of the ludic system as a simulation into the background, since game play and narrative provide strong imperatives of purpose motivating player action. This sense of purpose may be implicit but strongly suggested within a simulation game. For example, *Sim City* implicitly conveys the game objective of growing your city, and doing so may result in the emergence of repetitive play patterns. But this can be varied, and it is possible to have one's city destroyed by a natural disaster, or to play with dysfunctional cities in different forms, or simply with very different kinds of cities to see how they develop. The game then functions as a "toy" as much as a game; for a simulation, play is much more of a matter of exploring the space of possible experiences supported by the simulation, in which case the purpose of play is provided much more strongly by the player. Authored and pre-specified time structures are then typically manifested by:

- discrete event modelling of physical phenomena, such as the motions of virtual physical objects within a 3D space subjected to modeled gravitational forces
- growth and decay of game world objects (eg. buildings within zones in Sim City)
- events manifesting probabilistically, such as arrivals or departures of game objects (eg. wandering monsters or enemies)
- functional modeling of complex systems (eg. vehicle simulators and models)

A model-based ludic system may involve *no* specific repetitive and goal-oriented activities, no obvious end state (other than the player getting bored) and no large scale predefined patterning of the play experience. Play patterns emerge over the course of running a model, can be completely different for different runs, and most likely have never been anticipated by the designers of the model. Repetitive action may be used to operate a model, but may not be directed to any specific final goal by the player/operator. In terms of engagement and immersion, this is a matter of how the player chooses to operate the model, and can include modes of play more typical of toys, or experiences of flow that may be associated with other kinds of activities than game play.

The extent to which a ludic system is structured and experienced predominantly as a model is reflected in the ability of players to define their own narratives and/or games and game systems within the modeled world. In this sense a model provides a *field of play*, within which it is up to the players to define *how* they will play. Integration of more specific narrative and game play patterns provides more ready-made purposes for interaction, but the model substrate of ludic systems always makes it an option for the player not to play the provided games or not to follow pre-structured narratives. For a game that is a functional model with little to no predefined narrative or game elements, players need to engage more heavily to create and sustain their own purposive behaviors. Narratives and games provide purposes and modes of action that can be activated in order to meet those purposes. Engagement in that case facilitates the discovery of schemas of game or narrative form (ie. for specific genres of games or narratives) that provide criteria for the development and/or selection of schemas of play or viewing.

6 Conclusion

This paper has considered the present of the formal systems of games, narratives and models within ludic systems. Each kind of formal system has schemas that make it recognizable in terms of temporal structure and interaction possibilities. The familiarity or unfamiliarity of schemas leads to either immersion or engagement in the ludic experience. It has also been discussed how learning to play a game is a matter of learning one or more gameplay gestalts, or game play schemas, in combination with selecting appropriate schemas already learned as play patterns applicable to making progress within a game of a particular type. Developing or selecting one or more appropriate gestalts or schemas for the lludic experience involve firstly an experience of engagement with the ludic system followed by and immersion within the ludic experience. Engagement and immersion facilate the player entering a state of flow, which provides a form of playing pleasure based upon the pattern of interaction.

These formal models do not rely upon issues of the *thematics* of a production. Themes suggest a mapping onto a real or fictional world; for example, one can have a fantasy chess set, a cat and dogs chess set, or an abstract chess set. Themes can obviously have a role in the appeal of a particular game to a particular player (otherwise all ludic systems would be abstract). However, the essential form of a game can be transferred across different themes, just as a particular narrative structure can be realized in different scenarios. Genres often involve thematic conventions, but these can be stretched; a strategy game could deal with historical scenarios, while the same mechanics can also be applied to fantasy scenarios, science fiction, farmyard animals, or just about anything else.

Similarly the context and situation of a ludic system can radically redefine its functions and meaning. This means that the basic mechanics, form and structure of a ludic system can be effective in terms of immersion, engagement and flow across many different thematic manifestations and functions. Ludic play is therefore seen to be a generic mechanism. It is, therefore, possible to regard ludic schemas with their implications for engagement, immersion and flow as a general design approach for human-computer interaction across a broad range of applications. Understanding the experiential implications of game play patterns is a contribution to understanding the broad appeal of computer games. But since these patterns are largely dependent upon the abstract system and mechanics of games, they could be adopted as interaction modes across many applications not traditionally regarded in terms of entertainment. The result is an approach to interaction design that renders interaction entertaining, whatever the overall functions and context of a system may be. The challenge in pursuing this paradigm lies within the many possible application areas, and consists of mapping abstract moves of games onto meaningful functions and useful effects within the domain, together with defining a purpose of interaction served by those moves and leading to the creative orchestration of moves into an immersive experience of play by system users who are also players. Play then does not need to be limited to purposes of entertainment, and repetitive processes of work can be transformed into experiences of optimal flow.

References

1. Aarseth E. J., *Cybertext: Perspectives on Ergodic* Literature, The Johns Hopkins University Press, 1997.
2. Csikszentmihalyi M., *Flow: The Psychology of Optimal Experience*, Perennial; Reproduction edition, March 13, 1991.
3. Dancyger K. and Rush J., *Alternative Scriptwriting*, Second Edition, Focal Press, 1995.
4. Douglas J. Y. and Hargadon A., 2001 "The pleasures of immersion and engagement: schemas, scripts and the fifth business", *Digital Creativity*, Vol. 12, No. 3, pp. 153–166.
5. Eladhari M., *Objektorienterat berättande i berättelsedrivna datorspel* ("Object Oriented Story Construction in Story Driven Computer Games"), Masters Thesis, University of Stockholm, http://zerogame.interactiveinstitute.se/papers.htm. 2002.
6. Juul J., "The Game, The Player, The World: Looking for a Heart of Gameness", *Proceedings, Level Up Digital Games Research Conference*, pp. 30–45, Copier M. and Raessens J., Eds., 4–6 November 2003, Utrecht.
7. Klabbers J. H. G., "The Gaming Landscape: A Taxonomy for Classifying Games and Simulations", *Proceedings, Level Up Digital Games Research Conference*, pp. 54–67, Copier M. and Raessens J., Eds., 4–6 November 2003, Utrecht.
8. Lindley C. A., "Game Taxonomies: A High Level Framework for Game Analysis and Design", Gamasutra feature article, 3 October 2003,
    http://www.gamasutra.com/features/20031003/lindley_01.shtml.
9. Turkle S., *The Second Self: Computers and the Human Spirit*, Simon and Schuster, New York, 1984.

Realization of Tai-Chi Motion Using a Humanoid Robot

Takenori Wama[1], Masayuki Higuchi[1], Hajime Sakamoto[2], and Ryohei Nakatsu[1]

[1] Kwansei Gakuin University, School of Science and Technology
2-1 Gakuen, Sanda, 669-1337 Japan
{scbc0057,x78072,nakatsu}@ksc.kwansei.ac.jp
http://www.ksc.kwansei.ac.jp
http://ist.ksc.kwansei.ac.jp/index.html
[2] Hajime Laboratory, Kobe, Japan
h_sakamoto@cam.hi-ho.ne.jp
http://www.hajimerobot.co.jp/

Abstract. Even though in recent years research and development of humanoid robots has increased, the major topics of research generally focus on how to make a robot perform specific motions such as walking. However, walking is only one of the complicated motions humans can perform. For robots to play an active role in society as our partner, they must be able to simulate precisely various kinds of human actions . We chose tai-chi as an example of complicated human actions and succeeded in programming a robot to perform the 24 fundamental tai-chi actions.

1 Introduction

Many companies and universities are currently doing research and development into humanoid robots. These robots are equipped with a certain amount of flexibility at their robotic "joints," making it possible for them to perform various motions. However, most of these studies investigate little outside of rising or walking actions, ignoring the rest of the actions that humans can perform. As a result, little research has fully investigated and utilized robotic flexibility. Indeed, since walking and rising are good examples of complicated and dynamic actions, it is valuable to study them. At the same time, however, it is expected that in the near future humanoid robots will be introduced into society to become our partner at home and in the workplace. Therefore, robots must not only walk or rise but also do various kinds of human-like operations naturally. Robots must also use these motions to communicate with humans. Based on this basic concept, we tried to reproduce smooth full body actions in a commercially available humanoid robot. We selected the motions of *tai-chi*, a Chinese martial art form, because smooth movements condensed from all human actions for exercising the entire body are essential to it. Therefore, our goal is to design tai-chi actions, install them, and develop a humanoid robot that can perform them.

M. Rauterberg (Ed.): ICEC 2004, LNCS 3166, pp. 14–19, 2004.
© IFIP International Federation for Information Processing 2004

2 Humanoid Robot

We decided to use a robot developed at the Hajime Laboratory to reproduce the smooth exercises of tai-chi. This humanoid robot was equipped with 22 servomotors, enabling it to simulate the smooth, human-like motions by simultaneously controlling all of these motors. The hardware specifications of the robot are shown in Table 1, and its appearance is shown in Fig. 1.

Table 1. Specification of the humanoid robot used for experiment

Size / Weight	34cm / 1.7kg
Flexibility	22 (leg 12, arm 8, waist 1, head 1)
CPU	SH2/7047F
Motor	KO PDS-2144, FUTABA S3003, FUTABA S3102, FUTABA S3103
Battery	DC6V

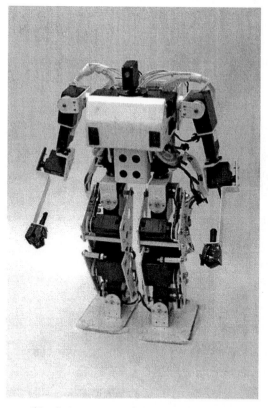

Fig. 1. Appearance of the humanoid robot

3 Tai-Chi

There are five major schools of tai-chi: Chin, Kure, Son, Bu and Yo, which is the most commonly practiced style. Yo's extended version has been officially established by the Chinese government. As an established tai-chi, there are 24 formula, 48 formula, 88 formula, and etc. In creating tai-chi motions, we chose the 24 formula tai-chi because even though it is the simplest form of tai-chi, it still contains the strong points of the other schools.

4 Motion Editor

A motion editor was used to design the robot's motion as shown in Fig. 2. Figure 2 also shows the *Front*, *Right*, and *Top* views for the robot's front, right, and above positions, respectively. In the *Perspective* view, we can rotate the robot image 360 degrees in any direction to gain a panoramic view. The angle of each motor is controlled by the parameter in the upper right part of the figure. The number in the left-hand side shows the data assigned to each motor, and the right-hand side number shows the angle of each motor. The transition time for each motion is decided by the parameter in the lower right part of the figure. Moreover, since we can create and store 32 motions in one file, 24 files were created to store all of the 24 formula tai-chi motions.

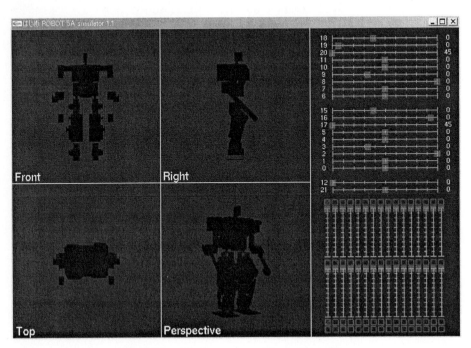

Fig. 2. User interface screen of the motion editor

5 Motion Design

Basically, each motion was created manually using a motion editor. By connecting each created motion, a series of smooth actions was generated. The detailed process is described below.

5.1 Creation of Motion with the Motion Editor

As described in Sect. 4, we exhaustively studied each tai-chi motion through magazines and videos. Then we divided each continuous motion into a series of short, key motions; key frames were decided for each motion. Next, a portion of each key motion was decided using the motion editor, which then output the control data for each servomotor. In the process, we had to create each motion, maintaining as much balance as possible.

5.2 Check of Continuous Action

Before connecting the motion created in Sect. 5.1 to a series of motions, it was necessary to investigate any incongruities by comparing the motion with that of human tai-chi motion from magazines and videos. Tai-chi, essentially, is comprised of a series of continuous actions that do not stop from beginning to end. When the robot does tai-chi, however, there is a short pause when the motion is connected because of the specifications of the motion editor that we used. However, if we concentrate on watching the tai-chi motion of the robot, however, there is no little sense of incongruity.

5.3 Motion Adjustment on an Actual Robot

Each tai-chi motion created in Sect. 5.2 was then installed into the robot and checked. Since the robot's center-of-gravity could only be checked during simulations with the actual physical robot, this whole process was the most important and time consuming. Sometimes small differences in the center-of-gravity between the computer graphics robot and the physical robot couldn't be recognized on the motion editor. If the robot fell down during a tai-chi motion, the motor angle had to be adjusted. A key frame between two key frames had to be carried out. In this way, we investigated for incongruity in the series of robot motions, eventually obtaining complete motion data.

6 Demonstration of Tai-Chi Motion Based on Human Robot Interaction

We extended our study and added a speech recognition tool called *Julian* to the robot, enabling it to perform a tai-chi demonstration based on communication with humans. When a user utters a command sentence, the key words are extracted by the speech

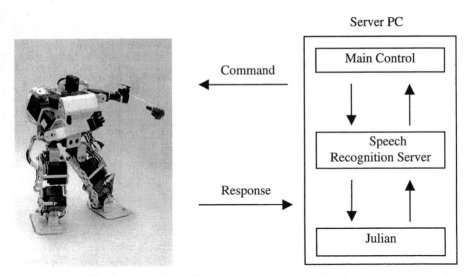

Fig. 3. Composition of the conversation system using the robot

recognition tool, converted into the control command for the robot, and sent to it (Fig. 3). The control data for each motion itself is loaded in the robot's microcomputer. Corresponding to the control command sent from the Server PC, the microcomputer reads out suitable control data to control the robot movement.

At various exhibitions we demonstrated our robot having easy conversations with the audience and showing them various tai-chi motions. In the future, various applications are possible based on such interaction between humans and this type of humanoid robot. For example, a robot can talk or chat with humans and act as their partner. It can also entertain humans by showing them tai-chi or dancing with them. Moreover, such forms of entertainment that currently use computer characters as fighting games and role-playing games could be performed with humanoid robots. In the near future there could be a growing market for such interactive games.

7   Conclusion

In this paper we investigated the realization of tai-chi motions for a humanoid robot and created a control data base of human-like tai-chi motions. However, tai-chi is only one of the complicated motions and actions of humans. A humanoid robot must be able to perform various human-like motions, so a robot needs to be capable of autonomous motion, action, and behavior.

For the autonomy of a robot, there are many research issues. We want to prepare a database containing various kinds of fundamental motions and achieve any desired motions and actions by combining these basic motion units. For the preparation of such a database, it is necessary for the motion editor to grasp the center-of-gravity balance and make it easy for the user to design robot motions. In addition, it is necessary to introduce new technologies for the humanoid robot. For example, if a robot encounters stairs, it must use image processing to recognize their height and inclination. Thus, research of image processing is also required. Research on accurate speech recognition is also needed.

At present the functions of humanoid robots are very limited. However, we believe that someday such autonomous robots as science fiction *Androids* from movies will emerge and be introduced into society.

Building Better Systems for Learning and Training: Bringing the Entertainment Industry and Simulation Technology Together

William R. Swartout

Institute for Creative Technologies, University of Southern California
13273 Fiji Way, Marina del Rey, CA 90265, USA
swartout@ict.usc.edu
http://www.ict.usc.edu

Abstract. In 1999, at the University of Southern California the Institute for Creative Technologies (ICT) was established. The ICT was intended to explore a question: what would happen if researchers who understood the technology of simulation and virtual reality worked in close collaboration with people from the entertainment industry who understood how to create compelling stories and engaging characters? What synergies would emerge? Would it be possible to create much more immersive simulation systems for training and learning? In the brief period since the opening of the ICT, we are starting to see the answers to these questions and understand the promise of this approach. In this keynote talk, I will describe some of the insights that have emerged from this collaboration, the major research efforts we have undertaken in areas such as graphics, artificial intelligence and sound, and the integrating virtual reality applications we have produced in areas such as training and leadership development.

M. Rauterberg (Ed.): ICEC 2004, LNCS 3166, p. 20, 2004.
© IFIP International Federation for Information Processing 2004

Game Intelligence: From Animal Play Behavior to Entertainment Computing

Marion Bönsch-Kauke

Ahrenshooper Str. 33/0501, 13051 Berlin, Germany
Marion.Boensch-Kauke@gmx.de

Abstract. Playing a game, cooperative, competitive or mixed motive, keeps our attention; good vibrations and a sense of humor 'arouse' interests; desire leads to approach (AIDA): this entertains you. This remark is only true if the state activities in play, gamble or game to achieve real "playing" from a psychological point of view. Profound, extended and long-lasting scientific studies from animal play behavior to progress in culture of mankind have investigated childhood, adolescence and late adulthood up to simulations in cyberspace century. The results of these studies show clearly that game behavior can be described in at least five stages: 1. Relaxed field; 2. Quasi-experimental operating; 3. Imitating and imagining a "make-believe" world; 4. Selection of regularities; 5. Fairness (respect for the rules: moral and responsibility). The peak or crown of game behavior is called "Game Intelligence". The social-psychological facts of entertainment computing must be taken into consideration when developing present and future inventions.

References

[1] Kauke, Marion (1992). *Spielintelligenz. Spielend lernen – Spielen lehren?* Spektrum Akademischer Verlag Heidelberg, Berlin, New York.
[2] Kauke, Marion (1998). *Kooperative Intelligenz. Sozialpsychologische und spielexperimentelle Grundlagen der Interaktivität zwischen Partnern*. Spektrum Akademischer Verlag Heidelberg

Effects of Violent Video Games on Aggressive Behavior, Helping Behavior, Aggressive Thoughts, Angry Feelings, and Physiological Arousal

Brad Bushman

Institute for Social Research, University of Michigan,
426 Thompson Street, Ann Arbor, MI 48106, USA
bbushman@umich.edu
http://www.umich.edu/~bbushman

Abstract. Meta-analytic procedures were used to review the results from 85 studies on violent video game effects. Violent video games increase aggressive behavior, aggressive thoughts, angry feelings, and arousal levels, and decrease helpful behaviors. The effects occurred for both children and adults and for both males and females. The more violent the video game, the stronger the effects. Violent video game effects are also increasing over time.

References

[1] Anderson, C. and Bushman, B., (2001). Effects of violent video games on aggressive behaviour, aggressive cognition, aggressive affect, physiological arousal, and pro-social behavior: a meta-analytic review of the scientific literature. *Psychological Science*, Vol. 12, No. 5, pp. 353–359.
[2] Anderson, C. and Bushman, B., (2002). Effects of media violence on society. *Science*, Vol. 295, No. 3, pp. 2377–2379.

M. Rauterberg (Ed.): ICEC 2004, LNCS 3166, p. 22, 2004.

New Behavioural Approaches for Virtual Environments

Marc Cavazza[1], Simon Hartley[1], Jean-Luc Lugrin[1], Paolo Libardi[2],
and Mikael Le Bras[1]

[1] School of Computing, University of Teesside, TS1 3BA, Middlesbrough, United Kingdom
m.o.cavazza@tees.ac.uk
[2] Department of Electronics for Automation, University of Brescia,
via Branze 38, Brescia, I-25123, Italy

Abstract. We describe a new approach to the behaviour of 3D environments
that supports the definition of physical processes and interactive phenomena.
The work takes as a starting point the traditional event-based architecture that
underlies most game engines. These systems discretise the environments' Physics by separating the objects' kinematics from the physical processes corresponding to objects interactions. This property has been used to insert a new
behavioural layer, which implements AI-based simulation techniques. We introduce the rationale behind AI-based simulation and the techniques we use for
qualitative Physics, as well as a new approach to world behaviour based on the
induction of causal impressions. This is illustrated through several examples on
a test environment. This approach has implications for the definition of complex world behaviour or non-standard physics, as required in creative applications.

1 Introduction

It is a common view in interactive systems research to consider that, while graphics
and visualisation have made significant progress over recent years, behavioural aspects are somehow lagging behind, and have not sustained a similar pace of progression. This generic statement concerns both the simulation of realistic Physics for 3D
worlds and the behaviour (generally AI-based) of autonomous entities populating
them.

One well-known instantiation of this statement consists in saying that the added
value of future computer games will derive increasingly from the AI technology they
incorporate, although this statement probably needs to be revisited from a more fundamental perspective. More realistic physical modelling also constitutes a challenge,
in particular in terms of computational resources. This problem is currently approached by discretising physical simulation to reflect the actual events taking place
in the virtual world, in particular those arising from interaction between world entities.

There has been, generally speaking, little research on the notion of integrated world
behaviour, which goes beyond the isolated simulation of object's physical behaviour
to consider the world's physical phenomena from a more global perspective. Such an
approach would be centred not only on physical objects but also on processes affecting objects, on the aggregation of objects into systems or devices whose behaviour

M. Rauterberg (Ed.): ICEC 2004, LNCS 3166, pp. 23–31, 2004.

cannot be deduced directly from simple physical simulation, but requires a higher level of conceptual modelling. It should also consider relations between events occurring in the 3D world, and how these can be perceived as causally related by the user.

In this paper, we introduce a novel approach to the integrated behaviour of virtual worlds, which is based on the use of AI techniques derived, among others, from qualitative simulation. We first describe the rationale for this approach and the system architecture, which is organised around the Unreal Tournament 2003™ game engine [1], whose event-based system serves as a baseline layer for integration of high-level behaviour. We then discuss two novel methods supporting 3D world's behaviour, which are qualitative physics and causal propagation, and how their basic components and formalism have been adapted to the specific constraints of real-time visualisation.

1.1 Physics Modelling, Event-Based Systems, and Interaction

Comprehensive modelling of all physical events in a virtual environment would be a formidable task, impossible to achieve in real time. In interactive virtual environments, basic physical behaviour is implemented in an interactive fashion to maintain a response rate which is acceptable for user interaction. This has led to the rationale, that in order to maintain this interaction rate, the Physical simulation is discretised. Kinematic aspects within these systems tend to be simulated through traditional numerical approaches, while more complex mechanical events (objects breaking or exploding) are pre-calculated. In other words, the overall dynamics of objects is subject to traditional physical simulation, while interactions between objects (collisions, etc.) constitute discretisation units. This saves considerable computation at the level of these events, whose pre-computed consequences can be triggered as a consequence of event recognition. The condition for such a system to work efficiently is the availability of an "event system", i.e. mechanisms for recognising in real-time the occurrence of such events and supporting the programming of cause-effects associations. In most cases, event systems are derived from basic collision detection mechanisms of the graphic engines. These systems are able to produce event primitives corresponding to collision or contact between objects, or objects entering and leaving areas or volumes in the 3D environment.

This is not specific to game engines, as event-based systems play an important role in VR software as well [2]. However, traditional game engines use their event system essentially as an API supporting the ad hoc development of object's behaviours associated with specific instances of events. The starting point for this research was to use the inherent discretisation of Physics in 3D engines to integrate high level behavioural mechanisms that could support complex behavioural simulation on a principled basis.

1.2 System Architecture

The system comprises a graphic environment, composed of the UT 2003 engine and an external physical simulation modules (called QP engine and causal engine, see below), developed in C++. The software architecture is based on UDP communication, supported through the UDPLink class in UT 2003. The messages exchanged between the UT 2003 environment and the behavioural modules correspond, on one side, to the activation conditions of various behaviour instances run by the engine. On the other side, the engine sends messages to update object states, which are interpreted by the Unreal Environment [3]. The Unreal Tournament engine extensively relies on event generation to support many of its interaction aspects and, most importantly, the mechanism for event generation is accessible to redefine specific behaviours. Formally, an event can be characterised as an encapsulated message, which is generated by an Event Source, this being an object of the environment. Examples of such basic events are:

```
Bump(Actor Other), Touch(Actor Other), UnTouch(Actor Other),
ActorEnteredVolume (Actor Volume), etc.
```

The Unreal Tournament Engine implements two different kinds of event: the basic (primitive) events, which are low level events defined within the game engine (derived from the collision detection procedures in the graphic engine), and the programmed events. The latter are events whose definitions are scripted and can thus be programmed by the system developer. This is a mechanism by which the system can parse low-level events into high-level events corresponding to a semantic description of the world.

1.3 Techniques for World Behaviour

The notion of *world behaviour* generalises that of virtual world Physics, to encompass any kind of dynamic generation of events in the virtual world. In traditional physical simulation, pre-defined consequences are triggered in response to specific events, such as a glass exploding when hit by a missile.

This approach can be generalised by considering the principles according to which events can be related to one another. For instance, physical simulation can be entirely discretised using laws of physics to produce causal chains of elementary events. This approach to symbolic reasoning on physical systems corresponds to an AI technique known as Qualitative Physics [3]. On the other hand, it is also possible to produce world behaviours by directly relating events to one another so as to create artificial causal chains. We describe both methods in the remainder of this paper. Like with any AI method, but more specifically with those modelling worlds, we should first discuss the knowledge representation formalisms that support their implementation.

2 Ontology and Representations

The principled definition of behaviour in a symbolic system relies on the appropriate description of action and processes, as well as object properties, which are determinants for their involvement in certain classes of actions and processes. It is thus necessary to develop an ontology for a given environment's Physics. Importantly, this ontology will describe both objects and relevant actions in the environment.

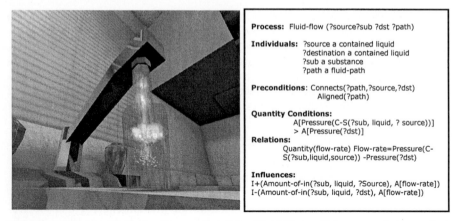

Fig. 1. An Example Qualitative Process describing Fluid Flows. This process is interactively triggered by moving the glass under to running water.

2.1 Representing Actions and Processes

The default mechanism for representing actions UT 2003™, which is representative of large class of interactive 3D system, consists in directly associating physical events to a set of possible consequences depending on the objects involved. For instance, the impact of a fragile object on a hard surface will be associated with this object being broken, through specific, ad hoc, scripting. This description should be supported by an appropriate formalism for change-inducing events, which should clearly identify actions and their consequences. The second step consists in defining an ontology of such events, i.e. describing the most important high-level events that can be recognised in the virtual environment.

We have termed these change-inducing events Context Events (CE) to reflect their semantic nature. Typically, a CE is represented using an action formalism inspired from those serving similar functions in planning and robotics, such as STRIPS [4] or the operator representation in the SIPE system [5].

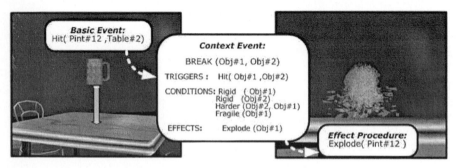

Fig. 2. Context Events constitute high-level descriptions of actions in the virtual environment. Here, a fragile object breaking on impact (instantiated to a falling glass).

These representations originally describe operators responsible for transforming state of affairs in the world. They tend to be organised around pre-conditions, i.e. conditions that should be satisfied for them to take place and post-conditions, i.e. those world changes induced by their application.

Our formalism for CE comprises three main fields, which are analogue to the SIPE representation. The first field, called trigger, contains the basic event from which the CE can be recognised and which prompts instantiation of the corresponding CE. The condition field is a formula testing properties of the objects involved in such as CE. The effect field corresponds to the consequence part of the CE and contains the effect to be applied to the objects affected by the CE (Figure 2).

Another kind of action representation consists of discretised physical processes such as those used by qualitative physics. These Qualitative Processes (QP) encapsulate the expression of physical laws relevant to a given high-level process, e.g. liquid flows, heat transfer, etc. An example qualitative process is shown on Figure 1. It formalises several relevant aspects, from the conditions that trigger the activation of a process to the formulas which determine the evolution of key variables (influence equations). The set of formalised qualitative processes constitute an ontology of physical transformations for a given virtual world.

2.2 Objects' Representation

Objects descriptions vary greatly depending on the kind of processing which is applied to them. Often, part-whole relationships and functional properties tend to dominate symbolic object descriptions. In our specific context, the main role of object descriptions is to determine the kind of actions and processes they can take part in, as well as relating an object's visual appearance to the transformations that can be applied to it. In the first instance, we have organised these representations according to several dimensions: i) the object's mechanical properties (e.g. breakable, movable, etc.), ii) its functional properties (e.g. object as container, fluid source, support, etc.) and iii) its visual properties (includes the object's appearance, but also the visual translation of certain of its behaviours, for instance for a glass to tilt, etc.). We have made a choice for the overall granularity of the representation, where direct relations can map properties of a given field onto another. This, in order to avoid the computational overhead of managing a complex semantic network .

Another aspect of object representation consists in relating them with the kind of qualitative processes they can take part in. The integration of Qualitative Physics in the virtual environments' basic mechanisms is achieved through the redefinition of a special class of physical objects: qualitative process objects, or QP objects. This follows traditional implementation techniques by which classes of objects are defined depending on the computations they can trigger from the interactions they participate in (i.e., in UT 2003, objects manipulated by the native physics engine, Karma™, are defined as members of the class of "Karma™ objects"). The QP objects have several properties: i) they are associated with an event interception mechanism that attaches data-driven procedures for the recognition of the pre-conditions of QPs in which they can take part, ii) their properties can be defined through qualitative variables, which are the key variables defined within QP's and are involved in qualitative proportionalities and influence equations, iii) they are associated physical states that have a visual translation, including in terms of transitions between states (e.g. animations showing a recipient filling, a liquid evaporating, etc.). These states correspond to landmark values for the qualitative variables.

3   Qualitative Physics in Virtual Environments

Of the various approaches that have been described in qualitative physics, we have opted for Qualitative Process Theory (henceforth QPT) [6], essentially for its representational properties. QPT descriptions are centred on physical processes (e.g. liquid flows, heat transfer, etc.) whose states are described through the values of qualitative variables. We have given a brief introduction to this formalism in previous sections. In essence, relations between variables are described through influence equations and qualitative proportionalities. The former correspond to the actual dynamics of the process; for instance, that the amount of liquid in a recipient increases with the inflow. The latter maintain "static" relationships between variables, such as the fact that the mass of liquid in the container is proportional to its volume. The QPT formalism is well adapted to its integration in virtual environments, for several reasons: i) the explicit description of a QP's pre-conditions supports the definition of procedures activating the QP simulation from physical events involving objects in the virtual world. This is the basic mechanism for integration of QP's in the interactive environment, ii) The kind of causality associated with QP descriptions can be matched to user interventions, and iii) QPT has been successfully used to define ontologies with a significant number of processes, representing a whole subset of physical processes for a given world.

In terms of their actual implementation, pre-conditions are encoded in specific UnrealScript™ (the programming language of UT2003 serving as an API) procedures associated to the virtual world objects' in order to trigger the activation of relevant QPs. In that sense, pre-conditions are not strictly speaking part of the actual QP representation implemented. However, all the other elements of the QP representations; qualitative variables, qualitative proportionalities and influence equations are implemented within the QP engine. Their actual use by the engine during simulations is discussed in the following sections.

Figure 3 shows the behaviour of the system simulating the filling of a glass from a running tap. When objects, which can behave as recipients, are aligned with a liquid flow (here the beer tap), this, corresponding to the pre-condition of a filling process, activates the corresponding liquid-flow QP on these objects. The process running in the QP engine updates the value of the amount of water in the glass, through its influence equations. In a similar fashion, qualitative proportionalities update the total mass of the glass, as well as the height of liquid. These variables transform the state of the filling glass in the virtual world by updating its physical properties (e.g. weight) as well as its appearance. The overall dynamics is dictated by the QP simulation process, the speed of the filling glass animation being an approximation of these dynamics. The overall simulation remains interactive, and at any time, the user can remove the glass from the running tap, which will interrupt the process while retaining the physical properties of the glass (amount of water/beer filled into the glass).

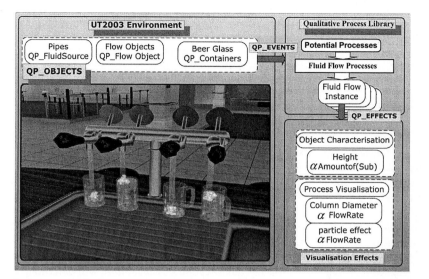

Fig. 3. Several Qualitative Processes operating simultaneously can be visualised in the virtual world.

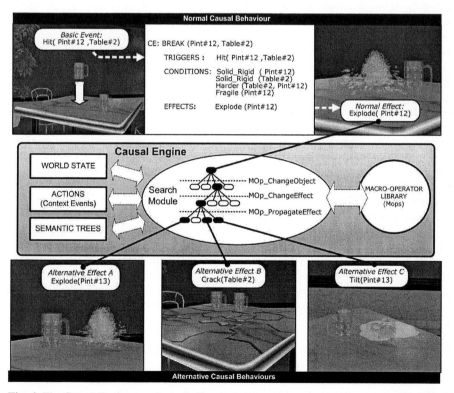

Fig. 4. The Causal Engine can dynamically generate new consequences for events taking place in the virtual world by inhibiting the default outcome and substituting it with alternative effects. It relies on semantic descriptions of the actions and objects involved.

A typical description of world behaviour contains many QP that can interact dynamically, so as to reflect the behaviour of complex systems or devices that would be difficult to model in an integrated fashion through numerical simulation.

4   Redefining the Laws of Causality

Causal Simulation normally relates one event occurring in the virtual world to its logical consequences. Causal simulation is a technique for generating behaviours using symbolic descriptions of causal chains relating physical events.
In that sense, qualitative physics, as introduced above, incorporates causality within the symbolic description of physical processes and the physical laws governing them.

However, if we consider the behaviour of a virtual world as the one *perceived* by human users rather than an absolute one, it should be characterised by the causal links attributed by the user to sequences of events. Hence, a mechanism that can generate event co-occurrences on a principled basis will elicit the perception of causal relations between these events. In return, the modification of causal laws will determine original virtual world behaviours.

This mechanism is implemented into a "causal engine", a system intercepting events in the virtual world and re-arranging their occurrence using specific knowledge about the desired behaviour of the virtual world [7]. The causal engine operates continuously through sampling cycles that are initiated by the occurrence of actions in the virtual world. Basically, the occurrence of events affecting world objects initiates a sampling cycle, during which the system recognises potential events and stores them while inhibiting their effects (it could be said that it "freezes" them). The causal engine then transforms these "frozen" events, by altering their effects, before re-activating them. This re-activation then initiates a new sampling cycle. The causal engine operates by recognising high-level events (introduced above as Context Events, or CE), whose semantic properties are used to generate new causal associations. These high-level events (such as breaking, filling, launching, etc.) are recognised from primitive events obtained from the graphics engine. For instance, the candidate CE for the glass breaking, is triggered by the glass hitting the table surface. This means that during a sampling cycle, a break(?glass) CE will be instantiated upon recognition of the hit(?table, ?glass) basic event, as the CE's conditions are satisfied. This CE will be the target for effects' modifications in the causal engine.

These modifications of CE's are carried out though the applications of specific knowledge structures, called Macro-Operators (Henceforth MOp). MOp use world knowledge (for instance on physical properties of objects) to modify appropriate CE's parameters. For instance, objects which should break up as an effect of the CE could be replaced by similar, "breakable", objects. We can illustrate the behaviour of the Causal Engine on a simple example. The test case we will consider is that of a glass being grasped, then dropped by the user for a certain height onto the surface of a table, which can also hold other objects, such as similar glasses. The default physical behaviour would consist for the glass to break on impact (Figure 4, top line), as would be directly encoded as an object behaviour in a Physics engine. Figure 4 represents several alternative behaviours. The default object of the break CE, i.e. the falling glass is substituted with the other glass standing on the table. The basis for this substitution being that the two objects are similar (actually identical), and in close spatial relation.

The resulting impression is depicted on Figure 4 (bottom line, left): the glass falls on the table and upon impact on the table, it is the adjacent glass which breaks up.

From the user's perspective, the normal cause-effect sequence is disrupted: the triggering event of a given CE, in this case the glass falling on a table, will be followed, not by its default consequence (e.g. the falling glass breaking), but by an alternative effect (e.g. a nearby glass breaking without being directly hit). The causal engine can generate multiple alternative behaviours for a given CE: in this example, the table can break rather than the falling glass (Figure 4, bottom line, centre), or the adjacent glass on the table could tilt, spilling its contents (Figure 4, bottom line, right). The causal engine can generate alternative cause-effects relationships for the complete set of events occurring in a virtual world, so as to redefine the overall physical behaviour experienced by the user.

5   Conclusion and Perspectives

We have presented a new approach to the implementation of virtual world's physical behaviour. This approach is based on the simulation of physical phenomena using symbolic computation rather than numerical integration. It uses established AI techniques, such as qualitative simulation as well as a novel approaches to explicit definition of laws of causality. This approach enables the description of the overall "laws of Physics" of a given world, supporting in particular the description of alternative laws of Physics. This simulation method is compatible with the operation of native Physics engines, which can still take charge on the non-discretised aspects of the simulation (e.g. object kinematics): in that sense, even as symbolic methods, they do not compromise the response time of the overall system.

Acknowledgements. This work has been supported in part by the European Commission through the ALTERNE project, IST-38575.

References

1. Lewis, M and Jacobson, Games Engines in Scientific Research. Communications of ACM, Vol. 45, No. I, pp. 27–31, 2002.
2. Jiang, H., Kessler, G.D and Nonnemaker, J. (2002). DEMIS: a Dynamic Event Model for Interactive Systems. ACM Virtual Reality Software Technology 2002, Hong Kong
3. Cavazza, M., Hartley, S., Lugrin J.-L. and Le Bras, M., Qualitative Physics in Virtual Environments, ACM Intelligent User Interfaces, pp. 54–61, 2004.
4. Fikes, R. E. and Nilsson, N. J., STRIPS: a new approach to the, application of theorem proving to problem solving. Artificial Intelligence, 2 (3-4), pp. 189–208, 1971.
5. Wilkins, D. E. (1988). Causal reasoning in planning. Computational Intelligence, vol. 4, no. 4, pp. 373–380.
6. Forbus, K.D., Qualitative Process Theory, Artificial Intelligence, 24, 1-3, pp. 85–168, 1984.
7. Cavazza, M., Lugrin, J.-L., Hartley, S., Libardi, P., Barnes, M.J. and Le Bras, M., 2004. ALTERNE: Intelligent Virtual Environments for Virtual Reality Arts. Smart Graphics 2004 Symposium, Banff, Canada, Lecture Notes in Computer Science vol. 3031, Springer Verlag.

Advanced Interaction Design

"*Kuru-kuru* Pitcher": A Game for the ^S_cha$_i$r^e Internet Chair

Kazuya Adachi, Michael Cohen, Uresh Duminduwardena, and Kayoko Kanno

Spatial Media Group, University of Aizu,
Aizu-Wakamatsu, Fukushima-ken 965-8580; Japan
{m5081101,mcohen,m5062101,s1090061}@u-aizu.ac.jp

Abstract. We have developed second-generation prototypes of the Internet Chair, a novel internet appliance. The first generation explored using the chair as an input device; "^S_cha$_i$r^e," the prototype described here, is a pivot (swivel, rotating) chair deployed as an output device, a rotary motion-platform information appliance. Its haptic display modality is yaw, dynamically synchronized with wireless visual displays and spatial audio in a rotation-invariant virtual space. In groupware situations— like teleconferencing, chat spaces, or multiplayer gaming— such orientation is also used to twist iconic representations of a seated user, avatars in a virtual world, enabling social situation awareness. Using its audio display modality, transaural speakers (without crosstalk), "nearphones" embedded in the seat headrest, the system can present unencumbered binaural sound with soundscape stabilization for multichannel sound image localization. As a haptic output modality, chairs with servomotors render kinesthetic and proprioceptive cues, twisting under networked control, to direct the attention of a seated subject, orienting seated users like a "dark ride" amusement park attraction or under active user control, local and/or distributed. The ^S_cha$_i$r^e, manifesting as personal LBE (location-based entertainment), can be used in both stand-alone and networked applications. We have developed a multiplayer game that exploits some unique features of our networked rotary motion-platform, loosely resembling a disk/disc access driver, in which "spindled" players race to acquire circularly arrayed dynamically arriving targets.

Keywords: {augmented, enhanced, hybrid, mediated, mixed} reality/virtuality, haptic interface, information furniture, location-based entertainment (LBE), motion platform, networked appliance, soundscape stabilization.

1 Introduction

There are more chairs in the world than windows, desks, computers, or telephones. According to a metric of person-hours used, and generalized to include couches, stools, benches and other seat furniture, the chair is the most popular tool on earth, with the possible exceptions of its cousin the bed, and eyewear. The Internet Chair[1] begins to exploit such ubiquity, as an instance of information furniture. The first generation explored using the chair as an input device [1]. (The introduction to that same

---

[1] www.u-aizu.ac.jp/~mcohen/spatial-media/IC/

M. Rauterberg (Ed.): ICEC 2004, LNCS 3166, pp. 35–45, 2004.

reference also surveys some instances of cybernetic chairs.) It determines which way a seated user is facing, adjusting dynamic maps and soundscape presentations accordingly. We have developed a second-generation prototype of our Internet Chair deployable as an output device, a motion-platform information appliance. Dubbed "Schaire" (and pronounced "schaire," for "share-chair"), our prototypes can twist under networked control, synchronized with panoramic visual displays and spatial audio for propriocentric consistency. Besides entertainment computing, this research belongs to fields variously described as or associated with calm technology" or "ubicomp" (for ubiquitous computing[2]), which containment hierarchy can be proposed as Table 2, driving displays at different scales, a taxonomy of which is shown in Table 1.

1.1 Soundscape Stabilization

The direction one's body is oriented differs from which way one's head is turned (a primary parameter for auditory directionalization), which in turn differs from which way one's eyes (and also often one's attention) point. Nevertheless, a system that tracks the orientation of a pivot (swivel, rotating) chair provides a convenient first-order approximation for all of these attributes. Informal experiments suggest that seated body tracking alone provides adequate parameterization of dynamic transfer function selection for auditory directionalization [6] while serving as a cue to others in groupware contexts (virtual conferences, concerts, and cocktail parties) about directed attention. The propriocentric sensation is linked with soundscape stabilization, invariance preserving the location of virtual sources under reorientation of the user for world-referenced spatial audio.

1.2 Social Situational Awareness

Gaze awareness is an understanding of the direction of another's attention [7,8]. Besides the usual reasons for turning around (to face an interesting direction), users can use rotation to disambiguate front→back sounds, for example, and to signal to other users a direction of regard. A networked chair can be linked to visual displays of virtual spaces, which iconify distributed users as avatars, as suggested by Table 4. Calibrating the Schaire to align real and virtual worlds amplifies natural situational awareness so, for example, teleconferees' voices can be directionalized to their actual location. With suitably acoustically transparent audio display, such signals can be registered with the actual environment for alignment of real and synthesized cues. In general, both an icon/avatar's visual presentation and audio manifestation are directionally dependent— icons by having non-symmetric attributes, and sources and sinks by being non-isotropic (non-omnidirectional). The multicast spinning of audio sources communicates to other users in a chat space, both visually and acoustically, as the loudness of non-omnidirectional sources changes when speakers face or turn away from sinks.

---

[2] www.didi.com/sorcerersapprentice

Table 1. Audio and visual displays along a private↔public continuum. The Schaire is an instance of the second row.

Proxemic Context	Architecture	Audio Display	Visual Display
Intimate	headset, wearable computer	*eartop* headphones, ear buds[3]	*eyetop* HWD (head-worn display) HMD (head-mounted display)
Individual	chair	nearphones	*laptop* display, *desktop* monitor
Interpersonal	couch or bench	transaural speakers (ex.: SDP [stereo dipole])	HDTV, "fishtank VR," VisionDome,[4] workbench
Multipersonal	automobile, spatially immersive display (Cave™, Cabin™)	surround sound (ex.: Ambisonics,[5] wave field synthesis)	projection
Social	club, theater "Reality Center"	speaker array (ex.: VBAP)	large-screen display CyberDome[6]
Public	stadium, concert arena	public address PSE with IMAX[7]	(ex.: Jumbotron)

Table 2. Ubicomp hierarchy— Saturated: distributed & pervasive, continuous & networked, transparent or invisible

smart spaces and aware environments
 cooperative buildings
  roomware (software for rooms) and reactive rooms
   media spaces
    immobots (immobile robots)
    spatially immersive displays
     information furniture
     networked appliances
      handheld/mobile/nomadic/portable/wireless/ambulatory
      wearable/intimate computing
       computational clothing (smart clothes)
       motes/smart dust (Pister)
        MEMS (microelectromechanical systems): "nanites"

---

[3] www.jabra.com/products/mobiles.htm
[4] www.elumens.com/produts/visiondome.html
[5] www.ambisonics.net
[6] www.mew.co.jp/cyberdome
[7] www.imax.com

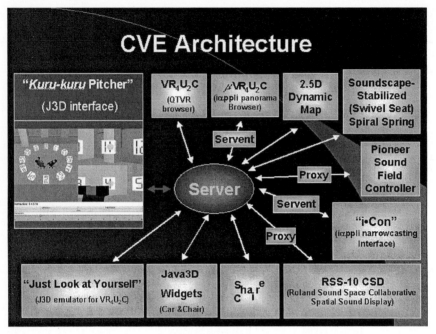

Fig. 1. CVE Architecture: groupware suite

2 Implementation: Session-Integrated Multimodal I/O Clients

We have designed and implemented an architecture and framework [9] to support a collaborative virtual environment (CVE), allowing distributed users to share multimodal virtual worlds. Our CVE architecture (as shown in Fig. 1) is based upon a client/server (C/S) model, and its main transaction shares the state of virtual objects and users (avatars) by effective multicast via replicated-unicast of position parameters to client peers in a session. The client/server architecture integrates multimodal control/display clients— including the haptic renderer, a spiral visualizer and intensity panner, and perspective renderer— described in the following subsections.

2.1 Azimuth-Display Output Modality

Our second-generation prototype, developed with partners Mechtec[8] and Yamagata University, features a powerful (with about 3–4 Newton·meters of torque, adjustable to limit maximum speed and force) servomotor for force display [11][12] and computer-mediated rotation of the chair— visceral sensation as it whirls around to direct the attention of a seated subject with adjustable insistence/forcefulness— like a "dark ride" amusement park attraction, or subtly nudging the user in a particular direction. As shown in Fig. 3, an arbitrary number of similarly equipped chairs can be net

---

[8] www.mechtec.co.jp

Table 3. Chair rotational degrees of freedom

DoF	Roll	Pitch	Yaw
Tumble	cartwheel	somersault	pirouette
Axis	back ↘ front	left ↔ right	up ↕ down
Chair	hammock 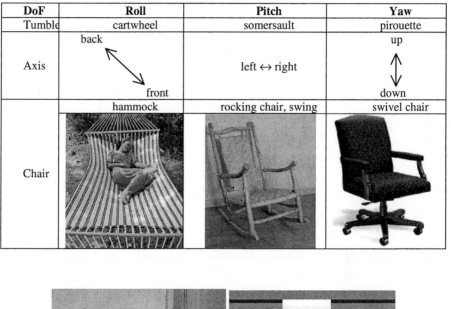	rocking chair, swing	swivel chair

Fig. 2. For its haptic output modality, servomotors render kinesthetic force display, rotating each Schaire under networked control. Note the nearphones straddling the headrest

worked, with application-determined distribution of cybernetic torque [13]. In practice, each Schaire uses two session channels, one to track its real time orientation and one to anticipate its rotational "target." (Details of the chair driver are the subject of a forthcoming article.)

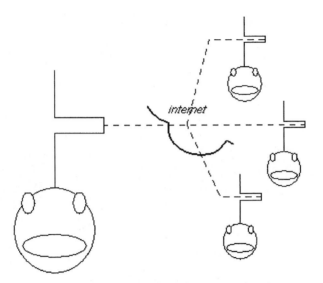

Fig. 3. Simplified concept: nearphone-equipped rotating seats exchanging torque via networked mutual tractor beams

2.2 S⁶ (Soundscape Stabilized Swivel-Seat Spiral-Spring): Spatial Audio Output Modality

We have developed interfaces for such a servomotor-equipped chair [14], one of which graphical instances is shown in Fig. 4. This GUI displays and controls the azimuth of the Schaire using a spiral spring metaphor, and also allows positioning of audio sources, directionalized from resident sound files or captured in realtime from analog streams. As an alternative to transaural loudspeakers (providing crosstalk-cancelled binaural cues), speaker arrays, and normal headphones, we are using "nearphones," external loudspeakers placed near but not on the ears, straddling the headrest of a chair: a hybrid of circumaural headphones (which block ambient sounds) and loudspeakers, as shown in Fig. 5.

Our groupware suite features other heterogeneous clients. Of particular relevance for the game described in the next section is a computer graphic rendering of a space, allowing various camera positions, including endocentric (1st person: from the point-of-view of the avatar), egocentric or tethered (2nd person: attached to but separate from the avatar), and exocentric (3rd person: totally detached from the avatar) perspectives [p. 125–147, 15]. For cable-less operation necessitated by the spinning chair, these clients run on laptop computers networked via Wi-Fi. (In our lab we use various Mac iBooks and Powerbooks with the AirPort[9] wireless option.)

---

[9] www.apple.com/airport

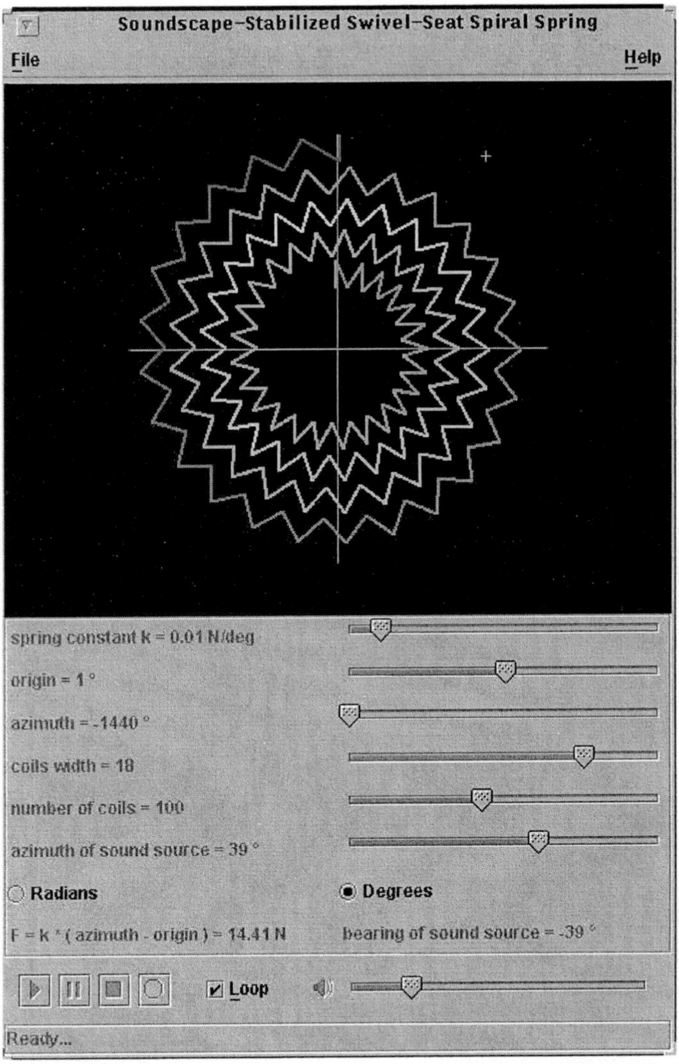

Fig. 4. Soundscape-stabilized spiral-spring swivel seat interface. A spiral spring metaphor is used to calculate restoration force delivered through a servomotor, and the yaw of the chair (as indicated by the total deflection of the spring) and azimuth of a virtual sound source (as indicated by the plus sign, set here at 0° (NW) are used to control intensity stereo panning for playback of audio files and streams. (Developed by Kenta Sasa and Shiyougo Ihara with Takashi Wada and extended by Newton Fernando with Dishna Wanasinghe.)

2.3 *Kuru-kuru* Pitcher Game: Graphical Output Modality and Input

We have developed a game called "*Kuru-kuru* Pitcher" featuring the ^s_cha^e_r motion platform, programmed using Java3D[10] [16] [17] [18]. ("*Kuru-kuru*" means "rotation" in Japanese.) Users seated in the Internet Chair shoot at blocks, arranged around the players like the hours a clock. (For example, the twelfth block is to the (logical) North, and the third block is to the East.) A software game manager streams instructions about which blocks should be targeted.

Players race to rotate their chairs, aiming at and shooting the targets, acquiring them in any order. The game's main graphical window includes three panes, as shown in Fig. 5. The left pane shows an exocentric view of both ^s_cha^e_rs; the right panes show egocentric views for both players. When the "Shoot" button is pushed, one's ball is pitched, which animation is displayed in the game windows (the yellow sphere). If one's ball hits a correct block, it disappears from the space (and displays) of both players.

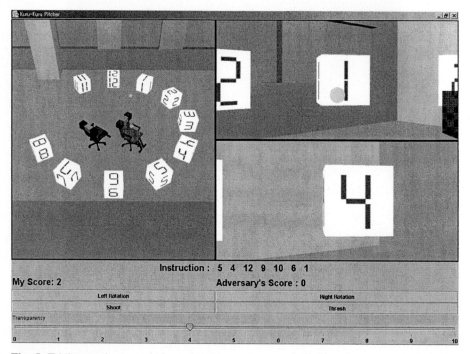

Fig. 5. Triple-paned game window, showing one exocentric (left) and two egocentric (right) views. The player has just pitched a yellow ball at a (missed) target, while the opponent has rendered his/her avatar semi-invisible (yielding the translucent occlusion seen in the bottom right of the top right pane).

---

[10] java.sun.com/products/java-media/3D/

Table 4. Hierarchy of (meta-)* simulation: If a real chair is thought of as a grounding "0th-order" simulation, our game can be thought of as combining 1st- and 2nd-order simulations— the 1st-order being the ^S_cha$_i$r^e which simulates a "real" chair, and the 2nd-order "metasimulation" being its virtual representation. A movie of a game session can be considered a 3rd-order "meta-metasimulation."

0th-order: Reality Real Chair	1st-order: Simulation ^S_cha$_i$r^e Internet Chair
2nd-order: Metasimulation Java3D model	3rd-order: Meta-metasimulation Time-slidable movie of meta-simulation

As a further situational cue to game state, each player's nearphones display music spatialized to the opponent's relative azimuth, using the "S^6" utility client described in the previous section. Mapping the twelve block positions to the twelve notes of a chromatic scale, we are experimenting with two styles of audio cues: playing the respective note as a rotating chair passes that azimuth, and spatializing a melody composed from the notes associated with the target blocks.

One's avatar transparency can be adjusted dynamically, to make one invisible, so that the opponent confronts a "ghost player." An exotic feature of our game is the ability of each player to swap positions with the other, using the "Thrash" button, naturally also swapping egocentric display panes on the right of the game window.

Even though the player chairs are shown adjacently in the game window, the coexistence is of course only virtual, as the chairs are in separate physical spaces. For instance, one can't shoot the other player. In this sense, then, the players can be said to inhabit separate but coextensive spaces. Player behavior can be likened to that of a disk/disc drive access algorithm, where the targets are circularly arrayed sectors of dynamically arriving page faults to access, and the players are the spindle. (The metaphor is limited, though, as there is no direct analog to our game's multiplayer competitive aspects, spatialized audio cues, transparency feature, or "Thrash"-swappable positions.) Strategy involves determining the most efficient acquisition order, in consideration of the other player and one's own position and motion, adjusted dynamically to accommodate newly arrived targets. The winner is the one with the most blocks at the end of a timed round.

3 Conclusion

Information furniture interpolates between the convenience of spatially immersive displays and the personalness of carried or worn interfaces. The ^S_cha$_i$r^e mediates between its occupant, a seatee, and information, networked multimedia, including real-time audio and data streams for groupware. Our game, platformed on the ^S_cha$_i$r^e rotary motion-platform, encourages propriocentric consistency, while allowing rejection of the perspective singularity characteristic of immersive systems. Its interface's multimodal, multiplayer features blur the distinction between endo-, ego-, and exocentric systems by integrating an egocentric audio display with fluid visual perspective control into inter-personal LBE that is literally sensational.

Acknowledgments. This research was supported in part by grants from the Gigabit Research Project and the Fukushima Prefectural Foundation for the Advancement of Science and Education.

References

1. Cohen, M.: The Internet Chair. IJHCI: Int. J. of Human-Computer Interaction 15 (2003) 297–311. Special Issue: Mediated Reality. ISSN 1044-7318.
2. Streitz, N.A., Siegel, J., Hartkopf, V., Konomi, S., eds.: Cooperative Buildings: Integrating Information, Organizations, and Architecture (CoBuild'99: Proc. of the Second Int. Wkshp.), Pittsburgh, Springer (LNCS 1670) (1999). ISBN 3-540-66596-X.
3. Lewis, T.: Information appliances: Gadget netopia. (IEEE) Computer (1998) 59–68. ISSN 0018-9162.
4. Mann, S.: Smart clothing: The wearable computer and wearcam. Personal Technologies 1 (1997) 21–27. ISSN 0949-2054 and 1433-3066.
5. Billinghurst, M., Starner, T.: Wearable devices: New ways to manage information. (IEEE) Computer 32 (1999) 57–64
6. Koizumi, N., Cohen, M., Aoki, S.: Japanese patent #3042731: Sound reproduction system (2000)
7. Ishii, H.: Translucent multiuser interface for realtime collaboration. IEICE Trans. on Fundamentals of Electronics, Communications and Computer Sciences (Special Section on Fundamentals of Next Generation Human Interface) E75-A (1992) 122–131. 0916-8508.
8. Ishii, H., Kobayashi, M., Grudin, J.: Integration of inter-personal space and shared workspace: Clearboard design and experiments. TOIS: ACM Trans. on Information Systems (Special Issue on CSCW'92) 11 (1993) 349–375
9. Kanno, T., Cohen, M., Nagashima, Y., Hoshino, T.: Mobile control of multimodal groupware in a distributed virtual environment. In Tachi, S., Hirose, M., Nakatsu, R., Takemura, H., eds.: Proc. ICAT: Int. Conf. on Artificial Reality and Tele-Existence, Tokyo: University of Tokyo (2001) 147—154. ISSN 1345-1278; sklab-www.pi.titech.ac.jp/~hase/ICATPHP/upload/39_camera.pdf; vrsj.t.u-tokyo.ac.jp/ic-at/papers/01147.pdf.
10. Cohen, M., Martens, W.L.: Spatial Media Research at the University of Aizu. JVRSJ: J. Virtual Reality Society of Japan 6 (2001) 52–57. ISSN 1342-6680; www.u-aizu.ac.jp/~mcohen/welcome/publications/spatial-media.ps.
11. Burdea, G.C.: Force and Touch Feedback for Virtual Reality. John Wiley & Sons, New York (1996). ISBN 0-471-02141-5.
12. Rosenberg, L.B.: A Force Feedback Programming Primer (for PC Gaming Peripherals Supporting I-Force 2.0 and Direct-X 5.0). (1997) www.force-feedback.com.
13. Brave, S., Ishii, H., Dahley, A.: Tangible interfaces for remote collaboration and communication. In: CSCW'98: Proc. Conf. on Computer-Supported Cooperative Work, Seattle, Washington, ACM (1998) 169–178. ISBN 1-58113-009-0.
14. Cohen, M., Sasa, K.: An interface for a soundscape-stabilized spiral-spring swivel-seat. In Kuwano, S., Kato, T., eds.: Proc. WESTPRAC VII: 7th Western Pacific Regional Acoustics Conf., Kumamoto, Japan (2000) 321–324. ISBN 4-9980886-1-0 and 4-9980886-3-7.
15. Barrilleaux, J.: 3D User Interfaces with Java 3D. Manning Publications (2001). ISBN 1-88477-790-2.
16. Sowizral, H., Rushforth, K., Deering, M.: The Java 3D API Specification. Second edn. Addison-Wesley (2000). ISBN 0-201-71041-2.
17. Palmer, I.: Essential Java 3D fast: developing 3D graphics applications. Springer (2001). ISBN 1-85233-394-4.
18. Walsh, A.E., Gehringer, D.: Java 3D API jump-start. Prentice-Hall (2002). ISBN 0-13-034076-6.

Fun and Sports: Enhancing the Home Fitness Experience

Wijnand IJsselsteijn[1], Yvonne de Kort[1], Joyce Westerink[2], Marko de Jager[2], and Ronald Bonants[2]

[1] Human-Technology Interaction Group, Department of Technology Management
Eindhoven University of Technology, P.O.Box 513, 5600 MB Eindhoven, The Netherlands
{w.a.ijsselsteijn,y.a.w.d.kort}@tue.nl
[2] Personal Care Institute, Philips Research Eindhoven
5656 AA Eindhoven, The Netherlands
{joyce.westerink,marko.de.jager}@philips.com

Abstract. The current paper describes research that is aimed to elucidate our understanding of technology factors that may help users of home exercise equipment to stay motivated for doing regular work-outs. In particular, we investigated the effects of immersion and coaching by a virtual agent on intrinsic motivation and the sense of presence of participants cycling on a stationary home exercise bike. A basic two-by-two within-subjects experimental design was employed whereby participants were presented with a virtual racetrack with two levels of immersion (high vs. low) and two levels of a virtual coach (with vs. without). Results indicate a clear positive effect of immersion on both motivation and presence. The virtual coach significantly lowered the perceived control and pressure/tension dimensions of intrinsic motivation, but did not affect the enjoyment dimension. The presence of the virtual coach also reduced negative effects associated with VEs.

1 Introduction

An object frequently encountered at yard sales, or gathering dust in the attic is the stationary exercise bike. This is most likely due to the fact that exercising on a stationary bike at home is usually quite boring. On the other hand, cycling outside can be time-intensive, uncomfortable (e.g. bad weather, smog), or even dangerous around places not well adapted to bikers. Thus, there appears to be a clear need for exercise equipment in the home that is more stimulating and more gratifying to use so that people's motivational levels will not plummet after the initial enthusiasm that led to the purchase of the exercise equipment has faded away.

The current study deals with the question whether virtual environments (VEs) and biofeedback presented via a virtual coach can help raise motivation for engaging in physical exercise. We hypothesized that offering a more immersive environment in which the user feels present would heighten the fun the user is having, and would thus have a beneficial effect on the user's motivation. Additionally, we expected that a virtual coach providing biofeedback information on training intensity, specifically heart rate, would increase the motivation as well, as it helps goal-setting and raises perceived control and competency, both of which help boost motivation.

M. Rauterberg (Ed.): ICEC 2004, LNCS 3166, pp. 46–56, 2004.
© IFIP International Federation for Information Processing 2004

1.1 Motivation

Motivation is the concept we use when we describe the forces acting on or within an organism to initiate and direct behavior (e.g. [1]). We usually discern between intrinsic and extrinsic motivation, where intrinsic motivation refers to engaging in an activity purely for the pleasure and satisfaction derived from doing the activity, whereas extrinsic motivation refers to engaging in a variety of behaviors as a means to an end and not for their own sake [2]. Intrinsic motivation is often considered more powerful and leading to more stable behaviour than extrinsic motivation and is highly relevant for sports. Below we will discuss how immersion and feedback are thought to influence intrinsic motivation.

1.2 Immersion and Presence

Slater & Wilbur [3] refer to immersion as the objectively measurable properties of a VE. According to them it is the "extent to which computer displays are capable of delivering an inclusive, extensive, surrounding, and vivid illusion of reality to the senses of the VE participant" (p. 604). Thus, immersion refers to the system's ability to shut out sensations from the real world, accommodating many sensory modalities with a rich representational capability, and a panoramic field of view and sound. Presence can be conceptualised as the experiential counterpart of immersion. It has been defined as the sense of 'being there' in a mediated environment (e.g. [4],[5]) and more recently as the "perceptual illusion of non-mediation" [6], which broadens the definitional scope somewhat, also including social factors.

Various empirical studies have demonstrated a positive effect of immersion factors on presence, including field of view, stereoscopic imagery, interactivity, pictorial realism, spatial audio, and haptic feedback [7-10]. Presence is generally considered a positive outcome of immersive environments, leading to engagement and more intense enjoyment. If presence could make fitness a more engaging and fun experience, this is likely to boost intrinsic motivation to train.

1.3 Biofeedback

The term biofeedback was originally used to describe laboratory procedures (developed in the 1940's) where trained research subjects were provided with information about their own brain activity, blood pressure, muscle tension, heart rate and other bodily functions that are normally not under our voluntarily control, with the purpose of exerting conscious control over them. Today, biofeedback is often used as a training technique in which people are taught to improve their health and performance by using signals from their own bodies.

In the current experiment, heart rate was measured and, based on this information, feedback was provided to the participant using a virtual social agent, who could either encourage participants to do better, tell them they were doing great, or tell them to slow down a little, if the heart rate became too high. In this way, the coach could both be an extrinsic motivator and at the same time provide feedback on the impact of the exercise. This information is likely to enhance the person's perceived control and competence and stimulates goal-setting and adherence: the information underlines the person's efforts and progress.

2 Method

2.1 Design

A basic two-by-two within-subjects experimental design was employed whereby participants were presented with two levels of Immersion (high vs. low) and two levels of Virtual coach (with vs. without).

2.2 Participants

Twenty-four employees of Philips participated in the study, none of whom engaged in frequent physical exercise. Male/female distribution was even; their average age was 41.3 years.

2.3 Equipment and Setting

The experiment was conducted in the HomeLab, at the Philips Research laboratories in Eindhoven, The Netherlands. HomeLab is a future home-simulation, a test laboratory that looks like a normal house and thus provides us with a relatively natural context in which to test the behaviour of the participants using the home fitness application. The experiment was conducted in a room, which was darkened for the purpose of the experiment to avoid bright sunlight unpredictably influencing the visibility of the screen. Participants were asked to seat themselves on a racing bicycle placed on a training system with variable resistance. The bicycle was placed in front of a wall-mounted screen on which the environment and the coach were projected with a beamer (see Figure 1).

Fig. 1. Composite photograph of the experimental setup, with the stationary racing bicycle placed in front of the wall-projected virtual environment. Participants' viewing distance was approximately 2.20m, with an image size of 1.60m by 1.10m.

You're heart rate is too low. Cycle faster.

Fig. 2. Immersive condition with virtual coach. Virtual environment generated by Tacx T1900 'i-magic' VR Trainer software. Virtual Coach kindly provided by Philips PDSL.

2.4 Stimuli

The high immersion condition showed a fairly detailed interactive computer-generated visualization of a person cycling on a racing bicycle through a landscape. Interaction with the environment took place via the handlebars (for direction) and biking velocity. The low immersion condition showed an abstract picture of a race-track in bird's eye view, with a dot indicating the position of the biker. Interaction with the environment was less rich since participants did not have to use the steer to stay on track, nor could they influence the velocity of the dot on the track (although most participants were not aware of this).

In the condition with virtual coach, an avatar-like female appeared every minute (see Figure 2). She gave feedback to the participant, based on heart-rate information measured with a special chest belt. In the condition without the virtual coach this image did not appear.

2.5 Dependent Variables

The main dependent measures were intrinsic motivation and presence. Motivation was measured using an existing, well-validated questionnaire, the Intrinsic Motivation Inventory (IMI), consisting of six subscales (interest/enjoyment – which is the most central one to motivation – perceived competence, value/usefulness, perceived control/choice, felt pressure and tension, and effort) [11]. For measuring presence various methods have been used or proposed to date (for a review, see [12]). The ITC Sense of Presence Inventory [13] provides sufficient sensitivity, while having proven reliability and validity. It consists of four subscales: spatial presence, engagement, ecological validity, and negative effects. Besides this, heart rate and velocity of the participant were also measured and recorded. The heart rate was used as input for the coach's directions; average speed was considered as a corroborative behavioural measure of motivation, since one would expect participants to work harder during their exercise when motivation is higher.

2.6 Procedure

Participants – in sports clothing – received a short introduction upon entering the exercise room. After putting on the chest belt for easy heart rate measurement, they mounted the bicycle for the first session. The total procedure consisted of four sessions, the order of which was fully counterbalanced. After every session participants filled out the IMI and ITC-SOPI, which also gave them 10 minutes to recover from their exercise. The total experiment took about 1.5 hours to complete.

3 Results

For both the ITC-Sense of Presence Inventory (ITC-SOPI) and the Intrinsic Motivation Inventory (IMI), components were computed based on the factor structures that were validated in earlier studies. Subsequently, repeated measures analyses of variance (REMANOVA) were performed on these components according to the full model, with Immersion (high vs. low) and Coach (with vs. without) as independent within factors. Results will be reported for intrinsic motivation components first, then for presence. Lastly we will report bivariate correlations between the various components.

3.1 Intrinsic Motivation

The six IMI components were all subjected to full model REMANOVAs. Four scales (interest/enjoyment, perceived competence, value/usefulness, and perceived control) showed significant effects of Immersion: all scores were higher for high immersion. These last two scales also showed a significant effect of the virtual coach, as did the pressure/tension scale: value/usefulness was higher, perceived control and pressure were lower with the coach present. Finally, the effort/importance scale did not show any significant results. Means of the most important scales are visualized in Figures 3-5 and reported in Table 1; statistics are reported in Table 2.

Average velocity was used as a corroborative behavioural measure of motivation. Indeed velocity scores showed the same pattern of results as the questionnaire data did. There was a main effect of Immersion $F(1,23)=65.73$, p<.001, with average speed higher in the high (v=23.8 km/h) vs. low (v=20.6 km/h) immersion condition. The virtual coach had no significant effects.

Table 1. Means of motivation components

	Immersion low		Immersion high	
	without coach	with coach	without coach	with coach
interest/enjoyment	3.30	4.17	4.98	4.88
perceived competence	3.95	4.14	4.40	4.35
value/usefulness	4.29	4.75	4.92	5.23
perceived control	3.98	4.11	5.10	4.04
pressure/tension	4.15	3.84	4.77	3.18
effort/importance	4.01	4.23	4.19	4.42

Table 2. Repeated measures analyses of variance of motivation components (IMI)

	Immersion		Coach		Imm xCoach	
	F	p	F	p	F	p
interest/enjoyment	29.14	**.00**	0.30	.59	1.49	.23
perceived competence	7.69	**.01**	0.68	.42	0.09	.77
value/usefulness	9.01	**.01**	6.61	**.02**	0.09	.77
perceived control	22.07	**.00**	37.41	**.00**	1.70	.21
pressure/tension	3.89	.06	21.78	**.00**	2.93	.10
effort/importance	1.17	.29	3.85	.06	0.09	.77

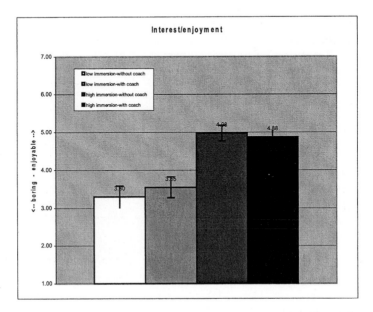

Fig. 3. Means and standard errors of Interest/Enjoyment component of the IMI, for all experimental conditions

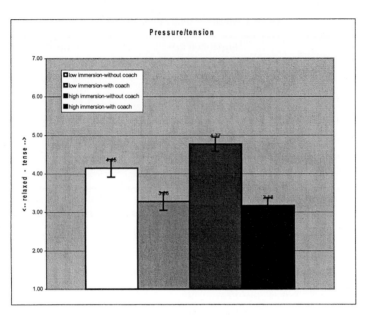

Fig. 4. Means and standard errors of Pressure/Tension component of the IMI, for all experimental conditions

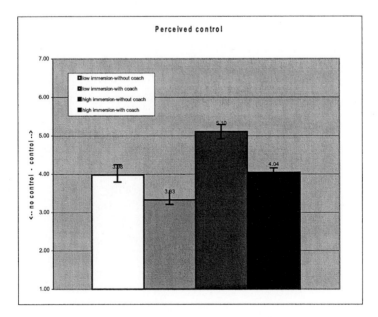

Fig. 5. Means and standard errors of Perceived Control component of the IMI, for all experimental conditions

3.2 Presence

Secondly, four separate REMANOVAs were performed with the components of presence (spatial presence, engagement, ecological validity, and negative effects) as dependent variables. Three components showed strong and highly significant effects of Immersion, indicating that spatial presence, engagement, and ecological validity were higher for high Immersion. The effect on the 'negative effects' subscale was smaller, but also significant. This component also showed a significant effect of Coach, as did spatial presence; participants reported more presence and less negative effects in the condition with the virtual coach present. No significant interactions were found. Means are visualized in Figures 6-9, results of the ANOVAs are reported in Table 3.

Table 3. Repeated measures analyses of variance of presence components (ITC-SOPI)

	Immersion		Coach		Imm xCoach	
	F	p	F	p	F	p
spatial presence	72.22	**.00**	9.45	**.01**	1.66	.21
engagement	90.20	**.00**	2.62	.12	2.85	.11
ecological validity	68.08	**.00**	1.53	.23	0.45	.51
negative effects	4.16	**.05**	13.49	**.00**	0.38	.54

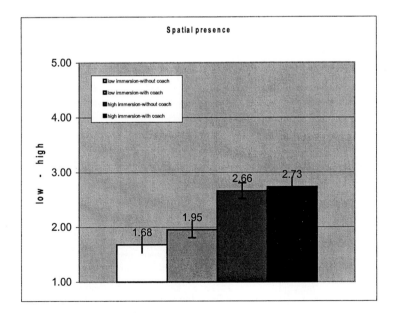

Fig. 6. Means and standard errors of Spatial Presence component of the ITC-SOPI, for all experimental conditions

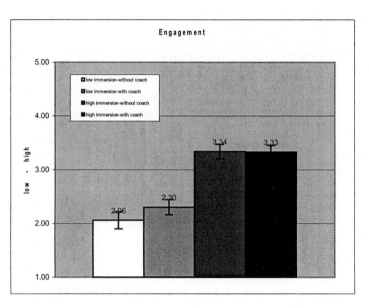

Fig. 7. Means and standard errors of Engagement component of the ITC-SOPI, for all experimental conditions

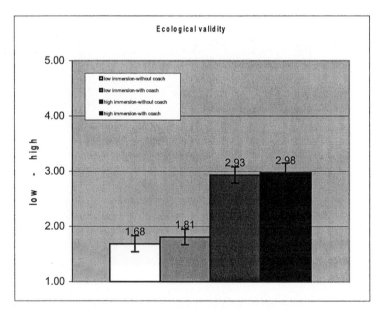

Fig. 8. Means and standard errors of Ecological Validity component of the ITC-SOPI, for all experimental conditions

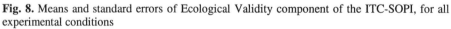

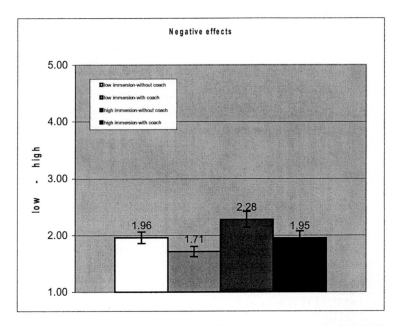

Fig. 9. Means and standard errors of Negative Effects component of the ITC-SOPI, for all experimental conditions

3.3 Correlations Between Motivation and Presence

We were also interested in testing relationships between the various components of motivation and presence. For this reason, bivariate correlations were computed. Space does not allow full coverage of all results. In summary we found considerable correlations between the motivation scales interest/enjoyment, perceived competence, value/usefulness, and perceived control (.39-.69, p<.01), high correlations between presence scales – spatial presence, engagement, and ecological validity (.77-.84, p<.001), and some moderate but significant correlations between presence components (spatial presence, engagement and ecological validity) on one hand and motivation components (interest/enjoyment, perceived control, pressure/tension) on the other (.24-.71, p<.05).

4 Discussion

The results of this study show that offering a more immersive environment in which the user feels present heightens the fun the user is having, and thus has a beneficial effect on the user's motivation. In the highly immersive environment, where the presence experience was stronger, participants reported more interest and enjoyment, more perceived competence and control and – perhaps even more importantly – they cycled faster! Additionally, we found some effects of the virtual coach providing biofeedback information, but not quite what we expected. Training intensity was not influenced and enjoyment was not higher with the coach. This could be attributed to the fact that the coach may act more as an extrinsic motivator than as an intrinsic one. The presence of the coach did lower perceived pressure and tension, which is good, and also perceived control. This last finding is somewhat striking since one would expect control to increase with feedback. Perhaps receiving directions regarding the intensity of your workout counteracted this effect. In future studies we hope to disentangle these effects further and continue our efforts to improve the home fitness experience.

References

1. Petri, H. (1981). Motivation: Theory and Research. Belmont, CA: Wadsworth Publishing Company.
2. Deci, E. L. (1975). Intrinsic motivation. New York: Plenum Press.
3. Slater, M. & Wilbur, S. (1997). A Framework for Immersive Virtual Environments (FIVE): Speculations on the Role of Presence in Virtual Environments. Presence: Teleoperators and Virtual Environments 6, 603–616.
4. Heeter, C. (1992). Being there: The subjective experience of presence. Presence: Teleoperators and Virtual Environments 1, 262–271.
5. Steuer, J. (1992). Defining Virtual Reality: Dimensions determining telepresence. Journal of Communication, 44 (2), 73–93.
6. Lombard, M. & Ditton, T. B. (1997). At the heart of it all: The concept of presence. Journal of Computer-Mediated Communication, 3(2). Available online at http://www.ascusc.org/jcmc/ vol3/issue2/lombard.html
7. Hendrix, C., & Barfield, W. (1996a). Presence within virtual environments as a function of visual display parameters. Presence: Teleoperators and Virtual Environments 5, 274–289.
8. Hendrix, C., & Barfield, W. (1996b).The sense of presence within auditory virtual environments. Presence: Teleoperators and Virtual Environments 5, 290–301.
9. Welch, R.B., Blackmon, T.T., Liu, A., Mellers, B.A., & Stark, L.W. (1996). The effects of pictorial realism, delay of visual feedback and observer interactivity on the subjective sense of presence. Presence: Teleoperators and Virtual Environments 5, 263–273
10. IJsselsteijn, W.A., de Ridder, H., Freeman, J., Avons, S.E. & Bouwhuis, D. (2001). Effects of stereoscopic presentation, image motion and screen size on subjective and objective corroborative measures of presence. Presence: Teleoperators and Virtual Environments 10, 298–311.
11. Intrinsic Motivation Inventory, (retrieved on 01-10-2003): http://www.psych.rochester.edu/SDT/measures/word/IMIfull.doc
12. IJsselsteijn, W.A., de Ridder, H., Freeman, J. & Avons, S.E. (2000). Presence: Concept, determinants and measurement. Proceedings of the SPIE 3959, 520–529.
13. Lessiter, J., Freeman, J., Keogh, E., & Davidoff, J. (2001). A cross-media presence questionnaire: The ITC–Sense of Presence Inventory. Presence: Teleoperators and Virtual Environments 10, 282–297.

Manipulating Multimedia Contents with Tangible Media Control System*

Sejin Oh and Woontack Woo

GIST U-VR Lab, Gwangju 500-712, South Korea
{sejinoh,wwoo}@gist.ac.kr

Abstract. We propose Tangible Media Control System (TMCS), which allows users to manipulate media contents with physical objects in an intuitive way. Currently, most people access digital media contents by exploiting GUI. However, it provides limited manipulations of the media contents. The proposed system, instead of mouse and keyboard, adopts two types of tangible objects, i.e. RFID-enabled object and tracker-embedded object. The TMCS enables users to easily access and control digital media contents with the tangible objects. In addition, it supports an interactive media controller which can be used to synthesize media contents and generate new media contents according to users' taste. It also offers personalized contents, which is suitable for users' preferences, by exploiting context such as a user's profile and situational information. Accordingly, the TMCS demonstrates that a tangible interface with context can provide more effective interface to fulfill users' satisfaction. Therefore, the proposed system can be applied to various interactive applications such as multimedia education, entertainment and multimedia editor.

1 Introduction

With rapid development of computing technologies, various media contents (e.g. music, image, graphic and movie, etc) are now available in the form of digital contents which can be accessed through computers. Thus, use of media contents has increased and they play an important role as entertainments in our daily life. However, many people still have difficulties in using the digital media contents even though Graphical User Interface (GUI) mitigates the problem to some extent. Especially, the elderly, who are not familiar with computers, feel uncomfortable while manipulating digital media contents with keyboard and mouse. Moreover, the GUI is not convenient enough to let users enjoy digital media contents and to manipulate the media contents according to their taste in the space of daily life, such as living room. Recently, in order to overcome such inconveniences, Tangible User Interface (TUI) [1] has been proposed as a new kind of interface since TUI allows users to intuitively control digital information by using physical objects.

Ishii et al.[1] proposed Tangible Bits, which allows users to present and control digital information by using elements existing in everyday life, such as sound, light, airflow and movement of water. For example, MusicBottle[2] and genieBottles [3]

---

* This work was supported in part by GIST and in part by MIC through ITRC at GIST.

M. Rauterberg (Ed.): ICEC 2004, LNCS 3166, pp. 57–67, 2004.

use glass bottles as interface for playing music or telling a story. They link digital media contents to physical glass bottles and exploit the human sense of touch. MusiCocktail [4] allows users to blend various kinds of music in the way they mix their beverages. Musical Trinkets [5] provides users with physical objects, e.g. dolls and finger rings, to play several music pieces and insert effective sounds. It allows users to generate synthesized music by using their hands. BlockJam[6] allows users to create as well as to control the tempo of the music by assembling blocks or exploiting several buttons onto the blocks. These applications provide users with an interactive music player and entertainment factors. However, they are limited in achieving users' satisfaction since they offer same media contents to all the users in same way without considering users' taste.

In order to improve the current TUI, we propose TMCS (Tangible Media Control System), which combines the concept of TUI with RFID tag [7] and tracker. The TMCS allows users to intuitively manipulate media contents by using tangible objects, such as CD, doll, etc, which are physical objects with RFID tags and a tracker. In addition, it offers personalized contents according to the implicit context, e.g. a user's profile or situational information using ubi-UCAM (a Unified Context-aware Application Model) [8]. The proposed system consists of three key components; tangible objects, context recognizer and media controller. Tangible objects, physical objects with RFID tags and a tracker, provide an intuitive interface to users. Context recognizer creates context [9] of a user and tangible objects; and media controller allows users to manipulate the media contents.

The proposed TMCS has following advantages. It provides novice computer users with an intuitive interface for media contents. Thus they can easily access and control digital media contents with tangible objects. In addition, it offers an adequate environment for users' satisfactions, by providing personalized contents according to users' preference. Furthermore, it enhances entertainment value of media contents since it allows users to naturally manipulate media contents according to their taste. Consequently, TMCS can be applied to various applications in the fields of interactive training, entertainment, education, media editing, etc.

This paper is organized as follows. In Chap 2, we describe architecture of the proposed TMCS, and in Chap 3, we show the implementation of TMCS. In Chap 4, we illustrate experimental set up and results about usefulness of the proposed system. Finally, we discuss the future works in Chap 5.

2   TMCS: Tangible Media Control System

As shown in Fig. 1, the proposed TMCS consists of three key components; Tangible objects, context recognizer and media controller. Tangible objects offer an intuitive interface for accessing and manipulating media contents. Context recognizer senses any changes in environment and creates contexts of users and tangible objects from the sensed signal. Media controller provides different media contents according to users' preferences and allows users to manipulate and synthesize the contents.

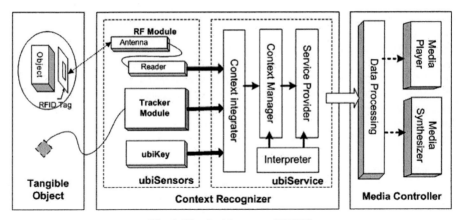

Fig. 1. The Architecture of TMCS

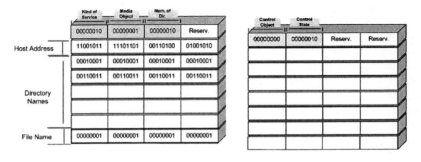

(a) Media object   (b) Control object

Fig. 2. The Memory of RFID tag in Tangible Object

2.1 Tangible Object

Tangible object links a physical object to digital media contents and allows users to easily access the digital contents by using the object. Additionally it offers an intuitive interface for natural manipulation of the media contents according to users' taste. It has two types of tangible objects, i.e. Media object and Control object.

Media object provides users with an intuitive interface for accessing digital media contents by using a physical object, which is commonplace in our daily life. Each object has an RFID tag. As shown in Fig. 2 (a), the RFID tag contains URL information of media contents. The contained information consists of the number of directories, a host address storing the digital media contents, metadata of directory and file, etc. Therefore, without knowing the explicit URL of the media contents, users can easily access digital media contents through the media object.

Control object allows users to naturally manipulate digital media contents in accordance with users' preferences through their hands. It has two types of objects; one is RFID-enabled object, and the other is tracker-embedded object. As shown in Fig. 2(b), the RFID tag attached to an RFID-enabled object contains control state information of a convenient media player. By rotating the RFID-enabled control object, users can control digital media contents, e.g. Play, Pause, Stop, Fast forward, Rewind, and Increase/Decrease Volume. On the other hand, a tracker-embedded control object is embedded with a tracker to a physical object. It also creates commands to execute complex manipulation of media contents, e.g. generating new music pieces, and changing musical instruments or note, according to changes of parameters of the tracker. Therefore, users can manipulate media contents naturally by using the two kinds of control object.

2.2   Context Recognizer

Context recognizer creates a meaningful context from sensed signals and translates it to an appropriate context for media controller. It consists of ubiSensor, an intelligent sensor that generates a preliminary context from sensed signals; and ubiService, an application that integrates the preliminary contexts to generate a final context.

ubiSensor senses changes in environment and generates a preliminary context in the form of 5W1H (Who, What, Where, When, How, Why). It consists of RF module, tracker module and ubiKey. The RF module reads data from an RFID tag of tangible object, e.g. URL information of media object or control state information of control object, and then creates a preliminary context for the tangible object. The Tracker module also detects changes of 6 parameters of tracker, and then generates a preliminary context of tracker-embedded control object by interpreting values of these parameters. Similarly, ubiKey creates a preliminary context of a user from his or her profile stored in the ubiKey. Table 1 shows the preliminary context created by each ubiSensor.

Table 1. The preliminary Context of ubiSensors

ubiSensor	Context (5W1H)	Context Information
RF module	What	Metadata of Directory and file name
	Where	Server IP address
	How	Control state information
Tracker module	What	Musical instrument / note/octave
	How	Control state information
ubiKey	Who	User name
	When	Entrance time

ubiService efficiently integrates preliminary contexts generated by ubiSensors. In addition, it creates an integrated context reflecting the user's intention as well as explicit commands. As shown in Fig.3, it consists of Context Integrator, Interpreter, Context Manager and Service Provider. Context Integrator collects preliminary contexts from RF module, Tracker module and ubiKey. Then, it computes "why" data representing a user's intention and creates an integrated context. Interpreter provides an interface to let users define context conditions and functions that must be executed according to the conditions. Context Manager creates a final context, which is suitable

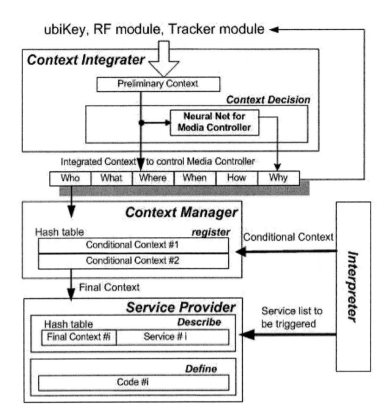

Fig. 3. The Data Flow between components of ubiService

for a media controller, according to context conditions defined by users. Service Provider executes the specified module of media controller according to the final context and the context condition. Fig. 3 shows data flow between the four components.

2.3 Media Controller

Media controller offers personalized contents, i.e. provides different media contents in accordance with users' preferences. It also allows users to control or manipulate the media contents according to their taste. It is composed of data processing module, media player and media synthesizer.

Data processing module analyzes final contexts generated by context recognizer. It extracts user's information and control state information or generates URL of digital media contents. In order to generate URL of digital media contents, it extracts IP address of digital media contents server from the final context. Then it accesses database of the server. It also finds substantial directory and file name by exploiting metadata of directory and file in final context. Finally, it combines them and then completes the URL of digital media contents.

Media player supports a simple control according to analyzed data by data processing module. Thus, it retrieves digital media contents by using the URL generated from data processing module. It also allows users to control the media contents according to control state information related to playing (e.g. Play, Stop, Pause, Fast forward, Rewind) and related to volume(e.g. Increase/Decrease Volume).

Media synthesizer provides an interactive environment which enables flexible manipulation of digital media contents according to users' taste, e.g. mixing several media contents, inserting sound effects and so on. Additionally, it allows users to change musical instruments, note and octave of the instrument. Furthermore, it provides users with "history service". That is, media synthesizer maintains a log of manipulation, such as media contents, selected musical instruments and note, etc. Then it analyzes user's preferences such as preferred musical instruments or media contents. When the user accesses it later, it provides personalized media contents and musical instruments according to the user's preferences. Therefore, it offers an environment which can efficiently satisfy user's expectations.

3 Implementation

As shown in Fig. 4, the proposed TMCS is installed in ubiHome, a test-bed of home appliances for ubiquitous computing. In order to allow users to experience TMCS in a smart home environment, RF module and Tracker module are attached under a table in a living room. Thus, users can naturally interact with digital media contents while sitting on a sofa. Additionally, it provides an environment where users can experience the results of manipulation through TV and speakers in living room.

As shown in Fig. 5(a), the Media object, one of tangible objects, is embedded with an RFID tag (Texas Instrument's [10] transponder, RI-I01-110A) to physical objects, such as CD, picture, doll, etc. Thus, digital media contents are automatically retrieved when users put the object onto the table. As shown in Fig. 5(b), the Control object, the

Fig. 4. Set up in ubiHome

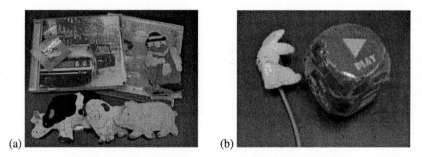

Fig. 5. Tangible Object (a) Media object (b) Control object

other kind of tangible objects, can be implemented in two ways; an RFID-enabled object and a tracker-embedded object. An RFID-enabled object attaches an RFID tag, which contains control state information, and a picture to each side of cube. The picture depicts control state information contained in the RFID-tag on opposite side of cube. Through the attached picture, users can easily know and select a control command. Additionally, as soon as a user puts the RFID-enabled object, with a picture representing the desired command, onto the table, the related control function is executed. A tracker-embedded object is embedded with a tracker to a doll which is easy to use. Thus, a user can manipulate media contents, such as various musical instruments or MIDI sounds, by weaving or rotating the object.

As shown in Figure 6, ubiSensors of the proposed TMCS consist of RF module, Tracker module and ubiKey. RF module is implemented by using RFID system of Texas Instrument (S6000 Reader/Antenna Set R1-K01-320A) and the Tracker module uses ISOTRACK II of Polhemus[11]. In addition, the ubiKey is implemented by exploiting USB Flash Drive 16MB.

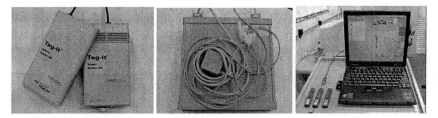

Fig. 6. ubiSensors (a)RF module (b)Tracker module (c) ubiKey

As shown in Fig. 7, Media Controller is implemented by using JDK 1.4 and JMF (Java Media Framework)[12] 2.1.1. Thus it supports various formats of digital media contents (e.g. wav, avi, mpeg, qt, etc) and MIDI. In addition, a Compag ML 370 Server (Pentium III 1G, Dual/IGB DRAM) manages media contents and MS-SQL 2000 Server is used as database to store information related to media contents.

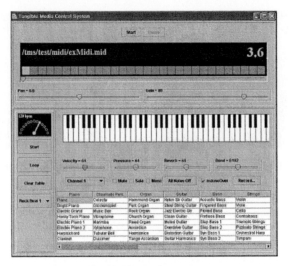

Fig. 7. Media Controller

Fig. 8. SONAR

4   Experiments and Results

To evaluate usefulness of the proposed system, we compared the TUI-based TMCS with the GUI-based SONAR [13]. As shown in Fig. 8, SONAR is a MIDI Synthesizer that needs mouse and keyboard for retrieving digital media contents, and selecting or playing musical instruments. In order to ensure an unbiased comparison between TMCS and SONAR, subjects used both two systems in ubiHome. Then, we performed qualitative and quantitative comparison between the two systems. 20 subjects participated in this experiment. One half (group A) of the subjects were in fifties, and not familiar with computers, while the other half (group B) were in twenties, with a good knowledge of computers. Though the number of subjects is not sufficient, we believe that evaluation results show a tendency at least.

4.1 The Qualitative Comparison

To qualitatively compare the TMCS with the SONAR, 20 subjects used each system and then we surveyed their satisfaction over the range from 0% (dissatisfaction) to 100% (satisfaction). It showed how much subjects were satisfied with the control method, media contents and services provided by each system. Table 2 shows the satisfaction for TMCS and SONAR.

Table 2. The satisfaction for TMCS and SONAR

	Elder group (A)		Younger group (B)	
	SONAR	TMCS	SONAR	TMCS
Control	29.5 %	84.5 %	68.5 %	74.5 %
Contents	68.0 %	83.5 %	70.0 %	75.0 %
Service	58.0 %	75.0 %	73.0 %	76.0 %

Since most subjects of Group 'A' were not familiar with computers, they faced difficulties in controlling digital media contents by using mouse and keyboard. Thus they showed low satisfaction (29.5%) for control method of SONAR. However, they expressed high satisfaction (84.5%) towards TMCS because they could naturally move their hands to control media contents with tangible objects. In addition, they expressed more satisfaction for TMCS (83.5%) than for SONAR (68%) since it provides different media contents according to their taste. Though two systems allow subjects to synthesize several media contents or modify the media contents, they were more satisfied with TMCS (75%) than with SONAR (58%). Therefore, through the results of group 'A', we found that they used tangible objects more easily than mouse and keyboard, and showed more satisfaction for TUI-based TMCS than GUI-based SONAR.

In case of Group 'B', younger subjects showed higher satisfaction about control method for TMCS (74.5%) than for SONAR (68.5%). This is because TMCS allows subjects to intuitively access media contents by using tangible objects without any information of the media contents. As group 'A', they were also more satisfied with the personalized contents provided by TMCS (75%) than contents of SONAR (70%). They showed slightly higher satisfaction for those services offered by TMCS (76%) than provided by SONAR (73%). Especially, they expressed higher contentment for natural interaction through tangible object when they manipulated media contents by using both systems.

As a result, subjects generally showed more satisfaction for the proposed TUI-based TMCS than for GUI-based SONAR. Most subjects were satisfied that they could naturally manipulate digital media contents by using tangible objects. They also expressed high satisfaction about providing personalized adaptive contents according to their taste and preference.

4.2 The Quantitative Comparison

To quantitatively compare the TMCS with SONAR, we measured learning time, selection time and control time. Learning time was the time taken by 20 subjects to learn how to use each system. Selection time was the time spent while selecting media contents. It was measured until digital media contents were actually displayed on a monitor or a TV. We also measured control time to manipulate keyboard and mouse or control objects for controlling digital media contents. Table 3 shows the average of each time for TMCS and SONAR.

Table 3. The learning /selection /control time for TMCS and SONAR

	Elder group (A)		Younger Group (B)	
	SONAR	TMCS	SONAR	TMCS
Learning time	801 sec	369 sec	100 sec	36 sec
Selection time	366.7sec	4.1 sec	25.6 sec	3.4 sec
Control time	99.4 sec	2.1 sec	2.0 sec	1.6 sec

As shown in Table 3, group 'A' took more than 13 minutes (801 seconds) to learn how to use SONAR. On the other hand, it took those about 6 minutes (369 seconds) to know how to use TMCS. Additionally, since most subjects of group 'A' made repeated mistakes while using keyboard and mouse, it took them more than 6 minutes (366.7 seconds) to select digital media contents. They also spent about 99 seconds to control digital media contents. In case of TMCS, since subjects could select digital media contents only by placing media objects onto a table, it took those about 4 seconds to do the task. They also spent about 2 seconds to manipulate digital media contents by using the control object. Through these results, we found that the proposed TMCS provides an effective interface to those who are not familiar with keyboard or mouse, such as the subjects of group 'A'.

In case of Group 'B', younger subjects took about 100 seconds to learn how to use SONAR. As shown in Table 3, their learning period for TMCS (26.5seconds) was much shorter than that for SONAR. Though most subjects of Group 'B' were familiar with computer, selection time for SONAR (36 seconds) was longer than that for TMCS (3.4 seconds). This was because they had to input URL of digital media contents with keyboard or mouse. However, there is little difference between control times of both systems, so the subjects did not observe much variation.

Therefore, the proposed TMCS offered more efficient methods for selecting and controlling digital media contents than SONAR. Most subjects spent less time to select and control media contents with TMCS than with SONAR. This is because TMCS allows subjects to easily access digital media contents without knowing URL of the media contents. By comparing learning times, we conclude that was easier to learn how to use TMCS than SONAR.

5 Conclusions

The proposed TMCS provides a TUI-based interface by using tangible objects such as CD, picture, doll, etc. Accordingly, the TMCS provides a convenient and an intuitive interface for users to easily access and manipulate digital media contents in smart home environment. It offers personalized contents to a user by utilizing contexts of both a user and his or her environment .The proposed system also provides an interactive environment in which users can manipulate digital media contents according to the their taste. Thus, the proposed system can be applied to various applications such as interactive education, entertainment and media editor. For the future works, we have a plan to do further qualitative analysis with more subjects, and then to improve the current design of tangible objects. Moreover, we intend to make "container" object which will enable users to store and carry the media contents.

References

1. Ishii, H., and Ullmer, B. Tangible Bits: Toward Seamless Interface between People, Bits and Atoms. Proc. CHI'97, 173–179
2. Ishii, H., Mazalek, A., and Lee, J. Bottles as a Minimal Interface to Access Digital Information. Ext. Abstract CHI 2001, ACM Press, 187–188
3. Mazalek, A., Wood, A., and Ishii, H. genieBottles: An Interactive Narrative in Bottles. SIGGRAPH'01, 189
4. Mazalek, A., Jehan, and Tristan. Interacting with Music in a Social Setting. Proc. CHI 2000, ACM Press (2000).
5. Paradiso, A. J., Hsiao, K., and Benbasat, A. Tangible Music Interface Using Passive Magnetic Tags. CHI 2001, ACM Press (2000).
6. Newton-Dunn, H., Nakano, H., and Gibson, J. Block Jam: A Tangible Interface for Interactive Music. Proc. NIME'03, 170–177.
7. Want, R., Fishkin, P. K., Gujar, A., Harrison, L. B. Bridging Physical and Virtual Worlds with Electronic Tags. Proc. CHI'99, 370–377, 1999
8. Jang, S., Woo, W. ubi-UCAM: A Unified Context-aware Application Model for ubiHome. Context'03, 2003
9. Anind, K.D. Understanding and using context. Personal and Ubiquitous computing, 2001
10. Texas instrument http://www.ti.com/tiris/
11. ISOTRACK II http://www.est-kl.com/hardware/tracking/polhemus/isotrakii.html
12. JMF http://java.sun.com/products/java-media/jmf
13. SONAR http://www.cakewalk.com/Products/SONAR/default.asp

"Tangible Influence": Towards a New Interaction Paradigm for Computer Games

Marco Vala, Ana Paiva, and Rui Prada

IST-Technical University of Lisbon and INESC-ID
Av. Prof. Cavaco Silva, IST, Taguspark, 2780-990 Porto Salvo , Portugal
{ana.paiva,marco.vala,rui.prada}@inesc-id.pt

Abstract. As AI techniques become more widespread in computer games, and the area of synthetic characters matures, avatars in such computer games also tend to gain autonomy and become more clever. However, this autonomy may bring also some change in the interaction between users and game characters. Players may become less in charge of their characters and lose the power of complete motion or behavior control. On the other hand, characters may become more clever exhibiting much more interesting autonomous actions and behaviors. This paper presents, defines and discusses the concept of *"influence"*, as an alternative to "direct" control of game characters, describing how influence can be achieved in computer games. To illustrate the notion of *" influence"* we will present a game called FantasyA where players interact with it by influencing the emotions of they semi-autonomous avatars using a tangible interface called SenToy. We show how *"influence"* was built into this game, the role of SenToy as an influencing device, and the reactions of the users to this type of control.

1 Introduction

Gaming is a highly relevant application area for Intelligent Agents and Synthetic Characters. Nowadays, computer games invade our life bringing us a set of new experiences, driving us into first person fantastic adventures. Although purely fictional, characters in such games have a personality, likes and dislikes, that pulls us into the story and make us feel part of it. As AI techniques become more widespread in computer games, and the area of synthetic characters matures, avatars in such computer games also tend to gain autonomy and become more clever. However, those AI techniques are going beyond the control of payer's opponents, as they are also becoming part of the avatar's behaviors. That is, instead of mindless bodies acting on behalf of the player, computer games characters are gaining life and autonomy. However, this autonomy does not come without some change in the interaction mode. Players become less in charge of their characters and lose the power of complete motion and control. On the other hand, characters may become more clever, less lame and deeper, exhibiting much more interesting actions and behaviors. But, do players buy it? Do they accept not to control completely their characters? What kind of control is the most appropriate in such case?

M. Rauterberg (Ed.): ICEC 2004, LNCS 3166, pp. 68–79, 2004.

This paper presents and discusses the concept of "*influence*", as an alternative to "direct" control of characters, describing how influence can be achieved in computer games. We will describe what is "*influence*" and where does it stand in range of possible types of communication between synthetic agents and humans. To illustrate the notion of influence we will present a computer game called FantasyA where players interact in the game by influencing the emotions of they semi-autonomous avatars using a tangible interface called SenToy. We show how "*influence*" was built in this game, the role of SenToy as a tangible influencing device, and the reactions of the users to this type of control. Finally we will provide some discussion on the topic.

2   Interacting with Characters by Influence

About a decade ago, Negoponte [8] introduced the notion of "delegation" as a new paradigm for human/computer interaction. By contrast with direct manipulation, the idea of delegation is inspired by the image of an English butler, where instead of directly controlling all the actions in the interface, the user delegates some of his, perhaps more boring, activities to an interface agent that is clever enough to execute them autonomously. Although it took some time to catch its momentum, interface agents are now becoming more established and trustworthy as a human computer interaction medium. Still, trusting the agents and accepting not to control every aspect of the interface is something that many users are reluctant to do. The same happens to computer game's players. The idea of an avatar as the image of oneself (*Your digital you* [10]) in a virtual world that performs as one would responding to all the demands of the user is being challenged by work such as [10], [2] or [7]. However, most games do not allow for the user to delegate activities and rely mostly on direct control of the avatars. Computer games that use characters follow several interaction patterns that we should consider:

- Action Games - the player completely controls a single avatar using either a first person (e.g. Unreal Tournament, Quake) or a third person view (e.g. Tomb Raider)
- Sports Games- the player usually controls a team of virtual athletes switching between avatars together with the ball (e.g. FIFA Soccer, NBA Live)
- Adventure Games the player guides characters (usually one) through a predefined storyline (e.g. Monkey Island, Grim Fandango)
- Role Playing Games - the player goes through several quests controlling one or more characters with well defined roles and abilities
- Real Time Strategy Games - the player acts as a god controlling multiple characters at a time in order to achieve a certain objective (e.g. Warcraft, Age of Empires)

Clearly most of these games do not allow for the user to delegate activities and rely mostly on direct control of the characters.

Action / Sports Games explore in depth the idea of avatar as the image of oneself in the virtual world, and require accurate control (aiming, dodging, passing, shooting) which the player is definitely not willing to share. But as for the team, every player would like to have an interesting cooperative play which leaves some room for the concept of "influence". Should the player be able to indirectly control other characters while in control of a specific avatar? Indeed. In FIFA Soccer the player can instruct computer controlled characters to run forward so that s/he is able to do a through pass and perhaps be alone in the face of the goalkeeper when s/he takes control of the character which received the ball.

Adventure / Role Playing Games have characters witch are an interesting mixture between the player's image of oneself and the actor in the story. The player feels as if it is inside the story and assumes the character's goals and objectives. But s/he is constantly reminded that s/he is controlling somebody else's body which is not willing to pick that nasty tarantula or to jump over a cliff. In a way the player has less control over the character than in action/sports game but it still decides which action to do next. Characters act always the same way leading to repetitive and tedious interactions. Wouldn't it be more challenging to let the character's personality take control in certain occasions? The problem would change from what should I do with the character to what should I do to make the character do something. And that is one difference between control and influence.

In *Real Time Strategy Games* the player does not see himself in any particular character. S/he plays the role of god who has absolute control over all characters and their lives, personalities or interests do not have any special meaning. Games like Warcraft or Age of Empires have characters with very limited autonomy and can only make small decisions like which path to follow to reach some place in the world (path-planning) or to hold still or engage the enemy at sight (defined by the stance). More intelligent behavior like running away towards the next city if the enemy sighted is stronger would be welcome, especially if the player isn't looking at that particular spot of the world at that moment. Majesty is a good example of an RTS with autonomous characters where the player can only "influence" their behavior and where the ability of delegating tasks clearly changes the way players interact with the game.

2.1 Influence

If characters in a computer game become autonomous and interact with each other and with the players in an intelligent fashion, actions of such characters can be seen at as social actions. Considering both players and characters in a game as a society of agents (humans and artificial), we can follow Conte and Castelfranchi's work [3] on cognitive and social actions as a base to describe the social relations established within the society.

This approach leads to a notion of influence that is a result of the heterogeneity of the agents (certain agents can influence other "weak" agents where the "weak" agents adopt the "strong" agents' goals and state of mind). In our case, such heterogeneity comes not only from the presence of the human agent with more capabilities than our synthetic characters but also from the autonomy of the character itself (the user's digital self [10]).

Given this basic concept, two main questions arise. The first one is related to the effectiveness of the *influence*. *Influence* cannot always succeed in controlling the behavior of the characters, otherwise it would be reduced to direct control. So, when do we say that influence is effective? The second question is architectural and is related to the types of properties that our agents must have in order to be able to be influenced by the user (rather than purely controlled by him). By answering these two questions we will be lead to a more concrete definition of a semi-autonomous avatar.

Influence is not direct control: When the user controls directly the character it bypasses any kind of decision making on the part of the character and determines all the actions it is about to execute. Differently, with influence, the user's digital self (the character) gains brains and acts autonomously as well. So, the user will try to "convince" the character to a certain behavior by influencing its mental state. Note that such influence may or may not succeed and the character may do the behavior we want or may decide otherwise. This indirection, at first annoying for some users, becomes a challenge later on in the interaction (as we will see in the results obtained). For example, the situation where the user may want the character to be aggressive and act accordingly may not succeed even if the user influences the character to become angry. The character by itself may decide that it is better for its own goals to be defensive and cautious.

What kind of influence? Influencing different aspects of the state of mind: Although Conte and Castelfrachi consider the mechanism of influencing a cognitive one, nothing prevents us from considering the influencing at an emotional level as well. Indeed, influence, specially influence from the user to the agent, can be done on different attitudes. For example, the interaction can be designed so that users may influence the interests of their characters of even their emotions (as we have done with FantasyA and SenToy).

Constraints on the agent's properties and architecture: Influence, as here described, presupposes autonomy on both parts, that is, users and agents. Thus, our agents must have their own goals and mental states. That is, for that autonomy, characters must have an internal state, which may include beliefs, goals, emotions, etc, explicitly managed and reasoned upon, leading to some goal oriented behavior independently from the user's control. This allows for the agent to be in control, but still be able to be influenced. On the other hand, building a character that admits control from several different sources may also require an hierarchical architecture with different control levels. For example, the architecture developed by Badler et. al. (see [2]) supports both graphical and language control.

3   Using SenToy as an Influencing Device for FantasyA

In FantasyA, users play the role of an apprentice wizard who is challenged to find the leader of her/his clan in the land of FantasyA where the game takes place. The game has an introductory phase, where the four clans (the ways of air, earth, fire and water), and the duels are explained. Then the player is placed in the "FantasyA World" where s/he will engage in exploration in order to find her/his leader. In our first prototype characters can only challenge and duel wizards of other clans and the game itself develops in duels taking place in a battle arena built for the effect.

The main different between this game and many other computer games is that players "influence" their characters by emotional control using a tangible interface (SenToy) for that effect. Characters in the game have sufficient autonomy to act even when such control is against their goals.

3.1 Influence with SenToy

To "influence" the character players use SenToy, a wireless tangible interface with sensors in its body that allows the user to control the emotions of the character. The user must express appropriate gestures with the doll representing one of the following six emotions: anger, fear, surprise, gloat, sadness and happiness. SenToy is equipped with three sets of sensors: the accelerometers, which measure the acceleration that the SenToy is subjected to; analogical sensors, used to determine the limbs position; and digital sensors, used to indicate whether the hands of the doll are placed over the eyes or not. Since the emotions cannot be obtained directly from the rather complex data received from the SenToy sensors, a signal processing module was required and implemented so that the adequate patterns of movement can be detected.

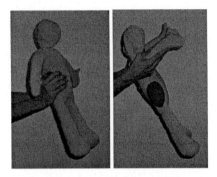

Fig. 1. First prototype of SenToy

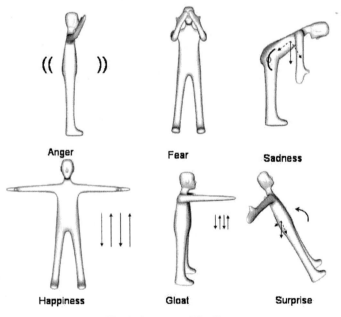

Fig. 2. Gestures of SenToy

The SenToy recognizes six different emotions (happiness, sadness, anger, fear, gloat and surprise) as described bellow (see Figure 2). Each of these gestures are performed as:

Anger: The most general form of shaking the doll is to move the doll back and forward in short but fast movements. These movements cause accentuated variations of the acceleration value given by the accelerometer on the X axis.

Fear: To detect the gesture associated with fear, the user must put SenToy's hands placed over the eyes, independently of the arms position.

Happiness: To express happiness with SenToy, usually the user makes the doll dancing and/or jump up and down as a continuous movement. For these movements, the variation of the SenToy's position is predominantly on the X axis, with wide and rhythmic variation.

Sadness: The sadness emotion is expressed by bending the doll forward, almost to the horizontal plan.

Surprise: The surprise emotion has an asymmetrical sequence of rules, corresponding to the movement of jumping back, and laying inclined backwards with its arms open slightly to the back.

Gloat: To express gloating the user has to perform the same gestures as happiness and at the same time point the right arm to the front. This gesture was inspired in cartoon's expressions.

These gestures are used by the user as the indirect mechanism to influence the character's behavior. Note that users may relate emotions to behavior but, as expected, such link does not succeed all the time.

3.2 Influencing and Action Cycle

Characters in the games must act. It is the action selection of the agents that will determine the dynamics of the game, and therefore its game play. In direct control, users shortcut the action decision and the process of deciding what to do is given to the user's control. So interaction and action are linked. However, to achieve influence in FantasyA, we had to design the interaction process in phases, separating the influence phase from the action phase. This is required so that, due to the indirect control, the influence phase can have an immediate feedback to the user in order for him to understand the action to be performed.

Let's consider a duel situation. To begin with, both characters are ready and placed in the arena for the duel to start. In the duel each character will cast spells that damage the opponent or defend themselves against the opponent. There are several offensive and defensive spells and each type can be further parameterized. The goal is to get the opponent endurance level equal to or below zero and at the same time keep its own endurance above zero.

- Influence phase – In this phase the player can influence the emotional state of his character. As soon as a new emotion is raised in the character, the influence phase ends and the the character may cast a new spell. In FantasyA this phase is done with SenToy. If the emotional state is not changed by the player the influence phase ends after a few seconds (and an appropriate spell is also cast taking into account the current internal emotional state of the character).

Fig. 3. A Duel

- Decision and Action Phases- After the influencing, agents decide whether to follow the suggested state of mind, and from then, select the appropriate action, or reject it. That is, action selection is separated from the influencing process. In FantasyA this means that the agent decides the spell to cast and executes it as a result of a new emotional state being triggered.
- Reaction phase - When the action is performed, the result affects both characters, that will react to it. A new emotional state will then be appraised for both characters, in particular for the controlled character.
- Permanent effects phase - Certain spells, such as heal or weaken, have longer influence in the character, in what we call the permanent effects. The changes on the endurance levels are made and then the combat continues with the next player action. Note that is phase was necessary to give some continuity to the game and to maintain the game play.

The phases described make a player's turn. Figure 3 shows on the left Alvegha's turn (the air character) in the moment when her influence phase has finished and she is casting a spell. On the right, it is Veronya's turn (the fire character), still in the influence phase.

3.3 Feedback on the Influence

Given that influence is not always effective, how does the player know that his or her character is acting under his influence? Indeed, the behavior of the agent will depend not only on its emotional state but also on some internal variables that define the agent's state of mind. Therefore, we need to provide immediate feedback to the payer.

In fact, in FantasyA one of the major aspects of the system is that any emotional state of the character is shown as expressive body movements portraying all the six different types of emotions. The body expression is an essential mechanism in the system for the user, although not completely in control, to interact with his or her character perceiving the response to the influence process. This problem was taken care not only with proper animations of the six emotional states, but also with an extension where the animations produced are generated by bending in real time all the characters actions with the current emotion posture. For example, to express an happy attack the character posture happy is blended with the attack animation. The body expression module of FantasyA has been described in detail elsewhere (see [11] for more details).

4 Autonomy and Semi-autonomy of the Characters

In the case of a computer game, the relation with the characters' autonomy and the user control is a serious issue and needs perfect equilibrium to keep the users engagement high. Our approach was to give the character an emotional dimension that the user could control and restrict the user accessibility to direct combat actions (e.g. spells). However, the characters had to act in a believable and sufficiently clever way for players to accept and understand their behavior. It was important for us to create believable behavior that would follow to certain extent the emotions induced by the user. In fact, characters in FantasyA select the action to perform based on the following elements: the character's current emotional state; the character's model of the world (duel); the opponent's emotional state; some personality parameters that are associated with the clan the character belongs; and some physical properties of the agent which includes the endurance level.

In this section we will first describe how the action decision works and how characters react emotionally to battle events.

4.1 Autonomy and Action Decision

The action selection of a character is influenced by emotions in two ways: (1) because the character's own emotions influence its action tendencies and decisions; and (2) because the character has to take into account the emotions of the opponent as well.

For the action selection mechanism, we decided to base our work on action tendencies that would guide the selection of the action to perform. However, some of the emotion theories, such as for example the well known OCC [9], while carefully addressing the appraisal process and how an emotion becomes active in an individual, leave out the effect that such emotion has in the behavior of the individuals. Further, given the limited choice of actions we had (several aggressive or defensive spells parametrized in different ways) it wouldn't make sense to explore deeply other more complex emotion theories (such as Scherer's theory for example). So, we have relied on three different emotion theories (Lazarus [6], Darwin [4] and Ekman [5]) to extract the relations between the emotion states and actions in the game.

Using these theories we have defined a set of action tendencies for our six emotions which then inspired the *first-level action selection rules* for our agents' behavior. These rules were implemented in Jess and can be translated into:

```
If EMOTION = "Happiness" then Character take an offensive behavior
If EMOTION = "Sadness" then Character take a defensive behavior
If EMOTION = "Gloat" then Character take an offensive behavior
If EMOTION = "Surprise" then Character take a defensive behavior
If EMOTION = "Anger" then Character take an offensive behavior
If EMOTION = "Fear" then Character take a defensive behavior
```

However, the behavior of the agent does not depend solely on the its own emotional state. It also depends on the opponent's emotional state as well as other internal factors. So, the *first-level action selection rules* have to be latter combined with the rules that depend on these other factors.

However, the influence of the others' emotions in an agent's own behavior is even a more difficult to address. There is not much research on the effects of emotion communication, but research on empathy, emotional contagion and social referencing [1] provided us with some hints on how to address the problem. Empathy and emotional contagion suggest mechanisms for transmitting emotions to others, while social referencing has been defined as the *process of using another person's interpretive message, or emotional information, about an uncertain situation to form one's own understanding of that situation [1].*

In our scenario the two agents' goals are opposite, and thus we can assume that if a situation is good for the opponent it will certainly be bad for the agent. Following the social referencing theory we can evaluate the situation and decide what to do based on the current emotion of the opponent. Thus, in order to appraise the situation, the agent must model the opponent's intentions. Given that the opponent decides what to do also depending on its emotional state, the agent models the emotional state of the opponent and simulates its action tendencies. This simulation is done following a mechanism similar to the one discussed above for the agent's own emotions. For example, if the opponent is happy this should mean that it feels comfortable about the current state of the duel and will attack, therefore the agent should defend to counter the opponent's confidence in the attack. In fact, based on the opponents emotions the agent predicts the opponent's next action and reacts accordingly.

Finally, we also considered that the reaction to the expectations on the opponent's actions depends on the personality of the agent. In the example above we described the behavior of a cautious agent, but if it were more aggressive it would respond to the attack tendencies of the opponent with counter-attacks and not defenses. This element of personality in the characters increases the richness of characters, their believability, autonomy, and thus, game-play.

4.2   Emotional Reactions and Emotional Influence

After acting, both characters react emotionally to the results. The emotional reaction depends on the action itself, its results (e.g. if it succeeded or failed) and on the previous emotional state of the character. Similar to OCC [9], where the appraisal mechanisms activate emotions on individuals according to event that she perceives, in FantasyA the emotion state creates an "action expectation" on the character based on the action tendency that the emotion has. This means that an angry character expects to attack her opponent and that attack to succeed. Characters will react differently to the action result if the action taken and its result was within her expectations or not.

5   Study and Results

We conducted a study to evaluate our approach to the presented problems. The items we wanted to check include the interaction issues associated with the notion of influence, and also some entertainment issues about the game. The study was developed in two different phases, first just with SenToy and afterwards with FantasyA and SenToy.

5.1   Emotional Reactions and Emotional Influence

The SenToy evaluation was made with a group of 34 subjects: 8 kids, 12 high-school students and 14 adults, from ages 9 to 45 - with the average age of 21.8. The subjects were introduced to the SenToy without any explanation of the gestures that it recognizes, and were asked to express each of the six emotions using it. The results were obtained through video analysis and some questionnaires. Tables 1 and 2 resume the results obtained.

Table 1. Number of subjects that could successfully express an emotion using the *SenToy*. Note that in case of gloat a very similar gesture was used with a very significant value.

Emotion	N. Succ.	Emotion	N. Succ.	Emotion	N. Succ.
Happy	22	Sad	16	Gloat	1(16)
Anger	28	Fear	10	Surprise	14

Table 2. The SenToy questionnaire results. Q1: "Did you like the Doll?" (Not like it 1 - Love it 7). Q2: "How easy was to express the emotions?" (Hard 1 - Easy 7).

Question	Kids	Students	Adults	Mean
Q1	6.1	4.8	4.4	4.9
Q2	5.8	3.8	4.7	4.7

Latter, after the first experience and when the recognized gestures were explained, all the subjects could easily manipulate the SenToy. We concluded that SenToy can be a good interface to express emotions but it would be improved if alternative gestures for some of the emotions were provided.

Fig. 4. One session of FantasyA's evaluation

5.2   Evaluation of FantasyA

The evaluation of FantasyA was conducted with 30 subjects: 8 kids, 12 high-school students and 10 adults - from ages 9 to 38 - with an average age of 20.6. The students and kids play computer games in an average of 10 hours per week, while adults almost didn't play at all. We run 15 sessions of 50 to 90 minutes each. Subjects were working in pairs and played an average of 20 duels in each session (Figure 4 shows the room layout and subject placement). The subjects were given two sheets with the game rules, but not with the emotion rules behind the combat logic. The results were obtained from three sources: video observation, open-ended interview and a questionnaire. The questionnaire included several questions focusing on three different aspects: the SenToy influence, the characters expressions and the game play.

In general the character expressions were well accepted and understood but the more exaggerated were better perceived. On the other hand the game logics seem too complex but some subjects got a few ideas about how influence worked. Some users were able to understand the indirection mechanism (see the following comment).
"I believe that you should check somewhat what the other guy [the opponent] does. What he expresses. [..] Yes, because he is probably expressing the same things as our guy is. Then you react to that. But we did not do that very much. [..]"(adult player).
Finally, and about the entertainment aspect of the game we got a complete success! All subjects were very pleased with the experience and some would even like to buy the game. One adult player said: *"This was a different game, enormously funny!"*, and one kid even asked *"It was a fun game that I hope will be released on the market sometime"* (13-year old).

6   Conclusions

In this paper we presented the concept of influence and how it was implemented in FantasyA and SenToy. The results show that influence can be an alternative to direct control of characters in games. However, the evaluation has also shown that we need to keep the balance between indirect and direct control of the avatar and that timing is very important. In fact, in FantasyA players are too much time inactive so one next improvement is to make a faster game cycle and even explore the idea of two influence phases one for attack an another for defense. However, in general, influence was a great success.

References

1.   M. S. Atkins. Dynamic analysis of infant social referencing. Master's Thesis. Eberly College of Arts and Sciences at West Virginia University, 2000.
2.   R. Bindiganavale, W. Schuler, J. Allbeck, N. Badler, A. Joshi and M. Palmer. Dynamically altering agent behaviours using natural language instructions. In Proceedings of the International Conference on Autonomous Agents (AA'2000), ACM Press, 2000.
3.   R. Conte and C. Castelfranchi. Cognitive and Social Action, UCL Press, 1995.
4.   C. Darwin. The Expression of Emotions in man and animals. 3rd Ed. By Paul Ekman, Oxford University Press, 1872/1998
5.   P. Ekman. Emotion in the Face. New York, Cambridge University Press, 1982.

6. R. Lazarus. Emotion and Adaptation. Oxford University Press, 1991.

7. I. Machado, A. Paiva and R. Prada. Is the wolf angry or just hungry? Inspecting, modifying and sharing character's minds. . In Proceedings of the International Conference on Autonomous Agents (AA'2001), ACM Press, 2001.

8. N. Negroponte. Agents: From direct manipulation to delegation. In J. Bradshaw, editor, Software Agents, MIT press, 1997.

9. A. Ortony, G. Clore and A. Collins. The Cognitive Structure of Emotions. Cambridge University Press, New York, edition 1988.

10. S. Penny, J. Smith, P. Sengers, A. Bernhardt and J. Schulte. Traces: embodied immersive interaction with semi-autonomous avatars, Convergence, 7(2), 2001.

11. M. Vala, M. Gomes, and A. Paiva Affective Bodies for Affective interactions. In Animating Expressive Characters for Social Interactions, Eds. L. Cañamero and R. Aylett (in print), 2004.

Computer Supported Collaborative Sports: Creating Social Spaces Filled with Sports Activities

Volker Wulf[1,3], Eckehard F. Moritz[2], Christian Henneke[2], Kanan Al-Zubaidi[1], and Gunnar Stevens[1]

[1] Institute for Information Systems, University of Siegen, Germany
{wulf,kanan,stevens}@fb5.uni-siegen.de
[2] SportKreativWerkstatt, Technical University of Munich, Germany
efm@sportkreativwerkstatt.de, christian.henneke@web.de
[3] Fraunhofer Institute for Applied Information Technology (FhG-FIT),
Schloss Birlinghoven, Sankt Augustin, Germany
volker.wulf@fit.fraunhofer.de

Abstract. We present the newly emerging research field of Computer Supported Collaborative Sports (CSCS). By applying innovative input and output technologies, it enables players to experience sportive activities in a shared computerized environment. Important dimensions in the design space of CSCS applications are discussed. Finally we present the FlyGuy, a prototypical realization of a CSCS device.

1 Introduction

Computer games have turned into a popular form of entertainment. An increasing number of people, specifically children, are playing computer games, thus converting them into an important leisure activity. When asked for the most fun entertainment activities in 2000, 35% of Americans mentioned computer and video games outranging alternatives such as watching television, surfing in the internet, reading books, or going to cinema [6]. So computer games fascinate and suck people's attention.

However, the success of computer games has always been critically discussed. Unsuitable content of the games, social isolation of the players, and lacking physical activities are mayor critical concerns with regard to computer games.

Quite a number of computer games deal with shooting or killing activities. An often expressed criticism with regard to this type of games is based on the assumption that killing activities within shooting games will lead to an increased aggressive behavior in daily life [20]. While empirical investigations with regard to this hypothesis show heterogeneous results [5], the design of ethically less problematic but fascinating game content is a big challenge.

Critics have pointed out that intense use of computer games may lead to social isolation of the players [19]. However, social arrangements such as playing single user games in a group or LAN parties where multi user games are played in physical proximity may compensate for this problem. Certain computer games address this issue by allowing playing together across local distances.

M. Rauterberg (Ed.): ICEC 2004, LNCS 3166, pp. 80–89, 2004.
© IFIP International Federation for Information Processing 2004

Another problematic issue with regard to computer games is lacking physical activity when playing – which offers a strange contrast to the "physical" content of many games. The typical input devices of computer games are system-specific push buttons, different types of keyboards, joy sticks, or mice. Output is typically provided to the players by audio and graphical means (e.g. loudspeakers and screens of different types). Only recently with the emergence of Ubiquitous Computing new input and output technologies have come up [3]. Other approaches take given sportive activities like skateboarding and karate as a base and augment them with information technology. By doing so existing sports activities get an additional 'game content' [10], [17], [16].

In the following we want to get one step beyond by further integrating computer games and computer augmented sports. We will postulate the approach of Computer Supported Cooperative Sports (CSCS). By applying innovative input and output technologies we want to enable users to gain new experiences in a shared computerized game environment.

The paper is structured as follows. First we will present the state of the art in computer games with computer augmented sportive interfaces. Then we will outline the concept of Computer Supported Collaborative Sports. A prototype of this design paradigm, the FlyGuy approach to enable flights in a shared 3D space, will be presented. We will conclude by discussing our findings.

2 Ubiquitous Games and Computer Augmented Sports

Ubiquitous computing offers interesting new options to interact with computers through real world objects and spaces. They offer new opportunities to create innovative games and sportive input devices. The STARS environment offers a platform to realize different board games on a computer augmented table. Real world objects, such as chess figures, can be moved on the board and their positions can be tracked. Based on this input, a game engine can compute appropriate output behaviour [12]. Based on rather similar input technologies, Harvard and Lovind [8] have developed toys based on a rather different conceptual idea. They try to encourage storytelling by moving away from the computer screen and take physical objects (typically simple plastic toys) as an interface that permits to explore the quirks of a story. Stories can be recorded and attached to different toys and their actual position.

A different approach is taken by Sanneblad and Holmquist [21]. They distribute a game area on different hand-held computers in a way that the whole area can only be seen by means of all the different displays. The players have to move towards each other to perform activities, e.g. stiring PacMan in the classic arcade game, on those parts of the game area which are not represented on their own hand-held. In this case physical activities of the players result from the need to see the whole game area.

Different approaches record human movements for navigation in virtual environments. Humphrey II[1], developed by the Futurelab in Linz, is a flight simulator where the user emerges into a 3D virtual space by means of a head mounted display. The behaviour of an avatar representing the users can be controlled by means of arm movements. In the Virtual Fitness Center (Virku) an exercise bicycle is positioned in

---

[1] www.aec.at/humphrey/

front of a video screen. The physical movements conducted on the exercise bicycle are used as input to modify the representation of 3D virtual environments from map information. Reversely, the map information affects the pedaling efforts. In an early implementation the players move this way along a hilly landscape in Finish Lapland [17].

Other approaches address collaborative sportive activities explicitly. They can be understood as early instances of CSCS research. AR^2 is an augmented reality air-hockey table with a virtual puck. The two players wear head-mounted displays to see a virtual puck on the table in front of them [18]. PingPongPlus is a system which augments traditional table tennis by means of a tracking device for the ball and a video projector. Different applications have been designed which project images on the table according to the location where the ball hits the table. When a ball hits the table in the water ripple mode, an image of a water ripple flows out from the spot the ball landed [10]. Mueller et al. [16] have developed a system which allows players to interact remotely through a life-size video conference screen using a regular soccer ball as an input device. Both players kick the ball against their local wall on which an audio and video connection with the other player is displayed. By tracking the position where the ball hits the wall specific single user games can be added on each player's side via an overlay technique.

While there are quite some interesting developments in the ubiquitous and entertainment computing fields, the sports engineering community has not come up with computer augmented sport devices. Most research is still restrained to analyse and model traditional sport devices or aspects of the human body (for a good summary see [23], [24]). There are few if any papers concerning the design of sport devices and none so far have touched the area of combining computers and sports in novel designs of sport equipments. If at all, respective contributions can be found in training science, but with the specific purpose to use the computer technology to achieve particular training objectives.

3   Computer Supported Cooperative Sports

Computer Supported Cooperative Sports investigates the design of computer applications which require sportive input activities to gain collective game experience. It is an interdisciplinary research field where sports engineers, computer scientists, designers, sport scientists, and social scientists need to cooperate, guided by a systematic design approach [15]. In the following we want to clarify the concept and discuss important aspects of the design space for innovative applications.

3.1   Integrating Sports with Games

In the following the hermeneutic and practical core of sports and games and their implications shall be identified, and related to one another. Sports in a traditional understanding has been defined as „organized play that is accompanied by physical exertion, guided by a formal structure, organized within the context of formal and explicit rules of behaviour and procedures, and observed by spectators" ([2], p.143). Still widely spread, this formalizing definition coerces sports into a specific scheme and strangely strangles the scope for innovation with respect to social and individual use value. However, there are also more context-sensitive approaches, defining sports as a "specific expression of human movement behaviour" ([7], p.8) that becomes "sports" only by "a situation-specific reception and an attribution of meaning" ([9], p. 34). Eventually it is the purpose an individual assigns to a movement which he considers being sportive (which in many cases encompass "physical exertion"), that defines sports. Reasons to do sports include fun, health, meeting with interesting people, maintaining fitness, and compensating for sedentary occupation [13], [14].

Doing sports and playing games have many similarities, especially the voluntary character of the activities motivated by a perception of fun. In the domain of computer games, sport genres have already been picked up. Players can simulate sport competitions, such as a soccer championship, on their computer. However, the aim of CSCS is not to simulate sports activities, but doing them.

3.2 Input and Output Devices for Sports Activities

An important dimension in the design space is obviously the type of sports activity which shapes the input and output interface to the computer augmented environment. Defining sports via the meaning individuals assign to a movement, one can imagine a wide scope of different activities. If we either presuppose the objective of fitness or at least like to reduce long-term physical harm, one of the essential requirements is balance in external load distribution, e.g. not to demand an over-utilization of the biceps and offering no stimulation to the triceps. Practical technical and bio-mechanical considerations and the wish to monitor progress furthermore suggest a reduction of movement complexity to a simple combination of translational and rotational movements – in which, however, one might have to compromise the natural feeling while moving around in a virtual world.

When becoming part of a computer augmented collaborative environment, existing sports may change their game idea altogether. Still less reference to an existing sport may finally be needed or wanted; save some examples where the similarity is explicitly aimed at (e.g. soccer in front of a video wall). So we can distinguish sport activities which already exist in the physical world from those which are newly designed within a computer-augmented environment.

With regard to the design of the input interface the question arises how to register sport activities appropriately. If this cannot be done by monitoring movements and forces in the device directly, e.g. the actual engine torque, then sensors of different kinds become an essential part of the design. These sensors can either measure the movements of the human body (e.g. stiring and pedaling an exercise bike) or of different types of sport tools (e.g. the ball in table tennis or the racket in hockey).

With regard to the design of the output interface in a distributed game environment one has to think of how to represent the activities of other actors and the physical texture of virtual space. This can either happen merely visually or also physically by means of forced feedback. For instance, in the Virku environment the physical texture of the virtual landscape translates into different levels of required pedaling efforts.

3.3 Collaboration

The concept of collaboration in CSCS environments needs some discussion. Sports, like many game genres, seem to imply competition either among individuals or among teams. However, in dancing or acrobatics it is the feeling of being together in combination with (joint) movements that people aim at. So in principle CSCS can be centred on cooperation or competition. Hence, the meaning of collaboration in CSCS can span the whole scope from multi user competitive settings (e.g. computer-augmented table tennis or a bicycles race in a virtual 3D environment), via settings of mere co-presence (e.g. playing soccer individually in a shared audio and video space or riding bicycles together in a virtual space) towards settings where cooperation is needed to achieve the common goals (e.g. moving in a game area distributed via different hand-helds or producing output loads that are converted into a stimulating input for the partner at a remote location).

From a computer science perspective, collaborative settings can be classified along the time-space dichotomy [11]. With regard to the space, players in CSCS applications can either interact at the same place (e.g. computer augmented table tennis) or at remote locations (e.g. soccer within a shared media space). With regard to time, most of the applications in the field of entertainment computing are synchronous in the sense that the players interact with each other at the same time. However, asynchronous applications such as community systems may help shaping social relationships among players. Seay et al. [22] and Friedl [4] describe how synchronous applications of computer mediated communication such as chat or e-mail can be integrated into Massive Multiplayer Online Games (MMOG). Friedl [4] stresses the importance of asynchronous features. Web pages allow, for instance, displaying information about player's performances in past games.

Another important dimension with regard to collaboration is the question whether the players know each other beforehand or whether they learn to know each other within the game environment. In the latter case specific technical features may be needed to introduce or match human actors [1]. Friedl [4] points out that personal information and information about players' performance and can stimulate social interactions.

3.4 Objectives and Vision

CSCS emerges in an interesting intersection of sports, game and innovative technologies. It may help to tackle problems which are of imminent importance to individuals and the society as a whole:

– "Animated fitness equipment" will greatly enhance the motivation to do something for one´s health and fitness, and to stick with it, by combining exertion with diversion (and diversity). It is further possible to address the wishes more directly and to pull the motivational triggers of different target groups.
– "Animated fitness worlds" will combine play, sports, and fitness: An overall leisure attraction may create an important offer to get kids away from stationary computer gaming, and thus to fight obesity and social isolation.
– "Computer controlled sports equipment" will allow monitoring movements and achievements, adapting training and rehabilitation, and enable remote supervision.

- "Computer enhanced sports equipment" may provide novel access to emotions and feelings, especially by combining movements and visual displays, which is not possible by purely mechancial sports equipment.
- "Computer supported collaborative sports equipment" will link people to do collaborative phyiscal activites; again enhancing motivation and opening up new physical communication channels for mates or even distributed teams.

To arrive at these objectives, however, puts high demands on how to conduct respective research and development projects. A project team heterogeneously assembled with engineers, computer scientists and sports experts will have to put their competences together, guided by a systematic approach to innovation in sports, and backed up by a distributed project management. A first pilot project in this area has been conducted and will be reported upon in the next section.

4 The FlyGuy Approach

We have developed a concept called FlyGuy[2] for an innovative CSCS device which combines effective fitness training with playful challenges, social interaction, and a versatile entertainment. The work was conducted in a multidisciplinary design team which consisted of researchers and students from Germany, Japan, Mexico, and the United States.

Other than PingPongPlus or the soccer game at the video wall, we wanted to design a collaborative environment for new physical experiences and sports activities. In a first face-to-face meeting of the project team, flying was identified as an interesting sports activity which humans can only experience in a computer augmented environment or by means of specific avionic devices such as hang gliders.

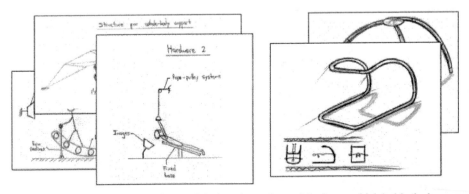

Fig. 1. First sketches of the FlyGuy and design alternatives of the frame which holds the human actor when flying

[2] The work on the FlyGuy was supported by the Japanese Ministry of Education in the project Tele Athletics New Experience (TANE). The work was conducted at the Technical University of Munich (Germany), Stanford University (USA), University of Siegen (Germany), Tokyo Institute of Technology (Japan), Tsukuba University (Japan), Universidad de las Americas (Puebla, Mexico), and University of Magdeburg (Germany).

Our concept looks as follows: The player immerses via a head mounted display into a 3D virtual environment. It controls a flight simulation by its body motion. In a first explorative realization two handles are grabbed with the hands; the flight direction can be changed via rotation of the torso, the height by pulling or pushing a lever horizontally. One of the reasons we chose to realize the flight movement in this "starfighter" fashion was that it appeared the most natural way to the test persons we asked to "fly" on a small table structure. Bird-like movements were less frequent – and above all would be more difficult to realize and to put into an efficient training regimen. The training effect is intensified by providing resistance for both concentric and excentric movements; thus it is possible to realize extreme intensity and early exhaustion. In further stages we plan to include the leg movements for acceleration and deceleration. The motions are captured by sensors located in the joints of the lever structure and transformed into electrical signals which are then being transmitted to a microcontroller and PC. These data are used as input to control the flight simulation which is perceived by the player via a head mounted display. The player so far is hanging in a frame made of aluminum similar to the frame of a hang glider.

In the virtual space, the sportsman has the possibility to solve different flight tasks and meet other persons and fly and exercise with them, even if they are in a far distant location in the real world. Whenever the players reach certain proximity in the virtual space, an audio channel is opened. Therefore different FlyGuy devices are connected via a local network or internet. The underlying technical infrastructure for communication is based on a dedicated server model architectures because it combines some peer-2-peer ideas with a client-server model and it will be possible to integrate an single-user or training modus.

For creating the virtual environment, we explored different popular 3D game engines and finally opted to tailor an existing game like Half-Life II for our purpose. This also helped to overcome the problem to arrive at a critical mass for efficient useage, as it makes it easier to integrate other players, which do not have the FlyGuy device, but nevertheless can use the FlyGuy game as well.

What mostly differentiates the FlyGuy from Humphrey II (Chapter 2) is the aspect that FlyGuy is a device for efficient fitness training, while Humphrey II focuses on entertainment only. This becomes apparent when looking at the rather non ergonomic pattern for user input. Moreover, Humphrey II is a single user environment which does not realize any collaborative feature.

Fig. 2. Experimenting with early prototypes of the FlyGuy

After defining the concept, the team separated again and worked on its realization (mechanics, mechatronics, network structure, virtual environment, output devices, biomechanics, game plan, sports scientific aspects, etc.) in a distributed fashion.

In a second face-to-face meeting a functional prototype was assembled and tested. This prototype was built to explore technical design issues such as the location of the hanging and the fix of the lever structure. We also tested whether the data conversion worked the way it was anticipated. Further functional design issues were explored such as the steering mechanisms. We also investigated which degree of freedom and what kind of support are necessary to provide the basis for efficient and safe training.

We evaluated our concepts internally during the design process. It turned out that some aspects of the prototype's design worked out better than others. For example the horizontal flight posture and the steering of the flight simulation were rated well and very intuitive, while the usage of a fixed and stiff lever structure was regarded suboptimal because it does not perfectly match the idea of "free" flight motions. Other aspects which need to be improved are the overly complicated access into the device and lacking adaptability with regard to different user anthropometries. We could not yet evaluate the game software and the virtual environment, as these were still rudimentarily adapted versions of software produced for completely different purposes.

5 Conclusion

We have presented the concept of Computer Supported Collaborative Sports and presented the FlyGuy, a first prototypical realization of a CSCS device. The FlyGuy prototype stimulated considerable interest from test users as well as from partners from industry. Obviously the attempt to transfer the excitement of computer games into a motivation for fitness training and thereby even allowing joint physical activities by partners far apart will mark an important trend in the future of entertainment computing and fitness-oriented sports alike.

The introduction of computers into cooperative sports equipment and settings does not only offer new areas of application for computers in entertainment but also opens up new dimensions in sports and fitness:

- There is a whole array of novel means to increase motivation to participate in sportive or health-sustaining activities.
- Linked via internet, people in different locations can do sports, share physical fun or follow rehabilitation schemes together.
- The development of virtual worlds and connected input-output devices provide for sensoric and emotional sensations that cannot be experienced otherwise; "flying" being just one example.

To explore this line of thoughts furthermore, we will need to realize a variety of different CSCS devices. Empirical evaluations of their appropriation by various groups of players will help us to even better understand the design space lined out in this paper.

References

1. Al-Zubaidi, K., Stevens, G.: CSCP at Work, in Proceedings of the Conference Mensch und Computer 2004 (MC 2004), Teubner, Stuttgart 2004 in press
2. Anshel, M.A. (Ed.): Dictionary of the Sports and Exercise Sciences; Human Kinetics Books, Illinois 1991
3. Björk, S.; Holopainen, J.; Ljundstrand, P.; Mandryk, R. (eds): Special Issue on Ubiquitous Games, in: Personal and Ubiquitous Computing, Vol. 6, 2002, pp. 358–361
4. Friedl, M.: Online Game Interactivity Theory. Hingham, Charles River Media 2003
5. Fritz, J.; Fehr, W. (eds): Handbuch Medien und Computer-Spiele, Bonn 1997
6. IDSA: Interactive Digital Software Association, http://www.idsa.com
7. Haag, H. (ed.): Sportphilosophie; Verlag Karl Hofmann, Schorndorf 1996
8. Harvard, Å., Løvind, S.: "Psst"-ipatory Design. Involving artists, technologists, students and children in the design of narrative toys, in: Binder, T., Gregory, J., Wagner, I. (eds) Proceedings of the PDC 2002 Participatory Design Conference, Malmö, 2002
9. Heinemann, K.: Einführung in die Soziologie des Sports; Verlag Karl Hofmann, Schorndorf 1998
10. Ishii; H.; Wisneski, C.; Orbanes, J.; Chun, B.; Paradiso, J.: PingPongPlus: Design of an Athletic-Tangible Interface for Computer-Supported Cooperative Play, in: Proceddings of CHI'99, May 15–20, 1999, ACM-Press, New York, pp. 394–401
11. Johansen, R.: Current User Approaches to Groupware, in Johansen, Robert (ed): Groupware, Freepress, New York 1988, pp. 12–44
12. Magerkurth, C.; Stenzel, R.: Computerunterstütztes kooperatives Spielen – Die Zukunft des Spieltisches, in: Ziegler, J.; Szwillus, G. (eds): Proceedings of Mensch & Computer 2003 (MC '03), Stuttgart, September 7–10, 2003, Teubner
13. Meyer, M.: Zur Entwicklung der Sportbedürfnisse; Dissertation, German Sports University, Cologne 1992
14. Moritz, E.F., Steffen, J.: Test For Fun – ein Konzept für einen nutzerorientierten Sportgerätetest; in: Roemer et al (eds) Sporttechnologie zwischen Theorie und Praxis; Shaker Verlag, Aachen 2003, pp. 43–63
15. Moritz, E.F.: Systematic Innovation in Popular Sports, in: 5th Conference of the International Sports Engineering Association, September 14-17, 2004, Davis CA, in press
16. Mueller, F.; Agamanolis, S.; Picard, R.: Exertion Interface: Sports over a Distance for Social Bonding and Fun, in: Proceedings of CHI 2003, April 5–10, 1999, ACM-Press, New York, pp. 561–568
17. Mokka, S.; Väätänen, A.; Välkkynen, P.: Fitness Computer Games with a Bodily User Interface, in: Proceedings of the Second International Conference on Entertainment Computing, Pittsburgh, Pennsylvania, May 8–10, 2003, ACM International Conference Proceeding Series, pp. 1–3
18. Ohshima, T.; Satoh, K.; Yamamoto, H.; Tamura, H.: AR2 Hockey, in: Conference Abstracts and Applications of SIGGRAPH'98, ACM-Press, New York, p. 110
19. Provenzo, Eugene F.: Video Kids: Making Sense of Nintendo. Harvard University Press Cambridge, MA 1991
20. Rauterberg, M.: Emotional Aspects of Shooting Activities: 'Real' versus 'Virtual' Actions and Targets, in: Proceedings of 2nd International Conference on Entertainment Computing (ICEC 2003); May 8–10, 2003, Pittsburgh, PA, ACM Digital Library
21. Sanneblad, J., Holmquist, L E.: Designing Collaborative Games on hand-held Computers, in: Proceedings of the SIGGRAPH 2003 conference on Sketches & applications: in conjunction with the 30th annual conference on Computer graphics and interactive techniques, San Diego, CA, July 27–31, 2003, ACM-Press, New York 2003
22. Seay, A. F., W. J. Jerome, et al.: Project Massive 1.0: Organizational Commitment, Sociability and Extraversion in Massively Multiplayer Online Games. LEVEL UP Digital Games Research Conference, Utrecht University 2003

23. Subic, A.J., Haake, S.J. (eds): The Engineering of Sport 3; Blackwell Science, Cambridge 2000
24. Ujihashi, S., Haake, S.J. (eds): The Engineering of Sport 4; Blackwell Science, Cambridge 2002

Optical-Flow-Driven Gadgets for Gaming User Interface

Zoran Zivkovic

Intelligent Autonomous Systems Group, University of Amsterdam,
1098SJ Amsterdam, The Netherlands
zivkovic@science.uva.nl
http://www.zoranz.net

Abstract. We describe how to build a VIDEOPLACE-like vision-driven user interface using "optical-flow" measurements. The optical-flow denotes the estimated movement of an image patch between two consecutive frames from a video sequence. Similar framework is used in a number of commercial vision-driven interactive computer games but the motion of the users is detected by examining the difference between two consecutive frames. The optical-flow presents a natural extension. We show here how the optical-flow can be used to provide much richer interaction.

1 Introduction

Vision-driven user interfaces are getting close to mass usage because computers are constantly becoming faster and cameras are getting cheaper. Facial and hand gesture recognition from video images remain therefore to be hot topics in the computer vision society [2]. Impressive results are reported and many applications seem possible. However, a real-world user-interface should fulfill a number of extremely difficult requirements: the interface should be very easy and natural to use, there should be no initialization and the system should work in difficult and changing environment conditions. It seems that the only actual commercial real-world vision-based interfaces are currently present in the gaming industry. The available games demonstrate rich and enjoyable interaction using just some simple computer-vision techniques. Although the techniques are often far away from the current state of the art in the computer-vision research, the used methods are fast and robust and fulfill the mentioned difficult real-world requirements. Furthermore, the gaming industry is particularly suitable for application of the computer-vision algorithms since the remaining imperfections of the vision-based interface are tolerated by the game players and often actually considered as an additional challenge.

There are a number of games and other systems that use a vision-based interface. We consider in this paper the "real" real-world systems that fulfill the mentioned requirements and can be actually used by anybody that has a web-cam attached to a PC. As we mentioned, it seems that the only actual commercial usage of the vision-based interfaces is present in the gaming industry. The currently available games use the VIDEOPLACE-like interaction model [9] where the users see themselves embedded into computer graphics with some computer generated objects that react to their movements. See section 2 for a detailed description. The IntelPlay Me2cam [12] and

M. Rauterberg (Ed.): ICEC 2004, LNCS 3166, pp. 90–100, 2004.

Vivid Group Gesture Xtreme [11] systems segment the player from the background in order to detect the user gestures. However, the segmentation requires initialization and a special setting. Another standard technique used for vision based interfaces is the detection of the skin colored regions in an image [21], but this is not robust to light conditions. The two commercial game suites of interest are the Reality Fusion Game Cam [3] and the Sony Eye Toy [4]. These games use simple difference between two successive images to detect the motion of the users (see section 3). The detected movements of the players are used to interact with the virtual objects. This is fast and robust and does not require initialization or a special setting. We should mention also the QuiQui game [8] where a computer animated avatar mimics user actions. This game is also using the simple image-differencing.

In this paper we describe a framework for building VIDEOPLACE-like vision-driven user interfaces using the "optical-flow" measurements. The "optical-flow" denotes the movement of an image patch between two frames of a video sequence. There are various techniques for estimating the optical-flow [13,14,20]. The mentioned currently available vision-driven games are using the image-differencing technique to detect user movements. The optical-flow presents a natural extension of the image-differencing. The optical-flow not only detects the movement but also gives us an estimate of the direction and the speed of the movement. This simple extension allows much richer interaction while the described requirements for the "real" real-world systems are still fulfilled. We implement a system that is using the standard image-differencing and a system that is using the optical-flow-based measurements. The two techniques are evaluated and compared both subjectively and objectively. We also present how optical flow can be used to perform some more complex tasks that are not possible using the standard image-differencing technique.

The paper is organized as follows. First, in Section 2 we describe the VIDEO-PLACE-like interaction framework that is used for various interactive systems and in the vision-driven computer games. In Section 3 we describe the image-differencing and how it is usually used to detect the movement of the user in the vision-driven games. We also describe a robust version of a standard technique for estimating the optical-flow and how it can be used for vision-based interaction. The experiments are reported in Section 4 and conclusions in Section 5.

2 VIDEOPLACE-Like Interaction Model

A VIDEOPLACE-like interaction involves an installation where the users see themselves, or some representation of themselves, on a video-projection screen together with some additional computer graphics. A realization is presented in the figure 1. Another simpler version would be just a computer monitor and a web-camera. First experiments using such interaction model were conducted by the artist Myron Krueger in his work VIDEOPLACE as early as 1969. See a description in [9]. This interaction model is used later by other artists for various installations [7], by computer-vision researchers to demonstrate their work [5,21] and finally in the gaming industry [3,4,11,12]. The futuristic interface from the movie "Minority Report"(2002) (designed by John Underkoffler) is another example.

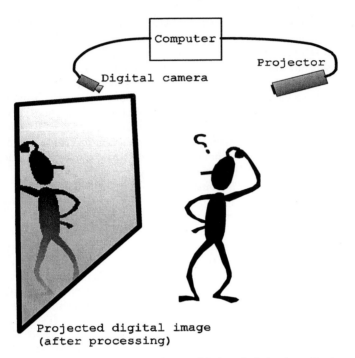

Fig. 1. VIDEOPLACE-like interaction model. A typical simple realization

2.1 Virtual Mirror Effect

The VIDEOPLACE-like interaction is based on the illusion of a mirror. Regular mirror is a common physical object in our environment and this makes a VIDEOPLACE-like virtual mirror a natural and easy to use interface [10]. It is also a simple way to provide the users with a certain level of immersion into a virtual world. There are some technical difficulties in realizing a completely realistic mirror illusion:

- If we move in front of a real mirror our view point is changing and consequently also the reflected image we see in the mirror. Since, the digital camera is static it is very difficult to simulate this effect. We would need to track the user's eyes position and to change the projected images accordingly. Even then, this would be possible only when there is a single user. To the best of our knowledge, there is no such a system that is able to compensate for the view point changes.
- Another related but simpler problem is the eye-contact. Having the eye-contact with yourself when you look at your reflection is important for the mirror illusion. An approximate solution is to use a semitransparent projection screen and to put the camera behind the virtual mirror somewhere at the eye height. See for example [5]. It is also possible to track the person eyes and apply the corrections [6];

Fortunately, in practice even the simplest realization with a web-camera and a computer monitor is enough to produce a reasonable effect and provoke interaction. Furthermore, in the early work of Myron Krueger there was just a shadow of the person and in the QuiQui game [8] there is a computer animated avatar.

2.2 Vision-Driven Gadgets

Beside the mirror-like image of the users, the VIDEOPLACE-like interaction involves some additional computer generated objects that are presented on the screen. The objects react to the movements of the users and we denote them as "vision-driven gadgets". There is a variety of types of such objects and we will mention the most common ones:

- **Static object**: These objects do not react to the user movements directly. For example there is often some static computer graphics present or there are numbers to show current score in the games etc.
- **Button**: This is the basic component of almost every user interface. In the VIDEOPLACE-like interaction the user should be able to use his movement to press a button. The current games are based mainly on this type of object or a variation of this type. The most common variation is the "moving button". The object moves around the image and when the user selects it the object changes its behavior. For example in a game from [4] bubbles fly around the screen and they explode when the user selects them. In some other games from [3] and [4] the objects bounce away when selected. The button is selected if there is a movement in the area of the image occupied by the button. In the current games the image-differencing technique is used to detect the movement and we will show how this can be improved by using the optical-flow.
- **Movable object**: Another common part in a user interface. For example the icons in the Windows user interface are dragged using the mouse. In the vision-based interface the user should be able to move the objects of this type using body movements. In the currently available games that use the image-differencing this is not possible. As we mentioned, in some games from [3] and [4] the objects bounce away when selected and this, in a way, controls the movement of the objects but very roughly. The interaction is still button-like. The optical flow provides also information about the direction and the magnitude of the movement and this can be used to move the objects and provide much richer interaction.

3 Detecting and Measuring Motion

A vision-based interface is driven by the movements of the users that are observed by a digital camera. Robust techniques are needed to detect and measure the motion of the users. We will discuss the common motion detection techniques in this section. The techniques are illustrated in figure 2. In the VIDEOPLACE-like framework the presented image consists of a mirror-like image of the users and a number of augmented computer generated vision-driven gadgets. The gadgets react to the user movements. We will denote the region of the image occupied by a "vision-driven-gadget" by W. We need to detect and measure the movement in this region.

a) a frame from an image sequence

b) the next frame from the sequence

c) the difference D between two frames

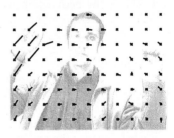

d) optical flow for some image points (lines present displacements)

e) skin color segmentation

f) background subtraction

Fig. 2. Common motion detection techniques used for vision-driven interaction

3.1 Image Differencing

We will usually have RGB images. Let us use $R_0(\mathbf{x})$, $G_0(\mathbf{x})$, $B_0(\mathbf{x})$ and $R_1(\mathbf{x})$, $G_1(\mathbf{x})$, $B_1(\mathbf{x})$ to denote the RGB values of a pixel at position $\mathbf{x}$ in two consecutive images obtained from the camera. Here $\mathbf{x}=[x\ y]^T$ is a vector, where x and y are the coordinates of the pixel within an image. The change of the image values within a region W can be described by:

$$D = \sum_{\text{all x within W}} \{(R_1(\mathbf{x})- R_0(\mathbf{x}))^2+(G_1(\mathbf{x})- G_0(\mathbf{x}))^2+(B_1(\mathbf{x})- B_0(\mathbf{x}))^2\} \qquad (1)$$

The motion can be simply detected by checking if D is greater than a predefined threshold value. The currently available games [3][4] use this or a similar technique to detect the motion of the users. The motion is used for a "button-like" interaction we described in the previous section. If motion is detected within W, the button is activated. Note that in this way we do not extract the direction of the motion and the value D is just weakly related to the magnitude of the motion. See figure 2c for an example.

3.2 Optical Flow

If a vision-driven-gadget covers a region W we would like to estimate the 2D displacement $\mathbf{d}=[d_x \ d_y]^T$ (optical flow) of this patch between two consecutive images that are captured by the camera. We will present a standard techniques for estimating the optical flow from [13][14] and modify it to get more robust results.

For simplicity we will use the gray intensity images. If we have RGB images we can get the intensity $I(\mathbf{x})$ of a pixel by $I(\mathbf{x})=(R(\mathbf{x})+G(\mathbf{x})+B(\mathbf{x}))/3$. For an intensity image I_0 and a patch W, the goal is to find the patch in the next image I_1 that is the most similar to the initial patch. If we put this into equations the goal would be to find the displacement $\mathbf{d}$ that minimizes:

$$J(\mathbf{d}) = \sum_{\text{all x within} W} (I_1(\mathbf{x}+\mathbf{d})- I_0(\mathbf{x}))^2 \qquad (2)$$

If we use a truncated Taylor expansion approximation of (2) we get:

$$Z\mathbf{d}=\mathbf{e}, \qquad (3)$$

where the 2x2 matrix Z and the vector $\mathbf{e}$ are given by:

$$Z = \sum_{\text{all x within} W} \begin{bmatrix} g_x^2 & g_x g_y \\ g_x g_y & g_y^2 \end{bmatrix} \qquad (4)$$

$$\mathbf{e} = \sum_{\text{all x within} W} (I_1- I_0)[g_x \ g_y]^T \qquad (5)$$

Here g_x and g_y present the derivatives of the initial intensity image I_0 in x and y direction. We compute the derivatives using a simple Sobel operator [19].

The procedure form [13] repeats the Taylor approximation (2) iteratively. If $\mathbf{d}(k)$ presents the estimated displacement at k-th iteration the iterative solution is given by:

$$\mathbf{d}(k+1) = \mathbf{d}(k)+Z^{-1} \mathbf{e}(k) \qquad (3)$$

At each iteration $\mathbf{d}(k)$ is used to wrap I_1 and recalculate $\mathbf{e}(k)$. The matrix Z remains the same. The procedure stops when the displacement estimate does not change any more or the maximum number of iterations is reached. The estimated displacement $\mathbf{d}$ can be used in various ways. See the experimental section for some examples.

Optical-flow estimates are often very noisy. Texture in an image is important to reliably estimate the position of an image patch W. This is known as the "aperture problem" [20]. However, we can avoid this in the following way. If the patch is in an area of the image with uniform intensity, the motion estimate will be very noisy. This can be detected using the eigenvalues e_1 and e_2 of the matrix Z. See also [15][16]. Both eigenvalues will be small and can set the motion to zero since it can not be reliably estimated. If the W is on a line-like structure in the image, the motion is only well defined in the direction normal to the line. This situation is detected when one of the eigenvalues is small and the other large. We then calculate the motion only in the direction of the eigenvector that correspond to the larger eigenvalue. This direction is the direction normal to the line. Only when both eigenvalues are larger than a threshold we calculate the full optical flow displacement as described.

Calculating the optical-flow in real-time for the whole image might require a lot of computing power. However, we only need optical-flow measurements for the visual-driven gadgets which can be done very fast.

3.3   Other Common Motion Detection Methods

Among other common techniques for detecting and measuring motion of the user, we will mention the "background subtraction" and the "skin color detection".

Background subtraction is a method that tries to distinguish the user from a static background. See an example in figure 2e. The IntelPlay Me2cam [12] and Vivid Group Gesture Xtreme [11] systems use this technique, but a special setting and initialization is needed. Background subtraction is also sensitive to environment changes and camera movements. In such cases the system should be re-initialized. Some automatic adaptive methods exist [22,23], but they are slow in adapting and they assume that the camera most of the time observes background which is not the case when a user is using a vision-based user interface.

Skin color detection is a common technique used for building vision based interfaces [21]. Regions in the image that have the color similar to that of the human skin are detected. These regions usually correspond to the hands and faces of the users. See figure 2f. The movement of these regions can be used for interaction. See [21] for some examples. Unfortunately, the observed colors depend heavily on the light conditions and also the camera that is used. Therefore, for good performance a careful calibration is required. In conclusion, both techniques do not fulfill the difficult "real" real-world requirements and will not be considered further in the experiments.

4   Experiments

In this section we will evaluate and compare the performance of the image-differencing and the optical-flow techniques.

4.1   Qualitative Comparison

Both techniques comply with the requirements for the "real" real-world algorithm mentioned in the introduction. Light conditions are not important, there is no initialization etc. This is probably why the commercial vision-driven games often use the image-differencing. Optical-flow measurements preserve the good properties of the image-differencing technique but provide more information. A summary is given in the table 1.

Both techniques present a simple low-level analysis of the scene. However, the optical-flow might be in perspective used also for some higher semantic level understanding the user actions. Jahansson, in his famous experiments [1], filmed people in darkness wearing small light bulbs on their body. Moving cloud of identical bright dots on a dark field was enough to detect people in the scene and even assess their activity, gender and age. Inspired by [1], computer vision algorithms for detecting human activities from optical-flow were reported in [17] and [18]. These results might be important for further extension of the interface we present in this paper.

Table 1. Qualitative comparison of the two simple methods. A summary

	Image-differencing	Optical-flow
No initialization	+	+
Works under different environment conditions	+	+
Simple to compute	+	+
Motion detection	+	+
Motion magnitude	≈	+
Motion direction	-	+

4.2 Buttons Experiment

We analyzed the performance of the two techniques on the basic element of any user interface, the button. (see section 2.2). We used simple static buttons that are selected when the movement in the area W of the button is detected. We implemented a system that is using the standard image-differencing technique. To filter out some possible noisy detection we wait until the motion is detected for two consecutive frames. We implemented also a system that is using the optical-flow. The button that is driven by the optical-flow will react only to the movement in the right direction. This filters out many unwanted motions. According to the users in our experiment, this is a very natural way of pressing a virtual button.

The experiments were performed using 14 people. The task was to press the button presented using green color. See figure 3. We counted number of well selected buttons and the number of wrongly selected buttons during a period of 30 seconds. After a button was selected there was a 0.5 second pause before a new button is randomly chosen and highlighted using green color. The users had 2 trials to learn to use the interface and the results from the third trial are reported in table 2. We observe a big improvement when the optical-flow is used. In the complex menu case (figure 3b) image-differencing was completely useless.

a) simple menu

b) complex menu with randomly distributed buttons

Fig. 3. Buttons experiment. Two situations are presented.

Table 2. Results of the experiments. We report the difference between the number of well selected buttons and the number of wrongly selected buttons. Mean value, standard deviation, maximum and minimum are reported

	Image-differencing (simple menu)	Optical-flow (simple menu)	Image-differencing (complex menu)	Optical-flow (complex menu)
Mean	11.2	19.2	-20.9	5.7
Std	6.6	2.9	17.8	4.9
Min	1	13	-54	1
Max	20	24	0	14

Fig. 4. Moving objects. Some images from a public performance are presented. Children sorted virtual objects on color and shape

4.3 Movable Objects

Optical flow can be used to perform another basic user-interface task: dragging a virtual object. A vision-driven-gadget is moved to the new position according to the calculated displacement **d**. We realized an interactive vision-driven game where the task was to sort virtual objects on shape and color. We had a large number of users during a set of public performances. It turned out that it was easy and fun for most people to use this interface. We had also a large number of children participants. The children enjoyed the game enormously and they were also able to learn to use the interface very fast. See some screen-shots in figure 4.

5   Conclusions

We proposed a way to use optical flow for vision-based user interfaces and presented how various basic user-interface tasks can be realized. The optical-flow calculation is fast, simple and robust. It does not require initialization or some special setting and it is potentially very interesting for making "real" real-world vision-driven user interfaces. An example is the gaming industry where optical flow presents a natural extension of the currently used simple and robust techniques.

References

1. Johansson, G.: Visual Perception of Biological Motion and a Model for its Analysis, In: Perception and Psychophysics, Number 14, (1973) 201–211
2. Gong S., Zhang, H-J. (eds.): Proceedings of the IEEE International Workshop on Analysis and Modeling of Faces and Gestures – in connection with the International Conference on Computer Vision 2003, (2003)
3. Sony Computer Entertainment Inc.: Sony Eye Toy, www.eyetoy.com, (2003)
4. Reality Fusion Inc: GameCam, (1999)
5. Darrel, T., Baker, H., Crow, F., Gordon, G., Woodfill, J.: Magic Morphin Mirror. Presented at SIGGRAPH 1997– Electronic Garden (1997)
6. Yang, R., Zhang, Z.: Eye gaze correction with stereovision for video tele-conferencing. In: Proceedings of the Seventh European Conference on Computer Vision, (2002) 479–494
7. Rokeby, D.: Transforming Mirrors: Subjectivity and Control in Interactive Media. In: Simon Penny (ed.): Critical Issues in Electronic Media, Leonardo Electronic Almanac, Vol. 3, No. 4 (1995)
8. Höysniemi, J., Hämäläinen, P., and Turkki, L.: Using peer tutoring in evaluating the usability of a physically interactive computer game with children. In: Interacting with Computers, Vol. 15, Issue 2, (2003) 141–288
9. Krueger, M., Gionfriddo, T., Hinrichsen, K.: VIDEOPLACE-An Artificial Reality, In: Proceedings of the ACM Conference on Human Factors in Computing Systems (CHI '85) (1985)
10. Ishii, H., Ullmer, B.: Tangible Bits: Towards Seamless Interfaces between People, Bits and Atoms, In: Proceedings of ACM Conference on Human Factors in Computing Systems (CHI '97) (1997) 234–241
11. Vivid Group Inc.: Gesture Xtreme System, www.vividgroup.com (1986)

12. D'Hoge H.: Game Design Principles for the IntelPlay Me2Cam Virtual Game System, Intel Technology Journal (2001)
13. Lucas B., Kanade T.: An iterative image registration technique with an application to stereo vision. In: Proceedings IJCAI81 (1981) 674–679
14. Baker S., Matthews I.: Lucas-Kanade 20 years on: A unifying framework part 1: The quantity approximated, the warp update rule, and the gradient descent approximation, In: International Journal of Computer Vision (2003)
15. Thomasi C., Kanade T.: Detection and tracking of point features. In: Carnegie Mellon University Technical Report CMU-CS-91-132, (1991)
16. Zivkovic Z., van der Heiden F.: Improving the selection of feature points for tracking, In: Pattern Analysis and Applications, accepted for publication
17. Davis J., Bobick A., The Representation and Recognition of Action Using Temporal Templates, In: Proceedings of IEEE Conference CVPR, (1997), 928–934
18. Song Y., Concalves L., Perona P.: Unsupervised learning of human motion. In: IEEE Transactions Pattern Analysis and Machine Intelligence, 25(7), (2003) 814–827
19. Horn B.: Computer Vision. Cambridge, Mass.: MIT Press, (1986)
20. Beauchemin S.S., Barron J.L.: The Computation of Optical Flow, In: ACM Computing Surveys 27(3) (1996) 433–467
21. Pentland A.: Looking at People: Sensing for Ubiquitous and Wearable Computing, In: IEEE Transactions Pattern Analysis and Machine Intelligence, 22(1), (2000) 107–119
22. Stauffer C., Grimson W.: Adaptive background mixture models for real-time tracking, In: Proceedings of IEEE Conference CVPR,(1999) 246–252
23. Zivkovic Z.: Improved adaptive Gausian mixture model for background subtraction, In: Proceedings of the International Conference Pattern Recognition, (2004)

The Human-Information Workspace (HI-Space): Ambient Table Top Entertainment

Andrew J. Cowell, Richard May, and Nick Cramer

Pacific Northwest National Laboratory
PO Box 999, Richland, WA 99352, USA
{andrew,richard.may,nick}@pnl.gov

Abstract. This paper introduces the Human Information Workspace (HI-Space) as a test-bed for evaluating new information exploration mechanisms. In moving from dated interaction devices and small computer monitors, we aim to utilize more natural surfaces such as tables and walls as our interaction space. In testing our theories, we have produced a number of gaming applications as test cases. Here, we report on our most popular application, Virtual Hockey.

1 Introduction

The key to developing next generation human-information interfaces is to move beyond the limitations of dated interaction devices and small computer monitors. Our physical information space should include new canvases such as walls, tables and other natural surfaces. We perform physical interactions with 'information' every day when we pick up a book, draw a diagram, or write notes on a page. Similar innate methods of interaction need to be developed for the electronic equivalents, providing users with the ability to interact more quickly, naturally, and more effectively in the broader context of information exploration. To test these theories, we have developed the Human-Information Workspace (HI-Space) [1]. This system utilizes knowledge from many areas of research, including Psychology, Human-Computer Interaction, Virtual Reality, Kinesiology, and Computer Science, to create a workspace that blurs the boundaries between physical and electronic information. The most desirable aspects of both the physical and electronic information spaces are used to enhance the ability to interact with information, promote group dialog, and to facilitate group interaction with information to solve complex tasks.

After discussing the technology behind the HI-Space, we introduce a gaming application, Virtual Hockey, which was developed to present the potential of the HI-Space system. While this application is fairly simple, users have found the game to be truly addictive, potentially due to its ease of use, simplicity and the users ability to directly manipulate the outcome.

M. Rauterberg (Ed.): ICEC 2004, LNCS 3166, pp. 101–107, 2004.

2 HI-Space Technology

In a HI-Space system, the sensors (camera, radio frequency tagging antenna and microphone array) are placed over the table to capture user interactions with a table display. For the purpose of this paper only a single video camera is used as the tracking sensor. The display itself is a rear-view screen being fed by a standard LCD projector. The HI-Space creates an interaction space between the sensor array and the 2D display surface, as depicted in Figure 1. This creates a 3D interaction volume that allows the user a much greater degree of freedom. The system has the potential to interpret gestures or actions anywhere in the interaction volume and respond accordingly, giving the HI-Space much greater potential for advanced interactions than technologies that only mimic touch screen type functionality. The emphasis of our research has been the development of new interaction techniques and technologies as well as creating the information workspace. Towards this objective, we are taking advantage of technologies that are already in the mainstream pipeline, including new projector technology, large-screen displays, and high-resolution cameras. Battelle has a working proof-of-concept HI-Space system at its facilities [2] and has a second system at the University of Washington's Human Interface Technology Laboratory (HITL) [3]. Other HI-Space systems are in use at other sites around the USA (e.g. the GeoVISTA Center at Penn State [4]).

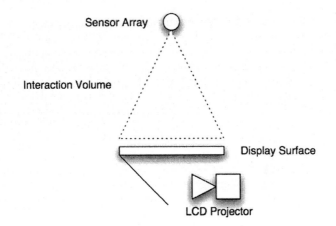

Fig. 1. The HI-Space System

The core of the HI-Space system is the underlying computer vision library that takes incoming video images and recognizes two new classes of input devices, pointers and objects. Pointers are anything that is reaching into the interaction volume. For example, a hand or hand held stylus. An object is something that has been placed on the display surface and left there. The use of objects in video tracked systems has been discussed extensively under the topic of tangible interfaces [5] and hand tracking has occurred in a variety of systems [6,7,8]. Hi-Space uniquely brings these and other functionality into a group environment where neither the user nor objects are instrumented or tethered in any way. All tracking and recognition is from physical characteristics derived only from the video camera. The system will track as many pointers and objects as are placed inside the interaction volume, however, there is a practical limit due to problems of recognizing when pointers overlap one another.

When a pointer or object is recognized by the HI-Space library routines, it passes to the application a set of characteristics about each and every pointer or object being tracked. These characteristics are updated with each new video frame. For pointers, the application is sent the location it entered the interaction volume, where the tip of the pointer is located, length of the pointer, how many fingers (in the case of a hand) are on the pointer, and if the pointer is in a recognized pose state. The pose is used for hands and is part of a gesture recognitions system. Each object has a list of characteristics including, location, size, and shape. Figure 2 shows an example a processed view with two points (one hand and one stylus) and one object. What applications choose to do with these new input devices is solely left to the discretion of the application programmer, just as is the case with any input device.

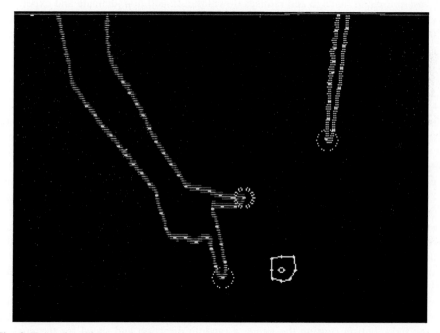

Fig. 2. Example pointers and object captured and processed by HI-Space. This is a view down from the camera over the table surface.

The main focus of HI-Space development has been to support a number of Human Computer Interaction (HCI) research issues such as investigating redundancy of multi-modal input and unencumbered work environments, direct manipulation as a mechanism for a more natural interface as well as collaborative group interaction of the same data at the same time and in the same physical space, as well as users at remote sites collaborating via matched tables. In conducting this work, we have produced a number of applications to evaluate theories and concepts. One specific example falls within the entertainment domain, and is presented here.

3 Entertainment Applications

The HI-Space system is in many ways ideal for entertainment applications. There is no equipment to be worn or calibration process to perform, allowing the experience to begin and end as simply as walking up to the system and walking away. This helps to maximize throughput of potential users. In addition, the number of players supported at one time is a function of the environment size. The larger the environment, the more players can interact at one time. For example, in 2001, three HI-Space tables were uses as part of an exhibit at the Seattle Art Museum[1]. The application and table size were designed to support up to 10 participants. This design allowed for 25,000 people to experience the exhibit over a 3 month period.

When interacting with the system, the only input device required are the players themselves (or in some cases non-breakable objects), while many other systems use fragile input devices such as mice, joysticks or buttons. This protects the hardware against abuse and damage and reduces downtime. In addition, delicate and expensive components are concealed away from players, meaning that spilled drinks or rambunctious players cannot damage the electronics. Here, we introduce our most popular gaming application written for the HI-Space system.

3.1 Virtual Hockey

Virtual Hockey is a fast paced, two-person game that combines aspects of an air hockey table and pinball. This style of competitive game dates back to the original PONG (http://www.pong-story.com) up to virtual reality versions like AR2 Hockey [9]. The Virtual Hockey game consists of three dynamic components: player paddles, a puck, and defenders. Figure 3 shows the playing field that appears on the table surface along with annotations indicating the various visual elements. Virtual Hockey supports two players with each player controlling a virtual paddle. The paddle automatically appears underneath the tip of the farthest finger when the player reaches over the playing field. Only one paddle is allowed on each side of the table and the game ignores any other hands over the space. The virtual paddle is just a circular graphic with a configurable pattern or image in the middle. As the player moves his/her hand over the table, the paddle follows.

The puck is also circular, slightly smaller than the paddles and controlled by the computer. Only one puck is maintained at a time. Initially, the puck rests in the center of the field, but on starting the game, a random direction and speed for the puck is defined. In addition to the paddles, each player has two defenders that can be placed on the table. Defenders are physical objects that the players manipulate in real time. The physical component is a 2.125" diameter wooden disk. The game looks for up to two defenders on each side of the table, and ignores objects that are not round with a diameter of 2.125 +/- 0.5in. When placed on the table, a ring appears around the wooden disk to indicate the defender is active and when activated by the player, the puck will bounce off the defender. When a defender is first placed on the field, a green ring is generated. Defenders are programmed to decay, however. As the puck hits the defender, the ring changes to yellow, then red. Finally, after enough hits by

---

[1] http://www.hitl.washington.edu/people/rmay/SAM/SAM.html.

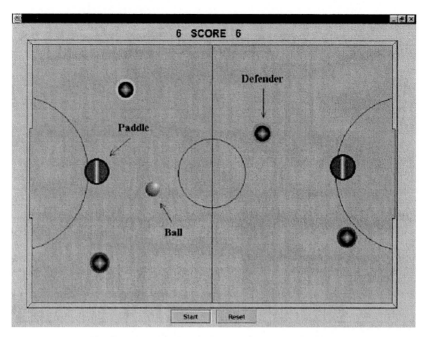

Fig. 3. Virtual Hockey playing field with annotations

the puck, the ring disappears altogether. When no graphical ring is around the defender, the defender is not activated and does not stop the puck.

In play, the puck can bounce off the walls, defenders, and paddles and a small amount of friction is applied to make the physics more realistic. The bounce equations also include a small amount of jitter to stop the puck from becoming trapped in a repeating bounce pattern. When, however, the puck bounces off a moving paddle, a percentage of the paddle's velocity is transferred to the puck, increasing the velocity of the puck. Virtual Hockey has a maximum puck velocity which serves as the upper limit when the puck speed is increased.

In addition to the visual feedback techniques already discussed, the game score is kept along the side of the screen. When a goal is scored, the updated score flashes in large print in the middle of the playing field. In addition, audio feedback plays a significant part in the game experience, providing both feedback to the player and generating excitement and interest in the game. Every time the puck bounces off a surface, a sound is made. The sound differs depending on whether the puck bounces off a wall, defender, or paddle. If the player imparts sufficient velocity to the puck, an additional "crack" sound is generated, implying a harder impact. When a player makes a goal, there is cheering.

The first version of Virtual Hockey was demonstrated at ACM-SIGGRAPH 2000 in New Orleans as part of the Emerging Technologies Venue. It ran for the five days of the conference and was a favorite among venue staff for holding after hours Virtual Hockey tournaments. Virtual Hockey was enhanced for showing at the ACM1 conference in March of 2001 at San Jose to include better graphics. ACM1 had a signifi-

Fig. 4. Virtual Hockey game in use

cant education component resulting in a large number of young adults and children attending. Figure 4 was taken at the ACM1 conference. Since the inception of Virtual Hockey it has become a main stay demonstration at both the Battelle and HITL facilities.

The response from players of Virtual Hockey has been extremely positive. One of the reasons for this is the performance of the game. Except for designed game pauses, the game at runs at 30fps on a Pentium III 800MHz system with a 16Mb graphics card (a very modest hardware platform by today's standards). This allows the players to respond quickly to the moving puck. Overall, the audio and visual feedback, combined with intuitive and direct physical interaction and a simple set of rules, has worked exceptionally well. While the game is not yet as fast as air hockey, it does generate a lot of energy, ingenuity, and competition. Figure 4 shows the game in use.

4 Summary

In this short paper we have introduced the HI-Space system, its technology and main research aims. We presented one of our main concept applications, a Virtual Hockey game that replicates much of the functionality of air hockey. We aim to continue the evolution of this technology to support collaborative scientific discovery for scientists across a number of disciplines – we hope whatever entertainment applications we develop to test our concepts continue to provide amusement as Virtual Hockey has done.

References

[1]   May, R. (1999). Hi-Space: A Next Generation Workspace Environment. Masters Thesis in Electrical Engineering Computer Science. Pullman, Washington, Washington State University.

[2]   http://showcase.pnl.gov/show?it/hispace-prod

[3]   http://www.hitl.washington.edu/hispace.html

[4]   MacEachren M.A., et al (2003) Visually-Enabled Geocollaboration to Support Data Exploration & Decision-Making. Proceedings of the 21st International Cartographic Conference, Durban, South Africa, pg. 10–16 August 2003.

[5]   Ullmer, B. and H. Ishii (1997). The metaDESK: Models and Prototypes for Tangible User Interfaces. UIST '97.

[6]   Matsushita, N. and J. Rekimoto (1997). HoloWall: Designing a Finger, Hand, Body, and Object Sensitive Wall. UIST '97.

[7]   Krueger, M. W. (1991). Artificial Reality II, Addison-Wesley Publishing Company.

[8]   Wellner, P. (1993). "Interactions with Paper on the DigitalDesk." Communications of the ACM 36(7): 87–96.

[9]   Ohshima, T., K. Sato, et al. (1998). AR2 Hockey; A Case Study of Collaborative Augmented Reality. VRAIS 98.

Game-Driven Intelligent Tutoring Systems*

Marco A. Gómez-Martín, Pedro P. Gómez-Martín, and Pedro A. González-Calero

Dep. Sistemas Informáticos y Programación, Universidad Complutense de Madrid, Spain
{marcoa,pedrop,pedro}@sip.ucm.es

Abstract. With the increase of computer capabilities, many learning systems have become complex simulators with advanced interfaces close to game quality. However, many games features have not been added to them. This paper focus on this area, listing what games can provide to simulation-driven tutoring systems. We also describe JV^{2}M as an example of a game-driven intelligent tutoring system to teach the compilation process of Java programs.

1 Introduction

Since computers have become popular, many tutoring systems have been developed. We can categorize them into animations, simulations, computer assisted instruction (also called computer-based training), Web-based learning, intelligent tutoring systems (ITS) and pedagogical agents.

In knowledge-domains where the student has to practice what she learns, simulators are the natural approach. But providing an almost perfect simulation is not enough without some kind of instruction and guide. Some ITS arise as improved simulators where intelligence has been added. Now the simulation *is* the learning environment, and the system provides guidance at the end of each iteration [1]. Case-base teaching (CBT), as a particular kind of ITS, is a learning method based on Case-based reasoning (CBR). Actually, CBT is a learning-by-doing approach where the student works on a task that pursues a pedagogical goal that profits from the expert experiences presented at the right moments. In order to do this, it confronts the student with more and more complex problems, and gives her contextualized explanations. When the system detects the student has enough knowledge to get over the next level, it presents the next exercise. A supplementary enhancement is to incorporate animated pedagogical agents (PA) who inhabit in the learning environments [7].

Most of those systems focused on learning factors are boring applications that the student uses because he has to. On the other hand, the rise of computer speed have increased the amount of entertainment software. Players are immersed in microworlds, not learning any particular domain but becoming part of the environment. Gaming shows us that long, traditionally tedious, and difficult tasks can be engaging and fun when they are part of a good story [5]. When we manage to make learning content blurs with game story, the concept of game-based learning is born. Thus, game-based teaching is used to describe the application of games to learn [10].

---

* Supported by the Spanish Committee of Science & Technology (TIC2002-01961).

M. Rauterberg (Ed.): ICEC 2004, LNCS 3166, pp. 108–113, 2004.
© IFIP International Federation for Information Processing 2004

We are not aware of any attempt to combine games (or game-base learning) with intelligent tutoring systems. This paper focuses on that attempt. In the next section we look for features in games that can be used in tutoring systems. We then describe one of such systems called JV^{2}M that we are developing to teach the Java compilation process, where we are integrating both fields. We conclude with an examination of related work and some conclusions.

2   What Games Can Provide to Learning-by-Doing

The basic relation between games and tutoring systems is the equivalence between game levels and exercises. In this section we analyse the consequences of this relation and how an ITS based on CBT can profit from the ideas already used in games.

With few exceptions, almost every game gets to an end. When the user reaches it, the game rewards her showing spectacular effects. This can motivate her, hoping to see where the game drives her. In learning environments where the concepts in the domain are clearly limited, the nature of the domain itself forces the application to finish when the user model indicates the learner knows all the domain concepts.

When playing entertainment software, the big reward is to win the game, but when the user starts playing, that is a pretty distant goal [9]. Thus to keep the player attention, many games add little rewards at the end of some levels (as cutting-scenes). Experience teaches us that these rewards cause users to play more. Learning applications can apply the same concept when the student resolves an exercise.

Usually, games manage to keep the user attention with a background story. In entertainment products, there is a common thread running throughout the entire game, giving the user the idea of unit. The cutting-scenes shown between levels are part of that story or tail, and they show the user the next challenge to overcome.

Therefore, when a tutoring system pretends to be as fun as a game, it is important to break the feeling of the application as a collection of independent exercises. It needs to keep some kind of relation between each exercise, in order for the user to perceive coherence in the application. The idea of using a background story can be taken from the game domain. Since every story must have an end, the ITS should finish. This contrasts with the fact that traditional intelligent tutoring systems do not have an implicit ending; the user does stop using it when she thinks she has learnt enough, when she gets bored or when the system does not introduce any new concept.

In order to obtain the story, a scriptwriter can compose an engaging script with a clear ending. As a basic constraint, the script has to be divided into different phases or levels, each one becoming an exercise proposed by the CBT. When the application considers the user knows all the concepts, it drives the story to its end, letting know the student that both, the game and the learning process, have finished. Ideally, the story has not to be *wire coded*, but can be created by a director system which dynamically generates it and controls it [3] according to the exercise progress. Whatever method is used to generate the script, the CBT cycle underlies the game process:

–   The script motivation is shown to the user, in order to engage her to proceed with the next exercise. It consists in presenting the goals of the story that the user will get if she manages to resolve the problem.
–   The pedagogical module chooses the next exercise using the student model.

- The virtual environment is shown, and the user is left on it to perform the exercise. If there is a pedagogical agent, he also receives information about the new exercise.
- Learner tries to resolve the problem while the pedagogical agent observes her and helps when she needs it. User model is updated with the information collected by the agent or system.

One potential drawback of hiding the CBT cycle is that the user cannot participate in the decision of choosing the next exercise, as some traditional tutoring systems allow. For example, in [11] the user can opt to repeat an exercise or ask for another similar one to practise the same concepts with a different problem.

However the idea also matches entertainment software. Nowadays more and more games allow the user to repeat a level. This behaviour can be kept in games with learning content, but now the user actually performs again the exercise when she is not very proud of her solution or time. The game could even have an option as "*play a level similar to this one which I have already passed*". Here the pedagogical module will select an exercise that involves the same concepts that those taught in this phase.

Using all these ideas, a set of relationships arises between the characteristics many games posses today and the kind of features a CBT system should have:

- Start a game: a new player is registered in the system. At the beginning, her user model will indicate that she has no knowledge on the domain.
- Game tutorial: more and more games include an initial tutorial to teach the user the basics of the application. In a learning environment this stage could be used to extract the learner's initial knowledge of the concepts and update her model.
- Accomplish a level (puzzle or quiz): it is equivalent to resolving an exercise selected by the pedagogical module.
- Save the game: in a CBT system, the save-points store the user model and the story state. The saved game also contains which exercises have been already resolved, to give a chance of repeating them.
- Load a game: it retrieves the user model and accomplished levels. The user is able to proceed to the next level or to repeat or to play in a similar one.
- Win the game: when all the levels have been accomplished, the user has finished the game. In a CBT system, the application states the user knows everything the system is able to teach. The script must be finished, and the user perceives that she has reached the end.
- Failed: when the user cannot accomplish the phase (she has been defeated), she must reload a previous game. In CBT systems, this action symbolizes the user performing an exercise incorrectly, and she must try again. Either the system or the pedagogical agent must provide some help to assure the student learns from her mistakes, and she advances towards the comprehension of the concepts.
- Checkpoints with automatic saving: in some occasions the game stores its state without an explicit order from the player. If the user happens to fail in her mission, the level starts over on that instant, rather than going back to the last user-saved point. However, these check points are not stored between sessions, so if the user closes the game it is not possible to start from this point. In a CBT system the application can use these places when the user has made too many mistakes in the exercise resolution, and it is not possible to recover from them.

Fig. 1. Student (right) approaching JAVY (left) to ask him a question.

3   JV²M Description

Currently, we are developing JV²M, an application where we aim at putting into practise the previous ideas about the relationship between games and ITS. JV²M uses ideas from CBT and pedagogical agents to teach programmers with Java knowledge the Java Virtual Machine (JVM) internals and how the compiler translates source code into object code (JVM code).

Specifically, student is immersed in a virtual environment where she can manipulate objects and interact with characters. The three-dimensional environment is an artificial site that simulates the JVM. User is symbolized as an avatar that interacts with the objects in the virtual world. She also owns an inventory where collected objects are stored in order to be used later.

The metaphorical virtual machine is also inhabited by JAVY (**Java** taught **Vi**rtually), an animated pedagogical agent who supplies hints, and who, eventually, can solve the exercise by himself. Each exercise consists of the source code of a Java program that must be compiled. User has to execute the *compiled object code* on top of the JVM represented by the metaphorical virtual environment.

The central part for a CBT becoming a game is a script that joins the exercises (levels) to keep them coherent. The story's background is the user avatar, who used to live in the real world, waking up with a hangover in a mysterious cartoon straw rick. He discovers he has been rammed into a virtual world, known as YOGYAKARTA, where he wants immediately run away. But he will be only able to leave when he understands the rules of that strange city. Obviously, YOGYAKARTA is our metaphorical JVM, so understanding it consists in executing Java program on top of it.

In the virtual world, our main character is not on his own. The environment is populated by other characters who are in similar horrible situation, locked in a world that is not theirs. They are oppressed peasants, who have neither time nor enough knowledge to unleash a war of liberation. And that is, specifically, the "auto impose" role of our pupil: he will study how that world works, in order to execute more and more difficult exercises to liberate more and more peasants of their oppressors and, eventually, to open the hidden communicating door with the free world.

In each level, a peasant asks the user to be freed. The student will have to execute a specific program to do it, and the slave will, eventually, join to the revolution. Clearly the exercise to solve is selected by the pedagogical module according to the estimated user knowledge.

The game (and the learning process) ends when the pedagogical module decides to face the user with the last level that joins every concept the user is supposed to have learnt. Instead of releasing a new peasant, this last exercise opens the secret door that let everybody leave YOGYAKARTA and, finally, come back to the real world.

4 Related Work

There are multiple commercial and academic attempts to teach specific concepts to children by means of computer applications that hide the learning process under a game. Even some commercial games have been recognized to promote beneficial skills and abilities as deductive reasoning, memorisation or co-operation. Teaching content which is of direct relevance to the school curriculum seems more difficult to teach [6]. Nevertheless, that has been achieved in some systems, as the commercial "Where is Carmen Sandiego?" game series.

"Monkey Wrench Conspiracy" [8] is a videogame tutorial, which teaches how to use a complex CAD program. Each level corresponds to an exercise in that program, but the system "decorates" them using a motivating script. Nevertheless, it does not seem to have a pedagogical module or a pedagogical agent: every game will be the same for each user.

The academic world has developed educational software to teach how some real and virtual machines work. A work similar to our system (about the way we teach the JVM) is CPUCity [1]. A pedagogical agent called WHIZLOW inhabits the virtual environment but the system has not a script to give a background story. Actually, the system is neither presented as a game at all nor had a clear exercise base or pedagogical module.

We are not aware of any other attempt to teach the compilation process, although there are some systems that aim at teaching computer programming. For example, ToonTalk [4] is a game to teach programming. Nevertheless, it is a system developed with children in mind, so it is supposed to teach programming concepts but users do not learn how to write source code.

Finally, Spion [2] has been used for years to teach German language using a textual adventure game about spies in the years previous to the unification of Germany.

5 Conclusions and Future Work

In this paper, we have analysed the different opportunities to improve intelligent tutoring systems using features of the game world, and vice versa. The main idea is to supply ITS with an explicit ending using a background story. We have also detailed how we are putting into practise this scheme in our own educational system, JV^{2}M.

This application teaches the Java compilation process using a virtual environment that simulates the Java Virtual Machine using a metaphor with buildings, characters and machines. Each exercise is the source code of a Java program the user has to compile and to execute on top of that JVM. A pedagogical agent called JAVY inhabits the learning environment and he supplies the user with help.

JV^{2}M is still under development and it needs more work. To gauge the effectiveness of our system, an evaluation will be conducted with students with Java programming knowledge when the program will be finished.

To conclude, an exciting point of open research that should be scrutinize is the real-time adjustment of the background story depending on the user interaction, in order to do each game even more different to others.

References

1. W. Bares, L. Zettlemoyer, and J. C. Lester. Habitable 3D learning environments for situated learning. In Proceedings of the Fourth International Conference on Intelligent Tutoring Systems, pages 76-85, San Antonio, TX, August 1998.
2. G. Culley, et al. A foreign language adventure game: Progress report on an application of AI to language instruction. CALICO Journal, 4(2):69–87, December 1986.
3. C. Fairclough and P. Cunningham. A multiplayer case based story engine. In 4th International Conference on Intelligent Games and Simulation (GAME-ON), pages 41–46, November 2003.
4. K. Kahn. A computer game to teach programming. In Proc. National Educational Computing Conf., 1999.
5. D. Klaila. Game-based e-learning gets real. Learning Circuits ASTD's Online Magazine. http://www.learningcircuits.org/2001/jan2001/klaila.html, January 2001.
6. A. McFarlane, A. Sparrowhawk, and Y. Heald. Report on the educational use of games. TEEM: Teachers Evaluating Educational Multimedia, 2002.
7. R. Moreno, R. Mayer, and J. C. Lester. Life-like pedagogical agents in constructivist multimedia environments: Cognitive consequences of their interaction. In Conference Proceedings of the World Conference on Educational Multimedia Hypermedia, and Telecommunications (ED-MEDIA), pages 741–746, Montreal, Canada, June 2000.
8. M. Prensky. Digital Game-Based Learning. McGraw-Hill Trade, First edition edition, December 2000.
9. A. Rollings and D. Morris. Game Architecture and Design. New Riders, Indianapolis, 2003.
10. L. Smith and S. Mann. Playing the game: A model for gameness in interactive game based learning. In Proceedings of the 15th Annual NACCQ, 2002.
11. R. H. Stottler. Tactical action officer intelligent tutoring system (TAO ITS). In Proceedings of the Industry/Interservice, Training, Simulation & Education Conference (I/ITSEC 2000), November 2000.

Practice! YUBIMOJI AIUEO for Japanese Hand Language Learning

Takao Terano[1], Fusako Kusunoki[2], Yasushi Harada[2], and Miki Namatame[3]

[1] University of Tsukuba, 3-29-1, Otsuka, Bunkyo-ku, Tokyo 112-0012 Japan
Tel:+81-3-3942-6855 Fax:+81-3-3942-6829
terano@gssm.otsuka.tsukuba.ac.jp
[2] Tama Art University, 2-1723, Yarimizu, Hachioji 192-0394, Japan
Tel: +81-426-79-5630
{hayaday,kusunoki}@tamabi.ac.jp
[3] Tsukuba Col. of Technology, 4-3-15, Amakubo, Tsukuba 305-0005, Japan
Tel: +81-29-858-9352
miki@a.tsukuba-tech.ac.jp

Abstract. In paper, we describe a PC-based Japanese hand alphabet learning system: Practice! Yubimoji AIUEO (PYA) to let ordinary elementary school pupils learn basic character expressions (AIUEO) of the Japanese hand characters (Yubimoji). PYA is a very simple system both from technical and educational points of view. Experiments in an elementary school shows that pupils have really enjoyed the system and learning, thus, we believe PYA is effective as an edutainment tool.

Keywords: Visual Interface, Edutainment for Elementary School Pupils, Learning Hand Characters, Classroom Experiments

1 Introduction

There are two main systems to communicate deaf people: hand alphabets and hand languages. Hand alphabets are used to (1) make exercise for pronunciations and (2) represent new words and/or proper nouns. Hand languages are commonly used in the conversation. However, in Japan, educational systems for deaf people commonly use both hand language and hand alphabets. This is different in the United States, where they recommend deaf people to read mouth shapes in conversation, thus, they do not often use hand the languages in education. The existence of such cultural differences, we believe we must promote the hand alphabets/language systems to ordinary people in Japan. Main objective of the research is to promote the essence of Japanese hand alphabets to ordinary school pupils.

Japanese sign language and Japanese hand alphabets or KANAs are not common for ordinary Japanese people. The language and alphabet system is a local one, and different from English one. Thus, we are conducting a project to develop a PC-based edutainment system for every pupil at elementary school ages as very beginners to learn Japanese hand alphabets.

M. Rauterberg (Ed.): ICEC 2004, LNCS 3166, pp. 114–119, 2004.
© IFIP International Federation for Information Processing 2004

Although the rapid development of computer technologies, until recently, the research on studying computer supports for hand languages or hand characters has not been a popular topic. Most of the current support systems focus on highly motivated users, therefore, they have a lot of sophisticated functions. For example, studies reported in [1] or [2] emphasize on the network communication functionality to use hand language systems. Mimehand or Mimehand II system in [3] utilize language representation movement of animated agents, which also requires very complex implementation. In S-Tel [4], they have implemented avatar type characters to transmit the representation of the hand language. Virtual RadLab [5] also provides school children with a large scale virtual environment for learning.

Therefore, from pedagogical and computer-human interaction points of view, few studies have been conducted. To envision an easy-to-use and interfaces for ordinary beginner pupils, we are developing the learning system: Practice! Yubimoji AIUEO (PYA). PYA aims at letting ordinary pupils learn basic character expressions (AIUEO) of the Japanese hand characters (Yubimoji). The main focus of the paper is to demonstrate the effectiveness of the simple but interesting system to attractively educate pupils.

2 Background and Objectives

Most of today's hand language learning support systems targets on highly motivated people. This means that their digital contents are usually manipulated via keyboards and/or menus from the equipped dictionary keyed by specified words or verbs. Some systems display continuous animation images to display the contents. They often emphasize the importance of the amount of contents and query processing functions.

Such functions are adequate for motivated and advanced users, however, the beginners are very hard to understand the language system. Contrary to such conventional learning support systems, we would like to motivate, introduce, and promote ordinary people, especially elementary school pupils, to learn the Japanese hand language system. As the first stage, we only focus on the Japanese Kana characters. Especially, the forms of the hand characters must be understood by the standpoints of both speakers and listeners. We often forget the forms are in the opposite relations from the both sides. The same requirements also hold to PYA.

On the other hand, for ordinary pupils or students, there are very few educational courses and only conventional textbooks. They are not attractive at all.

Based on the discussion, the principles of PYA are summarized as follows:

(1) Visual representation of the characters from both speakers and listeners;
(2) Simultaneous displays of the corresponding Kana characters, finger shapes, mouth forms, and sounds;
(3) Integration of finger shapes, sounding faces, and the corresponding animations;
(4) Animated graphics of the finger movement; and
(5) Explanation of the origin of the finger shapes of the characters.

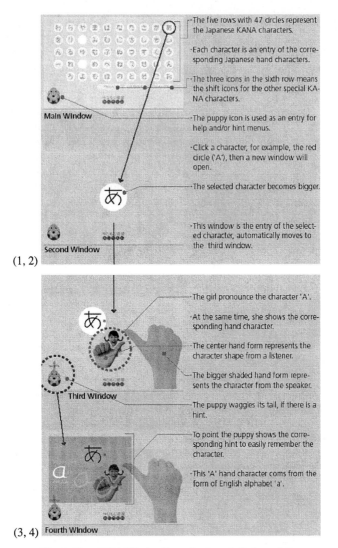

Fig. 1. How PYA Works (four displays 1, 2, 3, and 4)

3 Usage of PYA

This section describes how PYA works in a practical situation. Implementing the five principles in the previous section, PYA works as shown in Figure 3. The integrated visual interface supports the learning of the very beginners.

The first display in Figure 1 is the main entry of PYA, which shows all the Kana characters and three kind shift icons. Each Kana character is an entry to show the corresponding hand characters. The second display is shown when a user points the mouse to the place 'A', then PYA automatically shows the third display.

The girl appeared in the third display pronounces the sound of 'A'. At the same time, she shows the corresponding finger shape with appropriate movements. The center finger form represents the character from a listener, and the bigger finger form corresponds to the one from a speaker. These simultaneous finger forms enables a user to easily understand the correct form of 'A'. These displays are designed based on the principles of (1) through (4).

If there are hints about the origin of the finger shape, the puppy waggles its tail. Then, the fourth display will appear to explain how the form is determined. Such help information is essential because of the following reasons: 1) The hand characters are designed in ad hoc manner, thus, there are no fundamental principles; 2) Beginners tend to confuse the directions of each character shape, this makes difficult to memorize the shapes. The help information is the answer to the principle (5) in the previous section.

4   Experiments at an Elementary School

Using PYA, we have conducted three hours classroom experiments, which was held at Sumiyoshi Elementary School in Kobe as a special lecture on the "integrated courses" in December, 2003. The experiments consist of an oral lecture and a practice with PYA. The oral lecture was given by the first author, who is an expert of lectures to deaf students at Tsukuba College of Technology. She have much experience on the lectures of information technology and design courses to the students about 20 years old at the school . The second author, who is the designer of PYA, supported the computer exercise. He is also an expert of information design. The third author attended the experiments as a specialist on elementary school education programs.

4.1   Experimental Setups

Usually, in Japan, it is not allowed to carry out such experiments in an elementary school. Therefore, from experimental setting, the design plan was not sufficient. They required us to give the same contents and ways of the lecture to all the subjects. The 41 pupils with 11 or 12 years old are selected as the subjects of the experiments. They are all ordinary school pupils and the five of them have educational experience in the outside of Japan.

They are divided into the two groups Group 1 of 21 pupils and Group 2 of the other 20 pupils. We give Group 1 pupils PYA practice first, then an oral lecture. Group 2 pupils are given an oral lecture first, then PYA practice. We give them the same problems with different orders.

The oral lecture, which took 50 minutes, contains the explanation of the importance of the hand language system and the exercise to remember how to spell the subjects' own name and simple exercises of some popular words. In the oral lecture, the lecturers emphasize the importance both mouth forms and finger forms.

The PYA practice, which also took 50 minutes, consists of the free use of the system and simple exercises of some popular words. In the practice, pupils freely explore the visual interface of PYA under the requirements to memorize how to represent simple words and their own names.

After the practice and the lecture, we have conducted individual performance testing to uncover how they understand the language system. It took 2 to 5 minutes for each pupil to have the tests. The results have been evaluated the correctness of the forms of the characters (0-15 points), the directions of the forms (0-5 points), and the smoothness of the movements (0-5 points).

4.2 Results

We have had 40 samples (21 form Group 1 and 19 from Group 2). The summary of the sum of the evaluation items (0-25 points) are shown in Table 1. The total average score is 7.00and its standard deviation is 4.43. The subjects are divided into two or three categories according to the groups, understandability, difficulty, and interestingness: From the performance tests, we have had 40 samples (21 from Group 1 and 19 from Group 2). The summary of the sum of the evaluation items (0-25 points) is shown in Table 1.

The total average score is 7.00 and its standard deviation is 4.43. The subjects are divided into two or three categories according to the groups, understandability, difficulty, and interestingness.

Table 1. Summary of the Experiments

Category	Sub-cat	Average Scores	Category	Sub-cat	Average Scores
Group 1		6.33	Difficulty	High	6.50
Group 2		7.74	(1st Course)	Middle	7.24
PYA	Middle+	6.33		Low	7.33
understand	High	7.74	Interests	Middle+	7.77
PYA	Middle+	8.18	(1st Course)	High	6.63
interests	High	6.55	Difficulty	High	6.14
Lecture	Middle+	6.92	(2nd Course)	Middle	8.25
understand	High	7.04		Low	6.20
Lecture	Middle+	7.40	Interests	Middle+	8.36
Interests	High	6.87	(2nd Course)	High	6.48

From the experiments and preliminary statistical analyses, we have suggested that PYA is a good tool for the learning, however, more comprehensive analysis is necessary to reveal the characteristics of our learning courses. Although, the current implementation of PYA only supports individual learning, however, from the experiments, we have often observed that pupils are enjoying emerging collaborative practices. This would lead our projects towards total learning environments with mutual communications and collaborative environments [5], [6], [7], [8].

5 Concluding Remarks

In this paper, we have reported a PC-based Japanese hand alphabet learning system PYA and have discussed the effects of its visual interfaces. The current implementation of PYA is available from the web site [9]. PYA is a very simple system both from technical and educational points of view. However, from the experiments, the pupils have really enjoyed the system and learning, thus, we believe PYA is effective as an edutainment tool at elementary level courses.

The most important future work to be explored from the research is that we should develop a collaborative framework for the learning. This will help school teachers to conduct their courses more easily and effectively. Further research also includes enhancing the functionality of PYA to be able to utilize 3-D visual interfaces. To uncover the characteristics of behaviors of pupils, furthermore, we will conduct experiments to observe detailed motions of the subjects using, for example, motion capture devices.

References

1. Magnussen, M. : Videotelephony in Intervention with People with Speech and Language Disabilities. 12th Annual Conference, Technology and Persons with Disabilities, MAGNU2_T.TXT (1997) 8.
2. Sperling, G. : Future Prospects in Language and Communications for the Congenitally. In Deaf Children: Developmental Perspectives, Academic Press (1978) 103–114.
3. Mimehand web-page (2001):
    http://www.hitachi-eu.com/egov/case_studies/mimehand1.htm (in English),
    http://www.hitachi.co.jp/Prod/comp/app/shuwa/ (in Japanese).
4. Kuroda, T., Sato, K., and Chihara, K. Development of S-Tel: Avatar-Type Hand Language Transmitting System (in Japanese). Journal of Virtual Reality Society in Japan, Vol. 3, No.2 (1998) 41–46.
5. Virtual RadLab Web-Page (2003): http://www.virat.nottingham.ac.uk
6. Hammond, N., and Allinson, L. Travels around a Learning Support Environment: Rambling, Orientating or Touring? Proc. CHI 1988, (1988) 269–273.
7. Hudson, J. M., and Bruckman, A. Effects of CMC on Student Participation Patterns in a Foreign Language Learning Environment. Proc. CHI 2001, (2001) 263–264.
8. Sherman, L., et al. StoryKit: Tools for Children to Build Room-sized Interactive Experiences. Proc. CHI 2001, (2001) 197–198.
9. Harada, Y.: PYA Web-Page. (2004) http://ss4.idd.tamabi.ac.jp/~haraday/yubimoji/

The Bush Telegraph:
Networked Cooperative Music-Making

Rodney Berry, Mao Makino, Naoto Hikawa, and Masami Suzuki

ATR Media Information Science Laboratories
2-2-2 Hikaridai, 'Keihanna Science City', Kyoto 619-0288, Japan
{rodney,mao,hikawa,msuzuki}@atr.jp
http://www.mis.atr.co.jp/~mao/ac/

Abstract. *The Bush Telegraph* is based on the *Music Table*, a system that allows people to make music by arranging cards on a table. Because the user manipulates a schedule for note events rather than directly initiating them, this schedule can be shared between two remotely linked systems. *The Bush Telegraph* allows remote players to play together without timing problems due to network delays. Shared music making is made very easy but still allowing for creative freedom. We see this type of system becoming a fixture in dance club environments.

1 Introduction

The Bush Telegraph is a part of the Augmented Composer Project, an ongoing effort to explore the creative possibilities of augmented reality and related technologies for the composition, performance and learning of music. The interface itself is based on the Music Table, [1] a system aimed at younger musicians, using a set of marked cards that are read by the computer using an overhead camera. The user places the cards on a tabletop, and the positions of the cards are interpreted as musical note events, much like a simple musical score. A large screen shows the live video image overlaid with computer-generated characters and gadgets to provide extra information to the user in an amusing form. As well as the Note cards used to define a musical pattern, other cards can be used to save and layer patterns as well as to select different instruments sounds. The recent focus of the Music Table project has been on music education. Our basic idea was that manipulating abstract elements of the music in the form of physical objects, through large muscle interaction, could aid the development of musical abstraction. However, to explore entertainment applications of the system, we decided to build a new version of the music table aimed at an older audience for the spontaneous creation of 'techno' dance music. We also wanted to network two remote systems together for shared music making between people at different locations. This led us to the name Bush Telegraph, alluding to music's early function as a carrier of messages over long distances. We envisage that such a system would provide opportunities for creative expression and novel social interaction at such public events as dance parties.

M. Rauterberg (Ed.): ICEC 2004, LNCS 3166, pp. 120–123, 2004.

2 Bush Telegraph

The Bush Telegraph, like the Music Table, is divided into two sub-systems, one for handling marker tracking and visual display, and the other for handling the playing of the music.

Fig. 1. Typical set-up of music table used in *The Bush Telegraph*

Fig. 2. CG characters and gadgets for melody (left) and drum (right) instruments

2.1 Visual System and Design

The central part of the interface is the arrangement of specially marked cards on a tabletop to create simple musical patterns. This is done by tracking the positions of the cards using the Augmented Reality Toolkit (ARToolkit) programming libraries.[2] The ARToolkit allows the software to know the identity, position and rotations of each card whose marker is visible to the camera. The ARToolkit can also composite computer generated characters and models into the original video image, seemingly at the same locations as the marker patterns. In this way, the video display

Fig. 3. Note card, Phrase card and Instrument cube

shows CG characters and gadgets that appear to be manipulated by the player as he or she moves the marked cards. The overall graphic style invokes 1980s video game graphics suited to the low resolution of the output and the cartoon quality of the dance music culture.

Individual notes are shown as characters that get longer and shorter in response to tilting from left to right. This also changes the length of the note. Rotating the card changes the character and makes the note louder. Once a pattern is made on the table, a Phrase card can be introduced to store the pattern. In this way, several layers or tracks can be made. Once saved, a phrase card can be moved around to pan sounds from left to right or apply various effects by moving or tilting it. This kind of live control was a feature of The Augmented Groove, [3] an earlier project at our lab that allowed mixing of pre-recorded dance music tracks. A cube made with a marker on each face allows us to select which instrument sound or drum-set we want to hear, depending on which marker is facing the camera. This replaces the old Instrument card from the music table that most players found difficult to use.

2.2 Sound and MIDI

The midi sequencing component of the Music Table is built using Pure Data, a graphical programming environment. [4] For each note, values for pitch, loudness (MIDI velocity), length (time between MIDI note-off and note-on), as well as the note's timing, are all stored in arrays. When a card is moved, removed or added to the table, the arrays are updated immediately. Meanwhile the sequencer reads the updated values and, plays them. This means that the interface does not generate any real-time musical events. It produces updates and reads a schedule that is played to the beats of the internal clock. The original reason for this was to deal with the inherent latency in the camera-based tracking part of the interface. However, we decided that this asynchronous architecture could also be modified to link two Music Tables over a network.

2.3 Jamming over a Network

The schedule-sharing model used in the Bush Telegraph is inspired by Phil Burke's WebDrummer, a web jamming environment. [5] Unlike, WebDrummer, which uses a special server, we communicate directly via UDP sockets, and are limited to two remotely-connected stations. The remote player's note positions are indicated by clusters of stars on the local screen. The stars change color and shape according to the length and loudness of the other person's notes. Although the system has had only minimal user testing, players confirm that they feel they are playing with another person, and that the changes in the music feel 'live' and immediate without a sense of there being a delay. Importantly, the players said they liked the music being produced and that there was some creative freedom considering the simple operation. Of course the repetitive nature of dance music favors the short looping phrases made by the system.

3 Conclusions and Future Plans

Our physical interface adapts well to a networked situation but we now need to test it in a social environment such as a nightclub to expose and remedy flaws in the design (effects of lighting on tracking for example). We see this project differing further from the Music Table in the future, possibly even moving off the table and onto the dance-floor itself, and further exploiting the network and social aspects of the design.

Acknowledgements. This research was funded in part by a grant from N.I.C.T. Japan.

References

1. Berry, R., Makino, M., Hikawa, N., Suzuki, M., The Music Table *Proc. 2003 International Computer Music Conference,* Singapore. International Computer Music Association, (2003) 393–396. http://www.mis.atr.co.jp/~mao/ac/
2. Kato, H., and Billinghurst, M.. "Marker Tracking and HMD Calibration for a Video-based Augmented Reality Conferencing System", *Proc. of 2nd Int. Workshop on Augmented Reality,* (1999) 85–94
3. Puckette, M.. "Pure Data." Proceedings, International Computer Music Conference. San Francisco: International Computer Music Association, (1996) 269–272. http://crca.ucsd.edu/~msp/Publications/icmc96.ps http://crca.ucsd.edu/~msp/software.html
4. Poupyrev, I., Berry, R., Kurumisawa, J., Nakao, K., Billinghurst, M., Airola, C., Kato, H., Yonezawa, T., and Bald-win, L. 2000. "Augmented Groove: Collaborative Jamming in Augmented Reality". *Proceedings of the SIGGRAPH'2000 Conference Abstracts and Applications.* ACM. (2000) 77
5. Burke, P., Jammin' on the Web – a new Client/Server Architecture for Multi-User Musical Performance In Proc. International Computer Music Conference, International Computer Music Association, (2000) http://www.transjam.com

Art, Design, and Media

Live Role-Playing Games: Implications for Pervasive Gaming

Jennica Falk[1] and Glorianna Davenport[2]

[1] PLAY – Interactive Institute, Göteborg, Sweden & Media Lab Europe, Dublin, Ireland
jennica.falk@tii.se
[2] Interactive Cinema – MIT Media Laboratory,
Massachusetts Institute of Technology, Cambridge, Massachusetts
gid@media.mit.edu

Abstract. Live role-playing (LRP) games stand as powerful metaphorical models for the various digital and ubiquitous forms of entertainment that gather under the term pervasive games. Offering what can be regarded as the holy grail of interactive entertainment – the fully immersive experience – LRP games provide a tangible and distributed interface to a gaming activity that is emergent, improvised, collaboratively and socially created, and have the immediacy of personal experience. Supported by studies of LRP games, specifically aspects of costume, set design and props, we outline the interface culture specific to LRP and in which ways this culture may inform the design of pervasive games.

1 Introduction: Pervasive Games

Pervasive games make up a relatively contemporary area for academic inquiry. These are digital games that move beyond the traditional computer interfaces and into the physical world to occupy time and place on a human scale. These post-desktop games inhabit our physical surrounding and objects within it, employing human senses in ways that differ greatly from that of other electronic games. They take on ubiquitous and tangible forms – properties that contribute to the blurring of the lines between player and game character, game world and real world, and game artifacts and real world objects. These games have matured into experiences of personal immediacy, granting privilege to the skills with which we act and interact in our physical environment. *'Pirates!'* is an early example of such a game. It is a multi-player game played on networked handheld computers equipped with radio-frequency proximity sensors. The sensors make it possible to detect the players' relative position within a physical space, which they must navigate in order to explore the game world that unfolds on the computer screen [1]. In the *M-Views* project at MIT Media Laboratory's Interactive Cinema group, researchers are creating content and technology for what can be described as narrative treasure hunts. Equipped with handheld media machines, users navigate triangulated WLAN areas to follow movie characters around in a narrative taking place in the physical world [11]. This *mobile cinema* delivers motion picture stories based on the users' absolute location in time and space, catering for the participation of an audience immersed in context-aware multimedia. Blast

M. Rauterberg (Ed.): ICEC 2004, LNCS 3166, pp. 127–138, 2004.

Theory's gaming events *Can You See Me Now?* and *I Like Frank* explore the hybrid space between virtual and physical worlds through a mixed reality approach [2], employing human engagement in the physical world as an interaction mode for pervasive game play.

Designers of pervasive games face a number of challenges, most of which they share with designers of other ubiquitous computing applications. Notable are issues of technological nature, such as how to enable context-awareness and content delivery and issues of social nature; the impact of the application on society, privacy, and its integration with public spaces; issues of designing unambiguous functionality and how to interface content, and so forth. It is the subject matter of interfaces that we are currently focusing on; studying the interface model of *live role-playing (LRP)* games. This paper describes the nature of LRP, reports on observations from a set of games, and suggests implications for the design of ubiquitous game interfaces.

2 Live Role-Playing Games: Definitions

It is not straightforward to define what live role-playing games are – there are likely as many definitions as there are games. As Daniel Mackay observes about role-playing games, "each [game] is performed in a different way, and the performances that result are circumscribed by different boundaries." [8]. This is not necessarily an unfortunate thing but rather a good indication that the game genre offers great depth and variety in style to players. However, the situation calls for our own definition to be articulated. The following definition is applicable to the games we have studied in the past few years:

A live role-playing game is a dramatic and narrative game form that takes place in a physical environment. It is a story-telling system in which players assume character roles that they portray in person, through action and interaction. The game world is an agreed upon environment located in both space and time, and governed by a set of rules – some of which must be formal and quantifiable.

Purposefully uncomplicated, our definition highlights a number of features of special importance, which require some extra attention. Firstly, the definition indicates that LRP is about gaming. Like other games, they have a system of rules, context for advancement and goals, as well as obstacles and threats to those goals. This makes LRP different from some deceivingly similar activities, specifically living history and re-enactment events that may provide the same sort of spectacle but not the formal rules system. Secondly, they are also story-telling systems. The collective and individual game activities both have narrative qualities with emergent, collaborative, and mostly unpredictable outcomes. In this aspect LRP displays similarities with improvisational theatre, with the important difference that live role-playing games are devoid of the audience concept. Thirdly, LRP games take place in physical environments, bound by specific locations and time-frames. This is of course directly relevant to a discussion on how the physical world can be said act as an interface to the game, but more specifically it offers an appropriate metaphor for researching design implications for pervasive games.

Janet Murray describes live role-playing games as "games in which [fans of fantasy literature] assume the roles of characters within the same fictional universe."[10]. Further she elaborates, "players share a sense of exploring a common fictional landscape and inventing their stories as they go along." Her definition draws attention to an active audience literary genre and the dramatic exploration of a narrative reality.

It should be said that even if some definitions of LRP games (including our own) emphasize their game nature, this is not a widely accepted categorization. In the Dogma 99 [15] manifesto, Lars Wingård and Eirik Fatland argue that it is a "form and a method of individual and collective expression", that it is a medium rather than a genre and a "meeting between people, who through their roles, relate to each other in a fictional world." Their definition calls attention to LRP as performing arts, centering on the characters and what happens to them.

Mike Pohjola further supports the notion of active participation with his statement, "the creative side and the receptive side are no longer separate. The experience of role-playing is born through contributing. No-one can predict the events of a session beforehand, or recreate them afterwards." [12]. His statement reflects the improvisational nature of LRP games, while also emphasizing that it is very difficult (if not impossible) to tell pre-determined stories through LRP.

Fig. 1. Live role-playing games take place in the physical world

One principal objective of LRP games is the dramatization of a make-believe world. Offering social and emergent narrative co-creation, they encourage and depend on the players' active commitment and inter-personal participation. Daniel Mackay captures some of its essence, pointing to its peripatetic style: "The live action role-playing game is distinguished by the players' bodily movement through space and their assumption of costumes and other tools or techniques of naturalistic theatre. The live-action role-playing is both an environmental and improvisational performance." [8, p. 182].

All LRP games of our definition take place within an agreed upon theme or narrative setting that provides the context for players' actions and character roles. This theme can be pretty much anything you can imagine; the possibilities are inexhaustible. To give some obvious and common examples, it may be fantasy and involve magic, heroes, and fantastic creatures, much like the game world settings of the classic tabletop role-playing games. Or, it may be realistic, based on historic events or contemporary life. Or it can be futuristic post apocalyptic environments, involving mutants and cyborgian characters dwelling in deserted cities. Or, it can be any combination of these! Whatever the theme, the players will act on and within that context, creating their characters' costume, background stories, personalities and ambitions that fit into and contribute to it.

2.1 Live Role-Play and Theatre

It is possible to draw parallels between LRP and theatre, at least metaphorically. One can liken the physical environment in which the role-play takes place to the theatre's stage, upon which the players are actors and where the use of props and set-design enhances and supports the interplay between them. However, a critical difference between LRP and theatre fails the comparison. LRP games are devoid of the audience concept. It may seem an unlikely detail, especially since it is a spectacle coming across hundreds of people in costume and fake weapons behaving in mysterious ways. It is probably true that LRP is quite a show for some part of the display, but it is likely to end there. It is immensely difficult to get anything more than a flavor of what is actually going on during a LRP event, and trying to grasp or capture the story as an outsider would be an impressive feat. The most important reason for this is the participatory nature of the event. The story emerges out of the active participation of and interaction between characters. The only way to experience it with some level of coherency is really to be personally involved. From a narrative perspective, this is why LRP is different from for historical re-enactment events.

2.2 Why Do People Play LRP Games?

It is beyond the scope of this paper to analyze, or even speculate, why people play LRP games. There are many sociological studies that are devoted to this subject – primarily in the case of table-top role-playing games [e.g. 4, 8] – that suggest reasons ranging from escapism and the safe exploration of anti-social behavior (such as violence) to the need for pure and simple fun. This is certainly true also in live role-playing games. For the purposes of our work however, we direct our attention to the game mechanisms – that is, mechanisms that have little to do with the personality of the individual player – that enable immersion and engrossment within the game and its narrative theme. In other words, we are interested in how the very design and set-up of the game play affects players' commitment and engagement.

3 The 'Lorien Trust' Game World

We have followed live role-players in the United Kingdom for two years, primarily in the Lorien Trust (LT) LRP system [7]. During the summer months each year, LT organizes four main events at Locko Park in Derbyshire, each of which attracts thousands of players. We participated in a total of four of the main LT events during 2002 and 2003, each of which engaged between approximately 3500 and 4500 people. We also participated in a number of smaller events (25-100 participants) sanctioned by the LT. Each of these events typically takes place over the course of four days of continuous game play. Each event is part of a longer campaign that has been running for over ten years. In this study we are looking specifically at aspects of costume, physical props and set design with the aim to examine how they support or interface with the game play. The following analysis, although based on observations in the LT system, is not intended to be specific to this system; however, it should be noted that aspects of our analysis may not always be applicable to LRP games in general.

3.1 Costume as Interface

In mask theatre, actors act with masks covering their faces. To the actors, the masks work as tools of transformation into an often trance-like state of mind where they are not simply acting with a mask on, but are "possessed by the mask" [6, pp. 143-146]. In many ways, costume has the same effect on a live role-player, allowing them to enter into a persona separate and often different from themselves but yet one that is an extension of their selves. The LRP player, like a stage actor, is a person who undergoes a transformation into a character. The character's costume and accessories, or *kit*, aids this transformation, functioning as an interface on a number of different levels. First, it is an interface between the player and the character, i.e. it is something to 'get into character' with. The following anecdote illustrates this interface function of costume and kit. Player A is asking player B to change character from the one he is currently playing to make a brief appearance as another character:

A: *"Can you bring him into play?"*
B: *"Nah, I didn't bring any of his kit."*
A: *"Don't worry about it. There should be lots of stuff you can borrow."*
B: *"You don't understand, I can't be, and don't want to be him without his stuff."*

What A and B disagree on is the importance of costume as a tool for transformation. On the one hand, B feels that it would be a disservice to his character to portray it without the signature apparel, and on the other hand he suggests that it would be difficult to do even if he decided to try. It would be like expecting Charlie Chaplin to be The Tramp without the baggy pants, the too tiny jacket, the too big shoes, the hat and the stick. It would not be The Tramp and Chaplin would not be able to – nor would he likely want to – portray him!

Costume is also an interface between players. Consider the following dialogue:

A: *"Where is Bray?"* (Bray is the name of player B's character)
B: *"She is in my bag still. I haven't had a chance to get into kit..."*
A: *"Well, go get her! I need to talk to her!!"*

Here, A has already transformed into his character, while B has not. A feels that B needs to get into her character so that he can interact with it. It is not sufficient that B is there in the capacity of a playing person – she must become the character. A as a character is somehow unwilling to relate to the B unless she is Bray. This is likely directly linked to the fact that as long as you are 'out of character', i.e. if you are the person and not the character, the things you say, hear, see or do has no meaning within the game context. Only the character's actions and experiences are sanctioned and considered to be true. Costume signals when a person has entered into the mode of playing the game and therefore is eligible "prey" so to speak. In this capacity costume both contextualizes and endorses players' actions and behavior.

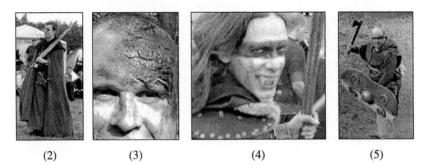

(2)   (3)   (4)   (5)

Fig. 2.–5. Samples of costume and personal props such as weapons and make-up

3.2 Set-Design and Props as Interface

The integration of game space and physical space creates a graspable game environment, the stage on which the game takes place. Physical structures may be used as game locations, and sometimes even purposely constructed to enhance the game world. This physicality contributes to creating a highly immersive, tangible and location-specific interface to the game. Allowing the game to extend in this way into the real world fosters coherent and meaningful role-playing relationships between characters and the game world. Figure 7 shows a library setting, which players would have to visit to gain some specific knowledge. In figure 8 is a magic mushroom that is one out of seven or eight like it, positioned in a circle on a field. The mushrooms form a transportation circle – an LT specific apparatus used to move characters great distances, and from which monsters are cloned and poured into the game world[1].

(6)   (7)   (8)

Fig. 6.–8. Props and physical structures support location-specific interaction and functionality

Players frequently use physical artifacts as props and tools in their role-play, primarily to back up their character roles. Commonly referred to as physical representations, or *physreps*, they represent game objects with tangible presence and functionality in the game. Mechanisms named *lammies* (laminated pieces of paper) formalize physreps' functionality in the game. Figure 10 shows an example, an amber talisman

---

[1] We are aware that this is unlikely to make much sense. This device is an illogical construct to logically justify the act of traveling distances in a time-frame that defies laws of physics.

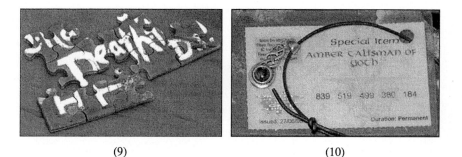

(9)   (10)

Fig. 9.–10. Samples of *physreps*, physical representations of game artifacts

that protects its wearer from certain diseases. Numbers are printed on the 'lammie', making up a codified reference to intrinsic properties such as monetary value, origin, magical nature, and so forth. Players with characters that have the appropriate skills can check these codes against so called 'lore-sheets', a mechanism that manages and sanctifies knowledge in the game. In this fashion, a 'lammie' enables plug-and-play features and offers a way to transform arbitrary objects into official game artifacts.

The most important difference between live role-playing games and computer games is that LRP players interact with and experience the game world directly. The physical environment allows for sophisticated sensory engagement. The players' perception of and navigation through space, and manipulation and organization of artifacts, can be transformed into game-related actions. The physical world interface is not a metaphor for interaction, but the medium for interaction.

3.3 Monsters as Interface

The Lorien Trust and many other systems use a supporting cast of characters to interact with the player characters. They may function as opposition and threat for the players to overcome: sometimes through violence, sometimes through politics and diplomacy. The degree of creative and improvisational freedom they have in their roles can vary. These characters have names like *monsters, non-player characters (NPC), scripted- or directed player characters,* or *crew characters*. They are part of the game environment, like extras in a movie set, often played by members of the organizing team. The least autonomous are controlled and directed in terms of behavior and motivation – they are told what to do, when and how to do it. They are quick injections into the scenery and the plot – e.g. the beggar that the players pass on their way to the village, or the wise woman that appears at their campfire at night to pass on a message and then disappears to never be encountered again, and so forth.

In contrast, NPCs and other scripted characters may also have a continuous presence amongst the player characters. As such they often have complex roles that are important in the overarching plan for the narrative progression and are often devised by the organizers and assigned to a person to play. While they may have a higher degree of freedom in their roles, they often must report to and accept being controlled by the organizing team. All of these characters add scenery and tangible points of interaction. They are the organizers' most potent, real-time interface to the players, allowing them to seamlessly infuse the game with in-character events on the fly.

Fig. 11. Battles contributes in part to the experience of personal immediacy

In the Lorien Trust system, most characters carry one weapon or another and many characters have fighter characteristics and skills. It is beyond the scope of this paper to argue for or against the pros and cons of violence or the affect the battle mechanism has on individuals, but it should be noted that the potential threat that armed conflict poses contributes to creating an experience of strong personal immediacy, particularly in the battle situation itself. The presence of this type of threat – the danger of exposing ones character to injury and mortal wounds – is of course a beautifully simple way of maintaining that tension required by the definition of a game. Further, it conditions many of the social interactions, is reflected in the costumes people choose for their characters, and most certainly adds to the spectacle!

3.4 The 'Magic Circle' in LRP

The *magic circle* is a term referring to a place in time and space that game players enter into when they agree to play a game together [13, pp.93-99], marking the beginning and the end of the game. It is also an abstract place that provides context to game actions, and as such allows a safe and lucid place for the players to submit their behavior. This is both a tangible (like the board of a board game) and an intangible (like house rules in a card game) construct in most games. As described by Salen and Zimmerman, special meaning is assigned to objects and to behavior within the magic circle, effectively creating a new reality and a cognitive frame for understanding this new reality. In games that constantly re-negotiate properties of a physical space into properties of a game space, as LRP games do, the magic circle is effectively blurred. To remedy this, LRP games must rely on some core unambiguous principles, or suffer from confused players who fail to distinguish the game from the real world. Costume is of course one of the most powerful mechanisms to signal when a person is playing the game, but lammies, the use of language, hand gestures and such tangible symbols are of equal importance.

Since the magic circle is meant to provide a safe place to submit play behavior, some may argue that the blurred and dissolved magic circle in LRP games poses the danger of anti-social addictions and players mistaking serious real life issues as part of playing a game. It is difficult to fend off those fears when these mistakes occasionally are made. However, in our experience, LRP players are more often than not sensitive to the fact that they are indeed playing a game. Jane McGonigal, describes sitive to the fact that they are indeed playing a game. Jane McGonigal, describes this very well when she points out the difference between the 'performance of belief', and the 'suspension of disbelief' [9]. Performing with belief is a social, active, expressive, and externalized act, while the suspension of disbelief is a solitary, passive, submissive, and internalized act. This is something that happens regularly in theatre and in cinemas. Immersive play, she argues, is foremost a desire of gamers for their virtual play to become real and rather than asking "to what extent players come to believe in the fictions they perform, we should ask: To what ends, and through what mechanisms, do players pretend to believe their own performances?"

4   Implications for Game Design

LRP games take place in a magical domain somewhere in the cross-sections between imagination, physical reality and fantastic fiction. They offer the kind of immersion that most games and interactive narratives promise as a technical goal but have yet to deliver. In an LRP game there is no physical division between player, character, and narrative, or between the real world and the game world. Some might argue that this level of immersion is the holy grail of interactive entertainment, where the content and the interaction with it is embedded in physical locations and in objects around us, creating a tangible, ubiquitous, and sensual interface to the game activity.

Pervasive games face many design challenges in order to meet the expectations on their ability to immerse players in a game world that is distinct but yet indistinguishable from the real world. It is our position that on the level of interface design, one possible and potentially potent approach begins to reveal itself when observing LRP games. Our study so far has been directed towards understanding the principles by which LRP interfaces contribute to making the game work and we argue that it is because they are believable, tangible, seductive, and part of a ubiquitous game environment. LRP interfaces come together as mechanisms that create social interaction, deliver content, contextualize the game, structure the narrative, and create immersion and engagement. We believe that this points in a direction of great importance to the design of pervasive game interfaces.

4.1   Ubiquitous: Games in Place

Mark Weiser's widely accepted definition of ubiquitous computing is the integration of a computational layer with the "fabric of everyday life" [14]. Its most obvious relevance to work on pervasive games is technological – the emphasis on embedding computation in our physical environment. From an interface perspective, ubiquitous computing also provides a compelling model that supports the notion of immersion. The argument that ubiquitous computing environments allow people to concentrate on interacting with each other rather than with computers carries additional appeal that would suggest social and cultural benefits.

Because the immediacy of the physical world is so pertinent, because of LRP games integration with the time and space of the physical environment, and because they incorporate game interfaces that are *part of* the physical world rather than *apart from* it, LRP games and the physical environments they are situated in make up some of the most powerful examples at hand when considering the design of pervasive games.

4.2 Tangible: An Interface That Touches

Tangible user interfaces [5] provide physical form, or embodiment, to digital content and controls, and thereby grant privilege to the sophisticated skills with which we interact with and make sense of the world. The term *tangible* does not refer only to the physical properties of the interface. It is not sufficient that it is graspable or that it has a presence in the real world. Rather, the word tangible in the context of tangible interfaces emphasizes control and representation of digital information as properties of the same artifact. It is not merely the case that a tangible interface can be touched – it also touches you back. In LRP, the physical props, dedicated physical game-locations, and perhaps most importantly, the characters themselves, are examples of interfaces that grant the players the opportunity to experience game content directly as opposed to abstractly, using the world as a *medium* for that interaction as opposed to a *metaphor*.

4.3 Believable: Lucidity in Representation

Computer gaming environments are increasingly realistic in their use of the physical world as a model for their game worlds. Many games have as a feature next to photo-graphic graphical representations of the game environment in their attention to detail in scenery. LRP environments are founded on a different attention to detail, where the game world is believable and convincing because there is no separation between the game world and the physical world. We can note that physreps, costume, and props rarely take token shapes or forms, but are instead carefully crafted to convey their dedicated purpose through their physical manifestation. These mechanisms contribute to supporting the performance of belief, helping the player express and display themselves, enabling them to share their performance in a meaningful way with other players. Elaborately dressing the environment with theatrical props and tangible game artifacts, as exemplified by the library setting in figure 6, is one way to make the players believe in and agree with what happens around them.

4.4 Magic: Interfaces That Seduce

While believability is important, what makes LRP worlds spellbinding is that they are typically rendered fantastic rather than realistic. The touch and feel of the game, the magic dust that has been sprinkled over it, the engrossing stories that you partake in when you are inside it, the mind-boggling consequences of your decisions sparking curiosity and seducing you, beckoning you to interact within the game world and with other players. As a simple example, take the puzzle in figure 9, which when solved not only spells out a message, but also functions as a key that unlocks the vessel containing a particularly nasty creature. In this example, the player will know what to do or how to interact with the puzzle, but cannot be certain what the result of that interaction is. The fact that it begins to suggest its functionality – the word "Death" is being spelled out when the pieces are put together – is part of encoding this particular artifact's magical message. The puzzle and its initially concealed functionality is part and parcel to the alluring, if not seductive, LRP environment that strengthens players' interest and even commitment to engage with the game world. Interestingly, players are habitually sensitive to the fact that messing with game artifacts often have unexpected effects, which is reflected in a typically curious but careful approach to them.

5 Conclusion

There is an unmistakable trend within the human-computer interaction community that points in the direction of pervasive technologies and ubiquitous interface cultures; a trend that is currently making rapid advances on entertainment domain. Future electronic entertainment applications – specifically future computer games and interactive narratives – will move participation and interaction into the physical world. These will be profound gaming experiences in which the real virtuality of the game world is manifest in physical locations and objects around us. This is the holy grail of interactive entertainment – pervasive, tangible, and sensory-intense digital interface design.

Acknowledgements. This research has been supported and financed by Media Lab Europe. A heartfelt Thank You goes out especially to the members of the Story Networks group. Lastly, we want to acknowledge the players in the Lorien Trust LRP system for valuable discussions.

References

1. Björk, S., Falk, J., Hansson, R., and Ljungstrand, P. Pirates! Using the Physical World as a Game Board. In *Proceedings of Interact'01*, Tokyo, Japan, 2001.
2. Blast Theory http://www.blasttheory.co.uk/
3. Falk, J. Interfacing the Narrative Experience. In *Funology: From Usability to Enjoyment.* Blythe, M.A., Overbeeke, K., Monk, A.F., Wright, P.C (*eds.*), Kluwer Academic Publishers, 2003.
4. Fine, G.A. *Shared Fantasy: Role-Playing Games as Social Worlds*, The University of Chicago Press, 1983.
5. Ishii, H., and Ullmer, B. Tangible Bits: Towards Seamless Interfaces between People, Bits, and Atoms. In *Proceedings of CHI 1997*, Atlanta, GA, ACM, 1997.
6. Johnstone, K. *Impro: Improvisation and the Theatre.* Methuen Publishing Limited, London, UK, 1989.
7. Lorien Trust. http://www.lorientrust.com/
8. Mackay, D. *The Fantasy Role-Playing Game – A New Performing Art*, McFarland & Company Inc., 2001
9. McGonigal, J. A Real Little Game: The Performance of Belief in Pervasive Play. In *Proceedings of DiGRA's Level-Up*, 2003.
10. Murray, J. *Hamlet on the Holodeck*, pp. 42, MIT Press, 2001.
11. Pan, P., Kastner, C., Crow, D., and Davenport, D. M-Studio: An Authoring Application for Context-Aware Multimedia. In *Proceedings of ACM Multimedia 2002*, Juan-les-Pins, France, 2002.

12. Pohjola, M. The Manifesto of the Turku School. In *As LARP Grows Up – Theory and Methods in LARP*, pp. 32-41, Projektgruppen KP03, 2003. Available at: http://www.laivforum.dk/kp03_book/classics/turku.pdf
13. Salen, K., Zimmerman, E. *Rules of Play*. MIT Press, 2004.
14. Weiser, M. The Computer for the 21st Century, *Scientific American*, pp. 94–110, 1991.
15. Wingård, L., and Fatland, Eirik. Dogma 99 – A programme for the liberation of LARP. Available at: http://fate.laiv.org/dogme99/

Animating Conversation in Online Games

Hannes Högni Vilhjálmsson

Information Sciences Institute[1], University of Southern California
4676 Admiralty Way, Marina del Rey, CA 90292, USA
hannes@isi.edu

Abstract. When players in online games engage in conversation with each other, often through a chat window, their graphical avatars typically do not exhibit interesting behavior. This paper proposes using a model of face-to-face communication to automatically generate realistic nonverbal behavior in the avatars based on what is going on in the conversation. It describes Spark, a flexible XML based architecture that makes this possible and reports on a user study that shows how such avatars could significantly improve online conversations.

1 Introduction

The term *avatar* refers to the graphical embodiment of a user in a virtual environment. In the same way that the avatars of Hindu mythology allowed the gods to walk among the humans by giving them corporeal form, graphical avatars allow human players to navigate and interact with electronic game worlds. To provide the illusion of presence in those worlds, the avatars need to obey the laws of the game, often including those of physics. For example avatars explode when hit or fall when driven off a ledge. As game worlds get richer, the avatars interact with it in richer ways, while keeping the player controller reasonably simple. For example, to make the avatar leap into a nearby vehicle, close the door and start the engine, a simple click of the mouse on the vehicle should suffice. Avatars have become more than simple puppets under the direct control of players and instead require intelligent behavior to carry out the player's intent and react to the world around them.

Different kinds of game environments require different kinds of intelligent avatar behavior. Shooter avatars know how to switch to the next best weapon when the current weapon is out of ammo, and adventure avatars know how to navigate around furniture to reach a chest across the room. In general, avatars are pretty good at handling dangerous situations, including dexterous locomotion and all manners of dying. But what about social interactions? When people meet face-to-face in the real world, their bodies spontaneously exhibit a range of highly coordinated behaviors that carry out their communicative intent. Yet, when players meet in an online game, their avatars typically cease all motion because they don't know what behaviors to exhibit and their players are too busy typing messages to each other to actually direct them.

---

[1] The paper describes research done by the author at the MIT Media Lab

M. Rauterberg (Ed.): ICEC 2004, LNCS 3166, pp. 139–150, 2004.

This paper describes how avatars can be brought to live during conversations between online players. By deriving communicative intent from the text that is typed using natural language techniques and consulting empirical models of typical human conversational behavior, avatars can generate something that approximates what the conversation would look like if the players were having it face-to-face. By providing behavior that supports the interaction, rather than using no motion or randomly generated motion, the avatars could even make in-game communication between players more effective.

The next section will discuss relevant background and then the paper will propose an approach and a system architecture called Spark to automatically generate conversational behavior in avatars. The following section describes how an implementation of this architecture was evaluated and finally the paper wraps up with conclusions.

2   Background

2.1   Face-to-Face Conversation

When people meet in the real world, they follow certain protocols without even thinking about it. These protocols both help them coordinate their actions and effectively communicate what they want to say. The former process has been referred to as interactional, while the latter has been referred to as propositional in nature [6]. There is certainly more going on in interactions face-to-face than these two types of processes, but they provide and maintain the underlying channel for communication and are therefore fundamental to human conversation.

On the interactional side, two important functions are turn management and feedback. Properly managing turns is necessary to ensure that everyone is not speaking at the same time, and can therefore be clearly heard. Turns are requested, taken, held and given using various signals, often exchanged in parallel with speech over nonverbal channels such as gaze, intonation, and gesture [10, 15]. Taking or requesting turn most often coincides with breaking eye contact [2] while raising hands into gesture space [17]. A speaker gives the turn by looking at the listener, or whoever is meant to speak next, and resting the hands [10, 14, 22].

Speakers often request feedback while speaking and expect at the very least some sign of attention from their listeners. Feedback requests typically involve looking at the listeners and raising eyebrows [9]. To request a more involved feedback, this behavior can be supplemented with pointing the head towards the listener or conducting a series of low amplitude head nods ending with a head raise [22]. Listener response to feedback requests can take on a variety of forms. Brief assertion of attention can be given by the dropping of the eyelids and or slight head nod towards the speaker. A stronger cue of attention may involve a slight leaning and a look towards the speaker along with a short verbal response or a laugh. A speaker's ability to formulate messages is critically dependent on these attentive cues, and therefore, even if only one person is speaking, everyone present is engaged in some kind of communicative behavior.

The propositional side deals with how we make sure those who are listening pick up what we are saying. Three types of communicative function play an important role here: emphasis, reference and illustration. Emphasis signals to listeners what the speaker considers to be the most important contribution of each utterance. It commonly involves raising or lowering of the eyebrows and sometimes vertical head movement as well [3, 9]. A short formless beat with either hand, striking on the stressed syllable, is also common [20]. Reference is most commonly carried out by a pointing hand. The reference can be made to the physical surroundings such as towards an object in the room, or to imaginary spots in space that for example represent something previously discussed [20]. References through pointing are also made towards the other participants of a conversation when the speaker wishes to acknowledge their previous contributions or remind them of a prior conversation [5]. Illustration is the spontaneous painting with the hands of some semantic feature of the current proposition. The particular features may lend themselves well to be portrayed by a visual modality, such as the configuration or size of objects, or the manner of motion [18, 20].

2.2 Avatars

Avatars in some form have been around in games since the virtual paddles in the original Pong, but the more human-like avatars used for online social interaction date back to the 2D sprites used in the first online graphical recreational world of Habitat in 1985 [21]. Since then online avatars have appeared in a wide variety of applications ranging from graphical chat rooms and networked games, to collaborative virtual environments and military training simulations. The model for generating communicative behaviors in avatars has generally relied on explicit user input, such as key presses or menu selections. For example, the pioneering online 3D communities *Blaxxun Contact* and *Active Worlds* allowed users to gesture with their avatars by clicking on labeled buttons. In popular online shooters such as *Unreal Tournament*, players can exhibit nonverbal taunts by pressing a key and in massively multiplayer games like *EverQuest*, special emote commands in the text chat window produce corresponding behaviors in the avatars.

This approach is fine for acting out deliberate displays of affect or insult, or to issue orders, but as was argued in [26], requiring the users to think about how to coordinate their virtual body every time they communicate places on them the burden of too much micromanagement. When people communicate face-to-face, they are not used to think about gesture production because it is something that happens spontaneously without conscious effort [17]. In the same way that avatars should animate walk cycles so that players won't have to worry about where to place their virtual feet, avatars should also provide the basic nonverbal foundation for communication.

Several innovative avatar interfaces have been developed, though few have made it into the gaming mainstream. Perhaps the best known technique for animating avatars during player conversation, pioneered by *Oz Virtual* and *OnLive!*, is to generate mouth movement based on the amplitude or even phoneme analysis of a speech signal. While this is a good way to see who is talking and get some idea of how intense the speaker is, it requires a voice link between players and focuses on very limited movement, leaving out important communicative behaviors such as gesture and gaze.

Animating gesture in avatars has been attempted through special input devices including a pen [4] and physical puppets [16], which may provide more intuitive interfaces than menus, and even generate personal motion nuances, but they still require deliberate effort to use. Bringing the avatar control to a much higher level, to avoid micromanagement of behavior, has been suggested by several researchers including [23]. This is a very good idea which still needs work, since it is not clear exactly how the player would best indicate their intent while playing a game, perhaps calling for ways to somehow automatically derive intent.

Automating the generation of communicative nonverbal behaviors in avatars was first proposed in BodyChat where avatars were not just waiting for their own users to issue behavior commands, but were also reacting to events in the online world according to preprogrammed rules based on a model of human face-to-face behavior [26]. The focus was on gaze cues associated with the interactional communicative processes. A study showed that the automation did not make the users feel any less in control over their social interactions, compared to using menu driven avatars. In fact, they reported they felt even more in control, suggesting that the automated avatars were providing some level of support [7].

If the avatar behavior is to be automated, one can ask how important it is that the behavior be carefully modeled to reflect the communicative intent of their users. Wouldn't it be enough to automatically generate some randomized nonverbal behavior to appear life-like? After all, that is an approach that many of today's systems take. According to several studies that compare algorithmically generated gaze behavior, taking into account speaker and listener roles, to randomized gaze behaviors in avatars, the algorithmic behaviors have proven more effective [11, 24].

So far, the automated behaviors have still mostly been restricted to gaze and mouth movement, and supported interactional management only. While some interesting work is being done on posture generation as a function of attitudes between users [12], no work to date has attempted to support both the interactional and the propositional procceses of conversation through real-time analysis of communicative intent.

3   The Spark Architecture

3.1 Overview

Spark is a new online messaging architecture that builds both on the previous BodyChat work [26] and the work on generating gesture from text in the BEAT system [8]. Lets first look at an example interaction to explain what Spark does.

Two players are having a conversation through their avatars, a wizard and a druid, when a third player comes running with a ranger avatar. As the ranger approaches, the wizard and druid look at her, the wizard raising his eyebrows in recognition and smiling as an invitation for her to join the conversation. The player of the ranger moves her avatar closer to the others and starts typing a message while her avatar nods in salutation and raises her hands in the air in preparation to speak, momentarily glancing away as if she needed to gather her thoughts. When the ranger starts speaking, voicing the words her user just typed, she looks at the wizard and begins gesticulating: "I just came back from the mountain pass". A brief nod of emphasis occurs on the coming back part and a glance and a hand wave towards the mountains behind her when mentioning the pass. The wizard and druid both glance up towards the mountains and then look back at the ranger nodding. She continues with eyes wide and raised eyebrows: "I noticed an Ogre headed this way, he had a group of goblins following him!". Her animated hands go up to indicate the tallness of the Ogre and then sweep low when mentioning the smaller goblins.

The players here did nothing but maneuver their avatars into place and then type what they wanted to say. Their avatars synthesized both their voices and nonverbal behavior not only to make it look like a believable conversation was taking place, but also to add some visual emphasis to what was being said. Spark accomplishes this by analyzing written messages in terms of their communicative intent, annotate them using tags that the avatars will understand, and then pass the message back to all the avatars engaged in the conversation so they can all generate associated communicative behaviors. The speaking avatar needs to generate behavior that communicates the intent while the listening avatars need to generate proper reactive behavior. The following sections describe the parts of this process in greater detail.

3.2 Frames

All interaction related events that pass through the Spark architecture are represented by an XML data structure termed a frame. A frame holds the actual event description, such as a written message, along with some additional context that can be used to interpret the event. A frame is a dynamic entity that can have its event description expanded and an interpretation added as it passes through a sequence of analyzing processes (see Figure 1). There are action frames and utterance frames. An action is a communicative event that occurs in the absence of a verbal message, such as when someone starts to type (but hasn't pressed ENTER yet) or selects something on the screen (perhaps picking an object or a person). An utterance contains words and eventually any nonverbal behavior that are associated with the delivery of those words.

3.3 Analyzer

The Analyzer sits on the server side and interprets all incoming frames, annotating their communicative function. It consists of two modules, one to process action frames and one to process utterance frames. Both modules have access to a special data structure called discourse context to help with the interpretation.

Action Module: The action module interprets the action described in the frame and maps it from an interface event to a communicative action. For example it would map the event when a player starts to type a message into an action requesting a turn in a conversation.

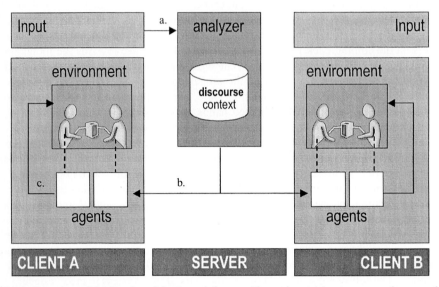

Fig. 1. Overview of the Spark architecture. A frame with raw input (a) enters an analyzer on the server-side, which annotates the frame with XML tags describing communicative function. The functionally annotated frame (b) is distributed to all clients where avatar agents transform those annotations into behavior annotations according to rules. The behaviorally annotated frame (c) is finally used to render the whole synchronized performance in the environment

Discourse Module: The discourse module carries out a series of linguistic and discourse analyses to identify and label how the various units of discourse within the utterance text, such as words, phrases and clauses, contribute to the conversation processes described in 0. It passes utterance frames to specialized methods that each focuses on one communicative function and adds only one new type of XML tag to the frame. This way new or improved methods can easily be plugged in without changes to the rest of the module. The methods currently implemented in Spark represent some known heuristic methods as well as some new ones. These are all described in more detail in [8] and [25], but are summarized here in Table 1.

Discourse Context: An action or words alone don't tell the full story, they always occur in some context crucial for determining their communicative function. The discourse context in Spark is represented by three main data structures: Discourse Model, Domain Knowledge and Participation Framework. The Discourse Model describes how information gets shared over the course of an entire conversation [1]. It contains a Discourse History that holds all the utterances exchanged so far. Discourse entities, corresponding to the unique objects referred to by noun phrases, are also kept track of in a list where the last entity referred to is moved to the top. The Domain Knowledge is a static structure that describes the ontology of a particular domain that relates to the conversation. It describes visual features of objects and actions that can be used for gestural illustration. The Participation Framework is a dynamic structure that keeps track of who is present and what their roles currently are in relation to the current utterance [13].

Table 1. A summary of methods that annotate frames with communicative function

Method	Description
Information Structure	Finds the most information rich part of a clause
Discourse Entities	Matches noun phrases with objects in ontology
Reference	For each discourse entity marks a possible visual (can be seen) or textual (has been mentioned before) reference
Emphasis	Uses information structure to mark special focus
Contrast	Uses a dictionary to tag contrasting words like antonyms
Illustration	Tags visual features of identified entities using ontology
Topic shifts	Places a tag where a new topic starts
Grounding	Finds places where listener feedback should be requested
Turn taking	Inserts floor negotiation markers

3.4 Avatar Agents

Now that a frame has been analyzed and annotated with a rich description of a communicative event in the context of the current encounter, it can be sent to all the clients where the delivery itself can draw from this representation to coordinate a believable and effective performance by all the avatars present.

When a communicative frame arrives at a client, it is first handed to the Avatar Agent that represents the player that originated the communicative event, the *actor*. The actor's job is to now annotate the frame with actual behaviors that nonverbally carry out the communicative functions described by the XML tags. This is a matter of translating functional annotations into behavior annotations according to a set of translation rules that represent empirical findings in the human communicative behavior literature reviewed in section 2.1.. Some example mapping rules are shown in Table 2. The frame is then passed around to all other Avatar Agents, participating in the scene, that then get a chance to add reacting behaviors. This way, everyone represented in a scene can have their avatars spontaneously react to what is going on. In fact, other agents than Avatar Agents could also participate in this reaction phase, for example a special Camera Agent could add camera moves, based on what is happening.

The output from the Avatar Agents is a frame that now is a detailed description of a performance that involves one or more avatars in the environment. This performance has to be carried out in the game world. The frame is given to a scheduler that converts any utterance to speech, retrieves the onset time for each word and thereby the onset and duration of each behavior spanning one or more words (see [8] for details) and then hands out timed behavior scripts to the individual avatars for execution.

Table 2. An example how avatar agents map communicative function tags into behavior tags

Function Tag	Speaker Behavior	Listener Behavior
EMPHASIS_WORD	HEADNOD	
	GESTURE_BEAT	
EMPHASIS_PHRASE	EYEBROWS_RAISE	
GROUNDING_REQUEST	GLANCE(addressee)	GLANCE(speaker)
	EYEBROWS_RAISE	HEADNOD
TURN_GIVE	LOOK(addressee)	LOOK(addressee)
TURN_TAKE	GLANCE_AWAY	LOOK(speaker)
TOPICSHIFT	POSTURESHIFT	
REFERENCE_TEXTUAL	GLANCE(last ref. speaker)	
REFERENCE_VISUAL	GLANCE(object)	GLANCE(object)
	GESTURE_POINT(object)	
CONTRAST	GESTURE_CONTRAST	
ILLUSTRATE	GESTURE_FEATURE	

4   Evaluation

The Spark approach was evaluated by implementing a scenario where three players had to get together in a special map room after being told they were prisoners in an enemy stronghold and had to plan their escape. This scenario was chosen because it involved conversation about a complex visual object, the map, and because it involved collaboration, which could provide some insight into whether the avatar behaviors contributed to the conversation process and a successful outcome. Besides, players coming together to strategize, is something that is a common occurrence in today's multiplayer games, but something that hasn't been animated before.

First, to evaluate how well the rules that the avatars possessed mimicked the real world, a physical mockup of the scene was created and videotaped with three live subjects performing the task. The utterances from a random 40-second segment of the video were fed through the Spark architecture and the resulting avatar behavior compared to that of the real people, which was annotated using Anvil [19]. The analysis involved emphasis gestures, pointing gestures, gaze direction and head movements. Overall Spark did well, making exact predictions of behavior more than half the time, with the wrong predictions mainly due to excessive emphasis and feedback generation. That makes sense, because the avatars in Spark generate a behavior every time a rule indicates a logical opportunity. If Spark took into account factors such as personality or affect, it might be able to use that as a principled way of reducing overall avatar liveliness. This is something to consider as future research.

50 subjects were signed up for 2 sessions each with the Spark system, where a session involved the group selecting what they believed to be the quickest escape route on the map in front of them. Each subject was briefed on a different set of helpful facts about the map prior to a session to ensure they needed to work together. In half of the sessions the subjects would just see the room and the map, and receive each other's messages without the avatars. In the other half, everything would be the same except they would see each other as animated avatars standing around the map see Figure 2. In both kinds of sessions the subjects could highlight parts of the map to indicate their choice of path. Two other conditions, crossed with the avatar versus no-

avatar conditions, were the use of synthesized speech versus scrolling text. Apart from noting that people typically didn't like the synthesized voices, this part of the study won't be discussed further here.

Fig. 2. Subjects discussing their escape from the stronghold

The fact that each subject was assigned to 2 instead of all conditions (although balanced for order effects and only assigned to adjacent cells) of the 4 conditions in this 2x2 design, made the analysis of the data more difficult and contributed to lower power than with standard within-subject experiments, which suggests a simpler design for future studies. But nevertheless, some clear results emerged.

The 14 subjects that tried both an avatar system and a system without avatars were asked to compare the systems on a 9 point likert scale from a high preference for no avatars to a high preference for avatars along 6 dimensions including which system was "more useful", "more fun", "more personal", "easier to use", "more efficient" and "allowed easier communication". One-tailed t-tests showed that the preference for avatars was significant ($p<0.05$) for all but the "easier to use" question where no significant preference either way was found. These subjective results clearly indicate that people find the avatars compelling and helpful.

To test the hypothesis that the avatars automating communicative intent would improve the overall process of conversation, compared to non-embodied communication, 11 different measures of quality of conversation process were taken. 7 were objective behavioral measures from the chat logs, including the portion of utterances without explicit grounding (i.e. verbal verification of reception), portion of utterances that got requested replies, portion of non-overlapping utterances and portion of on-task utterances. 4 were subjective likert scale questionnaire measures, including sense of ability to communicate and sense of control over conversation. All but one measure was found higher in the avatar condition and a t-test of the grand mean (across all 11 normalized measures) showed that indeed it was significantly higher ($p<0.02$) in the avatar condition than in the non-avatar condition, supporting the hypothesis.

To test the hypothesis that the avatars automating communicative intent would improve the actual outcome of player collaboration, compared to the non-embodied communication, 8 different measures of the quality of task outcome were taken. 2 were objective measures, one being the quality of the escape route that the subjects chose together and the other being the completion time (which ranged from 5 to 40 minutes). 6 were subjective likert scale questionnaire measures including "How well did you think the group performed on the task?", "How strong do you think the group's consensus is about the final solution?" and "How much do you think you contributed to the final solution?". Again, all but one measure was higher in the avatar condition, and again, a t-test of the grand mean (across all 8 normalized measures) showed that it was significantly higher ($p<0.02$) in the avatar condition than in the non-avatar condition, supporting the hypothesis.

5   Conclusions

The Spark architecture provided a flexible framework for animating the avatars in a collaborative game setting, using behavior generation rules that provided a reasonably realistic performance by drawing from research into human communicative behavior. A study showed that these avatars compel players and that the avatar behavior may in fact be supporting the conversational activity. While the overall results were encouraging, a follow-up study is needed to really look at the effect the avatars had on individual measures. Work remains to be done in extending the set of rules to include more aspects of social interaction and to embrace research into personality and emotion to broaden the range of expression and avatar intelligence.

Acknowledgements. The author would especially like to thank Justine Cassell for her guidance throughout the project and Amy Bruckman, Cynthia Breazeal, Bruce Blumberg and Dan Ariely for feedback that helped shape this work. Many thanks go to Joey Chang, Kenny Chang, David Mellis, Ivan Petrakiev, Vitaly Kulikov, Alan Gardner, Timothy Chang and Baris Yuksel for technical assistance on the character animation system. The author is grateful to Ian Gouldstone and Nina Yu for beautiful artwork and to the entire GNL team and Deepa Iyengar for input along the way. Last but not least, the author would like to thank the many sponsors of Digital Life at the MIT Media Lab for their support.

References

1.   Allen, J. Natural Language Understanding. The Benjamin/Cummings Publishing Company, Inc., Redwood City, CA, 1995.
2.   Argyle, M. and Cook, M. Gaze and Mutual Gaze. Cambridge University Press, Cambridge, 1976.

3. Argyle, M., Ingham, R., Alkema, F. and McCallin, M. The Different Functions of Gaze. Semiotica., 1973

4. Barrientos, F., Continuous Control of Avatar Gesture. in Bridging the Gap: Bringing Together New Media Artists and Multimedia Technologists, First International Workshop, (Marina del Rey, CA, 2000), ACM.

5. Bavelas, J.B., Chovil, N., Coates, L. and Roe, L. Gestures Specialized for Dialogue. Personality and Social Psychology, 21 (4). 394-405.

6. Cassell, J., Bickmore, T., Billinghurst, M., Campbell, L., Chang, K., Vilhjalmsson, H. and Yan, H., Embodiment in Conversational Interfaces: Rea. in CHI, (Pittsburgh, PI, 1999), ACM, 520-527.

7. Cassell, J. and Vilhjalmsson, H. Fully Embodied Conversational Avatars: Making Communicative Behaviors Autonomous. Autonomouse Agents and Multi-Agent Systems, 2 (1). 45-64.

8. Cassell, J., Vilhjalmsson, H. and Bickmore, T., BEAT: the Behavior Expression Animation Toolkit. in SIGGRAPH01, (Los Angeles, CA, 2001), ACM, 477-486.

9. Chovil, N. Discourse-Oriented Facial Displays in Conversation. Research on Language and Social Interaction, 25 (1991/1992). 163-194.

10. Duncan, S. On the structure of speaker-auditor interaction during speaking turns. Language in Society, 3. 161-180.

11. Garau, M., Slater, M., Bee, S. and Angela Sasse, M., The Impact of Eye Gaze on Communication using Humanoid Avatars. in CHI 2001, (Seattle, WA, 2001), ACM, 309-316.

12. Gillies, M. and Ballin, D., A Model of Interpersonal Attitude and Posture Generation. in Intelligent Virtual Agents, (Irsee, Germany, 2003), Springer-Verlag.

13. Goffman, E. Behavior in public places; notes on the social organization of gatherings. Free Press of Glencoe, [New York], 1963.

14. Goffman, E. Forms of Talk. University of Pennsylvania Publications, Philadelphia, PA, 1983.

15. Goodwin, C. Conversational Organization: Interaction between speakers and hearers. Academic Press, New York, 1981.

16. Johnson, M.P., Wilson, A., Blumberg, B., Kline, C. and Bobick, A. Sympathetic Interfaces: Using a Plush Toy to Direct Synthetic Characters. Proceedings of CHI'99. 152-158.

17. Kendon, A. Conducting Interaction: Patterns of behavior in focused encounters. Cambridge University Press, New York, 1990.

18. Kendon, A. On Gesture: Its Complementary Relationship With Speech. in Siegman, A.W. and Feldstein, S. eds. Nonverbal Behavior and Communication, Lawrence Erlbaum Associates, Inc., Hillsdale, 1987, 65-97.

19. Kipp, M., Anvil - A Generic Annotation Tool for Multimodal Dialogue. in Eurospeech, (Aalborg, 2001), 1367-1370.

20. McNeill, D. Hand and Mind. The University of Chicago Press, Chicago and London, 1992.

21. Morningstar, C. and Farmer, F.R., The Lessons of Lucasfilm's Habitat. in The First Annual International Conference on Cyberspace, (1990).

22. Rosenfeld, H.M. Conversational Control Functions of Nonverbal Behavior. in Siegman, A.W. and Feldstein, S. eds. Nonverbal Behavior and Communication, Lawrence Erlbaum Associates, Inc., Hillsdale, 1987, 563-601.

23. Shi, J., Smith, T.J., Graniere, J. and Badler, N., Smart avatars in JackMOO. in Virtual Reality, (Houston, TX, 1999), IEEE.

24. Vertegaal, R. and Ding, Y., Explaining Effects of Eye Gaze on Mediated Group Conversations: Amount or Synchronization. in CSCW 2002, (New Orleans, LA, 2002), ACM, 41-48.

25. Vilhjalmsson, H., Augmenting Online Conversation through Automatice Discourse Tagging. in HICSS Sixth Annual Minitrack on Persistent Conversation, (Hawaii, Under Review).
26. Vilhjalmsson, H. and Cassell, J., BodyChat: Autonomous Communicative Behaviors in Avatars. in Autonomous Agents, (Minneapolis, MN, 1998), ACM, 269-276.

From Artistry to Automation: A Structured Methodology for Procedural Content Creation

Timothy Roden and Ian Parberry

Department of Computer Science & Engineering, University of North Texas
P.O. Box 311366, Denton, Texas 76203-1366 USA
{roden,ian}@cs.unt.edu
http://www.cs.unt.edu/~roden/esrg/researchgroup.htm

Abstract. Procedural techniques will soon automate many aspects of content creation for computer games. We describe an efficient, deterministic, methodology for procedurally generating 3D game content of arbitrary size and complexity. The technique progressively amplifies simple dynamically generated data structures into complex geometry. We use a procedural pipeline with a minimum set of controls at each stage to facilitate authoring. We show two examples from our research. Our terrain generator can synthesize massive 3D terrains in real-time while our level generator can be used to create indoor environments offline or in real-time.

1 Introduction

In the short history of computer games the primary technique used in the development of computer game content has been artistry. Game content, including 3D models, bitmapped graphics, levels and audio, have all been, for the most part, handcrafted by artists and designers working with a variety of software, often custom created. This approach has enabled game developers precise control over their creations in a manner similar to the way in which feature films are created. In fact, many in the game industry have long predicted that game development would increasingly mirror film development. Due to several compelling factors we believe this trend is at an end. Procedural content creation will soon become the dominant form of content creation for games software.

1.1 The Limits of Art

Handcrafted game content currently has at least four drawbacks. First, advances in technology mean artists need increasingly more time to create content. Secondly, handcrafted content is often not easy to modify once created. In a typical game development environment, game content is created at the same time that programmers are working on the game engine (rendering, networking code, etc.). Changes in specification or design of the game engine can dramatically alter technical requirements for content, making content already produced obsolete. Thirdly, many

M. Rauterberg (Ed.): ICEC 2004, LNCS 3166, pp. 151–156, 2004.

widely used content creation authoring tools output content in a different format than that used by proprietary game engines. Developers typically build conversion utilities that can suffer from incompatibilities between what artists view in an authoring tool and how the content appears in the game engine. This difference can lead to repeated create-convert-test cycles which can be costly when the conversion process is time-intensive, such as creating a BSP tree from the output of a level editor. Finally, interactive games have the potential to become much more expansive than even the most epic film. If games are to reach this potential then humans can no longer continue to function as the predominant content creators.

1.2   Related Work

The use of procedural techniques in 3D graphic applications, including games, is not new. Particle systems have been used to model a variety of effects including smoke and fire. Procedural textures have also gained in popularity due to the work of Ken Perlin and others [1,7]. Procedural game textures have primarily been created offline using tools such as Darkling Simulation's Darktree, which allows the author to connect together a network of small procedural algorithms to generate the final texture [2]. With the advent of programmable graphics cards procedural textures will increasingly be synthesized dynamically. Researchers at MIT have experimented with systems to synthesize architectural 3D geometry from 2D floorplans [3] as well as methods to automatically populate buildings with furniture [4]. Inspired by studies into predictable random number generation and infinite universe techniques [5] procedurally generated virtual cities have been explored [6]. Fractal terrain generation and synthesis of vegetation has been the subject of much research, although most work has focused on offline generation [1,8].

2   Procedural Content Creation

Procedural techniques hold great promise yet harnessing that power can be difficult. Procedural methods typically use a set of parametric controls that enable a procedure to generate many different outputs. To make a procedure more useful, additional controls can be added. While the power of a procedure may be enhanced in this way, the resulting interface can become overly complex. In the case of a human using the interface, coming up with good results from a powerful procedure often degenerates into an authoring processing of trial and error. The challenge that is shaping the evolution of procedural content creation is to apply procedural techniques efficiently to meet demands for game content that is increasing both in quality and quantity.

An important premise of our procedural content creation systems is that we want to begin by generating very simple data. The data is then amplified in one or more steps, making use of predictable random number generators. Our terrain generator begins by synthesizing a relatively small 2D map while our level generator begins by creating a simple undirected graph. By using simple data as the foundation for the content we wish to generate, we achieve several goals at once including, 1) we can quickly generate a simple version of the content which allows our algorithms to run in real-time, 2) we achieve a significant savings in storage requirements for the content since we only amplify that portion of the data needed at any given time, 3) the set of amplified data acts as a hierarchical representation that can be useful for a variety of processing such as level of detail, visibility determination and path finding, and, 4) data sharing becomes more efficient since only top-level data need be exchanged since more detailed data is available via the amplification process.

We use procedural pipelining as an efficient, controllable methodology for building procedural content creation systems.   A primary goal is to structure the pipeline so that individual procedures can be constructed with the minimum number of controls necessary and each procedure can be authored somewhat separately from other procedures.   Such systems exhibit a high degree of reusability and enable fast authoring.

3   Terrain Generation

The motivation behind our terrain generator is to dynamically synthesize massive 3D maps in real-time. For example we want the ability to create a 100 square mile map where individual vertices are 10 feet apart. Given an estimated storage size of 20 bytes per vertex the resulting data would occupy over 67 terabytes for the textured height mesh alone. Even more space would be needed to store terrain features such as trees. This requirement is prohibitive for a personal computer. However, we observe that in many games with large maps a player often moves about in a small geographical area and typically explores a large map incrementally.

Given these observations and the limitation of incremental exploration, our terrain generator first creates a high level representation of the map and creates detail as needed according to the player's location. Data at the finest level of detail, including low-level terrain features such as vegetation, are only created in the immediate vicinity of the player. As exploration proceeds, detail is generated as needed using a caching scheme that purges data unlikely to be needed in the near future.

Our terrain generator uses a rule-based system to first create a high-level 2D representation of the map (Fig. 1). In contrast to techniques that directly create 3D content we begin with 2D data for several reasons. First, we want to synthesize our terrain at the highest level of abstraction possible for efficiency reasons. Major terrain features on the 2D map are easily encoded using a minimum set of rules and include ocean, river, swamp, grass, forest, desert, hills and mountains. Second, since many of these terrain features naturally imply elevation, height data is essentially created for free. Third, our 2D map forms the basis for both synthesized elevation data and low-level terrain features such as vegetation.

Parametric controls in the 2D map generator include number of continents, ratio of land to ocean and percentage of various terrain types (river, swamp, forest, and hills) to amount of total land. Placement of terrain is governed via separate rules for each terrain type that attempt to mimic terrain patterns found on earth. For example, hills are placed along randomly generated fault lines with dense groupings of hills transformed into mountains. Currently, we are experimenting with scale of 2560 square feet per 2D map square (approximately one half square mile). A 100 square mile map thus requires a 2D map approximately 200 x 200 squares.

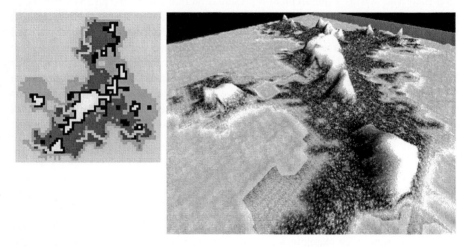

Fig. 1. 'Non-viewable' top-level coarse 3D height field (right) amplified directly from auto-generated 64 x 64 terrain map (left). Note: 3D textures have been applied for illustration only.

The second procedure in our terrain generation pipeline is a rule-based system that extrudes the 2D map into a high-level coarse 3D representation (Fig. 1). Parametric controls include an elevation scaling factor as well as controls for setting approximate elevation ranges for low-level terrain features such as different varieties of trees, grasses and rocks, altitude for snow, etc. A set of internal rules attempts to mimic earth-like elevation patterns. The coarse 3D map forms the root of a sparse quadtree with as many levels in the tree as needed to synthesize the required detail. The bottom level of the tree and several levels above form the viewable levels, enabling continuous-level-of-detail rendering.

The third procedure in the terrain pipeline is a recursive algorithm to subdivide a coarse 3D mesh into a series of higher detail meshes. The procedure uses a simple fractal method called midpoint displacement that subdivides an edge into two edges where the elevation of the midpoint is randomly chosen between the elevations of the endpoints of the original edge. Multiple subdivisions of the coarse map also serve to break up what would otherwise be unnatural looking contours.

Additional procedures add low-level terrain features to the viewable layers of the 3D mesh. As in previous procedures a set of rules attempts to mimic earth. For example a distribution of trees is based on several pieces of data. The 2D map provides a general description of the density of trees found in a larger square area of the map. Adjacent squares on the 2D map can also affect tree density including the presence of adjacent forest or river squares. Elevation data can be used to select a suitable variety of tree. A set of parametric controls provides customization in tree type, size, density and growth patterns.

4   Level Generation

A game level is generally an area of Euclidean space with corresponding 3D geometry and associated objects contained within the space including geometric objects and sounds. It is not unusual for game levels to represent space enclosed entirely indoors such as a building or an underground maze. For our initial experiments we chose to generate indoor environments. Example environments our level generator can synthesize are underground mazes or interior compartments and rooms of a spaceship, among other things. Our motivation is to dynamically create levels of size and complexity typically found in current games.

The level generator begins by creating a simple undirected graph in three dimensions. This first stage in the level pipeline can be controlled with several parameters including topology and a set of constraints. Some of the basic topologies are tree, ring and star. Additionally, multiple sub-graphs, with different topologies, can be connected together to form hybrid topologies. Each node in the graph represents a portion of the actual level geometry. Constraints on graph generation are given as rules relating to one or more fixed nodes with parameters such as min/max distance from terminal nodes (entry/exits), fixed connections to adjacent nodes and prefabricated geometry to be used for rendering the nodes. In addition, constraints can enable sequences of nodes that can only be visited by the player in a certain order.

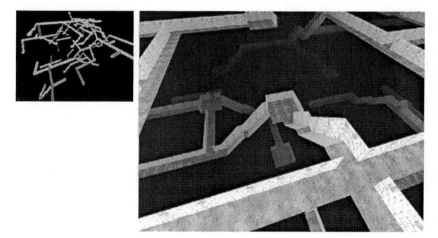

Fig. 2. Graph (left) amplified into full 3D geometry (right).

The next stage in the pipeline constructs basic geometry for each node (Fig. 2). We used a modeling program to build a limited set of prefabricated geometry sections that can be interconnected to produce a larger level. A similar method was used by Epic Games with level designers manually fitting together the prefabs [9]. To construct the geometry for a node in the graph we gather the appropriate set of prefabs and combine them to create the final geometry for the node. We found that it was much easier to construct a very basic set of prefabs that could be combined to produce more detailed geometry than to create larger prefabs for every possible geometric node configuration. For example, our 'basic-dungeon' set consists of ten prefabs including corridors, stairs and rooms.   Each prefab is textured in the modeling program. Completed node geometries are placed in a list that is instanced by nodes in the graph since multiple nodes in the graph may be structurally identical which allows them to share geometry.   Additionally, at this stage of the generation, nodes may have been flagged with a constraint that forces their geometry to be assigned from a dedicated set of prefab enabling the level author to insert special rooms into the level.

The final stage in the pipeline involves adding objects to the level.   Objects can include static 3D geometry in addition to movable 3D objects such as furniture. Sounds can also be added and would typically correspond to geometric features.

5   Conclusion

We believe the way forward for game developers to successfully incorporate procedural content into their games will begin by following a structured approach. Amplification of simple data structures in a pipelined architecture is a structured methodology that will enable procedural content creation systems to be built in a minimum amount of time, facilitate testing and debugging, and most importantly enhance authoring.

References

1. Ebert, David, et al: Texturing and Modeling: A Procedural Approach, 3rd edition. Morgan Kaufmann Publishers, San Francisco (2003).
2. Theodore, Steve: "Product Reviews: Darkling Simulations' Darktree 2," Game Developer Magazine, pp. 6-7 (March 2002).
3. Wehowsky, Andreas: Procedural Generation of a 3D model of MIT campus, Research Project Report, Massachusetts Institute of Technology Graphics Laboratory (May 2001). http://graphics.lcs.mit.edu/~seth/pubs/WehowskyBMG.pdf
4. Kjolass, Kari Anne Hoier: Automatic Furniture Population of Large Architectural Models, Master Thesis, Department of Electrical Engineering and Computer Science, MIT (2000).
5. Lecky-Thompson, Guy: Infinite Game Universe: Mathematical Techniques, Charles River Media (2001).
6. Greuter, Stefan, et al: Real-time Procedural Generation of 'Pseudo Infinite' Cities, in Proceedings of the 1st International Conference on Computer Graphics and Interactive Techniques in Austalasia and South East Asia, pp. 87 (2003).
7. Perlin, K: An Image Synthesizer, in Proceedings ACM SIGGRAPH, pp. 287-296 (1985).
8. DeLoura, Mark, ed.: Game Programming Gems, Charles River Media (2000).
9. Perry, L: "Modular Level and Component Design," Game Developer, pp. 30-35 (Nov 2002).

Commedia Virtuale: Theatre Inspiration for Expressive Avatars

Ben Salem[*]

Industrial Design, Technische Universiteit Eindhoven, The Netherlands
b.i.salem@tue.nl

Abstract. We are investigating face, hand and body expressions to be applied to avatars to improve their communication capabilities and enrich and facilitate their perception by users of a virtual environment. We support the idea that avatars have to be designed in such a way as to express state of mind, mood and emotions that are easily understood. We report on our work based on obtaining inspiration from the world of theatre. In this perspective Commedia dell'Arte and Noh theatre have been the focus of our attention. The outcome of this work is a visual language for avatars made up of postures, gestures and appearances.

1 Introduction

We are attempting to design avatars that would make the experience of participating into the CVE closer to real life. To do so the avatars have to perform easy to understand gestures, postures and expressions. Such avatar design will also facilitate the awareness of other participants in the CVE, although it is relevant to point out that it is not just the avatars that will make participants aware of each others but also the interaction and dialogues between users [1].

The Commedia Virtuale work is part of the ReLIVE [2] project. In Commedia Virtuale we first look at human communication and the importance of gestures, postures, and expressions for an affective exchange.

2 Human Communication

Communication between people involves the exchange of a spoken discourse along side a series of expressions rendered by the face, the hands and the body. These expressions, gestures, postures are called Non-Verbal Communications (NVC). NVC can be used to express emotions and moods (anger, happiness), communicate interpersonal status (friend, acquaintance, stranger), support speech (emphasis, illustration), identity assertion (appearance, status, group membership) and to perform rituals (greetings, etiquette) [3]. NVC is also used to strengthen the communication and support the spoken discourse [4] and the exchange of information [5]. NVC is not

---

[*] The author was formerly with Polywork Ltd., Sheffield Science Park, England.

M. Rauterberg (Ed.): ICEC 2004, LNCS 3166, pp. 157–162, 2004.

simply a complement to speech but carry a message on its own which is quite distinct and help social relations [6]. When used in combination with speech it helps establish flexible and robust communication [4]. NVC conveys real-time responsiveness between conversation participants, it lets people influence others and acknowledge influence attempts [7].

2.1 Perception of Other Participants

The awareness of other participants in the virtual environment is a combination of three components occurring in chronology [8]. They are pre-judgement, prediction and attachment. The first part is about attributing the person certain characteristics and quickly evaluating them. Pre-Judgment is about gaining first impressions of a person. The prediction is about generalising to all situations, the behaviour and characteristics of a person from what has been observing in one situation. The predictions are therefore directly the result of the pre-judgement one makes of another person. The attachment is the emotional response one has to another person in terms of liking, sympathy, and so on.

2.2 Body Location

Body location is about the distance between participants that should reflect the kind of relationship that links them. It is also about the invasion of territory (intimate for couples or in a medical practitioner/patient situation, personal for very close people, social for friends, professional with colleagues and public).

During communication; participants establish a small territory in which their discourse will occur [9]. The participant orientation, and the distances separating them as well as the amount of body contact and touching are all part of communication and the establishment of a social order between participants.

2.3 Role and Identity

A role is a set of appearances and behaviours characteristic of one or a group of persons in a context. It is important to ignore those characteristics of a person that do not define a role, for example the eyes colour of a police officer. There are three role genres: social roles, (e.g. the middle class married couple), contextual roles (e.g. the patient in a hospital), and functional roles/roles associated with tasks, (e.g. the postman delivering mail).

Three key elements of an avatar have to be considered during their design as the embodiment of an environment agent or participant. They are: the avatar role, its interaction mode, its representation and its personality [10]. Another important issue is the credibility and relevance of the avatar and the expression of its competence and expertise. The embodiment of avatars does also reinforce the environments users experience of presence [11].

3 NVC for Avatars

There are three kind of NVC, which we have used: appearances, postures and expressions. Some work has been done in the area of facial expressions and presentation engine for avatars [12]. There also has been some work on the setting of a system for the autonomous behaviour for avatars [13]. Looking at CdA and Noh/Kabuki theatre the exaggerated features the characters possess in these theatre styles make them very relevant for our design choices.

3.1 Facial Expressions

Facial expressions are of great importance for the conveying of messages for social interaction and are one of the first forms of communication we rely on [14]. They are used for close range encounter, and are particularly relevant during a conversation. Facial expressions can communicate effectively a multitude of emotions [15]. The key elements of a facial expression are the mouth, the eyes which help modify an expression, and the brows to a lesser degree [16].

3.2 Hand Gestures

Hand gestures are a powerful means for non-verbal communication [17]. Gestures are used for commands, dialogues, to quantify and describe, as well as to perform static and dynamic signs as with the American and British Sign Languages. They are also used to indicate objects and direction and to illustrate properties of objects such as size. Hence the suitability of hand gestures for expressive avatars.

3.3 Body Postures

Human communication is also about the understanding of the other's mental state, beliefs, desires, moods and personality [18]. Body postures are essential in interpersonal communication when people are trying to understand more than just the spoken discourse. There is no reason why avatars should not be capable of performing postures and gestures to emphasise their discourse, to inform about their status and tasks.

Body postures are perceived at the farthest range they can be used for someone wishing to attract attention or indicate his status. The postures are however limited in the number of mood they can express. We have also developed the concept of conversation circle as a structure in the virtual environment for social encounters and collaboration [19]. Further to the body postures, joining a conversation circle is a clear indication of the avatar's owner interests.

4 Avatars Masks

A part from few exceptions facial expressions are culturally universal, and seven expressions are identified easily, they are: happiness, sadness, surprise, anger, fear, disgust/contempt and interest [20]. Some key features are used to generate these expressions.

4.1 Commedia Masks

CdA masks are always half masks. They are the most efficient and powerful way of giving the identity of the character[21]. In Commedia Virtuale we have made two kinds of masks, low and high resolution. Low-resolution masks are used for system agents such as Il Dottore as a help agent. The mask is modelled out of simple shapes, circles and cones. Yet the overall aspect is still preserved as shown in figure 1.

   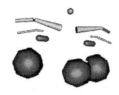

3a. Mask   3b. Model

Fig. 1. Il Dottore

High-resolution mask are used for avatar of greater importance representing an application agent, e.g. Pantalone and the environment manager, e.g. Brighella .

4a. Pantalone Mask   4c. Pantalone Model   4b. Brighella Mask   4d. Brighella Model

Fig. 2. Pantalone and Brighella

4.2 Noh Masks

The Commedia Virtuale system is designed for westerners, therefore Noh/Kabuki masks may not portray personalities easily recognisable in our society. We have selected the demons masks to represent agents delivery messages related to bandwidth bottlenecks, security, and system failures.

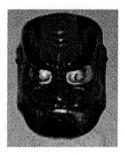   

5a. Kiri Mask   5c. Kiri Model   5b. Tengu Mask [22]   5d. Tengu Model

Fig. 3. Kiri and Tengu

5 Conclusion

Commedia Virtuale is an inspiration from theatre styles in our drive to implement avatars that possess a certain degree of expressiveness, a useful quality for interpersonal communication. Inspiring the design of avatar from the world of theatre can be productive, and it is easy to understand why CdA and Noh are popular and still successful theatre styles. The Commedia Virtuale is at crossing point between the world of entertainment and the world of virtual environments.

Acknowledgements. Commedia Virtuale was funded with a grant from Yorkshire Arts, RAL Program # 5-2080.

References

1.   Robinson M., Pekkola S., Korhonen J., Hujala S., Toivonen T., Saarinen M.-J., Extending the Limits of Collaborative Virtual Environments, *In Collaborative Virtual Environments (CVEs): Histories, Perspective and Issues*, Churchill E., Snowdon D., Munro A., Editors, Springer-Verlag, London, England, 2001, pp. 21-42.
2.   ReLIVE website:www.relive.org.uk
3.   Argyle M., *Bodily Communication*, Routledge, London, England, 1990.
4.   Olveres J., Billinghurst M., Savage J., Holden A., Intelligent, Expressive Avatars. *In Proceedings of IEEE Workshop on Embodies Conversational Characters*, IEEE, pp. 47-55.
5.   Watanabe T., Okubo M., Virtual Face-to-Face Communication System for Human Interaction Analysis by Synthesis, *In Proceedings of HCI INT 99*, 2, pp. 182-186.
6.   Chovil N., Discourse-Oriented Facial Displays in Conversation. *Research on Language and Social Interaction*, 25, 1991/1992, pp. 163-194.
7.   Wiemann J.M., Harrison R.P., Non-Language Aspects of Social Interaction, In *Nonverbal Interaction,* Wiemann J.M., Harrison R.P., Editors, Sage Publications, Beverly Hills, CA, USA, 1983.
8.   Warr P., Knapper C., *The Perception of People and Events,* John Wiley & Sons, London, England, 1968.

9.   Scheflen A.E., *Body Language and the Social Order*, Prentice Hall, Englewood Cliffs, USA, 1972.

10. Churchill E., Cook L., Hodgson P., Prevost S., Sullivan W., *Embodied Conversational Agents,* MIT Press, Cambridge, MA, USA, 2000.

11. Gerhard, M., Moore, D., Hobbs, D., Embodiment and copresence in collaborative interfaces, *Int. J. Human-Computer Studies*, (2004), Article in press, available at www.elseviercomputerscience.com.

12. Muller, W., Spierling, U., Alexa, M., Rieger, Th., Face-to-face with your assistant. Realization issues of animated used interface agents for home appliances, *Computer & Graphics*, 25, (2001), 593-600.

13. Cassell, J., Vilhjalmsson, H., Fully Embodied Conversational Avatars: Making Communicative Behaviors Autonomous, *Autonomous Agents and Multi-Agent Systems*, 2, (1999), 45-64.

14. Izard C., Facial Expression, Emotion, and Motivation, In *Nonverbal Behavior: Applications and Cultural Implications,* Wolfgang A., Editor, Academic Press, New York, NY, USA, 1979.

15. Fabri M., Gerhard M., The Virtual Student: User Embodiment in Virtual Learning Environments, *In International Perspectives on Tele-Education and Virtual Learning Environments*, Orange G. and Hobbs D., Editors, Ashgate, Aldershot, England, 2000, pp. 32-55.

16. Fleming B., Dobbs D., *Animating Facial Features & Expressions,* Charles River Media, Rockland, MA, USA, 1999.

17. Salem B., Gestures, *In Interface technology the leading Edge*, Noyes J. M. and Cook M. Editors, RSP, Hertfordshire, England, 1999, pp.73-96.

18. Bruce, V., What the human face tells the human mind: some challenged for the robot-human interface, *Advanced Robotics*, 8, No 4, (1994), 341-355.

19. Salem B., and Earle N., Designing a Non-Verbal Language for Expressive Avatars, *In Proceedings of CVE'2000* (San Francisco, CA, USA, September 2000), ACM Press, 93-101.

20. Anderson, A.H. The Human Communication Research Dialogue Data Base, *Journal of Child Language*, 19, 1992, 711-716.

21. Grantham, M., *Playing Commedia: A training guide to commedia techniques*, Nick Hern Book, London, UK, 2000.

22. Photo from : www.pasar5.com/NOH_MASK/mask/tengu.html

Take the Money and Run? An Ethical Approach to the Relation Between Game Research and Game Industry

Miguel Sicart

Department of Digital Aesthetics and Culture, IT University of Copenhagen, Denmark
miguel@itu.dk

Abstract. This article tries to give some light to the ethical issues concerning the relationship of research and industry in the field of computer game research. No conclusive answers are reached. The ethical issues addressed here concerned basically the independence of academic institutions as a key feature for the quality of research. While the most common ethical approach, *consequentialism*, seems not to provide meaningful answers to this questions, a *deontological* approach seems to be a possible option. Nevertheless, much is yet to be done. Perhaps the most important conclusion of this paper is the relevance of *independence* for the well developing of the discipline.

1 Introduction

The field of Computer Game Research is now living its third year of existence [1]. In these years we have experienced a flourishing of games research centres, masters programs, and associations of researchers. This challenging panorama reveals the emergent interest on computer games from traditional academic institutions.

This paper will provide a basic introduction to different ethical positions that researchers and academia can assume concerning their relation with game industry, a topic not sufficiently well researched yet. This article will focus on some possible economic issues concerning these relations, and their ethical interpretations and consequences.

The theoretical framework of this article is grounded both on the philosophical tradition of ethics, and in its application to Internet Research. Due to its integration of the traditional ethical discourses and the specificities of the digital media, the Association of Internet Researchers' (AoIR) guidelines [5] are a source of inspiration for this paper.

This paper does not intend to give any conclusive answers to the problems that it examines. The ethical research, as far as this paper is concerned, consists on pointing out problematic issues and giving a possible framework for meaningful answers.

2 Game Research – Game Industry: Where Are the Problems?

Where do these ethical issues appear? Given the facts that academic disciplines usually require external funding for their development, not to say an object of study,

M. Rauterberg (Ed.): ICEC 2004, LNCS 3166, pp. 163–167, 2004.

and that the computer game industry can actually provide both, it is in that relation where this paper finds its groundings for an ethically framed analysis.

If the role of academia is to develop knowledge independent from funding sources, valuable for the community, its relation with an industry so strongly based on revenues and profit makes questions arise: can computer game research establish interesting relations with computer game industry without loosing independence, and therefore loosing academic credibility? Is it possible for a researcher or an academic institution to receive economic and material support from the industry without compromising their results? Is the industry's need for social acceptance so important that can blur the academic approach to the products they develop, via direct or indirect influence? These are some of the questions that this paper intends to analyze.

3   In the Game for the Pay: Academic Institutions and Game Industry

Academic institutions with a special interest in computer games research face several problems when it comes to their relationships with industry. Among these issues, these seem to be some of the most relevant: The costs of the software are high, and the possibility of an alliance of an academic institution with a publisher might lower those costs. If the academic institution is interested in developing products with research interest, it will need to purchase expensive middleware. Thus, a similar alliance might be considered.

Given the need of social recognition that game industries have, a direct funding of a game research institution might be seen as a win-win situation for both the industry and academia. So far, some conclusions can be drawn: academia might be interested in cooperating with the industry for economic reasons, as the field requires some major expenses in order to achieve excellence in research. On the other hand, computer game industry is interested in this collaboration as it provides both a test bank and a social recognition of which they are very needed.

Applying a consequentialist perspective, it is possible to say that, as long as these relations are inside the boundaries of economic laws, there is no apparent risk of harming individuals, institutions or the research field by agreements between academia and industry. Both would achieve their expectations.

Nevertheless, for academia there are some problems that have to be taken into account. The need for funding might derive in a loss if independence of the field. Some of the possible negative outcomes of these relations are:

- Limitation of the scope of research.
- Becoming an underpaid R&D division of a major company.
- Abuse of the social recognition in publicity for the major funding company.

Given the risks that we have pointed out, a consequentialist approach, following the ethical basic concept of "do no harm", suggests not to relate with game industry unless further discussions clarify the negative outcomes. And even in that case, more negative or unforeseen consequences can tear apart any choice we have taken with an ethical perspective.

This means that, despite the interesting mapping of the future that consequentialism suggests, it is not a reasonable exclusive ethical framework for the developing of a new academic field in relation with industry. Even though it is useful, it cannot be let alone to answer all the ethical issues in this field. A broader, complementary perspective seems to be necessary.

This approach, though, has revealed one of the most relevant ethical issues concerning this relationship between game research and game industry: the independence of academic research. In order to create knowledge an academic institution shall (or should) be at least partially independent from the source of its research. If that independence is threatened, then the value and the prestige of the research may be damaged. It is not risky to say that independence is a key component of academic identity.

4 Deontology: The Need for Codes

So far, this article has focused on a consequentialist ethics approach to the relations between game research and game industry. The limitations of consequentialist ethics call for a new perspective. But first of all, it is needed to explain more clearly the main problem that this brief research on the ethics of game research has pointed out: the independence of academic milieus.

Academia is traditionally considered an independent source for knowledge. Despite their focus on industrial and economic items, academic research must preserve a certain kind of integrity to have their results validated as valuable knowledge. If an academic institution's independence is threatened by the possible collaboration with companies that seek for economic benefit, the usual responses are to moderate, or annul, that cooperation.

In the case of computer game research, the establishing of a relation with industry seems to offer great possibilities to develop the emerging field. The threat to independence, though, is still present. A positive ethical approach would try to deal with this issue in order to provide a framework in which both institutions and industry could benefit from the collaboration, without loosing identity.

The answer this paper suggests to this issue is derived from the application of deontological ethics to other fields of research, like medicine or Internet Research. Deontological ethics assumes that every person has a set of rights and duties to follow in order to justify ethically their decisions. If the individual sets his or her actions within this framework, then the choices taken have a substantial moral ground, despite the possible negative outcome they might have.

Therefore, a suggested ethical approach to solve the issues concerning game research relations with game industry is the elaboration of a deontological code including the ethical issues that are debated, and how the researchers can act upon them. In other words, game research as a discipline is in need of a deontological code, which may contribute to clearing and solving the problem concerning independence as threatened by possible collaboration with the industry.

What does this need tell us about computer game research as a discipline? To ensure the health and prosperity of the discipline, an ethical ground is needed. It is time for game research to start developing and identity beyond the mere object of study, reflecting upon itself and the possible consequences in the academic panorama. Only then infancy will be over, and computer game research will become a mature, well-defined discipline.

5 Conclusions

This article has tried to give some light to the ethical issues concerning the relationship of research and industry in the field of computer game research. No conclusive answers were reached, but the outlines for the future can be relevant in future discussions on the topic.

The ethical issues addressed here concerned basically the independence of academic institutions as a key feature for the quality of research. While the most common ethical approach, consequentialism, seems not to provide meaningful answers to this questions, a deontological approach, imitating the relevance that the ethical guidelines have in other research fields, seems to be a possible option for the future.

Nevertheless, much is yet to be done in this young field of research. Perhaps the most important conclusion of this paper is the relevance of independence for the well developing of the discipline. Many mistakes were done in other research fields in the past. As game researchers, we have the unique possibility to foresee problems, and act before they become unsolvable. That is also a part of becoming a relevant, meaningful academic field.

References

[1]   Aarseth, Espen. Cybertext. Perspectives on Ergodic Literature. Baltimore: The John Hopkins University Press, 1997.
[2]   Baird, Robert M., Reagan Ramsower, and Stuart E. Rosenbaum, ed. Cyber-ethics: Social and Moral Issues in the Computer Age. Amherst, New York: Prometheus Books, 2000.
[3]   Copier, Marinka and Joost Raessens. "Level Up. Proceedings of the Digital Games Research Conference 2003." Paper presented at the Level Up, Utrecht 2003.
[4]   Ess, Charles, ed. Philosophical Perspectives in Computer Mediated Communication. New York: SUNY, 1996.
[5]   Ess, Charles, and the AoIR Ethics Working Committee. Ethical Guidelines for Internet Research 2003 [cited 3/2 2004]. Available from htpp://www.aoir.org/reports/ethics.pdf.
[6]   Floridi, Luciano. "What Is the Philosophy of Information?" In Cyber-philosophy: The Intersection of Computing and Philosophy, edited by James H. Moor and Terrell Ward Byrum. London: Blackwell, 2002.
[7]   ———, ed. The Blackwell Guide to the Philosophy of Computing and Information. London: Blackwell, 2003.
[8]   Floridi, Luciano and J.W. Sanders. "Internet Ethics: The Constructionist Values of Homo Poieticus." In The Impact of the Internet in Our Moral Lives, edited by R. Cavalier. New York: SUNY, 2003.
[9]   Hayles, Katherine. How We Became Posthuman: Virtual Bodies in Cybernetics, Literature, and Informatics. Chicago: University of Chicago Press, 1999.

[10] Ihde, Don. Technology and the Lifeworld. From Garden to Earth. Edited by Indiana University Press, The Indiana Series in the Philosophy of Technology. Bloomington and Indianapolis: Indiana University Press, 1990.

[11] Moor, James H. and Terrell Ward Bynum, ed. Cyber-philosophy: The Intersection of Computing and Philosophy. Oxford: Blackwell, 2002.

[12] NESH. "Guidelines for Research Ethics in the Social Sciences, Law and the Humanities." Norway: National Committee for Research Ethics in the Social Sciences and Humanities, 2001.

[13] RESPECT. "Code of Practice." 2003.

[14] Reynolds, Ren. Playing a "Good" Game: A Philosophical Approach to Understanding the Morality of Games 2002 [cited 3/2 2004].
Available from http://www.igda.org/articles/rreynoldsethics.php.

[15] Spinello, Richard. Cyber-ethics: Morality and Law in Cyberspace. Boston: Jones and Bartlett, 2000.

[16] Wolf, Mark J.P. "The Video Game as Medium." In The Medium of the Video Game, edited by Mark J.P. Wolf. Austin: University of Texas Press, 2001.

[17] Wolf, Mark J.P., ed. The Medium of the Video-Game. Austin: University of Texas Press, 2001.

Moved by Movements: How Character Movements Cue Us to Form Specific Genre and Affective Impressions

Valentijn Visch

Cultural Studies: Word & Image, Faculty of Arts, Vrije Universiteit Amsterdam
Technical University Delft: Faculty of Industrial Design: StudioLab
Netherlands Institute for Animation Film, Tilburg
vt.visch@let.vu.nl

Abstract. When we see a feature film scene, it is usually not very hard to tell to which genre the film might belong. Our research focuses on the role of bodily movements of actors in the genre recognition process. We aim to identify by means of empirical experiments using 3-D animated scenes, which parameters of bodily movements – and which configurations of these - are responsible for what generic and affective viewer impression. The following set of parameters is varied in an animated and abstracted "running chase" scene: *velocity, efficiency, fluency, detail* and *body proportion*. As the experiment is running at this moment of writing, the results shall be presented during the conference.

1 Introduction

When we see a feature film, it is usually not very hard to tell to which genre the film might belong. Viewers can differentiate easily between a horror and a drama or between a comic and an action movie. From an analytical perspective there is no doubt that genres do have a substantive function in film comprehension: viewers use genre cues from the films they are watching to shape their expectations as to the genre-specific development and outcomes of major actions and events [5]. Next they match their expectations with their perceptions in order to structure, facilitate and contextualize these [1] [6]. When perceptions do not match anymore with the expectations the viewer will eventually adjust the recognized genre into another or a new genre (Altman 1999). According to these film theoreticians, genre cues act in the viewers' conscious attempts to find the best fitting genre. Additionally, given the body of evidence on media priming, genre cues may be expected to act at a less conscious level of processing. They may prime viewer attention, perception, inferences and expectations [7]. However, hardly any specific research is performed on genre cues, such as plot, movements, iconography or film style, that viewers use to arrive at genre categorizations [3] [4]. Our research tries to reveal the working of the genre cues that ensue from the actor's body movements. In a series of experiments we aim to identify which parameters of actor movement are responsible for what generic and affective viewer impression.

M. Rauterberg (Ed.): ICEC 2004, LNCS 3166, pp. 168–171, 2004.

2 Procedure

As we wanted to know which body parameters are specific for what generic and affective viewer impression, we had to find film scenes that occurred in different genres while its bodily realisation varied. Scenes like *happy reunion* or *running chase* would meet this request. We gained our fiction film material from diverse mainstream and art house feature film throughout the 20th century. Our non-fiction film material was taken from news items and documentaries and in part shot by the author at an airport arrivals terminal.

2.1 Body Movement Parameters

When we analysed the material we traced the following five body movement parameters on which each generic realisation differed: velocity, efficiency, fluency, detail and body proportion. We performed two experiments testing the effect of velocity and body proportion on genre recognition - its conclusions are described below. At this moment of writing we are conducting an experiment using a 3D animation which test all five parameters independently on five levels. The results of this experiment will be presented at the conference.

In the animated chase object A chases object B - figure 1. When the distance between the objects becomes shorter, object B increases the amount *and* the sharpness of its corners. The movements of A are varied while the movements of B - as well as the camera, duration, setting and color - remain constant.

Efficiency is defined as the amount of energy, imagined by the viewer, that A has to use to reach its goal (B). Efficiency is varied in the animation by adjusting the track of the chaser: efficiency is positive when A takes the inner corners (A anticipates the movements of B), negative when A takes the outer corners (A is distracted by B) and neutral when A follows B's track.

Fluency is defined by the nature of A's velocity shifts. The fluency is positive when the velocity shifts are continuous. The fluency is negative when the velocity shifts are step-wise combined with a few some stop motion frames.

Detail is defined by the amount of movements. In the animation the amount of keys of A, each defining a velocity shift, is varied ranging from 2 to 26.

2.2 Velocity

In study 1 [8] we took a genre prototypical and a genre non-prototypical *happy reunion* scenes from the comic, dramatic, action and non-fiction genre. This selection included happy reunion scenes from films ranging from *The English Patient* (e.g.; a prototypical drama scene where two former lovers reunite in a romantic room) to *Reservoir Dogs* (e.g.; a non-prototypical action scene where two friends reunite in a classy office) and from a prototypical (non-fiction) news items showing a reunion of a released Bosnian Serbian criminal with his family, to a non-prototypical scene where a Rwandan father reunites in a quietly with his 8-year old daughter he had supposed to be dead.

The velocity of the scenes was varied on three levels: acceleration by a third, deceleration by a third and its original speed. 44 participants were presented with all the scenes and were asked to judge the fittingness of the scenes on a 5-point scale in *each* of the four genres. In order to focus the viewer's attention on the body movements of the actors we distorted the image quality of all the scenes . Genre cues like lightening, the actor's face, color and setting details were in this way minimized, while the actor's bodily outlines were maximized (figure 2). Repeated measure analyses of the data provided the following conclusions:

- film velocity has a significant effect on genre recognition;
- accelerated fragments are judged to fit significantly better in the comical genre than non-accelerated fragment;

with the following exception:

- the comical prototype contains an optimal velocity: when the velocity of that scene is varied the judged comical fittingness decreases significantly;
- decelerated scenes, as opposed to un-manipulated scenes, are judged to fit significantly better in the drama genre and significantly worse in the comical genre.

Fig. 1. Animation example.   **Fig. 2.** Image distortion example.

2.3 Body Proportion

In study 2 we varied the body proportion of the chaser A in the above described animation. While the body-volume remained constant, its proportion was varied on five levels: from narrow and high through square to wide and low. 46 participants were asked to judge the genre fittingness on a 5-point scale of each variations for each of genres (comic, drama, action and non-fiction). Repeated measure analyses provided the following conclusions:

- the two extreme proportions (narrow high and wide low) were judged to fit significantly better in the comic genre than in any other genre.
- the wide low proportion was judged to fit significantly better in the comical genre than the narrow high proportion.

3   Conclusions

In study 1 we asked participants to judge the genre fittingness of happy reunion scenes which were taken from diverse genres. The genre judgments of the velocity un-manipulated and genre prototypical fragments allowed us to make the following explorations concerning genre relations:

- the non-fiction genre serves as an export genre, i.e. a non-fiction scene fits better in other genres than scenes from other genres fit in the non-fiction genre. This conclusion hints to the statement that non-fiction representations function as a neutral basis for fiction.
- the comical genre serves as an import genre, i.e. scenes from non-comical genres fit better in the comical genre than a comical scene fits in any of the non-comical genres. The comical genre thus has the ability to parody the other genres.

In an additional experiment 3, we presented 46 participants with genre prototypical running chases taken from the four genres and asked the subjects again to judge the genre fittingness of the fragments. We manipulated the images the same way as in study 1 (figure 2). This experiment confirmed the above described exporting nature of the non-fiction genre and the importing nature of the comical genre. A remarkable effect of the two narrative episodes was that the non-fiction happy reunion scene was judged to fit second to best in the dramatic genre while the running chase scene was judged to fit second to best in the action genre (- both scenes were judged to fit best in the non-fiction genre). This effect can be explained by the neutral cinematic representation of the non-fiction genre in combination with a specific generic viewer impression that is cued by a specific narrative episode.

References

[1] Allen, R. (1995). Projecting Illusion: Film Spectatorship and the Impression of Reality. Cambridge, UK: Cambridge University Press.
[2] Altman, R. (1999). Film/ Genre. London: British Film Institute.
[3] Austin, A. (1989). Immediate Seating: A Look at Movie Audiences. Belmont, CA: Wadsworth Publishing Company.
[4] Bordwell, D. & Thompson, K. (1997). Film Art: An Introduction. NY: McGraw-Hill Companies.
[5] Grodal, T. (1997). Moving Pictures. Oxford: Clarendon Press.
[6] Neale, S. (2000). Genre and Hollywood. London: Routledge.
[7] Roskos-Ewoldsen, D.R., Roskos-Ewoldsen, B., & Dillman-Carpentier, F.R. (2002). Media priming: a synthesis. In: J. Bryant & D. Zillmann (Eds.) Media Effects (2nd ed., 97- 120.) Mahwah, NJ: Erlbaum
[8] Visch, V.T. & Tan, E.S.H (2003). Effect of Film Velocity on Genre Recognition. Manuscript submitted for publication.

Improvisation in Theatre Rehearsals for Synthetic Actors

Tony Meyer and Chris Messom

IIMS, Massey University, Auckland, New Zealand
T.A.Meyer@massey.ac.nz

Abstract. Although the use of computers to create otherwise impossible characters has long been a staple of film, corresponding use in live stage performance is uncommon, and such characters have typically been only electronic puppets. Improvisation is an essential part of rehearsals for a live stage (scripted) performance, providing development of character and plot; in addition, the rehearsal process provides a training ground for the actors involved with the performance. The author aims to develop synthetic characters capable of taking full part in this process. Initial experiments (dynamically adding an affect component to scripted speech, and evolving variations of movement) have been promising, and form the beginnings of the larger system, which will autonomously build up a model of the character that the synthetic actor is portraying, with the aim of presenting continually improved performances.

1   Synthetic Actors

Although the use of computers to create otherwise impossible characters has long been staple of film, corresponding use in live stage performance is uncommon. Within this project, the aim is both to assist the development of synthetic actors within live stage performances, and also to progress synthetic characters so that they are more truly autonomous.

From 1996 to 2001, Claudio Pinhanez at the M.I.T Media Lab produced various experiments in computer theatre, concentrating on computer, or synthetic, actors. In 1996's *SingSong*, four disembodied heads interacted with a human conductor to perform a short musical item in front of a live audience [1]. All the characters were completely autonomous, working off a known script, and able to adapt to (limited) changes in the performance by the human actor. 1998's *It/I* told the story of a computer actor (*It*) who tries to keep the attention of a human actor (*I*) by presenting various images, generating sounds, and changing lighting. Pinhanez's actors were able to adapt to temporal changes in the performance, and, to a certain extent, vary their performance each time it was presented [1].

The Virtual Theater project at Stanford University aimed to provide a multimedia environment in which users could fill all the roles associated with putting on a play in an improvisational theatre company, including producer, playwright, casting directory, set designer, music director, real-time directory, and actor. Those roles not filled by the user were filled by intelligent agents. The focus of the Virtual Theater

M. Rauterberg (Ed.): ICEC 2004, LNCS 3166, pp. 172–175, 2004.
© IFIP International Federation for Information Processing 2004

project was on improvisation in the classical mode of improvisation first practiced by the Commedia dell'Arte during the Italian Renaissance, rather than performances that were scripted [2].

Ideally, synthetic actors are capable of following a script, but also reacting according to its own role. This is far more important than achieving lifelike or realistic characters – as Reilly and Bates state: "We are not necessarily interested in lifelike or realistic agents. We don't really care if our characters only have four fingers or are talking animals. The arts have always abstracted away from reality and created characters that were 'larger than life' and that were much more interesting than any mere 'real' people or animals we might know" [3].

2   Aims

Improvisation is often used to refer to performance "with little or no preparation" [4], although it has an additional meaning – "to play ... extemporaneously, especially by inventing variations" [4]. In fact, many improvised performances are often created by inventing variations, with the aim of **appearing to have** carried out no preparation. The other key role of the rehearsal process is practice: sections of the play are performed, feedback is gained from the director, and, using that feedback to alter the performance, the section is performed again, until an optimum performance is achieved. This project aims to improve synthetic actors so that they are able to take part in these two key elements of the rehearsal process.

3   Preliminary Results

One aspect of the synthetic actor's performance is the spoken lines of dialogue. Audio analysis of line delivery by the human actors is computationally expensive, and so not available to the current system, so the synthetic actors must utilise other methods to determine a variation of the line appropriate to the current situation.

Using a statistical method with a relatively simple set of tokens, comprised of the words in the lines (case-normalised, without punctuation, and stemmed), the name of the character delivering the line, details of the parts of speech used in the line, and the words in the previous line, the system suitably classifies forty to fifty percent of lines, and tags another fifteen to twenty percent as unsure. In a rehearsal situation, where the synthetic actor is able to make three attempts at each line of dialogue, the system succeeds 65 to 75 percent of the time, is unsure another ten percent, and incorrect with only ten to fifteen percent of lines (see Figure 1). With training, during the rehearsal process (alongside human actors), success quickly approaches one hundred percent, while still allowing variation of performance through the combination of the various scores.

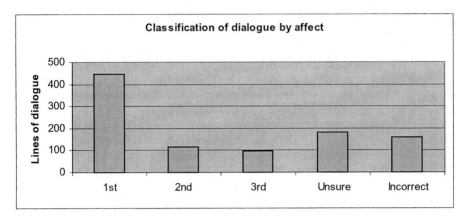

Fig. 1. Suitable classification of lines of dialogue, given three attempts.

In addition to inventing variations in the way that lines are delivered, the synthetic actors must vary their movement. The current system has the synthetic actors in a three-dimensional virtual world, which is projected onto screens at the rear and side of the theatre stage. Within this world, the characters can move and perform various animations (we are interested in high-level movement, so these animations are fixed). In order to vary these movements, without losing the overall purpose of each movement, evolutionary methods were used. Using a hierarchy of seeded generators (where early generators are fast, but poorly tested, and later generators are slow, but comprehensively tested), the synthetic actor is able to present a small number of variations of each movement in the rehearsal setting. The feedback from the director is then able to be used to evaluate the fitness of these individuals, to further generate improved movement.

4   Conclusion

Autonomous synthetic actors should be capable of introducing variations into rehearsal performances, as a method of developing an optimal performance; the actors should then be capable of learning from the limited feedback provided in a rehearsal setting to improve the variations offered in future. An example of such variation is the manner in which synthesised speech is delivered (for example, varying pitch, volume and rate of speech). Although the synthetic actors have a very limited amount of data available (particularly in early rehearsals), it is possible to extract enough information from this data to produce generally acceptable performances. Use of a simple statistical technique, primarily based on the words in the lines of dialogue, allows synthetic actors to select an appropriate speech delivery method for two thirds of all lines, without any specific training. Similarly, use of evolutionary methods enables the synthetic actors to invent variations of known movements, without losing the purpose of each movement.

References

1. C. Pinhanez, "Representation and Recognition of Action in Interactive Spaces," Massachusetts Institute of Technology, 1999.
2. D. Rousseau and B. Hayes-Roth, "Improvisational Synthetic Actors with Flexible Personalities," Department of Computer Science, Stanford University, Knowledge Systems Laboratory Report 97-10, December 1997.
3. W. S. Reilly and J. Bates, *Natural negotiation for believable agents*. Pittsburgh, Pa.: School of Computer Science Carnegie Mellon University, 1995.
4. Houghton Mifflin Company, *The American Heritage® Dictionary of the English Language*, 4th Ed. ed: Houghton Mifflin Company, 2000.

Enjoyment and Entertainment in East and West

Matthias Rauterberg

Department Industrial Design, Technische Unversiteit Eindhoven,
Den Doelch 2, 5600 MB Eindhoven, The Netherlands
g.w.m.rauterberg@tue.nl
http://www.ipo.tue.nl/homepages/mrauterb/

Abstract. From a users' perspective entertainment is based on enjoyment in using these products or services. How and which cultural differences between eastern and western cultures are influencing enjoyment and the design of entertainment technology is described in this paper. In particular the underlying religious structures are discussed and compared.

1 Introduction

Entertainment related to leisure activities is -in opposition to work- increasing in most industrialized countries. Even modern knowledge intensive work has to rely on intrinsic motivation, while traditional work is primarily extrinsic motivated (e.g. salary, bonus, extras, etc). In this respect all industrialized countries have to face similar challenges, but regarding enjoyment and entertainment cultural differences between western and eastern countries seems to be obvious. This paper address the issue of cultural differences and discuss possible underlying reasons.

1.1 Playing

Playing is one of the dominating factors of human cultures, even work, law, war, science and art contains elements of playing [5]. Playing is a specific activity in which 'learning' and 'creativity' (incl. fantasy) can come together [8]. Playing of children is an important necessity to get acquainted with reality [6]. Playing for learning is primarily process oriented, while playing for being creative is product oriented [8]. Csikszentmihalyi [4] could show how human activities can be based on intensive enjoyment, called 'flow experience'; the following conditions should be met: (1) make it a game ("look at your task as a game, establish rules, objectives, challenges to be overcome, and rewards"); (2) establish powerful goals ("as you play the game, remind yourself frequently of the overriding spiritual, social, or intellectual purpose that drive your efforts"); (3) focus ("release your mind from all distractions, from within or without; focus your entire attention on the game"); (4) surrender to the process ("let go; don't strive or strain to achieve your objective; just enjoy the process of work"); (5) accept ecstasy ("this is the natural result of the preceding four steps; it will hit you suddenly, by surprise; but there will be no mistaking it"); and (6) achieve

M. Rauterberg (Ed.): ICEC 2004, LNCS 3166, pp. 176–181, 2004.

peak productivity ("your ecstasy state opens vast reservoirs of resourcefulness, creativity, and energy; your productivity and quality of work shoot through the roof"). Of course, this flow experience is not always possible or even acceptable, but still very attractive and sometimes very productive.

In the past, several attempts are done to define 'playing'. According Rubinstein [15] (pp. 727-728) is human play "a result of activities that enables the human to redesign reality and to change the world. The nature of human play consists of the ability to redesign reality through mental representations". Scheuerl [19] characterized play as the origin of any activity based on the following six basic motives: (1) freedom, (2) internal infinity, (3) illusion, (4) ambivalence, (5) closure, and (6) presence. Play is at the same time familiar and alien, known and unknown. Playing was and still is an anthropological necessity for human development [6]. Play in its pure sense is 'anti-dogmatic' and 'anti-authoritarian', and can be characterized by the following three principles: (1) freedom (free choice to take part in a game), (2) equality (all players have to follow the same rules), and (3) democracy (games are open to change there rules on negotiations among players).

1.2 Working

In western societies an academic interest in the differences between working and playing started in the 19th century, when the political, economical and social conditions developed into a separation of play from work [10]. This was the begin –at least in the western, industrialized societies- for establishing childhood and youth as a separate phase in child development (e.g., deliberated from child work).

The German word 'arbeit' for work has possibly its roots in the Arabic word 'arebeit' that means 'drudgery' or 'strain'. Work and in particular labor is defined by 'difficult or arduous work or effort' and related to 'pain' [20].

Table 1. The different profiles of work versus play (see Rauterberg and Paul [13])

Work	Play
paid	not paid
laborious	enjoyable
product oriented	process oriented
external controlled	internal controlled
alienating	empowering

2 Enjoyment, Religion, and Culture

Playing has meaning only in relation to non-playful activities such as work or sleep. Historically, play has been associated with joy or even ecstasy [4], wherein a kind of transcendence is experienced. Play may create an openness to a dimension of enjoyment outside the boundaries of the mundane. Berger [2] has even developed an argument for God and the supernatural from the social fact of play. The nature of play evokes a kind of timelessness and innocence that Berger takes to a "signal of transcendence" even within the essential patterns of human culture. Lewis [9] also argued that experiences of deep "joy" indicate a reality beyond the material, to which our souls are sometimes exposed and in which they gratefully delight.

To achieve a 'mentally enriched society' Nakastu [11] expressed clearly, that entertainment industry has to aim for a kind of entertainment technology that enable users to grow mentally (e.g., enlightment) and to avoid known pitfalls (e.g., addiction, pornography, violence, etc). Rauterberg [14] summarizes the state of the art of positive effects of existing information and communication technology (including entertainment technology) on human behavior (e.g., learning and development).

2.1 Enjoyment and Religion

Saroglou and Jaspard [16] have hypothesized that humor (as one aspect of enjoyment) may be negatively affected by religion. In an empirical study, Saroglou found that religiosity and religious fundamentalism (contrary to 'quest' religiosity) were negatively associated with humor creation. Saroglou and Jaspard [16] investigated in an experiment whether this association reflects causality: 85 western students were tested in their propensity to spontaneously produce humor as a response to hypothetical daily hassles after exposure to a religious video or to a humorous one vs. a non-stimulation condition. They found significant effects of experimental condition, gender, and interaction in the hypothesized direction: religious stimulation inhibited humor, while humorous stimulation promoted it. Participants' religious fundamentalism and orthodoxy predicted low humor creation in the religious condition but not in the humorous one.

Saroglou [17] could find in another study (based on pencil evaluation of humorous stimuli by 118 western participants), that religious fundamentalism and orthodoxy were found to be negatively correlated to humor appreciation in general and to appreciation of incongruity-resolution and nonsense humor in particular, whereas religious historical relativism was positively correlated to appreciation of nonsense humor (=unresolved incongruity). However, religiosity was unrelated to humor appreciation and no religious dimension predicted low appreciation of sexual humor.

Berecz [1] discusses critically the relationship of Christian sexuality and intimacy: in a western culture obsessed with sexuality as entertainment, the followers of Christ call others to view human sexuality not primarily in terms of eroticism, power, or procreation, but rather in terms of psychological intimacy.

Saroglou et al. [18] investigated 181 western adults, who were approached at the exits of bookstores to evaluate themselves on the following dimensions: adult attachment (anxiety and avoidance), 'need for closure' (preference for order and predictability), religion (classic religiosity and spirituality/emotion-based religion) and 'reading interests'. The authors found that 'need for closure' (but not attachment dimensions) predicted classic religiosity, whereas anxiety in relationships (but not avoidance) and 'preference for order' (but not predictability) predicted interest in spirituality/emotional religion. Finally, adults high in anxiety reported high interest in reading spirituality books. The authors discuss critically the 'correspondence model' (secure people are more religious) and emphasize the need for distinguishing between anxiety and avoidance when studying religion.

2.2 Religion and Culture

The western religion of Christianity was introduced into Japan in the middle of the 16th century. Christianity was generally tolerated until the beginning of the 17th century, but the Tokugawa shogunate (1603-1867) eventually proscribed it and persecuted its adherents. When relations with the west were restored in the middle of the 19th century, Christianity was reintroduced and has continued to exist in Japan till today. But still, in popular Japanese perception Christianity is regarded as a 'foreign' creed, recommending and preaching admirable ideals but unsuitable for ordinary Japanese. Because of it's 'foreign' nature, Christianity has been persecuted when demands for national unity were strong; it has been widely accepted during period of social instabilities (16th century, Meiji era, Post World war II) but once social and economical stability was reestablished interest came back. Apart from the Nagasaki region Christianity seems to be most attractive to the urban, professional classes. Various aspects of Christianity differ fundamentally from the traditional pattern of Japanese thought and outlook (e.g., monotheism versus traditional polytheism; the concept of a transcendent God versus the immanent Japanese deities; a western individual ethic versus a eastern group-orientated ethic). It is difficult to estimate whether organized Christianity can accommodate itself to the established concepts in Japan as much as Buddhism, but there still remains much potential for expressing Christian concepts in a more Japanese form (transcription from Kondansha's Encyclopedia of Japan [3] [7]).

(a)   (b)   (c)

Fig. 1. Three pictures of Jesus' death (a), Jesus' ascension (b), and Buddha's enlightment (c).

One of the major difference between Christianity and Buddhism seems to be the use of important symbols: Christianity prefers the crucified and dying Christ (Fig. 1 a) while Buddhism prefers the enlightened person (Fig. 1c). At the beginning of Christianity in the western world the symbol of the ascension of Christ (Fig. 1 b) was used, but changed later to the crucified Christ. A speculative conclusion seems to be that modern Christianity relies more on anxiety than on enjoyment (see also the results of Saroglou et al. [16] [17] [18]).

Onishi and Murhpy-Shigematsu [12] could find that, unlike in Japanese society, where religion plays a relatively small role in people's everyday lives and in their conscious way of thinking, in Muslim societies religion has a pervasive effect on all aspects of life. In Japan, people rarely use religion to represent themselves or to categorize others. While in many western and/or eastern societies where major religious groups exist, the persons in Onishi and Murhpy-Shigematsu's study may have been socially categorized as 'Muslim immigrants', in Japan they were categorized as 'foreign workers' or just 'Asians' (coming from Bangladesh [N=13], Pakistan [N=7], and Iran [N=4]; age 28-35, all male, coming to Japan at age 16-28). Although their religion is salient in Japanese society, it was not an aspect of interest for Japanese people, race and nationality assume much more importance. This focus in turn influenced the foreign respondents to emphasize these same aspects of their non-Japanese identity (e.g., getting a deeper understanding of the own religious roots).

3 Conclusions

We presented and discussed several interesting and important results, mainly based on scientific investigations to explore the relationships among enjoyment, religion and culture. Some of the possible conclusions are somewhat speculative: (1) Japanese strengths in entertainment technology can be related to social openness and lack of religious constrains towards enjoyment; (2) while the western entertainment industry is more focusing on the technology, the eastern is focusing on the content and narrative structure too [21]; and (3) probably entertainment technology will challenge the social and cultural norms and values more than any information and communication technology so far [22]. If content really matters (and there is sufficient evidence for) then we better take a closer look to our future vision how society should develop and aim for, and how entertainment technology can help to achieve these aims.

Acknowledgments. I have to thank the following people for our very fruitful discussions: Ryohei Nakatsu, Brad Bushman and Ben Salem.

References

[1]   Berecz, J. (2002). Is there such a thing as "Christian" sex? Pastoral Psychology, Vol. 50, No. 3, pp. 139-146.

[2]   Berger, P. (1990, 2nd ed). A Rumor of Angels: Modern Society and the Rediscovery of tile Supernatural. New York.

[3]   Christianity in Japan, transcription from Kondansha's Encyclopedia of Japan, retrieved May 26, 2004 from http://www.baobab.or.jp/~stranger/mypage/chrinjap.htm

[4]   Csikszentmihalyi, M. (1990). Flow: the psychology of optimal experience. Harpercollins.

[5]   Huizinga, J. (1962). Homo ludens-vom Ursprung der Kultur des Spiels [Homo ludens-the origin of play cultur]. Hamburg (1938 first edition).

[6]   Kauke, M. (1992). Spielintelligenz: spielend lernen-spielend lehren? [Play intelligence: playful learning-playful teaching]. Heidelberg.

[7]   Kondansha's Encyclopedia of Japan (2004) via http://www.ency-japan.com/

[8]   Leontjew, A. N. (1973). Probleme der Entwicklung des Psychischen [Problems of mental development]. Frankfurt.

[9]   Lewis, C. S. (1965, re's ed.).The weight of glory and other addresses. New York.

[10] Nahrstedt, W. (1969). Die Entstehung der Freizeit zwischen 1750-1850-dargestellt am Beispiel Hamburg [The appearence of freetime between 1750 and 1850, described at Hamburg city]. PhD Thesis, University of Hamburg, Germany.

[11] Nakatsu, R. (2004). Entertainment Computing. Presentation, retrieved May 25, 2004 from http://www.ipo.tue.nl/homepages/mrauterb/presentations/Nakatsu(2004)/ Nakatsu[2004].htm

[12] Onishi, A. & Murhpy-Shigematsu, S. (2003). Identity narratives of Muslim foreign workers in Japan. Journal of Community & Applied Social Psychology, Vol. 13, pp. 224-239

[13] Rauterberg, M. & Paul, H.-J. (1990). Computerspiele - Computerarbeit: Spielerische Momente in der Arbeit [Computer game-computer work: play aspects in work]. In: F. Nake (ed.), Ergebnisse der 9.Arbeitstagung "Mensch-Maschine-Kommunikation" (Informatics Report No. 8/90, pp. 13-49). Bremen.

[14] Rauterberg, M. (2004) (in press). Positive effects of entertainment technology on human behaviour. In: Proceedings IFIP World Computer Congress (Vol. Topical Day 2). Kluwer.

[15] Rubinstein, S. L. (1977). Grundlagen der Allgemeinen Psychologie [Foundations of General Psychology]. Berlin.

[16] Saroglou, V. & Jaspard, J.-M. (2001). Does religion affect humour creation? An experimental study. Mental Health, Religion, and Culture, Vol. 4, pp. 33-46.

[17] Saroglou, V. (2003). Humor appreciation as function of religious dimensions. Archiv für Religionpsychologie, pp. 144-153.

[18] Saroglou, V., Kempeneers, A., & Seynhaeve, I. (2003). Need for closure and adult attachment dimensions as predictors of religion and reading interests. In P. Roelofsma, J. Corveleyn, & J. van Saane (Eds.), One hundred years of psychology and religion (pp. 139-154). Amsterdam.

[19] Scheuerl, H. (1959). Das Spiel [The Play]. Weinheim.

[20] Word Reference (2004) via http://www.wordreference.com/

[21] Shirabe, M. & Baba, Y. (1997). Do three-dimensional realtime interfaces really play important roles?. In: M.J. Smith, G. Salvendy & R.J. Koubek (eds.) Design of Computing Systems: social and ergonomic considerations. Advances in Human Factors/Ergonomics, Vol. 21B, pp. 849-852.

[22] Vorderer, P., Hartmann, T. & Klimmt, C. (2003). Explaining the enjoyment of playing video games: the role of competition. In: Proceedings of 2nd International Conference on Entertainment Computing, ICEC 2003, ACM Digital Library.

Augmented, Virtual, and Mixed Reality

Interactive Props and Choreography Planning with the Mixed Reality Stage

Wolfgang Broll[1], Stefan Grünvogel[2], Iris Herbst[1], Irma Lindt[1], Martin Maercker[3], Jan Ohlenburg[1], and Michael Wittkämper[1]

[1] Fraunhofer-Institut für Angewandte Informationstechnik FIT,
Schloß Birlinghoven, 53754 Sankt Augustin, Germany
{wolfgang.broll, iris.herbst, irma.lindt, jan.ohlenburg,
michael.wittkaemper}@fit.fraunhofer.de
[2] Laboratory for Mixed Realities, Institute at the Academy of Media Arts Cologne,
Schaafenstr. 25, D-50676 Köln, Germany
gruenvogel@lmr.khm.de
[3] plan_b media ag, Schaafenstr. 25, 50676 Köln, Germany
maercker@planb_media.de

Abstract. This paper introduces–the Mixed Reality Stage–an interactive Mixed Reality environment for collaborative planning of stage shows and events. The Mixed Reality Stage combines the presence of reality with the flexibility of virtuality to form an intuitive and efficient planning tool. The planning environment is based on a physical miniature stage enriched with computer-generated props and characters. Users may load virtual models from a Virtual Menu, arrange those using Tangible Units or employ more sophisticated functionality in the form of special Tools. A major feature of the Mixed Reality stage is the planning of choreographies for virtual characters. Animation paths may be recorded and walking styles may be defined in a straightforward way. The planning results are recorded and may be played back at any time. User tests have been conducted that demonstrate the viability of the Mixed Reality Stage.

1 Introduction

During the planning process of an event such as a theatre performance, a concert or a product presentation the creativity and imagination of the people involved are in demand. Various ideas are discussed and revised or discarded. To illustrate an idea planners typically use sketches and/or specifically built 3D models. A common practice is to employ a downscaled model stage including props, real stage lights and jointed dolls representing actors. The physical models - usually at a ratio of 4:1 – are elementary components of the planning process and their arrangement visualizes the current planning status. Within the model stage planners can easily compose stage setups and test different lighting arrangements. However, physical models are not very flexible when it comes to the planning of more dynamic aspects of a stage event.

A higher flexibility in modeling the dynamic as well as the static aspects of a stage show may be reached by Virtual Reality technology. Typically, in VR planning tools,

M. Rauterberg (Ed.): ICEC 2004, LNCS 3166, pp. 185–192, 2004.

planners can choose from a large variety of virtual models that can be easily modified to fit into the stage setup. Animation tools are part of most VR systems and allow the modeling of changes in stage settings, choreographies or light shows. A stage show that was created with VR technology may give the spectator a good impression of the planning result. A disadvantage, however, is that VR technology is not very well suited for the planning process itself.

In order to support collaborative planning, a system needs to provide an appropriate user interface and it must respond to user interaction in real time. Many VR user interfaces do not facilitate the cooperative editing of virtual objects, nor do they consider a face-to-face collaboration among participants. In addition, the support of multiple users is often disappointing in terms of immersion (e.g. in CAVE-like environments). The real time capabilities of most VR systems are also very limited. A sufficient visualization of material properties is not yet feasible in real time. The same is true for professional lighting simulations which are often based on several hundred independent light sources. An example for a VR based planning environment that has successfully been used to plan stage shows is X-Rooms 0. The systems uses stereo-projection and polarized filters to visualize 3D computer graphics and touch screen, joystick, mouse and steering wheel for interaction. A drawback of X-Rooms is the separation between working and presentation space, though.

Fig. 1. The real model stage without virtual objects (left) and virtually enhanced as Mixed Reality Stage (right).

Mixed Reality planning tools, on the other hand, seamlessly combine real and virtual objects to overcome the individual limitations of real and virtual planning environments. Mixed Reality is a more viable technology for applications that require complex manipulation of three-dimensional information 0. The Luminous Table project 0, for example, supports urban planning using paper sketches as well as physical and virtual 3D models. Other Mixed Reality planning tools such as the AR Planning Tool 0 or the Build-It project 0 mainly use virtual objects as elementary planning components. Real objects serve as placeholders that are connected to virtual 3D models to form Tangible User Interfaces (TUIs) 0.

In the Mixed Reality Stage, physical models are used for a realistic presentation of typical components such as the stage itself, the props, or the stage lighting fixtures. The stage is extended by interactive computer graphics using Augmented Reality technology 0. Arbitrary virtual objects such as props or virtual characters are visualized and may easily be manipulated within the Mixed Reality Stage.

For each user the head position and its orientation are tracked 0 and the synthetic scene is visualized by means of semi-transparent Head Mounted Displays (HMDs). The point of view is egocentric, which serves to deepen the user's sense of immersion. A hybrid collaborative user interface was developed by employing a variety of techniques - such as TUI - where they best suited the different interaction tasks. A real control desk for stage machinery and a real stage lighting control board are also part of the user interface and allow planners to work in a familiar way without the need to learn new interaction mechanisms. With its intuitive user interface the Mixed Reality Stage provides multiple users with the means to creatively plan stage shows and to flexibly experiment with different ideas.

2   The Mixed Reality Stage User Interface

The Mixed Reality Stage is a collaborative AR environment 0 supporting face-to-face collaboration. Based on the positive experience and successful implementation of social protocols for group collaboration our interface approach focuses on providing powerful awareness mechanisms rather than limiting the user's freedom by rigid synchronization and locking mechanisms.

In cooperative planning situations a production design is analyzed from a high level perspective that follows from an institution's aesthetic and commercial strategies. Intricate details of a prop are, as a rule, not at issue. Therefore, users are primarily concerned with basic but expressive tasks such as arranging objects in space and time. The interaction design of the Mixed Reality Stage facilitates this approach by emphasizing simple, direct and reliable mechanisms to implement fundamental modeling operations:

- **View Pointer:** An object is selected when it is directly in a user's line of sight, i.e. users select objects by looking at them. A crosshair shown in the HMD helps users "aiming". The selection is visualized using the object's bounding box.
- **Virtual Menu:** Virtual objects have menus that contain those operations which are applicable to the specific type of object. The user opens a menu by issuing a single, modal voice command. Navigation in the menu hierarchy and invocation of operations is accomplished by selecting menu entries via the View Pointer and activating them by voice command.
- **Tangible Units:** A Tangible Unit (TU) realizes an interaction mechanism that provides direct and seamless manipulation of the position and orientation of a virtual object. A TU is composed of a tracked physical object (*realoid*) and an associated virtual object (*virtualoid*). To create a TU, the user collides the realoid with the virtualoid and links them by applying an explicit voice command. Another way to build a TU is to select the virtualoid, apply the command, select the realoid and apply a second command. The final voice command moves the virtualoid to the realoid and binds the two objects as a TU. This second method is provided as an alternative that obviates having to place the realoid at the same position as the virtualoid in order to form a TU.

- **Tools:** The operations in a menu are tied to the virtualoid operand for which the menu was opened. Tools, on the other hand, are independent representations of individual operations in the workspace. They allow the user to configure an operation's parameters once, applying that operation to any number of virtualoids afterwards, and customizing the workspace by loading and positioning tools as desired. Tools can be made part of a Tangible Unit where the movement data is interpreted as parameters to the operation. Realized tools so far are: a scale tool to adjust the size of virtualoids, a texture tool to change the texture of a virtualoid, and time tools to control the playback of animations (e.g. play, stop, rewind, fast forward).

Fig. 2. Selecting an entry from a Virtual Menu using the View Pointer.

Fig. 3. Positioning a virtual couch that is part of a Tangible Unit. The Tools on the right side can be used to play back animations.

The use of voice commands is consciously limited to avoid the cognitive burden of having to learn many different symbols as well as to minimize interference with the communication between users. Voice commands are used solely to trigger functions and can be replaced by alternative trigger mechanisms, e.g. a pressed button of a wearable input device, depending on the individual requirements of the user or the particular environment.

3 Interaction with Virtual Characters

A vital feature of the Mixed Reality Stage is the support for the development of choreographies. As a first step, planners create a rudimentary motion sequence for the actors. This can be used, for example, to verify whether an actor will reach a particular position within a certain time span or to prevent it from colliding with a prop while walking about the stage. As potential users made clear from preliminary requirements analysis onwards, real time animation of the character's motion is the decisive requirement for sophisticated choreography planning, playing a much greater role than the ability to render particular details of the animation (such as finger or face animation).

3.1 Creating a Choreography

The interaction mechanisms introduced in the previous section provide the basis for creating high level choreographies. Major tasks include the creation and assignment of walking paths and stage directions to a virtual character. To determine the path an actor should follow on the stage the planner links a virtual character to a TU. After activating the path recording operation from the character's menu, the movement of the TU is recorded. The same mechanism is used to finalize the path. The recorded path is displayed as a spline on the stage. The control points of the spline are displayed as well. The spline can be edited afterwards by linking individual control points to a TU.

Fig. 4. Virtual character and its path (green line), control points (blue cubes) and assigned stage directions (grey bar and cube) in relation to time (orange bar and cube, cube not visible here)

Moreover, planners have to consider stage directions. Therefore, some basic movements for characters are provided. Planners are able to assign different walk styles, e.g. running. It is also possible to assign different basic gestures such as waving, pointing or squatting. These choreography elements are created using the character's virtual menu.

In order to correlate stage directions with time a time bar is displayed on which the current time is denoted by a virtual *Now Point*. In addition, a bar is displayed for each character with knobs that represent the stage directions given for that character. The position of the knob on the bar indicates when the character is to execute the stage direction. The knob can be part of a TU as well, enabling planners to move the characters' tasks in time. Fig. 4 shows a virtual character and additional handles for editing an existing choreography.

3.2 Character Animations

The creation and the editing of choreographies are implemented by a two-layered model. The upper layer is adjoin to the user interface component of the Mixed Reality Stage system. The upper layer is responsible for creating and deleting the characters and to manage their choreographies. The lower layer realizes the creation of the animations in real time 0. Each visible character is represented in the upper layer as an abstract object with reactive behavior, independent from the appearance or the skeleton of the character. If a stage direction is given via the user interface, a command is sent to the character which is responsible for the corresponding realization of the task in form of so called subtasks 0.

During the editing of choreographies each character also resolves conflicts which can emerge between different tasks. For example, if a character that is walking receives the command to stand, a conflict results because both tasks (walk and stand) can not be executed at the same time. In principle it would be possible to warn the user, to point him to the conflict and to offer him alternatives to resolve the conflict. In the large majority of cases, however, the system can deduce the required modifications of a character's task by means of (configurable) heuristics and avoid a disruption of the users' workflow. Thus a walk cycle, for instance, is automatically stopped by the system if the user activates a task which results in a movement of the character in space (e.g. jumping).

Synchronization points are used to synchronize the character animation and the stage animation. They are user defined space-time constraints, i.e. they ensure that the character is at a specific position at a specific time. A character's task list settings may be such that they do not allow the character to immediately comply with newly set synchronization point constraints. The system then amends the task list of the character with special animation sequences. For example, if the character is too fast and reaches a synchronization point before the associated time then it waits and enters an idle animation loop. If it is too slow it does a comic-book-like "zip" to reach the required position at the designated time. Users can, of course, choose to modify the task list to reduce the role played by special animations in enabling the character to meet synchronization point constraints.

The subtasks realizing the tasks which are activated by the user interface (such as walking along a path) control the creation of the animation. For each character this is implemented at the lower layer by an *animation engine*. The animation engine gives access to dynamic motion models at the upper layer and sends the animation data to the skeleton of the character. Dynamic motion models are abstract descriptions of motions (e.g. walking) having their own sets of parameters. Examples for parameters are the style and the speed of walking or the direction for pointing. The parameters can be changed dynamically while the animations are created in real-time and the animations are then adapted dynamically. The animations are created by manipulation and blending of small pieces of pre-produced animation data 0.

4 User Tests

User tests were performed in the Mixed Reality Laboratory of Fraunhofer FIT. A Mixed Reality Stage based on a downscaled four-to-one model stage (2m x 2m) was used. The tests were focused on the evaluation of the user interface mechanisms.

Seven people participated in the tests. All participants were from the theatrical preproduction domain with an average professional experience of 13 years. Two of them were permanent employees of (different) theatres, the other five were freelancers. They described their computer skills as above average, especially in regard to 3D modeling software.

In the beginning of each trial session the interaction mechanisms of the Mixed Reality Stage were introduced. The participants were then asked to describe typical problems from their everyday practice. These scenarios served as a foundation for experimentation within the individual areas of functionality as well as with the Mixed Reality Stage as a whole. The participants were assisted by a member of the project team as collaboration partner. The sessions closed with a discussion of the strengths and weaknesses of the system. During the tests interviewers took notes and the tests were videotaped. The sessions lasted two and a half hours on average. The main feedback received from these user tests was:

- Selecting objects with the view pointer was easy to understand and to use.
- The voice input to activate a selected command was facile to understand. The analogue to a mouse was obvious, and every participant controlled this interaction mechanism at once.
- The possibility to arrange virtual objects with a TU was novel for all participants and they were impressed when the virtual object followed the movements of the realoid. The participants readily accepted this mechanism for spatial operations and emphasized the sensual aspects of the interaction as playing an important role in their assessment.
- The participants appraised the creation of a character animation as a vital feature of the Mixed Reality Stage. The editing of animation splines using TUs was observed as straightforward and rated as being much easier than using a 3D modeling software.

5 Conclusions and Future Work

In this paper we presented a new approach for interactive props and choreography planning using the Augmented Reality environment Mixed Reality Stage. We introduced the individual interaction mechanisms with an emphasis on props and choreography planning support. Finally, we presented the initial results of ongoing user tests, confirming the validity of our approach. In our future work we plan to continue the evaluation with professional users and extend the user tests into field trials at different locations. The Mixed Reality user interface will be enhanced and adapted according to the feedback received. Additionally, we will investigate possibilities for using the technology and mechanisms in new application areas.

Acknowledgements. This work is part of the mqube project and has been partially funded by the German Federal Ministry of Education and Research. We would like to thank the partners of the mqube project for their fruitful collaboration.

References

1. Azuma, R. T.: A Survey of Augmented Reality, Presence: Teleoperators and Virtual Environments 6, 4 (August 1997), 355-385
2. Billinghurst, M., Kato, H.: Collaborative Augmented Reality, Communication of the ACM Vol.45, No.7, 64-70 (2002)
3. Fitzmaurice, G., Ishii, H. Buxton, W. Bricks: Laying the Foundations for Graspable User Interfaces. Proceedings of the Conference on Human Factors in Computer Systems (CHI'95). 442-449 (1995)
4. Gausemeier, J., Fruend, J., Matysczok, C.: AR-Planning Tool – Designing Flexible Manufacturing Systems with Augmented Reality. Proceedings of Eurographics Workshop on Virtual Environments 2002
5. Grünvogel, S. Schwichtenberg, S.: Scripting Choreographies, T. Rist et. al. (Eds.), IVA 2003, Lecture Notes in Artificial Intelligence 2792, pp 170-174, 2003, Springer-Verlag Berlin Heidelberg, 2003
6. Grünvogel, S.: Dynamic character animations, International Journal of Intelligent Games & Simulation Vol.2 No.1 (2003), pp. 11- 19
7. Isakovic, K., Dudziak, T., Köchy, K.: X-Rooms. A PC-based immersive visualization environment, Web 3D Conference, Tempe, Arizona, 2002.
8. Ishii, H., Ullmer, B.: Tangible Bits: Towards Seamless Interfaces between people, Bits and Atoms. CHI'97, Atlanta, Georgia 1997
9. Ishii, H., Underkoffler, J., Chak, D., Piper, B.: Augmented Urban Planning Work-bench: Overlaying Drawings, Physical Models and Digital Simulation. In Proceedings of ISMAR'02 (2002)
10. Krüger, H., Klingbeil, L., Kraft, E., Hamburger, R.: BlueTrak - A wireless six degrees of freedom motion tracking system. In Proceedings of ISMAR'03, Tokio, Japan, Okt. 2003
11. Rauterberg, M., Fjeld, M., Krüger, H., Bichsel, M., Leonhardt, U., Meier, M.: Build-IT: A Planning Tool for Construction and Design. In Proceedings of CHI'98 (1998)
12. Schmalstieg, D., Fuhrmann, A., Hesina, G., Szalavari, Z., Encarnação, M., Gervautz. M., Purgathofer, W.: The Studierstube Augmented Reality Project. In PRESENCE - Teleoperators and Virtual Environments, MIT Press, 2002

The Interactive and Multi-protagonist Film: A Hypermovie on DVD

André Melzer, Sebastian Hasse, Oliver Jeskulke, Inga Schön, and Michael Herczeg

Institute for Multimedia and Interactive Systems, University of Luebeck,
MediaDocks, Willy-Brandt-Allee 31a, D-23554 Luebeck, Germany
{Melzer, Schoen, Herczeg}@imis.uni-luebeck.de

Abstract. The interactive and multi-protagonist (IMP) film is a novel concept that extends the hypermovie genre. The IMP film is based on the common structures of linear narrative storytelling and provides the viewer with various decision points within the evolving story that support an active choice among different protagonists' views. The viewer will thus be elevated to the role of a decision maker. They individually and actively determine the story flow. The IMP film substantially extends the currently offered interactivity of DVDs which is primarily limited to navigation. The production process of an IMP film will be illustrated by presenting *Deine Wahrheit* (Your Truth), a DVD-based movie. The results of an empirical study support the advantages of the IMP film compared to a traditional single-protagonist version of the film. The potential of the IMP film as a new genre in hypermovie will be discussed.

1 Introduction

People have a natural and intrinsic ambition to broaden their knowledge and to enhance their abilities [1]. This motivation energizes behaviour with regard to acquisition of specific skills, as well as it supports explorative behaviour per se. In social contexts, for example, actively gathering as much information as possible is extremely functional. Exploring other peoples' points of view reduces the likelihood of misinterpreting human behaviour. Exploratory behaviour needs curiosity as a motivational prerequisite, and both curiosity and exploration depend on environmental conditions [2]. The key principle is to establish and maintain an optimal amount of incongruence. Perceptions of a discrepancy between present cognitive structures and environmental conditions may lead the viewer to experience a given situation as novel, entertaining or challenging. The issue of incongruence and motivation is already important in current extensions of interaction design, specifically experience design [3; 4]. Various forms of interactive or participatory narrative concepts [5] were used to attract and maintain the attention of users or viewers.

The tendency of humans to gather information by exploring different points of view is also addressed in numerous movies, for example in *Citizen Kane*; a movie masterpiece directed and co-written by Orson Welles in 1941. Welles introduced a novel concept in movie storytelling, in which the story evolved in a series of

M. Rauterberg (Ed.): ICEC 2004, LNCS 3166, pp. 193–203, 2004.
© IFIP International Federation for Information Processing 2004

flashbacks. Each flashback sequence's narrator was different, and they presented their subjective point of view concerning the main character in the plot.[1] Moreover, the movie did not transport any "final truth" – it was totally up to the viewer to interpret the chain of events. *Citizen Kane* conforms to traditional storytelling methods, however, in that the different views were always presented in predetermined succession and, thus, the viewers' role was "passive".

In this paper, we will describe *Deine Wahrheit* (Your Truth), an experimental interactive and multi-protagonist (IMP) film on DVD that uses a multiple points of view approach. By carefully integrating the interactive elements within the evolving story, the IMP film enables the viewer to choose actively among different competing views at various key points, thus extending structural and functional aspects of the DVD as a hypermedium. However, *Deine Wahrheit* does not deviate from common structures of linear narrative storytelling.

The IMP film, as a hypermovie, stems from the concepts of hypermedia [6] and hyperfiction [7; 8]. The basic principles of hypermedia and hyperfiction have already been realised in various forms of digital or interactive television. These productions have failed as successful commercial products due to various technical inadequacies (e.g., missing or deficient feedback channels), as well as the unavailability of new marketing and distribution strategies (e.g., Video-on-Demand (VoD)).

The DVD is technically predestined to be used as a medium for interactive and multi-protagonist films. The general availability of DVDs on the consumer market creates an opportunity for easy accessibility for hyperfilms.[2] It is possible that the DVD-based hyperfilms will corner a market alongside the already established interactive gaming industry. To date there are few conclusive empirical studies which address the effects of hyperfilms on the viewer's motivation. The present study considers these effects.

2 Interactivity and DVD as a Hypermedium

DVD was initially developed as a mass storage device: principally for high-quality digital video information. It also offers a potential for a wide range of interactivity. The implementation of interactivity on present DVD productions is often limited to navigational functions (e.g., chapter selection). These functions are in principle the same options offered in the outdated analogue videotapes. The DVD's interactive menus offer unique opportunities for the viewer to participate individually and actively in the navigation of the narration.

Technically these menus are implemented as so-called sub-picture overlays. These overlays can be positioned anywhere on top of any screenshot throughout the film. In the project *Deine Wahrheit* we tested whether adding an additional interactive navigational level (choosing between protagonists' views in the DVD menu) to the currently used function level positively influenced the viewer's media experiences.

---

[1] To describe a narrative that presents a plotline in multiple versions, Murray [5] suggested the term *multiform story*.

[2] Tua [9] lists other possible concepts for hyperfilms.

3 Production of the Interactive and Multi-protagonist Film *Deine Wahrheit*

From the outset, the rise of new media was accompanied by the desire for the interactive aspects in the medium of film [10]. Attempts to establish interactivity in film and cinema benefited from the rapid development of digital technology. The *Future Cinema* exhibition at the ZKM, Karlsruhe [http://www.zkm.de/futurecinema/ Access May 27 2004], offered numerous contemporary, as well as visionary, approaches in the field of interactivity in new media.

Three Angry Men, an augmented reality (AR) environment developed by MacIntyre and his colleagues [11], follows the setting of a jury trial in the Hollywood classic *Twelve Angry Men* (USA, 1957). In *Three Angry Men* users may choose among different competing levels that all share the common timeline of a fixed plot. Within the AR environment, the viewer "occupies" one of the virtual characters that were added to a physical room. The viewer may follow conversations between the characters, but also hears the thoughts of his present virtual character. Changing characters supports the active gathering of information and, thus, enables the viewer to develop a better understanding for the other characters' points of view. Another system that used the multiple viewpoint approach within an AR environment was proposed by Mazalek, Davenport, and Ishii [12]. In the present paper we describe a DVD-based implementation of interactive elements in the film that support an active choice among different protagonists' views.

3.1 Requirements Analysis

In an extensive analysis process prior realization of an IMP film, we identified the critical requirements in navigation, technical aspects, as well as the narrative parameters.

The final product should allow the viewer great latitude in making their own choices throughout the film. At the same time, the viewer should be given as little guidance as possible. However, it had to be ensured that they would always have an idea of the approximate length of the entire film. Decisions that lead to dead-ends had to be avoided. The film should reach a high external validity and therewith acquire the standard TV movie qualities in visual elements, sound and narrative content. In addition, redundancies had to be avoided, so that repeated viewings of the film, in a different order, should still be as interesting as the initial viewing. Most important, the interactive elements had to be implemented in such a manner that a relatively direct transport of contents is assured. All distractions from the contents, such as noticing the presence of the media being used, should be avoided.

In the IMP film *Deine Wahrheit* the interactive elements were integrated as cyclic elements within the story (i.e., leaving an apartment). The viewer's interactions step in the story at the end of each episode which represents a natural transition to the next chapter. Gansing [10] stresses the importance of deliberately designing the interactive elements in the film genre for the viewers' actions:

"(…) we cannot ignore the importance of interaction design as it enters into dialogue with narrative structures. Just as stylistic conventions regulate narrative understanding, interaction design regulates possible actions." [10, p.40]

3.2 Concept

The basis of the IMP film *Deine Wahrheit* is a uniform story that is narrated independent of the viewer's interaction. Their natural motivation for gathering new information should be supported by the implementation of interactive elements, without directly influencing the story line, and still keeping the linear character of a feature film.

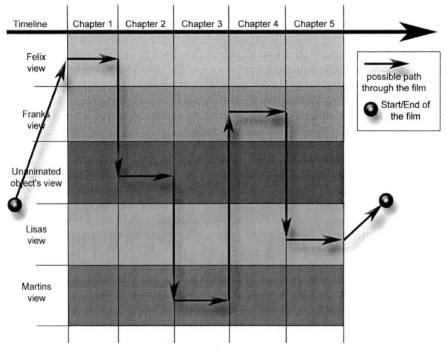

Fig. 1. The structure of the IMP film *Deine Wahrheit*

The use of different camera filters is an important technique in film-making. Filters are chosen selectively to affect the viewer's impression of an ongoing story. The filter technique was adopted for the multiple viewpoint approach in the IMP film. Each view presented in *Deine Wahrheit* represented a filter to the story. The view-filter analogy is supported by findings from cognitive psychology that filters affect human perception. This is due to the fact that human perception is the result of complex and interdependent processes that are mediated by characteristics of the perceiving subject (for a review see [13]). Among other things, individual characteristics include attitudes, feelings, and knowledge. These characteristics, however, are subject to the continuous flow of information. Thus, what is thought to be "true" may change with additional perceptions. The interactive key points in the IMP film *Deine Wahrheit* serve as an interface, or filter, that enable the viewer to choose actively among competing subjective perceptions of the same events. By way of reflecting the perceived events, a deeper understanding for the story and the acting characters evolves. The viewer will thus be elevated to the role of an active decision maker. Lastly they need to realize that they are responsible for the interpretation of the story.

The story of the IMP film *Deine Wahrheit* splits into five chapters. Prior to each chapter, a menu with a choice of five different perspectives from which to watch the following chapter is displayed. Overall the film can thus be watched in five to the fifth (3125) different ways. It could also be entirely watched from only one perspective (ongoing), without considering any of the other four. Figure 1 illustrates the structure of the IMP film.

3.3   Story, Main Characters, and Script

Deine Wahrheit depicts a type of crime story, regarding the missing main character Tracy. Tracy's brother is accompanied by the viewer while looking for an explanation for his disappearance. The key is that the viewer decides which person from Tracy's surroundings the brother will meet and will describe the events, which will be shown in flashbacks, of the individual chapters. Together, at the end of each chapter, the viewer and Tracy's brother leave the person's place, and again a perspective will be chosen for the chapter thereafter. In doing so the viewer is taking the place of the brother and will make a choice on his notebook (see Fig. 2).

Fig. 2. Interaction menu in the IMP film *Deine Wahrheit*: Choosing the protagonist's view

Out of the various mentioned concepts, most of the importance, in the conception and forming of the IMP film's script and story, was put on the authenticity of the dialog and presentation of the film characters. The main character Tracy is the centre of the story. The different characters, such as his two friends Felix and Martin, his counterpart Frank, and his girlfriend Lisa, form a circle of various perspectives around him. In addition to the four characters' view there was an unanimated object's view called Tracy's apartment (*Tracy's Wohnung*). In each of the five perspectives a certain, and each time a different, aspect on Tracy's personality is brought to the light (see Fig. 3). The previously invented personalities, such as the motivations and emotions, of the characters were then combined with the situations in the story to form the scenes and dialogs of the script.

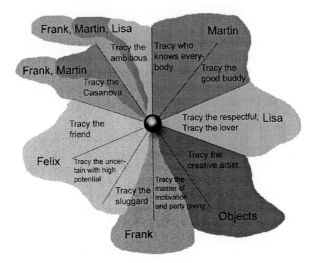

Fig. 3. The main character Tracy in the view of the sub characters

3.4 Film-Shooting, Editing, Post-production, and DVD-Authoring

Due to the complexity of the project and the planning of the film-shooting, it was essential to create a database for the efficient scheduling of the scenes, the roles, and availability of the actors. The film was shot with Sony Mini-DV cameras. Sound was recorded with an external microphone onto DAT-tapes.

The 25 film episodes (an episode is a chapter covering a certain perspective) vary in lengths between eight and thirteen minutes each. After the editing and post production, the parts of the film were exported and converted into MPEG-II format.

Consumer DVD-burners are currently limited to CDs with the smallest capacity (DVD-5). For an average video data rate of 3.5mbits, the film had to be divided up onto two DVDs. This requires the viewer to switch DVDs half way throughout the film and they will therewith be taken back down to the user's level. However, any reduction of the film's length, or picture and sound quality would have resulted in a greater distraction from the reception of the film.

For the storyboard the sublevel menus after each chapter should not be realized by the viewer to be a direct interaction. They were hence integrated into the film in a manner that suits the normal course of the story. After the selection of a perspective for the following chapter, the film continues at the same spot at which it was actually interrupted (see Fig. 4).

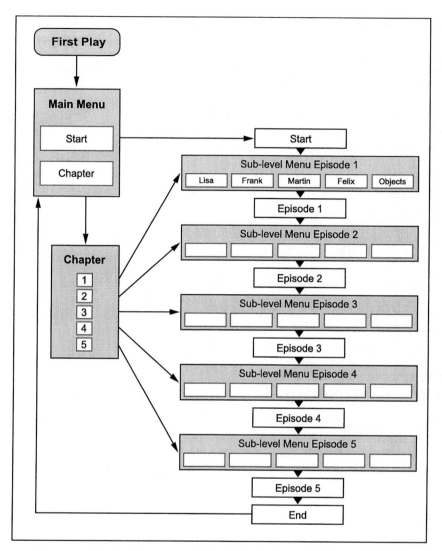

Fig. 4. The storyboard of the IMP film *Deine Wahrheit*

4 Empirical Evaluation

Do viewers of an IMP film differ from viewers of a traditional film in terms of their film ratings? What are the specific advantages of the IMP film? To address these questions, 28 participants were invited to watch the IMP film *Deine Wahrheit* on DVD under single testing conditions. On each of three consecutive trials, the whole film was shown on a PC or notebook. Prior testing, participants were randomly assigned one of two groups. Members of the first group (subsequently referred to as *interactive condition*) were told to switch between points of view at the beginning of each chapter as often as possible. They were given no further specifications. For the second group (subsequently referred to as *linear condition*), the presented point of view was fixed within each trial, but differed between trials. Thus, participants in the linear condition watched a traditional multiple point of view version of the IMP film, with different views being presented in succession.

Following the third trial the participants were given a questionnaire with 19 items that concluded the evaluation (see Appendix). In the interactive condition there were eight additional items to evaluate the navigation and interactivity in the IMP film.

4.1   Results

For each item, participants' ratings were recorded on a four-point scale, ranging from 1 (*"I don't agree at all"*) to 4 (*"I totally agree"*). The following details represent mean group ratings that were further analyzed by means of unpaired *t*-tests ($df = 26$, $\alpha = .05$).

Substantial group differences were observed in the ratings of the questionnaire. Though mean ratings were on a high level in both conditions, indicating that most participants liked *Deine Wahrheit*, there was a significant advantage for the interactive condition ($M = 3.71$) compared to the linear condition ($M = 3.07$; $t = 3.11$).

The IMP film also seems to be important for viewers' feelings of familiarity with the different characters shown in the film. In the interactive condition ($M = 3.07$), participants agreed more strongly to the fact that they felt familiar with film characters in a way similar to characters in well-known TV series ($M = 2.50$, for the linear condition; $t = 2.66$).

In spite of the repetitive events in the film, participants in both conditions welcomed the availability of different points of view. Interestingly, ratings in the linear condition ($M = 3.64$) significantly surpassed those of the interactive condition ($M = 3.21$), for the respective item ($t = 2.10$). Participants in the linear condition ($M = 3.50$) also tended to miss more strongly the availability of all points of view or episodes in the film ($M = 3.00$, for the interactive version of the IMP film; $t = 1.84$, $p = .08$).

For the interactive condition, participants strongly agreed to the item that the concept of interactivity had been successfully implemented in the navigational structure of the DVD ($M = 3.79$). The ratings also indicated that the IMP film neither offered too few ($M = 2.07$), nor too many ($M = 1.43$), key points to choose among different competing views.

4.2   Discussion

The comparison of the two versions of the film revealed that participants favoured the additional interactive elements in the IMP film that supported an active choice among different protagonists' views. In addition, using these elements was simple and not confusing.

Viewers of the interactive version of the IMP film reported an outstanding feeling of familiarity with the characters shown in the film. This finding illustrates one of the IMP film's major advantages; it seems especially suited to induce a deep understanding of the different acting characters. We interpret this result as evidence that, by adding interactive elements to a popular hypermedium, the natural tendency of humans to gather information actively may be successfully supported.

5 Conclusion and Future Research

Deine Wahrheit, an example of a DVD-based IMP film, reflects and extends current trends in media. The IMP film follows common structures of linear narrative storytelling, but offers an additional interactive navigational level to the currently used function level of the DVD as a hypermedium. The IMP film integrates the concepts of hyperfiction [7; 8], participatory narration [5], and experience design [3; 4].

Various interaction points that were carefully implemented within the evolving story of the IMP film support the active role of viewers. Choosing among different protagonists' viewss enables the viewer to determine individually and actively their information flow. The IMP film, thus, follows the notion of interactivity in digital media as a way of externalising mental processes [14].

In this paper, we have demonstrated that the DVD-based IMP film successfully contributes to entertainment computing. The IMP film provides the viewer with an interactive basis that supports their natural motivation to gather additional information. To choose among different competing views is found attractive and challenging, and, eventually, helps to make complex human behaviour more transparent. It is assumed that the DVD-based hyperfilms will corner a market alongside other forms of interactive media, specifically the already established gaming industry.

An additional concept for the IMP film is the multi-viewpoint film like discussed during the introduction of high-performance graphic boards for PCs. These systems allow for different spatial viewpoints via realtime rendering of cinematic sequences of computer animations. The concept has been called *cinematic computing* [15]. This method might be used in future mainly digitally produced films together with the IMP film concepts described in this paper. Multiple spatial viewpoints combined with multiple story threads can be expected to be extremely entertaining for an active audience looking for an interactive narration-based visual experience.

References

1. White, R. W.: Motivation Reconsidered: The Concept of Competence. Psychological Review, 66 (1959) 297-333
2. Piaget, J.: The Development of Thought: Equilibrium of Cognitive Structures. Viking Press, New York (1977)
3. Shedroff, N.: Experience Design. New Riders Publishing, Indianapolis, IN (1995)

4.   Shedroff, N.: Information Interaction Design: A Unified Field Theory of Design. In Jacobsen, R. (ed.): Information Design. MIT Press, Cambridge (1999) 267-292
5.   Murray, J. H.: Hamlet on The Holodeck: The Future of Narrative in Cyberspace. Free Press, New York (1997)
6.   Woodhead, N.: Hypertext and Hypermedia: Theory and Applications. Addison-Wesley Longman, Boston, MA (1991)
7.   Sassòn-Henry, P.: Jorge Luis Borges: A Forerunner of the Technology of the New Millennium. In: ACM Hypertext 1999. Doctoral Consortium Final Report, Aalborg University Technical Report AUE-CS-99-03 (1999) http://www.daimi.au.dk/~pnuern/ht99dc/sasson/final.pdf /Access Mar 02 2004
8.   Zellweger, P. T.; Mangen, A.; Newman, P.: Narratives and Literary Hypertext: Reading and Writing Fluid Hypertext Narratives. In: Proceedings of the thirteenth ACM conference on Hyper-text and Hypermedia. College Park, Maryland, USA (2002) 45-54
9.   Tua, R.: From Hyper-Film to Hyper-Web: Continuation of a European Project. In: Cappellini, V.; Hemsley, J.; Stanke, G. (eds.): EVA 2002 Proceedings, Bologna (2002)
10.   Gansing, K.: The Myth of Interactivity or The Interactivity Myth?: Interactive Film as an Imaginary Genre. In: Proceedings of the Fifth International Digital Arts and Culture Conference. RMIT, Melbourne, Australia (2003) 39-45 http://hypertext.rmit.edu.au/dac/papers/Gansing.pdf/Access Mar 02 2004
11.   MacIntyre, B.; Bolter, J.; Vaughan, J.; Hannigan, B.; Moreno, E.; Haas, M.; Gandy, M.: Three Angry Men: Dramatizing Point-of-View using Augmented Reality. In: SIGGRAPH 2002 Technical Sketches. San Antonio, TX (2002) 268
12.   Mazalek, A.; Davenport, G.; Ishii, H.: Tangible Viewpoints: A Physical Approach to Multimedia Stories. In: Proceedings of the Tenth ACM International Conference on Multimedia. Juan-les-Pins, France (2002) 153-160
13.   Goldstein, E. B.: Sensation and Perception. Wadsworth Publishing, Belmont, CA (2002)
14.   Manovich, L.: The Language of New Media. MIT Press, Cambridge, MA (2001)
15.   Kirk, D.: Graphic Architectures: The Dawn of Cinematic Computing. In: Proceedings of the 1st international conference on Computer graphics and interactive techniques in Australasia and South East Asia. Melbourne, Australia, ACM Press, (2003), 9

Appendix

Table 1. Items used in the questionnaire during the empirical evaluation of the IMP film *Deine Wahrheit,* together with mean group ratings (*M*) and standard deviations (*SD*) in the *interactive* and *linear* condition.

	interactive		linear	
Would you agree that	M	SD	M	SD
1 ...you liked the movie?	3.36	0.74	3.14	0.36
2 ...the characters of the film were authentic?	3.07	0.62	3.00	0.39
3 ...the story was credible?	2.93	0.62	3.00	0.55
4 ...you always knew where you were in the course of the story?	2.79	0.80	2.64	0.74
5 ...the story was comprehensible?	3.07	0.27	3.36	0.50
6 ...you regret not having been able to see all parts of the film?	3.00	0.88	3.50	0.52
7 ...your impressions of the events in the film deepened after the reruns?	2.71	0.47	2.54	0.52
8 ...you liked the form of presentation (choosing among the protagonists' views within the story vs. different narrators between trials)?	3.71	0.47	3.07	0.62
9 ...you would prefer another form of presentation (only one	1.86	0.53	2.29	0.99

Would you agree that	interactive		linear	
	M	*SD*	*M*	SD
narrator's view per trial vs. choosing among the protagonists' views within the story)?				
10 ...you were bored because of the constantly repeating events?	2.07	0.83	1.79	0.58
11 ...it was the small but important differences between repetitions that made it interesting to watch the film again?	3.21	0.56	3.64	0.48
12 ...the different protagonists' views complemented well?	3.21	0.58	3.14	0.53
13 ...you became familiar with the film characters in a way similar to characters in your preferred TV series?	3.07	0.47	2.50	0.65
14 ...you would appreciate watching the film with other people and share the responsibility for choosing among perspectives?	2.36	1.15	2.64	0.63
15 ...watching the film with other people would prevent you from making decisions on your own?	2.50	1.16	2.29	0.61
16 ...you prefer movies that do not force you to make a decision what to view next?	2.07	0.47	2.14	0.66
17 ...the presented type of film is definitely interesting and you would like to watch more of this kind?	3.50	0.52	3.64	0.50
18 ...movies should provide the opportunity to control the story, but without requiring a choice among different protagonists' views?	2.79	0.43	2.86	0.77
19 ...movies should provide both the opportunity to control the story and to choose among different protagonists' views?	2.79	0.97	2.86	1.10
20 ...the navigation (names on the notepad) was easy and well integrated within the ongoing events?	3.79	0.43		
21 ...it was easy to choose a specific view for the next episode?	2.86	0.95		
22 ...it was difficult to choose a specific view because you were afraid to miss important information?	2.21	0.89		
23 ...you were always in total control of what is going on in the story?	2.21	0.97		
24 ...choosing among different views was annoying because the story evolves independently of your decision?	1.71	0.73		
25 ...choosing one view was annoying because you felt uncertain about the goal of the story?	1.93	0.73		
26 ...that there were too many decision points for choosing among the competing views?	1.43	0.65		
27 ...that there were too few decision points for choosing among the competing views?	2.07	1.07		

Apply Social Network Analysis and Data Mining to Dynamic Task Synthesis for Persistent MMORPG Virtual World

Larry Shi and Weiyun Huang

Atlantic Drive, Atlanta, GA 30332-0280,Georgia Institute of Technology
{shiw,wyhuang}@cc.gatech.edu

Abstract. This paper describes a new scheme for designing MMORPG virtualworld that assigns dynamically synthesized tasks and scripts to avatars in a MMORPG. Different from most current MMORPGs, the new scheme tries to bridge the gap between a real social world with a virtual RPG social world by introducing social relationship, social structure, and avatar personality into the game play. Adaptation of social network analysis to MMORPG virtual world design is also discussed. The objective is to increase a game's long term appeal to players. Moreover, the paper also proposes a method to use data mining technique for intelligently selecting dynamically synthesized tasks so that the tasks will be most likely interesting to the players. The paper represents an endeavor to forge a common research ground for virtual world game design, social network analysis, artificial intelligence, and traditional data mining research.

1 Introduction

Persistent MMORPGs (massively multiplayer online role-playing games) have become increasingly popular since the commercial success of Ultima Online. Today, millions of players engage in online persistent virtual worlds every day. Players trade virtual artifacts of popular MMORPG on the web and other online auction sites. The popularity of MMORPG has captured imaginations of sociologists, psychologists, computer scientists, and telecommunication service providers. Sociologists view it as another media for studying social communication. Computer scientists wonder how to manage the vast volume of data generated by online players. Psychologists ponder human behavior in a virtual world. Service providers are amazed by its market potential. Although there have been recent studies on different aspects of MMOPRGs in academia, most of the studies only scratch the surface of its richness for scientific research and few people have tried to bridge the gap of different disciplines for designing next generation MMORPG. This paper is aimed to meet the challenge by proposing a new scheme for MMORPG design that combines the techniques of social network analysis, dynamic task synthesis, relational data mining to construct future persistent MMORPG world that is more socially structured, more interesting in terms of providing unlimited computer synthesized storylines and scripts uniquely tuned for each player.

M. Rauterberg (Ed.): ICEC 2004, LNCS 3166, pp. 204–215, 2004.

One of the challenges of designing persistent MMOPRG is that it should have long lasting appeal to players. Since hosting persistent MMORPG is service oriented, the success of a MMORPG to a great extent determined by its long term attraction to the players. Most current MMORPG designs are not sufficient to provide such long term appeal due to,

1) lack of the ability to facilitate social construction. Few MMORPGs allow complicated social structures and relationships. Although some games enhance player interactivity through assigning co-operative tasks to a group of players each one may have a different role such as using a different weapon. None of the MMORPGs, as to our knowledge, apply social analysis to the social relationships of avatars and allows in-game avatar personality development. Moreover, none of the games takes the rich information of social analysis into game logic and creates human drama.

2) lack of rich sets of storylines and tasks to keep player hooked into the game. Most MMORPGs are designed based on similar recipe of game play and tasks. Players engage in never ending camping and resource collecting. Players may easily get bored by such game design. Pre-defined highly crafted stories and game scripts maybe ideal for single player game where its long term appeal is not a concern. But for MMORPGs, one promising solution could be dynamical creation of in-game stories and tasks based on current context of game state.

3) lack of the ability to provide unique in-game experience to players. In-game scripts and tasks are mostly pre-defined and not specifically designed for a virtual figure and tuned according to each player's interests. Data mining based dynamic task synthesis proposed in this paper is a promising technique to allow unique tasks "intelligently" created for each player and provides unique experiences of game play and character development.

Different from the current MMORPG design, the scheme proposed in this paper has the following characteristics,

1) introducing multi-dimensional social structures/relationships, avatar personality into game design, social structure/relationship aware game logic, personality aware task and script generation.

2) in-game personality development of virtual figure (avatar).

3) dynamic, automatic task and script synthesis for avatars.

4) data mining based task synthesis that generates unique avatar task tuned for character development.

5) relative high fidelity of an online persistent MMORPG world to the real social world.

The contributions of this paper can be summarized as, 1) create a new research area where traditional social network analysis/modeling and data mining technique could work jointly for designing new types of persistent MMORPGs; 2) apply social network analysis to understand social structure of MMORPG virtual world; 3) propose data mining based task synthesis and selection techniques that enrich experience of game play and facilitates in-game character development. In this paper, we use the terms virtual figure, avatar, virtual character exchangeably.

The paper is organized as follows. The next section describes how to encode social relation/social structure in MMORPG and how to incorporate social relation into game logic. Then in section 3, we introduce social network analysis and its application to MMORPG. In the section after that, we present the concept of automatic task/script synthesis, followed by a section on how to adapt relational data mining technique to help selecting tasks for avatars so that player friendly task generation could be achieved. In section 5, we discuss future work and the last section concludes the paper.

2 Emulating Social Relationships/Structures in Persistent MMORPG

To emulate and model the complexity of social structure in a persistent MMORPG world, three problems have to be addressed,

1) There must be ways to encode social relationships and social networks in a digital MMORPG world. Both formal and informal social relationships in a virtual world can be created, updated, and queried.

2)There must be ways to analyze social relationships and networks to extract second order knowledge about the virtual society. Examples of second order knowledge are leaders of a virtual group, group or clique of closed avatars, personality of avatars.

3) The game must be designed in a way to encourage construction of social network. Social relationships, social structures, and their second order knowledge are incorporated into game logic and rules of game play.

In this section, we describe how to represent social relationships and their second order knowledge in a MMORPG and how to design game logic that is social relationship aware, or avatar personality aware in two sub sections. In the next section, we address how to apply social network analysis to extract second order knowledge from encoded social relationships.

2.1 Multi-dimensional Avatar

In most MMORPGs, there is a set of attributes associated with each avatar. Examples of these attributes are strength, experience level, magic power, class of avatar (e.g., a warrior, a magician, a monster), etc. Aside from these attributes, there maybe virtual artifacts possessed by the avatar such as armors, treasures, magic objects, etc. To encode social relationships, its second order knowledge, avatar personality, etc, we introduce several new dimensions of avatar attributes listed as follows,

Social relationships. Social relationship between avatars can be represented as directed graph or network, in which a node typically represents an avatar, a directed edge from one node A to another node B denotes a relationship between the two avatars represented by the two nodes.

There could be three possible relationships, A connects to B (e.g., A likes B), B connects to A, or A and B are both connected (e.g., A and B are mutual friends). The third case is called reciprocal relationship. Each directed edge can have a weight value representing the strength of the relationship. Furthermore, there can be multiple relationships between two avatars. For example, avatar A may be a leader of avatar B. But at the same time, B may dislike A. In a MMORPG, relationship can be either formally defined and ordained by the game rule or created in an informal way or entirely derived or inferred from analysis.

In a RPG of clan warfare, formal relationship can be defined such as clan leader, warrior, magician, etc. Informal relationships can also exist such as friendship and attraction between avatars. Some types of relationship can not be created by players explicitly. Instead they are derived from analyzing avatar behavior according to certain pre-determined gaming rules. For example, for a MMORPG where attraction between avatars can be expressed by one avatar through giving virtual objects as gifts to another avatar he/she feel attracted to, the relationship can be derived from analysis how many virtual objects are given as gifts and their virtual value. The directed graph made by avatars and their relationships in a MMORPG is called MMORPG social network.

Social & personal characteristics of avatar. The Characteristics or personality of avatar can be also encoded as avatar attributes. Personality of avatar is derived knowledge based on either social network analysis or analysis of avatar behavior. Examples of traits of avatar personality are, trustworthiness of an avatar, leadership, selfishness, attraction, etc. Aside from personality, there are derived social characteristics associated with each avatar such as popularity, influences, importance of avatar.

Table 1. Example Social & Personal Characteristics of Avatar

Attributes	Definition	Computation
trustworthiness	extend the virtual payer can be trusted as friend	behavior analysis
selfishness	disparity between the received and given by an avatar	helps behavior analysis
attraction	attraction of avatar to other avatars	behavior analysis
popularity	center of a friendship network	social network analysis
Importance	impact of removing an avatar to a social network	network analysis

Most social characteristics and personality of avatar can be derived from social network analysis described in the next section. Some characteristics such as trustworthiness are determined based on understanding of avatar's behaviors. Later in this section, we will present example on how to compute trustworthiness for avatars.

Information possessed by avatar. Beside tangible virtual artifacts owned by avatar, we define information as another set of virtual "objects" that can be possessed by avatar. Different from the tangible artifacts, information can be passed and shared by avatars. Information may become invalid or destroyed after it is out of date or no longer valid. Examples of types of information in a MMORPG are listed in table 2.

There are many sources of information. First, information can be created by avatars. Second, information can be derived from social network analysis described in the next section and avatar behavior analysis. Examples of such information include, who is the most popular avatar in an avatar group, who is the most trustworthy avatar, etc. Third, the information can be an assertion of a fact in a MMORPG virtual world such as who kills whom, or who owns what virtual objects. Finally, the game can reveal some of the game plot or storyline as information such as who is assigned what tasks, who is going to meet whom where according to game script. Avatars can talk with one another freely. It is entirely upto the avatar who possesses the information on whether the information will be passed to another avatar. An avatar can ask for reward for giving information to another avatar and sometimes, refuse to give certain information if the information is considered as secret to a group of avatars.

Table 2. Types of Information Flowed in Virtual World

Type	Definition	Source
announcement	statement of in-game events	in-game event log
oracle	statement of future or planned in-game events	task scripts
virtual fact	avatarinformation about avatars	results of analysis
player created information	information created by player	player
...	...	...

Social structure. Asides from these new attributes associated with avatar, social structure is encoded separately as virtual world context and state. Social structure in a MMORPG involves many avatars. Among the many possible social structures, one of the important ones is group or clique of avatars. A group is a subset of avatars who share strong ties among them in the social network of MMORPG virtual world. Small cohesive avatar group and its "leaders" (avatar who is the center of the group and whose removal would most likely disintegrate the group) can be identified through social network analysis described in the next section. As we will show later, specific tasks or scripts can be synthesized around identified avatar group.

2.2 Social Relationship/Personality Aware Game Logic

Attributes of avatars and other game states are updated during game play. The rules for updating are part of game logic. To emulate the effects of human relationship and personal characteristics in a MMORPG virtual world, we need to incorporate social relationships, social and personality characteristics of avatar, and social structure into MMORPG game logic. The resulting game logic is called social relationship or personality aware game logic. Here we describe some example design scenarios about how to take friend relationship and trustworthiness personality into a simple MMORPG.

Social relationship. Use friendship as an example, given friendship is encoded in a MMORPG social network, then it can be somehow incorporated into game logic by enforcing friendship related game play rules. For example, an avatar is obligated to help his/her friends when they need help. Such help can be, defending a common enemy, collaborating to complete a task, locating a resource, and etc. Giving help to another avatar will positively reinforce the friendship between two avatars and refusal of help will negatively affect the friendship and optional punishment (e.g., deduction of points) can be issued to avatars who refuse to help his/her friends. In a MMORPG social network, the weight associated with each directed edge connecting two virtual avatar friends can be used to indicate the likelihood one avatar will help another when the other is in need of help. The likelihood value can be estimated based on history data of the involved avatars. For example, if avatar A has called 20 times help from B and B only helped 5 times, then the likelihood will be 20%.

"Popular" avatar can be defined for a MMORPG social network. They are local centers of the friendship social network. Often these "popular" avatars have far more friends than their friends. Removal of a "popular" avatar may also have far greater impact on the social network than removing a non-popular avatar.

Like real social relationship, a virtual relationship has both pros and cons. Using friendship as an example, although virtual friends are obligated to help one another but they are also vulnerable to one other. MMORPG game logic can be designed in a way that a friend has less defending power against attacks made by his/her friends. The closer is the friend, the greater is the vulnerability. This means that in a MMORPG world, virtual friends may betray one another. The personality trait, trustworthiness, is used to measure the extent a virtual friend can be trusted. A high quantity of this trait can mean that the avatar never or rarely turn against his/her friends and a low quantity can mean that the avatar frequently betrays his/her friends for personal gains. Personality too can be incorporated into game logic as discussed next.

Personality. Characteristics of avatar can be either measured based on avatar's behaviors or extracted from MMORPG social network analysis. They can also be used to define game playing rules and incorporated into the game logic. For example, the trait of trustworthiness can be taken into the game logic to affect how virtual friends interact. As presented earlier, virtual avatar friends can be obligated to help one other. But the obligation can be modulated by how trustworthiness the avatar is. Refusal of helping a friend may bring punishment to an avatar. But if the avatar who needs help is an un-trustworthy one who often betrays his/her friends, the punishment can be very small or none.

In this section, we described how social relationship and characteristics of avatar can be encoded and incorporated into game logic using examples. The same principle not the detailed implementation can be carried out to different MMORPG design. The objective is to increase MMORPG's entertaining value and make it closer to emulate a real human society.

3 Social Network Analysis

Social network analysis has a long history [4,5,8] and is a fundamental tool used by social scientists to understand real human society. Many theories and techniques have been proposed, for example, identify "stars" of a social network, informal leaders, subgroup of influential figures, cliques, etc. How to adapt these methods to MMORPGs for understanding virtual society and helping to design better games that has long last appeal is less understood by both social scientists and game designers. In this section, instead of going through many techniques in details, we just briefly define these techniques and give references for interested readers.

There are some differences between a real human society and a MMORPG virtual world. For example, human society is very much an opened system while a MMORPG virtual world is a very closed system where a strict set of game play rules apply. Another difference is that human relationship in real world is not quantified. But in a virtual world, everything is digitized and quantified with a number. Here we briefly introduce some popular techniques for social network analysis, please note that this is not a comprehensive list.

Similarity. The greater the similarity of the attributes of two avatars, the greater the likelihood they may like one another or become friends. Similarity can be measured by measuring the difference of avatar characteristics.

Centrality of social network. Leaders or popularity of an avatar can be measured by counting in-degree, out-degree edges of social network [1].

Clusters, cliques, or circles. Densely connected subgraph, cliques, clusters, or small circles can be discovered through social network analysis. Techniques have been proposed to find dense regions of networks such that the connections within the region are more dense and cohesive than the connections outside the region [7].

4   Automatic Task Synthesis(ATS)

There are several MMORPG design choices related to tasking. One alternative is to have no task, another choice is to have fixed in-game storyline and tasks, and the third choice is to have computer dynamically to synthesize tasks and assigning them to avatars. There are pros and cons for each choice. Also, as studies show that certain group of people or certain culture may favor one choice over another. The benefit of dynamic task synthesis is that,

1) It can increase the challenge of game play. Challenging tasks may help keeping players hooked to the game.

2) It can give variety of game play experiences. This may help increasing the long term appeal of a MMORPG game to players because players may feel bored by repeative play experience such as forever camping and resource collection in some "taskless" MMORPGs.

3) It broads possibly game play paths players can explore. In a "taskless" MMORPG, some players may always play the game the same way or in the same pattern. By giving them different tasks, they can explore alternative ways on how the game can be played. This again may help increase the game's long term appeal to the players.

As we have discussed before, fixed in-game storyline and tasks is not appropriate for persistent MMORPGs. This leaves dynamic synthesis of tasks and scripts a very attractive choice for designing MMORPG virtual world. The challenges of dynamic task synthesis are many folds,

1) It must be non-repeative and flexible. Repeative tasks may easily make player feel bored.

2) It must be appropriate for the game context. The automatically synthesized tasks must be consistent with the current state of the RPG virtual world and make sense to the players.

3) The tasks must be interesting to the players.

In this section, we describe how task can be automatically generated according to the current game context using some examples. In the next section, we will address how to select and tune task synthesis to the need of avatars using data mining technique.

4.1 Categories of Tasks

There are many types of tasks that can be assigned to avatars in a MMORPG world. Different types of tasks may incur totally different game play experiences. For example, tasks can be categorized as either co-operative tasks or competitive tasks. Co-operative tasks often require avatars to work together to complete it while competitive tasks often mean the opposite. In competitive tasks, one avatar (or one group of avatars)'s success often means failure of other avatar (or other groups of avatars)'s task. Both competitive and co-operative tasks can be applied in a MMORPG game. Furthermore, tasks can be alternatively categorized for its objective. For example, tasks can be used to encourage social network construction, such as a task requiring an avatar to make three friends of other avatars. Tasks can also be used for character construction, such as tasks to collect certain resources. Another way to differentiate tasks is to categorize them as enforced-tasks or non-enforced-tasks. Enforced tasks are tasks that avatars have to complete before he/she can continue and non-enforced-tasks are tasks that avatar can choose to complete or not. However, there can be a penalty associated with refusing completion of an assigned task.

4.2 Task Template

The most critical concept for task synthesis is task template. It is task template that enables unlimited number of game context dependent tasks dynamically generated on the fly. A task template is a task abstraction that can be instantiated into many tasks according to a game context. A MMORPG can have hundreds or thousands of task templates organized in a task database. Each task template has some pre-conditions that must be met before a task can be instantiated. These pre-conditions are evaluated based on the current game context. If the conditions are satisfied, the task template is enabled. New tasks can be generated from enabled task templates and assigned to avatars.

When there are many more task templates enabled than the number of avatars, a task selection mechanism is required to decide which enabled task template will be instantiated. A simple selection mechanism is randomly selecting one enabled task template for an avatar. More complex selection mechanism can be developed such as the one described in the next section using data mining to choose one task that is most appropriate for an avatar.

Aside from the pre-conditions, a task template can contain a number of free parameters (or slots). These free parameters are bound to real values during task template evaluation and task instantiation. The following code illustrates one simple task template.

Table 3. Help Task Template

```
task_template('help_friend', ...){
  preconditions:
    exist avatar p, and
    p->help_received > k*p->help_give;
  var:
    avatar p;
    int help_cnt = 0;
    int reward = ...
  task_script:
    issue a task to p that he/she has to help three
      of his/her friends;
  task_event_trigger:
    if (p helps one of his/her friends) help_cnt++;
    if (help_cnt == threshold)
      give reward to p;
      task completed;
    endif
}
```

In the above example, avatar p is a free parameter. The task template's precondition says that it is applicable to avatars who has a large disparity between help received and help he/she gives. The body of the task template specifies that the avatar who is assigned this task is supposed to give help to his/her friends. In the game, everything an avatar has done is represented as an event. Events associated with each avatar are evaluated by tasks assigned to him/her. In the above example, after pre-defined number of helps are given by the avatar, the task is considered completed.

The above code illustrates another task template called "assassin". Pre-condition of the task is more complex than the first example. Relationship between the two involved avatars are evaluated. First, p must be a valuable avatar. Second, p and q must belong to two antagonist groups. To make the game play more interesting, p can be informed about the assassin task but not who will do the job. P can call his/her friends to help locating the avatar who receives the task. The task template makes this job achievable because the information that q is about to assassin p is known by some avatars. The examples show that MMORPG designers can represent a rich set of in-game stories, scripts using task templates and have them assigned to avatars on the fly. The pre-conditions associated with task templates guarantee that the synthesized task will fit with the current game context. For example, the trait popularity of p is evaluated through social network analysis and kept up with the constant change of social network.

Table 4. Assissin Task Template

```
task_template('assassin', ...)
{ preconditions:
    exist avatar p, and
    p->popularity > threshold, and
    exist avatar q, and
    q belongs to a group that is an enemy
      of p's group, and
      no assassin task been created with p as target;
  var:
    avatar p;
    avatar q;
    int reward = ...
  task_script:
    issue an assassin task to q with p as target;
    create information about the fact that q is about
      to assassin p;
    spread this information to some avatars;
    optionally, inform p that a rumor that somebody
      is about to assassin him/her;
    p may ask his/her friends to locate q first;
  task_event_trigger:
      if (p is killed by q) task completed; endif
      if (q is killed first) task failed; endif
}
```

Beside tasks synthesized by computer, avatars can also instantiate tasks from task templates and assign them to other avatars. In this case, free parameters will be filled by avatars who instantiate the tasks. To give some example, in a clan warfare MMORPG, leaders of a clan may be entitled the ability to assign certain tasks to warriors of the clan. Such tasks can be attacking enemy's stronghold, defending the clan's properties, etc.

5 Data Mining Facilitated ATS

As addressed in the previous section, tasks can be dynamically synthesized and assigned to avatars. A task selection mechanism is used to choose enabled task templates. The purpose of task selection are two folds,

1) There can be more enabled task templates than avatars who need a task.

2) Avatar can either accept the task, complete it and receive the associated reward, or refuse the task and receive a punishment. This makes task selection important for choosing the right tasks that may most likely appeal to the players.

Data mining is an entrenched technique developed by both artificial intelligence and database research communities to understand large volume of data [2,3,9]. At first, it is used for automatic discovery of statistically significant patterns in propositional database records. Specific data mining techniques targeted for understanding networked and relational data are also developed in recent years.

Data mining techniques are especially promising for designing a better task selection mechanism so that the selected candidate tasks will have higher acceptance rate and are interesting from the players' point of view. The rationale of data mining based task selection is that game players and virtual figures controlled by them are often biased in accepting tasks. Certain tasks are more likely to be accepted by players with certain traits. Instead of coming up with a comprehensive theory on the connection between traits of players and their favored tasks, data mining can be applied to discover significant relationship between traits of players and favored tasks automatically. Figure 1 shows an example of a task-selection decision tree (only part of the model is presented). To train such models, we can analyze data such as the personality of an avatar, the history of the avatar's behavior, and the relationship between this avatar and other avatars. For instance, the model in figure 3 shows that an avatar that owns only a few artifacts tends to accept an artifact-collection task; and when he/she owns more, he/she may be more interested in human-rescue type of tasks.

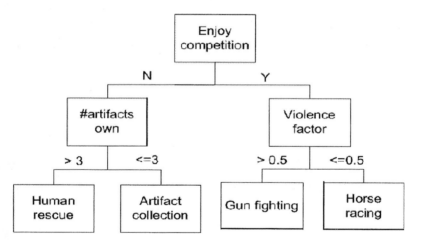

Fig. 1. Part of a Task Selection Decision Tree.

The history of avatars' behavior is a very good data collection for supervised learning. The assumption is that a player tends to make similar choices. However, it's also possible that the player will like to pursue a different career for his/her avatar. In such case, a probabilistic model is favored over deterministic models. For example, for an avatar that likes to fight, we can offer a competitive task with 70\% probability, and in the rest of the cases a co-operative task can be provided. Besides decision trees, other models and data mining algorithms can also be employed to analyze the data. Relation between tasks and traits of real game players and traits of the associated avatar can be discovered. Given a task, a player, and the associated avatar, probability of task success can be estimated. Corresponding adjustments due to a task success/failure can be arranged. The learned models can even help the game designers to introduce new avatars and task templates so as to make the game more attractive.

6 Future Work

We are experimenting the design of social network analysis, automatic task synthesis, and data mining for an experimental MMORPG game. A script language embedded in the game is developed for describing task templates and a script interpreter is implemented. A graphical interface is under development and in-depth player study will be conducted.

7 Conclusion

In this paper, we described a new design scheme for MMORPG that introduces social network analysis and in-game avatar personality development into MMORPG. We addressed how MMORPG can be designed to be social relationship and avatar personality aware. Furthermore, we discussed how tasks and scripts can be dynamically synthesized on the fly to enrich game play experiences. Finally, we introduced the concept of data mining based task selection to improve the playbility of synthesized tasks. The objective of this paper is to create a common ground for multiple-disciplinary study of MMORPG virtual world design so that it can have long lasting appeal to players.

References

1. Freeman, Linton.: Centrality in Social Networks: I. Conceptual Clarification. Social Networks 1215-39.
2. A Blockeel, H., and De Raedt, L.: Top-down induction of first-order logical decision trees. Artificial Intelligence, 101, 285-297, 1998.
3. S. Dzeroski and N. Lavrac.: editors. Relational Data Mining. Springger-Verlag, 2001.
4. Wellman, B., and S.D. Berkowitz.: Social Structures: A Network Approach, Cambridge: Cambridge University Press, 1988.
5. Wasserman, S. and K. Faust.: Social Network Analysis. Cambridge: Cambridge University Press. 1994.
6. White, Boorman, and Breiger.: Social Structure from Multiple Networks I: Blockmodels of Roles and Positions. American Journal of Sociology {\bf 81} (1976):730-779;
7. White, Douglas R. and Frank Harary.: The cohesiveness of Blocks and Social Networks: Node Connectivity and Condoitional Density. Sociological Methodology 31305-59. 2001.
8. Burt, R.S., and M. Minor.: Applied Network Analysis: A Methodological Introduction, Newbury Park: Sage, 1983.
9. Tom Mitchell.: Machine Learning. McGrawHill, 1997.

How Realistic Is Realism? Considerations on the Aesthetics of Computer Games

Richard Wages, Stefan M. Grünvogel, and Benno Grützmacher

NOMADS Lab, Piusstr. 40, D - 50823 Cologne, Germany
{wages, gruenvogel, gruetzmacher}@nomadslab.org

Abstract. One of the major goals in the development of virtual environments in recent years has been to create more and more realistic scenery, characters and natural human forms of interaction with the environment. We question this approach especially for the domain of computer games for two main reasons. Firstly we argue the following: When the absolute difference between reality and virtual environments decreases one would expect the latter to become increasingly believable for a spectator. Paradoxically often the opposite is true since the attention of the spectator gets drawn to the remaining differences to a greater extent. Secondly we ask ourselves why of all things computer games which are created for entertainment should be limited with real world constraints and are not used to experience features that are only possible in virtual environments. We conclude with a 'manifesto' for the renovation of computer games.

1 Introduction

An examination of earlier and current developments in the domain of computer games suggests that a great deal of all effort is concerned with creating ever higher degrees of 'realism' and photorealism in particular. The straightforward reason behind this tendency is the strong and seemingly natural belief within the industry and among many artists that the resulting productions will consequently be more believable and immersive for the user. While doing so the term realism itself is taken as self-evident as well as the conviction of the causality that somehow 'more realism equals higher believability'.

In this paper we will at first have a quick closer look at this often misconceived term with regard to computer games in particular. We will then give several reasons for our strong belief that the approach to 'reproduce realism' in computer games will fail and is the wrong track in the attempt to create better or the best possible games. Beside own considerations these reasons are based on findings in biology, ethology, robotics and character animation. The results even suggest that realism works counterproductive for immersion of the user. We will then proceed with stating our core matter of concern: The need for a formulation of new and specific *aesthetics for computer games*. Hence we list examples from inside and outside the domain of computer games and propose some first principles, knowing that this task has to be challenged by a broad community involved in the development of virtual

M. Rauterberg (Ed.): ICEC 2004, LNCS 3166, pp. 216–225, 2004.

environments in general and computer games in particular. In order to initiate a future and hopefully passionate debate on this issue we conclude by putting together a first *Manifesto for the Renovation of Computer Games* as a starting place.

2 Realism

What have players and marketing departments in mind when they are speaking of computer games being realistic? Surely they do think of the quality of the audio and visual presentation, the simulation of physical properties but also of the behavior of non player characters which should act naturally or like 'being real'. But can a fire-breathing dragon really be 'realistic' when there is of course no counterpart in nature?

The notion of reality often refers to the 'world itself' containing everything, the nature as well as the culture. But when talking of computer games the term 'realism' is often interpreted in a comparable or a partial sense. The notion of realism is used here to relate to a reference point. For example: If the reference point is a fantasy world equipped with trolls, dragons and magic, the appearance of a tax man from a fiscal authority like in our real world would be regarded as extremely unlikely and unrealistic. On the other hand if we speak of realistic graphics the point of reference will be the sense-impressions we receive with our eyes from the real world and the graphics on the screen will be compared with those.

Hence the question comes up how to measure the degree of realism of a computer game. To this question we do not expect an overall answer because there are finally different measures for various aspects of computer game worlds and their representation. In addition the notion of realism can always be regarded relative to a chosen point of reference. But if we took for an example the audio visual representation of the game world as well as the behavior of a non player character as a measure of realism, two different points of reference – belonging to perceptual realism or social realism respectively – are brought together, which have nothing to do with each other in the first place. Moreover there are some aspects which are barely measurable because the representation of the game world finally creates a representation of the game world inside the player's head, which is not comparable in an inter-subjective way.

Beside the term realism also other terms, which are closely related to the notion of realism, can be used to judge the quality of computer games and to classify them or particular aspects of them. *Presence* as 'illusion of nonmediation' [5] describes the experience that a medium is not perceived by a person while this person is dealing with it. As Lombard figures out the 'illusion of nonmediation' can be found in two different ways. Firstly the medium can appear invisible and transparent and the user as well as the content of the medium share the same physical environment. Secondly the medium can be transformed into something like a social entity. It is interesting to see that the expression of reality is not used in this examination (and is actually regarded in opposition to social and perceptual realism) and the focus is put only on the medium itself.

3   Drawbacks of Producing Realism

There is a desire to attain more and more realistic virtual worlds, characters and forms of interaction in computer games. This desire is driven by several reasons (one of them might be the competition in the game industry forcing companies to search for unique selling points for their products which are very often assumed in the graphical domain). One reason which is pointed out very often is the believe that the reduction of the absolute difference between real and virtual environments leads to a increase of presence and makes the virtual worlds more believable. We disagree with this point of view and do present in this paper some examples to support this opposition.

3.1   Essential and Non-essential Information

The attempt to 'simply copy nature' neglects the fact that the information contained in different stimuli for human senses divides into *essential* and *non-essential* information. It is safe to say that the vast majority – definitely more than 90 percent, maybe even more than 99 percent – of this information is non-essential insofar that it is filtered out physiologically and mentally. Hence it will not be used at all by our senses and mind to create an inner image of the 'real world'. Findings from research on behavior control rather suggest that in fact animals' attention predominantly is confined to relatively few certain specific features and stimuli. A famous example for this are the studies on stimuli releasers by Niko Tinbergen and Konrad Lorenz. Among other Tinbergen [7] studied the herring gull chickens' pecking on their parents' beaks which hold a noticeable red spot. The chickens perform this to beg for food. The pecking behavior towards the real head of a parent (Fig.1) was set to be the normal rate. For our considerations the results then were twofold:

Fig. 1.-2. Different degrees of abstraction of a Herring Gull's head and beak: 1. Original. 2. Stuffed animal.

Firstly increasingly realistic models (e.g. stuffed gull head, Fig. 2) were no more effective at eliciting pecking than a simple painted strip of cardboard (Fig.3). Secondly exaggerated sign stimuli sometimes lead to exaggerated responses (Fig.4, supernormal releaser), i.e. work better than the original although they are far from being realistic.

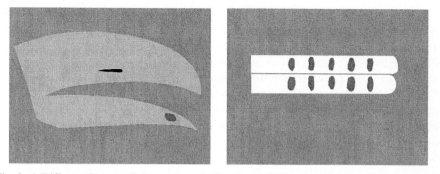

Fig. 3.-4. Different degrees of abstraction of a Herring Gull's head and beak. Painted cardboard with: 3. Similar shape and colors. 4. Exaggerated length and numerous red spots.

We do not want to suggest here that complex human behavior can be explained by or should be reduced to a small set of easily measurable actions. Rather we would suggest that creators of computer games should keep in mind two things: Firstly copying nature is costly out of proportion since one has to produce *all* the information including non-essential parts. While decreasing Δ *stimulus*, which here stands for the difference between artificial and real, (i.e. moving from left to right in the above diagram) the costs to do so simply explode. But even if one does so it is secondly not at all guaranteed that the results are the best ones possible. The use of certain specific aesthetics for computer games will most likely lead to stronger responses and emotional involvement of users. We will give further existing examples for this instance in chapter 4.

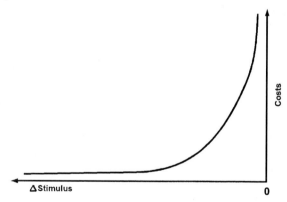

Fig. 5. The *costs* of a production in dependence of the size of Δ *Stimulus* given through the deviation of the stimuli from the virtual world related to those of the real world

3.2   A First Paradox – Single Stimuli

Mimicking real stimuli gives rise to an additional drawback. Humans undoubtedly are optimized for the perception of certain details (e.g. faces, movements). The discrepancies compared to stimuli from reality often are increasingly weighted by our cognition the closer (but not identical) the artificial stimuli are to reality. Metaphorically speaking the 'recognition of reality' awakes our 'wardens of reality' too who instantly detect incongruities and for example judge facial movements as spastic. Hence an increase in realism might paradoxically lead to a *decrease* in believability.

A similar effect has earlier been recognized and described within the realm of robotics by the Japanese roboticist Masahiro Mori while he did psychological experiments on human responses towards humanlike robots. A good formulation of this observation into a principle in English language is given by Dave Bryant [1]. Roughly the principle states that humans respond the more emphatically towards robots the more anthropomorphic the robots are – but only until a certain degree. Now a surprising thing happens: For robots (and all other characters) which are designed even more humanlike the formerly positive reaction of the users declines and becomes strongly repulsive. Only when the robots become (nearly) indistinguishable from real humans the user reaction reaches highest positive (human-human-like) levels again. The described dip of the empathy curve is called the 'Uncanny Valley'.

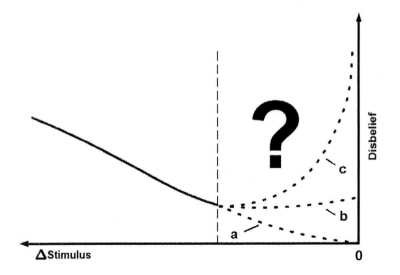

Fig. 6. The degree of *Disbelief* of a spectator in dependence of the measure of *Δ Stimulus* given through the deviation of the stimuli from the virtual world related to those of the real world

Obviously in the above principle the claim that the empathy for the robot or character will reach the highest possible rates can be regarded as an optimistic prediction since neither in robotics nor in any other field completely humanlike beings have been created to date. In the below figure we list the three possible scenarios. The most optimistic one (a) is that indeed from a certain point on the decreasing difference between the real and the artificial stimuli (Δ stimulus) leads to a continuous suspension of disbelieve of the user, finally reaching 0 and hence leads to full believability and immersion. The most pessimistic scenario (c) is that whenever humans detect even the smallest difference to reality they will refuse the artificial creation – the closer to reality the more – since an increasing number of 'wardens of reality' are awoken.

Of course any other outcome in between the two extremes (b) is possible too. We too have to leave this question open although we strongly fear that for the future (c) will be the most likely scenario. In addition to the concerns already stated in this chapter we want to list yet another observation.

3.3 A Second Paradox – Stimuli Interdependencies

The created total stimulus of a virtual environment is a composition of a number of different stimuli. Advances or even perfection of a single stimulus (e.g. photorealism) or a certain category of stimuli increasingly reveal the shortcomings in other categories of stimuli (e.g. social interaction, movements). This again leads to a paradoxical growth in the spectator's disbelieve.

The results presented by Hodgins et. al. in [4] demonstrate that an improvement of a virtual character's visual presentation must not automatically go along with an increase of it's realism. In an experiment three different figures of one character were presented to different subjects. The presented figures varied in the richness of detail of their visual presentation. The simplest figure was consisting only of simple sticks representing the character's skeleton, another figure had a body based on a polygon model and the third figure featured the highest degree of detail and showed the movement of muscles too. All characters where moved by the same sequence of animation. The resonance of the different subjects demonstrated the following: Shown the simplest figures (stick and polygon) the subjects did not recognize the subtleties of the animations. Consequently manipulated and unrealistic animations were recognized only with the most detailed figure. This means, that the increase of one aspect of realism (visual presentation) can rapidly lead to much more weight of another aspect (animations). Therefore flaws in one aspect might not appear until another aspect gets optimized to some extend.

4   Principles for Computer Games Aesthetics

In the before chapter we gave several reasons for our conviction that on the long run the approach 'reproducing realism' will not be successful at all in enhancing immersion in computer games. But what are the alternatives? We believe that for the still young art form computer games the goal must be to develop own aesthetics. We too believe now is the time to start postulating principles. Methods used in other (visually driven) media like movies or comic books for example may serve as a valuable source for insights.

4.1   Principle: (Mis)Use Well-Known Elements Even If They Seem Foreign to the Subject

Numerous examples for the method of creating instant understanding and a high degree of believability with the help of – on first look – inadequate elements can be found within the movie industry. The makers of Shrek used this method deliberately and very successfully throughout the entire movie. When for example Shrek and Donkey enter the arena of Lord Farquaad's castle within a short sequence one can observe the following:

The bright sun creates a lens flare, an effect not known to humans from a natural environment but the better known from nearly any movie one has seen (and hence build into some computer games already). But the makers came up with more than pure technical tricks. For the story's progress Shrek has to be named the winner of a competition. But who knows (or cares) what an original knight tournament looked like. So they finally decided to make the fight a nowadays well-known one, namely a mixture of ice hockey and wrestling. A further and very subtle solution was found for a sound problem. Just about nobody knows how it sounds when a battery of crossbows is drawn. But this very noise is needed to create an atmosphere of threat within a fraction of a second after Shrek's victory. Hence for the scene it was decided to simply use the well-known sound of cocking rifle shutters.

4.2   Principle: Use Principles Found Within Biology and Ethology

In the previous chapter we argued that acquainted or inborn reaction towards certain biological features or stimuli might for different reasons work unhelpful regarding the believability of a character or setting. On the other hand it was shown that reducing the number of features while exaggerating certain ones can have a stronger effect than a genuine stimulus. Hence we suggest that these very behavioral tendencies and principles should be exploited for the creation of believability, empathy and immersion. Keeping this in mind it is very comprehensible why for example the characters created by Walt Disney work so well in representing human behavior although not even being humans in the first place. Steven J. Gould [3] points out Lorenz' findings that humans have the ability to react biologically adequate towards animals as well as inanimate objects by projecting human characteristics onto them. The examination of the appearance of the character Mickey Mouse over a fifty years period leads him to the following conclusion: Knowingly or unknowingly the artists at the Disney Studios eventually have equipped their character along the exactly same principles as 'nature would have done' if the intention had been to create empathy and fondness. Only, the 'evolution of Mickey Mouse' went backwards resulting in an ever more youthful, nearly childish character (e.g. size of head and eyes, volume of arms and legs, behavior, relative positions of eyes and ears).

4.3 Principle: Amplification Through Simplification

In his examination of comics [6] Scott McCloud explains why realistically drawn pictures are not used in comics by the concept of amplification through simplification. An image of a face can be stripped down to its essential meaning through simplifying and cartooning. This allows artists to amplify the meaning of the image (e.g. the expression of a face) in a way that would not be possible with a realistic presentation. Another aspect is the universality of a simplification. In contrast to a realistic picture which represents only one individual person an abstract cartoon image might represents millions of people and is therefore more suitable for identification.

Within the domain of computer games Shigeru Miyamoto is not only the creator for the all time game classics Donkey Kong, Super Mario Bros. and The Legend of Zelda but also the one who has created the game industry's only instantly recognizable aesthetic – with a very colorful, cartoonish and whimsical look. Instead of using a particle system in the game Zelda the clouds of explosions are of a simplified flowery and spiral look.

4.4 Principle: Get Rid of Real World Constraints

In parallel to the issues whether or not it will at some point be possible to perfectly copy nature and whether this will at all lead to the intended breakthrough in terms of believability and immersion we question this approach for yet another reason: Our possibility to build highly sophisticated computer games – or more general, virtual environments – is an option to create *fantastic* worlds, the very worlds we can never visit in reality. Hence it was already argued for the formulation of 'qualitative physics' which are consistent but not necessarily an adaptation of real physics (e.g. by Marc Cavazza et. al. [2]) to create non-realistic or surreal behavior. Art and in particular VR art should not routinely and self-evidently be restricted with real world constraints.

4.5 Manifesto for the Renovation of Computer Games

Of course the above short list of principles cannot at all be more than a first start. To provoke further impetus to some of the topics to be scrutinized we end our first list of principles with further demands on future computer games.

Manifesto:

Contra:	Personalization by Figures, Humans, Aliens,...
Pro:	Representation as Protoplasm
Contra:	Nonverbal Communication by Gestures, Grimaces,...
Pro:	Communication by Colors, Emotions, Time, Sound,...
Contra:	Solid Body Stature
Pro:	Novel Organs and new Sense Organs, Developed by oneself
Contra:	Long Range Weapons
Pro:	Inner Fight
Contra:	Gravity and Thermodynamics

Pro:	New Forms of Viscosity
Contra:	Ethnical Debates and Transfiguration
Pro:	Multiple Egos
Contra:	Walking, Flying, Driving
Pro:	Crawling Wriggling, Flowing, Sliming, Dripping, Floating, Evaporation, Osmotic Motion…
Pro:	Reproduction, Sprouting and Vegetative Growth
Contra:	Hemispheric Visual Field
Pro:	More Arms, Legs, Eyes, Organs
Contra:	Walls and Dungeons
Contra:	Edges and 90° Angle
Contra:	Euclidian Space
Contra:	Surface with Characteristic 0
Pro:	Möbius Strip and Klein Bottle

5 Conclusion

The claim 'more realism equals higher believability' was proven wrong with the help of several examples and findings from different realms of media and science. An 'increase of realism' often leads to an at first paradoxical increase of disbelieve for the user. On the other hand several successful examples and approaches exist which deliberately turn down realism. This article does not want to condemn efforts to create realism but rather wants to emphasize the fact that other approaches lead to very good or even better results for computer games. Production can and should be freed from the 'corset of realism'. We hope that this text helps to incite a continuative discussion about the aesthetics of computer games and an extension of this discussion to other media and sciences.

Acknowledgements. The authors would like to thank Otto E. Rössler, Michael Mateas and Andrew Stern for valuable comments on the topic during personal conversations.

References

1. Bryant, D.: The Uncanny Valley. http://vcl.ctrl-c.liu.se/vcl/Authors/Catspaw-DTP-Services/valley.pdf
2. Cavazza, M., Hartley, S., Lugroin, J.-L., Le Bras, M.: Alternative Reality: A New Platform for Digital Arts. ACM Symposium on Virtual Reality Software and Technology, Osaka, Japan (2003) 100-108
3. Gould, S. J.: The Panda's Thumb. More Reflections in Natural History. W. W. Norton & Company, New York (1980)
4. Hodgins, J. K., O'Brien, J. F., Tumblin, J.: Judgments of Human Motion with Different Geometric Models. IEEE: Transactions on Visualization and Computer Graphics, Vol. 4, No. 4. (1998)

5.   Lombard, M., Ditton, T.: At the Heart of it all: The Concept of Presence. Journal of Computer-Mediated Communication, Vol. 3, No.2, http://www.ascusc.org/jcmc/vol3/issue2/lombard.html (1997)
6.   McCloud, S.: Understanding Comics. 2nd edn. Kitchen Ink Press INC, Northampton (1993)
7.   Tinbergen, N.: The Herring Gull's World; A Study of the Social Behavior of Birds. Collins, London (1953)

Read-It: A Multi-modal Tangible Interface for Children Who Learn to Read

Ivo Weevers, Wouter Sluis, Claudia van Schijndel, Siska Fitrianie,
Lyuba Kolos-Mazuryk, and Jean-Bernard Martens

Design School of User System Interaction, University of Eindhoven,
Den Dolech 2, 5600 MB Eindhoven, The Netherlands
{i.weevers, r.j.w.sluis, c.h.g.j.v.schijndel, s.fitrianie,
l.kolos-mazuryk}@tm.tue.nl, j.b.o.s.martens@tue.nl

Abstract. Multi-modal tabletop applications offer excellent opportunities for enriching the education of young children. Read-It is an example of an interactive game with a multi-modal tangible interface that was designed to combine the advantages of current physical games and computer exercises. It is a novel approach for supporting children who learn to read. The first experimental evaluation has demonstrated that the Read-It approach is indeed promising and meets a priori expectations.

1 Introduction

In primary school, children aged five to seven years old start to learn how to read and write letters and words. The most frequently-used Dutch reading method, called *Veilig Leren Lezen* (VLL – Learning to Read Safely) [9], uses classroom activities, such as storytelling and verbal repetition, in combination with physical games and computer exercises, to practice reading. Currently, these latter exercises are assumed to be performed on a desktop computer. Since children at this age cannot read and write well, they mostly interact with the computer by means of the mouse. They, however, often experience difficulties while selecting, dragging and moving the cursor in a controlled way [15]. Although some argue against this by stating that these problems relate to the graphical user interface design and that children are more familiar with the mouse nowadays [10], interviews we carried out with primary school teachers, indicate that mouse handling problems occur frequently. Smets et al. [13] report that the interaction problems on a desktop computer are further increased by the fact that action (for example, the mouse movements) and perception (for example, the visual feedback on the screen) are spatially separated. The teachers whom we interviewed tend to confirm this point of view. Most importantly, however, desktop computers are based on a single-user/single-computer paradigm [14], and hence do not effectively support co-located, multi-user interaction. Scott et al. [12] have shown that children greatly enjoy technology that supports concurrent activities, and that forcing children to share one input device contributes to off-task behavior and boredom. Social interactions in a learning environment have also shown to lead to significant learning benefits [4,7]. Research by Inkpen et al. [5] demonstrates that

M. Rauterberg (Ed.): ICEC 2004, LNCS 3166, pp. 226–234, 2004.
© IFIP International Federation for Information Processing 2004

children exhibit a significantly higher level of engagement and tend to be more active when working in parallel. Unfortunately, the face-to-face setup that is most often preferred for effective group interaction is prohibited by a desktop setting.

As indicated before, current reading methods use real card and board games to exercise reading skills within playful group activity. However, this game approach suffers from at least three problems. First, supervision by teachers is often lacking during such games, so that assistance and verification are not available. Second, the unique orientation of letters and words can cause perception problems. For example, children sitting on opposite sides can perceive the same letter as either a /d/ or a /p/. Third, most of these games are purely visually-oriented (for example, use only pictures and letters/words), so that the children mostly exercise the picture-word association, but not the letter-sound association.

It seems that the computer exercises and the tangible board games suffer from largely complementary problems. In our view, recent developments towards multi-modal tangible interfaces offer the opportunity to combine the advantages of both methods, while avoiding the drawbacks. We developed the Read-It application: an interactive game that was inspired by the traditional card game "memory". Since it is a computer game, it can offer multi-modal feedback, consisting of written and spoken letters and words, in combination with pictures. Its interface allows for multiple simultaneously active interaction elements, and therefore allows for multiple simultaneous users, hence collaboration. Moreover, this tangible interface suits the motoric needs of the children.

2 Previous Work

Existing research projects have already explored many issues concerning the required technology, usability and possible applications of augmented tables (for example, Ishii and Ulmer [6], Fitzmaurice et al. [3], Rauterberg et al. [8], Aliakseyeu et al. [2]). Most of the presented applications have however only been tested with adult (usually, even highly professional) users. A much more challenging test for augmented table systems in our view is whether or not much less-experienced and trained subjects can also use and profit from such systems. Very young children as a user group, together with the identified problems of desktop computers and reading methods, influenced our choice for the design of an application with a clear educational goal.

There are only few existing projects in which tangible interfaces are used for creating collaborative learning experiences for children. One such prototype system is TICLE [11], which was designed for children that are "turned off by math and science" and shows promising results. Our prototype is different in at least two respects. First, our application is learning to read rather than solving mathematical puzzles. Second, we extend TICLE's design principles to a face-to-face setup and a coinciding action and perception space. In this way, we intend to establish more natural interaction between the children and between each child and the system.

Another project that we know off, but on which we have only limited information (see http://www.fit.fraunhofer.de/projekte/kiwi/), is the ZOOMlab. It was developed for the Vienna Children's Museum, and is intended to be used by up to 20 children simultaneously. It is implemented on the Assembly Table and focuses on assembly tasks, for example, on positioning multiple virtual objects on a large floor plan. The platform seems to be mostly intended for demonstrating the principle of tangible interaction. As far as we can deduce, no clear educational goals are pursued.

3   Read-It Design Rationale

Since the focus of our project is not on technological development, but on designing and testing an educational application, we have chosen to implement the Read-It prototype on an existing augmented tabletop environment, the Visual Interaction Platform (VIP) [2]. The platform consists of a computer, one beamer, an infrared light source, an infrared-sensitive camera, and a table with a reflective surface. The beamer projects the computer screen output onto the horizontal table. The infrared light source illuminates the action-perception space on the table. The light is reflected towards the infrared-sensitive camera by means of retro-reflecting tags. These tags are attached to physical bricks that are positioned on the table. The computer runs computer-vision software to analyze the images from the camera. The software output consists of tag – and thus brick – positions, orientations and unique tag identifications. Each brick has a unique tag, which pattern is defined by a number and the position of non-reflecting holes in the tag.

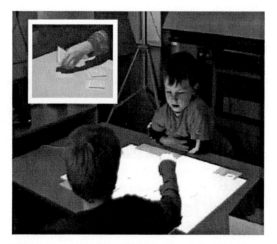

Fig. 1. Two children playing the Read-It game. Top-left: Flipping a tangible brick.

Our application is inspired by the traditional game of "memory". It uses twenty tangible bricks, each associated with a virtual memory card. The virtual cards are projected on top of the physical bricks. The sides of the bricks that are facing upwards when the game is started are associated with the blind sides of the virtual memory cards. The invisible sides are associated with the pictures (and words). By flipping a brick, the corresponding virtual memory card is flipped and the system shows or hides the card's picture. Figure 1 shows a child flipping a brick and thus a virtual card.

3.1 The Game

The goal of the Read-It game is to find all matching picture pairs. Two pictures match when their related words have either identical first, middle or last letters (depending on the game type). For example, the Dutch words "<u>v</u>is" (fish) and "<u>v</u>os" (fox) match in their first letter, while "<u>v</u>is" and "<u>p</u>en" (pen) do not. Children play in couples and they are encouraged to collaborate. When the children think two pictures match they have to press a large button next to the projection area. If their decision is correct, they receive a carrot picture as a reward. If their decision is incorrect, the virtual cards show a red border and the children have to turn them back over before continuing. The game ends when the children have found all matching pairs. A large animated carrot is the final reward.

3.2 Multi-modality

Training through different senses benefits the children's reading skills. Especially in early reading education, children need to acquire knowledge about the correct grapheme (the graphical character /v/) to phoneme (the sound [v]) mapping. Read-It offers the children the opportunity to practice this mapping by offering both audio and video feedback. When the children reveal a new picture by flipping a brick, the Read-It application displays and spells the associated letters and word visually and auditory, in a synchronized way.

3.3 The Orientation Problem

Reading displayed letters from opposite sides of a table raises an orientation problem. For example, one child might see a /d/, while the child sitting on the opposite site will perceive the same letter as a /p/. Such a situation is especially troublesome for novice readers and is hence to be avoided. We solved the problem by separating the projection area into one shared and two personal workspaces. Figure 2 shows the image being projected onto the table by the Read-It game. The shared workspace holds the virtual cards and displays only pictures. When a new picture is revealed, the system displays a smaller version of the same picture, together with the corresponding spelled word, in each personal workspace. This prevents that the children have to shift their attention from the personal to the shared workspace while reading a word. We expect this to benefit the picture-word mapping.

3.4 Movement of Focus

The focus of attention is purposely shifted around during the course of the game, by involving different areas when flipping the cards, by spelling the words both visually and auditory, and by the need to press the confirmation button. Acuff [1] has pointed out that children like to be busy and entertained and react positively to frequent stimulation. With Read-It, children do not need to keep still and concentrate continuously on the same thing. We expect this to favor their engagement.

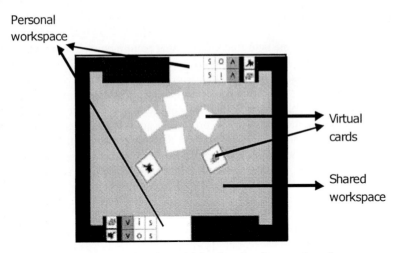

Fig. 2. The Read-It interface with its shared and personal workspaces.

3.5 Tangible Objects

Bricks avoid two of the above-mentioned desktop problems. First, they match the children's motoric skills better than a mouse. Second, the bricks on the augmented table realize a combined action-perception space. Another advantage, as indicated by some of the teachers, is that bricks agree with many children's preference towards brick toys, such as LEGO. In order to obtain reliable brick recognition, the brick size was fixed at 5.5x5.5 cm. We tested bricks with varying heights (2, 6, 8, 16, 18, and 22 mm) with 37 five-to-seven-year old children to select a brick height that suited the children's motoric skills and preference. Furthermore, we tested bricks with and without a notch along the sides. Such a notch makes it potentially easier to grasp and turn the brick. On average, the brick with a height of 6 mm and with a notch was preferred.

3.6 Collaboration

Unlike desktop games, the Read-It application is a cooperative game that promotes natural face-to-face communication. Since the game uses twenty bricks that are scattered around the table, collaboration benefits the children in reaching their goal. They can collaborate both mentally, in order to remember the locations of the pictures, and physically, in order to reach the bricks to be flipped and to press the confirmation button. This collaboration is further strengthened by the fact that the Read-It application supports parallel activity by the children through simultaneously active interaction elements. We expect that education styles for children that support such daily social interactions result in learning benefits [4,7].

3.7 Support for Learning

Teachers use reading games in class to strengthen the recall and rehearsal of words and letters. Both learning mechanisms are essential in the process of learning how to read and are supported by Read-It. Children flip the same card multiple times, which makes them read the corresponding letters and hear the related sounds more than once. Although children will find some matching cards fairly fast (by shear luck), the game holds multiple instances of each letter, so that all letters/sounds are rehearsed.

4 Experimental Evaluation

Before setting up a large longitudinal study to find out about Read-It's effects on reading skills, we needed to evaluate whether or not our system meets first requirements. We designed an experiment to evaluate whether or not five-to-seven-year-old children are able to understand and work with the augmented application. We also wanted to find out whether or not face-to-face collaboration within the couples is established, which we consider to be an indication for achieved social communication.

4.1 Experimental Design

The experiment involved 15 children between five and seven years old. Twelve of them formed 6 pairs. Three children were paired with a member of the research theme. The observations for these three children were only used for analyzing how they handled augmented reality, not for analyzing collaborative behavior.

All children knew the traditional memory game, which has the goal of competing against each other. However, with Read-It the children are encouraged to collaborate. Therefore, in order to get acquainted with the new game rules, the couples started by playing a memory game with Read-It game rules using real cards. Next, in order to become familiarized with the augmented environment of the Read-It system, and in order to adjust to the laboratory setting, the children played an introductory Read-It game with three card pairs. Afterwards, the children played a full game with ten card pairs. Finally, the children had to explain to their parents with another three-pair-game what they had experienced. The parents could not observe their children during the previous sessions. The sessions were taped (two camera's recording each child from the front and one camera recording the children's action space). We used the tapes to observe peculiarities and to analyze the children's behavior with the coding schemes explained below.

4.2 Results

Augmented Reality. We used the number of explorative acts to quantify the children's understanding of the concept of augmented reality, for example, real bricks being combined with virtual cards. Children show an explorative act when they (1) pick up a card and look at it without flipping it, (2) peak under a card before turning it, and (3) express that they understand the match of the brick with the projection of the virtual card. We divided the explorative acts into four timeslots across each game. The total time, which is measured from flipping the first card to all cards facing downwards again after successful matching of all cards, varied. It took the couples on average 23 turns to finish the ten-pairs-game. Figure 3 plots the average number of explorative acts across all 15 children as a function of game quarter. It demonstrates that the explorative behavior of the children decreases fast. It is already reduced to 50% towards the end of the relatively short game.

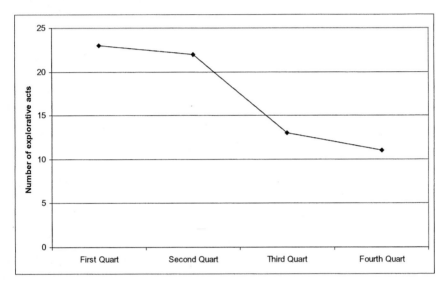

Fig. 3. Total number of explorative acts of the children as a function of the phase within the game.

Collaboration. We used four indicators for collaborative acts: (1) discussion about which card to flip, (2) discussion about which letter to match with, (3) making a gesture to direct the other child's attention to a specific card, and (4) looking at each other for confirmation. During the game we observed an average of 5.5 collaborative acts per couple. Large differences, however, occurred between couples, probably due to differences in dominance between the children within a couple.

5 Discussion

We think that the Read-It game will support the process of learning how to read in the long run. The pilot study confirms that the children are able to grasp and use the major system concepts, such as augmented reality and the multimodal environment.
All children finished the game and their exploratory behavior reduced quickly. Also, seven out of fifteen children read aloud along with the visual and auditory spelling by the system. The study also demonstrated that the children enjoyed playing and

learning with the applied technology. One could argue that the appearance of personal workspaces triggers the players towards an individualistic game strategy. However, a certain degree of collaboration between the children was clearly established.

6 Conclusion

We presented Read-It, a novel approach for supporting young children in the process of learning how to read. Read-It overcomes some identified problems of current desktop exercises and board games that support the reading method VLL. The game uses tangible bricks on a tabletop for improved interaction and applies different mechanisms – collaboration, recall and rehearsal – to support the learning process. Read-It was designed for enriching the process of developing reading skills. As such, the contribution of the system to the children's reading experience is a critical aspect. Understanding the true effect on reading skills would require a longitudinal study. Before conducting such a study, we performed a short pilot experiment to evaluate: (1) whether or not children of five-to-seven-years old are able to work with the concept of combined real and virtual elements, and (2) whether or not collaborative behavior was manifested. The conclusion on both aspects was positive, so that we can argue that we have indeed created a rich learning environment that encourages children. Altogether, the presented design and evaluation provide a good foundation for further research.

References

1. Acuff, D. S. What Kids Buy and Why: The Psychology of Marketing to Kids. Free Press, Detroit (1997).
2. Aliakseyeu D., Martens J.B., Subramanian S., Vroubel M. and Wesselink W, "Visual Interaction Platform", Proc. Interact 2001, Tokyo (2001) 232-239.
3. FitzMaurice, G.W., Ishii, H. & Buxton, W., Bricks: Laying the Foundation for Graspable User Interfaces, Proc. Of CHI '95, ACM Press (1995) 170-177.
4. Hymel S., Zinck B., Ditner E., Cooperation versus Competition in the Classroom. Exceptionality Education Canada (1993) 3:1-2, 103-128.
5. Inkpen, K.M., Ho-Ching, W., Kuederle, O., Scott, S.D., Shoemaker, G.B.D. "This is fun! We're all best friends and we're all playing.": Supporting children's synchronous collaboration. Proc. of CSCL '99, ACM Press (1999) 252-259.
6. Ishii, H., and B. Ulmer. Tangible Bits: Towards Seamless Interfaces between People, Bits, and Atoms. Proc. CHI '97, ACM Press (1997) 234-241.
7. Johnson D.W., Maruyana G., Jonhson R.T., Effects of Cooperative, Competitive and Individualistic Goal Structures on Achievement: A Meta-Analysis, Psychology Bulletin, (1981) 89(1), 47-62.
8. Rauterberg, M., Fjeld, M., Krueger, H., Bichsel, M., Leonhardt, U & Meier, M., BUILD-IT: a video-based interaction technique of a planning tool for construction and design, Proc. Work with Display Units (WWDU) '97, (1997) 175-176.
9. Reitsma, P. & Verhoeven, L., Acquisition of Reading Dutch, Foris Publications, Dordrecht, the Netherlands (1990).

10. Romeo G.I., Edwards S., McNamara S., Walker I., & Ziguras C., Investigating the Potential of Touchscreen Technology in Early Childhood Education, Proc. AARE '01 (2001).
11. Scarlatos L.L., TICLE: Using Multimedia Multimodal Guidance to Enhance Learning, Information Sciences 140 (2002) 85-103.
12. Scott S.D., Mandryk R.L., Inkpen K.M., Understanding children's collaborative interactions in shared environments, Journal of Computer Assisted Learning (2003) 19, 220-228.
13. Smets, G.J.F., Stappers, P.J., Overbeeke, K.J. and Van der Mast, C., Designing in virtual reality: Perception-action coupling and affordances. In: Carr, K., and England, R. (eds.), Simulated and Virtual Realities. Elements of Perception, Taylor & Francis, London (1995) 189-208.
14. Stewart J., Bederson B.B., Druin A, Single Display Groupware: A Model for Co-present Collaboration. Proc. CHI '99, ACM Press (1999) 286-293.
15. Strommen E. Children's Use of Mouse-Based Interfaces to Control Virtual Travel, Proc. SIGCHI on Human Factors in Computing Systems '94, ACM Press (1994) 405-410.

Exploiting Films and Multiple Subtitles Interaction for Casual Foreign Language Learning in the Living Room

Victor Bayon

Fraunhofer Integrated Publication and Information Systems Institute (IPSI),
Smart Environments of the Future (AMBIENTE)
Dolivostrasse 15, 64293 Darmstadt, Germany
bayon@ipsi.fraunhofer.de

Abstract. Films at the cinema, at home or on the computer screen are a fundamental part of today's entertainment culture. The careful listening and watching of foreign films with or without subtitles is often used as an aid for the learning of foreign languages. This paper presents the ongoing development of an entertainment/learning computer based DVD subsystem for the home environment that has been extended with the aim of further enabling the learning of foreign languages while watching films. By providing a "DualSubsView" of subtitles of 2 languages (native and foreign) as the film plays, users can become more familiar with the vocabulary of the foreign language that they want to learn. With this approach, vocabulary in a foreign language is presented as extra information embedded into the film and learners can exploit the information directly or indirectly for entertainment and for learning. Potential users of the system were involved in the initial design stages and in the informal evaluation process of the initial prototypes.

1 Introduction

Computers, in general, have a long and evolving history as tools or aids to support entertainment [1] and the learning of foreign languages [2]. As computers evolve, they are continuously adopting new form/factors and functionality, "disappearing" from their current appearances and contexts and "reappearing" into different ones with different form/factors and new application domains [3].

One of the areas where computers are converging and reshaping the home entertainment is towards their integration as multimedia hubs for the home [4], where computers can be shaped into "Home Media Appliances" to offer sophisticated entertainment. Such functionality can include capabilities for storing, organising, pre and post processing, replaying and interacting with all types of media and media sources, pushing fully featured computers into the living/entertainment spaces of households.

Standard home Audio/Visual equipment (A/V), such as radio, broadcast TV, Video/DVD, interactive TV, etc, are commonplace in living rooms with the potential and the tradition of being used as an entertainment and learning tool [5,6]. DVD players, with their interactive and multi-track capabilities, can already, for example,

M. Rauterberg (Ed.): ICEC 2004, LNCS 3166, pp. 235–240, 2004.

display a film in multiple languages and with subtitles and can be used this way to practise listening and reading a foreign language.

As learning a foreign language can be a very long and complicated process where many skills have to be developed, intrinsic motivation for learning plays a very important part in the process [7]. Film watching is an entertaining, proactive and intrinsically motivating experience and with the integration of home media appliances into the household new applications to support foreign language learning can be developed.

The paper describes the development of a system with the purpose of supporting the advanced used of subtitles in films for language learning. First of all, ideas and user requirements were gathered conducting an informal survey amongst learners of foreign languages. With this input, two integrated applications and one prototype have been initially developed: a "DualSubsView" DVD player where 2 subtitles in 2 different languages are shown, and a movie recommender system that determines which films might be more suitable for the learner to watch by comparing the words/vocabulary used in film and the vocabulary used in the language course and a PDA based remote control application. Finally the applications have been evaluated using an expert review and user feedback in order to gather initial impressions of the system as part of the user-centred design process. The paper concludes with a summary and ideas for future work based around the concepts presented in this paper.

2 Designing the System

In order to design the system and to gather initial ideas and user requirements, an informal survey was conducted via interviews and moderated discussions between the designers and members of a language course for mature students in a local college. The purpose of the survey was to find out what "out-of-class" materials and activities of a structured (course materials) and un-structured nature (that are not part of the language course) students used to reinforce their structured learning at the college.

The conversations among the designers and the mature students revealed that although DVD of foreign films with subtitles were commonly used as an un-structured learning aid (among many other activities), it presented several challenges for the students, especially amongst the ones at the beginner's level. Although the survey highlighted some issues that are typical and expected of foreign language students, it provided enough design input and discussions among the designers and students to generate the first ideas for the initial application prototypes and to try to tackle some of them within the context of watching films in the home.

2.1 "DualSubsView"

The application improves on the current subtitles and sub-captioning of standard DVD technology by enabling the possibility of visualising subtitles in 2 languages at the same time (Fig 1). The initial contact with the students revealed the need for shortening the gap between the language knowledge required to understand and the ability to follow a film with subtitles.

With the inclusion of the 2 subtitles channels, the students can view a film with the option of seeing the subtitles in two different languages (the native and the target language) and try to follow and understand the dialogues, the subtitles, or both. In fig 1 the screenshot of the "DualSubsView" DVD player shows two channels for text, top text for the English subs and bottom text for the German subs.

Students can follow several strategies in order to understand and learn from the conversation and find out ad-hoc which ones are more suitable for them depending on their foreign language skills. A typical strategy is matching the foreign audio/foreign track and rely on the native text to match the words that are unknown. Following this strategy, the students can reinforce listening skills, the vocabulary that they already know and acquire new vocabulary.

Fig. 1. "DualSubsView".

2.2 Movie Recommender

As all movies can differ in types of context, discussions, dialogue structures and vocabulary used, the task of selecting which movie to watch in order to practise listening and reading according to the student's language level can be a difficult task without external recommendation (such as the lecturer on the course or other students who know the films already).

A simple movie recommender application has been built in order to provide basic advice and complexity awareness to the students about which movie might be more suit-able for them to watch It focuses on the most basic feature of the films: the vocabulary used. The movie recommender holds a database of the vocabulary learned by the students in the course and each student has a personal electronic dictionary where new words are added each time the student searches for one. The vocabulary held in the dictionary is then compared with the vocabulary used in the films to determine how complex films are in relation to the course's vocabulary. A standard foreign language course can contain, for example, from 1200 basic words to many thousands.

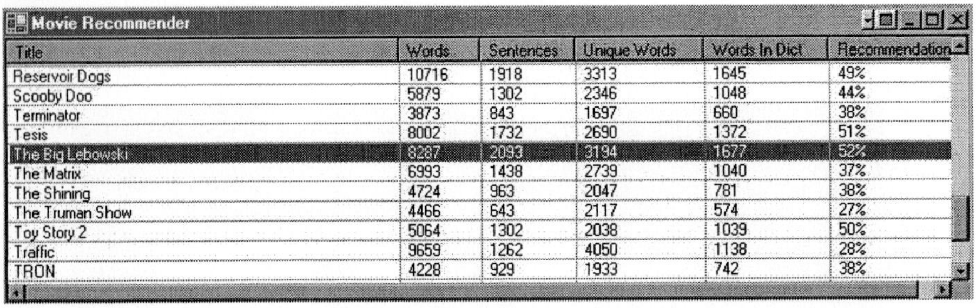

Movie Recommender					
Title	Words	Sentences	Unique Words	Words In Dict	Recommendation
Reservoir Dogs	10716	1918	3313	1645	49%
Scooby Doo	5879	1302	2346	1048	44%
Terminator	3873	843	1697	660	38%
Tesis	8002	1732	2690	1372	51%
The Big Lebowski	8287	2093	3194	1677	52%
The Matrix	6993	1438	2739	1040	37%
The Shining	4724	963	2047	781	38%
The Truman Show	4466	643	2117	574	27%
Toy Story 2	5064	1302	2038	1039	50%
Traffic	9659	1262	4050	1138	28%
TRON	4228	929	1933	742	38%

Fig. 2. Movie Recommender Desktop Interface.

Fig 2 shows the interface front-end of the recommender system, where the film "The Big Lebowski" is the film that contains most words or word repetitions (52%) from the user's dictionary and therefore has the highest recommendation percentage and, in principle, the student could have more possibilities to see/hear the vocabulary that is part of his/her course. The column "Words In Dict" represents the number of matches (with repetitions) between dictionary words and those in the film.. The column "Unique Words" represents the number of words in the films (without repetition). The comparisons are made using an approximate/fuzzy word by word comparison using the tool agrep.

Although there are existing recommender approaches and movie recommenders based on advanced text categorisation techniques [8], the basic heuristics employed here can be sufficient for the purpose of helping the students to identify the elemental features of the vocabulary in each film and help them to make a decision. The main purpose of the recommender is to make the students aware of how complex the vocabulary in a film is in relation to the vocabulary on their course.

2.3 Remote Control

The application, as it is designed for the living room, must have means of being controlled remotely. The PDA based Remote Control (RC) application includes the basic functions of a normal DVD player (start/stop/play, etc.). This functionality is accessible via the hardware buttons on the PDA. The RC connects to the main application on the computer via a wireless network. Further functionality of the RC is in a mock-up/prototyping stage in order to provide further interaction with the subtitles via the RC.

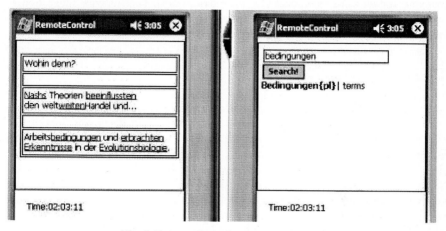

Fig. 3. Remote Control mock-up interface.

One more feature that is currently being prototyped, is to produce an interface that is able to display the subtitles on the PDA RC during the film. The aim of this interface is to enable the students to pause and to interact with the (foreign) text and read it as well from the PDA. For example, students can have the possibility of including the words that are not in the database (Fig 3) by selecting them with the PDA. As the film plays, the subtitles are displayed on the PDA.

When a word is selected on the PDA, the DVD pauses and the word is looked up in a dictionary, its meaning is retrieved and the database gets updated with the word. This interaction modality allows the students to further explore the meanings of words, allowing them to pause the film and reflect on the language used by the film.

3   Evaluation of the Initial Prototypes

With the current stage of development, the prototypes have been evaluated using an expert walkthrough and user feedback. A lecturer reviewed the system indicating the potential of the system as a complementary learning tool. As both subtitles are shown, students can learn new words and reinforce the ones that they already know with the possibility of observing how grammatically and semantically the expressions in both languages are constructed. Another observation that the lecturer remarked upon is that as the spoken dialogues can differ from the subtitles, students could reflect on these differences and that the system has the potential to be used as a complementary activity and aid on top of a structured foreign language course.

Students have also reviewed informally and used the system. The students commented that the system could have the potential of giving further use and bring a new dimension to their DVD collections as movies can be watched again not just for their entertainment value but also for their learning potential. However, students pointed out that having two subtitles displayed at the same time requires a lot of concentration in order to be able to follow the text and the audio track if there are many un-known words/sentences or if the movie is new. The students' suggestion was to watch the movie more than once in order to focus on different aspects of the movie first (story line, characters, etc) and then on the languages afterwards.

4 Summary and Future Work

This short paper has described the initial design of a system for complementing the study of a foreign language course based on the concept of displaying subtitles in 2 different languages during the viewing of a DVD based movie with the objective of vocabulary acquisition and reinforcement, complemented with listening and reading skills. The system incorporates a recommender system that facilitates the task of determining the richness of the vocabulary of a film in relation to the vocabulary used on the course and a PDA based remote control application. The system has been developed using an iterative design process involving practitioners, users and designers with the goal of producing an application that can be   used both for entertainment and for foreign language learning, and can be integrated into the living room and lifestyle of the students. Although the system is currently in a prototype stage and undergoing development, the stakeholders involved have shown interest in the concept and in the prototypes. Future work will include the enhancement of the functionality and usability of the remote control and the recommender system and further evaluation of the system as a learning aid. This work has been funded under the ERCIM Fellowship Program Num. 2003-20. The author would like to thank to all the members of IPSI-Ambiente for their ideas, suggestions and comments on early drafts of this paper and to all the learning stakeholders that participated directly or indirectly in this research.

References

1. Holmquist, L.E., Bjrk, S., Falk, J., Jaksetic, P., Ljungstrand, P., Redstrm, J.: What About Fun and Games? In Ljungberg, F. (ed.): Informatics in the Next Millennium, Lund: Student-litteratur, 1999.
2. Chapelle, C. A., Long, M. H., Richards, J. C.: Computer Applications in Second Language Acquisition. Cambridge University Press (2001).
3. The Disappearing Computer Initiative. http://www.disappearing-computer.net/.
4. Bell, G, Gemmell, J.: A Call For The Home Media Network. Communications of the ACM. 45(7), July 2002, 71-75.
5. BBC Learning. http://www.bbc.co.uk/learning/broadcast/
6. Pemberton L. 2002. The Potential of Interactive Television for Delivering Individualised Language Learning Future TV Workshop ITS 2002 conference in San Sebastian/Biarritz, June 2002.
7. Nakanishi, T.: Critical Literature Review on Motivation. Journal of Language and Linguistics. Vol. 1 No. 3 (2002).278 – 287.
8. Mak, H., Koprinska, I., Poon, J,: INTIMATE: A Web-Based Movie Recommender Using Text Categorization. IEEE/WIC International Conference on Web Intelligence (WI'03). October 13 - 17, 2003. Halifax, Canada.

CLOVES: A Virtual World Builder for Constructing Virtual Environments for Science Inquiry Learning

Yongjoo Cho[1], Kyoung Shin Park[2], Thomas Moher[3], Andrew E. Johnson[3],
Juno Chang[1], Min Cheol Whang[1], Joa Sang Lim[1], Dae-Woong Rhee[1],
Kang Ryoung Park[1], and Hung Kook Park[1]

[1] Sangmyung University, 7 Hongji-dong, Jongno-gu, Seoul, Korea
ycho@smu.ac.kr
[2] ICU Digital Media Lab, 517-10 Dogok-dong, Gangnam-gu, Seoul, Korea
[3] University of Illinois at Chicago, 851 S. Morgan, Chicago, IL, 60607, USA

Abstract. This paper presents the motivation, design, and a preliminary evaluation of a virtual world builder, CLOVES. CLOVES is designed to support rapid construction of data-rich virtual environments and instruments for young children's science inquiry learning. It provides a layered programming interface such as a visual design environment, scripting layer, and low-level application programming interface targeting for multiple levels of programming expertise. It is also intended to be a collaborative medium among interdisciplinary domain experts such as educators, modelers and software developers. A case study was conducted to evaluate the capabilities and effectiveness of CLOVES. The results showed that designers actively participated in decision making at every stage of the design process and shared knowledge among one another.

Keywords: Interactive learning, virtual reality environment

1 Introduction

While the real world offers myriad opportunities for children's scientific investigation, not all phenomena of interest are equally accessible. For instance, the curriculum topics that elementary school children might encounter in school—the possibility of life on Mars, the difference between ocean plant life in shallow and deep water, the way that bees communicate food sources—can only be experienced indirectly. Even when phenomena are readily accessible, nature does not always package them in ways that are conducive to student investigations. Consider visiting a local zoo to observe and take notes of chimpanzee's aggressive behavior and their response to aggression as part of a unit on animal behavior. A trip to a zoo does not guarantee that students will see instances of aggression within the context of "incidental" behavior. The teacher merely hopes that things would work out; it is beyond her power of control to make sure that the incidents happen.

These two issues—access and control—are the motivating forces behind a growing number of efforts to use virtual environments as a means of supplementing what nature makes readily available. Virtual environments hold out the possibility of doing

M. Rauterberg (Ed.): ICEC 2004, LNCS 3166, pp. 241–247, 2004.
© IFIP International Federation for Information Processing 2004

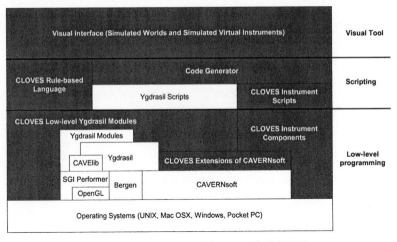

Fig. 1. Three tiered architecture of CLOVES

"first-person" science, investigating phenomena that would not otherwise be accessible, and focusing on the salient features of those phenomena that address curricular goals.

There have been many efforts of using virtual environments for education. Some results showed that the learning effects were at least equivalent to, and sometimes better than, that were achieved by traditional classroom methods. Despite the promise, children's access to virtual environments as a vehicle for formal learning is still limited to laboratory research projects and research augmented schools settings. This is partially due to the expense and fragility of contemporary VR systems, but it is not difficult to foresee a day when such technologies fall within the scope of real school budgets, and are sufficiently reliable for direct use by teachers.

The larger problem is the complexity of constructing the kinds of virtual environments that would support student learning in science. The development of the *Round Earth* application [4], for example, took almost a year, as application specifications evolved and programmers worked with low-level graphical tools to respond to requested changes in the application. The emergence of *world-builder* applications over the past decade has facilitated the construction of virtual environments. Systems such as Ygdrasil [6] and Alice [2] have been successful at raising the "level of discourse" to objects instead of computer graphics primitives; the use of Ygdrasil, for example, allowed the developers to build the *Field* [5] in half the time of *Round Earth*.

Traditionally, many world builders support the construction of virtual environments that are designed primarily to develop applications that highlight the experience of *being* in a virtual environment rather than *learning* in it. The construction of *learner-centered* [7] virtual environments, in contrast, necessarily begins with an analysis of the pedagogical requirements that in turn act as drivers for the features of those environments. From our experience of building several educational virtual environments, however, the most difficult problem we encountered was inviting educators into the design process and helping them understand and participate into the construction of virtual worlds. Due to the specialized complexity of construction process of virtual environments, the design was largely driven by software developers. This caused the isolation of educators who did not have enough knowledge to understand the distinctive vocabularies and processes of the construction.

This paper presents the motivation, design and preliminary assessment of a new virtual world builder, CLOVES (Construction of Layer Oriented Virtual Environments for Science inquiry learning). CLOVES is designed to help collaborative design among multidisciplinary designers such as educators, programmers, and modelers by providing construction affordances in terms of accessible across disciplines and by making visible the effects of design decisions at every stage of development. CLOVES allows designers to rapidly prototype and construct environments that either could not be built using contemporary world-builders or would instead require access to lower-level tools that would greatly extend the development time of such applications.

2 CLOVES as a Virtual World Builder

Fig. 1 shows the detail design and architecture of CLOVES. The main design features in CLOVES are a three-tiered toolkit that ranges from high-level authoring tool to low-level programming APIs and an integrated environment that supports creating virtual worlds, underlying simulation systems, and various sub-tools needed for investigating newly constructed virtual ambient environments. CLOVES implements three layers of interfaces and functionality that aim at different expertise of designers (Fig. 1). CLOVES provides a higher-level visual interface that allows novice users to build a simulated world with stock objects, rules, and scripts. CLOVES also serves a simple visual interface that helps users create the user-interface of virtual instruments by laying out existing instrumental components. Intermediate programmers can create more complex simulated worlds by using the scripting tools provided in CLOVES, Ygdrasil, and an instrument scripting system. The lowest level of CLOVES consists of a component-based framework that helps advanced programmers to extend the visual interface, scripting language, and versatile instrument components.

CLOVES supports the development of large and densely populated virtual environments. Populating the objects in a large virtual environment by hand is difficult and time-consuming process. CLOVES provides several ways, both visual and non-visual, to populate a large number of objects quickly. Its visual interface is inspired from other 2D drawing applications and allows easy population and manipulation of objects on a 2D-based workspace. It also allows more sophisticated and automated population through its rule-based scripting tool.

CLOVES supports the development of data-rich virtual environments in which objects and the environment itself have embedded properties, which form the grist for student investigations. Designers can bind constant property values to an object template and populate the instances of the object within the virtual world. CLOVES supports the design of virtual instruments. Not all phenomena of interest are visible to human eye; using CLOVES, designers can provide access to invisible phenomena to learners through the use of handheld instruments that "sense" the properties of the simulation.

CLOVES supports the creation of virtual environments which allow the investigation of three-dimensional phenomena. Using CLOVES, designers can create environments that consist of multiple levels, such as the *Ocean* application, which includes both shallow (coral reef) and deep-sea regions. CLOVES borrowed the concept of layers from other 2-D drawing applications and extended it to the 3-D worlds. A layer is defined as a block of area whose size must be the same as the size of the world and provides a way to organize the objects and regions within the CLOVES' visual interface. Layers can also be used to represent the different levels of a 3-D world (i.e., shallow and deep regions of an Ocean environment) that allows designers to construct a 3-D world using a 2-D interface.

CLOVES supports the participation of educators in the earliest stages of the design process. Virtual ambients are *not* instructional plans; they are spaces within which activities may be designed. It is nonetheless essential that educators inform the design of those spaces if they are to use them as components of instruction. CLOVES can act as a *medium* for collaborative design among educators, programmers, and modelers by providing construction affordances in terms accessible across disciplines, and by making visible the effects of design decisions at every stage of development.

3   Building a "Meteors on Mars" World Using CLOVES

A third grade elementary school teacher and a computer science graduate student participated in a preliminary evaluation of CLOVES. The elementary school teacher, Betty, was a naïve computer user, who reported that she mostly used her computer for checking e-mail and word-processing. Armando, the graduate student in computer science, had an especially strong background in the physical sciences; he was an undergraduate chemistry major, and had on several occasions given demonstrations to Betty's students. They both had prior experience with the use of virtual ambient environments in the classroom; Betty's third-grade class had used the *Bee Dance* [3] application, and Armando was responsible for the design of learning assessments associated with that unit. Neither had experience in the design of virtual worlds.

Betty and Armando had met eight meetings over the course of two months to construct the Martian world using CLOVES; each meeting lasted 60-90 minutes. The main author was present at each of the meetings, serving a dual role as application specialist and observer of the design process. At the end of each meeting, the designers completed a short survey form to describe what media they had used and what they had accomplished in the meeting. During the initial session, the designers were introduced to CLOVES, guided through all available resources for their uses, articulated learning goals, brainstormed a storyline and a new world based on the learning goals, and designed activity plans for students. During the four sessions, the designers constructed an activity plan that is following:

Is there life on Mars? Scientists believe that the presence of water is necessary to sustain life. To find water in Mars, we chose to dig up the softer areas of the planet first. One place where the surface gets "softened up" is where meteors strike on the planet. Unfortunately, most of the meteor impacts happened on Mars a long time ago, and erosion has made it difficult to see, with your eyes. Fortunately, when an asteroid hits the surface, it breaks down to small rocks that are spread around and creates certain elliptical contours around the impacted area. The rocks form the asteroid also shows higher value of iridium elements than other rocks that were already on Mars.

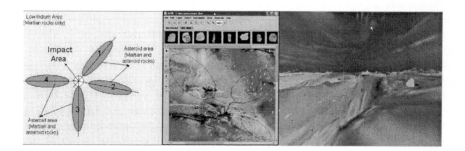

Fig. 2. Finding the impact area of asteroid (left), populated rocks in CLOVES (center) and the generated virtual world from CLOVES (right).

Thus, by checking the iridium values, children can find the contours on the Mars. When they find the elliptical contour, they are supposed to draw a line that crosses the furthest two points of the elliptical shape. When they draw lines from all elliptical shapes they find on the surface, they should be able to see the intersected points of those lines, which is the impact location of asteroid.

Then, during the sessions 4-7, the designers exclusively used CLOVES to build the Martian world and virtual instruments that would allow users to probe the values of chemicals of the rocks on Mars (see Fig. 2). A few deficiencies of CLOVES were found during the sessions, but the author of CLOVES was able to fix the problems or add new features to the environment between each session.

Betty faced a much more formidable learning task. In addition to her self-reported unease with using computers, she confronted new vocabulary both in programming (e.g., objects, properties) and mathematics (e.g., ellipses, polygons). Betty's notes and questionnaire responses reflect her process of getting acquainted herself with the terminology of CLOVES and the tool itself. During the first session, Betty began to use the term "object" freely, and (by the last of six pages of hand-written notes) she wrote about "populating the world" with objects, and that "properties or values are put in by us [the designers]." She made reference to a "rules box," but didn't seem to yet have a clear understanding of how rules related to the task at hand. During the next two sessions, Betty expanded her vocabulary markedly. She began to use terms such as "pixel," "properties," "pull-down," and "scale [an object]," and began to be familiar with concepts such as proximity-based sensing and the distinction between local and global properties.

Over the remainder of the design sessions, Betty continued to grow in her understanding of new vocabulary and concepts. While she preferred to let Armando do most of the direct user interaction with CLOVES, she was a full participant in each decision, and demonstrated a strong understanding of all of the sub-tasks (e.g., object placement, attribute binding, rule specification). Betty also made a suggestion to a problem of object attribute binding, which was adopted and used to resolve the problem. Her suggestion strongly shows that she understood and participated actively in the design process, which was a strong indication of making the "common ground" among designers.

This case study showed that Betty and Armando's experience was productive on several fronts. CLOVES got both functional and usability improvements through their design efforts. The most exciting outcome of the preliminary evaluation, however, was Betty's internalization of the concepts and vocabulary introduced in CLOVES, especially for someone who characterized herself as uncomfortable with technical materials. While Betty was a willing participant, there was relatively little expectation that she would adopt the language used in CLOVES, rather than requiring continuous efforts to "translate these things into her terms," as Armando put it. That she was able to articulate an innovative solution to a technical limitation of CLOVES reflected deep learning, in that she was able to take her new knowledge and apply it productively [1].

4 Conclusion

This paper described the motivation, design, and a preliminary evaluation of using CLOVES. CLOVES is designed to promote the non-programmer's participation in the design process of interactive learning environments even if they do not have enough knowledge in programming and virtual reality technology. To accomplish the goal, CLOVES borrowed the visual interface of 2D-based drawing tools and showed the effects of design decisions at every stage of development. The evaluation showed that the designers got to the point where they could construct the common ground of vocabularies and knowledge through CLOVES. Although it would be difficult to generalize the result of this study for other users, CLOVES' visual interface certainly helped educators be involved in the design process and share their knowledge with other designers. In particular, that Betty was able to understand and express the terms in a programmer level was remarkable. Further investigations will be made to evaluate and improve CLOVES and how it can help non-programmers understand and participate the development process of other educational virtual environments.

References

1. Bransford, J.D., Brown, A.L. & Cocking, R.R.: How People Learn: Brain, Mind, Experience, and School. Washington, DC: National Academy Press (1999)
2. Conway, M. J., Alice: Easy-to-Learn 3D Scripting for Novices. Ph. D. Thesis, School of Engineering and Applied Science, University of Virginia, December 1997.
3. Haas, D.: The Honeybee Dance: Classroom-based Science Discovery in a Simulated Environment, M.S. Thesis, University of Illinois at Chicago (2002).
4. Moher, T., Johnson, A., Ohlsson, S., Gillingham, M.: Bridging Strategies for VR-Based Learning. In Proceedings of ACM Conference on Human Factors in Computing Systems (CHI '99), pages 536-543, 1999
5. Moher, T., Johnson, A., Cho, Y., Lin, Y.: Observation-based Inquiry in a Virtual Ambient Environment. In Proceedings of International Conference of the Learning Sciences (2000) 238-245

6. Pape, D.: Composing Networked Virtual Environments, Ph. D. Dissertation, University of Illinois at Chicago (2001)
7. Soloway , E., Guzdial, M. and Hay, K.: Learner Centered Design: The Challenge for HCI in the 21st Century . Interactions;1(2): 36-48, 1994.

SEITV – Interactive Multimedia Leisure/Educational Services for Digital TV in MHP

Julián Flórez[1], Igor García[1], Iker Aizpurua[1], Céline Paloc[1], Alejandro Ugarte[1],
Igor Jainaga[2], Jesús Colet[3], and Xabier Zubiaur[4]

[1] VICOMTech, Visual Communication Technologies, Mikeletegi pasealekua 57,
Donostia – San Sebastian, E-20009, Basque Country, Spain
iolaizola@vicomtech.es
http://www.vicomtech.es
[2] Euskal Telebista, 48215 Iurreta, Basque ÿercede
[3] Redox ÿercedesÿa, Las ÿercedes 5, dpto1, 48930 Las Arenas (Bizkaia), Spain
[4] Euskaltel, Parque Tecnológico, 207-48170 Zamudio (Bizkaia), Spain

Abstract. Interactive TV is expected to revolutionize the TV market, providing a host of new services to the consumer homes. While being theoretically a promising technology, the design and implementation of interactive TV platforms are bringing new challenges to the IT society, due to the fundamental differences between TV sets and PCs environments. The SEITV project is presented in this paper, where a set of design considerations for interactive digital TV have been analyzed and applied to the creation of interactive services for entertainment and education.

1 Introduction

Digital Television allows the delivery of application data together with audio and video contents, which makes possible to provide interactive services using the TV sets. Interactive digital television (iTV) seems to be a very promising technology, providing a large range of new services to the TV user population. While several studies have predicted an explosion of the iTV market [1], the actual development of valuable applications presents several challenges which still need to be overcome.

Theoretically, digital TV offers a new platform for services which are currently supported by PC environments. However, the underlying technology differs in ways which greatly influence the iTV applications design strategy. Moreover, iTV applications target a far more diverse user population, whose demographics, skills and goals significantly differ from those of computer users.

As a consequence, the applications designed to be displayed in TV sets cannot be directly ported from PC-oriented designs. When developing an application for digital TV, one of the most important tasks is thus to identify the requirements and constraints of iTV environments.

There has been so far little work on developing applications specifically designed for iTV. Current research is mostly focused on qualitative studies, outlining the theoretical requirements for digital TV [2]. As for concrete applications, previous efforts have been mainly limited to merging TV with computers. The most popular are WebTV applications, which also have TV interfaces, but focus on TV as an

M. Rauterberg (Ed.): ICEC 2004, LNCS 3166, pp. 248–253, 2004.

appliance for web browsing and are limited by Internet to a reduced number of users [3]. On the other hand, the digital TV broadcast allows to transmit data to millions of users simultaneously. This opens new horizons for the multimedia content providers.

Digital TV is also opening up opportunities for interactive learning services to reach mass audiences. A new study, recently published by the European Commission, assesses the market potential for interactive TV learning services to the home [4]. The biggest challenge is making TV learning exciting and relevant enough to turn passive viewers into active learners.

The SEITV was a research project aimed at establishing a methodology for the creation of an iTV application focusing on adapting the technological and user differences from PC to TV environments. Our method was applied to the development of a prototype providing multimedia educational/entertainment interactive services through games and quizzes in order to motivate people to learn. Our application is currently being evaluated in real conditions by the main Basque TV company ETB and cable operator Euskatel.

2 Methods

The development of our iTV edutainment platform started with the implementation of a PC-oriented application of an educational game based on quizzes. Once ported to a TV set, this first version proved to be unsatisfying, and later versions were improved taking into account the constraints and requirements of TV environment.

One of the main tasks of the SEITV project was thus to analyze and evaluate the fundamental differences of design and implementation applications between TV and PC environments. As a result of our study, this section provides our guidelines to satisfy iTV constraints and the implementation details of our final edutainment prototype.

2.1 Hardware

Digital TV represents fundamentally new technology from the computer [5]. At the heart of iTV is the Set-Top Box (STB). The primary purpose of this box is to convert the digital signal it receives (via satellite, terrestrial broadcast or cable) into video and audio to play through the TV set [6].

Due to the need to minimize their manufacturing cost (they are usually provided by the subscriber at little or no cost), STBs have much less computing power than their home PC contemporaries. Furthermore, a TV set presents several differences to a computer monitor, which imply some rethinking of the interface design for iTV [7]. The considerations of these hardware differences in our implementation will be discussed in details in the next sections.

In the SEITV project, we focused on Phase Alternating Line (PAL) TV sets, as being the dominant European television standard. We chose to adopt an architecture based on Digital Terrestrial Television (DTT) network using standard DVB-MHP compliant STBs.

At each stage of the implementation, the application was tested in 4 different TV sets and 2 different STBs to ensure satisfying output, independently of the nature of the hardware devices.

2.2 Graphical Interface

Resolution and Overscan. The availability of screen real estate is an important issue in interface design. In iTV, it becomes an overriding concern, as TV sets have much lower resolution (720 x 576) than computer monitors (1054 x768). Moreover, the TV screen "safe area" is smaller than a computer monitor. This area also greatly varies on each TV screen. To avoid these problems, we chose to place all the important objects on the center area and keeping free about 10% of the outer area while filling the whole area with the background.

Visual acuity zone. Even more important than the physical screen size and resolution, another factor to be considered in the iTV design is the visual acuity zone. The effective resolution also depends on the viewing distance, measured by the so-called the visual angle (arctan of size/distance) providing a measure of image size on the eye's retina. Since TV users sit relatively far from the screen, their viewing area has a small visual angle even though the physical screen might be larger [8].

In the SEITV project, several attempts have been made in order to reach a high image quality on the TV screen and a comfortable reading. All of the combinations have been simultaneously tested on different TV screens, so that the final graphical interface can be viewed comfortably while sitting at several meters away.

Interlacing. The interlacing scanning of TV screens can produce flickering effects if the graphic design has not been adapted. Because of the two sets of scan lines, a very thin horizontal will flicker on video. All horizontal lines should thus be 3 or 4 pixels thick or greater to appear correctly on the screen. Our solution to reduce flicker consists of averaging lines or drawing parts of two horizontal thin lines simultaneously.

For the same reason, objects with hard horizontal edges also tend to flicker. To reduce the appearance of flickering, we applied a slight vertical blur of .5 or 1 to soften the edge. Anti-aliasing techniques can also help reducing flickering effects.

Colour. TV screens are not suitable for bright colours. Saturated colours must be also controlled [9] and not to exceed 80% in saturation level [10]. In the SEITV prototype, we adopted the use of pastel colours, which have given satisfying results on the TV screen. In order to insert text fields, we changed the luminance level between the background and the foreground colours.

Animation. As described previously, the hardware capabilities of STBs are currently limited. It is therefore difficult to obtain advanced animations for digital TV. However, additional techniques such as double buffering can help to perform simple animations. Within the SEITV project, a moving smiley have been implemented with satisfying results. Technical improvements of current STBs can expect to provide more advanced animations in the near future.

2.3 Input Device

The interface design has been a very important question in this project. In particular, the input device has been a major factor in the interface design. As keyboard or mouse are not appropriate for TV environments, the interactivity must be performed through the remote control keypad containing labelled buttons. Colour buttons provide an intuitive and fast way to interact with the application and the number buttons can be used if more options are required. 14 different options can easily be selected with one press event. Therefore, we believe that the remote control should not be a limitation if the interface is well designed.

In the last version of the SEITV project, careful consideration has been given to the layout and alignment of the navigation components in the game panel to enhance clarity, ease of use, and aesthetic appeal. For instance, the navigation buttons were placed in the order in which people read them and grouped together as logically related components. A clearer and most consistent layout streamlines the way users move through the application and helps them utilize its features efficiently.

2.4 Broadcast and Return Channel

In pure broadcast applications, the same information is transmitted by the broadcaster to all the receivers. But each user decides how to interact with the application. In this case, there are some limitations in the interactivity. For instance, it is not possible to upload any information and it is also almost impossible to personalize contents or service behaviours. The information flows in only one way and any feedback loop is not possible. The main advantage of pure broadcast applications is the fact that nothing more than the STBs is needed to run the application and that there are no costs associated to telephone connection. It is a good solution for information services like general news, games, etc...

When the return channel feature is added, the STB must have a modem or net adaptor connected to Internet. It increases the price of the devices and forces to make an installation before using the STB. However, the feedback loop allows to upload any information to a server and the interactivity level can be increased. It becomes possible to vote, to buy, to bet, to send the best scores obtained in a game, etc... The feedback loop can also be used to download the specific information requested by each user and all the services can then be personalized.

The application developed in the SEITV project can be run with or without any feedback loop. If the return channel exists, the application offers more possibilities and allows to send the scores obtained by each user. In this case, a server collects all the data and the broadcaster can transmit the winner's name er and the maximal score.

2.5 Application Size

As mentioned earlier, current STBs present limited hardware capabilities in comparison to PCs. For example, many home computers are operating over 1000 MHz, and 128Mb of RAM; in contrast, current STBs typically operate at up to50 MHz with a little as 8Mb of RAM available to applications. The different tests performed in the scope of the SEITV project showed that the application's size should stay under 1Mb to reach satisfying performance with standard hardware devices.

Another reason to keep the application's size low is to minimize the loading time of the transmission carrousel. Good carrousel designs can help to avoid delays.

In any case, the application should be designed to reach the best performance. In the SEITV project, the pictures have been optimized within the application, by reducing number of colours and resolution and by reusing the background when possible.

2.6 DVB-MHP Standard

Multimedia Home Platform (MHP) is the open and horizontal standard for interactive digital TV [11]. This standard is increasingly being supported by the international broadcasting industry as well as by governments. MHP has been combined with the Digital Video Broadcasting (DVB), the European standard for Digital TV [12].

In the SEITV project, several STBs have been tested to ensure that the developed applications are fully compliant to the DVB-MHP standard and that the current STBs are able to support these interactive services.

3   Prototype

As part of the SEITV project, the guidelines described in the previous section have been applied to the development of an iTV prototype. We focused on providing interactive services for digital television edutainment, i.e. a mix of entertainment content and other information to create a learning context. The project's ultimate goal is to establish the potential of interactive television as an entertainment and educational tool.

The application consists of a game whose content is enriched by a set of "tests", that the user has to pass to be able to go forward in the game. In the current implementation, each test corresponds to a question of general or specific knowledge. The user can select the nature of the questions. A snapshot of one of the game's pictures is shown in the Figure 1. In order to successfully complete this project, VICOMTech collaborated with the company Redox Multimedia (specialized in the development of multimedia content, mainly in CD support), Euskaltel (the most important telephone company in the Basque Country) and the Basque TV company EiTB. The final application has been tested in the Digital TV laboratory of VICOMTech in the DVB-C modulation and in a real DTT broadcast session made by ETB according to the DVB-T MHP standard. The different tests gave satisfying results, providing a valuable tool for digital television edutainment.

4   Conclusion

We described a set of guidelines for designing valuable iTV applications, focusing on the areas where digital TV differs significantly from computers, such as the hardware limitations, the TV sets constraints, and the greater population diversity.

Following these guidelines, a prototype was developed which aims at providing interactive services for edutainment context. The first testing of the current implementation has produced satisfying results. A fully integrated system can expect to provide a robust and valuable edutainment iTV platform for widespread use and to help bridge the digital divide.

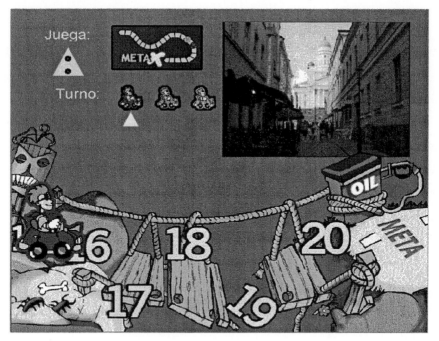

Fig. 1. Graphical Design example of the MHP application

References

1.   Srivastava,H.O.: Interactive TV technology and markets. (2002)
2.   European Conference on Interactive Television,
     http://www.it.brighton.ac.uk/interactive/euroitv
3.   Your website on television, http://www.e-envoy.gov.uk/
4.   Atwere D. and Bates P.: Interactive TV – a learning platform with potential (2003)
     http://www.lsda.org.uk/files/pdf/1443.pdf
5.   Benoit, H.: Digital Television, MPEG-1, MPEG-2 and principles of the DVB system.
     (2002)
6.   O'Driscoll, G.:The essential guide to digital set-top boxes and interactive TV. (2000)
7.   Poyton, C: Digital video and HDTV, algorithms and interfaces. (2003)
8.   Siggraph 2000 Introduction to the Human Visual System,
     http://www.vr.clemson.edu/eyetracking/sigcourse/
9.   Hartman, A.: Producing interactive television. (2002)
10. The MSN TV Developer Support Site, http://developer.msntv.com
11. DVB-MHP: Digital Video Broadcasting - Multimedia Home Platform (DVB-MHP)
     Standard, http://www.mhp.org/
12. DVB: Digital Video Broadcasting Standard, http://www.dvb.org/

Tangible Augmented Reality Modeling

Ja Yong Park and Jong Weon Lee

Sejong University, Digital Contents,
98 Gunja-Dong, Gwangjin-Gu, Seoul, 143-747 Republic of Korea
jayong95@hanmail.net, jwlee@sejong.ac.kr

Abstract. A Tangible Augmented Reality Modeling (TARM) system is a novel modeling system that uses Augmented Reality (AR) and Tangible User Interface (TUI). The TARM system provides users a unique interactive approach to create 3D models. AR and TUI are applied to mimic real-life interactions. A user creates models by manipulating physical blocks. The patterns in the real environment are captured and applied to models in real time to enhance reality. The system also provides a real pen to draw curves or surfaces directly on models. Using these approaches, the TARM system provides users natural ways to create models and allows novice users to create models easily and quickly with little practice.

1 Introduction

Augmented Reality (AR) adds virtual objects into real environment and displays the result in real time. Recently, many researchers are interested in AR, and the basic AR technologies are become feasible [1], [9]. Additionally few softwares providing basic AR functionalities are opened to public, so system developers can concentrate on developing applications without too much worrying about the basic AR technologies. Due to these changes, it has become possible to apply AR in various areas including medical, assembly, modeling, mobile and collaboration.

Few modeling systems have been developed using AR. Cheok et al. [2] create surface models by tracking user's hands. Fiorento et al. [3], [5] augmented virtual objects to real physical objects for the engineering and manufacturing evaluations. Lee et al. [7] proposes an AR-based modeling system that removes the mental separation between real and virtual workspaces. The system provides interactive methods to manipulate a model, to create new models or to deform existing models. ArtNova [4] applies textures onto 3D surfaces directly by brush strokes. These systems use free-form curves or curved surfaces or augmented virtual objects or texture information to real physical objects. In this paper, we present an innovative tangible AR modeling system that creates 3D models from manipulating real blocks.

There exist many modeling softwares. Users can create complex objects using these modeling softwares, but there is a high entry barrier. These modeling softwares are complicate and do not provide intuitive interfaces, so they require a lot of training even if a user only wants to create simple objects. In order to overcome these

M. Rauterberg (Ed.): ICEC 2004, LNCS 3166, pp. 254–259, 2004.

shortcomings, we developed a Tangible Augmented Reality Modeling (TARM) system based on AR and TUI.

The TARM system is a new modeling system with a low entry barrier. A user can create models with almost no training. The user creates models by stacking real blocks like a child uses LEGO blocks to create simple objects. The tangible user interface in AR environment enables the user to perform intuitive interaction and to understand spatial relationships of models. The TARM system also allows creating and storing partial models and then combining them together to model a larger object. A more complex object can be modeled by scaling partial models before combining them. To enhance the reality, the system provides the way to extract patterns from the real environment in real time and to apply the patterns to virtual objects. By applying this procedure, the user can create more realistic expression from a simplified model. When the details of the objects cannot be expressed by applying the described procedures, the user can add curves and surfaces using a real-pen interface.

The organization of the paper is as follows. After the introduction in section 1, section 2 describes the characteristics of the system. The way to model 3D objects is explained in section 3. The experiment results are presented in section 4, and the conclusion is given in section 5.

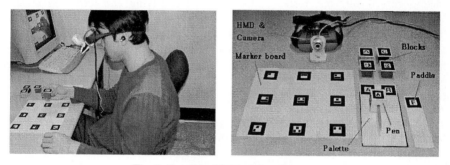

Fig. 1. Tangible AR Modeling System.

2   Tangible AR Modeling System

Tangible Augmented Reality Modeling (TARM) system is developed based on AR and TUIs and provides spatial perception to users (Fig. 1). The system allows the user to manipulate virtual objects by manipulating physical ones in real environment. The positions and orientations of markers and user's head are computed using ARToolKit [6], [10].

The proposed modeling system pursues to provide intuitive modeling to users and to create approximate models but with enhanced reality. The system offers natural interactions and spatial perception, so the modeling procedures are intuitive and easy. Novice users can use the system and create 3D models in relatively short time with brief introduction.

2.1 Tangible User Interfaces (TUIs)

The central characteristic of TUIs is the coupling of physical representations to underlying digital information and computational models [7], [8]. The physical embodiment of TUIs makes digital information directly manipulable with our hands and naturally perceptible through our peripheral senses. In the proposed system, these characteristics of TUIs are used to model 3D objects. The TUIs used in the proposed system are a block, a pen, a palette and a paddle.

Blocks. Real blocks are used to manipulate corresponding virtual blocks. The four cube blocks represent four basic types of virtual blocks of the TARM system, a cube, a cylinder, a cone and a sphere. Initially, the size of a virtual block is equal to the size of the real block for realistic manipulation, but the size of a virtual block can be adjusted according to the size of a model in consideration using a pen interface.

Pen. A pen is available for various user-system interactions. The interface is used to choose a palette menu, to choose a block, to apply the chosen menu and to draw a picture. The chosen menu is displayed on the head-part of the pen (Fig. 2).

Palette. A palette (Fig. 2(b)) is an interface that provides various menus. Providing functions are selecting colors and textures, drawing curves and curved surfaces, deleting curved surfaces, resizing block sizes, and saving and retrieving created models.

Paddle. A paddle is an interface that moves any displayed virtual models. The paddle has been used to move a model to the side areas of the working space, so a new job can be started at the main area of the working space. The paddle also brings the model back to the working space from the side area to combine it with another model to create a bigger one.

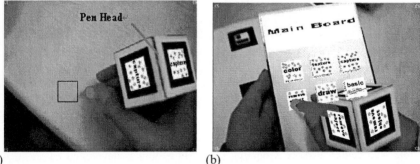

(a)   (b)

Fig. 2. Pen and palette interfaces: (a) capturing the texture in real environment and displaying the chosen menu on the head-part of the pen (b) selecting a menu of the palette using the pen.

3 3D Modeling Method

Modeling is achieved by manipulating the tangible user interfaces (TUIs). The user holds and manipulates real blocks to model 3D shapes. The user can also combine or move partial models for assembling or re-positioning. The system allows users to extract texture and color information from the real environment in real time (Fig. 2(a)) and then to apply the information to the virtual objects to enhance the reality. The system also offers additional functionalities to draw curves on the surface of the blocks or draw surfaces directly in the real environment.

3.1 Modeling Using Real Blocks

Because modeling is done by stacking or removing virtual blocks using a real block in the real environment, it can significantly improve accomplishment in a virtual manipulation task, and the spatial relationship is better understood by a user compared with using mouse or keyboard interfaces. When a physical block is close to a virtual block of the model, the face color of the virtual block is changed to indicate that the new block can be attached to that part of the model. If user stays the real block for a moment at the same location, a new virtual block is generated and attached on that face of the model.

3.2 Generating Curves and Curved Surface

A pen interface is used as an input device to draw curves and curved surfaces (Fig. 3). Using the computed positions of the pen interface, curves can be drawn on the surface of the virtual block, and curved surfaces can be generated on the working space. Because of the limitations on the accuracy of position measurements, only simple figures can be drawn currently.

Fig. 3. Drawing curves and curved surfaces.

3.3 Assembling Partial Models

The paddle is used to combine two small models to create a bigger one. In order to assemble two small models, the first model should be created and moved to the side by the paddle. After creating the second model, the relocated first model is assembled with second model by the paddle (Fig. 4). This assembling procedure can be repeated until creating a desired model. Because the virtual block generated by the system is equal to the size of the physical block and the system has the limited working volume on account of the limitations on the tracking, scaling is available for adjusting the size of a model or altering the parts of a virtual model. For generating a large or complex model, scaling and assembling procedures are employed.

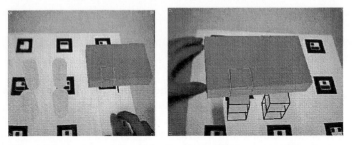

Fig. 4. Moving a partial model using the paddle to create a bigger one.

4   Experiments

Several users with little or no experience in modeling systems participate in the experiment, which tests the usability of the TARM system. The users had no difficulty with the interface. They used them naturally to generate 3D models. They were able to create interesting models using TARM system with little effort and training. A few examples of their work are given in Fig. 5. The video clip and some more examples are available at:
http://dasan.sejong.ac.kr/~jwlee/contents/TARM/TARM.htm.

Fig. 5. A sofa and the Dabotop, the national treasure tower in Korea

5   Conclusion

In this paper, we propose a new 3D modeling system using the tangible user interface on the AR environment. The Tangible AR Modeling (TARM) system has some limitations on modeling complex shapes, which is available in existing modeling programs. However, the TARM system allows users to model 3D objects easily and intuitively, so the system could be used by anyone with a short introduction. The system also enhances reality by acquiring a texture of the target object and by adding the texture to the model of the target object in real time. This is important because a simple model with appropriate texture could enhance the reality to the user. Mainly the TARM system is for a novice user who wants to create models quickly with little effort.

Acknowledgement. This paper was performed for the Intelligent Robotics Development Program, one of the 21st Century Frontier R&D Programs funded by the Ministry of Science and Technology of Korea.

References

1. Azuma, R., Baillot, Y., Behringer, R., Feiner, S., Julier, S., MacIntyre, B.: Recent Advances in Augmented Reality. In IEEE Computer Graphics and Applications, 25(6):24-35, Nov-Dec 2001.
2. Cheok, A. D., Edmund, N. W. C., Eng, A. W.: Inexpensive Non-Sensor Based Augmented Reality Modeling of Curves and Surfaces in Physical Space. Int. Symposium on Mixed and Augmented Reality (ISMAR'02) , September 30 - October 01, 2002.
3. Fiorentino, M., De Amicis, R., Stork, A., Monno G.: Spacedesign: A Mixed Reality Workspace for Aesthetic Industrial Design. Proc. of ISMAR 2002 IEEE and ACM International Symposium on Mixed and Augmented Reality, pp. 86-94, Sept. 30 - Oct. 1, 2002.
4. Foskey, M., Otaduy, M. A., Lin, M. C.: ArtNova: Touch-Enable 3D Model Design. IEEE Virtual Reality Conference 2002, March 24-28, 2002.
5. Ishii, H., Ullmer, B: Tangible Bits: Towards Seamless Interfaces between People, Bits and Atoms. In Proc. Of CHI'97, ACM Press, 234-241.
6. Kato, H.: Inside ARToolKit. http://iihm.imag.fr/fberard/ens/ensimag/ensi3srvra/download/docTechnique/ART02-Tutorial.pdf
7. Lee, J., Hirota, G., State, A.: Modeling Real Objects Using Video See-through Augmented Reality. University of North Carolina at Chapel Hill, 2002.
8. Ullmer, B., Ishii, H.: Emerging frameworks for tangible user interfaces. IBM System Journal, Vol 39, NOS 3&4, 2000.
9. Woodrow, B., Thomas, C.: Fundamentals of Wearable Computers and Augmented Reality. Lawrenge Erlbaum Associates, Inc., Publishers 2001.
10. Shared Space/ARToolKit Download Page, http://www.hitl.washington.edu/research/shared_space/download/

Human Body Tracking for Human Computer Intelligent Interaction

Jong-Seung Park and Sang-Rak Lee

Dept. of Computer Science and Engineering, University of Incheon,
177 Dohwa-dong, Nam-gu, Incheon, 402-749, Republic of Korea
{jong,srlee}@incheon.ac.kr

Abstract. For interactive mixed reality applications, a novel human body detection and tracking method is presented. The method automatically detects moving body regions and tracks them continuously until they disappear from the camera field of view. Two main cues, skin color and motion, are used to track visual attentions. The method can be used for applications of the attention based human-computer interfaces where attentions are mostly focused on human body parts. In our experiments, the method provided correct results whenever at least a patch of moving body parts was disclosed with skin color.

1 Introduction

To benefit human computer interface, it is important that both machine and human find the same sorts of perceptual features interesting. The use of human body motions, especially face motions and hand gestures, has become an important way of human computer interactions.

Human body tracking has been considered as a promising means in human-computer interaction and augmented reality [1]. The body tracking has been recognized as an essential prerequisite for robust human motion recognition. For the robust human body tracking system, both a stable bootstrap body detection module and a robust body tracking module are required. Since there are a great number of deformations and variations in body parts, postures, skin colors, lighting conditions, and clothes, human body detection and tracking has been considered as a difficult problem to put into practical use. To reduce the complexity, many previous works have focused on some specific topics such as face tracking, hand gesture tracking, and marker tracking. Most previous approaches make the assumption that people perform actions while they are in an upright-standing posture and researchers have been focused on detecting, tracking and understanding human actions [2][3].

In a human-computer interface a computer cannot handle every situations caused by human actions. For a real-time interactive application, to reduce the amount of computation, it is necessary for the computer to limit the visual field of interests to the attention focused regions. The motivation of our research is to find the most interesting body parts and focus the machine attention only onto the selected parts.

In our target applications the attention is limited to parts of human beings. Specifically our system finds some human body parts that are most interesting and

M. Rauterberg (Ed.): ICEC 2004, LNCS 3166, pp. 260–265, 2004.
© IFIP International Federation for Information Processing 2004

tracks them continuously until they disappear from the camera field of view. Our method detects human body parts from several consecutive image frames without any strict constraints on the environment. Recently it is shown that multi-cue tracking can increase the robustness of a visual tracking system [4]. In our system, two critical cues, skin color and motion, are used to track visual attentions. As well as the static camera, the moving camera is also supported with the same algorithm. The method is robust to occlusion of some body parts and insensitive to variations of skin boundaries.

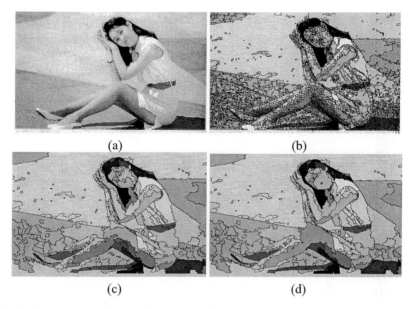

(a)   (b)

(c)   (d)

Fig. 1. Region segmentation and merging: (a) an input image frame, (b) Watershed segmentation results, (c) region merging results using region homogeneity, (d) region merging results using curve segments.

2   Detecting Human Body Parts

Since image frames are the only information available to find the region of interests, it is helpful to segment an image frame into homogeneous regions. Once the partition is available, it is less ambiguous to determine body parts since regions can be classified according to statistical region properties.

Since a digital image is often corrupted by noise, many segmentation algorithms use some form of smoothing operations as a preprocessing stage. To avoid blurring of information at the boundary, an edge-preserving smoothing technique, which average the value associated with a pixel with only those pixels in a local neighborhood that do not cross a high-contrast boundary, is recommended. At each pixel, a set of masks of different direction is used to compute the variance in that window. The pixels in the lowest variance mask are used to compute the new pixel average.

The gradient of the noise reduced image is calculated. Then the gradient magnitude $G(x,y)=\|\nabla I(x,y)\|$ is passed to the watershed segmentation algorithm, which produces an initial image partition. Our watershed algorithm is based on immersion simulations [5]. The high sensitivity of the watersheds algorithm to noise yields a large number of catchment basins, leading to over-segmentation [6]. One way to prevent over-segmentation is to increase the threshold value for the gradient magnitude image. However, if the gradient magnitude along their common boundary is not sufficiently high, high threshold values may cause merging of regions that correspond to different neighboring objects. Because our system only merges regions (no split process), initial segmentation must contain all the region boundaries desired in the final result. The over-segmentation cannot be avoided in the initial segmentation process.

After the over-segmentation step using the watershed algorithm, homogeneous regions are merged. The iterative region merging process starts with an initial segmentation and selects pairs of adjacent regions, which are candidates for merging into a single region. For each pair of regions a similarity score is assigned to the common boundary. If the score is below the global threshold T, the boundary is removed. This removal process repeated until no such boundaries are found. Removal of each boundary creates a new region from two old regions.

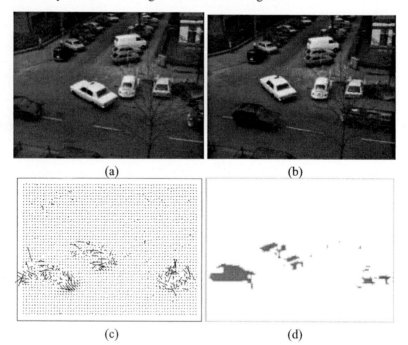

(a)   (b)

(c)   (d)

Fig. 2. Using motion fields to detect moving parts. (a) frame 0; (b) frame 20; (c) normal velocity field; (d) motion segmentation image.

The final step of human body region extraction works with curve segments and region color information. We first extract all curve segments. A curve segment is a list of boundary points with a smoothing curvature. Curve segments are representative features of human body boundaries.

Then prominent skin color regions are marked as possible regions of body parts. To extract skin regions, we use the hue, saturation, and value (HSV) color space. For the segmentation of skin-like regions it is sufficient to consider hue and saturation as discriminating color information. The range of hue is from 0 to 360 and the range of saturation is from 0 to 1. The empirical value for human skin color is [7]:

$$0 < h_{skin} < 50 \text{ and } 0.23 < s_{skin} < 0.68 .$$

The value component of HSV model is not used since it is sensitive to illumination and it is not effective to discriminate skin color.

Now the second region merging process is applied for the regions adjacent to the prominent skin color regions. As well as the region homogeneity property, the support by a common curve segment is regarded as a merging criterion.

We tested our method to real video streams and Fig. 1 shows an example of our segmentation experimental results.

3   Tracking Moving Parts Using Motion Fields

Visual motion appears to be a powerful cue for segmentation in the human visual system [8]. Although the importance of visual motion as a cue for segmentation is widely accepted, the emphasis of much of the recent work on optic flow has been on methods of reconstructing the three-dimensional scene from its two-dimensional flow field. Image flow algorithms have been developed with regularization, but the algorithms are not suitable for real world scenes because the algorithms cannot handle velocity field discontinuities. Results from psychology strongly suggest that the human vision system can estimate the image flow velocity field without blurring motion boundaries. This implies that a machine vision system should be capable of estimating the image flow velocity field with little distortion in the velocity field discontinuities.

We describe here how to estimate motion information. In the first step, a new image $\tilde{I}$ is computed by convolving the intensity image I at each pixel with the second derivative in time of the temporal Gaussian:

$$\tilde{I}(x,y,t) = \frac{\partial^2 G(t)}{\partial t^2} * I(x,y,t) \text{ where } G(t) = \frac{s}{\sqrt{\pi}} \exp(-s^2 t^2)$$

and s is a constant. The symbol * indicates convolution in time. The normal velocities are computed as follows. At each zero-crossing pixel, $\partial I / \partial x$, $\partial I / \partial y$, and $\partial I / \partial t$ are computed with numerical finite difference methods. The magnitude u_n of the normal velocity and the angle θ between the unit normal to the contour and the positive x axis were computed from

$$u_n = -\frac{\partial I}{\partial t} \bigg/ \sqrt{\left(\frac{\partial I}{\partial x}\right)^2 + \left(\frac{\partial I}{\partial y}\right)^2} \; , \; \theta = \tan^{-1}\left(\left(\frac{\partial I}{\partial y}\right)\bigg/\left(\frac{\partial I}{\partial x}\right)\right)$$

The normal velocity $\mathbf{u}$ is computed from u_n and θ :

$$\mathbf{u} = (u_n \cos\theta, u_n \sin\theta)$$

The computed normal velocity field is used as an initial estimate of motion field. We set initial motion boundary points by locating the spatial zero crossings in a single frame of $\tilde{I}$. We assume that neighboring points on a surface will have similar intensity (spatial intensity coherence), neighboring points on a surface will have similar normal velocity (spatial velocity coherence), and the image measurements change slowly over time (data consistency over time). Using the above constraints, motion vectors are computed by a non-linear iterative optimization method.

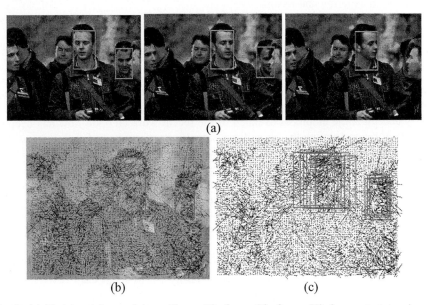

(a)

(b)   (c)

Fig. 3. (a) Test input image frames (frame 18, frame 20, frame 22) from a test movie and detected moving body parts, (b) motion vectors in frame 20, (c) tracking of moving body parts.

We formulate a simple model of image regions using local constraints on intensity and motion. The constraints account for surface patch boundaries as discontinuities in intensity and motion. Our approach differs from previous works in the point that the intensity information is used as well as the motion information to decide the motion boundaries. The method makes it possible to estimate the image flow velocity field with little distortion in the velocity field discontinuities. With each new image, current estimates are propagated by warping the grid of sites using the current optic flow estimate. During the warping process motion discontinuities are classified as occluding or not occluding. The estimates are then refined using some minimization techniques. Fig. 2 shows a result of moving object detection.

We have tested the implemented system extensively under various types of visual perturbations. The system has responded correctly even when colors of background regions are similar to skin colors. Only regions supported by the consistent motion fields are selected as candidates for body parts. Tracking of multiple moving body parts is also possible. An example of our experimental results is shown in Fig. 3.

4   Conclusion

A video-based human body tracking system has been developed which automatically detects and tracks human body parts. From the experimental results, we concluded that the proposed body parts tracking method is robust to self-occlusion of a human being and is not sensitive to the variation of body boundaries. Our method is also robust to background regions of colors similar to skin colors. Only regions supported by the consistent motion fields are selected as candidates for body parts. Experiments showed that our method is also robust to illumination changes and variations of skin colors.

In the current work, it is assumed that, when there are two or more human bodies in an image, a body region is not adjacent nor too close to other body region. As a future work, it would be practical to relax this constraint to track multiple attentions simultaneously.

References

1. Sherrah, J., Gong, S.: Vigour: A system for tracking and recognition of multiple people and their activities. In: Proceedings of the International Conference on Pattern Recognition. (2000) 1179–1182
2. Wren, C.R., Azarbayejni, A., Darrell, T., Pentland, A.P.: Pfinder: real-time tracking of the human body. IEEE Trans. PAMI 19(7) (1997) 780–785
3. Leung, M.K., Yee-Hong: First sight: a human body outline labeling system. IEEE Trans. PAMI 17(4) (1995) 359–377
4. Spengler, M., Schiele, B.: Towards robust multi-cue integration for visual tracking. Machine Vision and Applications 14 (2003) 50–58
5. Vincent, L., Soille, P.: Watersheds in digital spaces: An efficient algorithm based on immersion simulations. IEEE Trans. Pattern Anal. Machine Intell. 13 (1991) 583–598
6. Haris, K., Efstratiadis, S.N., Maglaveras, N., Katsaggelos, A.K.: Hybrid image segmentation using watersheds and fast region merging. IEEE Trans. Image Processing 7 (1998) 1684–1699
7. Sobottka, K., Pitas, I.: Segmentation and tracking of faces in color images. In: Proc. Second Int'l Conf. Automatic Face and Gesture Recognition. (1996) 236–241
8. Murray, D.W., Buxton, B.F.: Scene segmentation from visual motion using global optimization. IEEE Trans. Patt. Anal. Mach. Intell. 9(2) (1987) 220–228

A Graphical System for Interactive Rendering of Objects in an Augmented Reality Scenery

Uwe Berner, Norbert Braun, and Sofia Kolebinova

GRIS, Informatik, TU-Darmstadt, 64283 Darmstadt, Germany
{UBerner, NBraun, SKolebi}@GRIS.Informatik.TU-Darmstadt.de

Abstract. We describe the rendering functions of the Augmented Reality System GEIST. GEIST is a 3D based narrative education system, an installation at the castle of Heidelberg, Germany, based on digital storytelling, GPS localization and interactive rendering. The rendering is interactive, as it is driven by user interaction, e.g. GPS position, head movement and line of sight as well as direct interaction (yes/no to questions of Virtual Characters).

1 Introduction

The basic idea of the project GEIST [4] (*engl.* ghost) is the presentation of historical data to a young audience in a edutainment scenery. The user of the system get a complete portable AR system combined with a GPS position locator. The participant of the "game" can walk around the famous German city Heidelberg and look around to buildings and castles. On certain places, ghosts take their attention. The ghosts involve the users into a hundreds of years old story, belonging to the 30 years war and the destiny of Heidelberg and its citizens. While interacting with the ghosts and the environment, the users solve problems relating to the time epoch, increasing their historical knowledge while 'narrating' to the story. The story can evolve in various ways, in the end, the story comes to a happy ending with all the problems of the ghosts been solved. More information about the story processing can be found in [3].

The project GEIST combines two research areas, namely the geodata systems and the interactive computer graphics systems. Those areas handle complex problems, e.g. geodata systems handle position data and orientation of users and other objects in real space [5]; computer graphic handles real time animation to offer interaction with graphical data.

Our system is able to handle real time animations in relation to geo position data, as well it can handle pre-authored animations as well as on-the-fly generated animations. The user can interact in real time, influencing personally the behavior of the presented objects. The graphical sub system has to offer several functions (via an API) to the AR presentation system:

- The pre-authored animations have to be inserted into a graphical space, a scene graph.
- Capability to generate animations on the fly, in relation to geodata information, e.g point at or look at , with a corresponding body and head movement.

M. Rauterberg (Ed.): ICEC 2004, LNCS 3166, pp. 266–269, 2004.

- Capability to generate speech output, e.g. with several intonations and voice-emotions.

Based on the functions, every virtual object, e.g. the Virtual Characters or the buildings, are integrated into the AR scenes of the GEIST system. The next paragraph will give an overview on the basic scene graph functionality of the graphical subsystem. In paragraph 3, we give details on the additional geodata-based functions, as well as interaction functions of the subsystem. We give some graphical examples of our work, then we finish with a conclusion in paragraph 4.

2   The Basic Graphical Subsystem

The basic graphical subsystem is based on Open SG, see [6]. It is able to integrate the objects of pre-authored animations into a scene graph as well as to map the object's actions. So far, it allows the adding of geodata-specific, additional functionality via its C++ interface. This is an important feature, as it grants the possibility of the GEIST system's future development and evolution.

OpenSG is a portable scenegraph system to create realtime graphics programs, e.g. for virtual reality applications. It runs on IRIX, Windows and Linux and is based on OpenGL. OpenSG is not supposed to be a complete AR system. It is the rendering basis on top of which AR systems like the GEIST graphical system can be built.

OpenSG has the following properties: Multithreaded Asynchronous Scenegraph Manipulation , View Volume Culling , Portability, Loader: (VRML97, OBJ, OFF, RAW), Flexible Geometry, Runtime Changeable Type System, Reflective Structures. With these properties, OpenSG is an ideal candidate to be coupled with a geodata system to build AR scene graphs.

3   The AR Graphical Subsystem

A scene graph is structured via several nodes, defining the geometry and manipulations of the scene, see [1,2]. The basic nodes are implemented via the class GeistObject, the scene graph is implemented via the class GeistSceneManager.

The GeistSceneManager contains the following scene-manipulating functions: addObject, removeObject, removeAllObjects, setCameraPosition, getCameraPosition, setLightIntensity, update, addJob and jobDone. The method AddJob adds a manipulation of the scenegraph – at this point, the user interaction is inserted in the scene graph. Every user interaction property simply has to call this function to add an interaction job to the AR system.

A special class VRMLHumanoid is implemented for the presentation of Virtual Humans, to represent skeleton, skin and viewpoints, etc. Pre-authored animations of the GEIST system are stored as VRML graphs. VRML has an own scenegraph to represent the geometry of objects. In addition, VRML uses several nodes, defining actions onto the geometries. Those nodes are not directly translatable to an OpenSG node. For this reason, we implemented new nodes to OpenSG, simulating the functionality of VRML. The coordinates of real objects in the AR scene has to be translated into the coordinates of the virtual objects of the AR system, see Fig. 1. Afterwards, it is able to do the positioning of objects or the pointing of Virtual Characters using inverse kinematics.

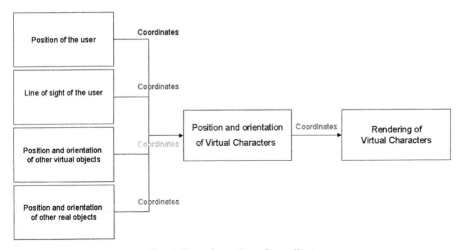

Fig. 1. Transformation of coordinates

Beside the positioning of the Virtual Characters in a way that users can see them it is significant to show pointing gestures in a way that the user can believe that the ghost can see what he is pointing at. When the Virtual Character is pointing, he should not point through his own body. We defined two spheres at the left and at the right of the Virtual Character. Pointing is only allowed in this spheres. If the pointing is going beyond the sphere, the Virtual Character moves in a way that it can point within the sphere.

4   Conclusion

The GEIST system is an installation at the castle of Heidelberg, Germany. Several evaluations of the systems were done, details can be found in [7]. Figure 2 gives an insight in the rendering of the AR system.

We presented the graphical subsystem of the AR presentation system of the GEIST project. We give insights into the structure and processing (e.g. animation loading and processing, coordinate-transformation, positioning) of pre-authored animations and on-the-fly generated animations in relation to geodata information, as well as their rendering into AR scenes. In the future we will advance the outdoor-located AR system to indoor-applications, therefore we will give the possibility to users to walk into the castle, as well as we will support more interaction properties.

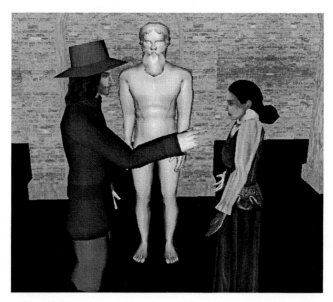

Fig. 2. Virtual Characters in the so called cave at the castle of Heidelberg, from left to right: Salomon, the River-God, Katarina

References

1. Braun, N.: GEIST ZE 2.5.3: Infrastruktur Körperposen und Gesten, report of the GEIST project (2003)
2. Braun, N.: GEIST ZE 2.5.4: Integration in das AR-Präsentationssystem, report of the GEIST project (2003)
3. Braun, N. and Schneider, O.: Suspenseful User Experiences in Collaborative Virtual Spaces, Enabled by Interactive Narration. Conference Proceedings of HCI International 2003, Greece (2003)
4. Holweg, D., Schneider, O.: GEIST : Mobile Outdoor AR-Informationssystem for Historical Education with Digital Storytelling. In: Federal Ministry of Education and Research: Virtual and Augmented Reality Status Conference 2004. Proceedings CD-ROM. Leipzig (2004)
5. Kretschmer, U.: Measuring Position of a User in Altering Settings. Bieber, Gerald (Ed.) u.a.: IMC Workshop 2003. Proceedings : Assistance, Mobility, Applications. Stuttgart : Fraunhofer IRB Verlag (2003), pp. 170-173
6. OpenSG Forum: OpenSG, http://www.opensg.org, (2003).
7. Schwarting, U.: GEIST AP 5.2.1 Evaluation, Inhaltliche Evaluation des Demonstrators, report of the GEIST project (2002)

Computer Games

TEAM: The Team-Oriented Evolutionary Adaptability Mechanism

Sander Bakkes, Pieter Spronck, and Eric Postma

Universiteit Maastricht, Institute for Knowledge and Agent Technology (IKAT),
P.O. Box 616, NL-6200 MD Maastricht, The Netherlands
Sander.Bakkes@student.tul.edu, {p.spronck,
postma}@cs.unimaas.nl

Abstract. Many commercial computer games allow a team of players to match their skills against another team, controlled by humans or by the computer. Most players prefer human opponents, since the artificial intelligence of a computer-controlled team is in general inferior. An adaptive mechanism for team-oriented artificial intelligence would allow computer-controlled opponents to adapt to human player behaviour, thereby providing a means of dealing with weaknesses in the game AI. Current commercial computer games lack challenging adaptive mechanisms. This paper proposes "TEAM", a novel team-oriented adaptive mechanism which is inspired by evolutionary algorithms. The performance of TEAM is evaluated in an experiment involving an actual commercial computer game (the Capture The Flag team-based game mode of the popular commercial computer game Quake III). The experimental results indicate that TEAM succeeds in endowing computer-controlled opponents with successful adaptive performance. We therefore conclude that TEAM can be successfully applied to generate challenging adaptive opponent behaviour in team-oriented commercial computer games.

1 Introduction

In the last twenty years commercial computer games (henceforth called "games") became increasingly realistic with regard to visual and auditory presentation. Unfortunately, artificial intelligence (AI) in games did not reach a high degree of realism yet [1]. In recent years, game developers started to improve AI in their games, focussing specifically on "opponent AI", i.e., the behaviour of computer-controlled agents [2] that compete with a human player.

Opponent AI is typically based on non-adaptive techniques [3]. A major disadvantage of non-adaptive opponent AI is that once a weakness is discovered, nothing stops the human player from exploiting the discovery. The disadvantage can be resolved by endowing opponent AI with adaptive behaviour, i.e., the ability to learn from mistakes. Adaptive behaviour can be imposed on agents by means of using machine-learning techniques, such as artificial neural networks [4] and evolutionary algorithms [5]. In state-of-the-art games, however, adaptive techniques are seldom used.

M. Rauterberg (Ed.): ICEC 2004, LNCS 3166, pp. 273–282, 2004.
© IFIP International Federation for Information Processing 2004

One area where AI in games can profit from adaptive behaviour is the organisation and interaction of opponents in team-oriented games. Even in state-of-the-art games this so-called "team AI" is barely challenging. The aim of our research is to create more challenging team AI by endowing the opponent AI with adaptive behaviour.

The organisation of this paper is as follows. Section 2 will discuss adaptive team AI in current commercial computer games. The TEAM artificial intelligence adaptation mechanism is discussion in section 3. In section 4, an experiment to test the performance of TEAM is discussed. Section 5 reports our findings, and section 6 concludes and indicates future work.

2   Adaptive Team AI in Commercial Computer Games

We define adaptive team AI as the behaviour of a team of adaptive agents that competes with other teams within a game environment. Adaptive team AI consists of four components: (1) the individual agent AI, (2) a means of communication, (3) team organisation, and (4) an adaptive mechanism. We discuss each of these four components below.

2.1   Individual Agent AI

Individual agent AI is, as the name implies, the AI of an agent which controls the agent's behaviour. Individual agent AI is game-specific.

2.2   Communication

Coordinated behaviour in a team requires communication. Typically, agents pass along messages containing information or commands. The information can be used to compute counteractions and distribute commands amongst the team-members.

2.3   Organisation

Internal organisation is required to establish team cohesion. Two distinctive approaches to organising a team are: (1) a decentralised approach, and (2) a centralised approach.

The decentralised approach is an extension of the individual agent AI. In the decentralised approach, agents operate in a non-hierarchical communication structure. Figure 1 (left) is an illustration of a decentralised group of agents. Team behaviour emerges through the combined interaction of all agents.

The centralised approach, schematically displayed in figure 1 (right), is strictly hierarchical and is specifically designed to create and maintain well-organised team cohesion. In this approach, the process of decision-making is centralised. Typically, a centralised decision-making mechanism observes agents, makes a decision and processes the decision into agent-commands. The implementation of the centralised mechanism varies in style from authoritarian (which focuses on team performance by forcing agents to commands) to coaching (which advises, rather than forces, agents).

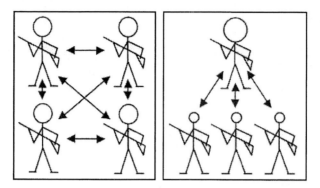

Fig. 1. Decentralised organisation (left) and centralised organisation (right) [6].

2.4   Adaptive Mechanism

To our knowledge an adaptive mechanism for team AI does not yet exist in any game. We decided to design and implement an adaptive mechanism for team AI. This mechanism, called TEAM, is discussed next.

3   Tactics Evolutionary Adaptability Mechanism (TEAM)

The Tactics Evolutionary Adaptability Mechanism (TEAM) is an evolutionary inspired adaptation mechanism that imposes adaptive team AI on opponents in games. In this chapter, the concept of TEAM is first laid out. Then, four features are discussed which distinguish TEAM from typical evolutionary approaches. These four features are: (1) a centralised agent control mechanism evolution, (2) a mutualistic-symbiotic evolution, (3) a delayed FSM-based evaluation, and (4) an evolution with history fall-back. A popular team-oriented game, the Quake III Capture The Flag (CTF) team-based game mode [7], is used for illustrative purposes.

3.1   Concept

TEAM is designed to be a generic adaptive mechanism for team-oriented games in which the game state can be represented as a finite state machine (FSM). An instance of TEAM is created for each state of the FSM. Each instance, in fact, is an evolutionary algorithm which learns state-specific behaviour for *a team as a whole*. In our experiment, the evolutionary algorithm was designed to learn optimal parameter values for each state's team control mechanism.

Cooperatively, all instances of TEAM learn successful team-oriented behaviour for *all states*. The concept of TEAM is illustrated in figure 2.

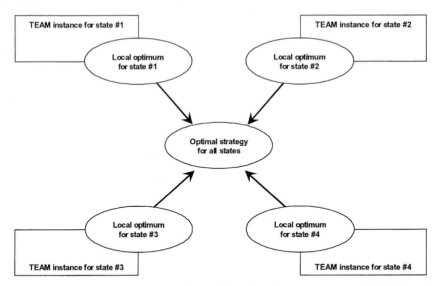

Fig. 2. Conceptually, TEAM learns adaptive behaviour for *a team as a whole* (rather than learning adaptive behaviour for each individual). Instances of TEAM cooperatively learn team-oriented behaviour, which is defined as the combination of the local optima for the states (in this example there are four states).

3.2   Centralised Agent Control Mechanism Evolution

TEAM evolves the agent team control mechanism in a centralised fashion. The choice for the centralised approach is motivated by the desire to evolve the behaviour for a team as a whole. The performance of a team's behaviour is assessed by performing a high-level evaluation of the whole team.

3.3   Mutualistic-Symbiotic Evolution

The evolutionary approach of TEAM is inspired by mutualistic-symbiotic animal communities [8]. In such communities, individuals postpone short-term individual goals in favour of long-term community goals.

The focus of TEAM's evolutionary mechanism lies on learning team-oriented behaviour by the cooperation of multiple evolutionary algorithms. For each state of the FSM controlling the team-oriented behaviour, a separate evolutionary algorithm is used. Each of these evolutionary algorithms learns relatively uncomplicated team-oriented behaviour for the specific state only. Yet, the behaviour is learned in consideration of the long-term effects on the other evolutionary algorithms. Subsequently, relatively complex team-oriented behaviour emerges in a computationally fast fashion.

3.4 Delayed FSM-Based Evaluation

We defined a delayed FSM-based evaluation function that postpones the deter-mination of the fitness value of a genome until a certain number of state transitions (the so-called "depth") after employing the genome have been processed. The delayed FSM-based evaluation function consists of two components: (1) a scaled fitness function, and (2) a delayed fitness function.

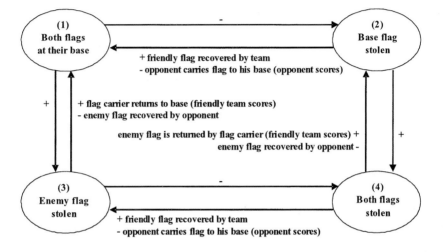

Fig. 3. Annotated finite state machine of Quake III CTF. Desirable state transitions are denoted with "+", whereas undesirable state transitions are denoted with "–".

First, the scaled fitness function is defined as:

$$
Scaled\_fitness = \begin{cases} 1.0 - \min\left(\dfrac{\sqrt{t} - \sqrt{t/3}}{10}, 1.0\right) & \{transition = +\} \\[3ex] \min\left(\dfrac{\sqrt{t} - \sqrt{t/3}}{10}, 1.0\right) & \{transition = -\} \end{cases} \tag{1}
$$

where t denotes the time before a state transition occurs, and *transition* is calculated by using annotations on the FSM which describes the states of a game. In figure 3, an example of annotations on the FSM of Quake III CTF is given. To realise the time-scaling, a damping square root is used, which has a substantial effect on short state transitions, and a clearing effect on long state transitions.

Second, the delayed fitness function for state transition M is defined as:

$$
Delayed\_fitness_M = \sum_{i=0}^{n} \frac{1}{i+1}\left(Scaled\_fitness_M + i\right) \tag{2}
$$

where i is the depth, n is a positive integer, and *Scaled_fitness* is the scaled fitness value of a genome. The delayed-reward is used to consider the long-term effects of genomes, because positive behaviour is only desirable if the team can retain or improve on the behaviour. In our experiment a two-deep delayed-reward is used ($n = 2$).

3.5   Evolution with History Fall-Back

The game-environment of team-oriented games is typically accompanied by a large amount of randomness. The randomness poses a problem for most adaptive mechanisms since one cannot be sure that a successful course of the evolution is the direct result of the genetic information in the population, or, of lucky circumstances. Consequentially, the evolutionary mechanism of TEAM is capable of reverting to an earlier state, if this is required. We implemented history fall-back with a fitness recalculation mechanism, which filters out unsuccessful genomes in due time.

4   Experiment: TEAM vs. Quake III Team AI

We tested the TEAM adaptation mechanism in a Quake III CTF game, where an adaptive team is pitted against a non-adaptive team. The adaptive team is controlled by TEAM. The non-adaptive team is controlled by the Quake III team AI, which offers non-static and fine-tuned, but non-adaptive, behaviour. The Quake III team AI changes its behaviour in such a way, that the adaptive team has to be able to deal with significant behavioural changes of the opponent. Both teams consist of four agents with identical individual agent AI, means of communication and team organisation, and only differ in the control mechanism employed (adaptive or non-adaptive).

4.1   Evaluation of an Experimental Run

An experimental run consists of two teams playing Quake III CTF until the game is interrupted by the experimenter. To quantify the performance of TEAM, two properties of an experimental run are used: the absolute turning point and the relative turning point.

We define the absolute turning point as the time at which the adaptive team obtains a win-loss ratio of a least 15 wins against 5 losses in a sliding window of 20. When the ratio is reached, the probability of the adaptive team outperforming the non-adaptive team is > 98% [9].

We define the relative turning point, which quantifies the noticeable effect of successful adaptive behaviour, as the last time at which the adaptive team has a zero lead with respect to the non-adaptive team, with the additional requirement that from this moment on the adaptive team does not lose its lead for the rest of the experimental run.

4.2   Results

In table 1 an overview of the experimental results is given. The average absolute turning point acquired is 108, and the average relative turning point is 71. TEAM merely requires several dozens of trials to evolve excellent behaviour, which is a good result especially considering that evolutionary algorithms typically require several thousands of trials to achieve successful results.

Table 1. Summary of experimental results.

	Absolute turning point	Relative turning point
Avg	108	71
StDev	62	45
StError	19	14
Median	99	50
Minimum	38	20
Maximum	263	158
Avg-StError	89	57
Avg+StError	127	85

To illustrate the course of a typical experimental run, we plotted the absolute and relative performance in figure 4. As shown in the top graph of figure 4, initially the adaptive team obtains approximately 10 wins against 10 losses; this is considered to be neutral performance. At the absolute turning point (point 99) a dramatic increase of the performance of the adaptive team is observed. In the bottom graph of figure 4, we observe that, initially, the adaptive team attains a lead of approximately zero. At the relative turning point (point 50) the lead of the adaptive team dramatically increases.

4.3   Evaluation of the Results

The experimental results imply that TEAM is able to successfully counter non-static opponent behaviour, as it defeated the non-static Quake III team AI. In the next section we will argue that this is the result of TEAM discovering and applying unforeseen dominant tactics.

Moreover, table 1 shows that the average relative turning point is much below the average absolute turning point. From this observation we may conclude that before we can reliably determine if the absolute turning point is reached, the opponent already notices the dominant effect of TEAM. Considering that in all runs we were able to determine relatively low absolute- and relative turning points, implying that TEAM learned to significantly outperform the opponent (in this case the Quake III team AI), we may draw the conclusion that TEAM is capable of successfully adapting to significant changes in the opponent behaviour. Figure 4 (below) reveals that TEAM learned to outperform the opponent without any significant degradation in the adaptive team's performance.

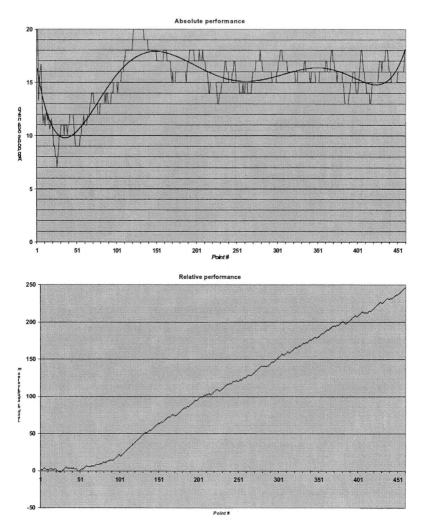

Fig. 4. Illustration of typical experimental results obtained with TEAM. The top graph shows the points scored by the adaptive team over a sliding window of 20 as a function of the amount of scored points. The bottom graph shows the lead of the adaptive team over the non-adaptive team as a function of the amount of scored points. The bottom graph reveals that the adaptive team outperforms the non-adaptive team without any significant degradation in its performance.

5 Discussion

Our experimental results show that TEAM is a successful adaptive mechanism for team-oriented behaviour. In sub-section 5.1 we will discuss to what extent TEAM meets the requirements necessary to allow it to be implemented in actual games. The behaviour learned by TEAM is discussed in sub-section 5.2.

5.1 Qualitative Evaluation of TEAM

TEAM is an online adaptive mechanism. For online adaptation to work in practice, we denote four requirements for qualitatively acceptable performance. It must be (1) computationally fast, (2) robust with respect to randomness inherent in the environment, (3) efficient with respect to the number of adaptation trials, and (4) effective with respect to the intermediate AI generated during the adaptation phase [10]. TEAM is computationally fast and is able to cope with a large amount of randomness inherent in the environment [11]. As argued in section 4.3, TEAM is efficient with respect to the limited number of trials required for an opponent to notice the effects of dominant adaptive behaviour. The effectiveness of TEAM is expressed by the fact that it outperforms non-adaptive AI without any significant degradation in performance. We may therefore conclude that TEAM is computationally fast, robust, efficient and effective, and can be applied in practice.

5.2 Learned Behaviour

Analysing the behaviour of TEAM, we observed that the population does not converge to merely one set of dominant tactics. TEAM is continuously adapting to the environment in order to remain dominant throughout the game. In our experiment, the adaptive team has learned risky, yet successful, tactics. These tactics can be best described as "rush" tactics, which are often applied in the real-time strategy game genre. Rush tactics aim at quickly obtaining offensive field supremacy. If rush tactics are successful, the opponent can seldom recover from the momentum of the offensive team. The original Quake III team AI uses only moderate tactics in all states. Therefore, it is not able to counter *any* field supremacy. This exemplifies the inadequacy of non-adaptive AI. Despite the fact that the original Quake III team AI is fine-tuned to be suitable for typical situations, it cannot adapt to superior player tactics, whereas TEAM can.

6 Conclusions and Future Work

We proposed the Tactics Evolutionary Adaptability Mechanism (TEAM) as a novel mechanism to impose adaptive behaviour on opponents in team-oriented commercial computer games. TEAM is based on evolutionary algorithms, but it possesses four features which distinguish the adaptive mechanism from typical evolutionary approaches. These four features are: (1) a centralised agent control mechanism evolution, (2) a mutualistic-symbiotic evolution, (3) a delayed FSM-based evaluation, and (4) an evolution with history fall-back. From the experimental results of our Quake III CTF experiment, we drew the conclusion that TEAM is capable of successfully adapting to changes in the opponent behaviour. TEAM adapted the team behaviour in such a way that dominant tactics were discovered. These dominant tactics outperformed the Quake III CTF tactics, which exhibit more cautious behaviour. Therefore, we may conclude that by creating a team-oriented mechanism capable of unsupervised and intelligent adaptation to the environment, we succeeded in creating challenging adaptive team AI.

Our future work aims at designing an adaptive mechanism capable of deciding which behavioural adaptations are required for endowing opponent AI with *entertaining* behaviour, and ultimately, designing a technique capable of learning meta-models for autonomously determining how to best accomplish an adaptation.

References

1.   Fenley, R.: Baby Steps to our Future. (2002)
      http://www.hal-pc.org/journal/02novdec/column/babystep/babystep.html
2.   FIPA: The foundation for intelligent physical agents. (2001) http://www.fipa.org
3.   Tozour, P.: The Perils of AI Scripting. AI Game Programming Wisdom (ed. Rabin, S.). Charles River Media. (2002) 1–547
4.   Mitchell, T.M.: Machine Learning. McGraw-Hill Science/Engineering/Math. (1997) 368–390
5.   Eiben, A.E.: Smith, J.E.: Evolutionary Computing Tutorial Part 1: What is an Evolutionary Algorithm? (2003)
      http://www.evonet.polytechnique.fr/CIRCUS2/valise/bcraenen/intro tut.pdf
6.   van der Sterren, W.: Squad Tactics - Team AI and Emergent Maneuvers. AI Game Programming Wisdom (ed. Rabin, S.). Charles River Media. (2002) 233–246
7.   van Waveren, J.P.M., Rothkrantz, L.J.M.: Artificial Player for Quake III Arena. 2nd International Conference on Intelligent Games and Simulation GAME-ON 2001 (eds. Quasim Mehdi, Norman Gough and David Al-Dabass). SCS Europe Bvba. (2001) 48–55
8.   Raven, P.H., Johnson, G.B.: Biology. McGraw-Hill Science/Engineering/Math. (2001)
9.   Cohen, P.R.: Empirical Methods for Artificial Intelligence. (HC) (1995)
10.   Spronck, P.H.M., Sprinkhuizen-Kuyper, I.G., Postma, E.O.: Online Adaptation of Computer Game Opponent AI. Universiteit Maastricht, The Netherlands (2003)
11.   Bakkes, S.C.J.: Learning to Play as a Team. Master's thesis. Universiteit Maastricht, The Netherlands (2003) 41–45

Size Variation and Flow Experience of Physical Game Support Objects

Loe Feijs, Peter Peters, and Berry Eggen

Department Industrial Design, Eindhoven University of Technology,
P.O.Box 513, 5600MB Eindhoven, The Netherlands
{l.m.g.feijs,p.j.f.peters,j.h.eggen}@tue.nl

Abstract. This paper is about designing and evaluating an innovative type of computer game. Game support objects are used to enrich the gaming experience [7]. The added objects are active but are simpler than real robots. In the study reported here they are four helper ghosts connected to a traditional Pacman game. In earlier projects we already found that children consider such type of additions attractive. We also found that the computer screen tends to draw the user's attention away from the support objects; therefore, the new set-up described here was designed to facilitate simultaneous screen and object-based interactions. The object interaction is essential for playing the game and not just an add-on. In order to develop a better understanding of this type of interaction and thus create future games more systematically, we did a formal user test in which we systematically varied one parameter. Three different versions of the system have been built and tested; they differ in the size of the ghosts (42cm, 15cm, 6cm high). We report on the playability of the new game, the embodiment of the interaction, the degree of flow that could be achieved and the effect of the size of the game support objects on both flow and scores. The lessons learned include a number of insights regarding the design of physical game extensions. The most important finding is that the size of the objects is relevant with respect to fun. No significant effects of size on flow were found. Visibility and distances are critical, however. Observations and interviews indicate that certain ergonomic aspects of the interaction, which are a consequence of the size parameter variation, are really decisive, not the perception of size as such.

1 Introduction

Computer games are important for entertainment and personal development. New games support rich interactions that are based on game support objects, in the future possibly even game support robots. The game support objects described in this paper take the form of four physical helper ghost characters. They are given an essential role in the game, which is a variant of Pacman, similar to the classic game "Puckman" created in 1980 by Toru Iwatani for Namco. By "essential role" we mean that the player *must* use the objects in order to get reasonable scores. We are able to build upon experiences with similar game support objects in earlier projects. We want to re-use these experiences and create a new version that is really fun to play. Moreover, an

M. Rauterberg (Ed.): ICEC 2004, LNCS 3166, pp. 283–295, 2004.

interesting question, not investigated so far is: "what is the effect of the size of the game support objects?" For example, larger game support objects could create a stronger feeling of immersion than small ones and hence make the game more fun. This idea relates to one of the findings by Reeves and Nass: that large faces on a screen can "invade" people's personal space [15]. In the work reported in this article, this idea is put to the test by means of a formal experiment. We created three comparable versions of the same game with one important difference: the size of the physical ghost characters. In addition to the outcomes of the experiment, we report some informal lessons learned based on observations and remarks made by the children that played the game.

2   Flow and Games

The concept of flow proposed by Csikszentmihalyi [2,3] is described by seven characteristics: (1) challenging (2) merging action and awareness (3) clear goals and feedback (4) concentration on task at hand (5) paradox of control, that is, feeling to be in control without fear of losing control (6) loss of self-consciousness, and (7) transformation of time. Flow is said to be autotelic, which means that the reward lies in the activity itself.

We assume that "flow" is an adequate description of the state a player enters when he or she is engaged in a computer game [5]. A flow questionnaire is considered a useful tool to measure the degree of flow in the game. Moreover, the subjects can be asked to rank game versions with respect to "fun". Both flow and fun are adopted as related, though possibly not the same, properties of successful and enjoyable games. We employ *reflection measures* for flow (the questionnaire) and for fun (the ranking) next to *behavior measures* (observing strategies and interaction styles). The scores could be taken as a *performance measure*.

3   Related Work

Extending computer gaming by adding new and rich types of interaction is a hot topic. An interesting development of this type is the Sony EyeToy camera; it connects to PlayStation2 using motion tracking to project the player into the screen, turning his or her movements into on-screen actions. A typical game is Ghost Catcher, which is about spotting ghosts as they appear and trying to hit them before they escape of the top of the screen. The interaction is not based on real objects or characters, however (the player usually is waving and hitting in the air).

Ullmer and Ishii [16] have developed a theoretical framework around the concept of Tangible User Interface (TUI). Whenever a physical artifact is added to a computer game, a TUI is created. Ullmer and Ishii's Model Control Representation physical-digital (MCRpd) model highlights the following characteristics of TUIs: Physical representations (rep-p) are computationally coupled to underlying digital information (model); physical representations (rep-p) embody mechanisms for interactive control

(control); Finally, physical representations (rep-p) are perceptually coupled to actively mediated digital representations (rep-d).

Fjeld et al. [8] describe an example of enriched interaction in a work-oriented application. They also propose the concept of interaction space. An interaction space is a place where action and perception coincide (in general it is ideal if they coincide).

Future versions of game support objects could develop into robots. A survey of robot-development for children is given in [4]. Two important observations are that children rapidly develop an understanding of the concept of robot and that interactive toys can become powerful tools for educational purposes, for example in storytelling.

Conversational interfaces such as Rea [1] and autonomous robots such as Aibo or Kismet offer complex perceptions and accept complex, multi-modal interactions. However, these provide a complete interaction on their own; they are not an add-on like physical game extensions or game support robots.

Christopher Kline and Bruce Blumberg [10] present a methodology for designing synthetic characters having intentions and thus being compelling, in the sense that people can empathize with them, and that the characters are understandable (their actions can be seen as attempts to satisfy their desires given their beliefs). The methodology combines sensor data by so-called transducers, accumulators and behavioral rules to let motivational drives emerge. Compared to our game support objects, the synthetic characters are more complex (the ghosts each have one sensor only). Yet there is a similarity to the Pacman game in the sense that the "eating or being eaten" narrative of the game indeed allows a motivational interpretation of the in-screen characters. Kline and Blumberg do not discuss the size issue, however.

Johnson, Wilson, Kline et al. [9] use a plush toy to direct synthetic (on-screen) characters. Like in our set-up, they assume that children enjoy touching objects. Their system can detect a variety of actions of the toy under user control, such as walk, run, fly, squeeze-belly, hop, kick and back flip. These are used to steer objects, but the relation between doll and object is variable (the software tries to infer which object has to be controlled). Compared to our game support objects, the plush dolls are used for navigation and steering whereas our ghosts are used to control game-related state information (rather than spatial information). Another difference is our idea of taking information out of the screen representation and putting it back to the physical interface, which plays no role in the plush toys.

Paiva, Andersson, Höök et al. [13,14] investigated the possibility to portray emotions through doll gestures. The investigation shows that it is possible to create a tangible sympathetic interaction device for affective input. Although our game support objects are simpler (they do not express emotions and are not bound by anthropomorphic needs), they do suffer from other limitations also encountered by SenToy's creators: the parameters determining the object's minimum size come mainly from the size and location of the hardware (sensors, switches, micro-controller) and the user's handling needs have a large impact on how the users experience the different ghost sizes. The fact that SenToy "pulls the user into the game" through the use of a physical interface is definitely noticeable in our Pacman setup as well.

4 Survey of Earlier Projects

We already gathered some experiences in extending Pacman-like games with game support objects in three previous projects. We summarize the set-ups used and the main findings of these.

Fig. 1. Mr. Ghost and Mr. Point, supporters of the ghosts and Pacman, respectively.

In a first project we added two game support objects (very simple robots) to an unmodified game. The objects, called Mr. Ghost and Mr. Point are shown in Fig. 1. The physical robots behave according to a supporter-like pattern based on the activities of the on-screen ghosts and Pacman, respectively. The main finding was that the children like the extensions and consider them fun, but once engaged in the game, they would hardly pay any attention to them [7].

Fig. 2. Character inviting to playful interaction preparing for stopping the game.

In other words, the computer (screen + keyboard) draws the attention away. Another view is that there are two *interaction spaces* and that the player has difficulties in switching between them. In a second project we explored ways to make fruitful use of the findings of the first project for a new goal: to help children get out of the flow and stop playing after a pre-programmed time period [6]. The forced, yet playful interaction with a physical character, as shown in Fig. 2, draws the player's attention away from the computer. The main finding was that children preferred this solution to other solutions (screen-based messages or removal of challenge).

In a third project we set up an experiment to improve our understanding of the two conflicting possible effects of adding game support objects: on the one hand they can add fun, on the other hand they introduce the problem of switching between interaction spaces. The computer is considered as one interaction space, the collection of game support objects is considered as the other interaction space. Therefore we built two different games, shown in Fig. 3 and Fig. 4, respectively.

Fig. 3. Ghosts, strongly coupled to the game   **Fig. 4.** Lanterns, weakly coupled to the game

In both cases the objects contain one lamp and one switch each and they are connected to a Pacman game. The four ghosts of Fig. 3 play an essential role in the game; they are based on forms and colors from the game; the timing of their interaction is critical when playing. That is why we say they are strongly coupled to the main game.

The lanterns of Fig. 4, however, although having the same complexity and comparable aesthetic qualities, are weakly coupled. They are a kind of stand-alone memory-game, which is played in an interleaving fashion with the main game. The main finding was that the children had difficulties in using the helper-ghosts. The lanterns did not suffer difficulties. The main difficulty was that the ghosts had white cloths; in order to identify a ghost the player had to look at the color of the pedestal.

For the new game set-ups described in the next section we set out to avoid these difficulties, adopting colored cloth for the physical ghosts. Also we decided to use stronger lamps.

5   The Four Ghosts Game

In this section we describe the four-ghost game in detail. The software does not differ from the software used in the third project mentioned before, but the objects do differ. The main objective of the game is like in the original Pacman game, except that the player is forced to use the four ghosts (unless he or she is willing to accept very low scores).

In order to fix our terminology we summarize the working of the ghosts in a traditional Pacman game. There are always four ghosts, called Pinky (pink), Inky (blue), Blinky (red), and Clyde (green). Each ghost can be in one of two states:

"aggressive" and "afraid". When the Pacman meets an aggressive ghost, the ghost "kills" the Pacman. If the Pacman meets a ghost that is afraid, the Pacman "kills" the ghost (and the player gets 20 points). If a ghost turns afraid, it loses its color and turns blue. This is very useful information for the player because it tells him or her whether it is necessary to avoid certain ghost. The transition from aggressive to afraid happens for all ghosts at once when the user eats a so-called energizer pill. Initially there are four energizer pills in each maze. After a while the ghosts turn aggressive again. Note that Inky does not really show its status: it is blue anyhow (an unpleasant surprise, usually discovered after a while by a novice player).

Next we describe the new game. The software is modified such that the status information is not visible anymore. The ghosts always have their natural color. Instead, the status information is made available through bright lamps underneath the colored cloth of the four physical ghosts, as shown in Fig. 5. There is one physical ghost in each of the four colors. The time-out that governs return of a ghost to the aggressive state is based on a random number generator. The time outs for the four ghosts work independently now. So, for example, if the on-screen Blinky is aggressive, the large physical red ghost will be illuminated. The player can also hit a physical ghost in its belly with the effect that its status changes to "afraid". The target area in the ghosts belly has a diameter of about one-fourth the ghosts' height. It is a foam ball mounted on a micro-switch, hidden behind the cloth. This is an alternative way of getting rid of dangerous ghosts, next to eating an energizer pill, which is still possible. The nice thing about hitting the physical ghosts is that its still works when all four energizer pills have been eaten.

Fig. 5. Game with four large ghosts.

The software is a modified version of the public domain Snack attack, which is available on the Internet as a part of Michael Packard's "crash course in game design" [12]. The software is written in Euphoria, a programming language with Pascal-like control and Lisp-like data structures. The software runs in a command tool under Windows 2000, using a sound-blaster simulator called VDMS. The four arrow keys of the computer keyboard control the game. The physical extensions are under software control via the serial port and two electronic interface boxes. The first interface box performs a series-parallel conversion. The second interface box contains the relays to switch the 230 Volts that is needed for the lamps.

The physical ghosts are positioned next to the notebook computer in such a way that the distance from the player's eye for the red ghost is roughly the same as the distance from the eye to the screen.

In order to study the effect of ghost size, we built three different versions. They differ in the size of the ghosts (42cm, 15cm, 6cm high). All proportions have been kept the same as much as possible. In particular the ratio between ghost size and target size is considered relevant. Also the distances between the ghosts are kept proportional to the ghost's size. A typical player uses the right hand for the arrow keys and the left hand for the ghosts (we found two left-handed children choosing this orientation too, although they were offered the option to change it). The medium-sized ghosts are shown in Fig. 6. The small ghosts are shown in Fig. 7. They contain 12 Volts lamps and are controlled by an alternative interface box containing transistors instead of relays to switch the lamps.

Fig. 6. Game with four medium-sized ghosts.   **Fig. 7.** Game with four small-sized ghosts.

6 Experiments

The purpose of this experiment is to find out whether the game brings children in the flow state and to investigate the effect of the ghost size on flow and fun. Therefore we adopt the following hypotheses:

- there is no flow during play (H0 hypothesis);
- the size of the game support objects influences the children's flow experience in the game;
- the size of the game support objects influences the children's preference with respect to the game considered most fun.

We adopted the "no flow" hypothesis based on our findings in a previous experiment. [6]. The second hypothesis was tested by an ANOVA and the third hypothesis was done by a ranking.

6.1 Participants

Twelve children, nine boys and three girls participated. They were between 8 and 10 years old. They were invited through personal contacts of university employees, such as children of a university-employee (not involved in the research) and classmates of children of the researchers. The children were asked whether they liked to participate in an experiment, which was "about a kind of new Pacman game" first, and next the parents were asked for permission (mostly in this order, but not always).

6.2 Materials

Three similar set-ups were used, each consisting of a notebook computer, four physical ghosts, two interfaces boxes and a digital video-camera on a tripod. Each set-up was on a table. The tables were 150x80 cm (for the large ghosts) and 100x100cm (for the other ghosts). The computers were NEC versa P520 Pentium notebooks, with no mouse attached, and Windows2000 operating system. The video cameras were in a fixed position in front of the subjects and focusing on their face. Soft drinks were available. Per subject a score-list, six flow questionnaires, and one ranking questionnaire were used. All flow questionnaires were identical. Six movie gift certificates complete the list of materials.

The flow questionnaire contains fourteen statements, which have to be assigned an integer score in a range from –2 ("I don't agree") to +2 ("I fully agree"). The statements are based on the seven characteristics of flow as described by Csikszentmihalyi. For each characteristic there are two questions, one describing the characteristic, the other describing the absence of the characteristic. For example: "time flies when I am playing" which describes the characteristic and "I have a quite accurate feeling of how much time has passed already when I am playing" describes its absence. The questions are presented in a mixed order such that the correspondence is not obvious to the subject. The characteristics are: Challenging, Merging action and awareness, Clear goals and feedback, Concentration on task, Paradox of control, The loss of self-consciousness, and Transformation of time.

The ranking questionnaire contained four questions: "which version of the game do you consider most fun?" (with three possible answers: large ghosts, medium ghosts, small ghosts), "why do you consider it to be most fun?", "which version of the game do you consider the least fun" (again three options: large ghosts, medium ghosts, small ghosts), and "why do you consider it to be the least fun?".

6.3 Procedure

Before conducting the experiment, a schedule was made to ensure that each of the six permutations LMS (Large ghosts-Medium ghosts-Small ghosts), MLS, SLM etc., was assigned to exactly two subjects. After a ten-minutes training session, each subject played six sessions, two times the same permutation. The training took place with the version of the first session (e.g. the large ghosts for a subject assigned the LMS permutation). There was a short break for soft drinks between the third and the fourth session (not counting the training session). Each session took ten minutes. The subjects were allowed to play until game-over, so occasionally the ten minutes became eleven or twelve minutes.

Before these six sessions the subjects were informed about the whole procedure: that he or she would play six sessions of ten minutes and fill out a questionnaire after each session. The subjects filled out the flow questionnaire themselves.

After the six sessions and the last flow questionnaire, the experimenter used a ranking questionnaire to conduct a short structured interview. The experimenter wrote down the answers. Several children said, "all three versions are fun", but then after some pressure they came up with a ranking nevertheless. Of course it was not allowed to mention the same version as being both most fun and least fun. The experimenter would sit next to the subject (not at the camera position). The experimenters answered questions and sometimes gave affirmative reactions to the subject's remarks or exclamations during the game sessions. The experimenters noted the scores and also made notes of any remarks made by the subjects.

The experiment took place in the faculty's exhibition space, which is an attractive open space containing several other technical or design-oriented demonstration tables. Two or three subjects would participate simultaneously. The tables for the three set-ups were about three meters separated so the children could keep in contact with each other. After the six sessions and the structured interview with the ranking questionnaire the subjects were thanked for participating in the experiment. Finally they were given movie gift certificates.

6.4   Quantitative Results

The subject's responses to the flow questionnaire were totaled per session, weighting the positive characteristic scores with a factor of +1 and the absence of characteristic scores with a factor of –1. From 14 questions ranging from –2...+2 a number between –28 and +28 is obtained for each session. Thus 72 flow scores were obtained, 6 for each of the 12 subjects, evenly distributed over the L, M and S versions.

Based on the measured overall flow score (averaged over all questionnaires) we can conclude that we can reject the H_0 hypothesis that there is no flow at the 0.01 level. This means on average subjects were in flow during the experiments.

Mean flow scores for the three versions are shown in Fig. 8. The intervals represent 95% confidence intervals (mean $\pm$ 1.96 σ_m). The averages, scaled back to the –2..+2 range, are 0.47, 0.50 and 0.46 for small, medium and large, respectively. The standard deviation of the mean, σ_m is 0.04 for all versions.

An analysis of variance for a repeated measures (within-subjects) design was performed on the flow scores. The analysis did not show significant differences between the 3 systems ($F(2,22)=1.90$; $p<0.25$).

The ranking questionnaires yielded 11 rankings (one subject was unable to choose) like for example L, M, S, which means that the large ghosts are considered least fun and the small ghost version is considered most fun. For this ordering, we determined the association among the 11 rankings by calculating the Kendall coefficient of concordance W (Siegel, 1988). The coefficient of concordance is significant at the 0.05 level of significance (W = 0.30; χ^2 = 7.17). This means the order L (least fun), S, M (most fun) is the best estimate of the 'true' ranking of the three versions. The scores were registered during the experiment but they show large variations (from 13 to 2500 points). It is interesting to note that the fun ranking yields the same order as the order of the flow scores as shown in Fig. 8 (although for the latter no significance can be shown, the trend is the same).

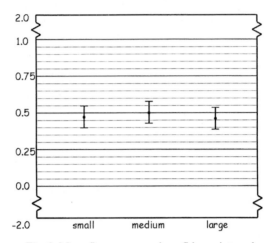

Fig. 8. Mean flow scores and confidence intervals.

6.5 Qualitative Results

A number of informal observations were made by the experimenters during the game sessions and afterwards during studying taped video fragments. They provide insights into the strategies the children develop. The first observation is that there are several clearly distinct strategies.

The first strategy is to focus on the screen and only hit a particular ghost on an as-needed basis. This is the initial strategy for most subjects. It does well until the player runs out of energizer pills. After that it is very hard to maintain this strategy in a pure form (the third strategy below is a natural follow-up).

The second strategy is to keep all ghosts in the afraid status. Most subjects try this strategy for a while. Some stick to it and get better and better at it, whereas others turn to another strategy. The disadvantage of this strategy usually is that the right hand cannot do complicated runs through the maze (probably because the mental energy goes to the physical ghost space). Typically the Pacman stays in the lower row of the maze for a long time (neither having dots to eat, nor being eaten by aggressive ghosts).

The third strategy is to focus on the screen, except for short periods of positioning the left hand to one of the ghosts. Once the hand is positioned, one or two other ghosts can be hit too without the need to look again. This skill improves after a few sessions. We did not observe a complete embodiment of the left-hand actions. Probably this would be easier if the targets would have been visible instead of being hidden behind the ghost's cloths. One child found that it became easier to hit the small ghosts when using his fist rather than his fingers, see Fig. 9. One child discovered a boring but technically perfect strategy: to enter the penalty box where the ghosts reincarnate, keep them afraid and eat them immediately upon reincarnation.

Also a number of informal remarks made by the subjects during gaming and as a reaction to the "why" questions of the ranking questionnaire were gathered. They show the same trend as the formal analyses, and they explain the children's preference for the medium-size version.

Fig. 9. Fist strategy for the small ghosts.   **Fig. 10.** Reaching toward the outermost ghost.

It is considered a disadvantage of the large ghosts over the other versions that the left hand must be lifted; for the others it can rest on the table.

The children complain about the large distance between the large ghosts. Also for the medium-size ghost some wanted the ghosts to be moved closer to each other (which was allowed during the experiment). Because of Fitt's law we decided to keep the ratio of distance between the ghost : size of the ghost constant.

Reaching the outermost large ghost was hard for the children; they could just reach it, as shown in Fig. 10. The small ghosts are considered too tiny for easy hitting, at least for some of the children. One child reports that he likes the large ghosts, just because they are so large. Visibility is a problem too; in particular, the blue ghost is harder to see because of differences in transparency characteristics of the different cloth colors (in all versions). In general the children are very positive about the game as a whole; for example, some ask when it will be available in the shops and one asks whether it will be for Mac or PC.

7 Discussion

The results of this experiment indicate that in our setup children prefer medium-sized game support objects to large or small versions. The preference seems based mostly on the version specific presence of difficulties in the player-object interaction, both the visual and the tactile interaction. The children consider the game fun and their reactions are very enthusiastic (some even wanted to go on playing after the total of 1+6 sessions). The limited impact of size on flow suggests that game size as such is not too important, provided the proportions are kept the same (i.e., the ratios between ghost size, target size and distance). We started the research with the original idea that larger game support objects create a stronger feeling of immersion and hence make the game more fun (this was the basis for the hypothesis that the size of the game support objects influences the children's flow experience in the game). However, even if the idea as such is applicable (it still is plausible), its effects seem weaker than other effects related to the player-object interaction such as reachability and ease of use. In this article we cannot compare the game with and without the support objects. It is clear that the children like the new game but a formal experiment would have to take care of the effect of novelty. Children may be interested in anything new and thus exciting as was also found in earlier work [6]. We leave the formal experiment as an option for future research.

8   Conclusions

Lessons learned: it is possible to design attractive games using game support objects. As can be learned from the qualitative observations in the previous section, all details related to visibility and all practicalities of hitting the ghosts matter. This does not mean that all difficulties should be removed: if the game is too easy, the flow and fun will be affected negatively. Difficulties that are obvious, for example when one ghost is harder to see or to reach than the others, will be sources of frustration. Such difficulties should be avoided, if possible. When designing the game, it is important to be aware of the significant effort it takes to switch from one action space to another. If we were to re-design the game, we would perform separate tests to make sure that, in principle, the left-hand actions can be embodied. We would also balance the lamp brightness to compensate for the different transparency of the different cloth colors.

Options for future work: it would be interesting to design a validated flow questionnaire that is applicable to children in playful situations. The existing flow questionnaires we know, such as Novak's web questionnaire [11], do not satisfy our needs; either they are not validated or they are too complex. It would also be interesting to design completely new games, extended with objects or robots.

Acknowledgements. We like to thank Ton van der Graft, Gert-Jan van der Wijst, Joep Frens, Carlijn Compen, Franka van Neerven and Don Bouwhuis for their support during this project.

References

1. Cassel, J., Bickmore T., Billinghurst M., Campbell, K. Chang, K., Vilhjálmsson, H., Yan, H., (1999) *Embodiment in conversational interfaces: REA.* Proceedings of CHI'99 pp.520-527.
2. Csikszentmihalyi, M., (1990) *Flow: the psychology of optimal Experience.* New York; Harper and Row
3. Csikszentmihalyi, M. (1992) *Flow: The Psychology of Happiness,* London: Rider.
4. Druin, A. and Hendler, (2000) J. *Robots for kids, exploring new technologies for learning,* Morgan Kaufmann.

5. Holt R. and Mitterer J., (2000) *Examining video game immersion as a flow state*. Paper presented at the 108th annual psychological association; Washington DC
6. Eggen, B, Feijs, L., de Graaf, M., and Peters, P. (2003), *Breaking the Flow: Intervention in Computer Game Play through Physical and On-screen Interaction*. In: Proceedings of the Digital Games Research Conference 2003 (DIGRA) To appear.
7. Feijs, L. and de Graaf, M., (2002) *Support robots for playing games: the role of player - actor relationships*. In: Faulkner X. et al. (Eds.), People and computers XVI. Springer, pp. 403-417.
8. Fjeld, M., Lauche, K., Dierssen, S., Bichsel, M. and Rauterberg, M., (1998) *BUILD-IT: A Brick-based integral Solution Supporting Multidisciplinary Design Tasks*. In: Sutcliffe, A., Ziegler, J. & Johnson, P. (Eds.) Designing Effective and Usable Multimedia Systems (IFIP 13.2), pp. 131-142. Boston: Kluwer.
9. Johnson, M.P., Wilson, A., Blumberg, B., Kline, C. and Bobick, A., (1999) *Sympathethic Interfaces: Using a Plush Toy to Direct Synthetic Characters*. In: Proceedings of CHI 99, pp. 152-158, Pittsburgh (PA), USA.
10. Kline, C. and Blumberg, B., (1999) *The Art and Science of Synthetic Character Design*. In: Proceedings of the Symposium on AI and Creativity in Entertainment and Visual Art (AISB), Edinburgh, Scotland.
11. Novak, T., Hoffman, D. and Young, Y. (1998), *Measuring the Customer Experience in Online Environments: A Structural Modeling Approach*, Vanderbilt University, http://elab.vanderbilt.edu/research/papers/pdf/manuscripts/ MeasuringCustomerExpOctober1999-pdf.pdf
12. Packard, M., Crash course in game design, http://www.berighteous.com/euphoria/
13. Paiva, A., Andersson, G., Höök, K., Mourão, D., Costa, M. and Martinho, C., (2002) *SenToy in FantasiA: Designing an Affective Sympathetic Interface to a Computer Game*. In: proceedings of Personal and Ubiquitous Computing, vol. 6, pp. 378-389. London: Springer-Verlag.
14. Paiva, A., Chaves, R., Moisés, P., Bullock, A., Andersson, G. and Höök, K., (2003) *SenToy: a Tangible Interface to Control the Emotions of a Synthetic Character*. In: proceedings of AAMAS'03, Melbourne, Australia.
15. Reeves, B. and Nass, C., (1996) *The media equation: How people treat computers, television and new media like real people and places*. Univ. of Chicago press.
16. Ullmer, B. and Ishii, H., (2000) *Emerging frameworks for tangible user interfaces*. IBM Systems Journal, vol. 39, nos 3&4, pp. 915-931.

Enhancing the Performance of Dynamic Scripting in Computer Games

Pieter Spronck, Ida Sprinkhuizen-Kuyper, and Eric Postma

Universiteit Maastricht, Institute for Knowledge and Agent Technology (IKAT),
P.O. Box 616, NL-6200 MD Maastricht, The Netherlands
{p.spronck, kuyper, postma}@cs.unimaas.nl

Abstract. Unsupervised online learning in commercial computer games allows computer-controlled opponents to adapt to the way the game is being played. As such it provides a mechanism to deal with weaknesses in the game AI and to respond to changes in human player tactics. In prior work we designed a novel technique called "dynamic scripting" that is able to create successful adaptive opponents. However, experimental evaluations indicated that, occasionally, the time needed for dynamic scripting to generate effective opponents becomes unacceptably long. We investigated two different countermeasures against these long adaptation times (which we call "outliers"), namely a better balance between rewards and penalties, and a history-fallback mechanism. Experimental results indicate that a combination of these two countermeasures is able to reduce the number of outliers significantly. We therefore conclude that the performance of dynamic scripting is enhanced by these counter-measures.

1 Introduction

The quality of commercial computer games is directly related to their entertainment value [1]. The general dissatisfaction of game players with the current level of artificial intelligence for controlling opponents (so-called "opponent AI") makes them prefer human-controlled opponents [2]. Improving the quality of opponent AI (while preserving the characteristics associated with high entertainment value [3]) is desired in case human-controlled opponents are not available.

In complex games, such as Computer RolePlaying Games (CRPGs), where the number of choices at each turn ranges from hundreds to even thousands, the incorporation of advanced AI is difficult. For these complex games most AI researchers resort to scripts, i.e., lists of rules that are executed sequentially [4]. These scripts are generally static and tend to be quite long and complex [5]. Because of their complexity, AI scripts are likely to contain weaknesses, which can be exploited by human players to easily defeat supposedly tough opponents. Furthermore, because they are static, scripts cannot deal with unforeseen tactics employed by the human player and cannot scale the difficulty level exhibited by the game AI to cater to both novice and experienced human players.

M. Rauterberg (Ed.): ICEC 2004, LNCS 3166, pp. 296–307, 2004.
© IFIP International Federation for Information Processing 2004

In our research we apply machine-learning techniques to improve the quality of scripted opponent AI. When machine learning is used to allow opponents to adapt while the game is played, this is referred to as "online learning". Online learning allows the opponents to automatically repair weaknesses in their scripts that are exploited by the human player, and to adapt to changes in human player tactics. While supervised online learning has been sporadically used in commercial games [6], unsupervised online learning is widely disregarded by commercial game developers [7], even though it has been shown to be feasible for games [8,9,10].

We designed a novel technique called "dynamic scripting" that realises online adaptation of scripted opponent AI, specifically for complex games [10]. While our evaluations showed that dynamic scripting meets all necessary requirements to be generally successful in games, we noted that, occasionally, chance causes adaptation to a new tactic to take too long. In the distribution of adaptation times, these exceptionally long adaptation times are outliers. The present research investigates two countermeasures against the occurrence of outliers, namely penalty balancing and history fallback.

The outline of the remainder of the paper is as follows. Section 2 discusses opponent AI in games and describes dynamic scripting. It also discusses the results achieved with dynamic scripting in a simulation and in the state-of-the-art CRPG NEVERWINTER NIGHTS. Section 3 presents the two countermeasures, and the results obtained by applying them in dynamic scripting. Section 4 discusses the results. Finally, section 5 concludes and points at future work.

2   Online Learning of Game Opponent AI with Dynamic Scripting

Online learning of computer game AI entails that the AI is adapted while the game is being played. In subsection 2.1 we present dynamic scripting as a technique that is designed specifically for this purpose. Those interested in a more detailed exposition of dynamic scripting are referred to [10]. Subsection 2.2 discusses online learning requirements for games and how dynamic scripting meets them. Subsection 2.3 presents the results of an evaluation of the effectiveness of dynamic scripting.

2.1   Dynamic Scripting

Dynamic scripting is an unsupervised online learning technique for commercial computer games. It maintains several rulebases, one for each opponent type in the game. The rules in the rulebases are manually designed using domain-specific knowledge. Every time a new opponent of a particular type is generated, the rules that comprise the script that controls the opponent are extracted from the corresponding rulebase. The probability that a rule is selected for a script is influenced by a weight value that is associated with each rule. The rulebase adapts by changing the weight values to reflect the success or failure rate of the corresponding rules in scripts. A priority mechanism can be used to let certain rules take precedence over other rules. The dynamic scripting process is illustrated in figure 1 in the context of a commercial game.

The learning mechanism in our dynamic scripting technique is inspired by reinforcement learning techniques [11]. It has been adapted for use in games because regular reinforcement learning techniques are not sufficiently efficient for online learning in games [12]. In the dynamic scripting approach, learning proceeds as follows. Upon completion of an encounter, the weights of the rules employed during the encounter are adapted depending on their contribution to the outcome. Rules that lead to success are rewarded with a weight increase, whereas rules that lead to failure are punished with a weight decrease. The remaining rules get updated so that the total of all weights in the rulebase remains unchanged. The size of the weight change depends on how well, or how badly, a team member performed during the encounter.

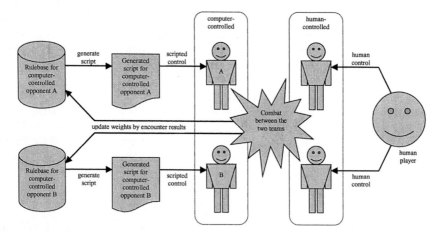

Fig. 1. The dynamic scripting process. For each computer-controlled opponent a rulebase generates a new script at the start of an encounter. After an encounter is over, the weights in the rulebase are adapted to reflect the results of the fight

2.2 Online Learning Requirements and Dynamic Scripting

For unsupervised online learning of computer game AI to be applicable in practice, it must be fast, effective, robust, and efficient. Below we discuss each of these four requirements in detail.

1. **Fast**. Since online learning takes place during gameplay, the learning algorithm should be computationally fast. This requirement excludes computationally intensive learning methods such as model-based learning. Dynamic scripting only requires the extraction of rules from a rulebase and the updating of weights once per encounter, and is therefore computationally fast.

2. **Effective**. In providing entertainment for the player, the adapted AI should be at least as challenging as manually designed AI (the occasional occurrence of a non-challenging opponent being permissible). This requirement excludes random learning methods, such as evolutionary algorithms. Dynamic scripting extracts the rules for the script from a rulebase, which contains only rules that have been manually designed using domain knowledge. Since none of the rules in the script

will be ineffective, the script as a whole won't be either, although it may be inappropriate for certain situations.

3. **Robust**. The learning mechanism must be able to cope with a significant amount of randomness inherent in most commercial gaming mechanisms. This requirement excludes deterministic learning methods that depend on a gradient search, such as straightforward hill-climbing. Dynamic scripting is robust because it uses a reward-and-penalty system, and does not remove rules immediately when punished.

4. **Efficient**. In a single game, a player experiences a limited number of encounters with similar groups of opponents. Therefore, the learning process should rely on just a small number of trials. This requirement excludes slow-learning techniques, such as neural networks, evolutionary algorithms and reinforcement learning. With appropriate weight-updating parameters dynamic scripting can adapt after a few encounters only. We have evaluated the efficiency of dynamic scripting with experiments that are discussed in subsection 2.3.

2.3   Evaluation of the Efficiency of Dynamic Scripting

To evaluate the efficiency of dynamic scripting, we implemented it in a simulation of an encounter of two teams in a complex CRPG, closely resembling the popular BALDUR'S GATE games (the simulation environment is shown in figure 2). We also implemented dynamic scripting in an actual commercial game, namely the state-of-the-art CRPG NEVERWINTER NIGHTS (NWN). Our evaluation experiments aimed at assessing the adaptive performance of a team controlled by the dynamic scripting technique, against a team controlled by static scripts. If dynamic scripting is efficient, the dynamic team will need only a few encounters to design a tactic that outperforms the static team, even if the static team uses a highly effective tactic. In the simulation, we pitted the dynamic team against a static team that would use one of four, manually designed, basic tactics (named "offensive", "disabling", "cursing" and "defensive") or one of three composite tactics (named "random party", "random character" and "consecutive party"). In NWN we pitted the dynamic team against the AI programmed by the developers of the game.

Of all the static team's tactics the most challenging is the consecutive party tactic. With this tactic the static team starts by using one of the four basic tactics. Each encounter the party will continue to use the tactic employed during the previous encounter if that encounter was won, but will switch to the next tactic if that encounter was lost. This strategy is closest to what human players do: they stick with a tactic as long as it works, and switch when it fails.

To quantify the relative performance of the dynamic team against the static team, after each encounter we calculate a so-called "fitness" value for each team. This is a real value in the range [0,1], which indicates how well the team did during the past encounter. It takes into account whether the team won or lost, and, if the team won, the number of surviving team members and their total remaining health. The dynamic team is said to *outperform* the static team at an encounter if the average fitness over the last ten encounters is higher for the dynamic team than for the static team.

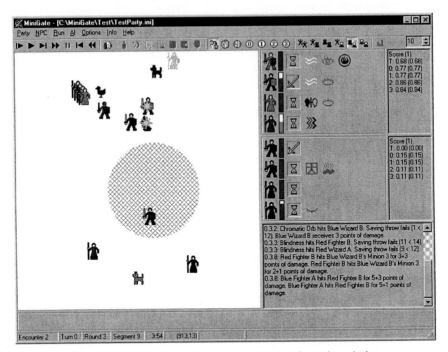

Fig. 2. The simulation environment used to test dynamic scripting

In order to identify reliable changes in strength between parties, we define the *turning point* as the number of the first encounter after which the dynamic team outperforms the static team for at least ten consecutive encounters. A low value for the turning point indicates good efficiency of dynamic scripting, since it shows that the dynamic team consistently outperforms the static team within a few encounters only.

The results of our evaluation experiments are summarised in table 1. Since the opponent AI in NWN was significantly improved between NWN version 1.29 (which we used in earlier research) and version 1.61, turning points have been calculated for both of them. From the results in this table we observe that the turning points achieved are low, especially considering the fact that rulebases started out with equal weights for all rules. We therefore conclude that dynamic scripting is efficient and thus meets all requirements stated in subsection 2.2.

However, from the surprising differences between the average and median values for the turning points, and from the fact that some of the highest turning points found are extremely high, we conclude that, although turning points are low in general, there occasionally are cases where they are too high for comfort. These so-called "outliers" are explained by the high degree of randomness that is inherent to these games. A long run of encounters where pure chance drives the learning process away from an optimum (for instance, a run of encounters wherein the dynamic team is lucky and wins although it employs inferior tactics, or wherein the dynamic team is unlucky and loses although it employs superior tactics) may place the rulebase in a state from which it has difficulty to recover. To resolve the problem of outliers, we investigated two countermeasures, which are discussed in the next section.

Table 1. Turning point values for dynamic scripting pitted against nine different tactics. The columns, from left to right, present the following: (1) the name of the tactic, (2) the number of experiments done with this tactic, (3) the average turning point found, (4) the median turning point found, (5) the standard deviation, (6) the standard error of the mean, (7) the highest turning point found, and (8) the average of the highest five turning points found

Tactic	#exp	$\bar{x}$	median	σ	$\sigma_{\bar{x}}$	highest	$\bar{x}_{top5}$
Offensive	100	58	53	35.0	3.5	314	155
Disabling	100	12	11	5.2	0.5	51	31
Cursing	100	137	35	333.6	33.4	1767	1461
Defensive	100	31	27	18.8	1.9	93	77
Random Party	100	56	34	74.4	7.4	595	310
Random Character	100	53	27	67.0	6.7	398	289
Consecutive Party	100	72	47	100.3	10.0	716	424
NWN AI 1.29	50	21	16	8.8	1.2	101	58
NWN AI 1.61	31	35	32	18.8	3.4	75	65

3   Reducing the Number of Outliers

To reduce the number of outliers, we propose two countermeasures, namely (1) penalty balancing, and (2) history fallback. Subsection 3.1 explains the first countermeasure, and subsection 3.2 the second. The results of the experiments used to test the effectiveness of the countermeasures are presented in subsection 3.3.

3.1   Penalty Balancing

The magnitude of the weight adaptation in a rulebase depends on a measure of the success (or failure) of the opponent whose script is extracted from the rulebase. Typically, the measure of success of an opponent is expressed in the form of an individual fitness function that, besides the team fitness value, incorporates elements of the opponent's individual performance during an encounter. The individual fitness takes a value in the range $[0,1]$. If the value is higher than a break-even value b, the weights of the rules in the script that governed the opponent's behaviour are rewarded, and otherwise they are penalised. The weight adjustment is expressed by the following formula for the new weight value W:

$$W = \begin{cases} \max\left(W_{min}, W_{org} - P_{max} \cdot \dfrac{b-F}{b}\right) & \{F < b\} \\ \min\left(W_{org} + R_{max} \cdot \dfrac{F-b}{1-b}, W_{max}\right) & \{F \geq b\} \end{cases} \tag{1}$$

where W_{org} is the original weight value, W_{min} and W_{max} respectively are the minimum and maximum weight values, R_{max} and P_{max} respectively are the maximum reward and penalty, F is the individual fitness, and b is the break-even value.

Penalty balancing is tuning the magnitude of the maximum penalty in relation to the maximum reward to optimise speed and effectiveness of the adaptation process. The experimental results presented in section 2 relied on a maximum reward that was substantially larger than the maximum penalty (namely, $P_{max}=30$ for the simulation experiments, and $P_{max}=50$ for the NWN experiments, while $R_{max}=100$ for both). The argument for the relatively small maximum penalties is that, as soon as an optimum is found, the rulebase should be protected against degradation. This argument seems to be intuitively correct, since for a local optimum a penalty can be considered equivalent to a mutation as used in an evolutionary learning system, and the effectiveness of a learning system improves if the mutation rate is small in the neighbourhood of an optimum [13]. However, if a sequence of undeserved rewards occurs, the relatively low maximum penalty will have problems reducing the unjustly increased weights. Penalty balancing, whereby P_{max} is brought closer to the value of R_{max}, gives dynamic scripting better chances to recover from undeserved weight increases, at the cost of higher chances to move away from a discovered optimum.

3.2 History Fallback

In the original formulation of dynamic scripting [10], the old weights of the rules in the rulebase are erased when the rulebase adapts. With history fallback all previous weights are retained in so-called "historic rulebases". When learning seems to be stuck in a sequence of rulebases that have inferior performance, it can "fall back" to one of the historic rulebases that seemed to perform better.

However, caution should be taken not to be too eager to fall back to earlier rulebases. The dynamic scripting process has shown to be quite robust and learns from both successes and failures. Returning to an earlier rulebase means losing everything that was learned after that rulebase was generated. Furthermore, an earlier rulebase may have a high fitness due to chance, and returning to it might therefore have an adverse effect. We confirmed the wisdom of this caution by implementing dynamic scripting with an eager history-fallback mechanism in NWN, and found its performance to be much worse than that of dynamic scripting without history fallback. Therefore, any history-fallback mechanism should only be activated when there is a high probability that a truly inferior rulebase is replaced by a truly superior one.

Our implementation of history fallback is as follows. The current rulebase R is used to generate scripts that control the behaviour of an opponent during an encounter. After each encounter i, before the weight updates, all weight values from rulebase R are copied to historic rulebase R_i. With R_i are also stored the individual fitness F_i, the team fitness T_i, and a number representing the so-called "parent" of R_i. The parent of R_i is the historic rulebase whose weights were updated to generate R_i (usually the parent of R_i is R_{i-1}). A rulebase is considered "inferior" when both its own fitness values, and the fitness values of its N immediate ancestors, are low. A rulebase is considered "superior" when both its own fitness values, and the fitness values of its N immediate ancestors, are high. If at encounter i we find that R_i is inferior, and in R_i's ancestry we find a historic rulebase R_j that is superior, the next parent used to generate the current rulebase R will not be R_i but R_j. In our experiments we used $N=2$.

Though unlikely, with this mechanism it is still possible to fall back to a historic rulebase that, although it seemed to perform well in the past, actually only did so by being lucky. While this will be discovered by the learning process soon enough, we don't want to run the risk of returning to such a rulebase over and over again. We propose two different ways of alleviating this problem. The first is by simply not allowing the mechanism to fall back to a historic rulebase that is "too old", but only allow it to fall back to the last M ancestors (in our experiments we used $M=15$). We call this "limited distance fallback" (LDF). The second is acknowledging that the individual fitness of a rulebase should not be too different from that of its direct ancestors. By propagating a newly calculated fitness value back through the ancestry of a rulebase, factoring it into the fitness values for those ancestors, a rulebase with a high individual fitness that has children that have low fitness values, will also have its fitness reduced fast. We call this "fitness propagation fallback" (FPF). Both versions of history fallback allow dynamic scripting to recover earlier, well-performing rulebases.

3.3   Experimental Results

To test the effectiveness of penalty balancing and history fallback, we ran a series of experiments in our simulation environment. We decided to use the "consecutive party tactic" as the tactic employed by the static team, since this tactic is the most challenging for dynamic scripting. We compared nine different configurations, namely learning runs using maximum penalties $P_{max}=30$, $P_{max}=70$ and $P_{max}=100$, combined with the use of no fallback (NoF), limited distance fallback (LDF), and fitness propagation fallback (FPF).

We also ran some experiments with NWN. In these experiments we used for the static team the standard AI of NWN version 1.61, and we ran also some experiments using so-called "cursed AI". With cursed AI in 20% of the encounters the game AI deliberately misleads dynamic scripting into awarding high fitness to purely random tactics, and low fitness to tactics that have shown good performance during earlier encounters. We did NWN experiments both with no fallback and fitness propagation fallback. We did not change the maximum penalties since in our original experiments for NWN we already used higher maximum penalties than for the simulation.

Table 2 gives an overview of both the simulation and the NWN experiments. Figure 3 shows histograms of the turning points for each of the series of simulation experiments. From these results we make the following four observations: (1) Penalty balancing is a necessary requirement to reduce the number of outliers. All experiments that have a higher maximum penalty than our original $P_{max}=30$ reduce the number and magnitude of outliers. (2) If penalty balancing is *not* applied, history fallback seems to have no effect or even an adverse effect. (3) If penalty balancing *is* applied, history fallback has no adverse effect and may actually have a positive effect. (4) In the NWN environment history fallback has little or no effect.

As a final experiment, we applied a combination of penalty balancing with $P_{max}=70$ and limited distance fallback to all the different tactics available in the simulation environment. The results are summarised in table 3. A comparison of table 3 and table 1 shows a significant, often very large reduction of the both the highest turning point and the average of the highest five turning points, for all tactics except for the "disabling" tactic (however, the "disabling" tactic already has the lowest turning points in both tables). This clearly confirms the positive effect of the two countermeasures.

Table 2. Turning point values for dynamic scripting pitted against the consecutive party tactic in the simulation and against the NWN AI 1.61, in different circumstances, which are specified in column 1. Columns 2 to 8 present equal information as in table 1

Situation	#exp	$\bar{x}$	median	σ	$\sigma_{\bar{x}}$	highest	$\bar{x}_{top5}$
Sim, P_{max}=30, NoF	100	72	47	100.3	10.0	716	424
Sim, P_{max}=30, LDF	100	99	49	229.3	22.9	2064	837
Sim, P_{max}=30, FPF	100	80	54	145.0	14.5	971	605
Sim, P_{max}=70, NoF	100	62	44	69.4	6.9	336	301
Sim, P_{max}=70, LDF	100	52	37	56.2	5.6	393	238
Sim, P_{max}=70, FPF	100	60	32	57.3	5.7	391	245
Sim, P_{max}=100, NoF	100	66	59	59.5	6.0	322	246
Sim, P_{max}=100, LDF	100	68	60	56.7	5.7	271	225
Sim, P_{max}=100, FPF	100	57	53	50.6	5.1	331	202
NWN, NoF	31	35	32	18.8	3.4	75	65
NWN, FPF	30	32	24	26.7	4.9	104	71
NWN cursed, NoF	21	33	24	21.8	4.8	92	64
NWN cursed, FPF	21	32	18	28.1	6.1	115	69

Table 3. Turning point values for dynamic scripting pitted against different tactics, using P_{max}=70 and limited distance fallback. The columns present equal information as in table 1

Tactic	#exp	$\bar{x}$	median	σ	$\sigma_{\bar{x}}$	highest	$\bar{x}_{top5}$
Offensive	100	53	52	24.8	2.5	120	107
Disabling	100	13	11	8.4	0.8	79	39
Cursing	100	44	26	50.4	5.0	304	222
Defensive	100	24	17	15.3	1.5	79	67
Random Party	100	51	29	64.5	6.5	480	271
Random Character	100	41	25	40.7	4.1	251	178
Consecutive Party	100	52	37	56.2	5.6	393	238

4   Discussion

In this section we discuss the results presented in the previous section. Subsection 4.1 examines the experimental results obtained using the countermeasures. Subsection 4.2 discusses the usefulness of dynamic scripting enhanced with the countermeasures.

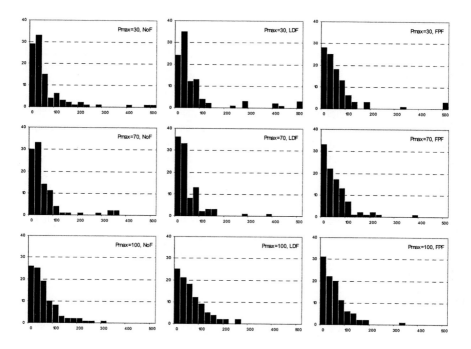

Fig. 3. Histograms of the turning points for the simulation experiments in table 2. The turning points have been grouped in ranges of 25 different values. Each bar indicates the number of turning points falling within a range. Each graph starts with the leftmost bar representing the range [0,24]. The rightmost bars in the topmost three graphs represent all turning points of 500 or greater (the other graphs do not have turning points in this range)

4.1 Interpretation of the Results

The results presented in table 2 indicate that penalty balancing has an undeniable positive influence on dynamic scripting, especially in reducing the number of outliers. In combination with penalty balancing, history fallback can have an extra positive impact. A qualitative explanation of the history fallback effect is the following. In subsection 3.1 we stated that penalty balancing runs the risk of losing a discovered optimum due to chance. History fallback counteracts this risk, and may therefore improve dynamic scripting even further.

In the NWN environment we observed that history fallback had little or no effect. This may be due to the following three reasons. (1) The effect of history fallback is small compared to the effect of penalty balancing. (2) Since even static opponents that use cursed AI do not cause significantly increased turning points, it seems that dynamic scripting in NWN is so robust that remote outliers do not occur, and therefore countermeasures are not needed. (3) Dynamic scripting in the NWN environment has two extra enhancements compared to the implementation in the simulation, namely the ability to decrease script length, and a rulebase that contains more general tactics as rules. These enhancements may also reduce the occurrence of outliers.

4.2   Usefulness

It is clear from the results in table 2 that the number of outliers has been significantly reduced with the proposed countermeasures. However, occasionally exceptionally long learning runs still occur in the simulation experiments, even though they are rare. Does this mean that dynamic scripting needs to be improved even more before it can be applied in a commercial game?

We argue that it does not. Dynamic scripting is ready to be applied in commercial games. Our argument is twofold. (1) Because dynamic scripting is a non-deterministic technique, outliers can never be prevented completely. However, entertainment value of a game is guaranteed even if an outlier occurs, because of the domain knowledge in the rulebase (this is the requirement of effectiveness from subsection 2.2). (2) Exceptionally long learning runs mainly occur because early in the process chance increases the wrong weights. This is not likely to happen in a rulebase with pre-initialised weights. When dynamic scripting is implemented in an actual game, the weights in the rulebase will not all start out with equal values, but they will be initialised to values that are already optimised against commonly used tactics. This will not only prevent the occurrence of outliers, but also increase the speed of weight optimisation, and provide history fallback with a likely candidate for a superior rulebase.

We note that, besides as a target for the history fallback mechanism, historic rulebases can also be used to store tactics that work well against a specific tactic employed by a human player. If human player tactics can be identified, these rulebases can simply be reloaded when the player starts to use a particular tactic again after having employed a completely different tactic for a while.

5   Conclusion and Future Work

Dynamic scripting is a technique that realises unsupervised online adaptation of opponent AI in complex commercial computer games such as CRPGs. It is based on the automatic online generation of AI scripts for computer game opponents by means of an adaptive rulebase. Although dynamic scripting has been shown to perform well, exceptionally long learning runs ("outliers") tend to occur occasionally. In this paper we investigated two countermeasures against the outliers, namely penalty balancing and history fallback. We found that penalty balancing has a significant positive effect on the occurrence of outliers, and that history fallback may improve the effect of penalty balancing even further. We conclude that the performance of dynamic scripting is enhanced by these two countermeasures, and that dynamic scripting can be successfully incorporated in commercial games.

Our future work aims at applying dynamic scripting in other game types than CRPGs, such as Real-Time Strategy games. We will also investigate whether offline machine learning techniques, which can be very effective in designing tactics [14], can be used to "invent" completely new rules for the dynamic scripting rulebase. Finally, since our main aim is to use online learning against human players, it is essential that we extend our experiments to assess if online learning actually increases the entertainment value of a game for human players. After all, for commercial game developers entertainment value is of primary concern when deciding whether or not to incorporate online learning in their games.

References

1. Tozour, P.: The Evolution of Game AI. In: Rabin, S. (ed.): AI Game Programming Wisdom. Charles River Media (2002) 3–15
2. Schaeffer, J.: A Gamut of Games. In: AI Magazine, Vol. 22, No. 3 (2001) 29–46
3. Scott, B.: The Illusion of Intelligence. In: Rabin, S. (ed.): AI Game Programming Wisdom. Charles River Media (2002) 16–20
4. Tozour, P.: The Perils of AI Scripting. In: Rabin, S. (ed.): AI Game Programming Wisdom. Charles River Media (2002) 541–547
5. Brockington, M. and Darrah, M.: How *Not* to Implement a Basic Scripting Language. In: Rabin, S. (ed.): AI Game Programming Wisdom. Charles River Media (2002) 548–554
6. Evans, R.: Varieties of Learning. In: Rabin, S. (ed.): AI Game Programming Wisdom. Charles River Media (2002) 567–578
7. Woodcock, S.: Game AI: The State of the Industry. In: Game Developer Magazine, August (2002)
8. Demasi, P. and Cruz, A.J. de O.: Online Coevolution for Action Games. In: Gough, N. and Mehdi, Q. (eds.): International Journal of Intelligent Games and Simulation, Vol. 2, No. 2 (2003) 80–88
9. Demasi, P. and Cruz, A.J. de O.: Anticipating Opponent Behaviour Using Sequential Prediction and Real-Time Fuzzy Rule Learning. In: Mehdi, Q., Gough, N. and Natkin, S. (eds.): Proceedings of the 4th International Conference on Intelligent Games and Simulation (2003) 101–105
10. Spronck, P., Sprinkhuizen-Kuyper, I. and Postma, E.: Online Adaptation of Game Opponent AI in Simulation and in Practice. In: Mehdi, Q., Gough, N. and Natkin, S. (eds.): Proceedings of 4th International Conference on Intelligent Games and Simulation (2003) 93–100
11. Russell, S. and Norvig, P.: Artificial Intelligence: A Modern Approach, Second Edition. Prentice Hall, Englewood Cliffs, New Jersey (2002)
12. Manslow, J.: Learning and Adaptation. In: Rabin, S. (ed.): AI Game Programming Wisdom. Charles River Media (2002) 557–566
13. Bäck, T.: Evolutionary Algorithms in Theory and Practice. Oxford University Press, New York (1996)
14. Spronck, P., Sprinkhuizen-Kuyper, I. and Postma, E.: Improving Opponent Intelligence Through Offline Evolutionary Learning. In: International Journal of Intelligent Games and Simulation, Vol. 2, No. 1 (2003) 20–27

Open-Source Game Development with the Multi-user Publishing Environment (MUPE) Application Platform

Riku Suomela[1], Eero Räsänen[1], Ari Koivisto[2], and Jouka Mattila[1]

[1] Nokia Research Center,
P.O. Box 100, 33721 Tampere, Finland
{riku.suomela, eero.k.rasanen, jouka.mattila}@nokia.com
[2] Tampere University of Technology,
P.O. Box 527, 33101 Tampere, Finland
borg@iki.fi

Abstract. The Multi-User Application Platform (MUPE) is a platform for rapid development of mobile multi-user context-aware applications. MUPE server implements a persistent user-authenticated service that can be customized into a game server. The game logic is written to the MUPE server and the end-users download the game User Interface (UI) to their terminals. This paper studies how MUPE can be used to create mobile multi-player games. This paper analyzes the important aspects of MUPE in game development and the different parts involved in developing games with MUPE. Two games made with MUPE are introduced and analyzed. The games presented in this paper and the MUPE system are available at the MUPE website http://www.mupe.net under the Nokia open source license version 1.0a.

1 Introduction

Mobile phones and devices are carried by millions of users worldwide. The devices are connected, thus enabling the construction of multi-player games that can be played by millions of mobile users. The development of multi-player games is a time and resource-consuming task as a multi-player game requires a solid software platform before the actual game development can start. Multi-User Publishing Environment (MUPE) is an open-source platform for creating mobile multi-user context-aware applications [1], such as mobile games. MUPE aims to lower the threshold of creating mobile multi-player games with a solid application platform that enables the application developers to directly concentrate on the game development.

The MUPE application platform has a client-server architecture, where the end-users use a MIDP 1.0 midlet to connect their mobile devices to the MUPE server in the Internet. A single MUPE client is used in all MUPE applications to enable easy connection to different MUPE applications and services. Any external information source in the Internet can be added to MUPE with the context components. The MUPE connection middleware connects the different parts of MUPE. The MUPE structure is seen in Fig. 1.

M. Rauterberg (Ed.): ICEC 2004, LNCS 3166, pp. 308–320, 2004.

MUPE applications are written to the MUPE server, which is the only component requiring programming in a basic application. The client User Interface (UI) is created with client UI scripts that the client downloads from the server. With the first connection, the client creates a persistent user account to the server and the client also stores the service address, username and password for enabling easy subsequent connection. Each application that the user connects to is displayed on the MUPE client services list.

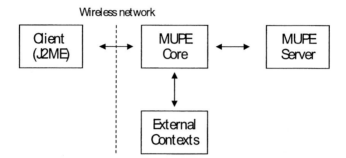

Fig. 1. The MUPE application platform structure

All parts of MUPE are available under the Nokia open source license version 1.0a [2]. Open sourcing the platform enables application developers to modify the system for their specific needs. Each game is different and has different requirement that can be well achieved with an open-source platform.

This paper studies how MUPE can be customized for mobile multi-player games. The application developers are free to modify MUPE and create their own games and services. The paper does not focus on game design, but rather looks into properties of MUPE that affect game design.

The paper is organized as follows. First, mobile and multi-player games as well as other technologies that influenced the development of MUPE are studied. After that the MUPE system and the essential parts to gaming are explained followed by two example games developed with MUPE. Finally, the work is concluded and future work is discussed.

2   Mobile and Multi-player Gaming

MUPE Platform is designed to enable easy creation of mobile multi-user context-aware applications. There are several systems that inspired and influenced the MUPE application platform design. The most important influences were the MUDs (Multi-User Dungeons) and MOOs (MUD Object-Oriented) [3] that were an early form of computer supported multi-player gaming. The first MUDs were developed already in the 1970s, being virtual worlds where people could interact with other users of the system. The MUDs have evolved over the years to support the new technologies in the Internet and today there are several hugely popular Massively Multiplayer Online Games (MMOG), such as Ultima Online [4] and PlanetSide [5]. The first MMOGs are making their way to mobile phones as well, as seen by games such as Tibia Micro Edition (TibiaME) [6]. Palm [7] gives a good overview of issues regarding the development of Mobile Massively Multiplayer Online Games (3MOG).

Mobile devices, however, are very different in nature compared to the desktop computers. The mobile devices are used in varying situations as the users move in the real world. The device's ability to react and adapt to changes in the users environment is called context-awareness. A good definition of context awareness is found in [8], which states that context is information that describes the situation of an entity. Context-awareness allows the environment to have an affect on the gameplay.

One of the oldest forms of context-aware gaming is the treasure hunt games played with a GPS receiver [9]. Several other context-aware games have also been built, such as the Pirates! [10], ARQuake [11], BotFighters [12] and Can You See Me Now? [13]. These games add new features to the games that truly take advantage of the mobility and the environment where the game is played. As the device is carried in the real world, the real world can and should influence the gameplay. A good study on how the real world can influence the gameplay can be found in [14].

MUPE is a platform for quick and easy development of new applications. MUPE contains the tools and ready-made technologies for creating new applications and games. The systems described here are good examples of how the games have evolved over time. The evolution will continue and MUPE aims to speed up the process of integrating new technologies to mobile gaming.

3   MUPE Application Platform for Mobile Gaming

MUPE application platform was designed to support different kinds of applications. This chapter explores the key technologies of MUPE that affect mobile game development. The key design issue when designing games with MUPE is the optimization of the client server communications.

Games, as all MUPE applications, are written to the MUPE server. The server is the main container for the application and it is the only component requiring programming when creating new games. The end-user client is a J2ME MIDlet that connects to the server. The client uses a custom script language that describes the UI and client side functionality. Any context source in the Internet can be connected to the system. The communication core of MUPE does not need any modification for a typical game application.

This chapter looks at how the MUPE application platform can be customized for mobile multi-player games. First, the client and its technology is discussed so we have a firm understanding on what kind of content can be shown to the end-users. After that, the server is analyzed and finally the context-awareness in the system is explained.

3.1   MUPE Client for Gaming

MUPE client is a MIDlet running on a mobile device such as a mobile phone. A single MUPE client is used in all different MUPE applications and the different UIs and functionality is achieved with the MUPE client script language. The client is based on MIDP 1.0 specifications [15] and it can be optimized in many different areas making it suitable for networked mobile applications. The main optimizations are done at the network level and with the client-side script language

In the network level, the communication is optimized for GRPS level data transfers, which mean high latency, and mediocre data transfer capabilities. MIDP 1.0 implementation uses only HTTP protocol, which restricts the choice of data exchange between the client and server. The client communicates with server by making requests and on each request the HTTP connection must be opened, which results in a high latency. Often the connection to the server takes longer than the actual data transfer. The HTTP connection sets restrictions on game developers, but with proper game design these should not matter too much. A good overview on mobile multiplayer game design can be found in [16]. The document also points out the latency problem and how the developers need to prepare for it.

The script language implements two different UI styles and some client side functionality enabling the client to be somewhat standalone. The two UIs supported by the client are canvas UI, which is a Graphical UI (GUI), and form UI, which is a text based UI. The two different UIs are both suitable for gaming purposes, but they are very different in nature. The client can contain several UIs at the same time and only one of them is active at a time.

The client script language uses hooks to catch different events in the UI, for example selecting an object or pressing a button. The hooks enable client-side functionality that work without a need for network communications. For example, the press of a button can move or hide objects on screen. The script language also defines attributes, timers, loops and a set of conditional statements that make the client-side functionality richer and more independent from the server.

The main point to remember when designing games with MUPE is that the transactions with the server create the most downtime and should be minimized. It is better to load the whole set of (or a certain subset of) user-interfaces into the client at one time than loading them on-demand all the time, since one can easily activate and disable UIs and UI widgets in the client-side when needed. This also applies to graphics, and all the required images should be loaded on startup, even though they are not all shown in the beginning. Naturally the client device's memory capacity sets some limitations on the size of these files. During the game, these pre-loaded images should be used, creating new image objects on the screen when necessary, and deleting them when they're not needed anymore. In some cases, rather than deleting, it's better just to hide the image objects, and show them again when they're needed. This removes the small delay in creating and deleting UI objects on the client side.

One can argue that a script language is not an optimal solution for the client side. However, the script language was implemented due to the limitations of MIDP 1.0 specifications, which do not allow the MIDlet to download Java classes over the network. This would be beneficial in many cases, as each game could use a dedicated client. One of the main goals of MUPE was to develop a single client that can be used in many applications. This eliminates the need to install a new client for every application.

MIDP was chosen for the client implementation due to its popularity. There are millions of client devices capable of running MIDP 1.0 MIDlets providing a wide range of end-user platforms that can run MUPE. MIDP is also constantly evolving, as many devices support MIDP 2.0. For detailed information on the client script language, refer to the MUPE website http://www.mupe.net.

3.2 MUPE Server for Gaming

MUPE server contains all of the game functionality and logic. The server knows the current state of the game and the connected players. The clients make requests and the server replies to the requests with a valid UI script. The UI script either generates a new UI or updates the existing UI. The reload of the whole UI should be avoided in games using a GUI whenever possible and only the changes should be updated. The server needs to know the state of each player in the system and be able to update the necessary changes to all.

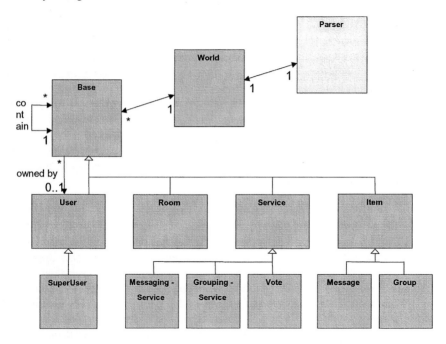

Fig. 2. The basic MUPE server structure

The basic MUPE server structure [17] contains a *World* class for storing the content inside the application and four classes representing the content: *User, Item, Service* and *Room*. The *User* class represents a single connected end-user in the system, the *Room* a location in the game world, *Services* provide add-on features for other objects, and an *Item* is any other data inside the application. The server structure can be easily mapped to common game elements: *User* for each player, *Room* for each game location, and *Item* for each object used by players or contained in the game world. *Services* provide add-on features to other objects, such as group forming. The game world can be in a single *Room*, or the game world is divided into several areas, each represented by *Rooms*. The *Item* class should be derived to add the necessary functions and items needed in the game. Different type of players in the game should be derived from the *User* class for the each different type of character needed in the game. The basic MUPE server structure is seen in Fig. 2.

As MUPE clients only support HTTP as the connection protocol, server cannot push any data to clients in order to update the UI. Instead, clients must poll the server constantly to fetch the latest updates. To make things easier, MUPE server has built-in commands for "pushing" data to users. Since current version cannot actually push the data to Clients, it is instead queued separately for each user, and returned to the Client with the next request the Client makes. Another built-in command also enables pushing data to every user within a certain *Room* in the game world to make updating the views even easier. The push times could vary for different users, depending on many things such as the network load. As the latency of each individual user can vary, the users push data queue can contain varying amount of information for various users.

The basic MUPE server contains several useful features that can be used in almost any game. As the user connects to the MUPE system, she/he creates an avatar into the MUPE server. This can be used as the game character creation service. The server also remembers the user state between the connections, and the MUPE communications middleware takes care of typical game communication needs. These features make MUPE an appealing platform for game creation. The virtual world and the user accounts can be easily modified to fit many kinds of multi-player games.

3.3 Context-Awareness

The context-awareness in MUPE is built into two separate parts. First, the connected user clients can send their context information to the server, as they are constantly connected to the service. Second, any information in the Internet can be sent to the MUPE application by writing a context producer that formats context information according to the Context Exchange Protocol (CEP) [18].

The connected user clients vary in their capabilities, so it is difficult to be sure that all the users have certain context capabilities present in their devices. If the game uses for example the location of the user, the capabilities of the different can vary a lot; some devices are not able to determine their location, while others have a varying accuracy for it.

The context producers on the Internet are not dependent on the client capabilities. They feed information to the MUPE applications no matter who is connected and also they can be totally controlled by the system administrators thus providing reliable information. External context producers can characterize the situation of any entity in the application, not necessarily that of an end-user. A single context producer can feed information to many MUPE services and when a producer is setup, other applications can also later connect to it.

Client-side context-awareness allows a lot more possibilities for the game developers. Each player can have personal context-information that describes his or her current state, which will be different for every user. At the moment though, the context producers are the only form of contexts that are supported by the MUPE application platform. There are several useful APIs for the J2ME platform that can be used, but at the time of writing this paper there were no devices available for us. The client script language will be updated with the context-aware features once they have been properly tested. At least the Bluetooth API (JSR-82) and Location API (JSR-179) for J2ME should be useful when determining context information on the client side. For more information on upcoming APIs for the J2ME platform, please refer to [15].

4 Games with MUPE Application Platform

We have developed two games with the MUPE application platform that explore the strengths and weaknesses of MUPE. They are both modified from the basic MUPE server found in the MUPE website. Both of these games are also available as open source software and they can be modified and extended by others.

The basic MUPE server does three things that are useful for the multi-player games. First, the basic MUPE framework takes care of all the communications. Second, the server creates a persistent user account for each user. Third, MUPE client and server remember these connections and allow the users to reconnect to the services easily, enabling a persistent game. These things enable the game developers to concentrate on the most important task, the game development. We hope that MUPE enables new mobile games to be made with less effort and resources.

The games have context-aware information already built into them and simulators for generating the data. However, currently the games presented here do not use this data for anything. If a proper connection with real world data to these games can be found, the context awareness is easy to add to these games.

4.1 MUPE Dungeon

MUPE Dungeon is a game of dungeon exploring, heavily influenced by the MUDs. The users take the role of one of four character types: Fighter, Gnome, Wizard or Thief and together the players explore the dungeon and fight horrendous monsters. The game screen seen by the players is composed of 9x9 tiles and usually less than half of the screen is occupied with the structures. Players, monsters and empty tiles take up the remaining space. Each game screen is a single *Room* in the MUPE world. The users move between the *Rooms* in the game world and encounter other users and monsters in them. There can be one or more players and the number of players is not restricted by the game, but the limited screen space makes it difficult to have a very large number of players at the same screen. The system will not support an endless amount of players as there will be limiting factors, such as cellular base station capacity and server hardware.

Three classes are created for the dungeon game: player, mapsquare and monster. Every player is a subclass of *User*, every 9x9 square view of the dungeon is a subclass of a *Room*, and all the monsters within the rooms are derived from *Item*. If the game was extended to contain weapons and other items, these could be derived from *Item* class and be picked up and carried by Users.

The game aims to showcase how MUPE can be used to build semi real-time multi-player games that have a varying number of players. Each player has a fixed time to make a move, which is set to five seconds. After that, each player updates his/her move to the server and the server responds with the new state of the UI. All graphics are downloaded at the connection time so graphics download does not slow down the gameplay. The communication between the client and server is done with HTTP, which usually takes a few seconds to get the response. During this time, the client animates the player's movement creating a feeling that something is constantly happening.

The user interface is shown in Fig. 3 and Fig. 4. The first screenshot in the Fig. 3 shows the login process where the user sets the password for connecting. The following image shows the user selecting the character for the game. The third image shows the four different player types and the three different monster types. There is also an animation shown on the screen that is marked with the star. The character next to the star has attacked a monster and while the client waits for the new updated information from the server, the animation is shown.

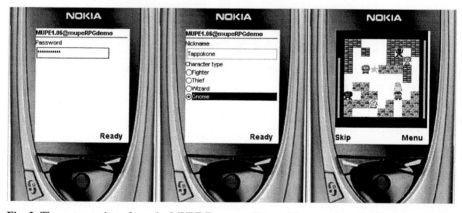

Fig. 3. Three screenshots from the MUPE Dungeon Game. All screenshots in this document are screenshots from the Wireless Toolkit 1.0.4_01 Emulator. The screen in mobile devices may vary

The animations are achieved by hooking the button presses of the device on the client side. As the user presses a button, the client knows what to do. If a monster is on the direction where the user is going to, the monster is attacked. If there is an empty space, the user is moved. This information is needed before the server data exchange to be able to create the animations while the user waits for the update.

The Fig. 4 shows two more images from the game. First, the character can see his or her stats by reverting to the character abilities screen. This screen and the game area are both contained in the memory of the client and no server connections are necessary when changing between the views. The user can also choose to say something to other players and the second image in Fig. 4 shows how the users see the comments of other players.

This game has been played several times with a varying group of players and the response has been the same. The user experience is heavily dependent on the latency of the connection, which varies a lot depending on many factors. As the user makes a move, the following move cannot be made before the server responds with the new state of the game. Whenever the latency is low enough, the update can be done while the animation is running on screen. If the latency is much higher than the animation time, the game is not very appealing.

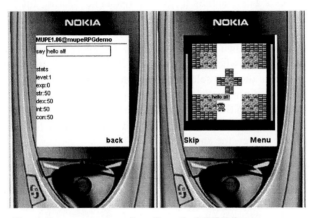

Fig. 4. Two more screenshots from the MUPE Dungeon game

4.2 First Strike

The second game made with MUPE is a turn-based strategy game for exactly four players and the game applies simultaneous turn taking. The players connect to the MUPE server and are placed in the game waiting room. The players select a color that represents them in the game and after enough players are connected, the game starts. When the four players start the game, the waiting room becomes empty and the next four players can start a new game.

First Strike contains four countries that are fighting for victory. Each player owns two cities and each player can choose one action from three options in a round. The choices are: 1. Attack another player's city. 2. Place shields on top of one city. 3. Hire the Nuclear Waste Army to visit a city (the result of the visit is unknown). Again, the users have a certain amount of time to select their actions after which the users data is sent to the server. During the update the user sees a notification: "waiting for other players". After the update is completed, the new game state is updated on screen, the actions are animated and the next round begins.

Fig. 5. Three screenshots of the First Strike game

The flow of the game can be seen in Figs 5 and 6. The first screenshot in Fig. 5 shows the character creation screen. After this, the user chooses a color and waits for other players to enter the game. The third image shows the actual gameplay, where the user selects a target for the military action.

Fig. 6. Three more screenshots of the FirstStrike game

The Fig. 6 shows more screenshots from the game. The first screenshot shows the user selecting what action is performed on the selected city, followed by the UI informing the user about the server update. Finally, an animation shows the actions taken this round.

The game server has been played several times and this game is not as dependent on the latency of the network as the MUPE Dungeon game. The user does many things in a turn, like assessing the status of the game and deciding what the next action will be. This also goes on during the update of the game state and thus the game tempo is better for this game.

The FirstStrike has a different server structure compared to the MUPEDungeon. The players are again *Users*, but this time the whole game is a single *Room*, and there are no *Items*. Even the *Users* are unchanged from the original MUPE release, making the whole First Strike game to be fit into only one *Room* subclass. Games such as FirstStrike can be moved to any MUPE application, where it is a special *Room* offering a gaming service. One idea of this game was to create a mini-game server, where several multiplayer games can be selected. At the moment the FirstStrike is the only game available but new games can be added in a similar way, that is, deriving from the *Room* object.

4.3 Analysis

This chapter presented two different games made with the MUPE platform. The games were designed differently, but both fitted well to the MUPE application platform. The MUPE server offers a flexible structure that can be exploited in many ways. The first game, MUPE Dungeon, creates a vast virtual world into the MUPE server where the users move between the game area rooms and explore the game world. The second game, First Strike, fits into a single room making it transferable to any MUPE server.

It seems simultaneous turn taking is a good strategy when designing games with the MUPE platform. Simultaneous turn taking is scalable, as the time for a round does not increase with the amount of players. Both of the games could use many features of the basic MUPE server, to speed up the development process. The user login is unchanged and the character creation only needs a little modification. The communications and client do not require any programming.

5 Conclusions

This paper presented how MUPE – the Multi-User Publishing Environment can be used to create mobile multi-player games. The platform enables rapid creation of multi-player games by providing ready-made architecture that connects the players to a server and creates a persistent player account for the end-users. The platform is available as open-source software allowing application developers to create their own mobile games with maximum flexibility.

The MUPE architecture fits well for games. The basic platform implements all connections and the creation of a persistent user account that are essential parts in multi-player gaming. The UI of the client can be completely customized and functionality can be uploaded to the client allowing the end-users to interact with the client device without a constant need for updates to the game server.

Two mobile multi-player games made with MUPE were presented to highlight the various aspects of the MUPE platform. The two games had a very different server structure highlighting how different games can be built with MUPE. The other game used several Room objects where the user can move to create a large game world, whereas the other game uses a single Room object for the game allowing easy addition of multiple games into the same server. Also, the game can be easily moved to other MUPE applications.

The MUPE game design was mostly restricted by the HTTP transport protocol used by the client. This causes high latencies in the data exchange between the client and the server. With proper design, for example applying simultaneous turn taking, such effects can be reduced.

6   Future Work

All parts of MUPE platform are under constant development. There are constantly new features and APIs available for the J2ME platform that will be integrated to the client UI scripts. The MIDP 2.0 version of the client will support other connection methods than HTTP, among other features. Java APIs for context-awareness, such as the Java location API (JSR-82) and the Bluetooth API (JSR-179) will be implemented in the future. These and new games will be further developed in the Nomadic Media ITEA (Information Technology for European Advancement) project. We aim to create games that support public screens in public spaces.

Acknowledgements. This work is funded by the Nomadic Media ITEA project.

References

1.   Multi-User Publishing Environment (MUPE) Application Platform. Available online at the MUPE website. http://www.mupe.net (2003)
2.   Nokia Open Source License Version 1.0a (NOKOS License). Available online at http://www.opensource.org/licenses/nokia.php
3.   Multiple User Dimension/Dungeon/Domain (MUD). Available online at http://www.moo.mud.org/
4.   ORIGIN Systems Inc: Ultima Online. Electronic Arts (1997)
5.   Verant Interactive: PlanetSide. Sony Online Entertainment (2003)
6.   CipSoft: Tibia Micro Edition (TibiaME). T-Mobile. (2003)
7.   Palm, T.: The Birth Of The Mobile MMOG. Available online at http://www.gamasutra.com/resource_guide/20030916/palm_01.shtml (2003)
8.   Dey, A.K.: Providing Architectural Support for Building Context-Aware Applications, Ph.D. thesis. College of Computing, Georgia Institute of Technology, (2000). Available online at http://www.cc.gatech.edu/fce/ctk/pubs/dey-thesis.pdf
9.   Geocaching. http://www.geocaching.com/
10. Björk, S., Falk, J., Hansson, R., Ljungstrand, P.: Pirates! - Using the Physical World as a Game Board. Proceedings of the Human-Computer Interaction INTERACT'01 (2001) 423-430
11. Thomas, B., Close, B., Donoghue, J., Squires, J., De Bondi, P., Morris, M., Piekarski, W.: ARQuake: an outdoor/indoor augmented reality first person application. Proceedings of the Fourth International Symposium on Wearable Computers. (2000) 139-146
12. It's Alive: BotFighters. It's Alive (2001)
13. Can You See Me now? http://www.canyouseemenow.co.uk/
14. Sotamaa, O. All The World's A Botfighter Stage: Notes on Location-based Multi-player Gaming. Proceedings of the Computer Games and Digital Cultures Conference, Tampere University Press (2002) 35-44

15. Java 2 Platform, Micro Edition (J2ME). http://java.sun.com/j2me/
16. Overview of Multiplayer Mobile Game Design. Available online at:
    http://www.forum.nokia.com/main.html (2003)
17. Koivisto, A.: Multi-User Publishing Environment Server. M Sc. Thesis, Tampere
    University of Technology. Available online at: http://www.mupe.net/ (2003)
18. Context Exchange Protocol. Available online at: http://www.mupe.net/ (2003)

Player-Centered Game Environments: Assessing Player Opinions, Experiences, and Issues

Penelope Sweetser and Daniel Johnson

School of Information Technology and Electrical Engineering,
University of Queensland, Australia.
{penny,uqdjohns}@itee.uq.edu.au

Abstract. Game developers have identified, explored and discussed many of the key issues that arise for players interacting in game worlds. However, there is a need to assess the thoughts and opinions of game-players on these issues, through structured, empirical studies. This paper reports the results of two player-centered studies aimed at investigating these issues from the player's perspective. The first study, a focus group, supports some of the issues identified by game developers; consistency, intuitiveness and freedom of expression, and identifies new issues; immersion and physics. The second study, a questionnaire, examined the relationship of these issues to game-type preference and game-playing experience. This paper represents important initial exploratory research that supplements the existing literature by focusing on the player's perspective and exploring which issues and context have the most impact on player enjoyment.

1 Introduction to Interactions in Game Worlds

Acquiring the player's perspective on game design issues is crucial in enhancing the gaming experience, by understanding, and ultimately meeting, the desires and expectations of the player. Although many game developers gather player feedback in some form, there is limited published literature on game design in terms of the aspects of game environments that affect player enjoyment. Furthermore, the majority of this literature is based on the personal experience and thoughts of game developers. This literature focuses on several major themes; consistency, intuitiveness, learning and freedom of player expression. Consistency is considered to be crucial for keeping players immersed in the game world [2]. If the game world seems to behave consistently and in ways that the player understands then the player has less difficulty immersing themselves in the environment and suspending disbelief [4]. Inconsistencies in games, such as getting stuck in a wall when adventuring in a dungeon, remind the player that it is just a game [2]. The second theme, intuitiveness, suggests that interactions with the game environment and objects in the game environment should be intuitive and meet player expectation. People who are less-experienced game players can be baffled by the physics of the game world and often need to relearn how to interact with the world like a child [4]. Game worlds are populated with objects that are visually similar to objects that we use every day, but

M. Rauterberg (Ed.): ICEC 2004, LNCS 3166, pp. 321–332, 2004.
© IFIP International Federation for Information Processing 2004

these objects are functionally different. Not only can these interactions be counter-intuitive for the player, but they can often confuse and frustrate the player [2]. An important benefit of making game worlds more intuitive is that they become easier to learn. The player is more likely to develop an intuitive understanding of the game elements if they are consistent with real world elements [3]. When the game environment is intuitive, the learning curve for the player is substantially decreased, which means that the player spends less time learning the game and more time playing the game [3]. The final theme identified in the literature is freedom of player expression or the possibility of emergent gameplay. In most games, the designers manually define a number of outcomes or interactions and allow the player to pick one, which restricts the player's freedom in interacting and removes the possibility of emergent gameplay [4]. A more pleasing experience for the player is theorized to result when the player has greater freedom in terms of deciding how to interact with the environment.

Although a great deal of insight can be gained from the thoughts and experiences of game developers, there is also a need to assess the thoughts and opinions of game players regarding the factors that affect their enjoyment of games. Previous empirical studies have provided insight into the player's perspective on non-player characters in games [5]. However, there is no published work on empirical studies conducted by game developers or researchers to ascertain player perspective on interacting in game environments. Therefore, the aim of the research reported in this paper is to investigate the aspects of game environments that affect player enjoyment from the player's perspective. The method employed in this study was to conduct a focus group with experienced game-players to identify the issues that they felt most affected their enjoyment of a game. The focus group was followed up by a questionnaire, which aimed to assess how these issues vary in importance across players with different game-playing experience and game-type preference.

2   Defining the Player-Centered Issues

The goal of this study was to collect the opinions and experiences of a group of experienced game players with respect to the issues that impacted upon their enjoyment of game environments. The method employed in this study was a focus group, consisting of four experienced game players who were brought together to discuss their experiences. The group members were aged between 21 and 25 and consisted of one female and three males. Each member of the group considered themselves to be an experienced game player and reported playing games on a daily basis with a minimum of five years experience playing games. The focus group involved several general points of discussion, but the group was mostly encouraged to freely discuss their experiences. An audio recording was taken during the focus group, which was later transcribed and analyzed using grounded theory [1]. This analysis gave rise to five major themes, consistency, immersion and suspension of disbelief, freedom of player expression, intuitiveness and physics.

2.1   Consistency

A strong theme arising throughout the focus group was the importance of consistency in games. Participants felt that it is highly important for objects that look the same to act the same. For example, one member was frustrated with "glass windows that break sometimes but don't break other times". Similar problems were identified for crates, barrels, lanterns and mirrors. These inconsistencies can cause difficulties for the player in learning the rules of the game, which appear to be constantly changing. Also, on the other end of this scale, it is important for objects that have different behavior to look different, signaling to the player that a different kind of interaction is possible. For example, "some games signal actions by having different colored walls for bits of wall you can kick out, e.g. *Bloodrayne*" and referring to the game *Dungeon Siege* "there were certain walls that looked a bit different, but you knew that you could shoot that wall out". However, it was also expressed that this visual difference shouldn't be in the form of something unrealistic, such as a big red circle around the section. Rather, it should be a subtle, realistic difference that the player can detect, such as a "worn-looking part of the wall" that might be more fragile.

2.2   Immersion and Suspension of Disbelief

Another major theme of the discussion was immersion and suspension of disbelief. The group agreed that audio is very important for keeping the player immersed in the game, in terms of a "powerful and moving soundtrack", as well as sound effects. The group thought that a game is immersive if it can cause an emotional response, such as fear or happiness. The group discussed how sounds can be used to build up suspense, such as in a horror movie when "you know that something is creeping up on you, to the point that you're afraid and shifting in your seat". Furthermore, audio was highlighted as being important for "drawing you into the game, but inconsistent graphics can quickly knock you back out again". The graphics don't need to be spectacular, but they do need to be consistent, ensuring "nothing catches your eye as being wrong or out of place". A good introduction and a strong narrative were also identified as being important for immersion. The introduction gives the player the storyline and background, tells them who their character is and what is going on. The player then feels like they are "part of the story and they want to find out more". As they play the game, the player is given more of the storyline, "similar to reading a book, except that they need to complete certain tasks" to be rewarded with more of the story.

2.3   Freedom of Player Expression

Another theme that arose was player expression, which is the freedom that the player has in expressing their creativity and intentions by playing the game in the way that they want, not the way that the designer had intended it to be played. The group discussed linearity in games and agreed that they are often forced to solve problems and perform tasks the way the designer had imagined, which sometimes relies on the player using trial and error. For example, many "quests aren't even quests, they're completely linear, you've been told exactly what to do, you just have to go pick this thing up and come back, you should be able to go out and do the quest your own way". One member said that it becomes "more like trial and error than playing and that it's not as fun as looking around at a collection of objects and working out how to use them to solve the problem". It was also felt to be important that the player has a range of interactions that can be performed with the environment and game objects and that each game should have some kind of new and unique interaction.

2.4 Intuitiveness

The group reflected on many experiences in games where their interactions with the environment had not been intuitive. A major source of frustration came from objects in games that were simply scenery and hence could not be used or affected. For example, furniture that cannot be moved as it seems to be bolted to the floor or "a flimsy little plastic chair that can be shot with a shotgun and it's resilient enough to take that and not be damaged". These interactions can also cause problems for gameplay, when the player cannot use objects in the way that they would expect in order to complete a quest or solve a problem. The group discussed the unintuitive nature of problem solving in some games. The group found that the way the designers intend the problem to be solved is often not intuitive for the player and that they "resort to trial and error". The group discussed this problem and suggested that "if it takes 10 hours to find a switch or the player needs to go to the internet to get a walkthrough then there is a serious problem with the game". Therefore, it is important to conduct extensive testing to ensure that the players' expectations are met and that they will be able to solve the problems in a reasonable time frame, rather than assuming the designer's intentions will be easily determined.

2.5 Physics

The group discussed their expectations of physics in games and reflected on their good and bad experiences. There was consensus that gravity in games is important for actions such as jumping, falling, taking falling damage, trajectory when launching rockets and so on. Modeling gravity can give rise to realistic effects such as bouncing grenades around corners, falling off a platform or rolling down a hill when shot. More importantly, the "gravity needs to behave consistently, even if it's not entirely realistic", such as in first person shooter games like *Unreal Tournament* and *Quake*, where the game may be in low gravity mode. Momentum was also identified as an important attribute of physics that needs to be modeled in games, especially in space simulations and first person shooters. For example, if the player shoots the enemy or is shot by the enemy then "being pushed backwards is natural". Another important aspect of physics concerns fire and explosions. Flammable game objects should burn and ignite when affected by a flamethrower or incendiary grenade. Also, when a flash grenade explodes next to a character it should adversely affect their sight and hearing, or when an explosion occurs the player "should be able to jump into a pool of water to be protected" from damage. Water was also identified as a substance that needs to be modeled more accurately in games. For example, there was considerable discussion about how most weapons shouldn't work under water, especially flamethrowers and fire-based weapons. Other attributes of water that the group decided were important were the effects of the flow and currents of the water, as well as visual effects such as ripples.

2.6 Conclusions

In summary, the focus group provided supporting evidence for the themes of consistency, freedom of expression and intuitiveness identified in the game design literature. First, players need consistency in games to be able to learn the rules of the game, to know when they can interact with game elements and to avoid frustration and confusion. Second, players want to be free to play games and solve problems in the way that they want, not the way the designer had intended. Third, counterintuitive interactions often result from game objects having no function or behaving in a way that conflicts with player expectation. Furthermore, this study provided insight into two new issues that affect player enjoyment in games, immersion and physics. Immersive games draw the player into the game and affect their senses and emotions through elements such as audio and narrative. Finally, consistent physics are important in games to ensure the physical elements of the game world, such as gravity, momentum, fire and water, behave in the way that the player expects, to allow the player to perform actions in an intuitive manner and to keep the player immersed in the game world.

3   Investigating the Player-Centered Issues

In this study, the results obtained from the focus group were used as a basis for constructing a questionnaire that aimed to further investigate the issues of consistency, immersion, freedom of expression, intuitiveness and physics in game environments. Whereas the focus group provided in-depth insight into the opinions and experiences of a small group of experienced game players with respect to these issues, the questionnaire was designed to provide a survey of the opinions of a large, diverse group of game players. The questionnaire was administered online [6] and invitations to participate were posted on several online game forums. The questionnaire was completed by four hundred and fifty-five participants, of which 421 (92.5%) were male and 34 (7.5%) were female. Participants ranged in age from 11 to 56 years, M = 24.8 (SD = 6.91). The sample consisted mainly of frequent game-players, with 94% playing computer games at least monthly. The distribution of game-playing frequency and age are shown in Fig. 1. There were two main aims of this study. First, to determine how the different issues (identified in the literature and from the results of the focus group) affect the enjoyment of people who play different types of computer games, such as role-playing games or first-person shooter games. The second aim was to determine how these issues affect the enjoyment of people with different levels of experience playing computer games. One question of particular interest is whether intuitive interactions with game environments and objects have a greater affect on the enjoyment of people with less game-playing experience. That is, do people who have less experience playing games (and aren't well-versed in the "rules" of game worlds) find that unintuitive interactions have a greater affect on their enjoyment?

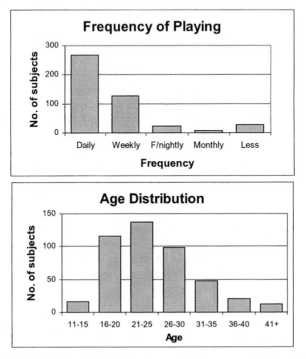

Fig. 1. The majority of subjects (94%) played gamed at least monthly. Participants ranged in age from 11 to 56 years, with the majority in their late teens to late twenties.

3.1   Method

There were three between-subject variables, gender, game-type preference and experience. The participants selected their preferred type of game from a list of seven common game types, with the majority of participants nominating role-playing games (41%), first-person shooters (28%) or strategy games (16%) as their preferred game type. The other four game-types, simulation, action, racing and sport accounted for twelve percent of the sample. The participants indicated their level of experience at playing computer games on a seven-point Likert scale, ranging from very inexperienced to very experienced, with the majority of participants rating themselves as experienced, M = 5.88 (SD = 1.37). The distribution of game-type preference and self-rated experience are shown in Fig. 2.

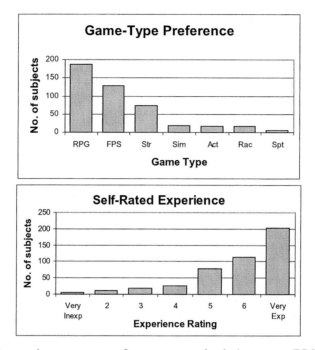

Fig. 2. The three major game-type preferences were role-playing games (RPG), first-person shooters (FPS) and strategy games (Str). The majority of participants rated themselves as very experienced.

The participants were required to complete 28 nine-point Likert scales to indicate the degree to which different aspects of games affect their enjoyment of their preferred type of game, where one indicated "much less enjoyable", five indicated "no effect" and nine indicated "much more enjoyable" (see Appendix for questionnaire items). All measures were assessed using multiple item scales and all negatively worded items were reverse-scored. Factor analysis via principal components was conducted to identify sets of variables that could be combined into scales. On the basis of eigenvalues greater than one criterion, a five factor solution was obtained accounting for 68.6% of the variance. Cronbach's coefficient alpha was used to assess the reliability of each scale. All scales were found to have acceptable reliabilities (.66 to .90). The five factors derived were physics, sound, narrative, intuitiveness and freedom of expression (see Table 1). The physics scale consisted of eight items related to gravity, momentum, life-like graphics and the behavior of water and fire. The sound scale consisted of three items related to a game's soundtrack and sound effects. The narrative scale was made up of two items related to a game's introduction and storyline. The intuitiveness scale was comprised of three items related to consistent behavior of objects, scenery and interaction with objects. The freedom of expression scale consisted of two items related to the variety of ways of interacting with objects and having new and unique ways of interacting with objects.

Table 1. Descriptive data for dependent measures

Variable	Mean	Standard Deviation	Possible Range	Actual Range	Reliability
Sound	7.53	1.26	1 - 9	1 – 9	.85
Narrative	7.20	1.31	1 - 9	1.5 – 9	.68
Physics	7.07	1.09	1 - 9	3.13 – 9	.90
Expression	7.40	1.29	1 - 9	1 – 9	.79
Intuitiveness	6.31	1.06	1 - 9	2.67 - 9	.66

3.2   Results and Discussion

Regression analyses were used to examine the main and interactive effects of gender, game-type preference and experience on each of the dependent measures (physics, sound, narrative, intuitiveness and expression). The main effect terms (gender, game-type preference and experience) were entered into the regression equation followed by the two-way interaction terms (gender-by-game-type preference, gender-by-experience and experience-by-game-type preference). The main effect terms, but not the two-way interaction terms, accounted for a significant increment of variance in physics ($F(3,385) = 3.185$, $p < .05$), sound ($F(3,384 = 6.662$, $p < .05$), freedom of expression ($F(3,385) = 5.287$, $p < .05$), and narrative ($F(4,387) = 2.788$, $p < .05$). Also, the main effect terms ($F(3,385) = 4.395$, $p < .05$) and the two-way interaction terms ($F(6,382) = 3.810$, $p < .05$) accounted for a significant increment of variance in intuitiveness.

Effects of Game-Type Preference. The first aim of this study was to investigate how game-type preference affects the aspects that make games more enjoyable for players. It was found that physics ($\beta = .095$, $t = 1.89$, $p = .06$), sound ($\beta = .117$, $t = 2.347$, $p < .05$) and intuitiveness ($\beta = .098$, $t = 1.937$, $p < .05$) have a greater affect on enjoyment for people who prefer first-person shooter games than people who prefer other types of games. This finding can be attributed to the centrality of these three aspects to first-person shooter games. First, physics is vital in first-person shooter games as typical behaviors include jumping, shooting and exploding, which need to be modeled with a certain degree of realism. Second, sound is important as it provides immediate feedback and information to the player about what is happening around them in this information rich environment, which includes fast gameplay, different enemies, rapid movement and numerous interactions with objects and the environment. Also, sound aids in setting the mood of the game and provides an additional level of immersion, by making the player feel frightened or excited. Finally, intuitive interactions with objects are important in first-person shooter games as this type of game requires far more direct interaction with the environment than any other type of game, such as direct manipulation of objects and interaction with scenery. Therefore, it is important that these interactions are intuitive as the player will be carrying out a greater number of interactions with greater frequency.

For people who prefer strategy games, it was found that narrative ($\beta = .112$, $t = 1.668$, $p < .10$) has a greater affect on enjoyment than for people who prefer other types of games. It might be expected that narrative would have a greater affect on the enjoyment of people who prefer role-playing games. However, this finding could be due to the fact that every role-playing game includes narrative, but it is uncommon in strategy games. Therefore, the addition of well-placed narrative in strategy games has a significant affect in increasing player enjoyment, whereas narrative is commonplace and expected in role-playing games and therefore the players fail to recognize it as something that affects their enjoyment.

Effects of Game-Playing Experience. The second aim of this study was to investigate how experience affects the aspects that make a game enjoyable. In particular, it was expected that the ability to interact intuitively with objects would have a greater affect on the enjoyment of people with less experience playing games. However, there was no evidence to support this theory. On the contrary, it was found that of the people who prefer role-playing games, the affect that intuitiveness has on enjoyment increases as level of experience increases ($\beta = -.804$, $\underline{t} = -2.841$, $p < .05$). Maybe more experienced game players expect to be able to interact with game environments and objects in a particular way, learned from their prior experience playing games, and find it annoying when the game doesn't behave in the way they have learned to expect. On the other hand, the inexperienced players have no concept of how the game objects should behave, rather they only have the concepts they have learned in real life. Additionally, it was found that the affect that sound ($\beta = .095$, $\underline{t} = 1.853$, $p < .10$), freedom of expression ($\beta = .179$, $\underline{t} = 3.448$, $p < .05$) and narrative ($\beta = .150$, $\underline{t} = 2.829$, $p < .05$) has on player enjoyment increases as level of experience increases. As with intuitive interactions, perhaps the player's expectations of these aspects are built up as they play more games. As a result, the more experienced game players know from experience that they have really enjoyed games with good sound and narrative. It makes sense that more experienced players should find freedom of expression more enjoyable, as their experience means that they are more likely to want to experiment, try different strategies and try to play the game in their own way.

4 Conclusions

The aim of this paper was to define the issues that have an impact on player enjoyment in a game environment from a player-centered perspective, by integrating the findings of a focus group and questionnaire with the insights of game developers. The focus group confirmed three of the themes identified in the game development literature. The first theme was consistency, which related to objects behaving in a consistent manner, enabling players to learn the rules of the game, to know when they can interact with game objects and to avoid frustration and confusion. The questionnaire, however, did not provide any further insight into this theme. The second theme from the literature that was supported by the focus group was freedom of expression, which refers to the ability of players to play the game and solve problems in their own way or a variety of ways, rather than the way the designer had intended. The questionnaire refined this theme by showing that the affect freedom of expression has on player enjoyment increases with level of experience. The third theme that was confirmed by the focus group was intuitive interactions with the game environment, which related to not being able to interact with objects or solve problems in the way that the player would expect. The findings from the questionnaire were that the affect that intuitiveness had on player enjoyment was higher for people who prefer first-person shooter games and people with more experience playing games.

Additionally, there were two new themes related to the enjoyment of players interacting in game worlds that were identified in the focus group. The first of these was immersion, which related to game aspects such as audio and narrative drawing the player into the game, enabling them to believe it is real or suspending their disbelief. The questionnaire further expanded this theme with the findings that sound has a significant affect on the enjoyment of people who prefer first-person shooter games and players with more experience. Also, it was found that narrative has a significant affect on people who prefer strategy games and players with more experience. The second new theme found in the focus group was consistent physics, which related to gravity, momentum and the basic laws of physics behaving consistently with player expectation, as well as more realistic behavior and interactivity in water, fire and explosions. The questionnaire showed that physics has a greater affect on the enjoyment of people who prefer first-person shooter games.

The background of the sample that participated in this study should also be considered. For the focus group, the participants were experienced game-players and as such their opinions and views may differ from a group of novice players. For the questionnaire, the majority of the sample consisted of experienced game-players and a large proportion of the participants were attracted from online game forums, such as Eve Online and EverQuest. As such, the results obtained from the questionnaire may more be biased towards these groups of players. Interesting and valuable future work would lie in investigating different groups of players and comparing their results to the results obtained in these studies.

In conclusion, the focus group provided supporting evidence from the player's perspective for some of the issues that were identified in game development literature, including intuitiveness, consistency and freedom of expression. Additionally, two new issues were defined in the focus group, immersion and physics. All these issues were then examined with relation to game-type preference and game-playing experience via the questionnaire. The two studies complement each other, as the focus group provided in-depth detail about how players feel about these issues, whereas the questionnaire provided empirical data about which groups of players these issues are most likely to affect. Particular insight was gained from the questionnaire with regards to first-person shooter games and also player experience. These studies also identify a number of interesting points that are worthy of further exploration in future player-centered studies.

References

1. Glaser, B.: Doing Grounded Theory: Issues and Discussions. Sociology Press, Mill Valley, CA (1998)
2. Hecker, C.: Physics in Computer Games. In: Communications of the ACM, Vol. 43 (7). ACM, New York (2000) 34-37
3. Smith, H.: Systemic Level Design. Presented at: Game Developers Conference, San Jose, CA, March 21-23 (2002)

4. Smith, H.: The Future of Game Design: Moving Beyond Deus Ex and Other Dated Paradigms. Available online at:
   http://www.planetdeusex.com/witchboy/articles/thefuture.shtml (2001)
5. Sweetser, P., Johnson, D., Sweetser, J. and Wiles, J.: Creating Engaging Artificial Characters for Games. In: Proceedings of the Second International Conference on Entertainment Computing. Carnegie Mellon University, Pittsburgh, PA (2003)
6. Available at http://www.itee.uq.edu.au/~penny/questionnaire.htm

Appendix: Questionnaire Measures

Each questionnaire item loaded on one of five factors (physics, sound, narrative, intuitiveness or expression) or was discarded if it did not load on a factor. The items that loaded on each factor and the discarded items are shown below.

Physics

- How does being affected by the laws of gravity affect your enjoyment of your preferred type of game (e.g. you can just in a realistic way or take falling damage)?
- How do objects that follow the laws of gravity in a realistic way affect your enjoyment of your preferred type of game (e.g. bouncing, falling, rolling down hills)?
- How does momentum affect your enjoyment of your preferred type of game (e.g. being pushed backwards when hit)?
- How does water that behaves in a realistic way affect your enjoyment of your preferred type of game (e.g. flows, wets, cools, current)?
- How do objects that are affected by water in a realistic way affect your enjoyment of your preferred type of game (e.g. weapons cannot work underwater)?
- How does fire that behaves in a realistic way affect your enjoyment of your preferred type of game (e.g. burns, ignites, heats)?
- How do objects that are affected by fire in a realistic way affect your enjoyment of your preferred type of game (e.g. flammable objects burn or explosives explode when they come in contact with fire)?
- How do life-like graphics affect your enjoyment of your preferred type of game?

Sound

- How does a moving and powerful soundtrack affect your enjoyment of your preferred type of game?
- How do sound effects that set the mood (e.g. build up suspense) affect your enjoyment of your preferred type of game?
- How do sound effects that cause an emotional response (e.g. fear or happiness) affect your enjoyment of your preferred type of game?

Narrative

- How does an introduction that sets the scene for the game affect your enjoyment of your preferred type of game?
- How does a strong storyline affect your enjoyment of your preferred type of game?

Intuitiveness

- How do objects that look the same but that cannot be used in the same way affect your enjoyment of your preferred type of game (e.g. one barrel can be broken but another cannot)?
- How does *not* being able to use game objects because they are only scenery affect your enjoyment of your preferred type of game (e.g. a piece of furniture cannot be moved)?
- How does *not* being able to use game objects in the way that you would expect to be able to use them affect your enjoyment of your preferred type of game (e.g. a bucket can be kicked but not picked up)?

Expression

- How does having a wide variety of possible ways to use objects in the game environment affect your enjoyment of your preferred type of game?
- How does having new and unique ways of using objects affect your enjoyment of your preferred type of game?

Discarded Items

- How does being able to use objects in the same way as you would in the real world affect your enjoyment of your preferred type of game?
- How does being able to use objects in the same way as you have in previous games affect your enjoyment of your preferred type of game?
- How do graphics with obvious inconsistencies (e.g. a body sticking through a wall) affect your enjoyment of your preferred type of game?
- How does only having one way to perform a task or solve a problem affect your enjoyment of your preferred type of game?
- How does needing to figure out what the game developer wanted you to do to perform a task or solve a problem affect your enjoyment of your preferred type of game?
- How does being able to perform a task or solve a problem in your own way affect your enjoyment of your preferred type of game?
- How does needing to use trial and error to perform a task or solve a problem affect your enjoyment of your preferred type of game?
- How does *not* being able to perform a task or solve a problem within a reasonable period of time affect your enjoyment of your preferred type of game?
- How does *not* being able to perform a task or solve a problem at all affect your enjoyment of your preferred type of game?
- How does needing to get help from the internet or another person in order to solve a problem affect your enjoyment of your preferred type of game?

An Application of Game-Refinement Theory to Mah Jong

Hiroyuki Iida[1,3], Kazutoshi Takahara[1], Jun Nagashima[1], Yoichiro Kajihara[1], and Tsuyoshi Hashimoto[2]

[1]Department of Computer Science, Shizuoka University,
3-5-1 Johoku Hamamatsu, 432-8011 Japan
{iida, cs9055, cs8066, cs6501}@cs.inf.shizuoka.ac.jp
[2]Department of Systems Engineering, Shizuoka University,
3-5-1 Johoku Hamamatsu, 432-8011 Japan
hasimoto@cs.inf.shizuoka.ac.jp
[3]Information and Systems, PRESTO, Japan Science and Technology Agency, Japan

Abstract. This paper presents an application of the game refinement theory to a class of multi-person incomplete-information games, especially in the domain of *Mah Jong* that is an old Chinese four-person incomplete-information game. We have developed a computer program to analyze some statistics on the number of the possible options and the game length. The results of the analysis show that the measure of the game-refinement for Mah Jong has an appropriate value as well as other refined games such as chess and Go.

Keywords: game-refinement theory, multi-person games with incomplete-information, and Mah Jong

1 Introduction

We have studied the property of the decision space in game playing [2] [3] [5] [6]. The decision space is the minimal search space without forecasting. It provides the common measures for almost all board games. The dynamics of decision options in the decision space has been investigated and we observed that this dynamics was a key factor for game entertainment. Then we proposed the measure of the refinement in games [3].

Interesting games are always uncertain until the last end of games. Thus the variation in available options stays constant all over games. Here the games are a kind of seesaw game between possible results. In contrast, one player quickly dominates over the other in uninteresting games. Here options are likely to be diminishing quickly. Therefore, the refined games are more likely to be in a seesaw game. We then call the *principle of seesaw games*.

Based on the principle of seesaw games, we proposed a logistic model of game uncertainty [4]. From the players' viewpoint, the information on the game result is an increasing function of time (the number of moves) t. We here define the information on the game result as the amount of solved uncertainty $x(t)$, such that

M. Rauterberg (Ed.): ICEC 2004, LNCS 3166, pp. 333–338, 2004.
© IFIP International Federation for Information Processing 2004

$$x'(t) = \frac{n}{t}x(t) \tag{1}$$

where constant n is the expected number of plausible moves that is determined based on the ability difference between the two players of a game, and $x(0) = 0$ and $x(D) = B$. Note that $0 \le t \le D$, $0 \le x(t) \le B$. The above equation implies that the rate of increase in the solved information $x'(t)$ is proportional to $x(t)$ and inverse proportional to t. Solving Equation (1), we get

$$x(t) = B\left(\frac{t}{D}\right)^n \tag{2}$$

Here we assume that the solved information $x(t)$ is twice derivable at $t \in [0, D]$. The second derivative here indicates the accelerated velocity of the solved uncertainty along the game progress. It is the difference of the rate of acquired information during game progress.

$$x''(t) = \frac{B}{D^n}n(n-1)t^{n-2} \tag{3}$$

A good dynamic seesaw game in which the result is unpredictable at the very last moves in the endgame stage corresponds with a high value of the second derivative at $t = D$. This implies that game is more exciting, fascinating and entertaining if this value is larger. We expect that this property is the most important characteristics of a well-refined game.

At $t = D$ (the last few moves of an endgame), Equation (3) becomes:

$$x''(D) = \frac{B}{D^n}n(n-1)D^{n-2} = \frac{B}{D^2}n(n-1) \tag{4}$$

In the second derivative of $x''(t)$, n is the constant related to the ability of players, $\frac{B}{D^2}$ or its root square $\frac{\sqrt{B}}{D}$ is the value related to the game property.

This measure should reflect some aspects of the attractiveness of games. We then compared a class of board games by means of this measure. We especially compare various chess variants by means of this measure and other characteristics [3]. The measure was $\frac{\sqrt{B}}{D}$ where B stands for the average number of possible moves and D stands for the average game length.

The rules and details of a game should have changed over the long history of games in most games and the current games are the evolutionary outcomes of a long history from the original games. For example, many variants of chess-like board games are known in history and the modern chess is the descendant of these variants.

Here consider the historical changes of refinement measure in chess variants. Suppose that a new variant is born from the old version of a game. If the old variant is less refined than a new variant, such a variant should be replaced by the new one, because it is less attractive [3].

Therefore, the game itself should be refined in a long history of a game, and the current game is the evolutionary outcome of the long history of games. The refinement measure should be expected to increase in a long history of a game. Consequently the history of games can be viewed as an evolutionary optimization of game-refinement factors as well as complexity. All mentioned above comes into the *theory of game refinement*.

In this paper we present an application of the game-refinement theory to a class of multi-person incomplete-information games, especially in the domain of *Mah Jong*. Even for the multi-person incomplete-information games, the proposed measure would be also a key factor for the attractiveness. The point is how to estimate the number of options and game length for such games.

Section 2 presents Mah Jong, a world-wide popular multi-person incomplete-information game with its basic rules. Section 3 discusses an appropriate estimation of decision space for Mah Jong. It also shows the implementation of a computer program to analyze the game scores to determine the possible options and game length, and the results are given. Finally, the concluding remarks are given.

2   Mah Jong

Mah Jong is an old Chinese game, which is now being played in many countries. The history of the game can be traced back about 2000 years, but its modern form is only about 150 years old [1]. Contrary to other classic games like chess and Go, there is no common rule set for Mah Jong. Actually there are countless different variations of the rules.

Fig. 1. The tiles of Mah Jong

2.1   Basic Rules

In Mah Jong, each player is dealt 13 tiles. An additional tile is picked up at the beginning of each turn so that the player has the opportunity to make four groups of three tiles and a pair. If this can be done, that player has won that game. The whole game of Mah Jong is played as 16 games, four east wind games, four south wind games, four west wind games and four north wind games. In each game, a banker is declared (in some versions, the person who is the banker stays the banker throughout the whole set of games) and they deal out the cards. If a banker wins a game, then an extra game is played.

Each player is trying to basically make a hand of four 3 of a kinds and a pair. If he gets a 4 of a kind, this may be placed down and an extra tile is collected from the rear. Normally, a person picks up a tile from the end of the wall (not the end with the two tiles on it) or from the middle and places the tile in their hand, making pairs, 3 and four of a kind. They then take a tile that they don't want and place it, face up, in the area in the middle of the walls so that people can see what it was. If someone can pick it up (either because it is their turn next or because they can make a 3 or 4 of a kind or the pair to win the game) then they can only do so before another tile is placed at the end of the discarded tile row. When the discarded tiles fill a row in the middle, that row is turned over and it is up to the memory of the players to remember which tiles have been placed down.

If you have a pair in your hand and you see a tile discarded, you can pick up out of turn to make a 3 of a kind but you must display this hand straight away (all tiles facing upwards). If you pick up a tile to make a 3 of a kind from the wall, you can keep it in your hand so that you can make a 4 of a kind if you are lucky. If you have a 3 of a kind in your hand and you pick up a tile that has been discarded, you must display it straight away and pick up a tile from the rear. The 4 of a kind that you have just made is called a visible four of a kind and is placed with all four tiles facing upwards.

If you pick up a season or a flower, you need to put it down straight away and pick up another tile from the rear. In addition to collecting tiles that are the same as each other, you can also collect runs of the same suit (such as a 3, 4 and 5 circles). These do not gain any points but they will count as equivalent to a 3 of a kind as far as going out is concerned. If you have 4 runs and a pair, you go out and, although you don't score many points, nobody else does.

Eventually, you or someone else will get enough runs or 3 or 4 of a kinds and a pair to go out (finish). In this case, the person who goes out is the only one that scores any points.

3   Estimation for Decision

In the Internet Mah Jong club ``Tonpuso'' (meaning east and west wind) [7], many games are played. Many game scores played there are stored at a web site [8]. There are 27,409 games. We developed a computer program to analyze the game scores to obtain the statistics on the average number of options and game length, based on our definition of the possible options and game length in Mah Jong.

3.1 Possible Options

In principle, Mah Jong is a game where each player plays turn by turn like chess. The remarkable point in estimating the possible options is that other players than one who is to play may play their moves, namely, jumping the turn of the player. It means that one may have the possibility of playing a move (*pong, kong* or *chee*) even at the turn of other players. In our implementation for computer analysis, the possible options are therefore counted as follows.

− When one has to place down a piece at his own turn, the number of options is estimated by the number of kinds of pieces at his hand. However, it is one option after he has declared the *reach*.
− When one is able to act the *pong* or *kong* at his own turn, the number of options necessary for acting the *pong* or *kong* is counted.
− When one has the possibility to act the *reach* at his own turn, the number of options to place down necessary for acting the reach action is counted.
− When one is able to act the *chee* at his own turn, the number of options necessary for acting the *chee* is counted.
− When one is able to act the *pong* at the turn of other players, an option is counted.

3.2 Game Length

In the computer analysis, the game length of a game is estimated by the number of the whole turns played in a game. It roughly corresponds to the number of pieces placed down plus the number of *pong, kong, chee* and *reach*.

3.3 Results and Discussions

We show, in Table 1, the results of the analysis using our computer program. We reproduce, in Table 2, the results of the analysis for three chess-like games [3].

Table 1. The average number of possible moves and game length for major chess variants.

Sample(n)	possible options (B)	game length(D)	$\frac{\sqrt{B}}{D}$
27,409	10.36	49.36	0.078

Table 2. Some characteristics for three chess-like games.

	B	D	$\frac{\sqrt{B}}{D}$
Western chess	35	80	0.074
Chinense chess	38	95	0.065
Japanese chess	80	115	0.078

4   Concluding Remarks

The results obtained by the computer analysis confirm the similarity of game entertainment impact of Mah Jong with other refiend games such as chess major variants. This means that multi-person incomplete-information games also follow the *principle of seesaw games*. If we can access to the strict rules of some historic variants of Mah Jong, we will see some more detail of the evolutionary changes of the game of Mah Jong. However, we expect that the current rules are the evolutionary outcomes of a long history from the original games [1].

Acknowledgement. The research was supported in part by the Grant-in-Aid for the Japan Society for the Promotion of Science Fellows (#2267 and #2289).

References

1. R. Asami (1999). A Brief History of Mah Jong, *The Study of Game's History*, No.11, pp.21-36.
2. H. Iida, T. Hashimoto, N. Sasaki, J.W.H.M. Uiterwijk and H.J.van den Herik (1999). A Computer Analysis: Towards a Classification of Games, *Proceedings of International Colloquium of Board Games in Academia III*, Firenze, Italy.
3. H. Iida, N.Takeshita and J.Yoshimura (2003). A Metric for Entertainment of Boardgames: its implication for evolution of chess variants, in R.Nakatsu and J.Hoshino, editors, *IWEC2002 Proceedings*, pages 65--72. Kluwer.
4. H. Iida and J.Yoshimura (2003). A Logistic Model of Game's Refinement, Technical Report, Department of Computer Science, Shizuoka University, Hamamatsu.
5. N. Sasaki, N.Takeshita, T.Hashimoto and H.Iida (2001) Decision-Complexity Estimate in Evolutionary Changes of Games, Game Programming Workshop 2001, *(IPSJ Symposium Series Vol.2001, No.14)*, pages 140--147.
6. N. Sasaki and H.Iida (2002). A Study on Evolutionary Changes of Shogi, *IPSJ Journal*, 43(10):2990--2997.
7. Tompuson, http://mj.giganet.net/
8. Sunemon, http://www.geocities.co.jo/Bookend-Shikibu/2873/

The Design and Implementation of Multi-player Card Games on Multi-user Interactive Tabletop Surfaces

Shwetak N. Patel, John A. Bunch, Kyle D. Forkner, Logan W. Johnson, Tiffany M. Johnson, Michael N. Rosack, and Gregory D. Abowd

College of Computing & GVU Center, Georgia Institute of Technology,
801 Atlantic Drive, Atlanta, GA 30332-0280, USA
{shwetak, bunch, dasbrute, logan, tif, michael.rosack, abowd}@cc.gatech.edu

Abstract. We present the design and implementation of a card game architecture for mulit-user interactive tabletop surfaces. Our system is built on the DiamondTouch, a touch-sensitive input surface that allows several users to interact with a program at the same time. We describe the software architecture and present Blackjack as a sample implementation using this framework.

1 Introduction and Motivation

Card games have been around for generations. From classic games like Poker and Blackjack to relatively recent ones like Magic the Gathering, card games have entertained and educated us in countless ways. Almost every card game has been digitized in some form or another; Blackjack is a good example of this. Most interactive systems for card games today are limited to the desktop where interaction is usually achieved indirectly through a mouse or keyboard. Systems that allow a more direct interaction have also been available for some time now like touch screen monitor overlays or touch screen laptops and PDAs. In addition, the latest Tablet PCs allow direct pen-based interaction. Smart technology also offers an interactive whiteboard called Smart Board [5], which employs a touch system similar to the Tablet PCs. However, these systems only allow for single user interaction. These systems could be extended so that they detect multiple inputs, but they would still lack the ability to differentiate between users and resolve multiple interaction points for a particular person. With these systems multi-user applications are limited to only sequential user interactions, making is unsuitable for many multi-player card games.

We describe our exploration of the DiamondTouch as a viable card game platform. The DiamondTouch is a touch-sensitive input surface that allows several users to interact with a program at the same time. Although current research has focused on collaborative workspace applications [1, 0, 4], we particularly focus on card gaming and show how we can create a rich gaming experience despite the loss of some physical affordances. We also present a software architecture written in Java that allows users to quickly implement a wide variety of card games on the DimondTouch, and we show Blackjack as an example.

M. Rauterberg (Ed.): ICEC 2004, LNCS 3166, pp. 339–344, 2004.

2   System Implementation

2.1   Hardware

The DiamondTouch, developed by Mitsubishi Electric Research Laboratory (MERL), is a multi-user touch sensitive input device that allows simultaneous interaction and can identify which user is touching where [0]. The DiamondTouch accomplishes this by using an array of antennas embedded in the touch surface. Each one of these antennas transmits a unique signal. In addition, each user is touching some receiver, a 3M electrostatic mat (Figure 1b) that is placed on a chair. When a user touches the surface of the DiamondTouch, the antennas near the touch point send a small amount of current through the user's body to the receiver mat that the user is sitting on. The current system supports up to 4 users. The unique signal determines where exactly the person is touching the surface. The effective resolution with signal interpolation is about 2550 by 1550, which is about .1 mm of accuracy. However, the projected top-down image has a 1025 X 768 pixel resolution.

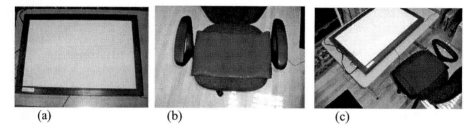

(a)   (b)   (c)

Fig. 1. a) MERL DiamondTouch. b) Conductive mat on chair c) DiamondTouch surface and mat

2.2   Software Framework

Figure 2 shows the overall high-level architecture for our tabletop card gaming system. The input layer provides an extensible programming interface for a variety of gestures common in card games such as hit, stand, or drag. All of the low-level Diamond Touch events are abstracted out into the input layer. The logical table provides hooks for implementing custom card games. Similar to the input layer, developers can create custom card games using generic archetypes. Finally, we provide a display layer for specifying how artifacts like chips and cards render or are graphically represented.

2.2.1   Generic Card Game Platform

We created *DTCards* as a multi-cardgame system, as well as an SDK for developing other card games. Pieces used for construction, interaction, and representation of a card game are largely reusable and thus are abstracted for game programmers. However, there is a great deal of variety in card games, and some aspects of any given game may not be reusable in another. Therefore our framework provides an interface to give developers the ability to extend commons archetypes and provide specialized, game-specific objects and interactions whenever necessary.

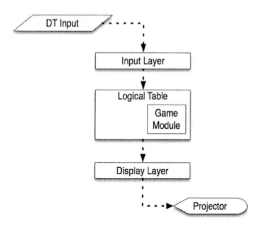

Fig. 2. High-level software architecture

2.2.2   Input and Gestures

The modularity of the *Input Layer* eases the burden of handling raw table events by the game developer. *Input Layer* reads events from the DiamondTouch and feeds them to *Gesture* objects. Each user has a copy of each *Gesture*, analyzes the event streams fed to them, and tries to recognize himself. Each user's *Gestures* compete among each other for recognition. When a *Gesture* matches a user's actions, it notifies the subscribed events. Our current implementation supports the following gestures, which were partly inspired by [6]:

1. **Hit** – a vertically motion on the tabletop
2. **Stand** – a horizontal motion
3. **Drag** – touch object and slide to another location
4. **Tap** – single quick touch
5. **Double tap** – two quick taps
6. **Private hand view** – a vertical hand is placed on the table and a message is projected on the palm of the hand so that only that player can view it

These are just a subset of potential gestures. Information flow through the system is essentially one-way. A user's gesture is picked up by the *Input Layer's* recognizer, which then sends it to the *LogicalTable*.

2.2.3   Game Module

The *LogicalTable* represents the binding (or "system") module. It ties the *Input Layer, Game module, and Display Layer* together. The *LogicalTable* contains a set of regions, which are areas on the game table that represent game objects, text strings, or special input areas. These regions are defined on the *LogicalTable* by the *Game module*, and when they are updated the *LogicalTable* notifies the *Display Layer* so that screen updates can be performed.

The *Display Layer* is represented to the rest of the system through the *CardTable* class. The *CardTable's* job is to receive updates from the *LogicalTable* and manage the on-screen game that the users see.

The rules for a game are supplied by a module that is represented to the rest of the system through a subclass of *Game*. This class -- in the case of our first demo, Blackjack (see Figure 3) -- manages players, game state, and game table contents. It receives players' *Gestures* from the *LogicalTable* and decides what, if anything, to do with them based on the rules of the game. This module is what a game author supplies to the *CardTable* system.

In constructing a game module, programmers must use or extend a variety of classes which comprise the *Game Kit*. This includes simple *Player objects, Cards, Suits*, and even specialized *Gestures* if need be. In the case of Blackjack, we needed a subclass of *Hand* that knew how to calculate the point value of a hand of cards in Blackjack. This in turn necessitated a subclass of *Player* which contained a *BlackjackHand* rather than a generic *Hand*. The *Game Kit* even provides an abstract *Gamepiece* class which game modules can subclass to introduce tokens, chips, or other game pieces not explicitly conceived and provided by the framework.

3 Blackjack Example

Figure 4 shows our example implementation of simple Blackjack (4a) and a more sophisticated casino version that involves betting (4b) built using the framework and toolkit described previously.

In the simple Blackjack version, the computer automatically deals two cards face up to each individual player. An indicator icon shows the player's turn. Each player can either hit by sliding a finger from the left to right on player's space. A player can stand by sliding a finger vertically, in which case the turn goes to the next user. On a bust, a message pops up and the player's hand clears. Figure 4b shows a version that includes betting. Players can drag chips from their stack and move them into the betting region very similar to casino style Blackjack.

4 Reflections and Conclusions

Despite the loss of the physical affordances of real cards, there are other advantages of an electronic tabletop card game system. Our implementation on the Diamond Touch allows gestures such as dragging and tapping for a richer gaming experience than traditional computer interfaces. In addition to the tabletop metaphor, users can directly manipulate digital artifacts by simple natural gestures on the table.

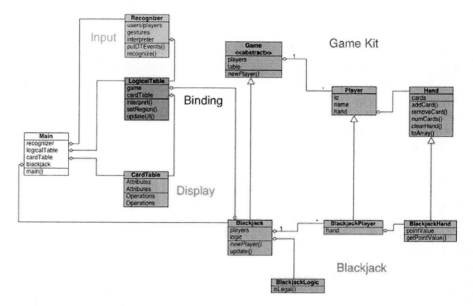

Fig. 3. Class diagram of Blackjack implementation

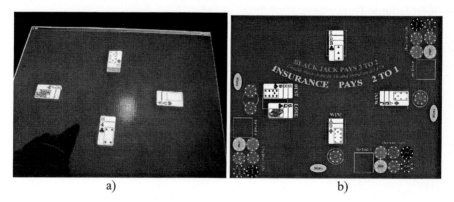

Fig. 4. Photographs of (a) simple Blackjack implementation and (b) Casino Blackjack that includes betting

The digital table can also provide novices with hints and rules as they play the game, making it an ideal learning system. Another interesting extension is the ability to remotely play others with a similar tabletop setup. For instance, a son could play with grandparents at a distance, while still retaining the tabletop metaphor. Now communities can emerge to resurrect long lost card games with this network capability. We are currently developing other multi-player games that require simultaneous interaction with the table such as Poker and Rummy.

Acknowledgements. The authors thank Mitsubishi Electronics Research Laboratory (MERL), and in particular Joe Marks, for the donation of the DiamondTouch for this research. We acknowledge that this work was done as part of an undergraduate senior design project with supervision by Bob Waters and Santosh Pande at Georgia Tech. This work is sponsored in part by National Science Foundation (ITR grant 0121661) and the industrial sponsors of the Aware Home Research Initiative at Georgia Tech.

References

1. Brodie, J. & Perry, M. *Mobile Collaboration at the Tabletop in Public Spaces.* Presented at Co-Located Tabletop Collaboration Workshop, CSCW 2002, New Orleans, November 2002.
2. Dietz, P. and Leigh, D. *DiamondTouch: a multi-user touch technology.* In proceedings of UIST 2001, pp. 219-226.
3. Rekimoto, J. and Saitoh, M. *Augmented surfaces: A spatially continuous workspace for hybrid computing environments.* In Proc. ACM CHI '99, Pittsburgh, PA, May 15--20 1999. ACM Press.
4. Shen, C., Everitt K., Ryall, K,: *UbiTable: Impromptu Face-to-Face Collaboration on Horizontal Interactive Surfaces.* In Ubicomp 2003, pages 281-288, Seattle, WA. USA, October 2003.
5. Smart Technologies Inc., *Smart Board.* http://www.smarttech.com
6. Wu, M., Ravin Balakrishnan. *Multi-finger and whole hand gestural interaction techniques for multi-user tabletop displays.* In proceeding of ACM UIST 2003 Symposium on User Interface Software & Technology. Vancouver, Canada. November 2003.

Entertainment Feature of a Computer Game Using a Biological Signal to Realize a Battle with Oneself

Shigeru Sakurazawa, Nagisa Munekata, Naofumi Yoshida, Yasuo Tsukahara, and Hitoshi Matsubara

Future University-Hakodate, System Information Science,
116-2 Kamedanakano Hakodate Hokkaido 041-8655, Japan
{sakura, c1100039, c1100081, yasuo, matsubar}@fun.ac.jp
http://www.fun.ac.jp/

Abstract. A novel computer game was developed in which a player challenges him- or herself using the skin conductance response to make the player aware of his or her own agitation. This game was developed as a paradoxical system in which their desire to win makes it more difficult to win. This type of game was found to have the following characteristics. First, players find uncontrollable themselves due to viewing their biological signals. In this situation, a kind of self-reference system is constructed. Second, the environments changed how the game was enjoyed. Third, the game system reveals differences of context between player and observer. From these characteristics, it is thought that the use of biological signals is attractive for entertainment computing.

1 Introduction

In most computer games, the player challenges either the computer or another human player. Players of these games try to find an opponent's weaknesses and conquer him or her. In such situations, the basic apparatus of the game is just a controller or actuator for the player. Exploring a new relationship between man and machine from the viewpoint of entertainment computing, a battle between the first person and him- or herself is an interesting development.

Electrical signals detected from the living body are objective and quantitative data reflecting psychological states and physiological functions of the human body. These signals have been used for diagnosis and treatment in medical care and have been used for the lie detector in police questioning.[1] The biological signal used in the lie detector is the skin conductance response (SCR), where changes in the conductance on the skin surface are induced by sweating due to mental agitation, surprise and excitation. [2-6] It was considered that a battle with oneself could be realized by introducing such signals into a computer game, and the present paper reports some initial testing of such a game.

M. Rauterberg (Ed.): ICEC 2004, LNCS 3166, pp. 345–350, 2004.

1.1 Involuntary Biological Signals

We have little awareness of the physiological functioning of our own body because most physiological functions are involuntary, and therefore uncontrollable. The SCR is a typical example. No-one is aware of the minute amounts of sweating during mental agitation unless there is an unusually large amount of mental stress. Therefore, observing one's own SCR produces a strange feeling that this is not a feature of one's own body but rather that of another person.

It is also generally believed that inner agitation during communication in daily life can be concealed. However, the SCR can reveal concealed agitation independent of one's intention to conceal. When someone is connected to a SCR indicator in situations such as a poker game, with a 'poker face' employed in an attempt to conceal excitation, the SCR indicator greatly amplifies the amount of involuntary signaling that can take place.

1.2 Synchronization Between Action and Reaction

A useful man-machine interface is one where the human has perfect control over the interface. To realize perfect control, each reaction of the machine should correspond to each human action. Perfect control is achieved by arranging for the man-machine interface to be synchronized from outside the system. However, a man-man interface in human communication basically has no externally applied synchronization because action and reaction occur by mutual observation during communication. [7] The system described here is a man-machine interface with features of a man-man interface, which generates synchrony by use of uncontrollable biological signals, forming the basis for a novel computer entertainment system.

2   Materials and Methods

Figure 1 shows the computer game system developed in the present study. The SCR occurs due to a change in conductance on the surface of the skin due to sweating. [2-6] Since eccrine sweat glands are most dense on the palm of the hand and sweating is an autonomic response that can be triggered by emotional stimuli, [2] the palm is an ideal site from which to obtain measurements of psychophysical activity using the SCR. The player holds a controller in one hand and the palm of the other hand provides the SCR via two electrodes (disposable electrocardiogram electrode J Vitrode, Ag/AgCl solid-gel tape, Nihon-Koden, Tokyo). The signal was amplified by a SCR sensor, fed into a PC through an A/D converter and can be displayed at the foot of the game monitor (see Fig. 2). Information from the player's psychological agitation is thus fed back to the player, which tends to result in the player becoming more agitated. A loop of positive feedback of this agitation often occurs with this system and to succeed in the game a player must overcome the effects of his or her own escalating panic.

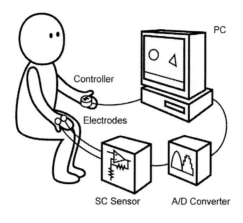

Fig. 1. System of the game

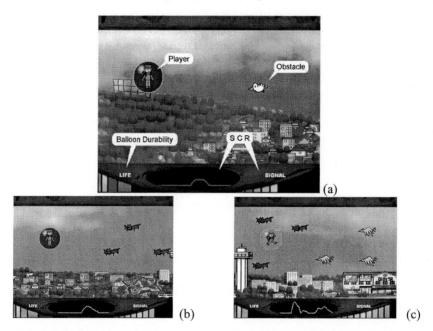

Fig. 2. Layout and progress of the game. A boy character (controlled by the player) makes a trip with a balloon that requires negotiation around various obstacles. Balloon durability and the SCR are displayed at the foot of the game monitor. The game scrolls to the right automatically. The number and kind of obstacles depend on the extent of the player's agitation. (a) start of game; (b) later in the game, showing evidence of increased agitation (SCR) and the consequent presence of more obstacles; (c) towards the end of the game, showing the player's panic due to the increased number of obstacles: the player is trapped in an escalating spiral of panic

The game developed in the present study was tested under various situations on subjects 5 to 68 years of age, with or without displaying the SCR on the game monitor, and in the presence or absence of an observer. For most trials, the players were in a closed room. Group A subjects (n=6) played the game alone 3 times with SCR displayed, then 3 times without; group B subjects (n=6) played the game alone 3 times without SCR displayed, then 3 times with; and group C subjects (n=8) played the game 3 times in the presence of an observer with SCR displayed. The SCR was recorded during play and the number of waves of SCR ('number of SCR changes'; Table 1) was estimated for each subject from the recordings.

Additional trials were also run where the player was in a more open situation, exposed to a number of observers watching his or her progress from an elevated observation gallery. Since this represented less controlled conditions, results from this open situation are presented only in anecdotal form in the Discussion.

3 Results

The results obtained with different trial regimes in the closed-room situation are summarized in Table 1. Paired t-tests revealed no significant differences (P≤0.05) between trials 1-3 of group A (with display) and trials 1-3 of group B (without display), nor between trials 1-3 of group B and trials 4-6 of group B. However, there was a significant difference (P≤0.05) between trials 1-3 of group A and trials 4-6 of group A. This suggests that displaying the subject's SCR caused it to increase. In other words, the player's level of agitation was increased upon watching his or her own SCR.

Table 1. Mean number of SCR changes per subject under different conditions. 'D' indicates trials with SCR displayed; 'O' indicates observer present

Group	Trials 1-3	Trials 4-6
A	16.5 D	11.8
B	16.6	13.4 D
C	22.6 DO	-----

Analysis of the SCR by autocorrelation (Fig. 3) showed a strong autocorrelation from 2.5 to 3.5 seconds when the SCR was displayed but little autocorrelation when it was not. Considering that the delay time for the SCR rising is about 3 seconds, this result suggests that the agitation induced by self-observation of the subject's own SCR induced the next stage in the escalation of agitation.

4 Discussion

In answer to a post-test questionnaire, 81% of the subjects indicated that they considered the game to be interesting. The results of the present study suggest that players of this game are surprised by observing their own body reaction, and that this system creates a new mode of communication by exposing conflicts between involuntary responses of the body and a person's own conscious awareness. In other words, players are able to simultaneously perceive their involuntary physical actions and their conscious psychological experience. The player recognizes the discrepancy by integrating these two kinds of perception as a self-reference concept, one of the characteristics of a living system. The requirement to solve the discrepancy produced here became the motivation to continue the game. This is a characteristic of game entertainment using biological signals.

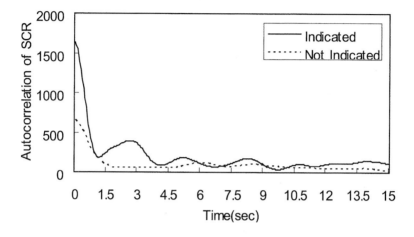

Fig. 3. Autocorrelation analysis of skin conduction response (SCR) while playing the experimental game with or without displaying the SCR on the game monitor. Solid line, with SCR displayed; broken line, without

Enjoyment of the game was different in different situations. In a closed room there were significant differences ($P \leq 0.05$) between the results of trials 1-3 of group A (Table 1) and trials 1-3 in group C, with group C showing larger SCR values. Subjects became more agitated when their SCR changes were pointed out by an observer. It was interesting to note that both player and observer found it amusing to observe the change in SCR following such comments by the observer. In this situation, the player's behavior remained consistent but the SCR showed more fluctuation.

However, in a situation where many observers were viewing the progress of a game player from a gallery, SCR changed frequently. Corresponding with this change, the number of obstacles on the screen increased (Fig. 2), raising cheers from the gallery, which in turn caused further changes in SCR. These subjects responded in questionnaires that they felt greatly agitated knowing that many people were watching them. In these experiments with several people observing from a gallery, these observers were regarded as enemies in the game context. This system therefore includes not only the computer and player, but also the environment. As such, the system involves the sharing of experiences between the player and other people and is a kind of communication system.

Generally, success at a computer game depends on the manipulative skills of the player. However, such advanced skills are not necessary in the game developed here.

A wide variety of people could enjoy this game and it is considered that such games using biological signals could form the basis for a new kind of communication.

With regard to observing and playing, the system exploited the two contexts by providing the opportunity for multimodal (physical and psychological) communication, producing an entertaining common experience (cf. Nakatsu [8, 9]). Although the effects of SCR display are expected to be complex, and interlinked with factors such as familiarization with the manipulations involved in the game, using such biological signals in a computer game enhances the entertainment experience and has opened the door to a multitude of other novel ways to combine physical and psychological experiences in the computer game context.

References

1. Geddes, L. A.: History of the Polygraph, an Instrument for the Detection of Deception. Biomed. Eng. 8 (1973) 154-156
2. Dawson, M. E., Schell, A. M., Filion, D. L.: The electrodermal system. In: Cacioppo, J. T., Tassinary, L. G. and Berntson, G. G. (eds.): Handbook of psychophysiology. 2nd edn. Cambridge University Press, New York (2000) 200-223
3. Ohman, A., Soares, J. J. F.: Unconscious anxiety, phobic responses to masked stimuli. Journal of Abnormal Psychology 103 (1994) 231-240
4. Gross, J. J. and Levenson, R. W.: Emotional suppression, self-report and expressive behavior. Journal of Personality and Social Psychology 64 (1993) 970-986
5. Gross, J. J. and Levenson, R. W.: Hiding feeling, the acute effects of inhibiting negative and positive emotion. Journal of Abnormal Psychology 106 (1997) 95-103
6. Petrie, K. J., Booth, R. J. and Pennebaker, J. W.: The Immunological Effects of Thought Suppression. Journal of Personality and Social Psychology 75 (1998) 1264-1272
7. Sakurazawa, S.: How is Communication of Molecules Possible? In: Diebner, H. H. & Ramsay, L. (eds.): Hierarchies of Communication. Center for Art and Media, Germany (2003) 197-204
8. Nakatsu, R.: Communication and Entertainment. IPSJ Magazine 4 (2003) 803-806 (in Japanese)
9. Kanda, T., Ishiguro, H., Ono T., Imai, M. and Nakatsu, R.: An Evaluation on Interaction Between Humans and an Autonomous Robot Robovie. JRSJ 20 (2002) 1-3 (in Japanese)

AI: The Missing Link in Digital Game Interface Design?

Darryl Charles[1] and Daniel Livingstone[2]

[1]Computing and Information Engineering, University of Ulster,
BT52 1SA. Northern Ireland
dk.charles@ulster.ac.uk
[2]School of Computing, University of Paisley,
Paisley, PA12BE. Scotland
daniel.livingstone@paisley.ac.uk

Abstract. The central problem that this paper addresses is how to manage dynamic change within game environments in response to variable player requirements and ability. In particular, we discuss the role of a game AI to enable game systems to learn about individual user patterns, behaviours, desires or moods in order to adapt the environment in reaction to the user's interaction with the environment. We discuss the role that AI may play in the design of the game interface in order to enhance the dynamic and responsive nature of the game system with respect to individual users and leading to more rewarding and immersive game experiences.

1 Introduction

There are many challenges for the use of artificial intelligence (AI) in next generation games [3], but as the power of computers and game consoles advance rapidly there are also many opportunities. In this paper we explore the role of AI within a game as facilitator for the gaming processes – the central goal being to intelligently enhance the interactive experience for individual players. While the concept of an adaptive game is a controversial topic among some gamers and developers, there are clear benefits to tailoring the game experience to particular player types – especially for educational games [2].

2 AI as an Interface Between Gamer and Game Environment

We propose that there are three aspects to an intelligent game interface that must be implemented so that a game may be effectively sensitive to player type. These are: modelling the player or player groups, recognising the player in order to adapt the game, and the verification that any adaptation is successful or appropriate.

Current games do little to automatically adapt to individual players needs or desires. However, it is a common feature of games to allow the player to adapt the game themselves; from simple examples like adjusting the difficulty level in games such as "Doom" and the tailoring of a character to a player's requirements at the start

M. Rauterberg (Ed.): ICEC 2004, LNCS 3166, pp. 351–354, 2004.

of a game as with "DeusEx", through to the player sculpting of a game world as happens in "The Sims".

Game developers have been most effective and imaginative in designing methods for dynamic assistance to a player – though examples are still relatively rare and most methods are far from providing intelligent support. One example that can be very effective is simply to track a player's progress and provide help to a player if he or she meets difficulty in a game. A straightforward scheme for this is demonstrated in "Crash Bandicoot". If the player repeatedly fails at a particular point, their character is awarded a magic mask – then no matter how badly the player does on the next attempt, their character will successfully negotiate the offending obstacle. This help is generally accepted willingly by the player; however this is not always the case, for example in "Mario Kart" the game provides a player who is losing the race with the most effective power-ups – which often frustrates their opponent who is normally disadvantaged by this positive discrimination.

Detecting when a player is having difficulty in a less linear games is often not as simple and may require more intelligent methods for understanding and detecting a player's difficulty. More advanced techniques may require the modelling of typical players and behaviours and mapping these to desired game responses, so that in-game we may track player patterns, identify behaviours and execute predefined actions. An example of where this might be useful is in a squad based game where players are able to ask other characters to carry out tasks. With an intelligent system analyzing the players' actions and intent, squad members may be able to pro-actively offer to carry out tasks. This would lead to less need for the player to micro-manage other characters – some element of control will be reduced to agreeing or disagreeing to offers of help. If implemented well it would also increase the perceived intelligence of the computer controlled squad members, and increasing the degree of immersion in the game overall.

3   Learning to Adapt to Individual Players

There are still relatively few well known games that use learning algorithms either in development or, even more rarely, within the game. Examples include "Colin McRae Rally 2" which uses neural networks to train to the non-player vehicles to drives realistically on the track, and "Black & White" which uses neural learning processes within modules to model an avatar's desire. Learning will become more important in next generation games because it will enable a more tailored experienced for individual game players and so we explore some of the issues related to learning.

Learning mechanisms may be offline or online. With offline learning we train the AI during the development process by forcing it to observe and model player behaviour [4] using learning algorithms such as artificial neural networks [6]. This may be used to create believable characters by imitation of a typical (or expert) player or combination of features from a variety of players, or perhaps offline learning may be used to model players in order to respond appropriately a player in-game. Online learning is a much more difficult prospect because it is a real-time process and many of the commonly used algorithms for learning are therefore not suitable.

There are two important aspects of learning that need to be considered within a game AI interface that is responsive to a player: that of the player learning to use the game system to its full potential and/or according to their needs, and that of the system learning to react to individual players' needs and desires. Both forms of learning are intrinsically linked in a game, i.e. by learning about the player then the game system should be more empowered in helping the player to play the game effectively. Intelligent methods may be built into the game to recognise player characteristics based on prior training performed during the game development and the game may continue to learn on the basis of new information.

However, adapting the environment based on our "belief" about the needs of the player is dangerous – if the change is very obvious or if it frequently disadvantages the player, then it may not be a popular technology. There are two opposing desires in players that we need to take into account: the desire of a player to learn the rules so as to master the game, and the requirement to avoid "sameness" or lack of variety of gameplay.

Even if we achieve this balance there are other issues due to the many difficulties in dealing with dynamic AI behaviours. The most significant issue with the implementation of this type of technology being that on-line learning can often produce very unpredictable results; sometimes these effects serve to enhance but more often it leads to erratic behaviour that may reduce the quality of experience for the user, and in worse scenarios will introduce dynamic software bugs [1].

4   How and What to Learn About the Player?

Knowing how and what to learn about a player is just as difficult as actually implementing the technology to perform the learning. One method that we may use to create typical player profiles is to cluster similar types of player together on the basis of player selected preferences and observing players during the game's development. We can then use these typical player groups to make decisions in-game that tailor the game experience better to an individual player. It is also possible for the game to learn how to react appropriately to a player dynamically as the game progresses. However, the question is: which aspects of the players' interaction with the game should we observe and when should the information gained be used? The information that the game has about a player may unambiguously point to a certain course of action but an incorrect transition in the game environment state may still be the result if we do not take into account player intension, desire or mood. These are difficult things gauge but if we were able to extract accurate information then it could vastly improve the performance of game state transition in response to player actions or behaviour.

Monitoring players' actions through input devices, such a mouse, keyboard or game pad is relatively easy. We can also track a players' progress, pattern of play and choices made, and all of this information may be used to form quite a clear picture of the player type. Using pre-constructed player profiles we can correlate the player patterns and make decisions on that basis. Using a pre-trained classifier within the game to identify player patterns can be very fast and efficient. However, these methods are not very good, by-in-large, for dynamic or adaptive learning purposes and a further difficulty is that player profiles ideally need to be adapted dynamically because a player's ability and way of playing will change as they play.

We may make even more accurate choices about the player state and therefore more informed decisions about the adaptation of the game environment in response to the players' needs if we gain information or at least clues about player intention, desire or mood. Devices similar to the EyeToy on the PlayStation 2 or a Web Cam on a PC may be used in the future to detect gestures and facial expressions that may provide valuable clues about a persons' mood. Similarly, the pressure exerted by pressing analog game pad buttons may provide information about a players' game style or current level of intensity or stress. Additionally, with simple modification of existing input devices temperature or pulse (i.e. heart rate) sensors may be added like those on a typical exercise bicycle.

Armed with information from standard sources such as the mouse or joy pad and more advanced sources such as a camera or other sensory devices, we have a wealth of information to make decisions that tailor the game to individual players.

5 Conclusion

Modern digital games are extraordinarily good at many things but even the best examples of these games are still not very capable at monitoring players, distinguishing between different player groups and altering the game state to meet individual players' needs. In this paper we have outlined the role that AI may play in the interface between player and game so as to respond to individual players and thus improve a players' game playing experience. The improvements that this may bring can be as straightforward as helping the player learning how to play the game or to react when the player becomes "stuck", through to encouraging gameplay innovation in digital games.

References

1. Barnes J and Hutchens J, "Testing Undefined Behaviour as a Result of Learning", AI Game Programming Wisdom, pp 615-623, Charles River Media, 2002.
2. Beal, C., Beck, J., Westbrook, D., Atkin, M., and Cohen, P., 2002, Intelligent Modeling of the User in Interactive Entertainment. In AAAI Spring Symposium on Artificial Intelligence and Interactive Entertainment. Stanford, CA.
3. Charles D, "Enhancing Gameplay: Challenges for Artificial Intelligence in Digital Games", Proceedings of the 1st World Conference on Digital Games 2003, University of Utrecht, The Netherlands, 4-6th November 2003.
4. Houlette R, "Player Modelling for Adaptive Games", pp 557-566, AI Game Programming Wisdom II, Charles River Media, 2004.
5. Livingstone D. & Charles D, "Intelligent Interfaces for Digital Games", AAAI-04 Workshop on Challenges in Game AI, (to be presented) 25-26th July 2004.
6. McGlinchey S, "Learning of AI Players from Game Observation Data", GAME-ON 2003, 4th International Conference on Intelligent Games and Simulation, pp. 106-110, Nov. 2003.

Engaging Game Characters: Informing Design with Player Perspectives

Penelope Drennan, Stephen Viller, and Peta Wyeth

School of Information Technology and Electrical Engineering,
University of Queensland, Australia
{pennyd, viller, peta}@itee.uq.edu.au

Abstract. The behavior of characters in current computer games is generally scripted and predictable. This paper discusses some issues related to creating game characters that enhance player engagement and identifies the need for a more player-centered approach to game character design. This paper reports the results of a focus group that was carried out with experienced game players to determine what game character behaviors would enhance their engagement in a game. The four general areas of concern that came out of this discussion were consistency with context, player expectations, social interactions and consistency with the environment. This paper discusses these issues and their implication for game character design with a view to creating engaging game characters.

1 Introduction

Non-player characters (NPCs) are a significant part of most computer games. They fill a wide range of roles, such as shopkeepers and barkeepers, and are an important aspect of making a fantasy game world seem more realistic to game players. NPCs can also take on more substantial roles that revolve around the player, such as the player's team-mate or opponent. NPCs are also an important aspect of Massively Multi-player Online Games (MMOGs), as there are many roles in these games that human players do not want to fill, such as blacksmiths, alchemists and other non-hero positions.

However, most NPCs have predictable behavior and completely scripted dialogue, which is not updated to take into account events that occur in the game world [1]. NPCs rarely show emotion or consistent personality, the lack of which can be enough to remind the player that they are playing a game, thereby lessening their engagement in the game. The importance of having engaging NPCs, as well as the recent growth in game-related research means that NPCs have become an interesting new field of study. The focus of most previous work on NPCs has been on realism not engagement. However, the assumption that people prefer playing against realistic NPCs has not been examined in detail. There is anecdotal evidence (for example, the proliferation of MMOGs discussed in [3]), as well as some recent empirical evidence [2], which indicates that players prefer playing games with human allies and opponents. This evidence is indicative of the assumption that players prefer realistic

M. Rauterberg (Ed.): ICEC 2004, LNCS 3166, pp. 355–358, 2004.
© IFIP International Federation for Information Processing 2004

NPCs. However, it is not enough to ask players if they prefer realistic NPCs, as realism may not be the most engaging behavior for the player. The underlying premise of this paper is that research needs to be undertaken to determine the types of behaviors and characteristics of NPCs that create the highest level of engagement for game players.

This paper describes the first step in a more player-grounded approach to designing NPCs. This step involved a process of eliciting player opinions through an online focus group. The focus group is part of a larger project that involves a range of player-centered studies, using a combination of qualitative and quantitative data gathering approaches. The end result of this project will be a detailed design guideline for creating engaging game characters. The aim of the focus group was to gather game players' opinions on and experiences with non-player characters (NPCs). In particular, players were asked to discuss those behaviors of NPCs that add to or detract from their engagement in a game. This paper reports on the issues that were raised during this focus group, and discusses research that needs to be conducted to further explore these issues.

2   Focus Group

Six experienced game players were asked to discuss the behavior of NPCs in a variety of computer games and how this behavior affects their engagement in a game. Each of the players considered themselves to be experienced players, stating that they had played computer games for five or more years. The genre preferences of the participants included First Person Shooter (FPS) games, Role Playing Games (RPGs), Strategy and Sports games, with many of the players indicating a preference for more than one of these types of games. There were five males and one female participant, aged between 22 and 26 years. All of the focus group participants were experienced computer users in general, as well as being experienced game players

The focus group was carried out online, via a private Internet Relay Chat (IRC) room, and lasted for approximately an hour and a half. Players were initially given an informal definition of engagement as "a feeling of deep emotional involvement in a game, where they tend not to notice time passing". They were then asked to discuss the behavior of NPCs in relation to engagement. The conversation was mostly open ended, although the moderator occasionally prompted the group members to move onto different genres of games, in order to make the discussion as broad as possible. The topics that were covered in each genre (such as combat and conversation) were not prompted by the moderator. Although the participants in the group expressed interest in a range of genres, the conversation generally centered on the NPCs in RPGs and FPS games.

The participants of the focus group felt that an NPC needed to have motivations, a range of actions, a variety of responses and a believable manner in order to add to their immersion in a game. In contrast to previous work on the design of NPCs, realism wasn't particularly important to the group. The group didn't focus on intelligence – they generally didn't mind if a character was stupid or smart - as long as the behavior of the character was consistent. During the conversation it became necessary to define what the group meant by engagement. The trend amongst participants was to mention frustration and annoyance, and when asked directly, they confirmed that they equated these emotions with disengagement and lack of immersion.

3 Outcomes

Based on the opinions of the participants in the focus group, the key points where engagement breaks down are:

- Consistent with Context: the actions, behavior and dialogue of a character should be consistent throughout the game, demonstrating personality and motivation. The character's behavior and dialogue should also be consistent with their purpose in the game
- Expectations: NPCs should behave competitively, have access to the same amount of information from the game environment as the player does, and meet certain stereotypes. Smarter NPCs should be more powerful than less intelligent characters.
- Social Interactions: NPCs should remember previous interactions, have a wide range of responses and display different behavior when interacting with other characters that are more or less powerful than them. They should also have goals and then act in a way that seems aimed at achieving their goals.
- Consistent with Environment: the behavior of the NPC should be suitable to the physical game environment, and their actions and reactions should demonstrate awareness of events in their immediate surroundings.

The information gained from this focus group has informed the development of a set of tentative guidelines for increasing player engagement:

- Determine the personality profile for an NPC and ensure that their behavior is consistent with this profile throughout the game
- Make sure that any actions or interactions that the NPC is involved in during scripted scenes are available to the NPC during interactive play
- AI for NPCs needs to be able to effectively perform actions such as intelligent pathfinding, looking for cover, accurately assessing combat situations, and not accidentally engage in friendly fire
- NPCs need to display the same level of intelligence throughout the game
- Social hierarchies of NPCs should reflect real-world dynamics, for example, smarter NPCs should have a higher status than less intelligent NPCs. NPCs should be able to display different demeanors to demonstrate their awareness of these dynamics
- NPCs should be able to display a wide range of human emotions and behavior and should also have a wide range of interaction possibilities
- Smarter, tougher NPC opponents should clearly have better AI than lesser opponents, instead of having more hit points
- Less repetition in the scripts used by background NPCs, ensuring that they have the appearance of memory of previous interactions

- NPCs should have goals and motivations and behave in a way that is clearly aimed at achieving these goals
- NPCs should respond appropriately to sights, sounds and events in their environment, by signaling awareness of the player or other characters.
- NPCs should be able to modify their approach to combat situations

Importantly, these guidelines are clearly grounded in the preferences of experienced game players. While further player-centered research activities are planned, this first step has produced a wide-ranging list of NPC behavior characteristics which have the potential to improve the overall quality of the game playing experience.

4   Conclusions and Future Work

The four major themes that came out of the focus group were that NPCs should be consistent with their context, meet player expectations, engage in a variety of social interactions with the player, and also be consistent with their environment. While these ideas need to be explored further through continued adoption of a player-centered approach, the design criteria generated as a result of the focus group are significant.

The next step in exploring these issues, following the player-centered process, is a questionnaire that is aimed at gathering more detailed and quantitative data on these issues. The questionnaire will be designed to confirm or deny whether these issues are important to a large percentage of game players. Following on from the questionnaire a number of observational studies will be carried out involving people interacting with NPCs in a game environment, to provide in-depth observational data to support the self-reported data from the focus group and questionnaire.

The combination of focus group, questionnaire and observational studies provides a multi-perspective approach to the problem of creating engaging NPCs. The reason for adopting this approach is that it leverages all the advantages of the different qualitative and quantitative methodologies involved. The data gathered during this project will be used to create detailed design guidelines for engaging game characters.

References

1. Drennan, P.: Conversational Agents: Creating Natural Dialogue between Players and Non-Player Characters. In Rabin, S. (ed): AI Game Programming Wisdom 2. Charles River Media Inc, Hingham, MA (2004).
2. Sweetser, P., Johnson, D., Sweetser, J., & Wiles, J.: Creating Engaging Artificial Characters for Games. In Proceedings of the International Conference on Entertainment Computing. Carnegie Mellon University, Pittsburgh, PA.(2003)
3. Zubek, R. & Khoo, A.: Making the Human Care: On Building Engaging Bots. In AAAI Spring Symposium on Artificial Intelligence and Interactive Entertainment, Technical Report SS-02-01. AAAI Press , Menlo Park, CA. (2002) 103-107.

Emergent Stories in Massively Multiplayer Online Games: Using Improvisational Techniques to Design for Emotional Impact

Brenda Harger, David Jimison, Eben Myers, Ben Smith, and Shanna Tellerman

Entertainment Technology Center, Carnegie Mellon University,
700 Technology Drive; 5th Floor; PTC, Pittsburgh Pennsylvania 15217, USA
{bharger, djimison, emyers, bjs1, shanna}@andrew.cmu.edu

Abstract. In this poster, we discuss the application of Theatrical Improvisational Techniques to address game design challenges of Massively Multiplayer Online Games (MMOGs), and we suggest how applying these techniques can create structure for emergent storytelling. We propose a common improv structure, CROW (Character, Relationship, Objective, Where), as a framework for designing MMOGs with compelling emergent stories.

1 Introduction

Massively multiplayer online games (MMOGs) are an emerging medium. Unlike in most single player video games, thousands of players simultaneously inhabit the same endless game world in MMOGs. Due to the colossal number of unpredictable human players, MMOGs must provide real-time, unscripted experiences. Story presents a framework that can help structure these experiences. However, because of the unscripted nature of MMOGs, the stories in them must also be unscripted. Game designers may be able to deal with this challenge by applying some techniques from improvisational theater (Improv), another real-time, unscripted medium. Improv creates stories that are generated on-the-fly through a series of rules and structures. Engaging stories can emerge by adapting and applying some of these improvisational rules and structures to the design of MMOGs.

2 MMOG Characteristics and Design Challenges

There are several defining characteristics of MMOGs. Attaining in-game goals is commonly a social encounter shared with other players. MMOGs take place in real-time and thus cannot be paused or restarted by the player. By removing the player's ability to halt their game's progression, MMOGs have developed a notion of shared history amongst the players. Players' interactions with each other and the game are unscripted. Players often do the unexpected or even try to subvert the game.

M. Rauterberg (Ed.): ICEC 2004, LNCS 3166, pp. 359–362, 2004.

Due to these characteristics, MMOGs present very explicit design challenges. The game must be structured in an unscripted fashion because the player's interactions are unpredictable and varied. Whereas most video games follow a single perspective, MMOGs allow many different perspectives to occur simultaneously. The inclination of each individual player to become the central hero when there is no single predictable story, poses a difficult design challenge. In addition, players of different skill levels and play styles must co-exist in the same game world, interacting with the world and each other without disturbing each other's enjoyment.

3 Creating Stories Through Improv

Traditionally, stories have been told in a linear fashion, generally following a dramatic arc. An introduction sets up conflict and builds towards a climactic point which is then resolved. In an MMOG-based story, the author has to create that same dramatic experience, but it has to be authored on-the-fly and remain cohesive across the collective experience of many players at once.

Emergence is the appearance of complex, unexpected behavior out of a set of simple rules, none of which has any explicit reference to the larger complexity [3]. If there were a set of rules that could give rise to stories when applied to an MMOG world, we would call those stories emergent. MMOGs require exactly this type of emergent story to sustain the excitement and interest of players.

Theatrical Improvisation Techniques (Improv) are a proven way of creating emergent stories. Game designers can use rules and structures from Improv to establish the emergence of strong, unscripted stories in their games. For this poster, we are focusing mainly on the Improv framework abbreviated as CROW.

4 CROW

CROW is a commonly used improv abbreviation for the four principle elements needed to begin a situation or story: Character, Relationship, Objective, and Where (location). In improvisational theater, these elements are established first and make up the building blocks for emergent stories. If the elements of CROW are the building blocks, then action and change are the mortar of an emergent story. When CROW is established, it should lead the character towards action, which should, in turn, alter one or more components of CROW. As these interrelated changes continually build up, more action is driven and a story will begin to emerge. The elements of CROW, in conjunction with action and change, are the fundamental pieces of emergent story. Though they do form the foundation of emergent stories, these fundamentals do not guarantee an engaging series of events. In order for satisfying stories to emerge, elements of CROW and the actions that they spur must exist within what Keith Johnstone terms the "circle of expectation." The circle of expectation is the realm of possible story outcomes that can result from a given situation [1]. Applied to MMOGs, the circle of expectation means creating a game system that allows players to act and react logically to events in the game.

4.1 Character

Character is the external and internal nature (or characteristics) of a character. For satisfying emergent stories, both player characters and non-player characters alike should be created with the following characteristics in mind: physicality, given circumstances, personality traits and inner needs [2]. For example, the way a character walks can impact the way that other characters perceive him, as can his personality and background.

4.2 Relationship

Every character has a relationship to every other character, whether biological, professional or social. A pair of characters can be family members, friends, enemies, or even strangers. Each category of relationship contains within it its own rules and expectations that govern the possible interactions and the meanings of those interactions. For instance, the expectations surrounding an encounter with your doctor are different from those surrounding a visit to your grandmother. In current MMOGs, relationships are commonly structured around players and not characters.

4.3 Objective

An objective is a physical and/or psychological goal, and is crucial to the creation of both satisfying stories and engaging game play. Objectives should be thought of as verbs, and must lead to action [4]. For instance, the psychological objective of "to save the damsel in distress" might lead to the action of slaying the dragon. Simple physical and psychological objectives can be combined and layered to create more complex and dynamic objectives. Physical objectives can be made more dynamic with the addition of psychological components. Psychological objectives can be made more concrete by adding physical goals.

4.4 Where (Location)

The final element of CROW is Where (or setting), which is the time period and the location of a story. Time (past, present, and future) and place introduce a circle of expectation. Cultural expectations shift and change according to the time period and location. The history of a given location will determine the way a society will behave within that environment. Characters should act and react according to the confines of their surroundings. In a crowded space, the player character might feel overwhelmed and have difficulty navigating. Wide open space creates a sense of isolation.

4.5 CROW Web

Although the main elements of CROW are separated into distinct categories, each category works to affect and define the others, even across multiple characters.

Often, there will be tension or conflict between two elements. These conflicts help to fuel a dynamic and intricate character and story. The CROW web is the interrelationship and integration of the different elements of CROW into character and story. Every combination of CROW is a single, distinct point in the web. When one aspect of CROW changes, it causes a shift in the web, and consequentially changes all the other aspects. Changes in CROW, that fall within the circle of expectation, can cause movement from one point in the CROW web to another.

5 Case Study: Status

One expression of character is status, which is the confidence and presence that a character displays physically in relation to others. Status is applied to a character's actions, movements, speech, interactions, and motivations [1].   Status can be arbitrarily represented as a numerical scale of 1 – 10. For instance, a character of low status, say 3 or 4, might shuffle their hands, act confused or lost, and become easily frightened. A character with highter status, such as 7, however, will be more relaxed, hold eye contact longer, blink less, and project their voice. A character of status 10, the highest status on the arbitrary scale, might take up a lot of space, command attention, speak clearly and directly, and even touch other people's faces. Status is dynamic and changing.   A character's status fluctuates depending on their relationships, objectives and locations. Likewise, interactions colored by status will affect relationships, objectives and even a character's location.

6 Conclusion

In the new medium of MMOGs, stories can be encouraged to emerge through techniques from improvisational theater. Establishing the elements of CROW early in a game experience will provide a web of interrelated components that will shift and change as action drives the game and the story forward. A well-defined circle of expectation will help actions in the game to make sense with respect to a consistent fiction, while at the same time aiding in the emergence of satisfying individual stories. These techniques form a method for approaching the design of MMOGs, allowing for the co-existence and interdependence of story and game play in a way that opens the doors to new creations and new audiences for MMOGs.

Referrences

1. Johnstone, Keith. Impro for Storytellers. Routledge/Theatre Arts Books, NY NY, 1994.
2. Seger, Linda. Creating Unforgettable Characters. Henry Holt & Company, NY, NY, 1990.
3. Smith, Harvey. The Future of Game Design: Moving Beyond Deus Ex and Other Dated Paradigms. IGDA. Oct. 2001. Sept. 2003 available at http://www.igda.org/articles/hsmith_future.php.
4. Stanislavski, Constantin. An Actor Prepares. Routledge, New York, NY, 1936.

Human Factors of Games

Towards a Framework for Design Guidelines for Young Children's Computer Games

Wolmet Barendregt and Mathilde M. Bekker

TU Eindhoven, Department of Industrial Design,
Den Dolech 2, P.O. Box 513, 5600 MB Eindhoven, The Netherlands
{w.barendregt, m.m.bekker}@tue.nl

Abstract. This paper describes a number of general design problems with adventure-like computer games for young children in order to demonstrate the need for specific design guidelines for this type of products. These problems were experienced by children participating in a number of user tests of existing computer games. By providing a generalization of these problems some first directions are given for the nature of the design guidelines that could be developed. Furthermore, a first proposal for a unifying framework to organize these guidelines is given.

1 Introduction

Computer games form a major part of the software market nowadays, and for young children (educational) games are probably even the biggest component of this market. The first experience with the computer for young children is also likely to be the playing of an (educational) game. Because this first experience can influence the attitudes of children towards computers it is very important to pay attention to the quality of these games. One way to enhance the quality of a game is by user testing it with real children from the envisioned user group. An additional way to ensure the quality is by translating the findings of these user tests into design guidelines or heuristics, and using these guidelines as input for the design process. Some well-known heuristics for work-related products are, for example, those of Nielsen [1] and Shneiderman [2]. Gilutz and Nielsen [3] created a highly detailed set of dedicated design guidelines for children's websites. Other guidelines focus specifically on the design of computer games, for example those created by Lepper and Malone [4], Pagulayan et al. [5], and Shelley [6]. Some of these guidelines, like Lepper and Malone's, focus primarily on creating fun or motivation in games and focus less on usability aspects of games. However, usability is an important prerequisite for pleasure [7]. As Pagulayan et al. [5] wrote: 'The ease of use of a game's controls and interface is closely related to fun ratings for that game. Think of this factor as the gatekeeper on the fun of a game'. Or as Clanton [8] stated: 'Problems should be in the game play, not in the interface, or game mechanics'. Other guidelines do focus on both fun and usability but are rather high level, for example Clanton's guideline 'Make it easy to learn' [8]. With guidelines at this level it is still difficult to determine

M. Rauterberg (Ed.): ICEC 2004, LNCS 3166, pp. 365–376, 2004.
© IFIP International Federation for Information Processing 2004

the concrete implementation in a game for a specific user group such as young children.

We think there is a need for detailed design guidelines for computer games for young children that enable designers to create both easy to use and fun products. To illustrate this we will discuss some examples of types of problems in this paper that are specific for computer games for young children. Furthermore, it is important that all guidelines are organized into a manageable framework [9], which keeps the relationship between these guidelines and an underlying theory about user system interaction. In this way it is much clearer which existing guidelines can be used, where they need to be made more specific for this type of product and user group and where possible gaps are. For designers it also provides an easy overview of all guidelines. The unifying framework that we propose is based on Norman's [10] theory of action model. This theory of action model is commonly used for the evaluation of non-entertainment products for adults but will be used in a novel way to help evaluate computer games for children and structure the design guidelines.

In the following sections we will first give some typical examples of problems in computer games for young children to illustrate the need for specific guidelines. Although (variants of) these problems can also be found in computer products for adults, the impact of these problems is often quite different for children and the solutions are not necessarily the same as for adults. Subsequently, we will describe the unifying framework to organize these guidelines, illustrated with further examples.

2   Age Group and Type of Games

In this paper we focus on computer games for children in the group 3 and 4 of primary school, around 5 to 7 years according to the Dutch school system. Many of the computer games for this young age group are adventure games. Prensky [11], a researcher of education through games defines adventure games as 'find your way around the unknown world, pick up objects, and solve puzzles' games. In this type of games children have to play a number of sub games in order to reach a certain goal. These sub games sometimes have an educational character, like choosing the right emotion to express how Grover is feeling in 'Sesame Street: Reading with Grover' ('Sesamstraat Lezen met Grover ©' in Dutch [12]), but they can also be more motor skill based, like saving the rabbit by clicking the wolves before they can eat it.

3   Examples of Problems in Games for Young Children

Our research group examines ways to evaluate children's computer products with children [13-15]. For this purpose we have tested a wide range of computer games over the last few years according to several different evaluation methods with children [14; 16]. Some of these games were tested with over thirty children, others were tested with fewer children but showed the same types of problems. Based on our experience we have selected some of the most salient examples of types of usability problems experienced by young children. These problems include issues related to starting up and closing down games, user/character perspective, cursor shapes, and modalities. While we are aware that for every problematic example we present there are numerous good design examples, we are convinced that specific design guidelines will contribute to even higher quality games. By using examples of problems in existing games we could give the impression that these games are not usable or fun to play. This is not our intention; by pointing out these problems in this article we would just like to illustrate the need for specific guidelines and a unifying framework without giving an overall judgement of the quality of any of the mentioned games.

3.1 Starting the Game

Many of these adventure-type games have an option to save the game. It is therefore possible that the player wants to open one of the saved games. When a game is started for the first time, a question like: 'Do you want to start a new game?' is often posed to distinguish between starting a new game and an already saved game. However, children often think that this question means: 'Do you want to play another game than this one?' Therefore they will answer 'No'. A reason for this misunderstanding could be that many children do not yet know that it is common to have saved games and that the game itself also does not make this clear before posing the question. Guidelines for starting a game should make the designer aware of the level of computer literacy and game experience that can be expected of this age group.

3.2 Perspective and Indirect Manipulation

Many adventure-type games apply one or more characters that the child has to help to achieve a goal. For example, in 'Milo and the magical stones' ('Max en de toverstenen ©' in Dutch [17]) the child has to help Milo and his friends to find magical stones on an island, and in 'Robbie Rabbit: Fun in the Clouds' ('Robbie Konijn: Pret in de wolken' in Dutch [18]) the child has to help Robbie and his friend Sam to prevent an island in the clouds from collapsing under a load of raingear. The characters are usually visible in the screen as companions, so it is clear that the child him/herself is not the character. However, in many games the instructions do not always maintain this separation between the character and the child. For example, in 'Milo and the magical stones' the child is instructed to 'catch the flies by jumping from one water plant leave to the next when a fly is in front of you'. To many children it is unclear that actually Milo has to jump the leaves, resulting in many children trying to catch the flies directly with the cursor without using Milo (see figure 1).

Guidelines about the wording of instructions to clarify the perspective could prevent designers from making such mistakes. However, clarifying the perspective is not always enough. In the above mentioned example, during a user test children were made aware of the fact that Milo was the one who had to catch the flies. Although this explanation helped many children for a while in trying to move Milo, there still was a tendency to return to trying to catch the flies directly by clicking them with the cursor, something that adults are less likely to do. It seems that this indirect way of manipulation is too unclear for some of the children, especially when there are moving objects attracting their attention. Guidelines for the appropriate level of (in)directness for manipulation for this age group should help designers.

Fig. 1. Children have to make Milo jump to the next water plant leave when one of the flies is in front of him. By doing this Milo will catch the fly. Instead the children just keep clicking the flies with the cursor. (Milo and the magical stones ©)

3.3 Cursor Shapes and Hotspots

Some games apply an alternative cursor-shape that is related to the game environment, for example a snake or some other animal. Normal arrow-shaped cursors have as their activation point the arrow tip, which is usually in the upper left corner. For these differently shaped cursors the actual activation point does not always comply with the perceived activation point. For example, in 'Milo and the magical stones' the cursor is shaped like a ladybird with the feelers as activation point (see figure 2). However, most children in our user tests used the body of the ladybird as the activation point, resulting in numerous wrong clicks and frustration about why the clicking did not result in any action. Some children even adopted a strategy of clicking so rapidly and wildly around the objects that they complained about an aching hand and had to shake it from time to time.

Of course, when the hotspots of the objects that have to be clicked are large enough there is probably less of a problem with such a cursor shape. Although adults may have the same problem with this type of cursor, children seem not to be able to overcome this problem on their own while adults can adapt their strategy more easily. Therefore, specific guidelines for children about the combination of cursor shape and the size and shape of the hotspots of objects should be created.

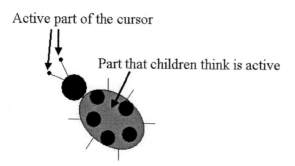

Active part of the cursor

Part that children think is active

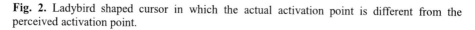

Fig. 2. Ladybird shaped cursor in which the actual activation point is different from the perceived activation point.

3.4 Modalities

Computer games for young children usually use mouse input as interaction technique. Sometimes they also require keyboard input but they are almost never equipped for speech input. Children can get quite confused about the expected modality when this is not clearly explained in the instructions that are given about how to play a subgame. For example, in 'Rainbow, the most beautiful fish in the ocean' ('Regenboog, de mooiste vis van de zee ©' in Dutch [19]) children are induced to try speech input due to the type of instruction the character gives. The character says: 'Would you help me count the scales that I still have to find?' and children spontaneously respond by starting to count verbally. While adults know this kind of input is probably not available, young children are sometimes quite confused that the computer cannot hear them. An instruction like 'Would you help me count the scales that I still have to find by clicking them?' would make the expected modality much clearer. Guidelines about how to indicate the right modality in instructions could prevent this type of problem.

3.5 Stopping the Game

Most games have some button or icon available on every screen to quit the game. Many children use this button in their search for the right way to play a subgame or to navigate to another screen. Usually, a question is asked like: 'Do you want to quit the game?' but many children interpret this question as 'Do you want to quit this *sub*game?' and because they are already puzzled about the way to play the subgame they click Yes, making them quit the whole game by accident. Guidelines that take in mind considerations about computer literacy of children should be developed about the way stop-options can be presented and explained more clearly.

4 Framework for the Organization of Design Guidelines

The examples above demonstrate the need for specific design guidelines for computer games for young children. Furthermore, there are numerous existing guidelines for other types of products and/or user groups that should be included. We propose to use a framework to organize these guidelines. There are many reasons why such a framework is useful and important. The first reason is the criticism on existing predictive methods, such as Nielsen's heuristic evaluation method.

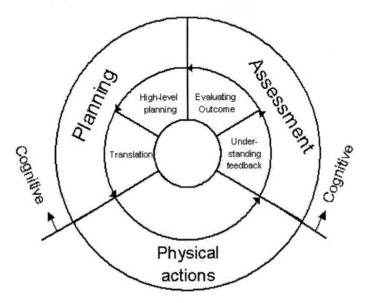

Fig. 3. The Interaction Cycle of Andre et. al's [23] User Action Framework describing how interaction between a human and any product or system happens in terms of cognitive and physical user actions.

The main point of critique to Nielsen's method is that the set is not clearly related to theory and that the rules are ambiguous and hard to interpret. A framework helps to keep the relationship between the guidelines and the underlying theory about user system interaction. The second reason is that the application of guidelines used for evaluation purposes relies heavily on the knowledge of the experts applying them [20]. By providing the experts with structured knowledge about the interaction and tasks the quality of the outcome may be increased. Finally, a framework makes it much clearer which existing guidelines can be used, where overlaps exist, where they need to be made more specific for this type of product and user group, and where possible gaps are. As a basis for our framework we use Norman's theory of action model [10] which applies to the interaction between humans and almost any kind of product or system. Many researchers have used this model in various ways for similar purposes [21; 22]. One of the frameworks that use the concepts of all Norman's stages is the User Action Framework [23] (see figure 3). This framework uses an adapted version of Norman's model, called the Interaction cycle, as an underlying structure to help think pragmatically about usability problems.

Fig. 4. The sandwich shop in 'Robbie Rabbit' where children have to buy ingredients to make a sandwich. (Robbie Konijn, Pret in de Wolken ©)

Although this interaction cycle is meant to model the interaction between a human and any kind of product or system, not specifically games, we think it can also be used for games. An example of interpreting this interaction cycle in the light of a subgame of an adventure is the following. In 'Robbie Rabbit: Fun in the Clouds' children have to buy a number of ingredients to make a sandwich (see figure 4):

- First, in the High-level planning phase, the children have to understand that the goal is to buy ingredients for the sandwich.
- In the Translation phase the children have to understand that to buy one ingredient they have to select it, put the right amount of money on the counter by clicking each coin and dragging it, and ring the bell to indicate that they are ready.
- Then the child has to actually select and drag the coins and click the bell in the Physical actions phase.
- When the child has rung the bell and the feedback comes whether the given amount of money is correct, the child has to perceive and understand this feedback in the Understanding Feedback phase
- Finally the child has to evaluate whether this is the desired outcome in the Evaluating Outcome phase.

So although the interaction cycle in the UAF is not specifically created for games, it is possible to use it to model the interaction in games. In the same way, specific guidelines for games fit well in this structure. For example, guidelines that deal with the level of indirect manipulation fit in the category Translation. In our example of a problem with indirect manipulation the child knows that flies should be caught, but the translation to the indirect manipulation by jumping with Milo from leave to leave is not clear.

4.1 What About Fun?

The examples of guidelines described above all covered aspects of making a game easy to use. However, computer games differ from productivity applications in a number of ways. One of the main differences is that games are designed to be pleasurable [24]. So, additional to the usability related guidelines we also need guidelines to help design fun. Fortunately many already exist [4; 6; 25]. The question is whether the proposed framework can also be used to organize these guidelines in order to create a complete set of guidelines to design easy to use and pleasurable games. We think it can, and even better, we think the framework can sometimes help to create much more specific guidelines. An important example of how the Interaction Cycle can help to make guidelines more specific is in the notion of Challenge. Many researchers agree that an appropriate level of challenge is one of the main aspects that make a game fun to use [4; 11; 24]. However, challenge can be created in different ways. For example by making the objects that have to be clicked very small or by letting them move very rapidly. Another example is by making the right way out of a maze not directly clear. In theory it is possible to create challenge by making any of the phases in the interaction cycle difficult. The first example is challenge created at the **'Physical actions'** level while the second example is challenge at the **'Translation'** level.

Fig. 5. Screen with fishes that have to be clicked to go to other parts of the game. While most of the fishes will guide the user to another part of the game when they are clicked once, the circled fish will only help after being clicked three times. (Regenboog, de mooiste vis van de zee ©')

By using the interaction cycle, guidelines about the appropriate level of challenge for young children can be more specific about the different ways to create challenge. For example, it is possible to create challenge by providing feedback that makes it difficult to determine whether the outcome is the desired outcome or not. In 'Rainbow, the most beautiful fish in the ocean' children have to click one of the navigational fishes three separate times to make it help them to go to another screen. The first two times that the child clicks the fish it says: I don't want to help you because I am hungry'. Children understand this feedback properly and conclude that by clicking this fish they will not get the desired outcome. However, the third time this fish is clicked it will be helpful, but the children have usually given up on trying to get help from this fish (see figure 5).

So, in this particular game, challenge is created by making the **'Evaluating outcome'** phase difficult. However, it is debatable whether this is the best way to create challenge for children at this age.

The Interaction Cycle helps to think of the different ways to create challenge and the specific guidelines for different kinds of challenge.

4.2   Adaptations to the Interaction Cycle

To make the Interaction Cycle more specific for use with games we propose to change some of the wording and split one of the phases in order to emphasize some parts of the cycle that are especially important for games. This adaptation is shown in Figure 6. The first change is the wording of the phase **'High level planning'** into **'Determining goal'**. For games goals are extremely important, especially to create challenge. In productivity applications goals are often defined externally, whereas games define their own goals. This implies also that goals should be clear and interesting to the user at all times. Some examples of games in which the goals are not always clear are 'Oscar the balloonist and the secrets of the forest' (Oscar de ballonvaarder en de geheimen van het bos ©' in Dutch [26]) and 'Witchstuff - With Hennie the Witch and the cat Helmer' ('Heksenspul - Met Hennie de Heks en de kat Helmer ©' in Dutch [27]). In 'Oscar' children can find information about different animals by clicking the animals in a forest. This is necessary to be able to play some games about what the animals are eating or when they are sleeping. However, this goal is not made clear beforehand so the children don't know why they should want to gather this information.

In 'Witchstuff' children can click objects in the rooms of Hennie's house. These objects then make a funny sound and show a little animation but there is no reason to click these objects other than that. One child in our test sessions therefore complained 'Actually, you cannot do anything here!'

By changing the wording of this phase from **'High-level Planning'** into **'Determining Goal'** the necessity of providing clear and interesting goals is made clearer. The other change in the Interaction Cycle is the addition of the phase **'Assess motivation to go on'**. While this assessment could be part of the phase **'Evaluating Outcome'** we feel it is important to make it more explicit. In games it is possible that although the user knows how to reach a goal he/she decides that reaching the goal is boring, too time-consuming or too stressful. In productivity applications, like for example a word processor, this is much less likely. An example of this assessment can be found in our test sessions of the educational adventure game 'World in Numbers,

The Fun-fair' ('Wereld in Getallen, Het Pretpark ©' in Dutch [28]). In this game, children have to perform three screens of arithmetic operations in order to help a ticket officer clean up his room. Some children in our tests, although able to perform the necessary arithmetic, stopped after one or two screens because they decided it took too much time to reach the end goal.

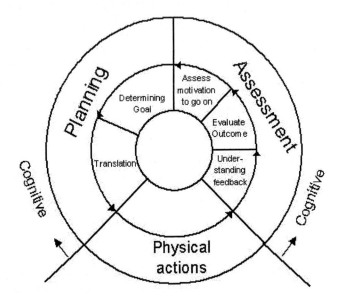

Fig. 6. Adapted Interaction Cycle for games describing how the interaction between a user and a computer game happens in terms of cognitive and physical user actions.

5   Discussion and Conclusions

Based on our experience we have argued for the need of specific guidelines for children's computer games. Subsequently, we suggested an integrated framework for organizing both usability and fun guidelines based on Norman's theory of action model. These guidelines can be either new or more specific guidelines for the user group, like the ones proposed in this paper, or existing guidelines [1; 2; 4; 8]. Although we propose to use this framework for adventure type computer games for young children it should be applicable for other types of games and user groups as well. For example, consider applying it to the design of a racing game:

- First, it must be clear what the goal is, for example reaching the finish first, or within a certain time, and/or with the highest score.
- Second, it must be clear how one should control the car to reach the goal, e.g. what is left, right, faster, slower etc.
- Next, the physical actions to control the car need to be performed. This is probably the most important challenge of the game.

- Then the feedback whether the car is moving, which way it is moving, or what is going wrong should be understood. E.g. after having slipped it should be clear which way to drive to reach the finish.
- Then the outcome should be evaluated: Am I taking the right steps towards the goal?
- Finally, the user should be able to assess whether the goals are reachable within the amount of time the user wants to spend on trying and practicing.

For different age groups it is likely that specific guidelines that relate to cognitive, emotional, and physical aspects of the age group should be adapted. However, the global organization of the guidelines in terms of the Interaction Cycle remains the same.

Finally, the way to represent the guidelines in this framework depends on the envisioned use, for example as an evaluative tool or as a design tool. Designers and evaluators are not necessarily the same people with the same background or the same working process. Therefore, more research on the best way to present the information for the different purposes of the framework is necessary. The way in which we want to proceed in developing this framework is in combination with a structured method for usability experts to evaluate games for children.

Acknowledgements. We would like to thank © MediaMix Benelux, and © Mindscape for giving us permission to use screenshots of their products. We would like to thank R. Gal, J. Geerts, L. Goorix, J. van der Linden, S. Crombeen, and M. Biesheuvel for conducting numerous user test sessions. Finally, we would like to thank the Innovation-oriented Research Program Human-Machine Interaction (IOP-MMI) of the Dutch government for providing the grant that has made this research possible.

References

1. Nielsen, J.: Usability Engineering. Boston: Academic Press Inc. (2003)
2. Shneiderman, B.: Designing the User Interface: Strategies for Effective Human-Computer Interaction. Reading, Mass.: Addison-Wesley. (1998)
3. Gilutz, S. & Nielsen, J.: Usability of Websites for children: 70 design guidelines based on usability studies with kids.(2002)
4. Malone, T. W. & Lepper, M. R.: Making learning fun: a taxonomy of intrinsic motivations for learning. In R.E.Snow & M. J. Farr (Eds.), Aptitude, Learning and Interaction III Cognitive and Affective Process Analysis. Hillsdale, N.J.: Erlbaum.(1987)
5. Pagulayan, R. J., Keeker, K., Wixon, D., Romero, R., & Fuller, T.: User-centered design in games. In J.Jacko & A. Sears (Eds.), Handbook for Human-Computer Interaction in Interactive Systems. Mahwah, NJ: Lawrence Erlbaum Associates.(2003) pp. 883-906
6. Shelley, B.: Guidelines for Developing Successful Games. http://www.gamasutra.com/features/20010815/shelley_01.htm . 15-8-2001.
7. Jordan, P. W.: Pleasure with Products: Human Factors for Body, Mind and Soul. In W.Green & P. Jordan (Eds.), Human Factors in Product Design: Current Practise and Future Trends.. Taylor & Francis UK.(1996)
8. Clanton, C.: An Interpreted Demonstration of Computer Game Design. Proceedings of the conference on CHI 98 summary: human factors in computing systems. (1998) pp. 1-2

9.   Hartson, H. R., Andre, T. S., Williges, R. C., & Rens, v. L.: The User Action Framework: A Theory-Based Foundation for Inspection and Classification of Usability Problems. HCI International 99. Munich, Germany: Aug 99. (1999)

10. Norman, D. A. & Draper, S. W.: User centered system design : new perspectives on human-computer interaction. Hillsdale: Erlbaum. (1986)

11. Prensky, M.: Digital game-based learning. New York: McGraw-Hill. (2000)

12. Sesamstraat: Lezen met Grover (Sesame Street: Reading with Grover) . [Computer software] TLC Domus (1999)

13. Bekker, M. M. & Kersten-Tsikalkina, M.: Evaluating Usability and pleasure of children's products. Proceedings of International Conference on Affective Human Factors Design. Singapore. (2001)

14. Barendregt, W., Bekker, M. M., & Speerstra, M.: Empirical evaluation of usability and fun in computer games for children. Proceedings of Interact Conference 2003. Zürich, Switzerland. (2003) pp. 705-708

15. Markopoulos, P. & Bekker, M. M.: On the assessment of usability testing methods for children. Interacting with Computers, 15(3), 227-243. (2003)

16. Bekker, M. M., Barendregt, W., Crombeen, S., & Biesheuvel, M.: Evaluating usability and fun during initial and extended use of children's computer games. Proceedings of the BCS-HCI, September 2004. Leeds. (2004)

17. Max en de toverstenen (Milo and the magical stones) . [Computer software] MediaMix Benelux (2002)

18. Robbie Konijn, Groep 3: Pret in de Wolken (Robbie Rabbit, Group 3: Fun in the Clouds) . [Computer software] Mindscape (2003)

19. Regenboog, de mooiste vis van de zee (Rainbow, the most beautiful fish in the ocean) . [Computer software] MediaMix Benelux (2002)

20. Cockton, G. & Woolrych, A.: Understanding Inspection Methods: Lessons from an Assessment of Heuristic Evaluation. In A.Blandford, J. Vanderdonckt, & P. D. Gray (Eds.). Springer-Verlag.(2001) pp. 171-192

21. Sutcliffe, A. G., Ryan, M., Doubleday, A., & Springett, M. V.: Model mismatch analysis: towards a deeper explanation of users' usability problems. Behaviour & Information Technology, 19(1), 43-55. (2000)

22. Vermeeren, A. P. O. S., den Bouwmeester, K., Aasman, J., & de Ridder, H.: DEVAN: a detailed video analysis of user test data. Behaviour & Information Technology. (2002)

23. Andre, T. S., Hartson, H. R., Belz, S. M., & McCreary, F. A.: The User action framework: a reliable foundation for usability engineering support tools. Int.J.of Human-Computer Studies, 54, 107-136. (2001)

24. Pagulayan, R. J., Steury, K. R., Fulton, B., & Romero, R.: Designing for fun: User-testing case studies. In M.Blythe, K. Overbeeke, A. Monk, & P. Wright (Eds.), Funology: From Usability to Enjoyment. Kluwer Academic Publishers.(2003) pp. 137-150

25. Federoff, M. A.: Heuristics and usability guidelines for the creation and evaluation of fun in video games Msc Department of Telecommunications of Indiana University. (2002)

26. Oscar en de geheimen van het bos (Oscar the balloonist and the secrets of the forest) . [Computer software] Lannoo (2000)

27. Heksenspul - Met Hennie de Heks en de kat Helmer (Witchstuff - With Hennie the Witch and the cat Helmer) . [Computer software] Karakter Interactive (2002)

28. Wereld in getallen, Groep: 3 Het Pretpark (World in numbers, group 3: The Fun-fair) . [Computer software] Malmberg Uitgeverij (2003)

Social Translucence of the *Xbox Live* Voice Channel

Martin R. Gibbs, Kevin Hew, and Greg Wadley

Department of Information Systems, The University of Melbourne,
Parkville, VIC 3010, Australia
{martinrg,gwadley}@unimelb.edu.au,
kevinhew@hotpop.com

Abstract. In this paper we use the concept of 'social translucence' to understand users' initial reaction to, and use of, the voice communication channel provided by *Xbox Live*. We found that although users expected voice to be an advance over text-based communication, in practice they found voice difficult to use. In particular, users experienced difficulties controlling the voice channel and these difficulties are indicative of usability and sociability problems with the configuration of the voice channel in some *Xbox Live* games. We argue that game developers will need to address these problems in order to realize the potential of voice in online multiplayer videogames. We believe these problems can be addressed by designing the voice channel so that socially salient information is made available to participants according to interactional affordances and constraints that are sensibly designed and well understood by users.

1 Introduction

Launched in the US in 2002 and in Europe and Australia in 2003, Microsoft's *Xbox Live* is a networking system allowing multiplayer gaming via the Internet using *Xbox* videogame consoles. *Xbox Live* brings together a novel cluster of features that includes: multiplayer gaming over the Internet; a console rather than a PC platform; voice communication using microphone and earphone headset; and a 'gamertag' system for the central management of online identity. In particular, and of interest in this paper, *Xbox Live* combines voice communication with a virtual environment, connecting users via broadband Internet for the purpose of computer mediated game play.

Typically, online communication has relied on typed text messages, and text is still the dominant medium for communication in computer games. However, *Xbox* consoles do not include keyboards, but users of *Xbox Live* can communicate with other players by voice in real time. This new mode of interaction makes *Xbox Live* an interesting technology to study. In this paper we address the following research question: *How do users react to their first encounter with voice communication in Xbox Live?*

To collect data we used a constructive interaction technique for usability testing [11], and focus group discussions, to gauge users' initial reactions to voice in multiplayer, online console videogames. We found that while participants expected voice to be an

M. Rauterberg (Ed.): ICEC 2004, LNCS 3166, pp. 377–385, 2004.

advance over text-based communication, in practice many found voice difficult to use due to inadequate facilities provided in the games tested to control what is heard and what is sent over the voice channel. Drawing on the concepts of sociability and 'social translucence' in computer mediated communication, we argue that this lack of control hindered the ability of participants in the study to ascertain socially significant information. As a result, their capacity to engage in convivial computer-mediated social interaction was inhibited. We conclude with a discussion of our findings and their implications for the design and configuration of voice communication in online multiplayer video games.

2   Sociability and Social Translucence

In the context of designing technologies to support online communities, *sociability* has been described as 'planning and developing social policies and supporting social interactions' [12: p605]. Sociability and usability are closely related yet usefully separated concepts for analyzing and designing technologies that support online communities. While usability concerns the interaction between a user and a technological artifact, sociability concerns the interactions between people that occur via the artifacts. Sociability includes the policies and social norms as well as the design features of the mediating technology that govern and influence behaviour online. While sociability concerns the interactions between people, the mediating technology must be usable if it is to support convivial social interactions [6].

We believe sociability is an important construct for understanding all computer-mediated communication, including instances of computer supported cooperative play [14] such as those found in online multiplayer game play. As Bannon has argued [1], consideration of the social layer of computing systems is crucial in systems design. This is further supported by Kutti [8], who argues that human-computer interaction needs to be understood in terms of social factors as well as the task-human-artifact dynamic. To successfully enable cooperative, sociable interaction in digital environments, close attention should be paid to the forms of social interaction afforded by mediating technologies. In terms of designing online multiplayer computer games, sociability emphasizes the importance not only of planning for the interaction between the player and the game, but also planning for the interactions between the people playing the game [14].

Xbox Live has a number of features designed to manage the sociability of the system. These include a fixed user-selected pseudonym ('gamertag') for player identity and accountability, player rankings for many games, and a friends list to allow players to find other players with whom they prefer to play. In addition, *Xbox Live* has introduced a voice channel for communication between players, and Microsoft has mandated that all *Xbox Live* games implement this form of communication. The configuration of the voice channel – the manner in which it is implemented within a particular game – and its resulting usability as a convivial medium, will significantly impact the sociability of games within the *Xbox Live* network.

We believe that voice communication can be a valuable addition to the game playing experience and the sociability of the game environment if it is 'socially translucent'. *Social translucence* is a design approach that emphasizes the importance of making socially significant information visible to participants in digital environments [5].

Social translucence has two dimensions. First, socially translucent systems make socially salient information available to participants. This *visibility* enables participants to be aware of others and their actions. This *awareness* helps bring the social rules, norms and customs that govern participants' actions and interactions into effect. It also allows participants to be held *accountable* for their actions. Visibility, awareness, and accountability are crucial to the sociability of digital environments because they enable participants to structure their interactions with one another in coherent and sensible ways [5]. Thus, in the design of sociable online games, it is important for users to be able to easily discern and identify the other users with whom they are interacting, and to be able to readily associate activity and actions with particular game identities and personas.

Second, socially translucent systems are not *transparent*; communication within these systems is constrained. In the physical world, 'physics' constrains communication and determines who can receive what information or communication in what circumstances. People use these constraints as a resource in social interaction. For example, it is far easier to see and hear a person standing by one's side than it is to see and hear someone across a crowded room and this proximity constraint is routinely used in a host of communicative acts such as raising and lowering one's voice depending on one's intended audience and social situation. Similarly, in designing socially translucent systems, attention needs to be paid to the 'physics', or rules, that govern communication within these digital environments. Furthermore, if participants share an awareness of the constraints that underlie the visibility of socially significant information in a digital environment they can use this understanding as a resource for structuring their social interactions. Thus, we would argue, sociability within online game environments is enhanced by making socially salient information available to participants according to interactional affordances and constraints that are sensibly designed and well understood by those involved.

3   Research Approach

Our research was conducted with six groups of three volunteers. Each group participated in one, two-hour research session. At the start of each session, participants completed a background questionnaire. They were then asked to play multiplayer games with other players over the Internet using *Xbox Live*. We observed their interaction both with other players via the network, and with other participants in the room. After the participants played games for an hour, a researcher led them in a focus group discussion. Open-ended questions sought the participants' opinions about their first encounter with *Xbox Live*. Questions focused on topics such as the voice headset, and playing online. The sessions were recorded using a single video camera directed at the participants. This data was analyzed to identify common themes across the groups through a process of open-coding, then closed-coding to refine and confirm prevalent themes.

Participants were aged between 18 and 27 years and both genders were represented. Participants reported that, on average, they played PC-based computer games more often than console games (6 hours per week versus 2 hours). Two participants played for over 20 hours per week. Only three participants played console games more often than computer games. Participants liked several different types of game. The most popular genres were first-person shooters (13), action games (13), sports (10), strategy games (10) and role-playing games (9). All participants owned or regularly used a computer and had Internet access.

Two games were used: *MotoGP* and *Unreal Championship*. *MotoGP* is a motorbike racing game that is packaged with every *Xbox Live* starter kit. *MotoGP* incorporates a 'lobby' area, outside the main racing arena, where players waiting for their race to start can converse in a party-line fashion. During a race, a proximity-based algorithm is used, allowing players to talk to each other if they are close together on the track. *Unreal Championship* is a first-person shooter allowing either all-against-all or team-based modes of play. In all-against-all play, each player can hear all other players speak. In the team games, all players on a given team can speak to and hear each other.

Groups were used in the observation sessions to encourage participants to express their views and describe their experience. This approach was based on the constructive interaction technique developed by O'Malley *et al.* [11] for usability testing. Also known as co-discovery learning [7], this technique aims to create an environment in which participants verbalize their thoughts more readily than does an individual 'thinking aloud' to a researcher [10]. The focus group discussions that followed each game playing session provided participants with an opportunity to discuss and reflect upon their initial encounter with *Xbox Live*. These discussions were used to provide insights into participants' opinions, feelings and attitudes about their experience playing with *Xbox Live* [9].

4 Findings

The primary purpose of connecting consoles via the Internet is to increase the opportunity to play with other people, rather than computer-generated opponents. The participants in our study all valued the social interactions entailed in playing with other people and cited three major reasons why they preferred to this form of play: unpredictability; fairness; and enjoyment of competition. Human players were regarded as being unpredictable because they are creative and do not follow a pre-programmed *'script'*. Some participants felt that the computer *'cheated'* or had an unfair advantage over them, particularly at high difficulty settings, because computer opponents could be unfairly fast, accurate, or omniscient. Participants reported deriving more satisfaction from beating human opponents than computer-generated ones, *'even though you can't see the person.'* Knowledge that there was another person in the game, even though they were not co-present, substantially increased enjoyment of the game.

Clearly users want to play against other people. One could assume that any feature that enhanced the social interactions of online multiplayer gaming would increase users' enjoyment. We might expect the addition of voice communication to game play to enhance social interaction. However, the voice system, as it was configured in the games used, often seemed to detract from the enjoyment of the game as a social experience. In the following sections we report on users' reaction to voice in *Xbox Live*.

Usefulness of Voice Communication – Perception vs. Practice. Participants expected that voice communication would enrich their multiplayer gaming experience. They expected voice would be an improvement on text-based messaging. In particular, many of our participants thought that voice would be beneficial in tactical team-based games, by better supporting the coordination of team members:

> *I quite like the headset, the fact that you can talk. Especially in Unreal where, well the fact that you're supposed to work as a team and you can sort of do that quite well. I think it's better than having to type or anything like that.*

An important advantage participants in the study cited for using the voice headset was freeing hands from the task of typing messages. Participants felt this would allow them to maintain control over their character's movements while they communicated with other players:

> *[Voice] was good because with network games on computers you have to type messages and that interferes with the game. But, [voice] was good because it didn't interfere with what you were doing.*

This assumed advantage created by voice over other forms of in-game communication was mentioned by the majority of participants. We, as researchers, certainly expected voice to positively augment the gaming experience. However, many participants stopped using the voice headset during observation sessions, effectively rejecting the technology. In practice, it would seem, our participants found voice communication to be unhelpful and not particularly useful or useable in the games used in this study due to a number of difficulties they experienced with the use of voice. These difficulties can be understood as being problems of channel control: controlling what is received, and what is sent, over the voice channel. We discuss these problems next.

Controlling What is Heard Through the Voice Channel. Participants reported two problems with what they heard through the headset: *'noise'* over the voice channel, and an inability to identify who was talking.

Participants felt that a lot of what was sent over the voice channel resembled noise more than conversation. Four types of noise were present on *Xbox Live*. First, the voice channel included speech that was not intended for the listener. Participants could hear conversations that they were not part of. Due to the configuration of the voice channel in the games used in this study, these conversations were as prominent in the voice channel as utterances directed at the participants. Second, participants overheard conversations that were apparently between groups of users co-located around consoles distant on the network. By leaving the microphone active, parts of these conversations were broadcast over the network. Third, participants encountered non-conversational sound such as television, vocalized motorbike sounds, and background music that was apparently transmitted unintentionally. Fourth, sometimes the non-conversational sound encountered by participants appeared to have been sent intentionally, to limit the usability of the channel for others. Some of our participants referred to this as *'spam'*. Examples included loud incoherent speech, relentless trash-talking, and music at a volume that suggested the sender's headset microphone was placed close to a hi-fi speaker. In response to noise of this kind, one participant suggested a preference towards typing over voice. He reasoned, *'that bit of effort in typing text just means you don't get crap on the airwaves.'* That is, the ease with which noise could be generated over the voice channel was seen as a negative feature once users had experienced a variety of irritating and anti-social examples of its usage.

Participants also had problems identifying who was talking on the voice channel. They were unable to link the voice they heard via the headset to the name of the user or the user's avatar on the screen:

> *It's hard to identify who you are talking to. I mean you can't get the sense of community if you are connected to all these people, [but] you can't really see them or you don't know who you are talking to.*

This was particularly pronounced in *Unreal Championship*, where the voice channel was configured in a broadcast, party-line mode, so that everyone could hear each other equally, regardless of their position in the game world. This effectively 'disembodied' the voice, because the volume and clarity of transmission was unrelated to proximity. *MotoGP* uses a coarse proximity-based algorithm that switches voices on or off according to the proximity of players on the racetrack. As a result, voices suddenly appeared, mid-sentence, with no sense of a person approaching or receding. Participants found these voices just as disembodied as those in *Unreal Championship*.

The ability of online gamers to connect socially with one another will depend on their ability to identify who is talking. However it is also important for a user to know who is *listening,* and we discuss this issue next.

Controlling What is Sent Over the Voice Channel. Participants experienced two problems involving transmissions they made over the voice channel: controlling who could hear what they said, and knowing whether their utterances were heard.

When participants spoke into the headset microphone, they could neither control nor know who was listening to their transmission. Participants desired the ability to direct their messages to specific people, but could not find this functionality. One said, *'I didn't know who I was talking to. There wasn't functionality to select who I was talking to.'* And another, in a different session, stated: *'One thing I didn't like was not knowing who you could or couldn't speak to.'*

Participants experienced the voice channel as chaotic and out of control. One participant suggested: *'It might be good if you could direct the speech, so you can specify before you talk who you want to hear it and who you don't want to hear it.'* Suggestions of this kind were made frequently by participants.

A related problem was participants' uncertainty over whether their utterances were being heard by the intended recipients. Participants often did not receive a response from other players in the game, and were uncertain whether they were being heard. One participant was heard to say: *'I'm hanging around the flag. Where are you? Can you hear me? Hello?'* During other sessions participants repeatedly asked: *'Is anyone there?'* or *'Hello, hello?'* in attempts to prompt a response from other players. Participants received no visual cues or other indications as to whether their transmissions were being sent or heard successfully.

5   Discussion

Our findings suggest that the potential to engage in computer mediated social interaction was hindered by the problems with the voice channel participants faced while using *Xbox Live*. Many participants rejected the voice headset, due to their inability to control both what they heard over the headset and who they were speaking to via the headset. Because voice is the only channel on *Xbox Live* through which players can communicate with other players, the rejection of the voice headset removed the participants' ability to engage other players in conversation. When participants did attempt to use the headset, they had problems identifying who was talking, and who they were talking to. Participants could not link utterances to people or their avatars and thus had difficulty interacting with other players on the *Xbox Live* network. This absence of social cues created disorder and chaos in the voice channel.

The inability to ascertain socially salient information – such as the identity of the person who was speaking, and an awareness of who was listening – reflects a lack of social translucence on *Xbox Live*. Kellogg and Erickson [5] suggest that we approach the design of socially translucent systems by first asking what properties of the physical world support graceful, coherent and nuanced communication between people. For example, if a metaphor of face-to-face conversation were used to guide the implementation of voice within a game, the volume of utterances would attenuate over distance, visual cues would be available to help determine who was speaking, and listeners would be able to perceive the direction utterances were coming from. Other features of a game environment might also constrain the ability to communicate, and limit the availability of social cues, such as only being able to communicate with other players within the same room or within close proximity. Other metaphors may also be appropriate in guiding how voice is implemented, depending on the game and its genre.

Xbox Live is new and our choice of games to use in this study was limited. It may be that the games used were not the most apt to encourage voice communication. The fast-paced and competitive nature of the games used may have limited social interaction. Social interactions are more prominent in multiplayer RPGs, and voice may be more suitable to this genre of game. However, it has been suggested that voice communication will detract from immersion in RPGs [2]. The genre of games in which voice will be useful and heavily used remains an open question at this early stage in the life of *Xbox Live*.

Our results suggest two directions for future research. Further work is required to determine how to implement socially translucent voice communication in online multiplayer video games. We are aware that researchers at Microsoft are working to improve the implementation of voice in *Xbox Live* games [13]. In pursuing this line of enquiry it will be necessary to bear in mind that different genres of games, and different styles of game play, will have different requirements in this regard.

Second, while our study has been useful for gauging participants' *initial* reaction to *Xbox Live* and for evaluating usability problems with current implementations of voice communication in games, further investigation of how voice communication is taken up and used by the game-playing community is also needed. Contextual interviews [3] with players, and ethnographically informed observations [4] of game play in settings where it naturally occurs, such as lounge-rooms, LAN cafes, and online digital game environments, should offer valuable insights into the adoption and appropriation (or otherwise) of the voice channel in online multiplayer games. We are currently pursuing both these avenues of inquiry.

6   Conclusion

The research reported in this paper represents the first stage of a longer study into the adoption, adaptation and integration of voice communication media into everyday online multiplayer gaming practice. It has provided an early look into how users react to their first encounters with *Xbox Live*. Our key findings were: (a) the participants' ability and willingness to engage socially with others on *Xbox Live* was hindered by the poor usability of the voice channel; (b) the voice channel's poor usability in the games we tested was due to lack of control over what is sent, and what is received, over the channel; (c) while participants expected voice communication to be an advance over text-based communication, in practice they often rejected it.

Our finding suggest that the current implementation of voice in some *Xbox Live* games is socially 'opaque' in that it is difficult to infer socially relevant information that would aid interaction, such as who is saying what to whom. In order for online videogames to be convivial places for social interaction we need to design systems that make socially salient information available to participants through carefully designed interactional affordances and constraints. The availability of socially relevant information should help participants to be aware of what is occurring in the social milieu of the online games they are playing, and accountable for their actions as a consequence of the public knowledge of that awareness. Furthermore, the rules or 'physics' governing the ways in which this socially significant information is made available need to be both sensible and easily discerned by participants. If this is the case, these rules can be used as a resource in social interaction by participants. We believe that voice communication in online games can be a valuable addition to both game play and the sociability of these digital environments. However, to realize this potential, the voice channel in online games needs to be implemented as a socially translucent mode of communication.

Acknowledgements. We would like to thank Conner Graham for his helpful advice, Steve Goschnick for supporting our use of the IDEA Lab, and the Interaction Design Group at The University of Melbourne for constructive criticism of earlier versions of this work.

References

1.   Bannon, L.: From Human Factors to Human Actors: The Role of Psychology and Human-Computer Interaction Studies in System Design. In: Greenbaum, J., Kyng, M. (eds): Design at Work. Lawrence Erlbaum, Hillsdale, NJ (1991) 25-44
2.   Bartle, R. Not Yet You Fools! Game+Girl=Advance. 28 July (2003): http://www.gamegirladvance.com/archives/2003/07/28/not_yet_you_fools.html

3. Beyer, H., Holtzblatt, K.: Contextual Design: Defining Customer-Centered Systems. Morgan Kaufmann, San Francisco (1998)
4. Blomberg, J., Burrell, M., et al.: An Ethnographic Approach to Design. In: Jacko, J., Sears, A. (eds): The Human-Computer Interaction Handbook. Lawrence Erlbaum, Mahwah, NJ (2003) 964–986
5. Erickson, T., Kellogg, W.: Social Translucence – An Approach to Designing Systems that Support Social Processes. ACM Trans. Computer-Human Interaction, 7 (2000) 59-83
6. Hew, K., Gibbs, M., Wadley, G.: Usability and Sociability of the Xbox Live Voice Channel. In Pisan, Y.: Proceedings Australian Workshop on Interactive Entertainment (IE2004), Creative and Cognitive Studios Press, Sydney (2004) 51-58
7. Kennedy, S. Using Video in the BNR Usability Lab. ACM Special Interest Group on Computer-Human Interaction Bulletin, 21, 2, (1989) 92-95
8. Kutti, K.: Activity Theory as a Potential Framework for Human-Computer Interaction Research. In: Nardi, B. (ed.): Context and Consciousness. MIT Press, London (1996) 17-44
9. Krueger R.: Focus Groups: A Practical Guide for Applied Research. Sage, Thousand Oaks CA (1994)
10. Nielsen, J.: Usability Engineering. Academic Press, Boston (1993)
11. O'Malley, C., Draper, S., et al.: Constructive Interaction: A Method for Studying Human-Computer Interaction. In: Shackel, B. (ed.): Proceedings of Interact 84, North Holland, Amsterdam (1984) 269-274
12. Preece, J., Maloney-Krichmar, D.: Online Communities: Focusing on Sociability and Usability. In: Jacko, J.A., Sears, A. (eds): The Human-Computer Interaction Handbook. Lawrence Erlbaum Mahwah, NJ (2003) 596-620
13. Terrano, M.: Lessons from Life: Designing More Immersive Games. Paper presented at the Australian Game Developers Conference, Melbourne, 20-23 November, (2003)
14. Wadley, G., Gibbs, M., Hew, K., Graham, C.: Computer Supported Cooperative Play, "Third Places" and Online Videogames. In Viller, S., Wyeth, P. (eds): Proceedings 2003 Australasian Computer Human Interaction Conference (OzCHI 2003), Ergonomics Society of Australia, Canberra (2003) 238-241

Artifact-Based Human-Computer Interface for the Handicapped

Ki-Hong Kim, Hong-Kee Kim, and Wook-Ho Son

Electronics and Telecommunications Research Institute,
161 Kajeong dong Yuseong gu Daejeon, Korea
{kimgh, hkimrock, whson}@etri.re.kr

Abstract. Artifacts mixed with EEG signals, which are measured from around the edge part of each eye, are used as the new interfacing means for the handicapped. Artifacts utilized in the experiment are the ones caused by chewing or biting teeth and blinking eyes. These signals might be generally eliminated while analyzing EEG signals because they are regarded as the unwanted ones or the noises. But from the viewpoint of developing an interface applicable in the real world, those signals can be more useful compared to the weak and subtle EEG signals because of their characteristics such as the easiness in creation and the clearness in shape. In this paper, the possibility and validity of using those signals for the communication with computer are examined.

1 Introduction

As a result of accident or disease, many people suffer from a severe loss of motor function. These people are forced to accept a reduced quality of life dependent on other individuals. Even if useful Human-Computer Interfaces based on speech or biometrics have been developed to communicate with computers, most of them are intended to give the normal people with more convenient or easier tools, not the individuals with severe disabilities. Thus, the needs for a novel interface to help the handicapped lead a more improved life have been addressed and the corresponding efforts have also been made in the related fields such as signal processing and UI(User Interface) development. Among various trials is the utilization of the physiological or biosignals obtainable from human's body as the means for communication with surrounding world. The signals widely used in this case are EEG(ElectroEnce-phaloGram), EMG(ElectroMyoGram) or EOG(ElectroOculoGram). While the interfaces based on EMG and EOG signals are used in a little bit limited application areas, the examples utilizing EEG signals are so various that they include the rehabilitation of the handicapped with loss of motor function, the control of VR-based games or electronic appliances. This comes from the advantage of EEG signals over the rest two signals, which means in EEG signals the intentions or emotions of a subject can be reflected. Hence, it can be said the number of commands created using EEG signals is more than that of EMG or EOG case. But, despite of this reason, the effectiveness and the performance of EEG-based interfaces have not been so

M. Rauterberg (Ed.): ICEC 2004, LNCS 3166, pp. 386–392, 2004.

satisfactory up to now. One of the problems is the lack of algorithms useful for eliminating the noises mixed with EEG signals such as signals resulting from any physical movement, eye-blinking or breathing etc. These kinds of noises are often called artifacts and regarded as the ones to be removed in most cases. But why should we always leave these artifacts out of consideration for the analysis of other signals? Are they really unwanted one? An approach to use the advantages of those artifacts over EEG signals such as the easiness in creation and the clearness in shape is introduced for the development of a special interface for the handicapped and their usefulness is examined in the experiment which will be described below.

2   Methods and Materials

Firstly, a preliminary experiment to find the optimal positions of sensors from which the artifacts are recorded while a subject makes some particular actions. When considering that the main users of the interface mentioned may be the handicapped with a severe loss of motor function, especially persons with all the parts of their bodies except over the neck paralyzed, the candidate positions of electrodes should be around the forehead, cheeks, nose, or eyes. Once several electrodes were attached to the appropriate positions described for data recording, a subject was asked to make the various actions prepared beforehand, such as chewing or biting teeth, raising forehead, blinking eyes, wrinkling nose or frowning. We wanted to find the optimal solution to the proper combination between the positions of electrodes and the actions the subject try to make. During such experiment, the positions of electrodes selected initially are fine-tuned gradually to be more appropriate ones by checking if some striking patterns unique to each action are observed or not. This comes from an assumption that although biosignals acquired naturally from the body are generally very random and complex, if some actions are made during recording, a unique pattern depending on the corresponding action can be detected from the signal acquired. Through many trials and errors, it was found that even though the signals recorded from around the nose or cheeks sometimes show somewhat noticeable patterns which are very different from the ones gathered from the other positions, many subjects appeared to be tired from making the repetitive actions like wrinkling nose or frowning and thus, the signals caused by those actions have lack of consistency in patterns as time goes by. In addition to this, many people are of opinion that those positions are not appropriate in terms of the usability and the appearance of the interface. Therefore by excluding those positions from the candidates, two parts around the temple, namely around the edge of each eye, are finally decided as the measurement positions. In such case, the actions like chewing or biting teeth or blinking eyes are found to be much to our purpose. The following figure 1 shows the positions of the two electrodes and a little bit distinct signals obtained through three kinds of actions, which are discriminated one another easily. In the figure, the two signals shown in the left side are the ones measured from around the left temple and the rest three signals, from around the right temple respectively.

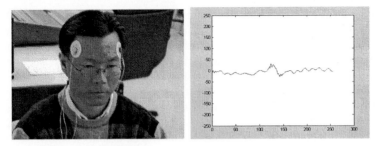

(a) The electrode positions and making no physical movement

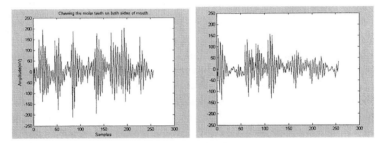

(b) Chewing or biting molar teeth in both sides of mouth

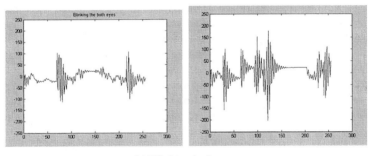

(c) Blinking both eyes

Fig. 1. The signals caused by the predefined actions

Thus, because two pairs of signals shown above represent the time-series obtained by the actions utilizing both sides of the face simultaneously, that is, chewing molar teeth in *both* sides of mouth or blinking *both* eyes, if a subject attempts to make an action like chewing molar teeth in the left side of mouth, the first signal in (b) and the second signal in (a) can be obtained from each electrode respectively. Therefore based on this kind of experimental paradigm, it is possible to acquire seven pairs of signals or patterns using teeth and eyes (1 pair of signal from no physical movement, each 3 pairs of signals from either chewing teeth or blinking eyes). But despite of the possibility like this, all the handicapped persons participating in the experiment don't always make actions correctly. This fact is true of the normal people. From the actual investigation of twenty people, we found that many people had difficulty in blinking only one eye rather than blinking both eyes at a time, and consequently, in case of blinking eyes, a subject was instructed to use both eyes. From the procedure having been described so far, the actions adopted in the experiment are finally classified into five kinds- making no movement, chewing molar teeth in either the left side or the right side of mouth, chewing molar teeth in both sides of mouth and blinking both eyes. The classification results of these five actions are converted to five commands and used to control the computer. In general, because it is well known that the artifacts produced by the contraction or relaxation of the muscles have their important information in the region below 200Hz in frequency domain, we set the sampling rate as 512Hz to avoid the aliasing effect. The 60Hz notch filter was also used to remove the power line noise in the preprocessing phase. The length of signal used in the analysis and classification phase was chosen as 0.5sec for a real-time processing.

2.1   The Analysis of Signals

Selecting the effective features and extracting them by the useful analysis technique are the most important work in the pattern classification. In this experiment, LPC (Linear Prediction Coefficients) and DAMV (Difference Absolute Mean Value) were adopted as features. While LPC is employed often to approximate a sample value at a certain time with several sample values preceding it in time aspect, namely, it can be expressed as the coefficient a_i, which reduces the error value e_n between the original signal s_n and the estimated signal $\tilde{s}_n$ to a minimum. The LPC order p selected in the analysis was 5, the reason of which will be mentioned in the experimental results.

$$\tilde{s}_n = \sum_{i=1}^{p} a_i s_{n-1}, p = 5$$

$$e_n = s_n - \tilde{s}_n = s_n - \sum_{i=1}^{p} a_i s_{n-1} \tag{1}$$

$$E = \sum_{n=1}^{N} e_n^2 = \sum_{n=1}^{N} s_n - \sum_{i=1}^{p} a_i s_{n-1}$$

DAMV is widely used to find how much the signal values are changed according to time change. As shown in the following equation (2), it is expressed as the average value of the absolute difference value between the adjacent samples.

$$\Delta \bar{x}_i = \frac{1}{N-1} \sum_{i=1}^{N-1} |x_{i+1} - x_i| \tag{2}$$

Where N means the number of samples and x_i means the sample value. To deal with a 0.5 second–long signal which has very random characteristics in a quasi-stationary mode, the signal is firstly segmented to become a sum of many consecutive frames.

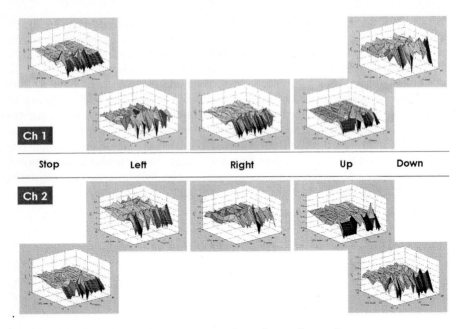

Fig. 2. The LPC patterns changed according to time

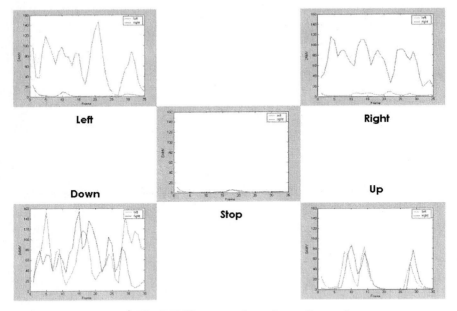

Fig. 3. The DAMV patterns changed according to time

Here, the window size corresponding to one frame was 30-50msec and the overlapping rate of window was 50%. The characteristics of samples within the same frame are assumed to be stationary and features are extracted from each frame. The figure 2 and 3 show how the forms of LPC and DAMV values extracted from all the frames in a signal are changed according to time. As seen in the two figures, the LPC and DAMV patterns are also distinctively discriminated one another for 5 classes.

2.2 Pattern Classification

HMM (Hidden Markov Model) was employed as the classifier in our experiment. It is because HMM is known to model signals with the random and non-stationary characteristics well through the stochastic processing. The one adopted here have a little simple structure with states whose number varies from 2 to 5 and 3 mixtures. The data set used consists of 500 data for training (100 data per each class) and 2500 data for testing (500 data per each class). Those data were recorded from 10 subjects (7 handicapped persons and 3 normal persons).

3 Experimental Results and Discussion

The LPC and DAMV feature vectors extracted from training data through the algorithms described in 2.1. were used to make 5 HMMs, each of which reflects the characteristics of signals belonging to each class and the classification work was carried out for the testing data. In case of LPC features, the investigation to find the optimal order of coefficients was also conducted. The following figure 4 shows the detailed results of the experiment made.

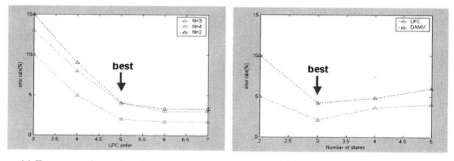

(a) Error rates for various LPC orders   (b) Error rates for different numbers of states

Fig. 4. The experimental results

As seen in the figure 4(a), the error rate in the classification phase decreases rapidly till the LPC order increases up to 5 and, after that, remains almost the same, about 3%, irrespective of the increase of order. Such result is also found even when the structure of HMM becomes more complex, that is, the number of states increases. The figure 4(b) indicates the performance of LPC is slightly better than that of DAMV in this experiment and moreover the error rate becomes the minimum, about 3%, when the number of states of HMM is 3. Therefore it is concluded that for designing an interface based on the artifacts caused by chewing or biting teeth or blinking eyes, HMM with 3 states in which 5th order LPC features are used can be applied effectively. Finally, through a demonstration of operating a maze game, it was found that the artifacts might become the good means for HCI.

References

1. Florian, G, Pfurtscheller, G.: "Dynamic spectral analysis of event-related EEG data", Electroenceph. Clin. Neurophysilol. 95, pp393-396(1995)

A Home Page Is Where the Heart Is: Using Games Based Design Techniques to Enhance Contact Centre Interfaces

Nicola J. Millard, Paul K. Buckley, Faye Skinner, and Rosita Venousiou

BT Exact, Adastral Park, Martlesham Heath, Ipswich, U.K.
nicola.millard@bt.com

Abstract. The demands for interface design for a time pressured and volatile environment such as a contact centre are not purely around usability and efficiency. Customer Service Representatives require interfaces that provide them with knowledge about the customer, products and services and company procedures in a way that is fast, easy to digest and easy to use. However, usability and efficiency have proved to be insufficient for such tools to be used in an operational environment. This study shows how the redesign of a knowledge system for a contact centre using designs inspired by computer games can be used to address issues of usage and acceptance. Two new designs were produced; one for use whilst online with the customer, emphasising the need for efficiency, speed and usability of knowledge access and another for use whilst offline which was more about having fun, knowledge sharing, personalisation and exploring the knowledge space.

1 Using the Contact Centre to Deliver "An Experience"

Contact Centres are regarded as a primary mechanism for businesses to talk to their customers. They are regarded as fundamental to enhancing relationships, improving the quality and consistency of customer contact and leveraging sales through service. As such, they have to deliver "an experience" to customers as a means for differentiation in a highly commoditised market [1]. However, the design of the contact centre environment often fails to address the affective aspects that are required to help customer service representatives (CSRs) deliver these experiences. Technologies designed for such environments tend to emphasise efficiency rather than experience and this is often reflected in low levels of customer satisfaction [2].

The goal of this research has been to develop contact centre systems that are easy to use and trustworthy but also enjoyable and fun in order to increase user acceptance and adoption. Contact centre systems are designed to achieve a defined pre-existing goal (meet the needs of a customer) but also have an affective component to them in that advisors need to deliver customer satisfaction and positive affect to the customer (termed 'emotional labour' [3]). We looked for inspiration from computer games design since games are designed to promote positive affect (because if they don't, they won't be used) [4]. We addressed some of these problems by applying both 'emotional usability' [5] (i.e. design that takes into account people's emotions) and traditional usability (emphasizing effectiveness and efficiency) in order to support both the CSR's task and emotional needs. Taking basic motivational psychology (for instance increasing teamwork and control) and innovative design inspired by

M. Rauterberg (Ed.): ICEC 2004, LNCS 3166, pp. 393–397, 2004.
© IFIP International Federation for Information Processing 2004

computer games, these interfaces aim to increase CSR engagement and participation as well as addressing effectiveness of the customer interaction (increasing customer satisfaction).

2 A Games Based Interface for Knowledge Management

CSR's provide an intermediary role in the contact centre between the customer and the system (Computer-Human-Human-Interaction (CHHI) [11]). They must not only maintain a coherent conversation with the person on the other end of the phone line but must also cope with a number of interfaces and interaction styles contained within the (often) multiple databases that they need to get information from and to.   In addition, they must adhere to all their quality procedures (on which they are monitored and incentivised) and control their emotional state [3]. During the dialogue process with the customer the CSR is constantly managing switches in salience between one stream of interaction and another [12]. The system is, therefore, a third partner in the dialogue with the customer and can heavily influence both structure and content [12].

This paper concentrates on a prototype interface employing games based techniques which was designed to enhance the usage of a recently introduced intranet based knowledge management system in a contact centre answering general customer service enquiries within a telecommunications company.

A survey of CSR systems usage showed that the new intranet knowledge system was only being used in 7% of customer interactions compared with 22% of interactions using an old, familiar (but outdated) database system. This was despite the fact that the intranet knowledge system was ranked favourably in terms of usability when a standard usability assessment (SUMI) questionnaire was administered.   The CSRs also generally perceived the new system to be a "good idea". Although users perceived it as being useful and usable, it was not sufficient for the system to actually be *used* [6] because it was not regarded as an essential part of the CSR's job. This was problematic because outdated or no knowledge guidance could compromise the accuracy of knowledge given out to customers.   Inaccurate information can impact negatively on customer satisfaction, cause a number of follow on calls into the contact centre and can, in the worst case, result in litigation.

Ethnographic observation of the CSRs showed that their requirements for knowledge use differed depending on whether they were on the telephone with a customer or doing work offline. It was decided that the prototype design should reflect these two distinctive modes. Whilst online with the customer the emphasis needed to be on efficiency, speed and usability of knowledge access. The emphasis whilst offline is less on efficiency and more on knowledge sharing, personalisation and exploration. In the latter mode, there needed to be more of an element of what Murray [7] describes as "orienteering" – pleasure in exploring and discovering things. In the former this becomes more akin to jet piloting – being able to retrace pathways to knowledge quickly. Yet intranet knowledge spaces tend to become what Murray [7] calls an "unsolvable maze". They can seem to be infinite with no end point, no way out and no landmarks showing paths towards discovery. It was decided to design two distinct sets of screens.

2.1 The Home Page

Factors for the adoption of systems have been identified as perceived usefulness, perceived ease of use and perceived enjoyment [14], along with perceived fun [15]. Fun is an example of intrinsic motivation, where the person performs an activity for no apparent reinforcement other than the process of performing the activity *per se* [16]. Increased ease of use of a system motivates the user to explore the system functionality, which may in turn increase intrinsic motivation, and result in greater enjoyment of the activity. This is often very much in evidence in the construction of the narrative of games [17].

The Home Page component of the interface needed to draw upon all these factors. The interface had to be friendly and familiar to draw them in but needed also to fit the individual CSR's way of working. In this service oriented contact centre the typical CSR was 25-35 and female so a user interface metaphor was selected to appeal to that demographic.   Due to the surfeit of home improvement programmes on British television at the time and the popularity of the game 'The Sims' it was decided to use the metaphor of a house as a home page.

Logan [5] stated that computer games are a good example of products with emotional usability. Since this interface is designed to engage the user, the decision to use a games-like home page was deemed appropriate because:

- The mode of interaction is both engaging and (relatively) intuitive.
- It implies that an element of play or exploration is allowed without the user being nervous that they will "break things".
- It fosters an atmosphere of discovery.
- It is less like the business-focused structure of the original version of the user interface and more friendly.

The page was constructed so that the artifacts in the house could be used as links to pages on the intranet.

It was also decided that the page would be fully customisable by the user to enhance their sense of ownership. Giving people a choice, or even the illusion of choice, often increases their motivation to do a task [8]. Wallpapers can be changed and artifacts can be moved. Although the fridge logically sits in the kitchen, the user can, if he or she wishes, move it to any room in the house. This again encourages a sense of play and ownership of the interface – but also starts to acknowledge that different people like to construct their information spaces in different ways. Peacock et al [9] discovered that different people managed information in different ways, some people were more organised than others and that people were reluctant to change the way in which they structured (or didn't) their information. By allowing an element of customisation it was hoped that some of these strategies could be better accommodated.

2.2 The Knowledge Portal

This used more conventional principles of usability to provide CSRs with fast and usable access to information about customers, products and information whilst online with a customer. Construction of the knowledge portal had to address the efficient access of knowledge, reduction of CSR cognitive load and increasing the usability and structure of the knowledge that CSRs had to read off the screen.

Peacock's [9] assertions about the different strategies that CSRs used in searching and navigating a knowledge space was very much in evidence from the ethnographic study. Individual search strategies were based upon training and personal preferences and, since time was a factor when they were on the phone, they were unlikely to explore unfamiliar search mechanisms.

The design of the first version of the system was very linguistic and relied almost entirely on naming and highlighted links. The only visual coding was on the menu structures but this added little to navigability. The redesign involved usage of space-semantic relationships to logically group related links together – such as tools to help CSRs price products and access general reference sources.

The redesigned interface also offered a number of ways in which CSRs could search for information to support different search mechanisms. This included a free text 'Find' function, a side toolbar of common pages using graphical icons, an A to Z and a bookmarking function on the page rather than in a pull down menu in the toolbar. The simplicity and familiarity of the search mechanisms were also designed to reduce cognitive load.

The most radical change in look and feel of the interface was introduction of colour on the front screen to provide a more definite grouping of product, procedural, service and customer information. These colour signposts were continued along a path to lower levels of the knowledge space.

3   Evaluation and Initial Results

The design prototype screens were taken back to the CSR user groups who had been involved in the ethnographic study in order to validate and evaluate the design. The research team allowed a selection of CSRs to conduct a guided tour of both the Home Page and the Knowledge Portal. They were asked to evaluate it both on a general usability level but were also asked to describe their feelings towards the system. These feelings were recorded as part of a free labelling method [10] as the CSRs wrote down their feelings as they went through the guided tour. Comments were recorded but, because emotional data can be difficult to verbalise, general demeanor and body language cues (e.g. facial expression [13]) were also recorded to assess emotional reactions to the prototype. Words such as "easy", "friendly", "encouragement", "clarity", "easier", "relaxed" and "fun" appeared frequently in the evaluation. Users asserted that they would want to use the new knowledge interface more than the old one which the CSRs described as "boring", "confusing", "intimidating" and "complex" using the same method. Reactions were generally positive with smiles and engagement.

However, this was under experimental conditions, so the research team returned to complete an ethnographic evaluation of the knowledge system use three months after changes had been implemented to assess whether the system was *actually* being used during calls. This evaluation showed that the games inspired intranet knowledge tool had increased usage from 7% to 49%. It is difficult to conclude that the design alone was responsible for the changes in usage pattern as there is likely to be influence simply from increased familiarity with the tool. Further study is required to look at the factors contributing to technology acceptance in this case.

4 Conclusions

This study has shown that designing for functional usability as well as for emotional usability provides a more complete user experience which, in turn, ensures that interfaces are not simply usable but are also used. These preliminary results have shown that the use of more games-like design principles in an environment where efficiency and usability are usually the only concerns can potentially engage and motivate people to actually *use* a system. The home page is still under consideration as a design for the live interface despite extremely positive user testing.

References

1. Voss, C. (2003), The Experience – Profit Cycle: Trends in the Experience Economy, *London Business School Report*, July 2003.
2. Hickman, M. and White, C., *Back to the Future,* The Henley Centre, January, 2004.
3. Hochschild, A. (1983) *The Managed Heart*, University of California, Berkeley.
4. Johnson, D. and Wiles, J. (2002), Effective Affective User Interface Design in Games, *Conference for Affective Human Factors Design*, Singapore.
5. Logan, R.J. Behavioural and Emotional Usability: Thomson Consumer Electronics. In M. Wiklind (Ed.), *Usability in Practice,* Cambridge, M.A: Academic Press, 1994.
6. Dix A. Absolutely Crackers, *Computers and Fun 4*. (York, UK) 29th November 2001.
7. Murray, J.H. *Hamlet on the Holodeck: The Future of Narrative in Cyberspace*, MIT Press, 1998.
8. Zimbardo, P.G. (1969), *Cognitive Control of Motivation,* Illinois: Scott & Foresman.
9. Peacock, L.A., Chmielewski, D., Jordan, P.W. and Jenson, S., User Organisation of Personal Data – Implications for the Design of Wireless Information Devices. In *Proceedings of Interact 2001*, Los Angeles: Chapman and Hall, 2001.
10. Philippot, P. (1993), Inducing and Assessing Differentiated Emotion Feeling States in the Laboratory, *Cognition and Emotion*, 7(2), 171-193.
11. Steel, A., Jones, M. and Apperley, M. (2002), The Use of Auditory Feedback in Call Centre CHHI, *Proceedings of CHI 2002*, Minneapolis: ACM Press.
12. Bowers, J. and Martin, D. (2000), Machinery in the New Factories: Interaction and Technology in a Bank's Telephone Call Centre, *Proceedings of CSCW 2000*, December 2-6, Philadelphia: ACM Press, 49-68.
13. Ekman, P. (2003), *Emotions Revealed: Understanding Faces and Feelings*, Weidenfeld & Nicholson.
14. Davis, F., Bagozzi, R. & Warshaw, P. (1992) Extrinsic and Intrinsic Motivation to Use Computers in the Workplace, *Journal of Applied Social Psychology*, 22,14,1111-1132.
15. Igbaria, M., Schiffman, S. & Wieckowski, T, The respective roles of perceived usefulness and perceived fun in the acceptance of microcomputer technology, *Behaviour & Information Technology,* 13, 6, 349-361, 1994.
16. Malone, T.W. (1981), What Makes Computer Games Fun?, Byte, December, 258-277.
17. Hopson, J. (2001), Behavioural Games Design, Gamasutra, April 27th , 2001.

Avoiding Average: Recording Interaction Data to Design for Specific User Groups

Nick Fine and Willem-Paul Brinkman

Brunel University, Department of Information Systems and Computing,
Uxbridge, Middlesex UB8 3PH, United Kingdom
{nick.fine, willem.brinkman}@brunel.ac.uk
http://disc.brunel.ac.uk

Abstract. Designing domestic user interfaces for broad user populations means designing for the average user. To design for more personally intuitive interfaces detailed interactive behaviours need to be captured and described in order to better inform the design process. By utilising technologies such as interface skins, log file analysis and user interface description languages, the PROSKIN project is developing an empirical tool for quantitative capture, description and analysis of interactive behaviour in a non-invasive and situated context. The purpose of the tool is to identify user groups by distinguishing behaviour or trait which will allow designers to develop more personally relevant user interfaces. The tool itself facilitates the analyses of large datasets of users and their interactive behaviours. This will allow designers to produce interface skins for user groups of similar interactive profile and subsequently providing a less average user experience.

1 Introduction

Interfaces are often boring by design because they have to be average. As individuals comprised of unique psychologies and physiologies with associated strengths and weaknesses, why are we often forced to use interfaces designed for the average user — designed to be average?

User-Centered Design seeks to "know the user" [3] but paradoxically once we know the user we tend to ignore them by designing for typical users. We create a single user interface that has to satisfy everyone, or at least 90% of them. This user-centered approach to design is widely accepted and is well documented in its effectiveness. The challenge for designers is to produce an interface that *all* users can effectively interact with. To design for 100% of your target population is very difficult to achieve, especially when the interface is used by a broad population. This is because there are too many design considerations and often the design compromises that are made either exclude certain members of the population or produce an interface that is confusing and inefficient.

Ergonomists often design for the 90th percentile as a more realistic design aim. This might be perfectly acceptable when designing an ATM or a car dashboard, but when it comes to entertaining users, 90% means a relatively boring interface. The industrial

M. Rauterberg (Ed.): ICEC 2004, LNCS 3166, pp. 398–401, 2004.

designer is not able to design for me, or people like me, because they do not have sufficient information about me. The resulting interface might functionally achieve its design aim but is unappealing — in other words effective but unaffective. Traditional definitions of design dictate both *form and function* but yet designing for broad target populations often means function without form. Logically in order to have both function and form one would need to understand the user population in great detail, even so far as individually. When it comes to entertaining and designing relevant interfaces (e.g. gaming and interactive digital television), an understanding of the *nature* of the individual serves not only to inform designers but to enhance the user experience beyond existing preference or history based personalisation.

The research project, named PROSKIN, is investigating ways to address these issues, of informing designers in detail about their user population and how to most effectively use skinning technology to enhance the user experience both aesthetically and functionally to provide for an interface more tailored to the individual and their differential traits, without having to design an interface for each and every user. PROSKIN seeks to establish and empirically validate a profiling tool to enable the identification of user groups within the general usage population based on large data collections of usage interaction. This information when fed back into the design chain enables designers to create user interfaces designed for particular types of users, rather than the average user.

2   Key Elements of PROSKIN

Three of the key tools to this investigation are interface skinning, log file analysis and user interface description languages.

2.1 Interface Aesthetics and Skinning

In order to achieve individual appeal designers have in recent years allowed the personalization of the user interface through interface skins. A skin is considered to be the appearance of the user interface, including graphic, haptic, and/or aural patterns. Skins are widely used to allow personalization of the interface and a number of different types of PC application are "skinnable" e.g. Winamp, Windows Media Player, ICQ, Internet Explorer and Messenger. Skins are used typically to change the "look and feel" of the interface components, often a cosmetic change alone (i.e. the colours change or a background image is applied, but the interface components remain unaffected in location, attribute or function). Changing skins (known as "re-skinning") allows not only the visual and interactive components of the interface to be changed but also aurally with personalised sound profiles. Interface reskinning can provide significant benefits to interaction for specific user groups, for example by changing interface colour to facilitate reading for dyslexic users [2]. The ability to re-skin an interface provides designers with the *means* to adapt the user interface to better suit individual preferences (in form and function) but does not inform them as to *how*.

2.2   Observing Interaction: Usability Evaluation Methods

Usability Evaluation Methods (UEMs) are one means by which interactive behaviours are investigated. Typically they involve the capture of snapshot data, require interviewing of the participant, or are performed away from the actual context of use. An ideal approach would involve continuous non-intrusive observation over a long period of time in the actual context of use. This provides a number of benefits to the investigation; longitudinal data allows for trend analysis over time and produces more realistic usage data than a snapshot or a low repetition sample. The resulting output describes behaviour over time and contributes towards more robust results. The issue therefore is how to observe user behaviour in context but in an unobtrusive way so as to observe and record natural behaviours.

A number of technological developments have facilitated such remote, non-invasive interaction logging. The increasing ubiquity of both computing resources and network communication means that home networks, which connect domestic devices together, are becoming more commonplace. To truly understand users, measurement of user behaviour should be based on interaction behaviours in their context of use and connected homes provide the means to extract such real life data.   Additional developments include broadband Internet access (i.e. "always-on" connectivity) to enable automatic long distance carriage of data back to investigators and programming tools and techniques enabling the description and recording of interactive actions within software applications.

2.3   Log File Analysis and User Interface Description Languages

Log file analysis is a computing tool that is frequently used by programmers and administrators. Logging in computing terms refers to the recording of data or events to a file, for example a security or event log. Other forms of logging include keystroke recording, where all user keypresses are recorded to a file and component message exchange logging, where communication between internal components is measured and recorded [1]. Logging techniques such as these provide the means for user behaviour to be recorded for remote analysis and provides for large participant populations without significant resourcing issues.

The system metrics to be measured are currently under review but typically could include low-level (keystrokes) and high-level user events [1], user event interval times, success/failure rates, frequency feature used and user skin configuration etc. This will provide quantitative datasets that in part describe the user and in part describe the system state, as well as indicators of user preference.

User Interface Description (UID) languages are forms of programming language that enable description of the interface components. By explicitly recording the interaction with these components it becomes possible to directly link the analysis with different interface components.

3 Approach

We envisage that increasingly connected homes and personal technology will mean increased availability of usage data and that existing evaluation methods, including existing UEMs, are not appropriate for the nature of the longitudinal data produced by online interaction logging. To this end we are developing a skinnable web radio application as a first prototype and a proof of concept for an empirically based tool for capture and analysis of user interaction logs. The radio will offer the user the ability to listen to a selection of Internet radio station, as well as features such as volume control, channel selection and skin selection. Being written into the program code are markers that allow for the required creation of log files for recording interaction. The log files will be periodically transmitted to a central database where it will be recorded for later analysis. All users of this application will have a detailed questionnaire to complete at installation of the software, to record a number of user metrics. These user metrics will be used to construct a user profile. Due to ethical limitations potential metrics are currently under review but may include: user age, user gender, personality dimensions, intelligence measures, domain experience, ergonomics/anthropometrics, perception, psychological classification metrics, geographical location etc. By correlating user profile with logged system behaviour we hope to establish an alternative means to enhance user profiling in a non- intrusive manner (i.e. not using user questionnaires). The output from these analyses will be given to designers and used to redesign skins based upon the results. The redesigned skins based will be redistributed to users with usage data logged to determine behavioural change. These analyses will provide user and group profile information designers currently lack. In so better understanding user and usage, designers are able to provide interfaces designed for particular user groups as opposed to general users, providing the means to design more towards the individual and away from average.

References

1. Brinkman, W.-P., Haakma, R., Bouwhuis, D.G.: Usability testing of interaction components: Taking the message exchange as a measure of usability. In Jacob, R.J.K., Limbourg, Q., Vanderdonckt, J. (eds.): Pre-Proceedings of CADUI'2004. Kluwer Academics, Dordrecht, The Netherlands (2004) 159-170
2. Gregor, P., Newell, A.F.: An empirical investigation of ways in which some of the problems encountered by some dyslexics may be alleviated using computer techniques. In Proceedings of the fourth international ACM conference on Assertive technologies. ACM, Arligtion, VA (2000) 85-91
3. Nielsen, J.: Usability Engineering. Academic Press, Boston (1993)

Physiological Response to Games and Non-games: A Contrastive Study

Karina Oertel, Gösta Fischer, and Holger Diener

Dept. Entertainment Technologies, Fraunhofer Institute for Computer Graphics Rostock,
Joachim-Jungius-Str. 11, 18059 Rostock, Germany
{Oertel, Fischer, Diener}@igd-r.fraunhofer.de

Abstract. We performed an experiment to verify the hypothesis that users are interacting more aroused and more pleased with games than with non-games. Therefore we used rating-scales and physiological measurements during a playing task in comparison with a writing task. The experiment, in which a total of 10 subjects participated, took place in a laboratory environment. Main finding is that playing a computer game causes that users feel emotional and physical stimulated, but do not imply a high physical arousal.

1 Introduction

Good HCI design means to develop usable, easy to learn and motivating interactive systems. A lot of methods and standards for the implementation of usability do exist, but a lack of adequate software applications still remains. Current studies show the relevance of computer games for user-centered design. They could be a good source to mediate functionality and motivate users [1] and are possibly one of the most successful application domains in the history of interactive systems. Assuming that self-reports are still a primary method for ascertaining emotion and mood, and the body usually responds physically to an emotion [4], we want to survey the following hypothesis: Users are interacting more aroused and more pleased with games than with non-games. Therefore, we set up an experiment using rating-scales and physiological measurements in different scenarios. In this paper we focus on a playing task in comparison with a writing task. We firstly introduce the circumplex model for assessment of effect and subsequently describe and analyze the obtained data.

2 Assessment of Effect

For a correlation between physiological variables and the affective dimensions of valence and arousal several studies have provided evidence [4]. To classify emotions, J. Russel [3] presents a circumplex model of affect as he calls his two dimensional model of valence and arousal (see fig. 1). The horizontal (east-west) metaphor is the pleasure-displeasure dimension, and the vertical (north-south) dimension is the arousal-sleep dimension. The different variables do not form discrete categories or even independent dimensions, but help to define the quadrants of space. To assess the effect of computer games, we place user feedback into this coordinate system.

M. Rauterberg (Ed.): ICEC 2004, LNCS 3166, pp. 402–405, 2004.
© IFIP International Federation for Information Processing 2004

3 Experiment

Method. To induce different emotions according to a more complex approach [2] five scenarios for interaction were developed. They were placed each in one quadrant of the coordinate system of valence and arousal, as expected (see fig. 1). During the experiment they were presented in a random order and every single scenario lasted approximately 10 minutes. We restrict this analysis to scenario 1 (writing task: tests participants had to write an official letter using MS Word) and scenario 4 (playing task: test participants could choose and play one (mini-)game of four (Pacman, Magic Balls, Smashing and Solitaire).

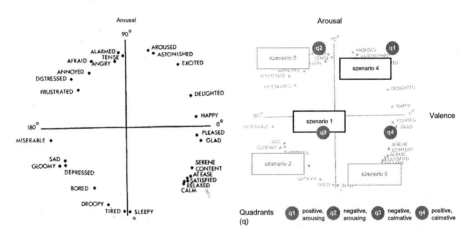

Fig. 1. Circumplex model of affect (left) for a placement of test scenarios (right)

A total of 10 subjects participated (7 males, 3 females). They mostly were students at the University of Rostock with an average age of 25,1 years. All participants had experiences with standard software and WWW and stated to use the computer often or very often. The experiment took place in a laboratory environment using the RealEYES-Setup.[1] It consisted of 10 sessions, in each of which one person participated at one time. All sessions began with a short introduction of the participant and closed with a questionnaire for individual data. A test observer controlled the task performance from a remote work station.

Measurements. To define the emotions we employed the Self-Assessment-Manikin (SAM) rating scale [2]. It is based on Russel's circumplex model of affect and consists of pictures of 5 manikins, each in different state of valence and arousal (see fig. 2). We used a 9ary instead of this 5ary scale to obtain more detailed self-reports. The test participants had to rate, arousal at first and valence after that, by pressing especially marked keys on the keyboard. For rating an acoustic signal sounded every 90 or 60 seconds or even more often whenever the observer watched abnormalities in face

---

[1] The RealEYES-System was developed for usability studies and allows a synchronous recording and playback of different user and system data; more at http://www.igd-r.fraunhofer.de.

video or physiological data. Physiological data, that means stress level (galvanic skin response) and heart rate (pulse), were recorded simultaneously and registered in log files. They were inspected as mean values of an interval of 10 seconds. These istarted each 10 seconds before the acoustic signal for self rating and ended with this signal.

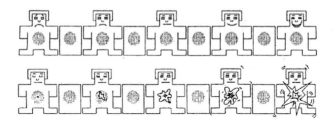

Fig. 2. The scales valence (top) and arousal (bottom) of the Self-Assessment-Manikin (SAM)

4   Findings and Discussion

To analyze the log files, we extracted the self-ratings and the physiological data[2] which go with them and found out (see fig. 3):
-   The self-ratings for playing are concentrated in q1 (positive, arousing).
-   The self-ratings for writing are concentrated in the middle of the coordinate system (neutral emotional and physical arousal).
-   Physiological data[3] show a medial value of heart rate and stress level during playing and high values during writing. Indeed the felt arousal in interaction with a computer game found no expression in these.

5   Conclusion

To summarize, our findings indicate that the physical load during a writing task could be considerable even though it was felt as a relatively relaxing work. This result should be taken seriously and examined in further analyses. Conversely, playing a computer game causes that users feel emotionally and physically stimulated, but do not imply a high physical arousal. Moreover computer games are obviously qualified to relax and to reduce physical arousal to an average value.

---

[2] To guarantee a comparability of data, we executed the z-transformation for heart rate and stress level of every participant.
[3] Between -1 and +1 are two third of all data for stress level and heart rate. The mean value is 0. We assume a normal distribution for stress level and heart rate.

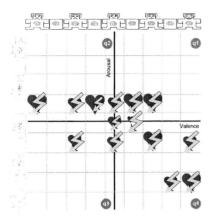
a) Heart rate and stress during writing

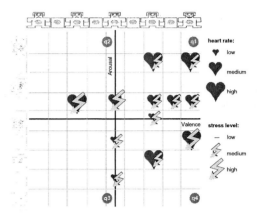
b) Heart rate and stress during playing

	self-ratings		physiological data	
	arousal 1.0 aroused - 4.5 medium - 9.0 sleepy	valence 11.0 pleased - 14.5 medium - 19.0 miserable	stress level > 0 = more stress than average	heart rate > 0 = higher heart rate than average
writing	5,543	14,304	0,761	0,459
playing	4,900	13,450	0,218	0,001

c) Mean values of self-ratings and physiological data

Fig. 3. Results within the coordinate system of valence and arousal (symbolic) for a writing task (a) and a playing task (b) and in terms of mean values (c)

References

1. Diener, H., Mainka, M.: *ContextControl – Complexity Bbecomes easy.* In: Proc. TIDSE'03 (2003) 403-407.
2. Peter, C., Herbon, A.: *On Defining the Structure of Emotion for Use in an Affective Computing Environment.* To be published 2004.
3. Russel, J.: *A Circumplex Model of Affect.* Journal of Personality and Social Psychology. 39 (1980) 1161-1178.
4. Zimmermann, P. et al.: *Affective Computing - A Rationale for Measuring Mood with Mouse and Keyboard.* Internat. Journal of Occupational Safety and Ergonomics. 9(2003) 539-551.

Intelligent Games

Probabilistic Opponent-Model Search in Bao

Jeroen Donkers, Jaap van den Herik, and Jos Uiterwijk

Department of Computer Science, IKAT, Universiteit Maastricht,
P.O. Box 616, 6200 MD Maastricht, The Netherlands
{donkers,herik,uiterwijk}@cs.unimaas.nl

Abstract. In Probabilistic Opponent-Model search (PrOM search) the opponent is modelled by a mixed strategy of N opponent types $\omega_0 \ldots \omega_{N-1}$. The opponent is assumed to adopt at every move one of the opponent types ω_i according to the probability $\Pr(\omega_i)$. We hypothesize that PrOM search is a better search mechanism than Opponent-Model search (OM search) and Minimax search. In this paper we investigate two questions: (1) to which extent is PrOM search better than OM search and Minimax search in the game of Bao? and (2) which opponent type is most advantageous to use? To answer the second question we constructed Five evaluation functions which we applied in a tournament consisting of 352,000 games. Our conclusions are twofold: (1) in Bao, PrOM search performs better than OM search and sometimes also better than Minimax search even when no perfect information of the opponent is available, and (2) for an adequate performance of PrOM search, emphasis on the own evaluation function in the opponent model should be higher than assumed so far.

1 Introduction

Probabilistic Opponent-Model search [6, 8] is an extension of Opponent-Model search (OM search). In OM search [3, 8, 13, 14], the opponent is assumed to use a weaker evaluation function than the player's own evaluation function. OM search tries to exploit the opponent's weaknesses. In fact, the opponent is modelled as precisely as possible by its evaluation function. PrOM search tries to exploit the weaknesses of the opponent too, but uses a more sophisticated model. In PrOM search the opponent is modelled by a mixed strategy of N known opponent types ω_i ($i = 0$, 1, ..., $N-1$), each ω_i is represented separately by an evaluation function. The mixed strategy is typified by a probability distribution $\Pr(\omega_i)$ over the opponent types. The opponent is assumed to adopt at every move one of the opponent types ω_i according to probability $\Pr(\omega_i)$, and to act like this opponent for the current move.

In brief, PrOM search works as follows. At max nodes, the child node with the highest value is selected, like in Minimax. At min nodes, two computations take place: (1) the value of the min node for every opponent type ω_i is established independently (using any Minimax-equivalent algorithm); (2) using the probabilities $\Pr(\omega_i)$, the *expected value* of the min node is computed. At leaf nodes, the player's evaluation function is used.

M. Rauterberg (Ed.): ICEC 2004, LNCS 3166, pp. 409–419, 2004.
© IFIP International Federation for Information Processing 2004

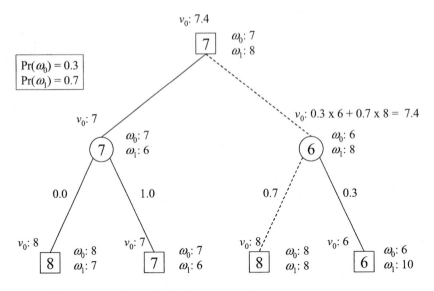

Fig. 1. PrOM Search and Minimax compared.

Figure 1 provides an example search tree in which PrOM search and Minimax are compared. The squares denote max nodes and the circles min nodes. The values inside the nodes are standard minimax values. In the example, there are two opponent types: ω_0 and ω_1 with probability 0.3 and 0.7, respectively. To the right of the nodes, the minimax values for these opponent types are given. The values for ω_0 are chosen to be equal to the minimax values. The PrOM-search values are mentioned above the nodes. At the right-hand min node, ω_0 would select the right-hand child ($v_{\omega 0} = 6$), but ω_1 would select the left-hand child ($v_{\omega 1} = 8$). The expected value of this min node is equal to 7.4, which is higher than the minimax value of this node and even higher than the minimax value of the left-hand min node (7). In passing we remark that ω_0 and ω_1 both select the right-hand node from the left-hand min node. Therefore we see that the distribution for the two branches is 0.0 and 1.0. In summary, at the root, PrOM search will select another move than Minimax does.

The mixed-strategy semantic of PrOM search as described above serves as an *approximation* of the real behaviour of the opponent. Although it is possible to approximate the opponent by a single evaluation function precisely tuned to the opponent's observed behaviour, as done by Carmel and Markovitch [4], the resulting plain OM search can lead to large risks, as pointed out in [9]. This is in particular true when the own evaluation function has a poor quality. The mixed-strategy approach of PrOM search incorporates an implicit kind of risk avoidance [6].

The individual opponent types (e.g., the evaluation functions) to be used by PrOM search can be achieved in two ways, either by *construction* or by *learning*. Construction can be based on a model of opponent behaviour or on a set of mistakes often made. Learning can be done by using previously recorded games [1, 10]. We hypothesize that it is a good idea to have the own (i.e., the MAX-player's) evaluation function as one of the opponent types, since this could prevent some of the fundamental problems that occur in OM search [9]. By convention we will denote this opponent type by ω_0. The larger the probability $Pr(\omega_0)$, the less PrOM search will yield results different from Minimax. When $Pr(\omega_0) = 1$, PrOM search is equivalent to Minimax.

In this paper we investigate two questions (1) to which extend is PrOM search better than OM search and Minimax search in the game of Bao? and (2) which opponent type is most advantageous to use? To answer these questions, we performed an extended experiment with PrOM search in the game of Bao. The experiment consists of a number of tournaments in which one player uses PrOM search and the opponent α-β search. The player using PrOM search applies in each tournament a different probabilistic opponent model. The goal of the experiment is to discover which opponent model gives the largest probability to win, under the circumstances given.

In section 2 we briefly introduce the game of Bao. Then in section 3 we explain the generation of five different opponent models for Bao. Section 4 shows how opponent-type probabilities have been obtained for six pairs of opponent types. The probabilistic opponent models are used in the experiment described in section 5. Section 6 ends the paper with two conclusions.

2   Bao

In large parts of the world, board games of the mancala group are being played in completely different versions (cf. [15, 16]). Whatever the case, most mancala games share the following five properties:
(1) the board has a number of *holes*, usually ordered in rows;
(2) the game is played with indistinguishable *counters* (e.g., pebbles, seeds, shells);
(3) players own a fixed set of holes on the board;
(4) a move consists of taking counters from one hole and putting them one-by-one in subsequent holes (*sowing*), possibly followed by some form of capture;
(5) the goal is to capture the most counters (for Bao it is to immobilize the opponent).

Mancala games differ in the number of players (1, 2 or more), the size and form of the board, the starting configuration of the counters, the rules for sowing and capturing, and in the way the game ends. The games of the mancala group are known by many names (for instance Kalah, Awari, Wari, Awele, Bao, Dakon, and Pallankuli). For an overview of different versions and the rules of many mancala games, we refer to [16].

Among the mancala games, (Zanzibar) Bao is regarded as the most complex one [17]. This is mainly due to the amount of rules and to the complexity of the rules. Bao is played in Tanzania and on Zanzibar in an organized way. There exist Bao clubs that own boards and that organize official tournaments.

The exact rules of the game are given in [8, 17]. Below, we summarize the properties that discriminate the game from the more widely known games Kalah and Awari.

North

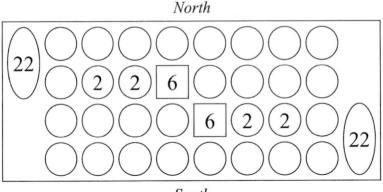

South

Fig. 2. Opening position of Bao.

Bao is played on a board with 4 rows of 8 holes by two players, called South and North, see Figure 2. Two square holes are called *houses* and play a special part in the game. There are 64 stones involved. At the start of the game each player has 10 stones on the board and 22 stones in store. Sowing only takes place in the own two rows of holes. The direction of sowing is not fixed. At the start of a move, a player can select a direction for the sowing (clockwise or anti-clockwise). During sowing or at a capture, the direction can turn at some point. This is regulated by deterministic rules.

In Bao, one is obliged to capture, if possible. It means that a position is either a capture position or a non-capture position. Captured counters do not leave the board but re-enter the game. Counters are captured from the opponent's front row. The captured counters are immediately sown in the own front row. It implies that the game does not converge like Kalah and Awari.

Moves are composite. For instance, at the end of a sowing, again a capture might be possible. Then the captured counters are again sown immediately at the own side of the board. In its turn, the second sowing can lead to a new capture, followed by a new sowing, etc. If a capture is not possible, and the hole reached was non-empty, all counters are taken out of that hole and sowing continues. This procedure stops when an empty hole is reached, which ends the move.

Moves can be endless because in a non-capture move, sowing may continue forever. The existence of endless moves can be proven theoretically [7]. In real games, moves that take more than an hour of sowing also occasionally occur, but players usually make small mistakes during sowing or simply quit the game. So, real endless moves never lead to endless sowing.

Bao games consist of two stages. In the first stage, stones are entered one by one on the board at the start of every move. In that stage, a game ends if the player to move has no counters left in the front row. As soon as all stones are entered, the second stage begins and a new set of rules applies. In this stage, a game ends if the player has no more than one counter in any hole of both rows. A draw is not defined in Bao. Note that the goal of Bao is not to capture the most stones, but to immobilize the opponent.

In [5], an analysis of the game properties of Bao is provided. The state-space complexity of Bao is approximated to be 1.0×10^{25}, which is much higher than those of Awari (2.8×10^{11}) and Kalah (1.3×10^{13}). The shortest game possible takes 5 ply, but most games take between 50 and 60 ply, which means that they reach the second stage. The maximum number of moves possible at any position is 32, but the average number of possible moves varies between 3 and 5, depending on the stage of the game. Forced moves occur quite often. The average game length (d) and branching factor (w) are normally used to estimate the size of a game tree that has to be traversed during search (w^d). For Bao the estimate is roughly 10^{34}. This number together with the game-tree complexity (10^{25}) places Bao in the overview of game complexities above checkers and in the neighbourhood of Qubic [11].

3 Opponent Types for Bao

In order to conduct the PrOM-search experiments, we created 5 different evaluation functions. We describe them below. (For operational reasons (see Section 5) we would like to have them ordered in increasing quality with respect to the strength of the resulting players.) Each of these five evaluation functions constitutes an opponent type. We will use two concepts of producing them: hand-made and machine-made.

The first two evaluation functions were created by hand. The first one, called MATERIAL, simply takes the difference in the number of stones on both sides of the board as the evaluation score.

The second hand-made evaluation function is called DEFAULT. This function incorporates some rudimental strategic knowledge of Bao. For instance, it is good to have more stones in your back row since this increases the mobility in the second stage of the game. The function awards 3 points to stones in the front row, 5 points to stones in the back row, and 5 additional points to opponent stones that can be captured. If the own house is still active, 200 extra points are given. The total score of the position is the score for MAX minus the score for MIN. There is a small asymmetry in this function: if MAX can capture MIN's house 100 points are rewarded, but if MIN can capture MAX's house, only 50 points are subtracted. This asymmetry is intended to produce a more offensive playing style.

The third evaluation function was created by using a genetic algorithm [12]. The evaluation function was represented by an integer-valued chromosome of 27 genes: one gene for the material balance, one gene per hole for the material in the own back and front row, one gene per hole in the front row for capturing, one gene for an active house, and another gene for capturing the opponent's house. The total score of a position was the score for the player minus the score for the opponent. The fitness of a chromosome was measured by the number of games out of 100 that it won against a fixed opponent. In these matches, both players used α-β search with a search depth of 6 ply. The genetic-algorithm parameters were as follows: the population size was 100, only the 10 fittest chromosomes produced offspring (using a single-point crossover), the mutation rate was 5 per cent for large changes in a gene (i.e., generate a new random number for the gene) and 20 per cent for minor changes (i.e., altering the value of a gene slightly). The genetic algorithm was continued until no improvement occurred anymore. We conducted three runs: in the first run, the opponent was DEFAULT. In the second and third run, the opponent was the winner of the previous run. The name of the resulting evaluation function is GA3.

To create the fourth evaluation function, we used TD-Leaf learning [2]. It is a temporal-difference method that is particularly suitable for learning evaluation functions in games. The evaluation function trained was a linear real-valued function with the same parameters as the genes in the chromosomes above, except that there were separate parameters for the two sides of the board. Batch learning was applied with 25 games per batch. The reinforcement signal used to update the parameters was the number of games in the batch that the player won against a fixed opponent, in this case GA3. The search depth used in the games was 10. The λ-factor and the annealing factor both were set to 0.99. The result was fourth evaluation function, called TDL2B.

The fifth evaluation function was also produced by TD-Leaf learning. This time we used a *normalized Gaussian network* (NGN) as evaluation function, similar to way in which Yoshioka, Ishii, and Ito [18] trained an evaluation function for the Othello game. The NGN had 54 nuclei in a 54-dimensional space. Every dimension correlated with a parameter in the previous evaluation function. The reinforcement signal was the number of won games out of 25 against a fixed opponent, being TDL2B. The search depth used in the games was 6, because the computation of the output for an NGN is relatively slow. No batch learning was applied here. The λ-factor was set to 0.8 and the annealing factor was set to 0.993. This evaluation function is called NGND6A.

Table 1 gives the outcome of a tournament between the five evaluation functions. Both South and North used α-β search with search depth 6. Per match 100 games were played, starting from a randomized opening position (these positions are provided in [8]). The table clearly shows that the evaluation functions differ in quality and that every evaluation function is indeed operationally better than any of the evaluation functions above them in the table.

Table 1. Results of the tournament between Five evaluation functions for Bao. Each cell shows the number of games won by South (the row) against North (the column). The three columns on the right show the number of games won by each evaluation function when playing South, when playing North, and in total.

S \ N	MATERIAL	DEFAULT	GA3	TDL2B	NGND6A	South	Score North	Total
MATERIAL	-	55	35	19	18	127	149	276
DEFAULT	48	-	54	30	28	160	146	306
GA3	55	61	-	36	30	182	179	361
TDL2B	69	65	57	-	39	230	255	485
NGND6A	79	73	75	60	-	287	285	572

4   Learning Opponent-Type Probabilities

In contrast to the assumption of PrOM search, an opponent is not likely to use a mixed strategy of opponent types $\{\omega_0 \ldots \omega_{N-1}\}$. Probably, the true opponent's evaluation function is not even in the set $\{\omega_0 \ldots \omega_{N-1}\}$. In the experiment of Section

5, we try to find for pairs (ω_0, ω_1) of opponent types from the set {MATERIAL, DEFAULT, GA3, TDL2B, and NGND6A} the probability distribution such that PrOM search plays best against a fixed opponent Ω. The opponent Ω uses α-β search with NGND6A, which is the strongest of the five evaluation functions according to Table 1. We call this distribution the best probability distribution.

The definition of PrOM search strongly suggests that the *best* probability distribution is identical to the probability distribution that best *predicts* the behaviour of NGND6A. The suggestion is straightforward, but only real game-playing can prove its correctness.

To learn the best predicting distributions, it is not necessary to perform actually and repeatedly an extended PrOM search. The procedure applied for learning was as follows. At every time step we randomly generated a legal Bao position. Then we used α-β search with a search depth of 4 ply to determine the move that Ω (NGND6A) would select and used α-β search with again a depth of 4 ply for both opponent types involved in the pair of potential opponents to determine the moves selected by those types. When either none or both opponent types selected the same move as Ω, the position was disposed. The process continued until 100,000 non-disposed positions were encountered. The estimated opponent-type probabilities were then computed using the formula of a maximum-likelihood estimator [8]:

$$\hat{\Pr}(\omega_i) = \frac{\#(m_i = m_\Omega)}{\sum_j (m_j = m_\Omega)} \qquad (1)$$

The sample size of 100,000 was chosen in order to ensure an estimation error of at most 0.3% at a confidence level of 95%. The random Bao positions were obtained by first taking a uniformly random number k from the range 3...30, and then generating and executing $2k$ random but legal moves, beginning at the official start position of Bao (see Figure 2). If an end position was reached before $2k$ moves were executed, the position was discarded and the random generation of moves was restarted.

Table 2 shows the learned opponent-type probabilities for six pairs of opponent types. (We did not investigate pairs with NGND6A since the probability for this type would always be 1.) A clear observation from this table is that the probability of an opponent type is higher when that type had a higher score in Table 1. The last two columns of Table 2 show the number of positions generated and the percentage of positions used. The estimation error is everywhere smaller than 0.3% with a confidence level of 95%.

Table 2. The probabilistic opponent models of the opponent NGND6A for all six possible pairs of the other opponent types.

Pair	Opponent Type				Positions	Used
	MATERIAL	DEFAULT	GA3	TDL2B		
1	49.28%	50.72%	-	-	351,124	28.48%
2	42.49%	-	57.51%	-	483,092	20.70%
3	33.04%	-	-	66.96%	410,509	24.36%
4	-	45/80%	54.20%	-	343,171	29.14%
5	-	36.93%	-	63.07%	338,066	29.58%
6	-	-	40.06%	59.94%	415,282	24.08%

5   Experimental Setup and Results

In the experiment, a tournament was held between PrOM search with opponent models constructed from pairs (ω_0, ω_1) of the five evaluation functions mentioned previously (MATERIAL, DEFAULT, GA3, TDL2B, and NGND6A) against a fixed opponent using α-β search with NGND6A. Since NGND6A was used by the true opponent in all games, it was not meaningful to use it as an evaluation function for MAX in PrOM search. It is obvious that if we would use NGND6A for MAX and thus also for ω_0, we would never be able to obtain better results than with Minimax search.

As a consequence, we did not use NGND6A for ω_0. For ω_1 we used all five evaluation functions. However, ω_0 and ω_1 were never the same. Hence we arrived at 4 × 4 = 16 different pairs of evaluation functions to be investigated.

With every pair (ω_0, ω_1) we played 2,000 games for each of the following eleven values of Pr(ω_0): 0, 0.1, 0.2, ..., 1.0. Every instance of such a pair and a probability value constitutes a separate probabilistic opponent model. So, we played 2,000 games for each of the 16 × 11 = 176 probabilistic opponent models, resulting in 352,000 games played.

PrOM search with one of these models was used by South, α-β search with NGND6A was used by North. The search depth was 6 ply for both players. The start positions were randomly generated in the same way as in the previous section, but the range for the start move was restricted to the range of 3 to 8 moves. Figure 3 shows the results of this experiment. Every square contains the results for a different pair of opponent types. The names of the two types in each opponent model are given in the squares. The first type represents ω_0, the second type is ω_1. The squares are arranged in such way that on every row, ω_0 is constant. On every column ω_1 is constant, except for the squares on the diagonal (which contain the results for the pairs that have the true opponent, NGND6A, as ω_1). On the vertical axis of each square is the win probability. On the horizontal axis of each square is the probability Pr(ω_0).

At probability Pr(ω_0) = 0 (at the left side of each square) PrOM search is equivalent to OM search; at probability Pr(ω_0) = 1 (at the right side of each square) PrOM search is equivalent to Minimax search (α-β search). The arrows indicate the opponent-type probabilities learned in Section 4. There are no arrows placed in the squares on the diagonal since ω_1 is the true opponent in those opponent models and therefore the opponent-type probabilities to be learned would be 0 for ω_0. The dotted lines above and below the straight lines indicate the 95% confidence interval for the win probabilities.

The win probability at Pr(ω_0) = 1 (the point where PrOM search is equivalent to Minimax search) should be the same in every square of each row since ω_0 is the same at each row. The figure shows small statistical fluctuations, but these are caused by the randomly chosen opening positions.

The win probability at Pr(ω_0) = 1 is the highest at the bottom row (where ω_0 is TDL2B). In all squares the win probability is the lowest at Pr(ω_0) = 0, which is the probability where PrOM search is equivalent to OM search. It means that for all cases that Pr(ω_0) was larger than zero, PrOM search performed better than OM search.

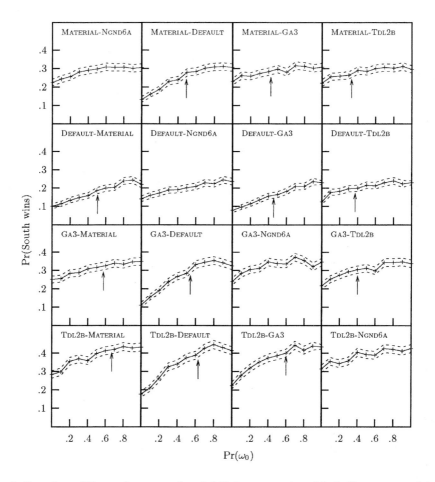

Fig. 3. Overview of the performance of probabilistic opponent models in Bao, expressed in South' win probability as a function of $Pr(\omega_0)$. The opponent models ω_0 - ω_1 are indicated inside the boxes. The arrows indicate the probabilities learned in Section 4. The dotted lines indicate the 95% confidence interval for the win probabilities.

There are four squares in which there is a probability $Pr(\omega_0)$ smaller than 1 at which the win probability was higher than the win probability at $Pr(\omega_0) = 1$ (where PrOM search is equivalent to Minimax search) with statistical significance. These are: DEFAULT-MATERIAL at $Pr(\omega_0) = 0.9$, GA3-DEFAULT at $Pr(\omega_0) = 0.8$, GA3-NGND6A at $Pr(\omega_0) = 0.7$, and TDL2B-DEFAULT at $Pr(\omega_0) = 0.8$. It means that in these cases, PrOM search performed better than Minimax search. Although only in these four cases an optimum above the value for Minimax is statistically significant, in all other cases, except one (GA3-MATERIAL), an optimum above the Minimax value is at least suggested by the graphs. However, we admit that the effect of PrOM search at these optima is small.

Two further observations on the results are: (1) all optima lie at probabilities considerably higher than the probabilities learned in Section 4 (indicated by the arrows) (2) some of the graphs in Figure 3 show a peculiarity (see below) that seems too regular to be explained by noise.

Observation (1) suggests that the learned opponent-type probabilities are not the probabilities with which PrOM search performs best: it seems that more probability should be assigned to the own evaluation function (ω_0).

Observation (2) suggests that there is a wave-like pattern in the graph of TDL2B-NGND6A. The waves have a length of 0.3. Moreover, a few waves of the same length are visible in the graph of Ga3-Ngnd6a and in the graph of Tdl2b-Material. Further research is needed to explain these waves.

6 Conclusions

From the experiments we conclude that in all cases PrOM search performed better than OM search. Moreover we may conclude that in some cases PrOM search performs better in Bao than Minimax search even when no perfect knowledge of the opponent is available. However, the gain arrived at by using PrOM search is not very large. Furthermore, we should note that the search depth was kept constant (six plies) for both sides. This means a considerable advantage for PrOM search since this search method evaluates many more leaf nodes than α-β search and therefore uses much more time for the same search depth. If we would allow both sides the same limited amount of time, matters may change.

The opponent-type probabilities learned off-line appeared not to be the best probabilities to use in PrOM search: the probability $\Pr(\omega_0)$ should have been larger than the current learned value. Here we may conclude that the opponent model should put more weight on the player's own evaluation function than was assumed to be needed so far. A possible explanation is that the additional weight balances the risks caused by estimation errors in the own evaluation function [8,9].

References

1. Anantharaman, T. (1997). Evaluation tuning for computer chess: Linear discriminant methods. *ICCA Journal*, Vol. 20, No. 4, pp. 224–242.
2. Baxter, J., Trigdell, A., and Weaver, L. (1998). KnightCap: a chess program that learns by combining TD(,) with game-tree search. *Proc. 15th International Conf. on Machine Learning*, pp. 28–36, Morgan Kaufmann, San Francisco, CA.
3. Carmel, D. and Markovitch, S. (1996). Learning and using opponent models in adversary search. Technical Report CIS9609, Technion, Haifa, Israel.
4. Carmel, D. and Markovitch, S. (1998). Pruning algorithms for multi-model adversary search. *Artificial Intelligence*, Vol. 99, No. 2, pp. 325–355.
5. Donkers, H.H.L.M. and Uiterwijk, J.W.H.M. (2002). Programming Bao. Seventh Computer Olympiad: Computer-Games Workshop Proceedings (ed. J.W.H.M. Uiterwijk), Technical Reports in Computer Science, CS 02-03, IKAT, Department of Computer Science, Universiteit Maastricht, Maastricht, The Netherlands.
6. Donkers, H.H.L.M., Uiterwijk, J.W.H.M., and Herik, H.J. van den (2001). Probabilistic opponent-model search. *Information Sciences*, Vol. 135, No. 3–4, pp.123–149.

7. Donkers, H.H.L.M., Uiterwijk, J.W.H.M., and Voogt, A.J. de (2002). Mancala games – topics in artificial intelligence and mathematics. *Step by Step. Proceedings of the 4th Colloquium 'Board Games in Academia'* (eds. J. Retschitzki and R. Haddad-Zubel), Editions Universitaires, Fribourg, Switserland.

8. Donkers, H.H.L.M. (2003). *Nosce Hostem: Searching with Opponent Models.* Ph.D. thesis, Universiteit Maastricht, Maastricht, The Netherlands.

9. Donkers, H.H.L.M., Uiterwijk, J.W.H.M., and Herik, H.J. van den (2003). Admissibility in opponent-model search. *Information Sciences*, Vol. 154, No. 3–4, pp. 119–140.

10. Fürnkranz, J. (1996). Machine learning in computer chess: The next generation. *ICCA Journal*, Vol. 19, No. 3, pp. 147–161.

11. Herik, H.J. van den, Uiterwijk, J.W.H.M., and Rijswijck, J. van (2002). Games solved, now and in the future. *Artificial Intelligence*, Vol. 134, No. 1–2, pp. 277–311.

12. Holland, J.H. (1975). *Adaption in Natural and Artificial Systems.* University of Michigan Press, Ann Arbor, MI.

13. Iida, H., Uiterwijk, J.W.H.M., Herik, H.J. van den, and Herschberg, I.S. (1993). Potential applications of opponent-model search. Part 1: the domain of applicability. *ICCA Journal*, Vol. 16, No. 4, pp. 201–208.

14. Iida, H., Kotani, I., Uiterwijk, J.W.H.M., and Herik, H.J. van den (1997). Gains and risks of OM search. *Advances in Computer Chess 8* (eds. H.J. van den Herik and J.W.H.M. Uiterwijk), pp. 153–165, Universiteit Maastricht, Maastricht, The Netherlands.

15. Murray, H.J.R. (1952). *A History of Board Games other than Chess.* Oxford University Press, Oxford, UK.

16. Russ, L. (2000). *The Complete Mancala Games Book.* Marlow & Company, New York.

17. Voogt, A.J. de (1995). *Limits of the Mind. Towards a Characterisation of Bao Mastership.* Ph.D. thesis, University of Leiden, The Netherlands.

18. Yoshioka, T., Ishii, S., and Ito, M. (1999). Strategy acquisition for the game othello based on reinforcement learning. *IEICE Transactions on Information and Systems*, Vol. E82-D, No. 12, pp. 1618–1626.

Agent Wars with Artificial Immune Systems

Gayle Leen and Colin Fyfe

Applied Computational Intelligence Research Unit,
The University of Paisley, Paisley, Scotland.
{gayle.leen,colin.fyfe}@paisley.ac.uk

Abstract. In this paper we discuss the use of concepts from Artificial Immune Systems (AIS) in computer games. The computer player in such games is typically called the AI but the AI is rarely truly intelligent which detracts from human enjoyment of such games. We illustrate making the AI truly intelligent in the context of simplified games by having two AIs play against each other when they are adapted using methods suggested by AIS.

1 Introduction

We have previously [5] shown how strategies may be dynamically created and utilised by an artificial intelligence (AI) in a Real Time Strategy (RTS) game; we used concepts from Artificial Immune Systems (AIS) to do so. In this paper we extend this research by having pairs of agents, each of whom adapts using AIS concepts, learn to play games. We develop as simple as possible RTS games in order to display the power of the method we use. Commonly in Real Time Strategy games, units are powerful against one type of unit and weak against another. In a typical game world, Scissors dominates Paper which dominates Stone which dominates Scissors. For example, in 'Rise of Nations' from Microsoft, cavalry are powerful against light infantry who are good against bowmen who are powerful against heavy infantry who in turn can overcome cavalry. Therefore knowing what strategy your opponent is going to use gives a player a very great advantage.

In these games, the computer player's strategy is often extremely predictable: typically, it will select what seems initially to be an optimal balance of each type of fighter but if that is known, it can be defended against. Thus the game reduces to the human player(s) simply identifying how the Artificial Intelligence (AI) will play and devising a strategy which will overcome the AI's strategy. The AI generally has no flexibility in its responses to the human strategies and so the game quickly becomes boring. At core is the fact that, for the AI, the strategies of the human player form an important part of an evolving environment: in giving it an *a priori* optimal strategy, the games developers may be giving it the best single static strategy but this will always be beaten by strategies which are learned during the course of the game and dynamically changed in response to the changing strategies met during the course of the game. We propose a system which allows the AI to respond dynamically to the strategies used by its human opponent; in effect, we wish to give the AI enough

M. Rauterberg (Ed.): ICEC 2004, LNCS 3166, pp. 420–428, 2004.

adaptability so that it may respond as a second human player would to the strategies of its human opponent.

In this paper, we create two AIs who learn to play against each other. This is of interest since multi-player games are becoming increasingly popular but, of course, are dependent on there being multiple human players on line at the same time. Thus our aim is to create games which have multiple truly-intelligent AIs and so we can have one human player playing a multi-player game off-line. Thus we propose to use Artificial Immune System [4] methods: the immune system response attributes of specificity, diversity, memory and self/non-self recognition are just what is needed in this situation. The next section discusses the immune system before we go on to describe the artificial immune system and how it may be used to optimise the AI's responses to human opponents. Finally we consider how the use of the immune system paradigm may allow us to develop more sophisticated games which are more like real life engagements.

2   The Immune System

We discuss only those aspects of Artificial Immune Systems which are relevant to this paper. For a fuller discussion, see e.g. [2,3,4]. The immune system is a complex system that enables a mechanism by which certain dangers to the organism can be identified. These dangers can be roughly classified as those which arise from dysfunction within the organism's own cells and those which are due to the action of exogenous pathogens. We will concentrate on the latter since we will consider the case in which the actions of one AI player are treated by the other AI as pathogens to which it must respond by creating actions which optimally confront those of the first player.

The root of the system we will be emulating is a set of cells known as the B-lymphocytes which are created in the bone marrow. They are responsible for producing specific antibodies in response to the identification of specific antigens: each antibody will respond optimally to a specific antigen rather like a key which fits into a keyhole. The key part of the antigen is known as the epitope and the keyhole part of the antibody is known as the paratope. The immune system itself is partly innate – we are born with an active immune system – and partly adaptive – the body learns to respond appropriately to the attacks which the organism meets in life. There are limited resources available for the production of antibodies so that in responding to a particular antigen by creating specific antibodies, the system inevitably has less resources available to respond to other antigens.

The adaptive immune system is believed to be continually creating antibodies in a somewhat random fashion: it is rather as though it is exploring the space of antigens always on the lookout for new dangers to the organism. This could be used in creating probing attacks on opponent's positions and in readying the AI for optimal response to new threats; we anticipate that a more intelligent response from the AI will lead to an arms race - its opponent will have to be continually changing his strategies in order to overcome the AI which in turn will be responding by developing new strategies.

One further feature of the immune system which is of interest in the current context is its memory: the adaptive immune system remembers which attacks the organism had to withstand and retains a response mechanism which is optimal for attacks of the same or a similar type in future. We will use this feature so that the AI learns typical tactics from the player(s) it meets most often so that it learns how to respond optimally to its opponents. It is worth noting at this stage that the adaptive response is often known as hypermutation which is a reference to the fact that the rate of mutation is very much greater than seen in evolutionary models. The antibody which is the most appropriate response to the current attack is cloned in greatest numbers but the cloning is accompanied by a rate of mutation which enables a very fast search of the antibody space. This very quick refining is the essence of the adaptive immune system. A final feature of the immune system in which we will be interested is based on Jerne's immune network theory[7]. This proposes that the various parts of the immune system itself recognise other parts of the same system and indeed affect the production or suppression of other parts of the system. A positive reaction between components can lead to cell proliferation and activation while a negative response can lead to cell tolerance and suppression

3   Artificial Immune System

Perhaps the definitive difference between traditional Artificial Intelligence and the studies which comprise contemporary Artificial Intelligence (which we take to encompass Evolutionary Algorithms, Artificial Neural Networks, Artificial Life and Artificial Immune Systems) is the emphasis on the program writer not solving the problem but merely creating conditions whereby a program, if exposed to sufficient training examples, will learn to extract sufficient information from a problem in order to solve it itself. The artificial immune system does just that.

4   Agent Wars

We stated above that Jerne had developed a theory that there were interactions between the various parts of an immune system: the production of one antibody can suppress or activate the production of a second type of antibody. To illustrate this feature we require to devise a game in which a resource of type A can dominate both a type B resource and a type C resource but which will be dominated by a joint attack from a (B+C) combination. Therefore we have A>B, A>C, B>C but (B+C)>A. We require to introduce a cost constraint rather than a constraint on number of pieces and so we have costs $C_A=4$, $C_B=3$ and $C_C=2$ so that it costs more to create a B+C combination than it does an A. Now we set up a game between two AI armies consisting of a number of As, Bs and Cs (the number must meet a certain cost constraint). When a unit from either group meets a weaker one it will prevail except when the unit is a type A in which case the weaker opponent (a B or C) will have the option of enlisting the support of a colleague (of type C or B respectively) *if such a colleague exists*. Thus we must use meetings of armies rather than individuals since we must model the situation in which there are finite resources. For the winning AI, we randomly delete one of the other units in the AI's resources and replace it with a new unit of the type which has just won. This is the AIS response: we have defeated this antigen but there may be more of the same around and so we therefore create similar antibodies. For the losing AI, we delete its resource and randomly select a new resource to replace it. If, during the game, a (B+C) combination wins, new copies of both B and C are put into the population.

Let one AI have 10 strategies initialised randomly while the other is initialised with noisy versions of a particular strategy {0.4,0.4, 0.2}. In order to create some inequality between the two AIs, we give one 5 times the exploratory capacity of the other i.e. when we clone the winner, we make the magnitude of the mutations 5 times greater for one AI than the other. Results are shown in Figure 1. We see that the two AIs perform a dance in which the actions of one is completely mirrored in the actions of the other. The left diagram is from the AI with the high mutation rate; the right diagram is from the AI with the low mutation rate.

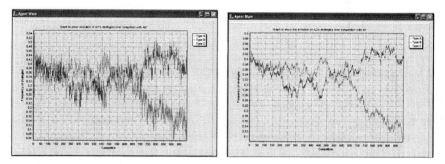

Fig. 1. Left: the strategies of the AI with the high mutation rate. Right: the strategies of the AI with the low mutation rate

This type of dance can be shown to continue for 100000s of iterations. However, if we explicitly ensure that, when one or other side has won no competition in the 10 contests, it takes random values as its new starting point, we get sudden transitions in one AI's strategies are followed by very fast transitions in the other AI's strategies. This is very close to human behaviour: if you are being beaten 10-0 in a game, you are clearly not in the sort of position in which fine tuning your strategies is going to be effective; only a major change in strategy-set is going to be effective.

When one AI has won 10 times out of 10, its opponent who won 0 of the last round is completely randomised. Rather counter-intuitively, if we decrease the rate of mutation, we increase the number of times this randomisation kicks in. This is due to the fact that a low mutation rate leads to more exploitation and less exploration and so the AI which finds a good niche first, is able to wipe out its opponent very quickly. The punctuated equilibrium of such simulations is clearly shown in Figure 2 in which we give one AI a much higher mutation rate than the other.

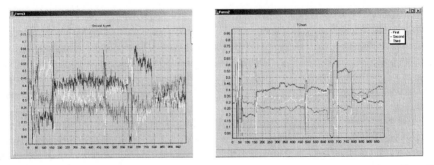

Fig. 2. A type of punctuated equilibrium is found when we use randomisation. For this simulation we used two different mutation rates.

5   Cooperating Strategies

Now we wish to investigate whether our AIs can learn to cooperate with each other. To do this, we create a typical game situation: we have three AIs each with slightly different interests. We create a payoff function discussed in [428], page 15. Let us have three AIs labeled 1, 2 and 3 and let the possible strategies be labeled A, B and C. The game consists of each of the AIs choosing a strategy and the strategy with the highest number of votes wins. If no strategy has a higher number of votes than any other, A wins by default. The payoff functions are

$$\mu_1(A)= \mu_2(B)= \mu_3(C)=2 \quad \mu_1(B)= \mu_2(C)= \mu_3(A)=1 \quad \mu_1(C)= \mu_2(A)= \mu_3(B)=0$$

where we are using $\mu_i(X)$ as the payoff for AI$_i$ on strategy X. At each stage, we give the AIs no global information: when it comes to updating the strategies, we select from each population of strategies separately a strategy which gives that particular AI the best payoff at that stage in the simulation. If there is more than one strategy, a strategy is selected randomly from the optimal ones.

The results of one typical simulation are shown in Figure 3. The figure shows one of the strategies during each round which was optimal for each agent.- AI$_1$ in red, AI$_2$ in green and AI$_3$ in yellow. Level 0 indicates strategy A, level 1 indicates strategy B, level 2 indicates strategy C. The AIs initially all compete, and then there is a short spell from round 200 to round 450 when each AI prefers its own optimal strategy to get a payoff of 2 each time. During this time, the diversity is being driven from the population till there comes a time when AI$_2$ can no longer find another B in the population to gain a payoff of 2. At this time its only chance of escaping the payoff of 0 is to switch to cooperate with AI$_3$ (i.e. vote for strategy C) to get a payoff of 1. This it does for the remainder of the simulation. At the end the population is totally converged to AI$_2$ and AI$_3$ voting for C while AI$_1$ continues to vote for A (there is no incentive for it to change).

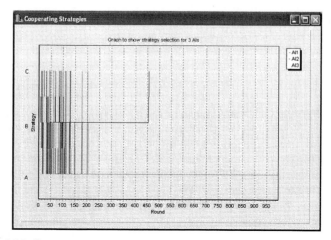

Fig. 3. Level 0 indicates strategy A, level 1 indicates strategy B, level 2 indicates strategy C.

Thus we have in effect a consortium involving AI_2 and AI_3 playing together against AI_1. AI_3 might be thought of as the stronger partner in this consortium since it is gaining greatest payoff each time but there is no incentive for AI_2 to change. If AI_1 were really intelligent, it would change to strategy B since then AI_2 would change its strategy to B to get a payoff of 2 and both AI_1 and AI_2 would gain. This might be done with randomisation.

6   Incomplete Information

Perhaps one of the most interesting aspects of modern computer games is the "fog of war" in which players are playing a game with incomplete information. We now investigate responses to incomplete information. We create a Russian roulette game in which the AI players' strategies are created by an Artificial Immune System. The AI takes turns with its opponent to pull the trigger of the gun (6 chambers, only one bullet) when the gun is pressed to the player's temple. Each player may opt out of the game but in doing so loses face which is however preferable to losing life if the player pulls the trigger and the bullet happens to be in that chamber. Thus we have three possible outcomes for the AI which in order of preference are:

- The AI wins either because its opponent has been killed or opted out; the AI does not care which of these it is since it wins in either case.
- The AI opts out of the game
- The AI is killed

Consider the AI who chooses whether to pull the trigger at rounds 1, 3 and 5. We initially set up a situation in which the AI has 10 random strategies and play the game 100 times. Each strategy will have two integer values: a 1 equivalent to pulling the trigger at this round, a 0 equal to opting out of the game at the current round. Each round of the game in which the AI pulls the trigger and is not killed, the AI gains one point. If the current strategy opts out of the game at any round, it gains 0.5. If it pulls the trigger and dies, it gains 0. The best strategy each round is cloned up to the death round. Figure 4 shows the results of 6 simulations. The first 100 columns show the total number of trigger pulls in each of the three rounds over the 10 strategies in the population when the bullet is in the first chamber. If the AI pulls the trigger the first time, it will die. Therefore the most successful strategy is to quit the game immediately. That this happens, is shown by the quick drop of the red line to zero. Since the other two strategies occur after the AI has dropped out of the race they remain at their original levels for the whole game. The second round shows the strategies of the AI when the bullet is in the second chamber (which will be used by the human). Now it pays the AI to pull the trigger on the first round and so the red line climbs to 10: the whole population of strategies opts to pull the trigger the first time. Again the second and third round strategies are unaffected since they come after the game has finished. The third hundred shows what happens during the third game when the bullet is in chamber 3. Now the AI pulls the trigger the first time but opts out of the game on the second round (the green line drops to 0 showing that the whole population have opted out of the game at that round.).

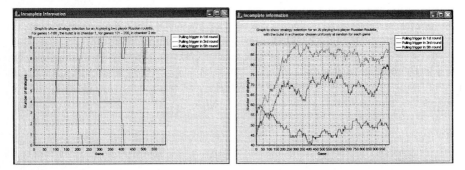

Fig. 4. Left: Each group of 100 shows the response of the AI to a game of 100 rounds when the bullet is in the first chamber (1-100), when the bullet is in the second chamber (101-200) etc. See text for discussion. **Right:** Playing more generally. The red line is the number of strategies out of 100 which pull the trigger in the first round. The green is the number of strategies who pull the trigger in the second round. The blue is the number of strategies who pull the figure in the third round.

Continuing in this way we see that for each game of 100 rounds the AI has found the optimal strategy for playing the game each time. Note that at no time are we giving the AI information as to where the bullet is. Clearly the AI is responding to the position of the bullet appropriately.

7   Dispensing with God

The game described above is somewhat unrealistic since God has decided where the bullet is and determined that the bullet is in the same position each time the game is played. Let us now alter that: for each iteration of the game, we use a different randomly chosen chamber for the bullet. The results for a simulation with 100 strategies over 1000 iterations are shown in Figure 4 (right). For the first round of each game, the probability of being killed if you pull the trigger is 1/6. Therefore the probability of not being killed is 5/6 ~0.83. We see that the red line which is the number of strategies out of 100 which pull the trigger first time is around this value. Similarly, if we get to round 3, there are 4 chambers left only one of which contains the bullet and therefore the probability of not being killed by pulling the trigger is ¾. The green line is around this value. Finally if we get to the fifth round, the probability of being killed by pulling the trigger is ½ and the blue line is around this value.

8 Duelling

The classic one-on-one shoot'em up game may be characterised as a duel between two opponents who are trying to kill each other as they move towards each other. Let us again abstract out the important features of this game. Let the opponents be initially at a distance $D=1$ from each other. Let each of two AIs have a set of binary strategy vectors each of length 10. Then if $AI_1[i]=1$, AI_1 will fire when it is at the ith position. If $AI_1[i]=0$, AI_1 will wait. Similarly with AI_2. Now we must give each a probability vector for hitting the other and this probability vector is dependent on the distance apart the two AIs are. Let $p_1(d)$ be the probability that AI_1 hits AI_2 when they are a distance d apart and $p_2(d)$ be the corresponding probability for AI_2 to hit AI_1. Let $p_1(d)=1-d$ and $p_2(d)=1-d^2$. Then, since $d <1$, AI_2 is a better shot than AI_1.

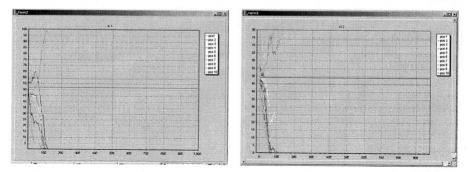

Fig. 5. Left: AI_1's strategy. 5 waits (0s) followed by one shot(1s). Some times corresponding to those distances smaller than the distance the shot is fired are unchanged; one is changed by chance. Right: the corresponding strategy for AI_2.

In our Artificial Immune System simulation, we give each AI 100 strategies and run the simulation for 1000 iterations. Each time we randomly select a pair of strategies, one from AI_1 and one from AI_2, to duel with each other. We clone the winning AI strategy up to the point that the shot is fired. Results are shown in Figure 5. From the left figure, we see that the preferred AI_1 strategy is to wait for 5 time intervals and shoot on the sixth. AI_2's strategy is slightly more complex. About 75% of the games, he also waits 5 times and shoots on the sixth. But on the other 25% of the games he waits 6 time intervals and shoots on the seventh. These figures accord well with the theoretical value derived in [1],page 132.

9 Conclusion

We have in this paper shown, in the context of a very simplified abstract Real Time Strategy game, how the concepts from the realm of Artificial Immune Systems can be used to give the AI more intelligence in dealing with an opponent who is creating novel strategies in the game in real time. In all simulations discussed in this paper, we have initiated the AI's strategy randomly yet shown that the AI's response to its opponent's strategy is approximately optimal and very fast. The fact that in each simulation we see that the AI response gets to approximately the correct level but oscillates around this level is, perhaps, no bad thing; after all, when two humans play, their play will not be exactly the same each and every day. Some randomness in the AI's response is liable to make its strategies appear more human-like. We consider that the method of this paper is not the only one from modern AI which games developers might profitably employ. Methods from evolutionary algorithms, artificial neural networks, ant colony optimisations and artificial life in general all share the capacity for adaptiveness. This perhaps is the distinguishing characteristic which differentiates modern Artificial Intelligence from its predecessors and it is this which game players require to make their games continually interesting. In this paper, we have had two AIs learning to play from each other. The next stage is to augment the games of [5] in which a human was playing with an AI with those of the current paper. We then have the possibility of having two or more AIs competing in what will appear as a multi-player game with the usual format of shifting alliances and non-stationarity.

References

1. Binmore, K. Fun and Games, DC Heath and Co, 1992.
2. De Castro, L. N. and von Zuben, F. J. , 1999 Artificial Immune Systems: Part 1 – Basic Theory and Applications, Technical report TR DCA 01/99, from ftp://ftp.dca.fee.unicamp.br/pub/docs/vonzuben/Inunes.
3. De Castro, L. N. and von Zuben, F. J. , 2000. Artificial Immune Systems: Part 2 – A Survey of Applications, Technical report TR DCA 02/00, from above site
4. Dasgupta, D. 2000, Artificial Immune Systems and their Applications, Springer-Verlag.
5. Fyfe, C. Dynamic Strategy Creation and Selection using Artificial Immune Systems, International Journal of Intelligent Games & Simulation, 3(1) 2004..
6. Fudenberg, D. and Tirole, J. Game Theory, MIT Press, 1991.
7. Jerne, N. K., 1974 Towards a network theory of the immune system. Annals of Immunology, 125C, 373-389.

MMOG Player Classification Using Hidden Markov Models

Yoshitaka Matsumoto and Ruck Thawonmas[1]

Intelligent Computer Entertainment Lab., Department of Human and Computer Intelligence,
Ritsumeikan University, Kusatsu, Shiga 525-8577, Japan
{matsumoto, ruck}@ice.ci.ritsumei.ac.jp
http://www.ice.ci.ritsumei.ac.jp/

Abstract. In this paper, we describe our work on classification of players in Massively Multiplayer Online Games using Hidden Markov Models based on player action sequences. In our previous work, we have discussed a classification approach using a variant of Memory Based Reasoning based on player action frequencies. That approach, however, does not exploit time structures hidden in action sequences of the players. The experimental results given in this paper show that Hidden Markov Models have higher recognition performance than our previous approach, especially for classification of players of different types but having similar action frequencies.

1 Introduction

The market size of Massively Multiplayer Online Games (MMOGs) continues to grow at a high speed. At the same time, competitions among MMOGs are also becoming very high. To keep players in the games, it is very important that the players' demands are grasped and the players are provided appropriate contents tailored for each player or each specific group of players. This kind of customer relationship management (CRM) [1] for MMOGs is inevitable.

In virtual worlds such as MMOGs, players are typically identified by their characteristics as "killer", "achiever", "explorer", and "socialiser" [2]. Killers just want to kill other players and monsters. Achievers entertain themselves by attempting all possible actions to grow their avatar characters up. Explorers roam around the game world to discover unknown things. Socialisers want to build and maintain social relations with other players. Following this categorization, a typical implementation of CRM for MMOGs can be depicted in Fig. 1. In this figure, players are categorized into pre-defined types based on appropriate selected features from the game logs, and are provided contents according to their favorites. Thereby, the players should enjoy the games more and hence play longer.

---

[1] The author has been supported in part by the Ritsumeikan University's *Kyoto Art and Entertainment Innovation Research*, a project of the 21st Century Center of Excellence Program funded by the Japan Society for Promotion of Science.

M. Rauterberg (Ed.): ICEC 2004, LNCS 3166, pp. 429–434, 2004.

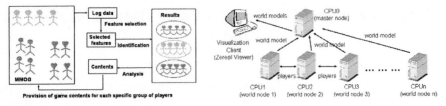

Fig. 1. Typical implementation of CRM for MMOGs

Fig. 2. Architecture of the MMOG simulator

We have reported in [3] a classification approach using Adaptive Memory Based Reasoning (AMBR), a variant of Memory Based Reasoning (MBR), based on the frequencies of player actions. That approach, however, does not exploit time structures hidden in action sequences of the players. Thus it is not suitable for classification of players of different types but having similar action frequencies.

In this paper, we propose an approach using Hidden Markov Models (HMMs) that mines time structures hidden in the action sequences. HMMs have been widely and successfully applied to a large number of problems, such as speech recognition [4], DNA and protein modeling [5], and gesture recognition [6]. We show in this paper that HMMs are also effective in classification of MMOG players, and, in particular, have higher recognition performance than AMBR based on action frequencies.

2   MMOG Simulator and Player Modeling

To acquire game logs in MMOGs, we use the version[2] of Zereal [7] released to us on June 14, 2003. Zereal is a Python-based multiple agent simulation system running on a PC cluster system. The architecture of Zereal and a screen shot of a game world are shown in Figs. 2 and 3, respectively.

In this study, we focus on two types of player agents, Killer and MarkovKiller, provided with Zereal, because they somehow behave like "killer" and "achiever", respectively. Each player agent has nine actions, i.e., 'walk', 'attack', 'chat', 'pickuppotion', 'pickupfood', 'pickupkey', 'leaveworld', 'enterworld', and 'removed'. The action 'removed' is outputted to the game logs when a player agent (or a monster) dies due to its hit point having reached zero. Killer and MarkovKiller have different characteristics as described below.

- **Killer (K)** has no sociability and will pursue the closest player or monster and kill it.
- **MarkovKiller (MK)** selects the next action from multiple candidates using a given Markov matrix. By manipulating the Markov matrix, we implement two types of MarkovKiller, InexperiencedMarkovKiller and ExperiencedMarkovKiller, described as follows:
- **InexperiencedMarkovKiller (IMK)** who equally attempts all possible actions in a given situation; all elements of the Markov matrix equal.

---

[2] This version of Zereal is different from the version that we used in our earlier reports in [1][3][8].

- **ExperiencedMarkovKiller (EMK)** who prefers particular actions over others in a given situation; the elements of the Markov matrix are not uniform.

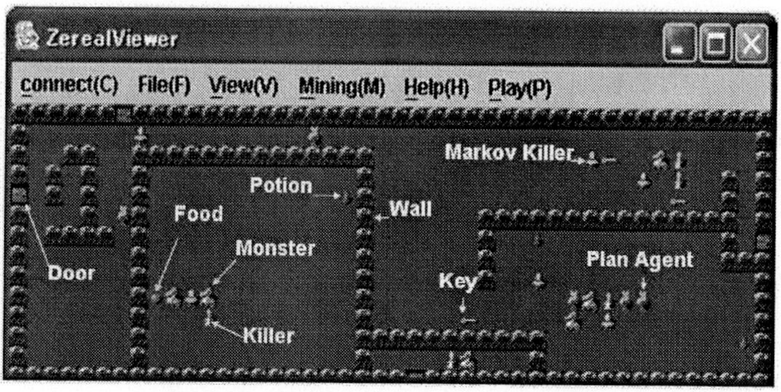

Fig. 3. Screenshot of a game world

3 Hidden Markov Models

HMMs [4] are a tool to statistically model a process that varies in time. From the set of observations, time structures hidden in the data are derived. An HMM can be specified by (1) the set of the possible hidden states $S = \{s_1,...,s_N\}$; (2) the transition matrix A whose elements a_{ij} represent the probability to go from state s_i to state s_j; (3) the set of the observation symbols $V = \{v_1,...,v_M\}$; (4) the emission matrix B whose elements b_{jk} indicate the probability of emission of symbol v_k when the system state is s_j; (5) the set of initial state probability distribution $\Pi = \{\pi_1,..., \pi_N\}$ whose elements π_i represent the probability for s_i to be the initial state. For convenience, we denote an HMM as a compact notation $\lambda = (A, B, \Pi)$.

Table 1. Initial emission matrix having 8 states and 9 symbols (w: walk, a: attack, c: chat, p: pickuppotion, f: pickupfood, k: pickupkey, e: enterworld, l: leaveworld, r: removed)

	w	a	c	p	f	k	e	l	r
fight	0.00	0.75	0.00	0.00	0.00	0.00	0.00	0.00	0.25
talk	0.00	0.00	1.00	0.00	0.00	0.00	0.00	0.00	0.00
hunt	0.70	0.00	0.00	0.10	0.10	0.10	0.00	0.00	0.00
transit	0.75	0.00	0.00	0.00	0.00	0.25	0.00	0.00	0.00
go for powerup	0.00	0.00	0.00	0.50	0.50	0.00	0.00	0.00	0.00
flee	0.75	0.00	0.00	0.00	0.00	0.00	0.00	0.00	0.25
bored	1.00	0.00	0.00	0.00	0.00	0.00	0.00	0.00	0.00
transported	0.00	0.00	0.00	0.00	0.00	0.00	0.50	0.50	0.00

The Baum-Welch algorithm was used to train HMMs, one for each player type, using the training data set. The training data set consists of both the action sequence and the type of each known agent player. To identify the type of an unknown player agent, the Viterbi algorithm was used. This algorithm computes the log probabilities using the trained HMMs, inputted by the action sequence of the unknown player agent. The unknown player agent will be assigned the type of the HMM with the highest log probability.

Table 2. Average appearance frequency of each action, and the average length of the action sequences for each agent type

	w	a	c	p	f	k	e	l	r	length
K	157.79	29.08	0.00	0.46	1.96	0.78	0.12	0.12	0.06	190
IMK	223.69	2.52	22.09	1.96	1.91	0.33	0.11	0.11	0.01	253
EMK	219.27	6.62	19.83	4.31	4.09	0.40	0.10	0.10	0.00	255

The performance of HMMs is in general dependent on the model structure and the initial parameters of λ. Here, we based on the model of MarkovKiller in Zereal. Namely, each HMM was constructed by 8 states ($N = 8$) and 9 symbols ($M = 9$), and the initial value of each element in B was shown in Table 1. An equivalent probability, i.e., $1/N = 0.125$, was assigned to each element of Π and A.

4   Results

In our experiments, we generated game logs by running 10 independent Zereal games with 300 simulation-time cycles. Each game consisted of 16 worlds, in each of which there were 50 player agents of each type, 50 monsters, and 50 items for each game object (food, potion, and key). The total number of each agent per game was thus 800. Next we transformed these raw game logs into sequences of actions for being used by HMMs. For performance comparisons, the game logs were also preprocessed by the feature selection algorithm originally proposed in [8] for being used by AMBR.

Table 2 shows the average appearance frequency of each action, and the average length of the action sequences for each agent type. It should be noted that InexperiencedMarkovKiller and ExperiencedMarkovKiller are relatively similar to one another, in terms of action frequencies, which would cause low recognition rates for any classifier that uses only this type of information.

We conducted experiments on hierarchical classification of players. First, upper-level classification was performed. Namely, we classified all agents into two agent types, Killer and MarkovKiller. Second, we conducted lower-level classification. MarkovKiller-type agents were classified into InexperiencedMarkovKiller and ExperiencedMarkovKiller. To reliably measure the recognition rates of the two classifiers, we used the leave-one-out method discussed in [9].

4.1   Upper-Level Classification

Figures 4 and 5 show the recognition rates of both HMMs and AMBR for classification of the player agents into Killer and MarkovKiller, respectively. Both classifiers give high recognition rates though HMMs slightly outperform its counter part for all games.

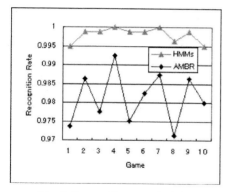

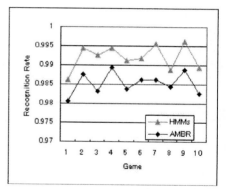

Fig. 4. Recognition rates for Killer   **Fig. 5.** Recognition rates for MarkovKiller

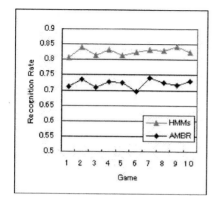

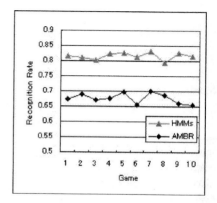

Fig. 6. Recognition rates for Inexperienced   **Fig. 7.** Recognition rates for   Experienced
MarkovKiller   MarkovKiller

4.2 Lower-Level Classification

Figures 6 and 7 show the recognition rates of both HMMs and AMBR for
classification of the MarkovKiller-type agents into InexperiencedMarkovKiller and
ExperiencedMarkovKiller, respectively. For this task, the performance of HMMs is
significantly superior to that of AMBR.

5 Conclusions

In this paper, we focused on time structures hidden in players' game logs of MMOGs,
and proposed an effective approach for player classification using Hidden Markov
Models. From the experiments, the recognition performance of HMMs is superior to
that of the previously proposed AMBR based on the frequencies of player actions. As

our future work, we will be researching on automatic generation of the optimal model structure of HMMs and the initial parameters. Moreover, we will be developing feature extraction techniques that preserve time structures. Eventually, we plan to apply our findings to real MMOG data.

References

1. Ho, J.Y., Matsumoto, Y. and Thawonmas, R., "MMOG Player Identification: A Step toward CRM of MMOGs", Proc. the 6th Pacific Rim International Workshop on Multi-Agents (PRIMA2003), Seoul, Korea, pp. 81-92, Nov. 2003.
2. Bartle, R., "Hearts, Clubs, Diamonds, Spades: Players Who Suit MUDs", The Journal of Virtual Environments, 1(1), May. 1996.
3. Ho, J.Y., and Thawonmas, R., "Episode Detection with Vector Space model in Agent Behavior Sequences of MMOGs", Proc. Future Business Technology Conference 2004 (FUBUTEC'2004), Fontainebleau, France, pp. 47-54, Mar. 2004.
4. Rabiner L.R., "A Tutorial on Hidden Markov Models and Selected Applications in Speech Recognition", Proceedings of the IEEE, Vol. 77, No. 2, pp. 257-286, Feb. 1989.
5. Hughey, R., Krogh, A., "Hidden Markov Model for sequence analysis: extension and analysis of the basis method", Comp. Appl. in the Bioscience, 12, pp. 95-107, 1996.
6. Eickeler, S., Kosmala, A., Rigoll, G., "Hidden Markov Model based online gesture recognition", Proc. Int. Conf. on Pattern Recognition (ICPR), pp. 1755-1757, 1998.
7. Tveit, A., Rein, O., Jorgen, V.I., and Matskin, M., "Scalable Agent-Based Simulation of Players in Massively Multiplayer Online Games", Proc. the 8th Scandinavian Conference on Artificial Intelligence (SCAI2003), Bergen, Norway, Nov. 2003.
8. Thawonmas, R., Ho, J.Y., and Matsumoto, Y., "Identification of Player Types in Massively Multiplayer Online Games", Proc. the 34th Annual conference of International Simulation And Gaming Association (ISAGA2003), Chiba, Japan, pp. 893-900, Aug. 2003.
9. Weiss, S.M. and Kulikowski, C.A., Computer Systems That Learn, Morgan Kaufmann Publishers, San Mateo, CA, 1991.

Expanding Spheres: A Collision Detection Algorithm for Interest Management in Networked Games

Graham Morgan, Kier Storey, and Fengyun Lu

School of Computing Science, Newcastle University,
Newcastle upon Tyne, NE1 7RU, UK
Telephone: + 44 191 222 7983, Fax: + 44 191 222 8232
{Graham.Morgan, Kier.Storey, Fengyun.Lu}@newcastle.ac.uk

Abstract. We present a collision detection algorithm (Expanding Spheres) for interest management in networked games. The aim of all interest management schemes is to identify when objects that inhabit a virtual world should be interacting and to enable such interaction via message passing while preventing objects that should not be interacting from exchanging messages. Preventing unnecessary message exchange provides a more scalable solution for networked games. A collision detection algorithm is required by interest management schemes as object interaction is commonly determined by object location in the virtual world: the closer objects are to each other the more likely they are to interact. The collision detection algorithm presented in this paper is designed specifically for interest management schemes and produces accurate results when determining object interactions. We present performance figures that indicate that our collision detection algorithm is scalable.

1 Introduction

Interest management has been used to satisfy the scalability requirements of computer supported collaborative work (CSCW) [5] and military simulations [7]. These environments provide similar functionality to networked games by presenting geographically distributed users with access to a shared virtual world. Therefore, we assume that such techniques may be employed by networked games to promote scalability by lowering the volume of message passing required to ensure players receive a mutually consistent view of the gaming environment. Ideally, interest management limits interactions between objects that inhabit the virtual world by only allowing objects to communicate their actions to other objects that fall within their influence. This is achieved via the spatial division of the virtual world with message dissemination among objects restricted by the boundaries associated with spatial division. Objects exchanging the same set of messages are associated to a group. To achieve message dissemination in this manner a multicast service is commonly used to manage group membership (objects leaving/joining groups) and the sending of messages to group members. As the membership of such groups is achieved via consideration of the geographic location of objects in the virtual world, a collision

M. Rauterberg (Ed.): ICEC 2004, LNCS 3166, pp. 435–440, 2004.

detection algorithm is required to aid in identifying an object's appropriate group membership.

Collision detection has been well studied in the literature and a number of algorithms have been proposed that perform better than $O(n^2)$ (e.g., [1] [2] [3] [4] [8]). Such algorithms commonly reduce the number of comparisons between objects via an ability to disregard many pairwise comparisons due to the large distances that may exist between objects. A number of these algorithms have been used to aid in determining appropriate object groups for interest management implementations [5] [6].

Collision detection algorithms are primarily designed to determine exact collisions between solid objects and are used to promote realism in virtual environments by making objects appear solid (e.g., objects should not pass through each other). However, in an interest management scheme it is common for the influence of an object to extend over the same virtual space that is occupied by other objects. Ideally, a collision detection algorithm suitable for interest management is required to identify the set of objects that may influence each other. This set provides the appropriate groupings for a multicast service. We believe that the development of a collision detection algorithm that performs better than $O(n^2)$ is required that is specifically designed for the purposes of interest management (i.e., identification of areas of the virtual world where area of influence of one or more objects coexist). Such an algorithm will provide the appropriate groupings of objects as expected by a multicast service and be able to more appropriately reflect the interest requirements of objects than existing collision detection algorithms.

The rest of the paper is organized as follows. In section 2 we describe our algorithm. In section 3 we discuss the performance of our algorithm and in section 4 we present our conclusions and future work.

2   Algorithm

We assume each object present in the virtual world to be a sphere. We consider these spheres to be auras associated with virtual world objects. An aura identifies an area of a virtual world over which an object may exert influence [5] [6]. All objects in the virtual world are members of the set VR. A collision between two objects, say O_a and O_b, is said to have occurred if O_a and O_b intersect (i.e., there exists an area of the virtual world that lies within the spheres of O_a and O_b). A *collision relation* (CR) identifies a set of objects that share, in part or fully, an area of the virtual world. Therefore, an object that belongs to a collision relation, say CR_i, collides with every other object that belongs to CR_i. Collision relations provide the appropriate groups that dictate the regionalization of the virtual world and provide a multicast service with appropriate group memberships. A set SU contains objects that are to be considered for collision; hence SU contains a subset of objects in the virtual world such that $SU = \{O_1, O_2, O_3, ..., O_n\}$. The determination of this subset is arbitrary, but will usually be equivalent to the full membership of VR at the start of the process of determining collisions. When an object, say O_a, from SU is being considered for collision it is said to be the *object under consideration* (*OUC* – when an object, say

O_a, becomes the object under consideration we write O_a^{OUC}). A set SC contains the collision relations between objects previously identified as the OUC. A collision relation is an element of set SC. For example, if $SC = \{\{O_a, O_b, O_c, O_d\}, \{O_a, O_e\}, \{O_f, O_g\}, \{O_h\}\}$ we may state that SC contains four collision relations that are made up from the objects O_a, O_b, O_c, O_d, O_e, O_f, O_g and O_h. A 2D graphical representation of the collisions between these objects is shown in figure 1 (the scheme is applicable in 3D virtual worlds but we limit our diagrams to 2D for clarity).

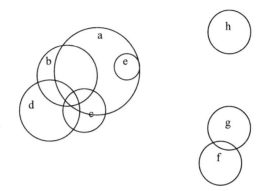

Fig. 1. Collision relations.

We now consider the identification of collision relations in more detail. We base our approach on determining if two spheres collide, say O_a and O_b, if the distance separating O_a and O_b is less than the sum of the radii of O_a and O_b. We assume an object's position vector and radius is known and may be described as O^{pos} and O^{rad} respectively. Additionally, our method also requires a CR to maintain position vector and radius information (CR^{pos}, CR^{rad}). CR^{pos} is taken from the first object identified in the CR and CR^{rad} is initially taken from the first object identified in the CR when the CR is created (i.e., CR only has one object within it). CR^{rad} is re-evaluated each time an object is added to a CR. Assume an object, say O_b, is to be added to a CR, say CR_i, the value of CR_i^{rad} is incremented using the following method:
1. Let SD be the separating distance between O_x^{pos} and CR_i^{pos}.
2. If $SD+O_x^{rad}$ is less than or equal to CR_i^{rad} then CR_i^{rad} remains unchanged.
3. If $SD+O_x^{rad}$ is greater than CR_i^{rad} then let CR_i^{rad} become $SD+O_x^{rad}$.
Extending CR^{rad} provides an opportunity to reduce the number of comparisons that need to be made in determining which objects intersect. We show how this can be possible by further considering the example shown in figure 2 when determining the collision relations of O_f (O_f is the OUC). Assume we have already deduced collision relations and calculated their associated CR^{rad} values for the first five objects considered in alphabetical order giving $CR_1 = \{O_a, O_b, O_c, O_d\}$ and $CR_2 = \{O_a, O_e\}$ (CR_2 is actually the true radius of O_a). It is clear that O_f does not intersect CR_1 and CR_2. Therefore O_f cannot intersect with any of the objects that lie within CR_1 and CR_2. By comparing O_f with CR_1 and CR_2 (two comparisons), we do not need to compare O_f with any of the objects within CR_1 and CR_2 (five comparisons). The pseudo code describing our algorithm is presented in figure 2.

```
Pseudo code main collision detection algorithm:
Algorithm CollisionDetection
Inputs  SU : Set of Objects;
Returns SC : Set of CRs // CR - Collision Relation;
Variables  Oₓ, Oₗ: Object; CL, CRᵧ: CRs; newCRs: Set of CRs

Begin
  SC:= Ø;
  for each Oₓ ∈ SU do
    newCRs:= Ø;
    for each CRᵧ ∈ SC do
      if (Oₓ collides with CRᵧ) then
        CL:= Ø;
        /** Find colliding objects in CR **/
        for each Oₗ ∈ CRᵧ do
          if (Oₓ collides with Oₗ) then CL:=CL ∪ {Oₗ} fi
        od
        /** Remove CRy if complete collision, add later **/
        if (card CL = card CRᵧ) then SC:=SC\{CRᵧ} fi
        if (CL ≠ Ø) then
          /** Turn CL into a CR by adding Oₓ **/
          CL:=CL ∪ {Oₓ};
          /** Add to set of new CRs for Oₓ **/
          /** Check for sub/super sets in newCRs **/
          newCRs:= addCR(CL, newCRs);
        fi
      fi
    od
    /** Add new CRs for Oₓ to SC **/
    if (newCRs = Ø) then /* Add singleton CR */
      SC:= SC ∪ {{Oₓ}};
    else
      SC:= SC ∪ newCRs;
    fi
  od
  return SC;
End
```

Fig. 2. Pseudo code describing the collision detection algorithm.

3   Performance Evaluation

Experiments were carried out to determine the performance of the expanding sphere algorithm. To enable comparative analysis of the performance figures a brute force collision detection algorithm with appropriate post-processing to determine collision relations was implemented. The number of comparisons is a count of the number of sphere-sphere (pairwise) intersection tests required to determine appropriate object group membership for all objects between two consecutive frames of animation. This measurement may not be influenced by implementation details (e.g., hardware configuration, memory management).

Object numbers were increased gradually from 1000 to 4000 with the number of comparisons recorded at each increment. The experiments were repeated with 3 different levels of aura coverage via the resizing of the virtual world. Each level identifies the percentage of the virtual world contained within auras given that no two auras overlap (low density (5%), medium density (10%), and high density (20%)). Experiments were conducted on a Pentium III 700MHz PC with 512MB RAM running Red Hat Linux 7.2.

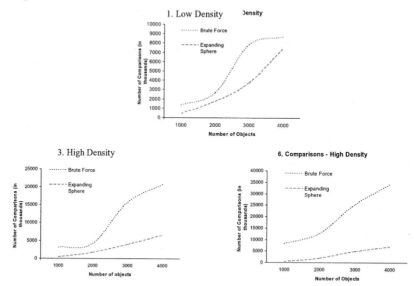

Fig. 3. Performance results.

An attempt is made to provide realistic movement of objects within the virtual world. A number of targets are positioned within the virtual world that objects travel towards. Each target has the ability to relocate during the execution of an experiment and objects may change their targets during the execution of an experiment Given that the number of targets is less than the number of objects and relocation and change direction events are timed appropriately, objects will cluster and disperse throughout the experiment. The auras of objects are uniform in size and their size does not change throughout the experiments.

Performance results are presented in figure 3. The first observation to be made is that expanding sphere outperforms brute force in all density types. Graphs 1, 2 and 3 show that expanding sphere carried out significantly less comparisons than brute force. This is particularly evident in medium and high densities. Furthermore, when object numbers increase to 4000 the number of comparisons performed by expanding sphere is approximately a sixth of the number of comparisons performed by brute force. This indicates that expanding sphere is scalable.

The performance increase provided by expanding sphere over brute force is not as noticeable in low density worlds as it is in medium and high density worlds. This can be explained by the fact that a low density world would have fewer collision relations with lower memberships, an environment that requires expanding sphere to carry out more comparisons (if there exists no aura overlap then expanding sphere will perform the same as brute force).

4 Conclusions and Future Work

We have presented a collision detection algorithm tailored to the needs of interest management schemes that rely on the aura based approach for determining object interaction. As we use aura overlap for determining spatial subdivision, our algorithm more accurately reflects the groupings of objects that may be interacting than existing collision detection algorithms. This has the added advantage that the number of groups that a multicast service is required to support when providing message dissemination services for interest management schemes is kept to a minimum. This is in contrast to existing interest management schemes that do not tackle this scalability problem. We have provided performance figures that show our algorithm to perform better than $O(n^2)$ and maintains such performance when large numbers of objects are present, indicating that our algorithm is scalable.

Future work will concentrate on further development of our algorithm. In particular, we want to apply our algorithm to our own interest management scheme [9].

Acknowledgements. This work is funded by the UK EPSRC under grant GR/S04529/01: "Middleware Services for Scalable Networked Virtual Environments".

References

1. M. H. Overmars, "Point Location in Fat Subdivisions", Inform. Proc. Lett., 44:261-265, 1992
2. P. M. Hubbard, "Collision Detection for Interactive Graphics Applications", IEEE Transactions on Visualization and Computer Graphics, 1(3) 218-230. 1995
3. S. Gottschalk, M, C. Lin, D. Monocha, "OBB-Tree: A Hierarchical Structure for Rapid Interference Detection", SIGGRAPH 93, p247-254, USA, 1993
4. M. S. Paterson, F. F. Yao, "Efficient Binary Space Partitions for Hidden-Surface Removal and Solid Modeling", Disc. Comput. Geom., 5, p 485-503, 1990.
5. C. Greenhalgh, S. Benford, "MASSIVE: a distributed virtual reality system incorporating spatial trading", Proceedings IEEE 15th International Conference on distributed computing systems (DCS 95), Vancouver, Canader, June 1995
6. C. Greenhalgh, S. Benford, "A Multicast Network Architecture for Large Scale Collaborative Virtual Environments", Proceedings of European Conference on Multimedia Applications, Services and Techniques (ECMAST 97), Milan, Italy, 1997, p 113 – 128
7. D. Miller, J. A. Thorpe. "SIMNET: The advent of simulator networking", In Proceedings of the IEEE 83(8), p 1114-1123, August 1995
8. J. D. Cohen, M. C. Lin, D. Manocha, M. K. Ponamgi, "I-COLLIDE: An Interactive and Exact Collision Detection System for Large-Scale Environments", In Proceedings of the 1995 symposium on Interactive 3D graphics, pages 189–196, 218. ACM, Press, 1995
9. G. Morgan, F. Lu, "Predictive Interest Management: An Approach to Managing Message Dissemination for Distributed Virtual Environments", Richmedia2003, Switzerland, 2003.

Electronic Augmentation of Traditional Board Games

Clim J. de Boer and Maarten H. Lamers

Leiden Institute for Advanced Computer Science, Leiden University, The Netherlands
clim@clim.nl

Abstract. Manufacturers of traditional board games are looking for ideas to innovate their products and keep up with the popularity of modern computer games. We developed an idea of how traditional board games can be augmented with modern technology and how electronics can increase the level of excitement and board game pleasure. The concept of a self-conscious gameboard is proposed and its viability demonstrated through a case study in which the popular board game *Settlers of Catan* was electronically enhanced.

1 Introduction

Modern technology results within the world of gaming almost solely in games that are targeted at the individual. On the contrary we find an enormous range of traditional board games that are played with family and friends around the table. Sales of board games in both Europe and the US have risen strongly since the year 1995 [1]. Some sociologists see this as a direct result of economic recession and the threat of terrorism and war [2]. Given the rise of computer games and the parallel relived interest in board games, crossover between both could be expected [3], but till now hardly seen.

In this paper we explore what value modern technology can add to the social-interactive character, the excitement and/or entertainment value, and also to the usability and flexibility of board games, played within the "traditional" context of family and friends. From our work we derived recommendations for electronically augmenting board games and we propose the concept of the *self-conscious gameboard*. Finally, these recommendations were applied to a case study in which we digitally enhanced the popular board game *Settlers of Catan* [4].

2 Exploring Electronic Augmentations

Trends in Board Games. From interviews and questionnaires that we conducted among the target groups of manufacturers, game authors and players, we identified trends in board games, market developments, past and future plans, opportunities and limitations of electronically augmented board games. Our findings are extensively reported in [5].

Possible Electronic Augmentations. Until recently, electronic game enhancements were limited to modest sound effects, lighting, or simple physical movements driven by servo motors. *King Arthur* of designer Rainer Knizia is currently one of the very few board games claiming to incorporate "intelligent electronics" that give feedback

M. Rauterberg (Ed.): ICEC 2004, LNCS 3166, pp. 441–444, 2004.
© IFIP International Federation for Information Processing 2004

depending on decisions made by players earlier in the game. Subjects in our questionnaire [5] were asked to consider among other things the following possible augmentations in board games: (1) integrated digital game rules enabling error detection and prevention, animated game examples, and electronic teaching of rules to players (2) randomization, e.g., changing the gameboard composition (3) automated administrative tasks, such as registration of time, scores, game movements, and player statistics (4) artificial intelligence, e.g., autonomously functioning game pieces, simulation of extra players, suggestions for game moves (5) audiovisual feedback in the form of light, audio effects, music, visual animations (6) saving and restoring game situations (7) automated physical tasks, like gameboard setup, dealing cards, actuating moves. These and additional possibilities are also discussed in [5] and [6].

Conclusions and Recommendations.   From our survey [5] we conclude that innovations should have a clear added value to the game concept and introduce new elements. Most importantly, the pleasure of playing a board game should be increased, while the existing physical elements of the game are preserved as much as possible. Summarizing, one could say that the added technology should fill holes in the game concept, that cannot be filled using traditional manners. The electronic enhancements desired most by our subject groups are: (1) randomly changing gameboard composition (2) integrated digital game rules, automatic error detection and prevention (3) simulation of additional players. One should keep in mind that electronic augmentations do not solely bring advantages. For example malfunctioning of the electronics can be expected. Also, unforeseen situations in pre-programmed game-logic could introduce problems. Further, a game should always stay transparent to its players. Obscured technology can give rise to confusion among players. To conclude, selling prices will be higher, due to increased costs for development and production. The conclusions from our survey are consistent with recommendations by Lundgren [6].

3   The Self-Conscious Gameboard

Given the results of our research we propose a conceptual framework within which future development of electronically augmented board games can be discussed: the *self-conscious gameboard*. It should be able to recognize the state and composition of all its elements: game floor, field tiles, and game tokens. The gameboard controller can identify all elements and request, set and communicate the state of these elements. A short explication of its elements:

- The *controller* is the computational unit, computer or microcontroller placed in or nearby the gameboard. It serves as the central "brain" in which the state of the gameboard is registered, user input analyzed, rules of game applied, scores registered and feedback initiated.
- The *game floor* is a matrix (or other fixed pattern of cells) on top of which the playfield is constructed. On each cell a field tile can be positioned. When there are no individual field tiles, the game floor can be seen as one field tile.
- *Field tiles* form the first layer on top of the game floor. Together they form the playfield. A field tile can have one or more states, based on its orientation/rotation,

type of tile and game tokens placed on top of it. Examples are the natural resource hexagons in *Settlers of Catan*.

- *Game tokens* are placed on top of the field tiles. As far as its characteristics are concerned, a game token is similar to a field tile: it can have several states that may be registered and altered by the controller. Its state may for instance be determined by its ownership, such as with hotels in *Monopoly* or the pieces in a game of *Chess*.
- *Game control elements* provide additional ways to supply the controller with event triggers and data (e.g., dice, configuration switches), but also means to offer feedback to the players (e.g., LCD display, LED, speaker).

Obviously, to implement a self-conscious gameboard, some minimal electronic infrastructure is essential for the controller to register the state of the game and give appropriate feedback. Given the scope of this short paper it is not possible to explicate physical wiring and electronics issues. For this we refer to [5], in which we describe how the number of required electronic contact points can be limited to $\lceil {}^2log(n*R+1) \rceil$ where n is the number of recognizable game tokens or field tiles, and R is the number of recognizable rotations of such elements. Once the hardware infrastructure is realized, more functionality can be added rather easily by extending the software in the controller. The state of the individual elements is changed appropriately in the controller and communicated to the players through the available channels of feedback.

4   Case Study with *Settlers of Catan*

To assess the weaknesses and strengths of our proposed concept of a self-conscious gameboard, a case study was undertaken. We chose to electronically augment an existing board game, as opposed to creating a new game. By this (1) we can compare the enhanced version to its original, (2) we ensure that the quality of the game itself is a proven fact, and (3) attention is focussed on the electronic enhancements, and not drawn away by a new board game.

Settlers of Catan [4] is a highly acclaimed multiplayer board game, and one of the best selling games of the last few years. The game presumes that its players are new settlers on the uninhabited island of Catan. During the game, settlers tap the land's natural resources to build roads, settlements, and cities. Resource production is controlled by two six-sided dice. A player's progress is recognized by victory points that are earned by building principalities and other. The first settler to declare that he has accumulated the required number of victory points wins.

In the traditional version of *Settlers of Catan* hexagonal field tiles represents one of six natural resources. A number between two and twelve is assigned to each tile indicating the dice value that must be tossed to earn that certain resource; their positions are unchanged during the game, after their (semi-)random initialization. In the electronically augmented prototype of *Catan*, each field tile has a seven-segment LED-display installed, showing its number. At the start of the game, the task of distributing the numbers on the board is automated. During a game the displayed numeric values may randomly change every ten minutes, or every ten turns. This results in a constantly changing gameboard and new opportunities for the players. Our board is fitted with a digital dice function that tosses between 2 and 12 using a selectable chance distribution (double-diced or uniform). The tossed number is indicated with a LED on each field tile that lights up on payout. The "robber" game token of *Catan* connects to a slot on every field tile, enabling the controller to recognize its position and thus inhibiting payout of resources (indicated by a red LED instead of green).

Several test teams of experienced *Catan* players played games on the prototype. The general opinion of the subjects was that the introduced randomization of numbers gives a strong added value to the level of excitement and game pleasure. The regularly changing gameboard altered player's opportunities, raised tension, and largely influenced player strategies. Although no real dice are used in the augmented version, their digital replacement was hardly mentioned by the testers, which points towards transparency of this technology. The choice between two chance distributions for the dice was deemed a unique feature. Because the original cardboard and wooden game elements were preserved in the prototype, the nostalgic feel of the game remained.

5 Discussion

The electronic augmentation of board games is still in its infancy. World leading board game manufacturers, although sceptic, are willing to invest resources in the development of such games. Important obstacles are the costs of development and production and the need for game designers to accumulate knowledge on modern technology. Our studies showed that for the consumer it is essential that the added technology is non-obtrusive and provides clear benefits in game pleasure, ease of use, and level of excitement. Through a case study in which *Settlers of Catan* was electronically enhanced, it was proved that the proposed concept of a self-conscious game board is viable and capable of heightening a board game's appreciation, particularly through dynamic changing of the game board. The case study also showed player's positive reception of the unexpected new possibilities to customize a game to their own likings. We trust that with the proposed concept of a self-conscious gameboard we contributed to future discussions regarding electronically augmented board games.

References

1. Barbaro, M.: *Beyond Monopoly*. The Washington Post, 07-07-2003 page F01
2. Murphy, L.: *Replaying Old Favorites*. 03-11-2002. Washington Times Corp
3. Mandryk, R.L., Maranan, D.S., Inkpen, K.M.: *False Prophets: Exploring Hybrid Board/Video Games*. Proceedings of CHI 2002, ACM Press (2002)
4. Teuber, K.: *Die Siedler von Catan*. Franckh-Kosmos Verlags-GmbH & Co (1995)
5. de Boer, C.J.: *Elektronische Toevoegingen aan Traditionele Bordspellen (Electronic Augmentations of Traditional Board Games)*. Technical Report 2004–05, Leiden University
6. Lundgren, S.: *Joining the Bits and Pieces*. MSc Thesis in Interaction Design, IT University of Göteborg, Sweden (2002)

Strategy Selection in Games Using Co-evolution Between Artificial Immune Systems

Donald MacDonald and Colin Fyfe

Applied Computational Intelligence Research Unit,
The University of Paisley, Scotland.
{Donald.macdonald,Colin.Fyfe}@paisley.ac.uk

Abstract. In this paper, we create a simple artificial computer game in order to illustrate a means of making software players in computer games more intelligent. Despite being known as AIs, the current generation of computer players are anything but intelligent. We suggest an algorithm motivated by concepts from Artificial Immune Systems (AIS) in which an attack from one opponent is met with a response from the other which is refined in time to create an optimal response to that attack.. We refine the AIS algorithm in that we model the response with a probability vector rather than a population of antibodies. Some typical results are shown on the simple computer game.

1 Introduction

One of the major disincentives to playing a game against a software opponent (the so-called AI) is that the AI is rarely truly intelligent. Any success which an AI has tends to be due to its ability to micro-manage resources. One might argue that the AI is simply playing to its strengths yet, nevertheless, this does not lead to a game in which the human player feels he is playing against an intelligent opponent. What is required is to enable the AI to learn so that it adopts strategies in response to its human opponent's strategies: both players are learning how to play against each other just as two humans learn to play a new game. In this paper, we propose that this learning is performed under the paradigm of Artificial Immune Systems: we will create an artificial computer game which is a simple abstraction of contemporary computer games and, under the influence of Artificial Immune Systems, have two computer opponents learn to play the game against each other.

Also in this paper, we extend the approach to modeling artificial immune systems (AIS) in a way which is reminiscent of the way that Population Based Incremental Learning (PBIL) extended Evolutionary Algorithms (EAs). We illustrate the use of these new methods on real time strategy Computer Games. First we describe Artificial Immune Systems and our extensions.

2 Artificial Immune Systems

The immune system is a complex of cells which are used to keep an organism healthy by repelling attacks both from exogenous pathogens and from internal malfunctions. We will be mainly modeling the former type of attack: thus, we will consider a situation in which a computer AI learns to adapt to the attacks of the other; the attacks will be considered as the antigens, the exogenous pathogens which are threatening the

M. Rauterberg (Ed.): ICEC 2004, LNCS 3166, pp. 445–450, 2004.
© IFIP International Federation for Information Processing 2004

organism, while the responses will be considered to be the antibodies, designed to repel the attacks from the antigens.

The immune system creates antibodies specific to the antigens the organism meets. However, prior to meeting any antigens, the immune system will be creating antibodies more or less at random rather as though it is searching the space of possible attacks while simultaneously being primed to respond to any threat which it identifies. Within its cohort of randomly produced antibodies, some antibodies will, by chance, be better able to respond to a specific antigen attack than others. Simply by being best able to respond, these antibodies identify themselves as those antibodies best able to keep the organism healthy and so these antibodies are cloned which leads to more antibodies in the population which are able to respond to the attacking antigen. However, crucially this cloning process is performed with a high rate of mutation. Thus, in the space of possible antibodies, the clones are centred round the responding antibody but in a rather diffuse cloud since the rate of mutation is typically very high. Since the initial response was from a randomly produced antibody, it is very likely that one or more of the clones is actually a better response to the antigen than the original antibody and it (or they) are now cloned with mutation in even greater numbers. The immune system is therefore now refining its response to the external threat. Thus in this way the immune system learns to identify the specific threat and respond optimally to it. One final feature of the immune system which is of interest in this context is its memory: having overcome the attacking antigen, the immune system retains a memory of the nature of the attack so that it is primed to respond optimally if the organism is attacked by the same or a similar antigen in future.

Notice that, from the antibodies perspective, the response of the immune system is rather stigmergic: stigmergy [7] is the process by which self-organisation emerges, for example, in insect populations who use the environment to regulate the behaviour of the population without the need to have any insect with a global plan of the regulation needed. This happens by changing some aspect of the environment in order to communicate with others: the most commonly cited example is the laying down of pheromone trails by ants in order to influence the behaviour of other ants. A complete ant trail leading from nest to food source can be created in a piece-meal fashion by such means even though at no time does an individual ant have the ability to direct the others towards the food source. In this paper, we will illustrate the stigmergic aspects of the artificial immune system in the context of a computer game. A more complete review of AIS can be found in e.g. [2,3].

3   Population Based Incremental Learning

Evolutionary Algorithms (EAs) such as the simple Genetic Algorithm are well known in the literature. They emulate the process of evolution and in doing so become generic problem solvers. Typically, we have a population of chromosomes which are potential solutions to a problem; some of these are better than others as solutions to the problem. The best solutions are selected for the next generation and allowed to breed which joins part of one good chromosome with part of another good chromosome. There is usually a mutation process at work also though the rate of mutation is usually very much lower than that of the Artificial Immune System described above. Repetition of this process over a number of generations has been shown to create a population of good solutions to the problem.

A recent innovation in genetically-motivated optimisation algorithms is the Population-based Incremental Learning (PBIL)[1,4] algorithm which abstracts out the GA operations of crossover and mutation and yet retains the stochastic search elements of the GA. The algorithm is

- Create a vector whose length is the same as the required chromosome and whose elements are the probabilities of a 1 in the corresponding bit position of the chromosome. When a binary alphabet is used for the chromosomes, the vector is initialised to 0.5 in every bit.
- Generate a number of samples from the vector where the probability of a 1 in each bit position of each vector is determined by the current probability vector.
- Find the fittest chromosome(s) from this population.
- Amend the probability vector's elements so that the probability of a 1 is increased in positions in which the fittest chromosomes have a 1.

The process is initialised with a probability vector each of whose elements is 0.5 and terminated when each element of the vector approaches 1 or 0. The update of the probability vector's elements is done using a supervised learning method.

$$\Delta p_i = \eta \ (E_{best}(chromosome_i) - p_i) \qquad\qquad (1)$$

where $E_{best}(chromosome_i)$ is the mean value of the ith chromosome bit taken over the fittest chromosome(s) and p_i is the probability of a 1 in position i in the current generation. η is a learning rate.

Therefore to transmit information from generation to generation we have a single vector - the probability vector - from which we can generate instances (chromosomes) from the appropriate distribution. Notice that

$$\Delta p_i \to 0 \Rightarrow p_i \to E_{best}(chromosome_i) \qquad\qquad (2)$$

Therefore if all the fittest chromosomes in each generation have a 1(0) in the ith position, the probability vector will also tend to have a 1(0) in that position.

4   The Artificial Immune System Algorithm

The Artificial Immune System (AIS) will be used by each of two competing AIs to learn to optimally respond to the attacks of the other. The first step (as with Evolutionary Algorithms) is to devise some coding of the problem, both the attacks and the responses. Because we are interested in computer games played by two AIs, the attack and response are anti-symmetrical but the two actions are drawn from an identical alphabet.

Previously, we [5] have developed computer games which learn using AIS such that, when an AI develops an antibody which can respond in some way to an attack, the antibody is cloned with a high rate of mutation. Thus we had a population of antibodies each of which represents a potential response to the attack. In this paper, we are motivated by the success of the PBIL to create a finer abstraction of the immune system so that at any one time, we have a vector whose elements represent the probabilities that each possible response has of being realized in a potential population of antibodies.

5 The Computer Game

To illustrate the above ideas, we create a simple conflict game between two armies each with elements from an alphabet of size three – horsemen, infantry and archers. We create a paper-scissors-stone type of conflict in that a horseman beats an infantryman, an infantryman beats an archer but an archer beats a horseman. Such conflicts are interesting because there is no *a priori* best strategy: one can only define a best response in the context of what one's opponent is doing. Indeed, under typical replicator dynamics [6], the time averages of such strategies converge not to a point (with a set number of each type of piece) but to a triangular cycle where the majority type of piece will rotate in order between horsemen, infantry and archers. In the current context, it is valuable that [6] have shown that such dynamics are equivalent to those of the Lotka-Volterra equations which model predator-prey interactions.

We create a square game grid with two opposing armies facing each other. Associated with each square is a probability vector which gives the probability that each type of element (horseman, infantryman or archer) will be created on that square. We introduce one further element to the conflict: if there are two neighbouring squares which contain two pieces of the same type, these two pieces can together overcome anything. This is done to encourage flocking-type behaviors which are more realistic in the context of armies' dispositions. Thus the system tends to reward local groups of troops all of the same type.

The game is initialized with a population of the three types drawn at random. As the armies engage, local battles are fought and winners declared for both sides. The probability vector is then updated so that those local battles which were won have their strategies rewarded by having the probabilities of similar responses made next time increased while the lost battles are given increased probabilities of a different random element next time round. From the current version of the probability vector, a new army is drawn each time and the process is repeated with the new armies.

The learning algorithm is similar to the PBIL algorithm but, since it is motivated by immune systems ideas rather than evolutionary algorithms, there is only one child. We have a specific constant learning rate, β, for the simulation so that, for the ith square, if p_{ij} is the probability of the jth element being selected then the change in the probability vector is given by $p_{ij} = \beta$ when j is a winning element and $p_{ij} = -\beta/2$ when j is a losing element.

Figure 1 (left) shows an example of an initial army deployment. Each troop has a line of sight, if there are no enemy units in line of sight then the troop will move closer, till a specific enemy unit is sighted, then each unit moves to engage one another. Archers and infantry move 3 units per turn, whereas horsemen move 7, which means that one of two things can happen: either the horseman moves and intercepts another horseman or the horseman moves quickly to intercept an archer killing him and giving the infantry time to intercept the infantry of the other side. By this time, the horsemen can sometimes be supporting the infantry leading to a victory for that side.

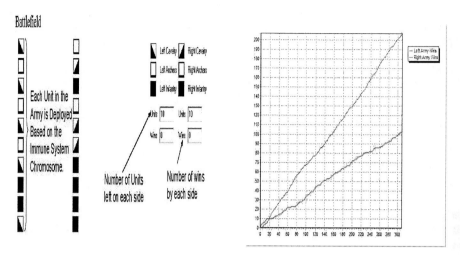

Fig. 1. *Left* an initial deployment of the two armies. *Right*: The number of wins by each army. The Left army is controlled by the Immune system with the higher learning rate.

In order to create some asymmetry between the players, we give one AI a learning rate which is five times that of its opponent. The chart in the right of figure 1 shows the number of battles won by each AI. The AI with the higher learning rate (left army) wins almost 70% of the battles though the slower learner eventually gains parity with the faster. A typical battle involves one opponent launching an attack either through the middle of the battle or down one flank and the opponent attempting to match this attack with a best defense.

6 Conclusion

We have shown that the Artificial Immune Systems paradigm can be used to give intelligence to a simple computer game. Further we have extended the AIS paradigm with an concept suggested by PBIL in that we only retain and train a probability vector rather than a population of antibodies at any one time. We have illustrated the results on a simplified war game though a better impression of the game is given by a demonstration of the software. Future work will investigate using the AIS paradigm on more complex games with the eventual aim of incorporating this type of learning into a real game's API.

References

[1]   Baluja, S. and Caruana, R. Removing the genetics from the standard genetic algorithm. In *Proceedings of the Twelfth International Conference on Machine Learning*, 1995.

[2] De Castro, L. N. and von Zuben, F. J. , 1999 Artificial Immune Systems: Part 1 – Basic Theory and Applications, Technical report TR DCA 01/99, and Artificial Immune Systems: Part 2 – A Survey of Applications, TR DCA 02/00, from ftp://ftp.dca.fee.unicamp.br/pub/docs/vonzuben/Inunes.

[3] Dasgupta, D. 2000, Artificial Immune Systems and their Applications, Springer-Verlag.

[4] Fyfe, C. Structured Population-based Incremental Learning. *Soft Computing,* 2, 191-198, 1999.

[5] Fyfe, C. Dynamic Strategy Creation and Selection using Artificial Immune Systems, *International Journal of Intelligent Games & Simulation,* 3(1) 2004.

[6] Hofbauer, J. and Sigmund, K. Evolutionary Games and Population Dynamics, Cambridge University Press. 1998

[7] Ramos, V. and Abraham, A. Evolving a stigmergic self-organized data-mining. 4th Int. Conf. on Intelligent Systems, Design and Applications, August 26-28 2004, Budapest, Hungary.

Level of Detail Modelling in a Computer Game Engine

Francisco Ramos and Miguel Chover

Department of Computer Languages and Systems, Universitat Jaume I
Campus Riu Sec, 12071, Castellon, Spain
{jromero,chover}@uji.es

Abstract. The representation of meshes at different levels of detail is an important tool in the rendering of complex geometric environments like video games. Most works have been addressed to the multiresolution model representation by means of triangle meshes and discrete representations in games. Nowadays, models that exploit connectivity have been developed and in this paper a multiresolution model that uses triangle strips as primitive is presented and implemented in a game. This primitive is used both in the data structure and in the rendering stage, which lowers storage cost and accelerates rendering time. This model was implemented in a game engine as a method of testing its suitability for video games.

1 Introduction

A common approach to solve the problem of complexity in large scenes consists of level-of-detail (LOD) or multiresolution modelling. Multiresolution models can be classified into two large groups: discrete multiresolution models, which contain various representations of the same object with different levels of detail, and continuous multiresolution models, which capture a vast range of approximations to a continuous object.

Discrete models store between five and ten LODs and suffer from popping artifacts when an LOD is changed. A number of graphics standards, like X3D or OpenInventor, use such models. In continuous multiresolution models, two consecutive LODs differ by only a few triangles. These small changes introduce minimal visual artifacts. On the other hand, the size of the model becomes smaller than that of a discrete model because no duplicate information is stored. Progressive Meshes by Hugges Hoppe [2] is currently the best known continuous multiresolution model. It is included in the graphics library DirectX 9.0 from Microsoft.

Although these models have offered excellent results in interactive visualisation, they work with isolated triangles. Recently, these models have been improved to include connectivity information and store the models as triangle strips or triangle fans that reduce the amount of information send to the graphics pipeline and increase the rendering frame rate [1][3][4].

M. Rauterberg (Ed.): ICEC 2004, LNCS 3166, pp. 451–454, 2004.
© IFIP International Federation for Information Processing 2004

2 Model

2.1 Overview

Recently, Ramos et al. [4][5][7] presented a multiresolution model that uses triangle strips as the primitive. This model was developed in order to manage uniform resolution meshes.

The model represents a mesh as a set of multiresolution strips. We denote a triangle strip mesh M as a tuple (V;S), where V is a set of vertices v_i with positions v_i $\in R^3$, and S is a collection of sub-triangulations $s_1,\ldots,s_m$, so each $s_i \in S$ is an ordered vertex sequence (1), also called a strip.

$$S = \{S_1 \quad \ldots \quad S_m\} \qquad V = \{V_1 \quad \ldots \quad V_n\} \tag{1}$$

Each item inside the S set represents a triangle strip. After some modifications, this set will be adapted to become a multiresolution triangle strip data structure so it can be used in our model. In this way, this data structure will change during level of detail transitions.

2.2 Rendering Improvements

Accelerating techniques has been applied to the model in order to improve the rendering stage. Mainly, coherence and hardware exploitation techniques were implemented.

It is important to underline the suitability of the LodStrips model [4] for applying hardware acceleration techniques. This model spends a small percentage of time on extracting the level of detail, which leads to good rendering times due to its lower extraction times, and it therefore benefits the application of those techniques.

3 Implementation

3.1 Fly3D Game Engine

The model was implemented in the Fly3D Game Engine [6], see figure 1, which consists of a 3D real-time rendering engine API that is well-suited for building games and all kinds of real-time 3D applications. Fly3D uses OpenGL as a graphics interface for rendering, and features a powerful object-oriented simulation engine implemented in C++.

The Fly3D engine has a plugin-orientation. With this new approach, it became simpler to add a new behaviour or feature to the software without having to recompile it again. All that is needed is to just make a plugin DLL and link it to the engine's main library. Moreover, a new game or application can be developed as a plugin DLL linked to the engine, while using all the engine's interface classes, methods and variables.

Software Architecture

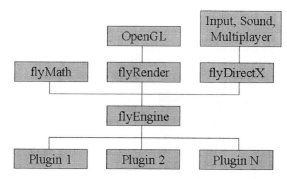

Fig. 1. Fly3D software architecture

The back-end part of the software is divided into four modules: the mathematics library, the DirectX library, the rendering library and the engine library. Each of these modules is a DLL, and the first three are linked to the engine module, which is the one that integrates them into a powerful rendering and simulation tool.

3.2 Integration of the Model

In order to insert the model in the Fly3D game engine, a new plugin that implements the behaviour of the model was created. The model consists in a C++ class which stores data and methods to retrieve the level of detail demanded and visualise it, and so a plugin interface was developed to interact with the application by means of the tools provided by the engine SDK.

Fig. 2. Tested model at a high level of detail   **Fig. 3.** Tested model at a low level of detail

4   Results

The model here presented was designed and implemented in a game engine. It was first tested with our own tool for designing models and, after that, it was implemented in the game engine. In Figures 2 and 3, it is possible to observe the modelling of the prototype in our tool; after prototyping it, it was implemented in the engine, and the criterion employed for managing the level of detail was the distance to the observer. Figures 4 and 5 show the behaviour.

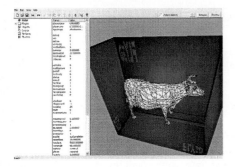
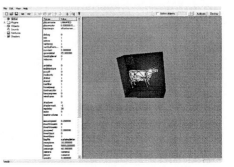

Fig. 4. Tested model implemented in the Fly3D Game Engine

Fig. 5. Tested model implemented in the Fly3D Game Engine

References

1. O. Belmonte, I. Remolar, J. Ribelles, M. Chover, M. Fernández. Efficient Use Connectivity Information between Triangles in a Mesh for Real-Time Rendering, Future Generation Computer Systems, Special issue on Computer Graphics and Geometric Modeling, 2003. ISSN 0167-739X.
2. Hoppe H. Progressive Meshes. Computer Graphics (SIGGRAPH), 30:99-108, 1996.
3. J. Ribelles, A. López, I. Remolar, O. Belmonte, M. Chover. Multiresolution Modelling of Polygonal Surface Meshes Using Triangle Fans. Proc.of 9th DGCI 2000, 431-442, 2000. ISBN 3-540-41396-0.
5. Ramos, J.F., Chover M. An approach to improve strip-based multiresolution schemes, in proceeding of WSCG 2004, Vol. 12, N°2, P. 349-354. ISSN 1213-6972.
4. Ramos, J. F., Chover, M. LodStrips: Level of detail strips. Submitted and accepted in CGGM 2004.
6. Fly3D Game Engine. http://www.fly3d.com.br
7. Ramos, J. F., Chover, M. Variable Level of detail strips. TSCG 2004, pp 622-630.

Mobile Entertainment

Networked Mobile Gaming for 3G-Networks

Amjad Akkawi[1], Sibylle Schaller[2], Oliver Wellnitz[1], and Lars Wolf[1]

[1]IBR; TU Braunschweig; Mühlenpfordtstraße 23; 38106 Braunschweig, Germany
{a.akkawi,wellnitz,wolf}@tu-bs.de
[2]NEC Europe Ltd.; Kurfürstenanlage 36; 69115 Heidelberg, Germany
Sibylle.Schaller@netlab.nec.de

Abstract. Mobile devices offer the opportunity to play games nearly everywhere. Moreover, networked games allow individual players to interact with other people and to participate in a larger gaming world, which also provides for new business opportunities. Hence, we currently see an increased interest from game developers, providers and players in mobile games. However, due to the inherent nature of wireless networks, many challenges have to be addressed. 3G technology combines two of the world's most powerful innovations, wireless communications and the Internet. This paper proposes an architecture for multiplayer games in 3G networks. It uses the capabilities and functionality provided by the IP Multimedia Subsystem (IMS). A prototype implementation demonstrates the feasibility of our approach.

1 Introduction

Until recently, most games where stand-alone applications designed for a single player only. This has changed lately, where many games are directed towards a multi-player scenario where people can interact and compete. Today, most of these networked multiplayer games are developed for PCs connected to fixed networks. Especially in the early days games had to cope with severe bandwidth limitations, e.g. due to narrowband modem links. Nowadays, many computers have access to broadband services (e.g. via ADSL).

Currently, game developers, providers and players get more and more interested in games that can be played everywhere. Thus, games must be available on mobile devices. Yet, in order to support games on mobile devices some challenges, which are due to the nature of wireless networks, have to be overcome. One issue is that in such a situation only limited bandwidth will be available. Additionally, because of the mobility of devices, locations can change frequently and introduce several according problems.

Various technologies for mobile networking and applications on mobile networks have been developed. There is no single mobile network technology that can serve all possible needs. Each of these solutions has its optimal place and purpose. Communication range, speed, latency, coverage as well as cost determine which technical solution should be used.

M. Rauterberg (Ed.): ICEC 2004, LNCS 3166, pp. 457–467, 2004.
© IFIP International Federation for Information Processing 2004

To support games in public and wide-spread areas, a wide-area mobile communication system such as a 2G or 3G system provides advantages. Furthermore, considering the huge base of end-systems, using such networks is interesting for providers and for users as well. Worldwide, the 2G GSM standard is used most often. GPRS is an evolution of GSM networks towards packet-switched data services. The GPRS speed is about ten times faster than current circuit-switched data services on GSM networks. GPRS fully enables mobile Internet functionality by allowing inter-working with the existing Internet.

Standards organizations and other related bodies have agreed to co-operate for the production of a complete set of globally applicable technical specifications for a 3rd Generation Mobile System based on the evolved GSM core networks and the radio access technologies supported by 3GPP (Generation Partnership Project [1]) partners. The technical specifications will be developed in view of global roaming and circulation of terminals. The first release of the 3GPP 3G standard has stabilised, and the first 3GPP compliant networks are going into operation. Work is currently ongoing for 3GPP Release 6. [2] From 3GPP specifications, a complete solution for the support of IP multimedia applications (including voice communications) shall be available. The solution consists of terminals, GERAN (GSM EDGE Radio Access Network) or UTRAN (UMTS Terrestrial Radio Access Network) radio access networks and GPRS evolved core network. [3] UTRAN is a new radio network architecture. It provides services with more bandwidth for data and better quality for voice as compared to GSM and GPRS. The 3GPP IP Multimedia Subsystem (IMS) enables a "platform" with capabilities like presence, multimedia conferencing, messaging, support for QoS (Quality of Service) for data traffic, etc.

Wireless LAN (WLAN) is another type of access network supported by the 3GPP IMS. WLAN according to the IEEE 802.11 standards family provides bandwidth from 2 up to 54 Mbit/s. The actual bandwidth available per device decreases proportional to the number of the connected, active devices.

By use of IMS service capabilities and standards protocols a new QoS for games as well as better performance and scalability can be achieved. Complex services can be created and integrated into a game; based on simple IMS services such as Instant Messaging and/or special services such as a scoring service. The availability of information like location, terminal capabilities and presence status can significantly ease the development and enhance the features of games.

In this paper we propose an architecture that enables games both to run on 3G networks and to use the capabilities and functionalities of the IMS. The focus is on networked, multiplayer games. A prototype implementation shows the feasibility of our approach.

In the next section "A General Game Service" we briefly introduce aspects of multiplayer games, depict a general game service, and explain its components. In the third section "Architecture for the Integration of Games over the IMS", we motivate the choice of the IMS for game services and introduce our game service architecture. After the description of our prototype implementation in section 4 "An Example Implementation", we conclude the paper in section 5 "Conclusions".

2 Related Work

It seems that there is no other work directly related with the topic of the paper: an architecture for mobile, networked games over the IMS. This paper proposes an architecture that enables games to run on 3G networks and at the same time to use the capabilities and features of the IMS. Current related work focuses on providing powerful mobile devices with different features for mobile games and wireless connectivity. Mostly, wireless connectivity for multiplayer games is limited to local area networks (e.g. Bluetooth). The architecture described in this paper is not tied to any game specific hardware. Also we took the approach to base the architecture on standardized components and interfaces.

The remainder of this section lists some commercial game platforms that allow for wireless networked games.

Nokia 0[4] has entered the mobile game arena with its N-Gage in September 2003. The Nokia N-Gage platform was designed for both games devices as well as mobile phones. The Nokia N-Gage games deck allows users to play multiplayer games connected locally via Bluetooth and/or remotely over mobile networks. The N-Gage device is a tri-band GSM 900/1800/1900 mobile phone which has, in addition to the large screen (176x208 pixels) supporting 3D-graphic, digital music player MP3, stereo FM radio, as well as.

The Game Park Inc device (GP32) [5] is officially available in Asia and parts of America. The device is equipped with USB and memory card slot and has a big screen. The GP32 is also equipped with a Radio Frequency Module enabling up to 4 players playing locally wireless games.

B'ngo is a mobile phone [6] with handheld functionality providing wireless games via Bluetooth. The B'ngo device provides up to 8 players in a single match.

Sony Computer Entertainment (SCE) described its Play Station Portable (PSP) as the "21st-century Walkman," showing confidence in the company's upcoming product, which utilizes a number of high-end components. In terms of communication, the PSP will come equipped with 802.11-standard LAN, IrDA, and USB 2.0. 802.11-standard. [7] SCE plans to release the PSP at the end of 2004 in Japan.

Gaming-hardware maker Nintendo, which claims 98 percent of the handheld console market with the Game Boy, has had a limited wireless-gaming offering. Customers of some Japanese carriers, including NTT DoCoMo, can attach their Game Boys to cell phones, which then act as a modem for Web-based play. The Nintendo wireless adapter will be launched in Japan during the first half of 2004. [8]

3 A General Game Service

After a brief introduction to aspects of multiplayer games, we describe a general game service and explain its components.

3.1 Aspects of Multiplayer Games

Multiplayer games allow two or more people to play together or against each other in the same game. Networked multiplayer games are playable over a network (e.g. the Internet). Since the first video game for computer (Space war) in 1961 and the first multiplayer game in 1969, the multiplayer game world has faced many challenges.

Despite both the network and hardware limitations, a variety of multiplayer games were produced. The communication range, speed, network coverage, bandwidth and latency, as well as parameters of the game client devices (processor, memory, graphics, etc.) have an influence on what kinds of multiplayer games can be developed. These technical issues can have a significant impact on the applicable techniques for specific types of games.

Independent of the type of network that connects the players with the game, the physical limitation of the network cannot be ignored. Important limitations are the scarcity of resources, interferences, etc. on the radio link, leading to small bandwidth and high latency. Several communication models and design technologies deal with these limitations.

The communication model can be Peer-to-Peer, Client-Server based, or Hybrid. [9, 10, 11] In the Peer-to-Peer model the game clients communicate directly with each other. In the Client-Server based model a game server is involved in all game-related communication. The game server also keeps the complete game state. In the Hybrid model a part of the game is implemented with the Client-Server model, especially the communication of the game clients with the server, and the remaining part with the Peer-to-Peer model. Table 1 shows the possible usage for the different communication models.

Table 1. Possible Usage of Game Communication Models

Number of Players	Communication Model
Small 1-16	Peer-to-Peer
Large 16-200	Client/Server & Hybrid
Super Large up 200	Hybrid

3.2 Components in a General Game Service

Fig. 1 shows the components used generally for game services. The Game Service is the sum of the contributions of all these components.

The central component in the Game Service is the *Gaming Service* that is a server-side platform providing network connectivity and general support for gaming. A *Game Provider* is a human, an organization, or a collection of humans and/or organizations that own a game application, or have the right to use and publish a game application (e.g. Tetris, Quake, Age Of Empires). The Game Provider publishes and distributes games via the Gaming Service.

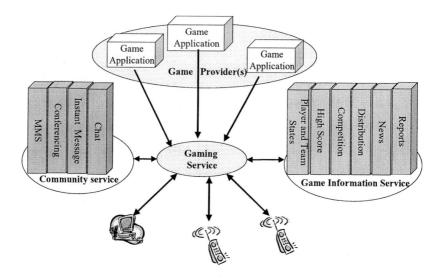

Fig. 1. Components in a General Game Service

Potential game players must install the game client(s) in their terminals. For mobile terminals, for example, this could be done with Over-the-Air provisioning. [12] An authenticated and authorized player can either join a (running) game of his choice or create a new game session. A game session is a single gathering of players to participate in an instance of a game. A game session lasts for some period of time.

The *Community Service* consists of different services that enable the players to communicate. Examples for Community Services are: Instant/Voice/Multimedia Messaging, Chat or Conferencing. One or more of these services may be integrated in a game and the player has the choice to use, join or leave them without having to interrupt the game.

The *Game Information Service* contains functionalities for the management of game related information. It may contain the information as listed in Table 2.

For the management, collection and distribution of game information the Gaming Service may use a Presence Service. Game presence information is a set of attributes characterizing the current status of a game such as score(s), player(s) and team(s), competition information, etc. The Game Information Service manipulates game presence information. Players and watchers of games can subscribe to all or parts of this information and may also be notified of any changes. Game watchers are users that do not (yet) actively participate in a game, but are interested in obtaining game related information and/or using game community services.

4   Architecture for the Integration of Games over the IMS

In this section we will briefly motivate the choice of 3GPP IMS for game services and introduce our game service architecture.

Table 2. Game Related Information

Type of Information	Description
Scores and Competition	Past and current scores, and competition information about past, current and future games. Each game may have one or more Score and Competition Information tables.
Players and Teams	Contains information about the game players and their teams. It may also contain information about a player's profile.
Downloading and Distribution	Information about new releases, new updates, demonstrations and levels. This information may also contain a download link.
News	Headlines, messages-of-the day, previews, screenshots, advertisement, etc.
Reports	A report may contain different information collected about games, e.g. during game launch. They give a game provider the possibility to make development and marketing decisions. Reports may contain statistical information about the players' requests and interests.

4.1 Why Games over 3GPP IMS

3G combines two of the world's most powerful innovations, the internet and wireless communications. Having access to the Internet in mobile devices will be of great value to many users.

The 3GPP IMS is a standardized infrastructure, able to run services of all categories while allowing ease of inter-working between (mobile) operators. [13] It will allow:

- Peer to peer, real-time and non-real-time services delivered over the packet switched domain
- Seamlessly combined services with different QoS categories
- Only one infrastructure is required for the support all types of services, keeping operators' CAPEX and OPEX low.

From a technical point of view, the IMS provides a horizontal approach to integrated, real-time, multiparty services for mobile networks. The Session Initiation Protocol (SIP) was chosen as the signalling protocol. It allows determining capabilities of user terminals, to negotiate QoS parameters, and to use and switch between media components as needed.

The first release of 3GPP architecture, Release 99 (R'99), defines the basic architecture of the network. R'99 was designed to be backward compatible with the existing GSM circuit switched infrastructure. The IP Multimedia Subsystem (IMS) is not part of this and the following release. The so-called Phase 1 IMS is specified in 3GPP Release 5 and contains the basic mechanisms for multimedia session management. The 3GPP Release 6 adds many new capabilities to the system and the IMS. Examples are: Presence, Conferencing, Messaging, WLAN-Interworking, and Group Management.

The IP Multimedia Subsystem (IMS) is an extension of the 3GPP packet-switched core network. It uses the Session Initiation Protocol (SIP) to setup, maintain and terminate voice and multimedia sessions. The 3GPP packet-switched core network is used to support the multimedia session bearer (data path) while hiding the terminal moves.

4.2 IMS Game Service Architecture

The IMS game service architecture was designed specifically for games based on the Client-Server communication model. Such games can be integrated with minimal effort. Peer-to-Peer or Hybrid games can also profit from some functions of the architecture.

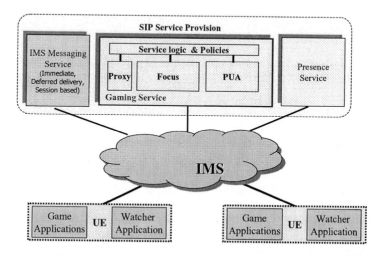

Fig. 2. Game Service over the IMS and Using IMS Capabilities and Functionalities

Fig. 2 illustrates the IMS game service architecture. The central component is the *Game Focus*. It maintains a SIP signalling relationship with each player in the game. Via IMS interfaces towards application servers the Focus can obtain the user location and his terminal capabilities, as well as authentication information accessing the 3GPP core networks HSS (Home Subscriber Server).

The game platform API is used for the information exchange between the focus and the respective *Game Servers*. This API is used to communicate the availability of game servers, accepted players, game sessions, etc. The game platform API is based on OMA Games Services version 1.0 (i.e. MGIF). [14]

The Focus serves the user's request, and forwards it to the "Service logic and policies" component. The game policy can be thought of as a database that contains policy information about how the focus should operate and may also contain player authorization information. It is the responsibility of the focus to enforce those policies. The focus also must both know about and eventually react to policy changes. Such changes might result, for example, in the termination of a dialog with a player by a sending SIP BYE message. Most policy changes will require a notification to subscriber(s) via the game notification service.

The Proxy component is needed when, e.g., a player wants to join a game's chat session. Thus the chat can be tightly integrated with the game, and the players need not to know/learn extra information (e.g. SIP-URI) about the chat service. In that case, the game service may also check the authorization.

The Presence User Agent (PUA) component is needed to inter-work with the IMS Presence Service for game and player related presence information. The IETF SIMPLE protocol is used to publish and obtain presence information. [15,16]

The game client (devices) and the game focus manage game sessions with the help of the SIP protocol. [17] SIP is also the signalling protocol in the IMS, thus the exploitation of the full IMS capabilities is possible. The session signalling also includes information needed for the provisioning of QoS for the game data traffic. The IMS provides the game client with an authorization token that can be used to do network reservations for the games data path. The games data path is set up directly with the games server. All game servers in this architecture will accept only data connections to game clients, which have been accepted previously via SIP signalling with the focus.

5   An Example Implementation

We implemented a prototype of the architecture described in the previous section (see also Figure 3). For our architecture two games were integrated: TetriNet and GNU VolleyBall. TetriNet was tested over GPRS as well as WLAN networks. TetriNet was playable over both types of networks. Because VolleyBall has most stringent requirements in regards to delay, the game was playable over WLAN, but not over the current GPRS network. In the GPRS network a delay is about one second was experienced. For our implementation we used NIST SIP stack implementation, which required Java Virtual Machine (JVM) 1.2. Due to restrictions of the JVM on the PDA, we had to modify the SIP stack to run on JVM 1.1.

The original TetriNet is a real-time multiplayer game and supports up to 6 players in each game session. For the client device a PDA (HP Ipaq) was chosen. Due to the small screen size of the PDA, we limited the number of possible players to 4. Sample screenshots of the game client can be seen in Figure 5.

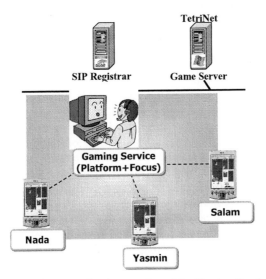

Fig. 3. A Prototype Implementation of the Gaming Service

The following entities were implemented:

1. A game client manager and the TetriNet game client on the PDA with the Windows PocketPC 2002 operating system. A graphical user interface (GUI) manages all games installed in the PDA. XML files are used for the configuration. With this GUI the user (player) can register himself at the SIP Registrar and join/leave game sessions. Our game client manager on the PDA automatically starts the respective game client after the user successfully joined a game session. See also Fig. 4 and Fig. 5.

2. The Focus of the Gaming Service on a PC running SUSE Linux 8.2. This component implements the functionalities of the Focus in the games architecture described above. The Focus manages the game sessions via SIP signalling with the game clients and with the game servers via the game platform API, enforcing the policies of the game provider.

3. The TetriNet game server on a PC running Windows XP. A so-called game agent supports the game server to register at the game focus. The game agent may serve all game servers on the host, and is able to trigger the initialisation of game servers.

4. Additionally a SIP proxy and registrar were needed. For this server we used the NIST SIP proxy/registrar on a PC running SUSE Linux version 8.2.

In our testbed, the TetriNet game server registers itself in the gaming service. The gaming service allocates resources, creates a SIP URI for the game and registers it at the SIP Registrar. Several TetriNet game servers may publish game sessions at the gaming service at the same time.

The client software on the IPAQ lists the published game session URIs, and then the user selects and joins a game session. Afterwards, the TetriNet game client starts automatically. It should be noted that the Focus is only involved with the game session management. The data path for the game is set up directly between the game client and the game server.

Fig. 4. Screenshot of the Game Client Manager GUI

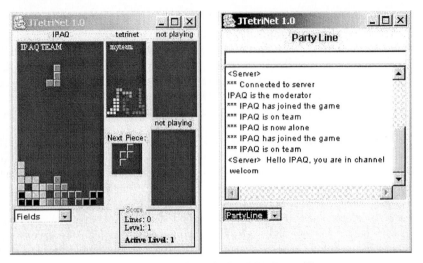

Fig. 5. Screenshots from the TetriNet Game Client

6   Conclusions

In this paper we presented a brief introduction to aspects of mobile multiplayer games. We also presented a view of a general game service and explained its components. Then we introduced our architecture for games over the 3GPP IMS and provided information about our prototype implementation. The prototype implementation of our architecture for Games over the IMS shows that games can be integrated relatively easily onto the 3GPP and IMS platform. The minimal changes that existing games will have to undergo are to enable them for SIP signalling to set up the game session before the data path for the actual game traffic is established.

Besides the porting and deployment of existing games, the presented architecture is suitable especially for the development of new games, since different (multimedia) services can be integrated and used easily. Overall, the IMS capable to support mobile, networked games. Of course, mobile devices may have restricted capabilities for running game applications. Such limitations cannot be solved completely by the IMS but it can help to overcome critical issues. The current prototype was evaluated on a SIP based network. The next step is to integrate the prototype with a real IMS system and to extend the prototype for using all available IMS functionalities (e.g. Presence Service, Conferencing). Security and charging issues are other topics that need more investigation.

References

1.   3rd Generation Partnership Project; www.3gpp.org
2.   3GPP TR 21.902; "3rd Generation Partnership Project; Technical Specification Group Services and System Aspects; Evolution of 3GPP System"

3. 3GPP TS 22.228; "3rd Generation Partnership Project; Technical Specification Group Services and System Aspects; Service requirements for the Internet Protocol (IP) multimedia core network subsystem; Stage 1"

4. http://www.heise.de/newsticker/data/daa-11.07.01-003

5. http://www.gampark.com

6. http://www.ttpcom.com/ttpcom/news/pr_03_bingo.htm

7. http://www.gamespot.com/all/news/news_6072659.html

8. http://www.nlgaming.com/nl/asp/id_1453/nl/newsDisp.htm

9. Yu-Chen "Internet Game Design" www.gamasutra.com

10. Joseph D. Pellegrino, Constantinos Dovrolis "Bandwidth requirements and state consistency in three multiplayer game architectures"; NetGames 2003

11. Jouni Smed, Timo Kaukoranta, Harri Hakonne, "Aspects of Networking in Multiplayer Computer Games"; http://staff.cs.utu.fi/~jounsmed/papers/AspectsOfMCGs.pdf

12. "Generic Content Download Over The Air Specification", OMA-Download-OTA-v1_0-20030221-C; www.openmobilealliance.org/tech/release.html

13. "Mobile Evolution Shaping the Future"; a White Paper from the UMTS Forum; August 2003; www.umts-forum.org

14. OMA Games Services version 1.0, Candidate Enabler Releases; www.openmobilealliance.org/tech/release.html

15. 3GPP TS 23.141; "3rd Generation Partnership Project; Technical Specification Group Services and System Aspects; Presence Service; Architecture and functional description (Release 6)"

16. "SIP for Instant Messaging and Presence Leveraging Extensions (SIMPLE)"; www.ietf.org/html.charters/simple-charter.html

17. "SIP: Session Initiation Protocol"; IETF RFC 3261

Mobile Games for Training Tactile Perception

Grigori Evreinov, Tatiana Evreinova, and Roope Raisamo

TAUCHI Computer-Human Interaction Unit, Department of Computer Sciences,
FIN-33014 University of Tampere, Finland
{grse, e_tg, rr}@cs.uta.fi

Abstract. Tactile interactive multimedia propose a wide spectrum of developmental games both for visually impaired children and adults. While some simulators can produce strong vibro-tactile sensations, the discrimination of several tactile patterns remains quite poor. Skin sensitivity is not enough for remembering and recognizing vibration patterns (tactons) and their combinations. Short-term tactile memory is the crucial factor in educational and vocational environments for deaf and blind people. We designed a vibro-tactile pen and software to create tactons and semantic sequences of vibro-tactile patterns on mobile devices (iPAQ pocket PC). We propose special games to facilitate learning and manipulation by tactons. The techniques are based on gesture recognition and spatial-temporal mapping for imaging vibro-tactile signals. The proposed approach and the tools implemented allow creating a new kind of mobile communication environment for deaf and blind people.

1 Introduction

There are many different games for training memory or musical skills, for instance "Senso" [10], but primarily they are intended for people without sensory problems. The games for visually impaired and blind users are based on Braille, tactile diagrams and speech synthesis. There is a small group of the deaf-blind users who also need special educational or training tools and access to novel communicative environments. Several attempts have been made to design vibro-tactile alphabet [4], [6]. As opposed to static spatial coding, as Braille, short-term tactile memory is the crucial factor in perception of dynamical signals, as Vibratese language [4].

There is a stable interest to use vibration signals in the games including small-size wearable devices like personal digital assistants and phones [1]. The combination of small size and low weight, low power consumption and noise, and human ability to feel the vibration when the hearing and vision are not accessible, makes vibration actuators ideal for mobile applications [2], [7].

On the other hand, the absence of moving components provides high mechanical reliability of input devices like touchscreens, but that impoverishes the primary feedback and makes interaction almost impossible for visually impaired users. Among recent projects, it is necessary to mention the works of Nashel and Razzaque [8], Fukumoto and Sugimura [3], Poupyrev et al [9]. The authors propose using small actuators, for instance, piezoceramic bending motor [3], [9] or shaking motor [8] attached to a touch panel or mounted on PDA. However, fingertip interaction has a

M. Rauterberg (Ed.): ICEC 2004, LNCS 3166, pp. 468–475, 2004.
© IFIP International Federation for Information Processing 2004

limited contact duration, as the finger occupies an essential space for imaging. In a case of blind manipulating by finger, the use of gesture technique is more efficient than absolute pointing through specific layout of software buttons. If the actuator is placed on the backside of the mobile device, vibration could be sensed at the palm holding the unit. In this case, the mass of the PDA is crucial and impacts onto spectrum of playback signals [2], [3].

From time to time vibro-tactile feedback has been added to a pen input device [11]. We also modeled different prototypes of the pen with embedded shaking motor. The vibro-tactile pen certainly has the benefits. In particular, the contact with fingers is permanent and has more touch surface; the pen has smaller weight and vibration is easily spread across this unit; the connection to mobile unit can be provided through a serial port or Bluetooth, that is, the main unit does not require any modification.

Based on vibro-tactile pen we designed the special technique for imaging and intuitive interacting through vibration patterns. Simple game scripts allow to simplify both the learning and usability testing of the system of the vibro-tactile icons (tactons) that might be used as awareness cues or non-verbal communication signals.

2 Method Design

2.1 Vibro-Tactile Pen

The prototype of vibro-tactile pen consists of a miniature DC motor with a stopped rotor (shaking motor), electronic switch and battery having the voltage of 3 V. Both the general view and some design features inside of the pen are shown in Fig. 1.

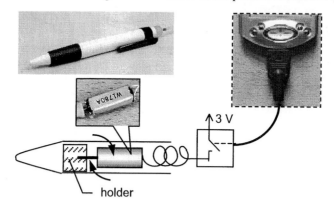

Fig. 1. Vibro-tactile pen: general view and schematics

There are only two control commands to start and stop the motor rotation. Therefore, to shape an appropriate vibration pattern, we need to combine the pulses of the current and the pauses with definite duration. The duration of the pulses can slightly change the power of the mechanical moment (torque). The frequency will mostly be determined by the duration of the pauses.

We used the cradle connector of Compaq iPAQ pocket PC which supports RS-232 and USB input/output signals. In particular, DTR or RTS signals can be used to realize the motor control.

2.2 Tactile Pattern Constructor

The software to create vibro-tactile patterns (tactons) was written in Microsoft eMbedded Visual Basic 3.0. Screenshot of the program is shown in Fig. 2.

This program allows shaping some number of vibro-tactile patterns which are composed of two serial bursts having different frequency of the pulses. The number of bursts could be increased, but the duration of the tactons shall be reasonable and shall not exceed 2 s. Corresponding labels called as "On" and "Off" define the duration of pulses and pauses measured in milliseconds accordingly. Clicking on the numerical label will increase the value or it will be decreased when label "–XX" was used. Number of pulses marked as "D1" or "D2" determines the duration of each burst. As it can be seen from the Fig. 2, the fourth pattern has the length of 1060 ms and consists of 10 pulses with frequency of 47.6 Hz (21 ms) and 10 pulses with frequency of 11.8 Hz (85 ms). All patterns are stored in the file "TPattern.txt" which can be loaded next by the game or another application.

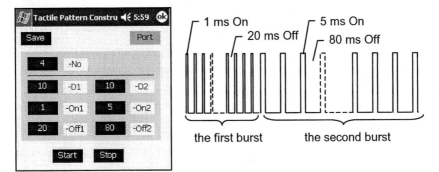

Fig. 2. Screenshot of the Tactile Pattern Constructor, and shaped signals

3 Game Scripts

3.1 "Locks and Burglars", the Version for Deaf Players

To feel imperceptible vibration (clicks) of the locks, burglars specializing on safes often wanted to increase fingertip sensitivity using sandpaper [5]. Fingertip sensitivity is extremely important for some categories of physically challenged people such as profoundly deaf, hard-of-hearing people and people who have low vision. Sometimes, only skin sensitivity is not enough to remember and recognize the vibration patterns and their combinations. While strong sensation depends on skin sensitivity, the discrimination of several tactile stimuli can remain quite poor. How long people can remember a tactile pattern depends on many factors, including both personal experience, making of the individual perceptive strategy, and the imaging system of alternative signals [4].

We propose special games and an approach to simplify learning and manipulation by the vibration patterns. The static script has own dynamics and does induce the player to make an individual strategy and mobilize perceptive skills. Let's consider a version of the game for able-bodied players or deaf users having a normal vision.

The goal of the "Burglar" is to investigate and memorize the lock prototype to open it as fast as possible. There are three levels of difficulty and two phases of the game on each level. In the "training" mode (the first phase), the player can touch the lock as many times as s/he needs. After remembering tactons and their positions, the player starts the game. By clicking on the label "Start" the key will appear, the game will start and the label will disappear (Fig. 3). When the player has the key in hand s/he can touch it as many times as needed. That is a chance to check the memory.

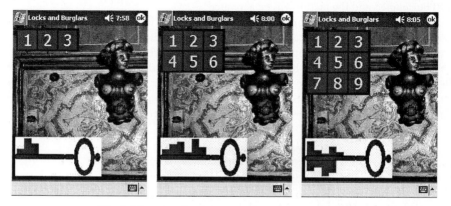

Fig. 3. Three levels of the game "Locks and Burglars"

After player had found known patterns and supposed in which position of the lock button s/he had detected these vibrations before, s/he can once click on the lock button. If the vibration pattern of the button coincides with corresponding tacton of the key piece, the lock will have a yellow shine. In a wrong case, a shine will be red. Repeated pressing of the corresponding position is also being considered as an error. That conditions a selection of the player strategy.

There is a restricted number of errors at each level of the game: single, four and six allowed errors. We assumed that 15 s per tacton is enough to pass the third level and the game's time was restricted by 2.5 minutes. All the data, times and the number of repetitions per tacton, in training phase and during the game were automatically collected and stored in a log file. Thus, we can estimate which of the patterns are more difficult to remember. Certainly, these data can be taken into account in the system of bonuses and penalties.

3.2 "Locks and Burglars", the Version for Blind Players

The script for blind interaction has several features. Screenshot of the game for non-visual interaction is shown in Fig. 4. There are four absolute positions for the software buttons "Repeat", "Start" and two buttons controlling the tacton number and the amount of tactons within playback sequence. Speech remarks support each change of the button state and arrow keys can be used instead of software buttons.

When the player should investigate and memorize the lock, s/he can make gestures along eight directions each time when it is necessary to activate the lock button or to mark once the direction by gesture and to press down the software button "Repeat" (or Down key) as many times as needed. The middle button (or Up arrow key) switches the mode of repetition. Three or all tactons can be played starting from the first, the fourth or the seventh position pointed by the last gesture.

To recognize gestures, we used the metaphor of the adaptive button. When the player touches the screen, the square shape automatically changes position and finger or stylus occurs in the center of the shape. After the motion was realized (sliding and lifting the stylus), the corresponding direction or the button position of the virtual lock will be counted and the tacton will be activated.

The button that appears on the second game phase in the bottom right position activates the tactons of the key. At this phase, the middle button (or Up arrow key) switches number of the tactons of the key within a playback sequence. However, to select the button of the lock by gesture the player should point before what piece of the virtual key s/he wishes to use. That is, the mode for playback of a single tacton should be activated. The absolute positions of software buttons do not require additional markers while some of players prefer to use arrow keys.

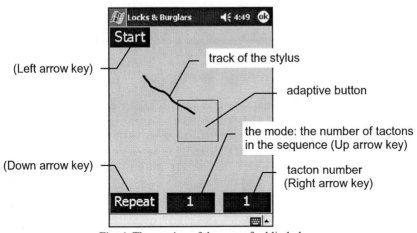

Fig. 4. The version of the game for blind player

3.3 "Tic-Tac-Toe", the Version for Blind Players

Since the technique for manipulating with nine buttons is very similar to another well-known game Tic-Tac-Toe, the script was realized using the same tools. In this game, only a single mode (the mode "all" of the middle button in previous game) is necessary to present the state of the game after each turn. All the tactons should be played starting from the upper left position. Only three tactons, which comprise a single burst of pulses, could be used to mark any position: empty (vibration frequency of 270 Hz), cross (square shape, vibration frequency of 20 Hz) and zero (round shape, 90 Hz). The interface supports the game between blind player and computer or the player having a normal vision (Fig. 5). Spatial-temporal mapping for vibro-tactile imaging is shown in Fig. 6.

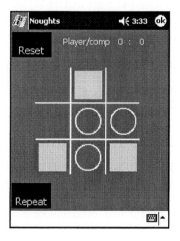

Fig. 5. Tic-Tac-Toe version of the game between computer and blind player.

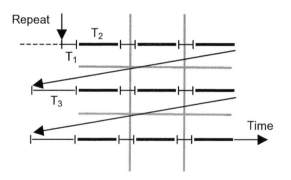

Fig. 6. Spatial-temporal mapping for vibro-tactile imaging: $T_1 = 60$ ms, $T_2 = 400$ ms, $T_3 = 300$ ms

Thus, the duration of each repetition of all the cells does not exceed 5 s including the earcon to mark the end of the sequence playback. This parameter is important and could be improved when stronger tactile feedback could be provided with the stylus having built-in actuator directly under the finger.

4 Evaluation of the Method and Pilot Results

The preliminary evaluation with able-bodied staff and students took place in the Department of Computer Sciences University of Tampere. The data were captured using the version of the game "Locks and Burglars" for deaf players. The data were collected concerning 267 trials in total, of 26 players (Table 1). While in tactons we used low frequencies of vibration (47.6 Hz and 11.8 Hz), we cannot exclude a weak acoustic effect, as the players had a normal hearing. Therefore, we can just summarize general considerations regarding the game difficulties and overall average results.

Table 1. The preliminary average results

Level (tactons)	Trials	Selection time per tacton	Total selection time	Repeats per tacton	Err, %
1 (3)	69	2.7 s	9.6 s	3-7	5.5
2 (6)	167	3.2 s	15.7 s	3-13	10.3
3 (9)	31	2-8 s	46.8 s	4-35	44.6

The first level of the game is simple as memorizing of 2 out of 3 patterns is enough to complete the task. The selection time (decision-making and pointing the lock button after receiving tactile feedback in corresponding piece of the key) in this level was about 2.7 s per tacton or 9.6 s to find matching of 3 tactons. The number of the repetitions to memorize 3 patterns was low, about 3-7 repetitions per tacton. The error rate (Err) was 5.5%. The error rate was counted as follows:

$$Err = \frac{[wrong\_selections]}{[trials] \times [tactons]} \times 100\% \,. \tag{1}$$

The second level of the game was not very difficult as well. However, the error rate was increased up to 10.3%. The one possible reason for this is the allowed number of errors (4). The third level of the game was difficult and only 11 out of 31 trials were finished by the win. While a selection time was about 30% of the entire time of the game, decision-making occupied much more time and players had lost a case, mostly due to the limited time. To memorize nine patterns in training phase the number of the repetitions was significantly varied. Thus, we can conclude that nine tactons require the special strategy to facilitate memorizing. The error rate was too high due to the allowed number of errors (6) and, probably, of the small tactile experience of the players.

Other games were briefly evaluated and showed a good potential to play and manipulate by vibro-tactile patterns even in the case when audio feedback was absent. The proposed approach and the tools implemented allow creating a new kind of mobile communication environment for deaf and blind people.

5 Conclusion

Tactile interactive multimedia propose a wide spectrum of developmental games both for visually impaired children and adults. Tactile memory is the major restriction for designing a vibro-tactile alphabet for the hearing impaired people. We designed a vibro-tactile pen and software to create tactons and semantic sequences of the vibro-tactile patterns on mobile devices such as iPAQ pocket PC. Simple game scripts allow to facilitate both the learning and usability testing of the tactons. Spatial-temporal mapping for imaging vibro-tactile signals has a potential for future development and detail investigating human perception of the long semantic sequences composed of the tactons. We suppose that after the play training, the tactons might be used like the system of non-verbal communication signals.

Acknowledgments. This work was financially supported by the Academy of Finland (grant 200761).

References

1.   Blind Games Software Development Project.
      http://www.cs.unc.edu/Research/assist/et/projects/blind_games/
2.   Chang, A., O'Modhrain, S., Jacob, R., Gunther, E., Ishii, H.: ComTouch: Design of a Vibrotactile Communication Device. In: Proc. DIS02, ACM (2002) 312-320
3.   Fukumoto, M. and Sugimura, T.: Active Click: Tactile Feedback for Touch Panels. In: Proceedings of CHI 2001, Interactive Posters, ACM (2001) 121-122
4.   Geldard, F.: Adventures in tactile literacy. American Psychologist, 12 (1957) 115-124
5.   Hampton, S.: Secrets of Lock Picking. Paladin Press (1987)
6.   Hong Z. Tan and Pentland, A.: Tactual Displays for Sensory Substitution and Wearable Computers. In: Woodrow, B. and Caudell, Th. (eds), Fundamentals of Wearable Computers and Augmented Reality, Mahwah, Lawrence Erlbaum Associates (2001) 579-598
7.   Michitaka Hirose and Tomohiro Amemiya: Wearable Finger-Braille Interface for Navigation of Deaf-Blind in Ubiquitous Barrier-Free Space. In: Proceedings of the HCI International 2003, Lawrence Erlbaum Associates, V4, (2003) 1417-1421
8.   Nashel, A. and Razzaque, S.: Tactile Virtual Buttons for Mobile Devices. In: Proceedings of CHI 2003, ACM (2003) 854-855
9.   Poupyrev, I., Maruyama, S. and Rekimoto, J.: Ambient Touch: Designing Tactile Interfaces for Handheld Devices. In: Proc. UIST 2002, ACM (2002) 51-60
10.   "Senso" game. http://www.tinysolutions.net/senso/
11.   Tactylus [tm] http://viswiz.imk.fraunhofer.de/~kruijff/research.html

Emotionally Loaded Mobile Multimedia Messaging

Timo Saari[1], Marko Turpeinen[2], Jari Laarni[3], Niklas Ravaja[3], and Kari Kallinen[3]

[1] Helsinki Institute for Information Technology and Center for Knowledge and Innovation
Research, Tammasaarenkatu 3, 00180, Helsinki, Finland
saari@hkkk.fi
http://ckir.hkkk.fi, http://www.hiit.fi
[2] Helsinki Institute for Information Technology,
Tammasaarenkatu 3, 00180, Helsinki, Finland
marko.turpeinen@hiit.fi
http://www.hiit.fi
[3] Center for Knowledge and Innovation Research,
Tammasaarenkatu 3, 00180, Helsinki, Finland
(Laarni, Ravaja, Kallinen) @hkkk.fi
http://ckir.hkkk.fi

Abstract. Mobile messaging is an increasingly important way of social interaction as people use their mobile phones for communicating with each other with textual and multimedia messages. Often with these messaging systems people have the need to communicate their own emotions or facilitate a given emotion in the receiver of their message. This paper will describe an information personalization system that may facilitate emotional communication especially in mobile multimedia messaging systems, thereby making the communication "emotionally loaded".

1 Introduction

When perceiving information via media and communications technologies users have a feeling of presence. In presence, the mediated information becomes the focused object of perception, while the immediate, external context, including the technological device, fades into the background [4, 28]. Various empirical studies show that information experienced in presence has real psychological effects on perceivers, such as emotional responses based on the events described or cognitive processing and learning from the events [36].

When using collaborative technology for computer-mediated social interaction, the users experience a state called social presence during which users may, for instance, experience intimacy of interaction or a feeling of togetherness in virtual space [28, 29]. During social presence users also experience various other types of emotional and cognitive effects, such as interpersonal emotion, emotion based on being successful in the task at hand and learning from shared activities or shared information. It is likely that when receiving and reading mobile messages with text or multimedia features users may experience presence with the message content and

M. Rauterberg (Ed.): ICEC 2004, LNCS 3166, pp. 476–486, 2004.
© IFIP International Federation for Information Processing 2004

social presence with the sender of the message. During and after the feeling of presence users may then experience emotions and moods based on the message.

Personalization and customization entails the automatic or semi-automatic adaptation of information per user in an intelligent way with information technology [see 38, 46]. One may also vary the form of information (modality for instance) per user profile, which may systematically produce, amplify, or shade different psychological effects [40, 41, 42, 43].

2   Modeling Short-Term Psychological Effects

Media- and communication technologies as special cases of information technology may be considered as consisting of three layers [2]. At the bottom is a *physical* layer that includes the physical technological device and the connection channel that is used to transmit communication signals. In the middle is a *code* layer that consists of the protocols and software that make the physical layer run. At the top is a *content* layer that consists of multimodal information. The content layer includes both the substance and the form of multimedia content [3, 40]. Substance refers to the core message of the information. Form implies aesthetic and expressive ways of organizing the substance, such as using different modalities and structures of information [40].

With the possibility of real-time customization and adaptation of information for different perceivers it is hypothesized that one may vary the form of information within some limits per the same substance of information. For instance, the same substance can be expressed in different modalities, or with different ways of interaction with the user and technology. This may produce a certain psychological effect in some perceivers; or shade or amplify a certain effect. In Figure 1 the interaction of media and communications technology and the user in context with certain types of tasks is seen as producing transient psychological effects. Media and communication technology is divided into the physical, code and content layers. The user is seen as consisting of various different psychological profiles, such as individual differences related to cognitive style, personality, cognitive ability, previous knowledge (mental models related to task) and other differences, such as pre-existing mood. [35, 40, 42, 43]

Media- and communication technologies may be called Mind-Based if they simultaneously take into account the interaction of three different key components: i) the individual differences and/or user segment differences of perceptual processing and sense making of different segments of users, ii) the elements and factors inherent in information and technology that may produce psychological effects (physical, code and content layers), and iii) the consequent transient psychological effects emerging based on perception and processing of information at the level of each individual. [44].

This type of system design approach may be of practical use, as it is known that individual differences in processing information (e.g., differences in working memory capacity, general intelligence or perceptual-motor skills) may produce sometimes quite large variance in the intensity or type of psychological effects, such as depth of learning, positive emotion, persuasion, presence, social presence and other types of psychological states and effects [13, 14, 40, 41, 42, 43]. It is also known that cognitive ability has an effect on computer-based task performance [e.g. 11]. For example, individual differences in memory capacity have an effect on people's behavior in many types of activities [48].

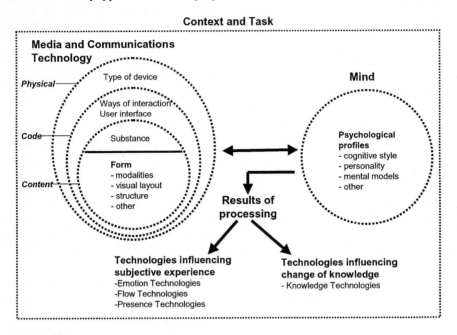

Fig. 1. Mind-Based Technologies as a framework for producing psychological effects. Adapted from [40].

As the task of capturing and predicting user´s psychological state in real time is highly complex, one possible realization for capturing user´s psychological state is to have the user linked to a sufficient number of measurement channels of various i) psychophysiological signals (EEG, EMG, GSR, cardiovascular activity, other), ii) eye-based measures (eye blinks, pupil dilation, eye movements) and iii) behavioral measures (response speed, response quality, voice pitch analysis etc.). An index based on these signals then would verify to the system whether a desired psychological effect has been realized.

Another approach would be to conduct a large number of user studies on certain tasks and contexts with certain user groups, psychological profiles and content-form variations and measure various psychological effects as objectively as possible. Here, both subjective methods (questionnaires and interviews) and objective measures (psychophysiological measures or eye-based methods) may be used as well interviews [for a review on the use of psychophysiological methods in media research, see 32]. This would constitute a database of design-rules for automatic adaptations of information per user profile to create similar effects in highly similar situations with real applications. Naturally, a hybrid approach would combine both of these methods for capturing and facilitating the user´s likely psychological state.

Table 1. Key factors influencing individual-centric emotional and cognitive effects of technology, adapted from [40].

Layer of technology	Key factors
Physical	**Hardware** - large or small vs. human scale - mobile or immobile - close or far from body (intimate-personal-social distance)
Code	**Interaction** - degree of user vs. system control and proactivity through user interface
	Visual-functional aspects - way of presenting controls in an interface visually and functionally
Content	**Substance** - the essence of the event described - type of substance (factual/imaginary; genre, other) - narrative techniques used by authors

	Form
	1. Modalities
	  - text, video, audio, graphics, animation, etc.
	2. Visual layout
	  - ways of presenting various shapes, colours, font types, groupings and other relationships or expressive properties of visual representations
	  - ways of integrating modalities into the user interface
	3. Structure
	  - ways of presenting modalities, visual layout and other elements of form and their relationships over time
	  - linear and/or non-linear structure (sequential vs. parallel; narrative techniques, hypertextuality)

Table 1 addresses the key factors, which may influence psychological effects of information. For instance, a user may wish to have certain substance of information with as much video material as possible and have the system completely take over the control and present a personalized tv-newscast-type of information flow. Another example would be that the user has a profile that indicates it is beneficial for him to receive information in textual modality and the system may try to alter the information flows presented to him accordingly. It should be noted that the amount of content substance may be important, especially in the case of mobile phones in which the displays are small and the optimal amount of information in preferred form per screen may be smaller than in a pc-environment, for example.

3 Systems for Psychological Customization

Psychological Customization is one possible operationalization of Mind-Based Technologies in system design. It can be applied to various areas of HCI, such as Augmentation Systems, Notification Systems, Affective Computing, Collaborative Filtering, Persuasive Technology and Messaging Systems. It can be hypothesized that the selection and manipulation of substance of information takes place through the technologies of the various application areas of Psychological Customization. Underlying the application areas is a basic technology layer for customizing design. This implies that within some limits one may automatically vary the form of information per a certain category of substance of information. The design space for Psychological Customization is formed in the interaction of a particular application area and the possibilities of the technical implementation of automated design variation [see 44]

The focus of this paper is on mobile multimedia messaging. Even though no actual system has been implemented yet for Psychological Customization related to mobile messaging content presented on small screens, empirical evidence supports the feasibility and validity of this idea.

There are individual differences in cognitive processes such as attention, memory and language abilities. These individual differences have a considerable effect on computer-based performance [e.g. 11]. This suggests the need for Psychological Customization Systems that optimize the presentation of information to different target groups having different psychological profiles. There is considerable evidence in literature that varying the form of information, such as modality, layouts, background colors, text types, emotionality of the message, audio characteristics, presence of image motion and subliminality creates for instance emotional, cognitive and attentional effects [9, 17, 18, 19, 20, 21, 23, 24, 25, 32, 35]. Some of these effects are produced in interaction with individual differences, such as cognitive style, personality, age and gender [16, 31, 32], or pre-existing mood [33]. The role of hardware should not be neglected. A device with a large screen or a portable device with smaller screen with user-changeable covers may also influence the emerging effects [e.g., 21].

To be able to conduct Psychological Customization the system needs a model of the user or users. In fact, customization is always based on some type of model of an individual, a group or a community. These three can be considered separately:

- *user modeling*, which includes a profile of an individual user,
- *group modeling*, which is based on similarities between user profiles and forming a user cluster using some form of automated technique, and
- *community modeling*, which includes a profile of the community as a whole, not as the sum or the average of its individual member's profiles.

A user model is computer-accessible presentation of information about an individual regarding specified domains of use. Both domain-specific (e.g., user preferences concerning the specific application) and domain-independent information (e.g., cognitive skills) should be represented in the user models [8]. Also community modeling, such as collaborative filtering techniques, psychological sense of a community, socio-economic profiles of local communities can be used [6, 43]. Communities are dynamic, but often the user has quite a stable feeling of belonging to her key communities [48]. Most communities also share some type of collective cognition around what they learn from one another's experiences, set common strategies, develop a shared vocabulary, evolve common norms and means, and evolve a distinctive and shared way of thinking [1]. Also, more or less intragroup and intergroup emotional patterns may be present in communities.

The user model can consist of data explicitly given by the user for the purposes of modeling or implicit observations of user's behavior. The personalization can also be based on inferred data about the user that is stored in the user model. For example, based on user behavior, the user can be assigned with some probability to belong to an identified segment. One may also classify users based on their personality, cognitive style and other psychologically relevant factors. The actual personalization is then done on a segment-by-segment basis. User modeling, group modeling and community modeling may be used simultaneously in customization in a hybrid manner [see 44].

4   Application for Emotionally Loaded Mobile Messaging

Emotional and cognitive effects of information are related to communication within social networks as follows: one may manipulate manually or with automated systems the substance and the form of information. It is obvious that in social interaction the users construct the substance of the messages. By varying the design of MMS (Multi Media Service) messages for instance one may be able to create emotional effects in the receivers of the message. This may be called emotionally loaded mobile messaging.

Saari (1998) has introduced the idea of Emotion Media as a type of digital media and computer interfaces that facilitate desired emotions or moods. This approach can be applied also to emotionally loaded mobile messaging. In accordance with particular emotional reactions or moods attention to external stimuli may be increased, memory may be influenced, performance in problem solving may be enhanced and judgment and decision making may be influenced [7, 15, 34]. One may focus on "primitive" emotional responses or emotions requiring more extensive cognitive appraisal and processing. Both of these types of emotions can be linked to various psychological consequences. Consequently, with Emotion Media one may focus on i) creating immediate and primitive emotional responses, ii) creating mood and iii) indirectly influencing secondary effects of emotion and mood, such as attention, memory, performance and judgment. In Table 2 immediate and primitive emotional responses are focused on from the point of view of form factors in MMS-messaging that may facilitate emotions.

Table 2. Possibilities for emotionally loaded mobile multimedia messaging.

Layer of Technology	Mobile Multimedia Messaging	Emotional Possibilities
1. Physical	Small device, larger color screen. Various multimedia capabilities: text, audio, graphics, video etc. Camera, video recorder, audio recorder. Local networking possibilities: infrared, Bluetooth etc. Buttons, voice and pen as inputs.	User changeable covers in colors and shapes that facilitate emotion (such as red)
2. Code	Menu or windows- type of user interface.	Shapes of navigation buttons and background colors and textures may be varied in real-time to facilitate desired emotions.
3. Content		
A. Substance	Fixed multimedia content created by the users.	Creating content that induces emotion, i.e. is generally arousing, funny, depressive etc.
B. Form Modality	Flexible modalities per substance, can be tailored to individual tastes. Text, audio, music video, graphics, photographs and animation may be used.	Modality may be matched to cognitive style or pre-existing mood of the receiver to create a feeling of ease of use and possible positive emotion. Background music, audio effects or ringing tones may be used as a separate modality to facilitate desired emotions and moods. Animated text can be used to create more efficient processing of text and also facilitate some emotional effects.
Visual presentation	Flexible visual presentation of substance, i.e. different layout schemes are quite easy to make and download. Larger color screen.	Emotionally evaluated and positioned layout designs and templates (colors, shapes and textures) may be offered to users.
Structure	Linear text, video, audio, graphics, animation etc.	Offering emotionally evaluated and positioned narrative templates for creating emotionally engaging stories.
Way of interaction and user interface	Flexible ways of interaction based on technological possibilities: pen-based input, speech, hardware and software controls.	Speech input and output may be used to create an intimacy, arousal or calmness or other effects (varying pitch, tone, background music, audio effects etc.) with the device that may facilitate emotions.

In order to a Psychological Customization system to function in emotionally loaded mobile multimedia messaging, the users would need to create a user profile (personality, cognitive style, other information) for the system to gain access to form factors that may create desired cognitive or emotional effects in the users. The users would also fill out a community profile that indicates which users have authority to utilize their profile to send emotionally loaded messages to them and vice versa. The system would need a database of design rules of probable psychological effects of each type of manipulation per type of user and some other functionality. Further, if the system could record the user´s psychological state, this may make the system more reliable by making it possible for the system to more objectively verify the psychological states of the user, such as pre-existing mood. Bluetooth- based networking with a heart rate measurement system worn on the wrist may be one possibility to provide a psychophysiological signal to the system.

Based on Table 2 it may be then said that for emotional effects, the system may offer the sender of messages graphical, video, audio or other types of MMS-templates to use in order to communicate a particular emotion of their own to the receiver or create a desired emotion in the receiver.

The system may automatically suggest for the sender of message a possibility to psychologically customize the message for a particular receiver. The user would select a desired effect, such as creating positive emotion in the receiver with a message in which the substance is written in text and the system would present the sender with ready-made and psychologically evaluated templates (consisting of graphics, animation, sounds, videos etc.) that with high probability may create the desired emotion for the receiver with a particular user profile. The sender would type in the text-message, record an audio message or shoot a video in the template, finalize the design and then send the message. The receiver would receive an emotionally optimised message and may then experience the desired emotion. Naturally, if the substance of the message and the form of the message communicate a different emotion, for instance the substance is hostile and the template is joyful, some effects may not be realized.

If the capture of user´s psychological states with psychophysiological and behavioral methods is realized with future mobile technologies, it may be possible to more objectively capture the effects of a given MMS template on the receiver designed to induce positive emotion, for instance. Such recording technologies would make the system more reliable and allow for fine-tuning of effects and allow the system to learn each individual´s patterns of responses in order to conduct better Psychological Customization over time. Naturally there are various technological challenges related to mobile phones related to such recording such as processor capacity, memory capacity and the non-intrusive integration of sensors into the phone either directly or over local networking with other smart devices. These issues are beyond the scope of this paper. However, it is clear that as mobile phones become more sophisticated, Psychological Customization systems may become more feasible.

5 Conclusion

According to the authors´ knowledge no other comprehensive framework of varying form of information to systematically create emotional and cognitive effects has been presented, specifically in emotionally loaded mobile messaging. Regarding usability studies, there is a growing conviction that, in order to ensure high user satisfaction usability alone is not sufficient [e.g., 10]. Hence, a psychology-based approach to user experience beyond usability, such as psychological customization, may be fruitful.

From the point of view of contribution to the field of computer mediated social interaction, Psychological Customization may provide a framework for creating systems for facilitating desired emotional effects more efficiently with mobile multimedia messaging systems. This may even result in more use of such systems as they become more fun to use. However, it is clear that privacy issues are important in creating user profiles for psychologically intelligent systems, such as giving the system access to one´s cognitive style and personality measures.

Finally, it is clear the validating the likely emotional reactions and moods per form factor per user profile remains a laborious task. It is even more complex in real-life contexts. Hence, it one may concentrate only on some selected application areas, such as facilitating selected emotions and moods with mobile multimedia messaging systems with selected modalities within given social and physical contexts. Further, international collaboration is evidently needed to test the results in different cultures and practices of using mobile multimedia messaging systems.

References

1. Agre, P. E. (1998). Designing Genres for New Media: Social, Economic, and Political Contexts, In Jones, S.G. (ed.) Cybersociety 2.0: Revisiting Computer-Mediated Communication and Community, Thousand Oaks: Sage Publications.
2. Benkler, Y. (2000) From Consumers to Users: Shifting the Deeper Structures of Regulation. Federal Communications Law Journal 52, 561-63.
3. Billmann, D. (1998) Representations. In Bechtel, W. and Graham, G. (1998) A companion to cognitive science, 649-659. Blackwell publishers, Malden, MA.
4. Biocca, F. and Levy, M. (1995) Communication in the age of virtual reality. Lawrence Erlbaum, Hillsdale, NJ.
5. Bödker & K. Kuutti (Eds.), Tradition and Transcendence. Proceedings of The Second Nordic Conference on Human-Computer Interaction, October 19-23, 2002, Arhus, Denmark (Pp. 217 – 220)
6. Chavis, D.M., Hogge, J.H., McMillan, D.W. (1986). Sense of community through Brunswick's lens: a first look. Journal of Community Psychology, No. 14.
7. Clore, G. C. and Gasper, K. (2000). Feeling is believing. Some affective influences on belief. In Frijda, N.H., Manstead, A. S. R. and Bem, S. (Ed.), Emotions and beliefs: How feelings influence thoughts (pp. 10-44). Paris/Cambridge: Editions de la Maison des Sciences de l'Homme and Cambridge University Press.
8. Console, L., Lombardi, G. I., Surano, V. & Torre, I. (2002). Adaptation and personalization on board cars: a framework and its applications to tourist services. P. de Bra, P. Brusilovsky & R. Conejo (Eds.), AH 2002, LCNS 2347, p. 112 – 121. Springer, Berlin.
9. Cuperfain, R. and Clarke, T. K. (1985) A new perspective on subliminal perception. Journal of Advertising, 14, 36-41.
10. Dillon, A. (2001). Beyond usability: process, outcome and affect in human computer interactions. Online: http://www.ischool.utexas.edu/~adillon/ publications/ beyond_ usability.html.
11. Egan, D. E. (1988). Individual differences in human-computer interaction. In: M. Helander (Ed.), Handbook of Human-Computer Interaction, p. 543 – 568. Elsevier, New York.
12. Erickson, T. (1995) Designing agents as if people mattered. In Bradshaw, J. M. (eds.) Software agents, 79-96. AAAI Press/The MIT Press, Menlo Park, CA, Cambridge, MA, London, England.
13. Eysenck, M. (1994) Individual Differences: Normal and Abnormal. New Jersey: Erlbaum.
14. Hampson, S. E. & Colman, A. M. (Eds., 1995) Individual differences and personality. London: Longman.
15. Isen, A. M. (2000). Positive affect and decision making. In Lewis, M. and Haviland-Jones, J. M. (Ed.), Handbook of emotions (2nd ed.) (pp. 417-435). New York: Guilford Press. Kallinen, K. (2001) Speakers versus headphones: preference, valence, arousal and experience of presence in audio PDA news. In Michitaka Hirose (Ed.) Human Computer Interaction INTERACT ' 01, Amsterdam: IOS Press, 805-806.

16. Kallinen, K., & Ravaja, N. (in press). Emotion-related effects of speech rate and rising vs. falling background music melody during audio news: The moderating influence of personality. Personality and Individual Differences.

17. Kihlström, J. F., Barnhardt, T. M. and Tataryn, D. J. (1992) Implicit perception. In Bornstein, R. F. and Pittmann, T. S. (eds.) Perception without awareness. Cognitive, clinical and social perspectives, 17-54. Guilford, New York.

18. Krosnick, J. A. , Betz, A. L., Jussim, J. L. and Lynn, A. R. (1992) Subliminal conditioning of attitudes. Personality and Social Psychology Bulletin, 18, 152-162.

19. Laarni, J. (2003). Effects of color, font type and font style on user preferences. In C. Stephanidis (Ed.) Adjunct Proceedings of HCI International 2003. (Pp. 31-32). Crete University Press, Heraklion.

20. Laarni, J. (2002). Searching for optimal methods of presenting dynamic text on different types of screens. In: O.W. Bertelsen, S.

21. Laarni, J. & Kojo, I.(2001). Reading financial news from PDA and laptop displays. In: M. J. Smith & G. Salvendy (Eds.) Systems, Social and Internationalization Design Aspects of Human-Computer Interaction. Vol. 2 of Proceedings of HCI International 2001. Lawrence Erlbaum, Hillsdale, NJ. (Pp. 109 – 113.)

22. Laarni, J., Kojo, I. & Kärkkäinen, L. (2002). Reading and searching information on small display screens. In: D. de Waard, K. Brookhuis, J. Moraal, & A. Toffetti (Eds.), Human Factors in Transportation, Communication, Health, and the Workplace. (Pp. 505 – 516). Shake, Maastricht. (On the occasion of the Human Factors and Ergonomics Society Europe Chapter Annual Meeting in Turin, Italy, November 2001).

23. Lang, A. (1990) Involuntary attention and physiological arousal evoked by structural features and mild emotion in TV commercials. Communication Research, 17 (3), 275-299.

24. Lang, A., Dhillon, P. and Dong, Q. (1995) Arousal, emotion and memory for television messages. Journal of Broadcasting and Electronic Media, 38, 1-15.

25. Lang, A., Newhagen, J. and Reeves. B. (1996) Negative video as structure: Emotion, attention, capacity and memory. Journal of Broadcasting and Electronic Media, 40, 460-477.

26. Lombard, M. and Ditton, T. (2000) Measuring presence: A literature-based approach to the development of a standardized paper-and-pencil instrument. Project abstract submitted to Presence 2000: The third international workshop on presence.

27. Lombard, M., Reich, R., Grabe, M. E., Bracken, C. and Ditton, T. (2000) Presence and television: The role of screen size. Human Communication Research, 26(1), 75-98.

28. Manovich, L. (2001) The language of new media. The MIT Press, Cambridge, MA, London, England.

29. Ravaja, N. (2004). Effects of a small talking facial image on autonomic activity: The moderating influence of dispositional BIS and BAS sensitivities and emotions. Biological Psychology, 65, 163-183.

30. Ravaja, N. (in press). Contributions of psychophysiology to media research: Review and recommendations. Media Psychology.

31. Ravaja, N., & Kallinen, K. (in press). Emotional effects of startling background music during reading news reports: The moderating influence of dispositional BIS and BAS sensitivities. Scandinavian Journal of Psychology.

32. Ravaja, N., Kallinen, K., Saari, T., & Keltikangas-Järvinen, L. (in press). Suboptimal exposure to facial expressions when viewing video messages from a small screen: Effects on emotion, attention, and memory. Journal of Experimental Psychology: Applied.

33. Ravaja, N., Saari, T., Kallinen, K., & Laarni, J. (2004). The Role of Mood in the Processing of Media Messages from a Small Screen: Effects on Subjective and Physiological Responses. Manuscript submitted for publication.

34. Reeves, B. and Nass, C. (1996) The media equation. How people treat computers, television and new media like real people and places. Cambridge University Press, CSLI, Stanford.
35. Riding, R. J. and Rayner, S. (1998) Cognitive styles and learning strategies. Understanding style differences in learning and behavior. David Fulton Publishers, London.
36. Riecken, D. (2000) Personalized views on personalization. Communications of the ACM, V. 43, 8, 27-28.
37. Saari, T. (1998) Knowledge creation and the production of individual autonomy. How news influences subjective reality. Reports from the department of teacher education in Tampere university. A15/1998.
38. Saari, T. (2001) Mind-Based Media and Communications Technologies. How the Form of Information Influences Felt Meaning. Acta Universitatis Tamperensis 834. Tampere University Press, Tampere 2001.
39. Saari, T. (2002) Designing Mind-Based Media and Communications Technologies. Proceedings of Presence 2002 Conference, Porto, Portugal.
40. Saari, T. (2003a) Designing for Psychological Effects. Towards Mind-Based Media and Communications Technologies. In Harris, D., Duffy, V., Smith, M. and Stephanidis, C. (eds.) Human-Centred Computing: Cognitive, Social and Ergonomic Aspects. Volume 3 of the Proceedings of HCI International 2003, pp. 557-561.
41. Saari, T. (2003b) Mind-Based Media and Communications Technologies. A Framework for producing personalized psychological effects. Proceedings of Human Factors and Ergonomics 2003 -conference. 13.-17.10.2003 Denver, Colorado.
42. Saari, T. and Turpeinen, M. (in press) Towards Psychological Customization of Information for Individuals and Social Groups. In Karat, J. and Karat. M.-C. (eds.) Personalization of User Experiences for eCommerce, Kluwer.
43. Shardanand, U., Maes, P. (1995). Social Information Filtering: Algorithms for Automating "Word of Mouth". Proceedings of CHI'95 Conference on Human Factors in Computing Systems, ACM Press.
44. Turpeinen, M. (2000) Customizing news content for individuals and communities. Acta Polytechnica Scandinavica. Mathematics and computing series no. 103. Helsinki University of Technology, Espoo.
45. Turpeinen, M. and Saari, T. (2004) System Architechture for Psychological Customization of Information. Proceedings of HICSS-37- conference, 5.-8.1. 2004, Hawaii.
46. Vecchi, T., Phillips, L. H. & Cornoldi, C. (2001). Individual differences in visuo-spatial working memory. In: M. Denis, R. H. Logie, C. Cornoldi, M. de Vega, & J. Engelkamp (Eds.), Imagery, language, and visuo-spatial thinking. Psychology Press, Hove.
47. Weitzman, L., Wittenburg, K. (1994) Automatic presentation of multimedia documents using relational grammars. In proceedings of Second ACM International Conference on Multimedia. 15-20 Oct. San Francisco, 443-451.
48. Wenger, E. (1998). Communities of Practice: Learning, Meaning, and Identity. Cambridge University Press, Cambridge, UK

"Why Is Everyone Inside Me?!" Using Shared Displays in Mobile Computer Games

Johan Sanneblad and Lars Erik Holmquist

Viktoria Institute, Hörselgången 4, SE-417 56, Sweden
{johans,leh}@viktoria.se
http://www.viktoria.se

Abstract. We have investigated the use of shared mobile displays to create a new type of computer games for mobile devices – Collaborative Games, which require players to physically coordinate their activities to succeed. Collaborative Games are played on mobile devices connected in wireless networks where users can start, join and leave games ad hoc. In a user study, one of these mobile games was made available in a café frequented by high school students for a period of two weeks. During the test period we noted several new forms of interaction emerging, such as players running away with their displays to avoid other players from accessing them. We also found interesting verbal exchanges, such as the use of "me" to refer to both the user's handheld display and her on-screen representation. We believe that these new ways of interaction is a result of using the shared display in a new domain.

1 Introduction

The use of handheld computers has increased rapidly over the past few years. Initially sold as replacements to pocket calendars, handheld computers are now being used for activities commonly seen on stationary computers, such as playing visually advanced computer games and surfing the web. With the invention of low-power and single-chip Bluetooth and Wireless LAN, wireless interconnectivity is becoming something of a de-facto standard on mobile devices. In fact, most current handheld devices has the ability to wirelessly connect to several other devices within the close proximity, a feature that has been explored in several recent research projects (e.g. proximity-based music sharing systems such as SoundPryer [2] and TunA [3]).

We believe that there are still areas related to the use of handheld computers in wireless ad hoc networks that are relatively unexplored. One such area is the sharing and combination of displays. In contrast to stationary computers, the displays of handheld computers can be moved, paired together, and re-arranged to form larger display areas of various sizes and forms. While some approaches for handheld computers have been made where people are required to *look* at each other's handheld displays to perform an activity (such as Geney [5]), most of them do not explore the possibility of synchronously *controlling* elements on another user's display using the wireless peer-to-peer network. Even though the use of mobile shared displays may seem similar to shared displays in stationary environments (e.g. multiple monitor use

M. Rauterberg (Ed.): ICEC 2004, LNCS 3166, pp. 487–498, 2004.
© IFIP International Federation for Information Processing 2004

[8], or face-to-face consultations [15]), the difference is that handheld computers can be used in any environment, and that users are not restricted by stationary technologies and can move about freely.

Fig. 1. An example of novel interaction triggered by shared display games: one player is running away with a display on which another user's game character resides

In a university course we recently supervised, students were given the assignment to create games for handheld computers that require players to share their displays with each other to advance in the game. The play area in the games was distributed across several screens, and players had to move their in-game character to the other displays to succeed. We call these games *Collaborative Games* since players are required to collaborate with each other to manage the sharing of the displays. We report from a user study where the Collaborative Games were handed out to high school students at a local café. Since our collaborative games use a wireless ad hoc peer-to-peer network with no requirements on infrastructure, we were able to evaluate the system in an environment already familiar with the students. Based on our study, we believe that the use of shared displays in mobile computer games has the potential to introduce new interaction models, which have not been previously explored in literature.

2   Shared Displays

The use of multiple and interconnected displays has previously been explored extensively in literature. While many studies have focused on developing new interaction techniques or designing new models for data sharing, it is only recently that usability studies of *mobile* shared displays has emerged. We believe that our approach with shared displays for Collaborative Games is a novel contribution.

2.1   Shared Displays in Pervasive Environments

One of the first systems for interacting across multiple displays was the *Pick-and-Drop* architecture [13]. Using the Pick-and-Drop interface, a person can "pick up" objects on one display using a pen, and then "drop" them onto another display by tapping with the pen on that display. The system used custom-designed software which connected the computers in a peer-to-peer network. The Pick-and-Drop architecture is asynchronous and only supports events being sent between peers, such as "picking up" and "dropping" objects. The choice of an asynchronous and event-based architecture would make it difficult to extend the platform with applications such as interactive computer games, or controlling events on another display interactively. Pick-and-Drop was thus later evolved into a system for interacting between displays and physical environments, such as described in [14].

One of the key motivations for designing systems with shared displays is to allow several users to interact with the same data set. One example of this is the *DiamondTouch* technique [6], where multiple users interact with the same display using location-dependent modulated electric fields. DiamondTouch is based around one large, front-projected horizontal display where several users can interact simultaneously. Another similar system is the *PointRight* [9] system where several users interact with several displays using a peer-to-peer pointer and keyboard redirection system. The major difference between systems such as these and our Collaborative Games is that users of mobile displays share their own *personal* displays with other users. When a person moves around in the room, so does the display. If people want to interact with objects on the user's display they have to move close to that person so they can see the contents of her display. Other differences are that Collaborative Games does not depend on any infrastructure or custom-designed hardware to operate.

The use of shared displays is often related to the use of multiple displays (as described in [8] or [15]). Technically, systems such as these comprise multiple monitors connected to one personal computer, where the desktop simply spans more than one monitor. With Collaborative Games it is possible to achieve a similar effect using peer-to-peer network technology, but also to provide the opportunity for users to dynamically re-arrange the displays as they see fit. Dynamically re-arranging displays in a stationary environment is more problematic due to cable restrictions and the sheer size of the displays.

2.2 Shared Displays in Mobile Environments

The *Pebbles* project [11] explored how handheld computers can serve as a useful adjunct to stationary computers. One set of applications supported meetings where the participants are co-located. Using the Pebbles software, all participants' PDAs are in continuous two-way communication with each other, and with the main computer. Output from the main computer can be projected on a screen to serve as the focal point of the discussion. The active work area for all users is restricted to that of the stationary PCs. In many cases, Pebbles is similar to systems for shared displays in pervasive environments. The option for peer-to-peer communication using the PDAs hints of a possible potential outside the meeting room. However, the architecture is server-based, and since Pebbles requires the use of actual cables to connect the PDAs to the server, moving about when using the system is very restricted.

An example of a collaborative educational application on handheld computers for children is *Geney* [5]. Here, children can explore genetic concepts through the use of multiple Palm devices and a central personal computer. The game differs from other similar games in that an entire class can play it, collaboratively, using multiple devices. Playing the game, students work together to produce, say, a fish with a particular set of genetics. They accomplish this goal by "beaming" genetic data between devices, producing offspring that comes closer to the end result. Each device only shows the local fish, and to send genetic data between devices students have to "beam" the information by aligning the infrared ports. While Geney might seem similar to our Collaborative Games by using an ad hoc wireless network, Geney differs that it requires an infrastructure for the "registrar" that manages all the clients. Furthermore, Geney does not support synchronous interaction on shared displays.

The closest to our model of shared displays is probably the context-aware game *Pirates!* [4]. This was played on a PDA equipped with a short-range radio and a medium-range Wireless LAN network card. The WLAN connection was used to communicate with the central server. The short-range radios were used to determine position, by detecting other radios in the vicinity (up to a range or 3-5 meters). In this way, devices could both detect when they were close to other players, and when they were close to "islands", which were represented by fixed radio beacons in the physical environment. To accomplish all tasks in the game, players had to travel to different islands by physically visiting them. During play, they could encounter other players and enter into combat with them. While this model frees the players from sitting at a stationary computer encouraging them to encounter each other face-to-face, preliminary user studies showed that most interaction was still being mediated by the screens of the individual players' devices.

3   Collaborative Games

For two years we held a course in software development on mobile devices at a local university. Using our *OpenTrek* platform [17], students were instructed to create games that required people to collaborate to succeed. An important requirement was that the games should not be playable as "normal" multiplayer games in stationary environments, where people use a personal computer and are often not even in the same location. The purpose was to create games that encouraged people to talk to each other while playing. For this reason, ordinary communication channels such as chat windows and voice-over-IP libraries were not allowed.

In each class the students created 12 different games, and after the second year we had a total of 24 games. To encourage people to talk to each other while playing the games, most of the students separated parts of the game interface and placed these parts across the displays of the different devices (c.f. [18]). For instance, in a game called "Earth Defenders", one display was assigned as the "map" device – showing where the players and the enemy ships are located. Other displays were assigned different roles such as "star fighters" and "orbital defense". To succeed in the game, the user with the map display had to look at the displays of the other players to see the status of their health, and if needed coordinate them to a safe place away from battle. The other players in turn had to keep an eye on the map to see where the enemies and other players are.

Every device participating in the game session had a locally stored database that was regularly synchronized with the other devices over a wireless network connection. Players could join any game at any time, at which time the database on their device got synchronized with one of the other devices in the session. In the following we will describe a typical Collaborative Game – Pac-Man Must Die.

3.1   Sample Game: Pac-Man Must Die

Pac-Man Must Die (Figure 2) is a game for two or more players. The game is a "reversal" of the classic arcade-game Pac-Man, which had the main character (Pac-Man) chased by ghosts of different colors. Here, each player instead controls a ghost and must collect "dots", while at the same time avoiding being captured by yellow Pac-Man monsters. To win the game, the player must collect all the dots matching the color of her own ghost. However, some of the dots are located on the displays of other players' devices! The player can enter another person's handheld display by using "doors" at the edges of the map. Each door has a unique color, matching the color of another player's ghost. When a player has entered the display of another computer she has to look at the other user's display to control her ghost.

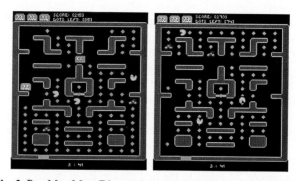

Fig. 2. Pac-Man Must Die running on two displays simultaneously

There are a total of ten different levels in the game, each with a unique layout. Each handheld device represents a unique virtual world to the other devices. If a player joins or leaves the game while others are playing, the colored dots are automatically redistributed across all displays. The game is entirely peer-to-peer, so players can join and leave the game session at any time (upon which the dots are re-distributed across the displays).

4   Collaborative Games in Use

To see how people would respond to and use Collaborative Games, we installed the game Pac-Man Must Die on six HP IPAQ Pocket PCs with Wireless LAN PC-Cards. The handheld computers were handed out to high school students (ages 16-18) at a student café, and no instructions on how to play the game were given. Since the games were designed to encourage people to communicate with each other while playing the game, we recorded everything that was said during the evaluation. For two weeks, two researchers sat at the café, handed out handheld computers, recorded audio and took pictures of the high school students playing the games [10].

Fig. 3. Running away with another player's display

Having transcribed the recordings we filed them into separate sessions, where a session in this case is a game of Pac-Man Must Die where people can join and leave the game ad hoc. The session ends when all players have left the game, one player has collected all her dots, or when the players where unable to collect all dots on all displays before a count-down timer was set to zero.

Below we highlight some of the interactions that took place during the sessions. We chose four categories that we believe represents the novel interactions that have resulted from the use of Collaborative Games: how displays become an active part of the interaction; how users share the display with others; understanding the Collaborative Games application model by example; and verbal definition of virtual places. In the transcripts, P1 refers to the first player, P2 to the second and so on.

4.1 Displays Become an Active Part of the Interaction

In one of the first sessions, four girls were playing the game. The girls had previously played several sessions, and knew how the Collaborative Games application model worked. During this session, the students did not try to coordinate where to stand in order to view each other's displays. They did however at several times make it difficult for each other by not allowing other people to access their displays.

```
[P3] -Asking P1- "Is Myra [P2] over with you?"
[P1] -Showing her display to P3- "Check, check this out!"
[P3] "Ok!!"
[P2] -Not being able to see her character that is residing on P1's
display- "THIS IS NOT FUN AT ALL!"
```

While playing the game, the girls regularly ran away with their displays, effectively preventing other players from playing the game when their ghost was located on that player's display (as shown in Figure 3). In another session with the same four girls, the girls express their issues with the sharing of the displays and how their actions of entering another display with their character could be synchronized.

```
[P1] -Asking P2- "Wait... Can you stand still with your display? Thank
you!" *laughing*
[P3] "Why can't I move?"
[P3] "Now I'm entering a new here..."
[P2] -To P1- "Watch it! I can't see!
```

```
[P1]  -To P3-  "Now I'm going into Jennifer… Give me the display!"
[P3]  *laughing*
[P1]  -To P3-  "Give me the display!"
[P3]  -To P1-  "I'm not giving you any display!"
[P1]  -laughing-
```

Thus, we could see how the physical properties and configurations of the devices became a vital part in playing the game. This is a feature of Collaborative Games interaction model, and is something that is not possible in traditional applications for shared displays.

4.2 Sharing Displays

Each device participating in a session of Pac-Man Must Die is assigned a unique color. The students playing the game did not know beforehand by what color each person was represented in the game – they had to figure this out through trial-and-error and asking each other. Colors are used for two purposes: the first is to indicate which other players have dots left on a person's display, and the second is to show where a player will end up if she enters one of the portals located at the edge of the map (i.e. moves her ghost to another display). Knowing which other players have dots left on one's own device is a strategic advantage, as those players sooner or later must enter that display to finish the game. As the following transcript shows, some of the students did not know each other by name before playing the game.

```
[P1]  "Who is blue?"
[P3]  "It's she!" -Points with her hand on P2-
```

After identities had been established, all players in the sessions seemed to remember what color each person was represented by. Furthermore, players often helped each other out when the player whose color was asked for was too busy to answer, as can be seen in the following transcript from another session:

```
[P1]  "Who is blue, who is blue? Who is BLUE? WHO IS BLUE?! Are you
blue?! Who IS BLUE?!"
[P1]  "Hellooooo, who is bluuuuue!?"
[P3]  "Alexandra!"
[P1]  "Alexandra is blue… And then…" - moves her ghost to Alexandra's
display- "I'm with you now Alexandra!"
```

Players also tried to help each other out when they thought they had mixed up each other's colors.

```
[P2]  "Who's red?"
[P1]  "Julia!"
[P3]  "No, I'm white!"
[P1]  "No, you're not! You are… Who is…" looking at P2's display "You
mean purple!"
```

Sometimes however, helping each other out proved to be not so successful.

```
[P1]  "Who is… Who is… Jennie, what color are you?"
[P3]  "I am pink!"
[P2]  -Answers simultaneously- "Like, the orange…"
[P1]  -Repeating what P2 said- "Like, the orange…"
```

```
[P3]  "But I am pink!"
[P1]  "Aaaaah…"
```

Another aspect of sharing displays is if several people are playing the game and one person suddenly has to leave the game. That happened in one session where two girls were playing and a male student joined the game. Unfortunately the male student had to quickly move on for a class, and both girls were then playing on his display (as seen in figure 4-b). He then simply left the display behind so that the girls could continue playing (Figure 4-c) without disrupting the game session.

Fig. 4. Sharing Displays: In one session two girls were playing where another student joined in. Unfortunately he had to leave early, and since both girls were playing on his display he had to leave it behind

4.3   Understanding the Collaborative Games Application Model

No student received instructions on how to play the game before the evaluation sessions started. Learning how to play the game also implies understanding how the Collaborative Games application model works, since displays have to be shared to complete the game. Students found it difficult to explain to each other how the game worked simply by explaining the rules, as can be seen in the following transcription:

```
[P3]  "Maybe you should begin by explaining how to play?" -laughing-
[P1]  -laughing- "I'm on her track"
[P4]  "Ah, I don't give a damn about that, you have to explain how it
is played first!"
[P1]  "I have tried to explain how it works!"
[P2]  "No, you have not!"
```

We found that students found it easier to teach each other the Collaborative Games application model by showing instead of telling.

```
[P1]  "No-one touches anything! Don't touch anything Alexandra!"
[P2]  -to P4- "Alexandra!"
[P4]  -to P3- "Ok, explain then!"
[P3]  "So I am red ghost Jennie? Taking my red items… But then I see
that I also have green, purple, and blue… And you are those colors…
So when I have taken all that are mine I am entering either the green
portal or…"
[P4]  "What happens if I take yours then?"
[P3]  "Silent! You can't take mine!"
[P4]  "But…?"
[P3]  "No, you can't take mine!"
[P4]  "But I have orange colors here…"
[P3]  "But you can't take them!"
```

```
[P4]  "Umm, ok…"
[P3]  -showing everyone her display- "Then I enter… Then I enter a
portal… I am entering the blue… Green! Or blue! I am entering yours!"
[P2]  "Can you enter the portals at any time?"
[P1]  "Yeah"
[P3]  -to P4- "Then I have to watch your display!"
[P4]  "Aha, and the one that gets… And since you got me with all your
items you won?"
[P3]  "Mmm… Mmm…"
[P3]  "You basically enter each other."
[P5]  "Now I want to try! Now that I have seen how it is done!"
```

Thus, despite this being a new interaction model, it seemed that the subjects of the study quickly caught on to the concept, even without any instructions.

4.4 Who Am I?

When playing the game, each player has to move their ghost to other people's displays to finish the game. During the sessions, players most of the time referred to the displays as the person using the display. Since both their devices and their virtual character in the game were referred to as "I", in some occurrences this caused some rather odd exclamations, such as when four players simultaneously were playing on one girl's display:

```
[P4]  "Why is everyone inside me?!"
```

In all sessions, most of the students new to the game referred to the physical device or display when talking with other players ("I am entering yours"). However, experienced players (who had played several sessions) and some of the new players always referred to the display as "he", "you", or "someone". Transferring the player's ghost to another display was always referred to as "coming over to you" and "coming in to you" by experienced players, which is exemplified below:

```
[P3]  "Who's green then?"
[P1]  "I am!"
[P3]  "Ok, then I'm coming over to you!"
[P1]  "Ah, ok… Now stay here…"
[P2]  *laughing* "But where am I coming then?"
[P3]  "But he's upside-down?"
[P1]  "Ah, it was my fault …"
[P2]  "Where am I?"
[P5]  "Eeeee… I don't know where you are …" … "Damn… Now I am inside
someone else …"
[P3]  "You're with me… Hang on a moment…"
```

Closely integrating a personal display with game mechanics has been previously explored (such as in Pirates! [4]). The difference with our approach is that the player provides an always "open door" to other players where they can use the display of that person any time, and it is up to the player using the display to allow that or not.

5   Discussion

Evaluating our Collaborative Games at the students' own local café probably had an impact of the results of the study. If we had setup a custom environment at a trade show or a conference to get feedback on the games, not only would most of the people evaluating the games not have know each other beforehand, they would also be limited in the way they could move around while playing the game (since we naturally would not want anyone to run away far with our handheld computers). We do not believe that evaluating the games this way had a negative impact on our results – in fact our choice of environment was based on how we believe Collaborative Games would be played if they were bundled with an off-the-shelf hardware device. We will now discuss some topics related to the evaluation: the use of ad hoc peer to peer networks in the study, the use of "I" when the students were relating to their devices and some of the issues related to knowing what person is using what device.

The Collaborative Games were all designed as peer-to-peer applications for ad hoc wireless network connections. Thanks to our OpenTrek platform [17], this has the effect that games can be played simply by turning on two devices and choosing what game to start and what people to play with on one device, and the game is then started automatically on all other devices, similar to Instant Messaging [7]. The ease-of-use and lack of infrastructure requirements made it possible for the students to move about freely when playing the games. While many systems for distributed and decentralized data sharing has been presented previously (such as Rendezvous [12] and GroupKit [16]) most of these systems are not applicable to the mobile realm since they still depend on central coordination to operate.

The students playing the game Pac-Man Must Die! often referred to their character in the game as "I" (e.g. "Ok, then I'm coming over to you!"). Using the Collaborative Games application model, each device had its own, unique labyrinth on the display. During play, this labyrinth also came to represent oneself, as expressed by one student "Why is everyone inside me?!" This apparent "personal connection" between the ghost, the device, the labyrinth and the player may have been strengthened due to the use of the Collaborative Games application model. By simply walking away with the PDA, a player is able to physically relocate the map as well as the representations of all other players in the room and on the same map in one simple movement.

When sharing the displays, the students needed to know what person was responsible for each device. Representing players by colors instead of names was chosen simply because we wanted the game to be playable if the people did not know each other beforehand. As seen in the evaluation, the connection between a color and a person required much verbal communication between the players. In other studies of recreational activities, unnecessary "coordination talk" between people who already knew each other well was not considered to be a positive thing [1]. In our case the need to communicate served as an "ice breaker" which forced people to talk to each other even if they did not beforehand know each other. With the new camera-enabled PDAs and phones that are now becoming available, it will be possible to begin each game session with the students taking pictures of themselves and allowing this picture to represent them in the game. While it would solve the question of what display was represented by what person, some of the communication between the players might also be lost at the same time: "Who is blue?" – "It's she!"

6   Implementation

We will now briefly describe some implementation details. All Collaborative Games were developed and tested on HP IPAQ Pocket PC devices with Wireless LAN expansion cards. These devices feature a large display and several input channels, such as button presses, pen input, and audio input. The provision for attaching a standard W-LAN card makes them well suited for prototyping of networked applications.

All games were written in C++ using two of our software platforms: *GapiDraw* and *OpenTrek*. GapiDraw (www.gapidraw.com) is a graphics toolkit for fast graphics, originally for PocketPC devices. It has now been extended to also support devices such as Palm and Symbian devices, and is today the most widely used graphics SDK for handheld computers and smartphones. Using GapiDraw, it is possible to create fast graphics on handheld computers without considering the differences between different graphics hardware implementations.

A complementary platform, OpenTrek [17] is primarily intended to assist the development of multiplayer networked games on handheld devices. Creating peer-to-peer networking applications for handheld computers can be difficult, since there are many hardware issues to consider. One example is limited network buffers, which require the developer to write meticulously timed programs with multiple threads managing incoming and outgoing network queues on the device. Developers also have to consider issues such as broadcasting information to other devices, forming game sessions on the wireless network, and showing the user what other people have their devices switched on. OpenTrek is specifically designed to abstract issues such as these.

7   Conclusions and Future Work

We have presented results from the use of Collaborative Games – computer games for mobile devices that require players to coordinate their activities physically. Based on the results from using the Collaborative Game Pac-Man Must Die!, we argue that Collaborative Games has the potential to introduce new forms of interaction between people. In times when almost every handheld device is equipped with some wireless connection (Wireless LAN or Bluetooth) we believe that the Collaborative Games interaction model may have significant impact on future mobile applications.

Future work involves exploring the use of different devices and different wireless connections, to enable the use of Collaborative Games on other devices than PDAs. We already have most of the games running on Smartphones, and we are in the process of creating network protocols that can be used for Bluetooth connections. We are also planning a more long-term study with several games involved, where different groups of people will be able to use the games in various situations and environments.

Acknowledgements. This project was financed by the Swedish Foundation for Strategic Research in the Mobile Services project. We would like to thank all our students who created all these fantastic games in such a short time frame. "Pac-Man" is a registered trademark of Namco, Inc.

References

1. Aoki, P. M., Grinter, R. E., Hurst, A., Szymanski, M. H., Thornton, J. D. and Woodruff, A., Sotto Voce: Exploring the Interplay of Conversation and Mobile Audio Spaces, in Proceedings of CHI 2002, Mineeapolis, USA.
2. Axelsson, F., Östergren, M., SoundPryer: Joint Music Listening on the Road, in Adjunct Proceedings of Ubicomp 2002, Göteborg, Sweden.
3. Bassoli, A., Cullinan, C., Moore, J., and Agamanolis, S., TunA: a Mobile Music Experience to Foster Local Interactions (poster), in Adjunct Proceedings of UbiComp 2003, Seattle, USA.
4. Björk, S., Falk, J., Hansson, R., Ljungstrand, P., Pirates! – Using the Physical World as a Game Board, in Proceedings of Interact 2001, Tokyo, Japan.
5. Danesh, A., Inkpen, K., Lau, F., Shu, K., Booth, K., Geney: Designing a Collaborative Activity for the Palm Handheld Computer, in Proceedings of CHI 2001, Minneapolis, USA.
6. Dietz, P. and Leigh, D., DiamondTouch: a multi-user touch technology, in Proceedings of UIST 2001, Orlando, USA.
7. Grinter, R. E., Palen, L., I M everywhere: Instant messaging in teen life, in Proceedings of CSCW 2002, New Orleans, USA.
8. Grudin, J., Partitioning digital worlds: focal and peripheral awareness in multiple monitor use, in Proceedings of CHI 2001, Minneapolis, USA.
9. Johanson, B., Hutchins, G., Winograd, T., Stone, M., PointRight: Experience with Flexible Input Redirection in Interactive Workspaces, in Proceedings of UIST 2002, Paris, France.
10. Larsson, J. and Skårman, J., Collaborative Games - Makes People Talk, M. Sc. Thesis in Informatics, University of Gothenburg, Sweden.
11. Myers, B. A., Stiel, H., Gargiulo, R., Collaboration Using Multiple PDAs Connected to a PC, in Proceedings of CSCW 1998, Seattle, USA.
12. Patterson, J. F., Meeks, W. S., Rendezvous: An Architecture for Synchronous Multi-User Applications, in Proceedings of CHI 1990, Seattle, USA.
13. Rekimoto, J., Pick-and-Drop: A Direct Manipulation Technique for Multiple Computer Environments, in Proceedings of UIST 1997, Banff, Canada.
14. Rekimoto, J., A Multiple Device Approach for Supporting Whiteboard-based Interactions, in Proceedings of CHI 1998, Los Angeles, USA.
15. Rodden, T., Rogers, Y., Halloran J., and Taylor, I., Designing Novel Interactional Workspaces to Support Face to Face Consultations, in Proceedings of CHI 2003, Ft. Lauderdale, USA.
16. Roseman, M. and Greenberg, S., Building Real-Time Groupware with GroupKit, A Groupware Toolkit, in Proceedings of CHI 1996, Vancouver, Canada.
17. Sanneblad, J. and Holmquist, L. E., OpenTrek: A Platform for Developing Interactive Networked Games on Mobile Devices, in Proceedings of Mobile HCI 2003, Udine, Italy.
18. Sanneblad, J. and Holmquist, L. E., Designing Collaborative Games on Handheld Computers, in Applications and Sketches Program, SIGGRAPH 2003, San Diego, USA.

Associated Emotion and Its Expression in an Entertainment Robot QRIO

Fumihide Tanaka[1], Kuniaki Noda[1], Tsutomu Sawada[2], and Masahiro Fujita[1,2]

[1] Life Dynamics Laboratory Preparatory Office, Sony Corporation, Tokyo, Japan
{boom, noda, mfujita}@pdp.crl.sony.co.jp
[2] Information Technologies Laboratories, Sony Corporation, Tokyo, Japan
tsawada@pdp.crl.sony.co.jp

Abstract. We human associate and memorize situations with emotional feelings at the time, and these experiences affect our daily behaviors. In this paper, we will present our attempt to design this character in an entertainment robot QRIO aiming for more genuine Human-Robot interaction.

1 Introduction

We consider that entertainment robots have broad potentials for making our life further enjoyable, and have developed several products and applications. After releasing AIBO [1], a pet-type quadruped robot, we also have been started a biped humanoid-type one QRIO [2,3,4] for years increasing its wide range of abilities. Among these manifold directions, we focus our target in this paper to the interaction domain between a human and a robot, especially in topics around emotion [5,6] as we consider it as an important factor realizing entertainment applications for humans. We set three issues: *"Realizing personalized interaction"*, *"Experience records dependency"*, and *"Clear expression of robotic emotions"*. First, to realize personalized interaction between a person and a robot, the latter should be able to recognize the former as an individual, and alter its behavior respectively. QRIO can recognize and identify humans by using its sensory information such as vision and audio [2], and this ability plays an important role here also. Secondly, the interaction process continues through our daily life, and therefore the robot should be able to accumulate experiences in its memories for affecting not only its behaviors but also emotions. This is one central point in this paper. As will be presented in Section 3 and 4, QRIO can associate the variation of its internal value variables with corresponding situation, and update its memories by accumulating many of the experience. This device makes it possible to create such kinds of behavior like *trauma*: just seeing an object scares QRIO, as there were dangerous experiences before about it. Finally, besides these abilities, the robot should be able to exhibit or express its emotions in clear ways. By exploiting its rich motion control system, we implemented above ideas to QRIO with vivid behaviors, which will be described in Section 5.

M. Rauterberg (Ed.): ICEC 2004, LNCS 3166, pp. 499–504, 2004.
© IFIP International Federation for Information Processing 2004

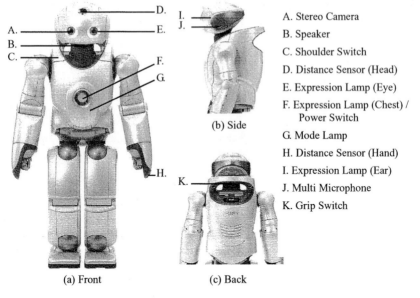

A. Stereo Camera

B. Speaker

C. Shoulder Switch

D. Distance Sensor (Head)

E. Expression Lamp (Eye)

F. Expression Lamp (Chest) /
    Power Switch

G. Mode Lamp

H. Distance Sensor (Hand)

I. Expression Lamp (Ear)

J. Multi Microphone

K. Grip Switch

(a) Front   (b) Side   (c) Back

Fig. 1. Appearance of QRIO

2   QRIO: A Small Biped Entertainment Robot

Fig. 1. illustrates the appearance of QRIO. It is a stand-alone autonomous robot interacting with people and the environment with various abilities: walking, running, dancing, singing songs, playing soccer, throwing a ball, making conversation, and so on. Please refer to [2,3,4] for more details about its specification and abilities.

3   Software Components in EGO Architecture

In this section, a brief overview of software components inside QRIO is presented (Fig. 2.). As a basic behavior and motion control architecture, we adopt the EGO (Emotionally GrOunded) architecture [7]. The main strategy of it is an ethological model [8,9]. Behavior control is based on homeostasis where a robot selects its behaviors to regulate and maintain its internal state within a certain acceptable range.

Perception part corrects all the input information from outside environment and inside QRIO by using various sensors. Some parts of it are processed by several recognition engines such as face recognition (FR) and general object recognition (OBJR). Memory part consists of the short-term memory (STM) and the long-term memory (LTM). STM integrates the results of perception in many ways. For example, it receives not only speech recognition results but also the sound source direction. LTM and Internal model part (DIA, ISM, and EMG) will be explained in the next section. Behavior and motion control part consists of the situated behavior layer (SBL) and the motion controller (MC). SBL [10] has multiple behavior modules and determines QRIO's actions processed by MC. Details in above are outside scope of this paper, and please refer to other literature [10] for more rich description.

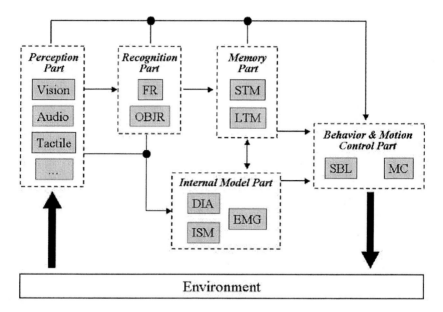

Fig. 2. Overview of the EGO Architecture

4   Emotion-Grounding in Internal Model Part

Internal model part (Fig. 2, 3.) takes charge of QRIO's internal states and emotions. Internal state model (ISM) maintains the former variables: HUNGER, FULLNESS, PAIN, COMFORT, FATIGUE, and SLEEPINESS [11]. They are varied with the passage of time and external stimuli such as "face detection". Some of the variables relate also to internal information like "battery volume" or "temperature".

Delta-Internal value associator (DIA) associates the variation of the internal state variables with the current situation that is composed of outputs from perception and recognition parts. When a variation (above a threshold) happens in ISM, it sends the variation (of the internal state variables) vector to DIA. Then DIA associates it with current outputs from FR, OBJR (and any other perceptual data). The association can be implemented by any function approximation systems like an artificial neural network or just a simple rule base that is stored at the long-term memory (LTM). After several learning (association) experiences, DIA can remind the variation of the internal state variables just seeing the corresponding person or object or both. Emotion generator (EMG) contains emotion model that is composed of 6+1 emotions: JOY, SADNESS, ANGER, SURPRISE, DISGUST, FEAR and NEUTRAL. Each emotion has an associated value that is determined based on the self-preservation values, SELF_CRISIS and SELF_CRISIS_EXPECTATION that in turn are calculated by values of ISM (and their variation vector from DIA in case there is).

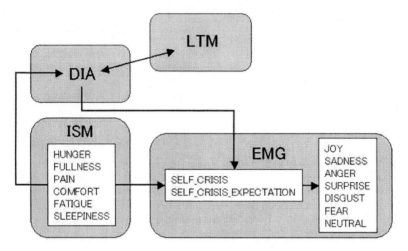

Fig. 3. Overview of the Internal Model Part

5 Expression of Associated Emotion

We applied above ideas to QRIO interacting with human. The far left in Fig. 4. plots a typical transition of emotion values (only NEUTRAL and FEAR are shown here) with time increases. A person comes and he twisted QRIO's hand (the 2nd picture). Observing his face, the ISM value PAIN stands up, and it leads up to increasing the value of FEAR at t=31. DIA learns the association between the face and the PAIN variation at the same time, updating LTM. After that, the person goes away and the value of FEAR decreases gradually. Then, he comes again in front of QRIO. DIA calculates the associated variation consulting LTM, and the value of FEAR is again stands up even without twisting hands at t=145. This change comes down to the behavior and motion control part, and QRIO expresses the gesture and voice of FEAR (the 3rd picture). We can also test continuous facial change in CG (the far right one).

Fig. 4. Association of PAIN and expression of FEAR

Fig. 5. Association of COMFORT and expression of JOY

Another person comes (the far left in Fig. 5.) stroking QRIO's head with chocolate in his hand. This time, COMFORT value increases (by the stroking) recognizing his face and the chocolate. This association is learned by DIA using a neural network stored at LTM. Thanks to its generalization property, here QRIO can remind the COMFORT variation and express the motion and voice of JOY in case not only showing the face and the chocolate (the 2nd picture) but also just the face (the 3rd one).

6 Conclusions

We are trying to develop entertainment robots for human in daily life. To this end, it is important for the robot to be able to identify himself with human, and vice versa. Associated emotion, that is, the one that is associated with the robot's situation at the time can be implemented by using the internal model presented in this paper. Emotion expression is another crucial ability, and we let QRIO do it by exploiting its powerful behavior control system. Regarding face expression [12], we will consider every technology after much debate for realizing further genuine interaction.

References

1. Fujita, M., Kitano, H.: Development of a Quadruped Robot for Robot Entertainment. Autonomous Robots, Vol.5, Kluwer Academic (1998) 7-18
2. Fujita, M., and et al.: SDR-4X II: A Small Humanoid as an Entertainer in Home Environment. Int. Symposium of Robotics Research (2003)
3. Ishida, T., and et al.: Development of Mechanical System for a Small Biped Entertainment Robot. IEEE Int. Workshop on Robot and Human Interactive Communication (2003)
4. Kuroki, Y., and et al.: A Small Biped Entertainment Robot Exploring Human-Robot Interactive Applications. IEEE Int. Workshop on Robot and Human Interactive Communication (2003)
5. Ogata, T., Sugano, S.: Consideration of Emotion Model and Primitive Language of Robots. In: Kitamura, T. (eds.): What Should be Computed to Understand and Model Brain Function?, World Scientific (2001)
6. Breazeal, C.: Designing Socialable Robots. MIT Press (2002)
7. Fujita, M., and et al.: Autonomous Behavior Control Architecture of Entertainment Humanoid Robot SDR-4X. IEEE/RSJ Int. Conf. on Intelligent Robots and Systems (2003)
8. Lorenz, K.: The Foundations of Ethology. Springer-Verlag (1981)

9.   Arkin, R., and et al.: Ethological and Emotional Basis for Human-Robot Interaction. Robotics and Autonomous System, Vol.42, Elsevier (2003) 191-201
10. Sawada, T., Takagi, T., Fujita, M.: Behavior Selection and Motion Modulation in Emotionally Grounded Architecture for QRIO SDR-4X II. IEEE/RSJ Int. Conf. on Intelligent Robots and Systems (2004, submitted)
11. Ekman, P., Davidson, R.J.: The Nature of Emotion. Oxford University Press (1994)
12. Takanishi, A.: An Anthropomorphic Robot Head having Autonomous Facial Expression Function for Natural Communication with Human. Int. Symposium of Robotics Research (1999)

Position-Aware IEEE 802.11b Mobile Video Services

Rafael Asorey-Cacheda[1], Francisco J. González-Castaño[1],
Enrique Costa-Montenegro[1], Ignacio López-Cabido[2], Andrés Gómez-Tato[2],
and José Carlos Pérez-Gómez[2]

[1]Departamento de Ingeniería Telemática, Universidad de Vigo,
ETSI Telecomunicación, Campus, 36280 Vigo, Spain
phone: +34 986 813788, fax: +34 986 812116
{rasorey, javier, kike}@det.uvigo.es
[2]Centro de Supercomputación de Galicia (CESGA),
Campus Sur, Avda. de Vigo s/n, 15705 Santiago de Compostela, Spain
phone: +34 981 569810, fax: +34 981 594616
{nlopez, agomez, jcarlos}@cesga.es

Abstract. In this paper, we present an experimental position-aware IEEE 802.11b mobile video service[1]. For example, it may be used to deliver TV channels to PDAs in airport terminals. Instead of implementing progressive encoding -which increases content bandwidth- we rely on transcoding rate adaptation to support position-awareness.

1 Introduction

The advent of IEEE 802.11 [1] has brought new services that rely on user mobility. In [2], we proposed a real-time DVB-S-to-IEEE 802.11b transcoding system to generate video contents for mobile networks. We also implemented and evaluated an indoor video service to deliver transcoded contents to wireless Pocket PCs via IEEE 802.11b multicast. In [3], we extended the system in [2] to support QoS and inter-LAN roaming. Multicast channel scheduling has been studied in the past [4, 5]. However, previous results are not directly applicable to IEEE 802.11b. For a given packet slot length, IEEE 802.11b modulation bitrate depends on user position (1, 2, 5.5 or 11 Mbps, *dynamic rate shifting*). This has interesting implications from the point of view of content channel rate. For example, transmitting a 1-Mbps stream at 1-Mbps bitrate requires 100% of access point (AP) bandwidth. However, a 1-Mbps stream at 11-Mbps bitrate only requires 10% of AP bandwidth, leaving room for more streams. Thus, content servers must set the fastest transfer rate possible for a given content channel rate, as far as user location admits it, or they must lower content channel rate to keep the number of content channels that fit into the service.

Previous research has focused on progressive encoding schemes (such as MPEG-4 FGS) that guarantee data validity regardless of terminal SNR (which depends on user location) [4, 6]. However, regarding bandwidth usage, progressive encoding is less efficient than fixed encoding, and it has been argued that it is not necessary to support most wireless applications [7].

---

[1] This research has been supported by project WIPv6 (CESGA, Spain).

M. Rauterberg (Ed.): ICEC 2004, LNCS 3166, pp. 505–508, 2004.
© IFIP International Federation for Information Processing 2004

2   Position-Aware IEEE 802.11b Mobile Services

Position-aware content channel scheduling:
1. If a user requests a content channel that is being transmitted at rate X and that rate is feasible at the user location, the user joins the multicast group of the content channel.
2. If the content channel is not being transmitted and there exists free bandwidth available, the server starts a new multicast group for that content channel. Let n_{AP} be the number of content channels the AP serves and let K be content channel rate (set for subjective quality). When a user in the X-Mbps region requests the content channel, there exists free space in the AP if $\gamma X/(1+n_{AP})$ K, where γ is the percentage of PCF mode time.
3. If there is no free space available, the server looks for an active content channel transmitted at the lowest rate $Y \le X$, sends a termination message to the users receiving that content channel and assigns it to the incoming request. Terminated demands re-enter the scheduling algorithm.
4. Finally, if it is not possible to find a content channel to terminate, the incoming request is blocked and leaves the system. Consequently, the *service planning goal* is to attain a negligible blocking probability.

We simulated a service scenario with 10 content channels, with independent demands requesting channels following a Zipf distribution with $\alpha=0.6$ [8]. Content channel bandwidth K is 500 Kbps [2] (multicast IEEE 802.11b, UDP, 1-KB data packets with 85 B PLCP+MAC+IP+UDP overhead) and $\gamma=90\%$. Content channel watching times are exponentially distributed with mean $\mu=5$ min. We determined the range of each IEEE 802.11b modulation from real measurements in open space. Requests come from user positions uniformly distributed within AP range (0-170 m). In these conditions, blocking probability is negligible regardless of system load if the minimum bitrate in the service scenario is 2 Mbps (e.g. by installing additional APs with non-overlapping bands to avoid the 1-Mbps modulation).

Prototype: Figure 1 shows the architecture of our prototype. The *server* is a PIII (800 MHz, 512 MB RAM) with Debian GNU/Linux 3.0 kernel v2.4.18. The PIII and two APs in non-overlapping bands (a D-Link DI-614+ and a D-Link DWL-1000AP, not shown) belong to the same Fast Ethernet LAN. A *stream server* generates "internal" UDP streams from the MPEG-2 TV channels captured by a Fujitsu-Siemens Activy 300 DVB SAT PCI board [9]. The *transcoder* process serves content channels at UDP sockets at rates depending on user position [10].

The *client* runs on a PIV notebook (2.6 GHz, 512 MB RAM) with Debian GNU/Linux 3.0 kernel v. 2.6.1. A *bitrate controller* monitors the modulation/bitrate of a D-Link DWL-650 PCMCIA IEEE 802.11b card [11]. Whenever the modulation changes (due to user movement within AP range or between APs), the client notifies this event to a *bandwidth controller* at the server via TCP signalling. *If necessary*, the transcoder changes content channel rate accordingly. Finally, the client displays transcoded UDP streams on a *vlc media player 0.7.2* screen [12] (Figure 2).

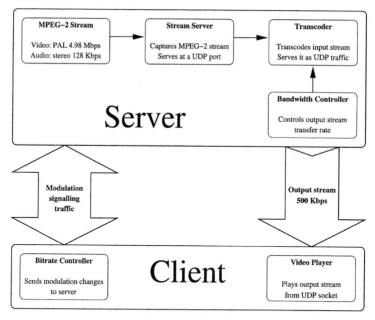

Fig. 1. Prototype

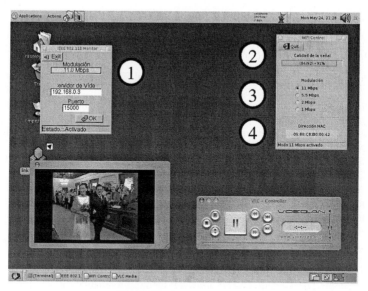

Fig. 2. Demonstrator screen

Figure 2 shows the demonstrator screen. It monitors (1) AP modulation bitrate, (2) wireless card signal quality, (3) wireless card modulation bitrate and (4) AP MAC address (for roaming tests). We performed several modulation change/roaming tests. For this purpose, we placed both APs at the same indoor location, and set a connection between the wireless card and the DWL-1000AP in the vicinity of that location -obviously, the server adapted content channel rate to a 11 Mbps modulation bitrate-. Then, we started moving away until we reached AP range overlapping boundary (the DI-614+ reaches a longer distance). At that point, the wireless card established a new connection with the DI-614+ at 5.5 Mbps modulation bitrate. As a result, flawlessly, the client roamed between APs and the server adapted content channel rate.

3 Conclusions and Future Work

In this paper, we have presented an experimental position-aware IEEE 802.11b mobile video system, as a continuation of the research in [2, 3]. For example, it may be used to deliver TV channels to PDAs in airport terminals. Instead of implementing progressive encoding -which increases content bandwidth- we rely on transcoding rate adaptation to support position-awareness. Future work is oriented towards *optimal* scheduling algorithms to minimize system resources (AP geographical density).

References

1. IEEE 802.11. [Online]. Available: http://grouper.ieee.org/groups/802/11/
2. R. Asorey-Cacheda, F.J. González-Castaño, "Real-Time Transcoding and Video Distribution in IEEE 802.11b Multicast Networks," in Proc. IEEE ISCC'03, 2003.
3. F.J. González-Castaño, R. Asorey-Cacheda et al, "QoS provisioning in mobile video services with satellite sources," in Proc. International Workshop of Cost Actions 272 and 280, ESTEC, The Netherlands, May 2003.
4. A. Majundar et al, "Multicast and unicast real-time video streaming over wireless LANs," IEEE Trans. on Circuits and Systems for Video Technology, June 2002.
5. J. Karvo, A study of teletraffic problems in multicast networks. Technical Report, Networking Laboratory / Helsinki University of Technology, Oct. 2002.
6. W. Li, "Overview of fine granularity scalability in MPEG-4 video standard," IEEE Trans. on Circuits and Systems for Video Technology, Mar. 2001.
7. T. Stockhammer, "Is fine-granular scalable video coding beneficial for wireless video applications?," in Proc. IEEE ICME'03, 2003.
8. L. Breslau, P. Cao, L. Fan, G. Phillips and S. Shenker, "Web caching and Zipf-like distributions: Evidence and implications," in Proc. INFOCOM'99, 1999.
9. dvbstream 0.4pre1 development software [Online]. Available: http://www.linuxstb.org.
10. ffmpeg cvs-2004-04-06 development software [Online]. Available: http://www.ffmpeg.org.
11. wireless tools 27pre18 development software [Online]. Available: http://packages.debian.org.
12. vlc media player 0.7.2 [Online]. Available: http://www.videolan.org.

A Human-Pet Interactive Entertainment System over the Internet

Lee Shang Ping, Farzam Farbiz, and Adrian David Cheok

Mixed Reality Research Laboratory, Department of Electrical & Computer Engineering,
National University of Singapore, 4 Engineering Drive 3, Singapore 117576
{eleleesp, eleff, eleadc}@nus.edu.sg

Abstract. We developed an interactive entertainment system for human and pet over the Internet. The system consists of a Backyard and an Office. The Backyard houses a rooster (the pet) and cameras which capture the movement of the rooster. The rooster wears a small wearable-computer dress equipped with vibrators and wireless camera. The Office has a mechanical positioning system which carries a doll, resembling the rooster. Inside the doll are touch-sensitive sensors. Both spaces are interconnected only by Internet. As the rooster walks, the doll is moved by the positioning system, imitating the path taken by the rooster. At the same time if the human at the Office fondles the doll, the rooster feels the tickling as the vibrators are activated. The video images of the Backyard and that as seen by the rooster, are constantly sent to the Office display.

1 Introduction

In days gone by most people lived on the land, or were hunter-gatherers, or nomads. People would spend many hours with their animal friends and helpers. For example, cowboys and their dogs on the prairie, aborigines hunting with dingoes in Australia, and Asian villagers keeping chickens in their homes. Pets not only bring warmness, but also provide entertainment to our family, such as those cats, dogs and hamsters in the *Planet's Funniest Animals* television show. However, in our modern, global city age people are too busy to spend time with their pets. This is part of the phenomenon of modern life, where people are getting farther from each other and from nature as well. Society's uncontrolled development results in modern human's feeling isolated and lonely and lacking a sense of value. Nowadays, one of the few things that bring warmness to our hearts and home are pets. They are the symbol of the nature with absolutely non-machinery behaviors. We can express our kindness feelings by fondling them and they can be used in human therapy setting to teach new skills or to reduce maladaptive behaviors. Thus in our modern lives, we need a mechanism to feel the presence and entertainment with our pets, no matter where we are, on work or business.

However while at work or having holidays aboard we are not able to bring our pets along. We need a solution that allows us to express our feeling to the pet in a tangible, entertaining manner. There are several possible approaches, such as using 2D video

M. Rauterberg (Ed.): ICEC 2004, LNCS 3166, pp. 509–512, 2004.
© IFIP International Federation for Information Processing 2004

monitoring, or 3D of 3D-Live augmented reality. But these are not interactive and lack the sense of entertaining.

We proposed and developed a system for human and pet that is both interactive and entertaining. The system consists of two sub-systems, namely Backyard and Office system. The Backyard is where the pet (a live rooster) resides, and the Office is a remote location where the human (pet owner) is. Both sub-systems are interconnected only by the Internet. Figure 1 illustrates the picture of the overall system.

The motion of the rooster is captured by a webcam, and is constantly tracked by the image processing algorithm in a Backyard computer. This information is constantly sent to the remote Office via Internet. In the Office, there is a mechanical X-Y positioning system which carries a doll. The doll is an avatar of the real rooster, and it is moved by the positioning system, following the path of the rooster in the Backyard. While the position information is sent to the Office constantly, the video images of the rooster and its view point (the rooster has a wireless camera mounted on its head) are sent to the Office at the same time. The rooster wears a small wearable-computer dress equipped with the wireless camera transmitter and small vibration motors.

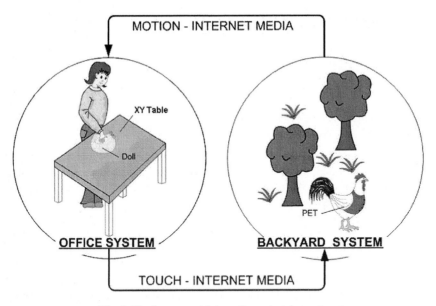

Fig. 1. The human-pet interactive entertainment system

The inside body of the doll is embedded with touch-sensitive sensors and wireless transmitter. As the pet owner touches the doll, the sensors sense the action and the wireless transmitter sends this 'touch information' to a computer. This is then sent via the Internet to the Backyard.

2   Technical Details

2.1   The Doll

The Office mainly comprises the doll and the mechanical positioning system. Figure 2a shows the doll and the touch-sensitive sensors, wireless transmitter, microcontroller board and a battery. The sensors project sense field through any dielectric glass, plastic, stone, ceramic and wood. It is designed specifically for human interfaces. The microcontroller reads the sense data and sends it through the wireless transmitter.

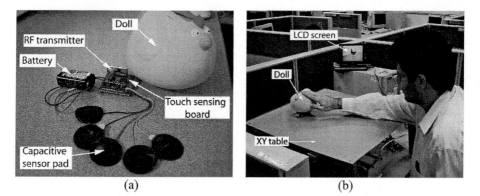

(a)   (b)

Fig. 2. (a) The doll with touch-sensitive sensors and wireless transmitter. All the devices are hidden inside the body of the doll. (b) A visitor playing with the doll in the Office. The doll is moved by the X-Y positioning system under the table. Together with the LCD screen our system provides total human-pet entertainment2.2   X-Y Sub-system

To move the doll on the table we designed and implemented a X-Y positioning system using two stepper motors for movements in X and Y direction and also one stepper motor for the rotation of the doll. These data are calculated based on the rooster motion in the backyard by computer vision tracking algorithm.

2.2   Wearable-Computer Pet Dress

The purpose of having pet dress is to make a system that receives touch information coming form the Office through the Internet and then transfer it to the rooster. The Office mainly comprises the doll and the mechanical positioning system. Figure 3 shows the rooster wearing the wearable-computer pet dress.

2.3   Video Streaming

As mentioned in Section 1, a webcam is used to capture the movement of the rooster. This video image is sent in real time to the Office and display in a small LCD. Also a small wireless camera is attached to the forehead of the rooster, and its view is also sent to the office. In this way we have a visual entertaining effect, in addition to the physical sense of rooster moving on the positioning system.

(a)   (b)

Fig. 3. (a) The rooster wearing the pet dress. (b) A fluffy toy chicken sitting on a Lego toy car; the vibrators and electronic devices are on the toy chicken and the pet dress on the floor

3   Experience

We set up the demonstration in our laboratory for a year-long demonstration. For the purposes of the conference demonstration we will show the demo using a fluffy toy chicken to simulate the real rooster. However the demonstration of the interaction effects are similar. The fluffy toy chicken is attached to a toy car and it is pre-programmed to move around, as shown if Figure 3(b).

As shown in Figure 2b, a visitor to our laboratory enjoys fondling with the doll. At the same time the LCD provides a life view of the rooster. It is a totally entertaining experience.

Developing and Evaluating Mobile Entertainment Applications: The Case of the Music Industry

Vasilios Koutsiouris, Pavlos Vlachos, and Adam Vrechopoulos

ELTRUN-IMES (Interactive Marketing & Electronic Services) Research Group
ELTRUN The Research Center - Department of Management Science and Technology
Athens University of Economics and Business, 47A Evelpidon Street, 113-62, Athens, Greece
Tel: +30-210-8203855, Fax: +30-210-8203854

Abstract. The rapidly evolving landscape in the music and mobile commerce industry fueled by the development of innovative commercial mobile music services calls for developing suitable evaluation frameworks towards measuring the performance of such kind of services. This paper elaborates on the Human Computer Interaction (HCI) established evaluation methods in order to provide a tailored evaluation framework to the peculiarities of the mobile music services. The framework provides an integrated view of the key variables involved the user-mobile interaction process both from a business and a technical perspective. Direct avenues for further research are provided at the end.

1 Research Background

A large amount of research work in electronic commerce applications evaluation methods employs the established knowledge derived through the human computer interaction (HCI) discipline [8]. They state, however, that practice has showed that the available literature appears to be highly diverse and ineffective when it comes to studying models tailored to the peculiarities and needs of each of the alternative digital shopping channels (e.g. interactive TV, vending machines, mobile commerce electronic services, CRM applications, call-centers, sales-force automation applications, etc.). The failure of WAP project, for example, shows the necessity of redefining the saturated principles in the evaluation frameworks. Similarly, Vlachos et al. [7] suggest that researchers should investigate each sector (e.g. tourism vs. banking) and each business model (e.g. web commerce vs. mobile commerce) separately, in order to develop theoretical frameworks and practical guidelines tailored to the peculiarities and needs of each of the given setting.

Along these lines, the dynamic and promising mobile music industry offers a challenging research opportunity for developing and applying "state-of-the-art" evaluation frameworks. Today, several mobile operators capitalizing on the third generation capabilities deliver music content to the end-users through innovative but not sufficiently tested applications [1]. To that end, the development of robust frameworks for evaluating such kind of applications constitutes a primary research

M. Rauterberg (Ed.): ICEC 2004, LNCS 3166, pp. 513–517, 2004.
© IFIP International Federation for Information Processing 2004

need in terms of improving business (e.g. price, promotion) and technical (e.g. interface, speed) aspects following a user-centered research approach [9].

Fig. 1. MUSICAL Mock-up Demo

Elaborating on the aforementioned research challenge, this paper aims to develop a generic evaluation framework for mobile music applications incorporating both technical and business dimensions. The work reported in this paper is partly funded by the MUSICAL project. MUSICAL aims to design and develop an innovative mobile application with extended personalization capabilities (Figure 1). The application enables the streaming of multicultural music content across new generation mobile networks (2.5 – 3G), addressing the needs of consumers, music professionals and local music content providers.

2   Human – Computer Interaction Evaluating Frameworks

The evaluation methods can be classified according to the stage of development in which they are carried out [2], [5]. More specifically, the designing evaluation targets the evaluation of the designing approach that was followed. There are various methods that can be utilized during the designing process either alone or in a combined form. The most important of those methods are summarized in Table 1. Evaluation during the implementation stage follows (Table 1). It includes the testing of the product against real users (e.g. consumers, administrators).

3   Evaluating Frameworks for the Music Industry

Based on a thorough interdisciplinary literature review and on the expertise provided through the design and development phase of the MUSICAL application, the proposed conceptual evaluation framework for mobile music applications stands upon

3 basic pillars: (a) User Interface Design, (b) End-users attitudes towards the mobile service and (c) Performance of the technology solution. The framework's dimensions and their corresponding descriptions are summarized in Table 2.

4   Implications, Limitations, and Further Research

The present research serves as a collection instrument of principles, metrics and dimensions that aim at evaluating applications in the field of mobile entertainment. This collection is a useful tool in the hands of researchers and practitioners that are interested in learning about the variables/dimensions that are directly related to the performance of a mobile commerce application. The total set of the dimensions included in the proposed framework, however, are probably not applicable in other business sectors (e.g. grocery retailing) or electronic shopping channels (e.g. interactive TV). To that end, further research should develop corresponding frameworks for different case settings tailored to their specific characteristics and peculiarities. However, several variables of the present framework are also applicable in any given research context. Finally, developing and testing research hypotheses through causal research designs (i.e. investigating cause-and-effect relationships) within laboratory or field experiments constitute a challenging future research approach.

Table 1. Evaluation Methods of Design and Implementation

Evaluation Methods	Main Characteristics	Criteria of Evaluation
Design Stage		
Cognitive walk	Discover how much the designed system supports the user in the execution of their tasks.	Analytical description of the system, user's goals, user's actions, user's information.
Heuristic evaluation	Evaluators examine the design of the system in comparison to known functionality criteria.	Simple and natural dialogue, usage of the user's language, consistency, esthetical and minimal design, instant recognition, diagnosis and correction of errors, help and documentation.
Evaluation based on the study of other evaluations	Utilizes the richness of knowledge provided from previous evaluation studies.	Use of previous evaluation studies' results. Time and funds saving.
Evaluation based on models	Cognitive and designing models (GOMS, KLM) provide indications of the users' performance.	Criteria based in models.
Implementation Stage		
Experimental evaluation	Use of a controlled experiment that allows basic sections of the whole, or of part of the system to be examined.	Existence of basic steps in every experiment.
Questioning techniques	They can pinpoint through the users point of view, system's sides that cannot be shown by using other methods.	Loud thinking, protocol analysis and afterwards walks
Observation techniques	Allow the users to directly express their opinion and the administrator to qualitatively observe their behaviour	Interviews and Questionnaires

Table 2. Conceptual Evaluation Framework for Mobile Music Applications

Evaluation of the User Interface Design	
Predictability	The support of the user in the prediction of the result of future actions judging from past results.
Possibility of synthesis	The support of the user in the realization of the results of previous actions in the current situation.
Familiarity	Whether the previous knowledge of the user with regard to other other real situations or calculating systems may be used in his interaction with a new system.
Possibility of generalization	The support of the user in the expansion of knowledge from certain cases in the same and other applications in relative situations.
Consistency	Similarity in the behavior during the input and appearance of data, that results from similar situations or targets.
Ability of observation	The ability of the user to appreciate the inner situation of the system from its outer appearance
Correspondence	The way in which the user notices the communication time with the system.
Ease of Use	How easy it is for the end-users to learn how to use the system and to explore the mobile services' features.
Informativeness	Informativeness deals with the amount of information provided in the system and the display of information and messages (e.g. error messages, position of messages in the screen).
Visibility of the systems status	Measure if the user knows the status of the system at any time. More specifically the user should know at any time where exactly he/she is.
Help for recovering from error	How easy is for end-user to recover from errors (e.g. information and guidance provided in error messages).
Effectiveness	Effectiveness deals with task completion, errors and abandonment rates.
Efficiency	Efficiency deals with the time and effort required for an end user to complete a key task.
Evaluation of the End-users Attitudes towards the Mobile Service	
Perceived Value	The value that end-users perceive that they will get out of a service/application (Zeithaml et al. 2002).
Overall Satisfaction	Overall satisfaction is defined as mobile's users overall "fulfilment response, the degree to which the level of fulfilment is pleasant or unpleasant (Kinnear and Taylor, 1996).
Usefulness	How useful is the mobile service in the customers' point of view.
Privacy/ security/ trust	Refers to the level of trust that end-users have to a service, to keep implicit and explicit personal data.
Reliability	Means delivering the mobile service dependably and accurately.
Willingness to pay	How willing are the potential users of a mobile service to pay for it.
Selection	Selection deals with the "product assortment".
Innovativeness	Users' sense regarding the innovativeness of the mobile service's functionalities.
Quality of the songs/video clips	Refers to the sonic quality of music songs and the quality of the video clips (high resolution).
Personalization	Refers to the level of personalization
Device characteristics	Which are the device's characteristics required for a mobile music service in the customers' point of view?
Payment model	End-users have to comment on the payment model that would like a mobile music service to have (e.g. flat rate, per event, ads based, hybrid).
Amount of Money	This variable is directly linked with the selected payment model.
Aesthetics	Aesthetics concern graphic style, colours, fonts etc.
Evaluation of the Technology Solution Performance	
Application loading time	Refers to the time needed for the application to load and to be ready for use.
Browsing/ Refresh Delay	This parameter refers to the amount of time needed to browse through the various menus of the application and the response time of the user – application transactions.
Initial streaming delay	This parameter represents the time needed for the song to start playing from the moment a user selects to hear a song.
Lag effect in streaming	High traffic in the mobile network causes the degradation of the mobile streaming application. It is obvious that the frequency of the appearance of gaps and delays when listening to the songs should be examined.
Number of errors/ crashes	The stability of the various modules of the system should be examined as well.
Network performance	The performance of the network under multimedia and streaming applications is a subject that requires deep study.

Acknowledgments. MUSICAL (Multimedia Streaming of Interactive Content Across Mobile Networks – *eContent* Program/European Commission – Contract No.: 22131Y2C2DMAL2 – Duration: 2002-2004.

References

1. Baldi, S. & Thaung, P. H., 'The Entertaining Way to M-commerce: Japan's Approach to the Mobile Internet-A Model for Europe?,' *Electronic Markets*, vol. 12, no.1, pp. 6-13, 2002
2. Dix A., Finlay J., Abowd G., Beale R., Human Computer Interaction, pp. 374-393, Prentice Hall International (UK), 1993.
3. Jones M., Marsden G., Mohd-Nasir N., Boone K., Buchanan G., Improving Web interaction on small displays, *Computer Networks* 31, pp.1129–1137, 1999.
4. Kinnear, T.C. and Taylor, J.R. (1996) *Marketing Research: An Applied Approach,* 5th edition, McGraw-Hill, Inc
5. Preece J., Rogers Y., Sharp H., Benyon D, .Holland S., Carey T., *Human Computer Interaction*, Addison Wesley, 1994.
6. Zeithaml, V. A., Parasuraman, A. & Malhotra, A. 2002, Service Quality Delivery Through Web Sites: A Critical Review of Extant Knowledge, *Journal of the Academy of Marketing Science*, vol. 30, no. 4, pp.362-375.
7. Vlachos, P., Vrechopoulos, A. & Doukidis, G. 2003, Exploring Consumer Attitudes towards Mobile Music Services in Europe, *The International Journal on Media Management*, vol.5, no.2, pp.138-148.
8. Vrechopoulos, A, O'Keefe, R., Doukidis, G. & Siomkos, G. 2004, Virtual Store Layout: An Experimental Comparison in the Context of Grocery Retail, *Journal of Retailing*, (in print).

An Entertaining Way to Access Web Content

Giacomo Poretti and Alberto Sollberger

3D-Enter SA, Pza. S. Franscini 5, 6900 Lugano, Switzerland
{gporetti, asollberger}@3denter.com
http://www.3denter.com

Abstract. This paper describes the 3D-Enter project's innovative findings. The project is aimed at simplifying the access to web content and at defining an entertaining way to make use of Internet and mobile services. This software application implements an interpreter and a graphic engine, which allows the interaction with business data to be searched and viewed as a "game-like" 3D graphical representation. It offers a feeling of involvement directly with a world of objects. It simplifies the usability of computer systems, improving information comprehension, thus increasing end-users' acceptance and immersion.

1 Introduction

This work is aimed at developing an innovative delivery of internet and mobile services allowing an entertaining way to interact with business objects using standard internet based PCs and future Java based mobile phones.

3D-Enter's patented method (Poretti, 2000) transforms traditional dialogue with Computer Systems' information in a three-dimensional virtual environment (VE) exploration, where 3D virtual worlds are used as a navigational interface. The information is embedded in animated and controllable three-dimensional VEs. This ensures an immediate visual understanding (looking instead of reading) and generates a sort of entertainment feeling, as well as an easier and more natural data-handling (navigating instead of scrolling).

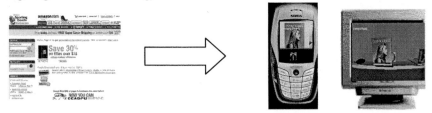

Fig. 1. 3D Amazon's Interface

The innovative elements of 3D-Enter's technology are the real time transformation of generic data entities to real life interactive objects (Fig. 1), the fact that two different users can interact with the same application through two complete different visuals, and the fact that the system can be applied to any existing web-based database or application.

M. Rauterberg (Ed.): ICEC 2004, LNCS 3166, pp. 518–521, 2004.

2 Case Studies

Selected cases of the method presented are available at www.3denter.com. The first case defines different 3D interfaces (Web and mobile) to the Amazon search engine. Search results are depicted as galleries, which can be explored following a physical movement metaphor (virtual reality). Individual data items (books and CDs) are represented as objects in the gallery and actions such as buying, reading reviewers, or resetting the search can be initiated by clicking on the objects.

The same technology has also been applied to another case modeled on the idea of sending a multimedia message. In this case the components of the message can be collected by exploring galleries and sent to a contact by exploring a "contacts space", where individuals contacts are represented by avatars. This technology defines a 3D cooperative and collaborative environment over the Internet where user devices (PCs and mobile phones) visualize actions and behavior of other users. A prototype shows the capacity to play a chess game between a PC and a mobile phone through two complete different visuals.

3 How Visual Are Created from Data

The core of the 3D-Enter's technology is the Visual Generator; a piece of software able to dynamically transform the result of a database retrieve operation into a 3D interactive VE. The Visual Generator is the combination of the "Visual Determination" and the "Population Way". The Visual Determination defines scenes' appearances and shapes of the result items of a database search. The VE appearance (scene) is assigned by the combination of the following input data; selected data (result-set), user's profile, and bandwidth (regularly measured during client server communication):

$$\text{scene} = f(\text{data, user's profile, bandwidth}) \qquad (1)$$

The shape of the selected objects is assigned upon the chosen scene, and upon the single items' attribute. The rule of the algorithm is the following:

$$\text{3D\_model} = f(\text{scene, data attribute}) \qquad (2)$$

The available interactivity on each object to be differentiated by data type, scene and display device:

$$\text{Interactivity} = f(\text{data type, scene, device}) \qquad (3)$$

The Population Way defines where single objects have to be placed inside a defined VE. Scenes are populated in a linear and repetitive way in order to allow the representation of an unknown number of entities inside unlimited spaces. The linear Population Way allows a simplified navigation avoiding traditional problems of the 3D navigation (Köykkä, 2000).

Pinhanez (2001) showed that consumers require watchable entertaining experiences on the web, i.e. "less clicking, more watching". 3D-Enter's technology implements the basic concepts of an automatic navigation in the same way as real world guided tours. In the virtual guided tours the system present information to the user continuously, from beginning to end, unless the user chooses to exercise control (e.g. pausing, interacting or manually navigating). Guided tours reduce active interactivity of the user (TV-like approach) simplifying the presentation of an unknown cardinality of queried data. This concept of guided tours was also developed based on Wilson's (1999) results, that spatial orientation is not affected by active exploration or passive observation.

4   System Architecture

The 3D Visual Server Technology has been developed using standard J2EE/J2ME Java technology (Fig. 2). The architecture is adaptable to most standard 3-tier models. The project defines a technical environment for the visualization and interaction with information accessible over the Internet from PCs and mobile phones. Through standards and open interfaces, the system can be easily applied to any existing Internet based application and database.

The Visual Generator runs at the mid-tier and this, in turn, interacts with a Java applet client and with the connected database, where data to be presented are defined. Navigation tools are standard: a computer keyboard and a mouse. Touch screen prototypes have also been tested, in order to be ready for most mobile phones without pointing devices. Mobile solution is under development, testing and refining.

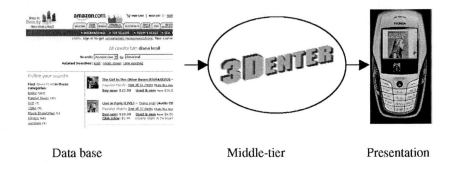

Data base   Middle-tier   Presentation

Fig. 2. Technical Architecture

5   Conclusion

3D-Enter's interface has been tested using MiLE usability method (Bolchini, 2002).
The purpose of the project was to define an entertaining way to make use of Internet services. The results suggested that this goal was achieved. The negative correlation between mouse interactivity and entertainment and engagement indicated that guided tours (TV-like navigation) are more entertaining.

The basic concepts of optimizing the distribution over the Internet of unlimited interactive VE reducing delays were well implemented. The simplification of 3D navigation inside 3D virtual environments were achieved: physical movement, viewpoint manipulation, target-based travel, and route planning. The concepts of accomplishing object selection, and object movements were tested with success. Traditional difficulty of visualization of unknown cardinality of data objects were solved thanks to the definition of linear populated scenes and thanks to the capacity of refining data searches inside generated VEs.

The capacity of freely changing visual representations increased fun, entertainment, and appeal. The visit time was also prolonged without set users becoming bored. Reducing user's active interactivity introducing a TV-like approach was positively judged: watching instead of reading, watching instead of clicking. The basis for an environment for the delivery and presentation of innovative and attractive services based on actual PC and on future Java-based mobile phones has been newly defined.

References

1. Poretti, G., Sollberger, A., 3D Virtual Landscape Database
   `http://12.espacenet.com/espacenet/`
   `viewer?PN=AU5517900&CY=ep&LG=en&DB=EPD` , European Patent Office, 2002
2. Köykkä, M., Usability Heuristic Guidelines for 3D Multi-user Worlds, Conference on Computer Human Interaction Special Interest Group of the Ergonomics Society of Australia - Wagga Wagga, Australia, 1999
3. Pinhanez C., "Less Clicking, More Watching": An Option for Entertainment in the Web, Results of the Iterative Design and Evaluation of Entertaining Web Experiences, Submitted to Interact'01, 2001
4. Wilson, P., Active exploration of a Virtual Environment dose not Promote Orientation, on Memory for Objects, Environment and behaviour 31(6), 752-763, 1999
5. Bolchini, D., DiBlas N., "MiLE: a Methodology for Usability Evaluation of Web Sites", VNET5 IST Workshop, Lugano, May 2002.

Design of an Interface for Technology Supported Collaborative Learning – The RAFT Approach

Lucia Terrenghi[1], Marcus Specht[1], and Moritz Stefaner[2]

[1] Institute for Applied Information Technology, Fraunhofer FIT,
Schloss Birlinghoven, 53754 Sankt Augustin, Germany.
{lucia.terrenghi, marcus.specht}@fit.fraunhofer.de
[2] Insitute for Cognitive Science, University of Osnabrück,
Katharinenstrasse 24, 49078 Osnabrück, Germany
mstefane@uos.de

Abstract. In the Remote Accessible Field Trips (RAFT[1]) project described in this paper, we aim to support high school students' field trips with mobile technology and to enable real-time remote collaboration with the classroom. therefore we look at the pedagogical issues and consequences for the interface design and propose a role-centred interface design approach, aiming at the development of dedicated tools and interfaces.

1 Introduction

The ongoing development of information communication technology, especially in the direction of wireless technology, puts the basis for new distributed scenarios and new forms of situated learning and knowledge management, together with new interaction patterns between users and environments, and between users and users.

In this paper we describe the design approach adopted in the ongoing European funded project RAFT[1] (Remote Accessible Field Trips). In order to accomplish the aim to deliver an enjoyable and engaging learning experience, we support the idea that consistent effort must be invested in acquiring knowledge of the domain, understanding the educational dynamics and identifying collaborative learning patterns to support the appliance design activity, both in terms of software and interface design.

2 The RAFT Concept and Its Pedagogical Ground

The main objectives of the RAFT project are to demonstrate the educational benefits and technical feasibility of remote field trips for high school students.

---

[1] The RAFT project is funded by the European Commission in the IST 5th framework programme under number IST-2001-34273

M. Rauterberg (Ed.): ICEC 2004, LNCS 3166, pp. 522–525, 2004.

It has become more and more difficult in many countries to organize field trips due to various reasons, including finance, staffing levels, health and safety. They usually have a high impact, though, on students' motivation because of the fun that is mostly associated with the field trip experience, and they can at the same time augment the curricula with additional material. RAFT envisions facilitating field trips for schools and enabling remote collaboration of schools. Web based video conferencing and wireless networking is used to enable an integrated, interactive system to link field trips and classrooms in real time, so as to establish extensions on current learning material standards and to exchange formats for contextualization of learning material.

Several fields related to experiential learning, education and training, rely on the idea that people can learn very effectively through direct, hands-on experience, as long as these experiences are well designed and facilitated (Dewey 1938) [0]. John Dewey's educational philosophy has inspired most of the experiential educational theories that are used in many outdoor educational programs. Experiential Learning Cycles [3] (ELC) are educational principles based on the idea that by breaking the fuzzy processes of learning into distinct stages we can better understand how the process of learning works.

Design patterns move on the same need to structure an activity by identifying an underlying framework based on recurring events, in order to draw generalizations and suggest solutions.

In order to recognize patterns and build a pattern language, domain knowledge is a main issue. In Computer Supported Collaborative Learning (CSCL) it is essential to gain an understanding of the learning activity so as to leverage new engaging learning experiences enabled by wireless technology.

In the first year of the RAFT project the different phases and functional requirements for supporting live collaboration and information access during field trips were worked out. The approach we adopted is in line with existing methodologies of scenario based design, contextual inquiry, evaluation of technology and participatory design.

A general RAFT scenario sees a teacher preparing a field trip as part of a course, structuring several modules including various tasks to be distributed among students in the field and in the classroom. The learners in the field and in the classroom work in teams in order to accomplish the assigned tasks. The groups going to the field are equipped with data-gathering devices (photographic, video, audio, measuring), wireless communication devices and a video conferencing system for direct interaction between the field and the classroom. Learners at school can ask questions, influence the behaviour of their peers in the field, and help them by providing information they request, analyze the collected data and eventually archive it.

By analysing learning scenarios, encountering main issues repeatedly occurring, we recognized and applied collaborative and pedagogical patterns. Because of the nature of the activities that make up a distributed field trip, including gathering of information in the field, answering questions, analyzing data from the field in order to provide immediate feedback, and communication taking place between the field and classroom, a wide spectrum of interaction between the participants needs to be enabled.

Referring to the work of DiGiano concerning collaborative learning patterns [0] we recognized in RAFT design issues consistent with the *Pipeline Workflow* activity pattern. This suggests a solution for the problem of "a teacher who needs to organize student activities in a complex task in a way that allows each student to play a meaningful role that requires cooperation with other students". The solution proposes that "Students work individually on a shared and accumulating data form. As each student completes his/her portion of the data calculations, he/she sends the revised form along to the next student in the sequence. The teacher initiates the activity by describing data collection procedure and rationale, forming students into groups, and distributing a base blank form to the first group member assigned to the first task in each group. Next, the teacher instructs students on how to operate within the sequence and how to save and send the form along, including to the final database."

This led us to draw a setting in which different users play different roles and perform different tasks to accomplish a shared goal.

The inquiry activities undertaken so far have been essential application design tools to recognize and apply patterns, identify workflows, specify roles and users' needs, evaluate technology and suggest interface design solutions.

3   The Design Approach

Given the dynamic set of devices that characterizes the RAFT Field Trips, the challenge is to provide a single GUI that runs on all the devices and yet accommodates the input, output and processing capabilities of each device. Our approach in this matter proposes a widget-based scalable and modular interface, which adapts to the role and to the device.

To clarify this approach and illustrate how some patterns identified can be realized on the basis of a flexible role-based architecture, we present the role of a Scout, getting involved in a task to detect a certain tree in the field. According to the related use cases, the Scout searches for interesting points in the field and needs to be informed about tasks; to be able to send information about interesting locations (hotspots); to communicate with other users in the class and in the field. A device suiting these requirements is a GPS, GPRS enabled handheld device, providing features of portability and trackability: the user interface for a Scout on a Gotive handheld device is shown in Figure 1, a.

The Scout mainly cooperates with the Task Manager in the classroom and the Data Gathering teams in the field. Therefore, the entities a Scout manipulates go into a consistent field trip object repository and can be seen and manipulated by other team members in the field and in the classroom.

The Scout starts to search for points of interest and scans the environment; as soon as he/she finds something interesting, he/she locks the position and a notification with the Point Of Interest (POI) record is stored in the shared field trip repository.

The repository automatically sends a notification to the team members and also to the Task Manager. Awareness about changes in the state of tasks and data collections for tasks plays an important role for the collaborative work and the design of the interface. The Task Manager evaluates the data and the metadata of the Scout and decides whether more scouting is needed or the data gathering and annotation can start. Figure 1,b shows the Task Manager's view on POIs in the filed, based on the status of the different tasks he/she is managing and on the scouts' notification.

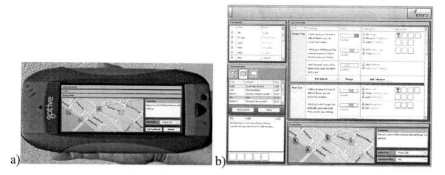

Fig. 1. a) the Scout's User interface on a Gotive device and b) the manager's interface on a desktop.

The Data Gatherer then works together with the Annotator in the field to collect samples and material that can be forwarded to the Task Manager and further elaborated by the students in the classroom. In this case the team players are distributed over different places and can use different devices due to the necessary mobility. Nevertheless different GUIs for the manipulation of POIs go back to a shared field trip repository.

4 Conclusions and Future Work

From the pedagogical point of view, the use of roles provides a clear methodology to start application design from educational and pedagogical functions the learners take in a realistic learning situation. The roles taken by learners can be described and mapped on to curricular goals. From a software engineering point of view this allows a clear mapping of functionalities and user requirements to interaction widgets. As – for example in UML – the use cases are often neglected when designing the user interface and interaction, this methodology provides an approach to design complex application with a clear relation to the use cases elicited.

References

1. Dewey, J.: Experience and education. Pocket Books (1938).
2. DiGiano, C. Yarnall, L., Patton, C., Roschelle, J., Tatar, D., Manley, M.: Collaboration Design Patterns: Conceptual Tools for Planning for the Wirless Classroom. *Proc. Workshop on Wireless and Mobile Technologies in Education 2002,* IEEE (2002)
3. Kolb, D. A.: Experiential Learning: Experience as the source of learning and development. New Jersey: Prentice Hall (1984).

Sound and Music

iFP: A Music Interface Using an Expressive Performance Template

Haruhiro Katayose[1,2] and Keita Okudaira[1]

[1] School of Science and Technology, Kwansei Gakuin University
Sanda 669-1337, Hyogo, Japan
{katayose, keita}@ksc.kwansei.ac.jp
http://ist.ksc.kwansei.ac.jp/~katayose/
[2] PRESTO, JST, JAPAN

Abstract. This paper describes a performance interface called iFP that enables players to play music as if he or she had the hands of the virtuoso. iFP is a tapping-style musical interface and refers to a pianist's expressiveness described in a performance template. The paper describes the scheduler that allows a player to mix her/his own intension with the expressiveness in the performance template and the user interfaces. The results of a subjective study suggest that using the expression template and the tapping-style interface contribute to the subject's joy of playing music. This result is also supported by a brain activation study that was done using near-infrared spectroscopy.

1   Introduction

Music has been an important form of entertainment since ancient days. Recently, interfaces for playing music have been incorporated into videogames. In 2003, the game "Taiko-no-Tatsujin" (Master of Drumming) manufactured by NAMCO ltd. sold more than 1.2 million copies, reaching 5th place in game sales for that year. Many people enjoy playing such music games. However, the object of most products is to have players compete over who displays the most rhythmic accuracy for a given piece of music, not to provide a pleasurable musical experience for the players.

Musical activities foster self-expression, acquisition of new skills, appreciation of good art, and sharing of experiences with others. Above all, the performance itself is the fundamental musical activity. Although it is fun to play a musical instrument, not a few people have experienced embarrassment due to their lack of skill in playing one. Sometimes this may even be the reason for a musician quitting and giving up a means of self-expression. Interactive musical instruments are meant to overcome this problem. They are expected to give users a chance to express what they would like to express even if they lack certain musical skills.

The score-follower based on beat tapping and proposed by Mathews [1] is a simple, intuitive music interface to express tempo and dynamics. It is intended especially for amateurs. Mathews' work has been followed by various conducting systems [2,3,4].

M. Rauterberg (Ed.): ICEC 2004, LNCS 3166, pp. 529–540, 2004.

If the note descriptions of the score given to the system are nominal (quantized), the players' expression would be limited to the tempi and dynamics. We designed a score-follower called iFP, which utilizes expression templates derived from virtuoso performances [5]. iFP enables its users to enjoy the experience of playing music, as if he or she had the hands of a virtuoso.

The next section outlines the design of iFP. We then describe the scheduler that realizes a mixture of the player's intention and expressiveness described in the performance template. After introducing the user interfaces, we discuss the effectiveness of using the expressive performance template as determined from a subjective evaluation and an observation of the test subject's brain activity.

2   System Overview

In this section, we briefly describe the iFP design and some of its functions. We then illustrate how the expressive performance template is utilized in iFP and describe its principal functions.

2.1   Utilizing a Template

Beat tapping is an intuitive interface to input tempo and dynamics to a performance system. However, the player cannot express the delicate sub-beat nuance with only beat tapping. The primary goal of utilizing the expressive performance template is to fill in expressions at the sub-beat level. The player's intention and the expression model described in the template are mixed as shown in Fig. 1.

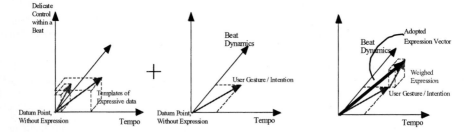

Fig. 1. Conceptual overview of performance calculation. The performance data are given by a mixture of the player's intention and expressiveness described in the performance template. In this three dimensional space, the vertical axis denotes the variance of deviations of all notes within the beat.

The player is allowed to vary the weight parameters dynamically by using sliders, each of which is multiplied with the deviation of tempo, dynamics, and delicate nuance within a beat. If all of these weight parameters are set to 0%, the expression of the template has no effect. On the other hand, if it is set to 120%, for example, the player can emphasize the deviations of the template.

iFP also provides a morphing function to interpolate (extrapolate) two different expressive performance templates of a musical piece.

2.2 Outline of Scheduling

Schedulers of interactive music systems have to calculate the timing of notes dynamically. iFP adopts a predictive scheduler, which arranges notes from the current beat to the next beat by using the history of the player's tap. One of the important points of using a predictive scheduler is that tap (beat) detection and scheduling of notes should be independent. This yields the merits of 1) compensation of the delay when using a MIDI-driven *robotic* acoustic instrument, and 2) easy implementation of the automatic performance mode (sequencer of the performance template). A predictive scheduler might produce undesired gaps between the predicted beat timing and the actual players' tap. Especially if the gap is a delay, it may be perceived as spoiling the performance. We prepared two countermeasures to improve the response; one is a function to urge the system when player's tap precedes the scheduled time, and the other is for receiving double taps for the given tactus (see the Expressive Performance Template section).

2.3 Functions

The features described above and the other characteristic functions are summarized as follows:
- Utilization of expressive performance template
- Real-time control of weight parameters regarding expressions
- Morphing of two different performance templates
- Predictive scheduling which allows the player to tap an arbitrary beat
- Pauses (breath) inserted based on release timing
- Real-time visualization (feedback) of expressiveness.
- Gestural input using a conducting sensor, a MIDI keyboard.

2.4 Expressive Performance Template

Fig. 2 shows a part of a performance template. The left row represents the start timing of the events. Information about each note, except for the start timing, is placed in brackets. Each bracketed term, in order, represents, the deviation regarding the start time, note name, velocity, duration, and the deviation of duration, respectively. In this format, the tempo is described using the descriptor BPM. The description is followed by the tempo (in bpm beat per minuets) and the beat name to which the tempo is given.

```
.....
2.00  BPM  126.2  4
2.00  (0.00  E3  78  3.00  -0.11)
=2
1.00  TACTUS 2 4
1.00  BPM  128.1  4
1.00  (0.00  C#4  76  0.75  -0.09) (0.04  E1  60  1.00  -0.13)
1.75  (0.10  D4  77  0.25  -0.14)
2.00  BPM  130.0  4
2.00  (0.00  B3  75  1.00  -0.03) (0.00  G#3  56  1.00  0.03)
3.00  BPM  127.7
3.00  (0.00  B3  72  1.00  0.00) (0.09  G#3  56  1.00  -0.12) (0.14  D3  57  1.00  -0.21)
=3
1.00  TACTUS 1 4
1.00  BPM  127.6  4
1.00  (0.00  B3  77  2.00  -0.05) (0.00  G#3  47  2.00  -0.05) (-0.06  D4  57  2.00  -0.32)
3.00  BPM  129.7  4
3.00  (0.00  F#4  75  1.00  -0.15) (0.00  D4  54  1.00  0.03)
=4
1.00  BPM  127.7  4
1.00  (0.00  D#4  73  0.75  -0.38) (0.02  C4  65  0.75  -0.08)
```

Fig. 2. Description of performance template.

iFP's predictive scheduler continues the performance, even if the performer does stop tapping. The player does not have to tap every beat. However, there often is the case that the players wish to tap to each note, instead of the beat. We introduced a descriptor **TACTUS** to explicitly describe how many taps are received for the beat. The following bracketed expression is an example of a **TACTUS** description. **(1.00 TACTUS 2 4)** This example means that after time **1.00**, two taps are received for quarter notes; in other words, the system receives a tap every eighth note, after time **1.00**. It is not easy to obtain quantized notation, because local tempi varies more than twice from the average tempo. Manual quantization is extremely troublesome. Therefore, we designed a tool which identifies the notes in the performance given only a sparse score and then assigns a canonical notation value and deviation to all of the notes [6]. The DP matching procedure is utilized for the 1_{st} step and a Hidden Markov Model (HMM) is used for assigning the 2_{nd} time value to the notes. This tool enables us to prepare error-free expressive performance templates by giving only 10% of the notes as guides. At present, we have made over 100 expressive performance templates.

3   Scheduler

In this section, we describe the scheduler that realizes a mixture of the player's intention and expressiveness described in the performance template.

3.1   Calculation of Tempo

The tempo is calculated using 1) the average tempo obtained from the recent history (tactus-count: α) of the tempo, 2) the tempo to which the player's veer is considered, using the differential of the two most recent tapping, and 3) the prescribed tempo in the performance template [**Tempo$_T$**]. Let **stdTEMPO** denote the overall average tempo of the template, and **w$_H$**, **w$_P$**, and **w$_T$** denote the weights for 1), 2) and 3) respectively. The tempo after **n$_{th}$** tactus, **BPM$_n$** is calculated as:

$$BPM_n = \left\{ w_T \times (Tempo_T - stdTempo) + w_H \left(\frac{1}{a} \sum_{k=n-a}^{n-1} BPM_k - stdTempo \right) \right\} \cdot \frac{1}{w_T + w_H} \cdot \left(\frac{BPM_{n-1}}{BPM_{n-2}} \right)^{w_P} \quad (1)$$

Fig. 3 shows an example of tempo calculation. If the player sets **w$_T$** to a bigger value, more template data will be imported, and the player can feel like conducting a pianist. Setting **w$_P$** to a bigger value quickens the response. By setting **w$_H$** to a bigger value, the tempo of the music will be stable, affected by the recent average tempo. The user can set the parameters as s/he likes.

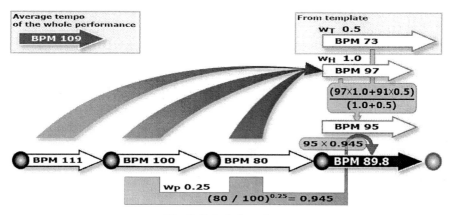

Fig. 3. Calculation of tempo

3.2 Improvement of Response and Estimation of Beat Position

The problem with using predictive control is the possibility of undesired gaps between the predicted beat time and the actual user input. We introduced the following procedures in order to fill the gap, when a player's tap for the next beat is prior to the scheduled (predicted) timing. Fig. 4 shows the scheduling status in the case of a) the player's tap is prior to the scheduled beat and b) the player's tap is after the scheduled beat. Here, the adjustment level is a parameter that stands for how much the scheduler has to shrink the gap between the scheduled (predicted) time and the player's real tap, when the beat is detected prior to the scheduled time. If the adjustment level is set to 50%, the system issues events that correspond to the note on the beat, at the middle position between the player's tap and scheduled time.

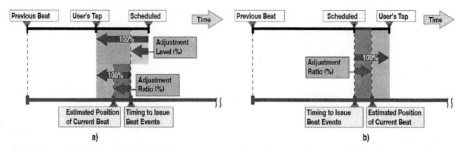

Fig. 4. Beat Position. A). Player's tap is prior to the scheduled beat, b) Player's tap is after the scheduled beat.

Estimation of the beat position in the music is one of the challenging unsolved targets in cognitive musicology. However, the scheduler has to estimate the position of the current beat in order to predict the next beat. iFP's scheduler estimates the position of the current beat by inter/extrapolating the timing of the player's tap and that the scheduler issues the events corresponding to the beat. The adjustment ratio, employed here, stands for the value for the inter/extrapolation. If the adjustment ratio is set to a higher/lower value the performance will tend to close to the player's/template's intention.

3.3   Calculation of Note Event Timing

The timing of each note event (note-on, note-off) is calculated using $\mathbf{IOI_n}$ given by the inverse of $\mathbf{BPM_n}$ (see the Calculation of Tempo section), as follows,

$$\mathbf{Time_{each\_note\_issue}} = \mathbf{IOI_n} \cdot (\mathbf{pos_{T\_each\_note}} + \mathbf{dev_{T\_each\_note}} \cdot \mathbf{w_{T\_dev}}) \tag{2}$$

where, $\mathbf{Time_{each\_note\_issue}}$ [s] is the time after the identified current beat, $\mathbf{pos_{T\_each\_note}}$ is the scheduled time of the note without deviation, $\mathbf{dev_{T\_each\_note}}$ is the value of the deviation term of the note, and the $\mathbf{w_{T\_dev}}$ is the weighting factor for the template. When $\mathbf{w_{T\_dev}} = \mathbf{0}$ is given, the temporal deviation under beat level will be mechanical.

3.4   Calculation of Velocity (Note Intensity)

The notes are classified into the control notes (note on the beat) and the remainder. First, the system decides the beat velocity $\mathbf{V_{beat}}$ for the beat. It is calculated, considering how loud/quiet the player and the machine (performance template) intend to play the note of the beat.

$$\mathbf{V_{beat}} = \mathbf{V_{std}} + \frac{(\mathbf{V_T} - \mathbf{V_{std}}) \cdot \mathbf{w_{T\_v}} + (\mathbf{V_U} - \mathbf{V_{std}}) \cdot \mathbf{w_{U\_v}}}{\mathbf{w_{T\_v}} + \mathbf{w_{U\_v}}} \tag{3}$$

where, $\mathbf{V_{std}}$ is the standard (average) velocity of the all notes of the template, $\mathbf{V_T}$ is the average of the note-on velocity within the beat, $\mathbf{V_U}$ is the velocity that the player gives, and $\mathbf{w_{T\_v}}$ and $\mathbf{w_{U\_v}}$ are the weights for $\mathbf{V_T}$ and $\mathbf{V_U}$, respectively. When $\mathbf{w_{T\_v}}$ and w_{U_v} are 0, the intensity deviation will be mechanical.

The velocity of the each note $V_{each\_note\_issue}$ is calculated as:

$$V_{each\_note\_issue} = V_{beat} \cdot (1 + V_{T\_each\_note\_dev} + V_{U\_each\_dev}) \qquad (4)$$

where, $V_{T\_each\_note\_dev}$ stands for deviation in the template, and $V_{U\_each\_dev}$ stands for the player's intensity veer.

$$V_{T\_each\_note\_dev} = (V_{T\_each\_note} - V_T) / V_T \cdot w_{T\_dev} \qquad (5)$$

$$V_{U\_each\_dev} = \frac{V_{Ucurrnt} - V_{Uprior}}{V_{Uprior}} \cdot (pos_{T\_each\_note} + dev_{T\_each\_note} \cdot w_{T\_dev}) \cdot w_{Ud\_v} \qquad (6)$$

where, $V_{T\_each\_note}$ is each note-on velocity within the beat, and V_{Un} denotes the velocity given by the n_{th} player's tap and w_{Ud_v} denotes the weight for the player's veer.

4   User Interface

4.1   GUI and Gestural Interface

Fig. 5 shows the standard GUI to characterize the performance. The users are given sliders so they can set the weight parameters regarding tempo (template/user), dynamics (velocity: template/user), and deviation (delicate control within a beat: template).

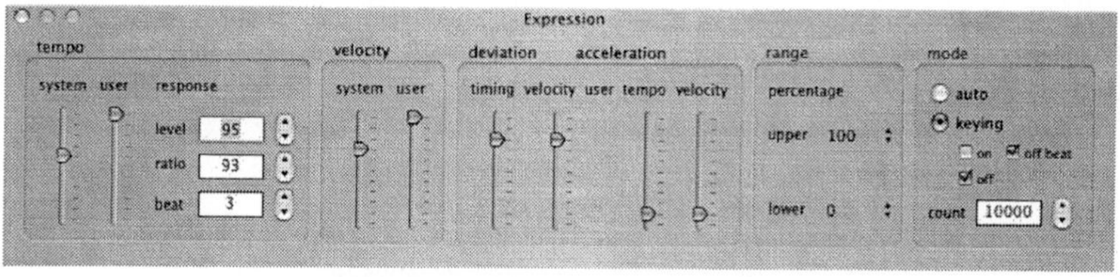

Fig. 5. Standard GUI for setting parameters.

iFP also provides a morphing interfaces of two templates of a music piece. The player can interpolate and extrapolate the performance using each of the morphing parameters. The player is also allowed to use peripherals of MIDI instruments instead of the software sliders. If the radio button "keying" is selected, the system accepts the player's beat tap. If "auto" is selected, the system does not accept the beat tap. The expressive performance template is played without the control of the player's beat tap (automatic mode). The gestural conducting sensor is based on capacity transducers (see Fig 6).

The beat signal is issued when the hand is located at the lowest position. The range of hand movement is assigned to the dynamics for the next beat. When the hand is lower than a certain threshold, the system holds the performance, i.e. gives a rest.

Fig. 6. With a conducting gestural interface using capacity transducers.

4.2 Visualization

iFP provides real-time visualization of the performance trajectory in three-dimensional space, as shown in Fig. 7. The axes are the tempo, the dynamics, and the summed variance of the expression deviation within a beat. The user can observe the trajectory from various viewpoints. If the player uses iFP with automatic (sequencer) mode, this visualization function should be the view of the expressiveness of the performance template.

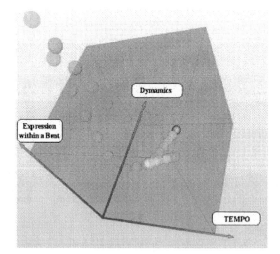

Fig. 7. Example of visualization of a performance. K.331 played by S. Bunin.

5 Evaluation

We conducted two experiments to verify the effectiveness of using expressive performance templates and gestural input devices. One was an evaluation regarding the players' introspection, and the other was a brain activity measurement using near-infrared spectroscopy (NIRS).

5.1 Introspection Evaluation

We focused on *"controllable"* and *"expressive"* aspects for the introspection study. *"Controllable"* stood for difficulty in playing music. *"Expressive"* stood for how well the player could express the music. For the experiment, we used a conducting interface and an expressive template for "When You Wish Upon A Star" for piano. The system parameters for this experiment were those of a music teacher who is also a conductor so that the performance taste would be close to conducting, as shown in Fig. 5. We interviewed forty subjects, whose music experience was 0~33 years. We asked them "Which performance (with / without the performance template) is more *"controllable"* or more *"expressive"*? We limited the time to practice to 10 minutes in this experiment. The results are shown in Table 1.

Table 1. Introspection Regarding Expression Template Use: The value in each column is the number of subjects who preferred the condition.

		Controllable		Sum
		Better: with Template	Better: without Template	
Expressive	Better: with template	13	15	28
	Better: without Template	0	12	12
	sum	13	27	40

We investigated the response of the 27 subjects who answered, "controllability is better without template", by changing the parameters affecting controllability. All of the subjects answered that the controllability was improved when the parameters of both adjustment level and ratio were 100%. This meant dis-coincidence of the player's own taps and heard beats makes the performance difficult. However, some of the subjects who are experienced in music commented that both adjustment level and ratio should not be so high in order to gain expressiveness, and the dis-coincidence played an important role for expressiveness. It is interesting to consider this point, related with what makes ensembles splendid.

Next, we investigated learning effects, for five of the 15 people who answered "expressive performance template contributes to *expressiveness*, but it does not contribute to *controllability*". Four people among five subjects changed their opinion to "prefer to use a template also for *controllability*" after learning. These results seem to indicate that the expressive performance template contributes to both *expressiveness* and *controllability*, after one has learned how to play the music using iFP.

5.2 Evaluation Using NIRS

Physiological measurements are good for verifying subjective introspection results. Brain activity is a most promising measure for what a subject is thinking and feeling. Recently, a relatively new technique, near-infrared spectroscopy (NIRS), has been used to measure changes in cerebral oxygenation in human subjects [7]. Changes in oxyhemoglobin (HbO) and deoxyhemoglobin (Hb) detected by NIRS reflect changes in neurophysiological activity, and as a result, may be used as an index of brain activity. It is reported that the brain in the Fz area is deactivated (HbO decrease), when a subject is relaxed, in meditation, or in immersion in playing games. We measured brain activities around the Fz area when the subjects played with the iFP, or did other musical tasks (control tasks).

Fig. 8 shows the results of experiments investigating the effects of using an expressive performance template and comparing input interfaces, for a subject who answered, "The expressive performance template contributes to both *expressiveness* and *controllability*." educated in music, and received her Master of Music degree from a music university. We can see the decrease in HbO, when the subject played with the expressive performance template. The decrease was most salient with the expression template and using the conducting interface. These results correspond very well to the reports of the subjects' introspection regarding pleasantness. The right data were obtained by chance. It is interesting to see the response of the subject when something unexpected happened.

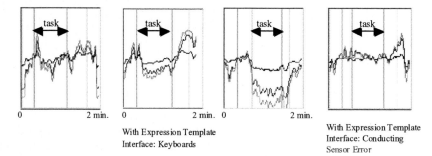

Fig. 8. Brain activity measured with NIRS. Measured during playing "When You Wish Upon A Star" using iFP. Arrows show the duration of the performance. A single emitting source fiber was positioned at Fz. The red line shows the sum of Oxi-Hb.

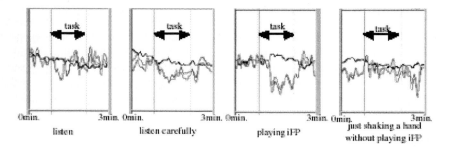

Fig. 9. Brain activity measured with NIRS. Measured during listening and playing with the iFP.

Fig. 9 is a comparison with other music activities. HbO was lower when the subject listened to the music carefully imagining the next musical progressions, and played with the iFP (subject A). The decrease was more salient with the iFP. The right data were obtained when the subject was shaking her hands without playing with the iFP. These results also correspond very well to the reports of the subjects' introspection.

We also conducted experiments regarding the learning effect for a subject who answered, "The expressive performance template contributes to *expressiveness* but not to *controllability*." This person is an experienced organist. In the first trial, there was no salient feature to the HbO while the subject used the conducting sensor, and the HbO fell while the subject used the keyboard. After the subject learned playing with the iFP for about one month, the behavior of HbO while using the keyboard was same as in the first trial. In contrast, the HbO increased while using the conducting sensor. The subject reported that it was difficult to control the conducting sensor. It seems that the subject became to be obliged to "think" how to control the conducting sensor. We should thus continue our experiments to assess the learning effect in this regard.

Although the interpretation of deactivation at Fz itself is still controversial [8], we can say that the results for subjects evaluating their own introspection when using the iFP match with the NIRS observation of brain activity.

In summary, the experimental results reported here suggest that 1) use of the expression template and 2) use of gestural input interfaces, contribute to a player's experience of pleasantness when performing a musical activity.

6   Conclusion

This paper introduced a performance interface called iFP for playing expressive music with a conducting interface. MIDI-formatted expressive performances played by pianists were analyzed and transformed into performance templates, in which the deviations from the printed notation values are separately described. Using the template as a skill-complement, a player can play music expressively over and under beat level. The scheduler of iFP allows the player to mix her/his own intension with the expressiveness in the performance template. The results of a forty-subject user study suggested that using the expression template contributes to a player's joy of expressing music. This conclusion is also supported by the results of brain activity measurements.

We are just beginning our experiments using NIRS. We would like to trace the changes of the subjects' introspection and brain activity, as they learn to play with the iFP. We are also interested in investigating interactions between brain regions when the subjects are playing music. We would like to propose a design guideline for music games, based on further investigations. Another important task is to provide more data to be used in iFP. So far, a tool to produce a performance template from MIDI-formatted data has been completed. We would like to improve the tool, so it can convert acoustic music into an expressive performance template.

Acknowledgement. The authors would like to thank Mr. K. Noike, Ms. M. Hashida, and Mr. K. Toyoda for their contributions to the study. Prof. Hiroshi Hoshina and Mr. Yoshihiro Takeuchi made valuable comments, and they were very helpful. This research was supported by PRESTO, JST, JAPAN.

References

1. Mathews, M.: The Conductor Program and Mechanical Baton, *Proc. Intl. Computer Music Conf.* (1989) 58-70
2. Morita, H., Hashimoto, S. and Ohteru, S.: A Computer Music System that Follows a Human Conductor. *IEEE Computer* (1991) 44-53
3. Usa, S. and Mochida, Y.: A Multi-modal Conducting Simulator," *Proc. Int. Computer Music Conf.* (1998) 25-32
4. Nakra, T. M.: Synthesizing Expressive Music Through the Language of Conducting. *J. of New Music Research, 31, 1* (2002) 11-26
5. Katayose, H., Okudaira, K.: sfp/punin: Performance Rendering Interfaces using Expression Model, *Proc. IJCAI03-workshop, Methods for Automatic Music Performance and their Applications in a Public Rendering Contest* (2003) 11-16
6. Toyoda, K., Katayose, H., Noike, K.: Utility System for Constructing Database of Performance Deviation, *SIGMUS-51, IPSJ* (2003 in Japanese) 65-70
7. Eda, H., Oda, I., Ito, Y. et al.: Multi-channel time-resolved optical tomographic imaging system. *Rev. Sci. Instum. 70* (1999) 3595-3602
8. Matsuda., G., and Hiraki, K.: Frontal deactivation in video game players, *Proc. Conf. of Intl. Simulation And Gaming Assoc.(ISAGA)* (2003) 799-808

Sound Pryer: Adding Value to Traffic Encounters with Streaming Audio

Mattias Östergren

Mobility, The Interactive Institute,
P.O. Box 24081, SE – 104 50 Stockholm, Sweden
mattias.ostergren@tii.se

Abstract. We present a novel in-car entertainment application that is inspired by listening to music and the social interaction of manoeuvring in traffic. The Sound Pryer is a peer-to-peer application of mobile wireless ad hoc networking for PDAs with the intent of adding value to mundane traffic encounters. In essence it works like a shared car-stereo. Besides playing your own music, it allows prying on the music played by other Sound Pryer applications in other cars close-by. It accomplishes this during brief traffic encounters by peer-to-peer RTP multicast streaming MP3 music files. Through field trial we found that user appreciated the concept, but the prototype needs some improvements, foremost in terms of audio playback.

1 Introduction

The Sound Pryer concept is based on two appreciated activities: driving and music listening. It provides joint listening among drivers in everyday traffic encounters adding a novel flavor to the experiential aspects of traffic encounters. In essence, it works as a shared car stereo. A user can hear the tunes played on his or her stereo, but also eavesdrop the music played at other stereos, in vehicles close-by. Sound Pryer is an implemented peer-to-peer application of mobile wireless ad hoc networking for PDAs, streaming MP3 files via the Real Time Protocol (RTP) [14]. It draws on the idea that people take an aesthetic interest in the surrounding traffic and they would not mind sharing music, as they are practically anonymous to each other. More so, we argue that hearing other people's music will spark curiosity about them. Being able to determine who is playing and see that person then further intensifies the experience.

We present the implementation of a prototype we used in a recent field trial. The architecture draws on two principal technologies. The first is Wireless Mobile Ad Hoc Networking (MANET) [12], which allows connections between cars without any further infrastructure. Ad Hoc Networking only allows connections within the radius of its wireless range. This we use to approximate the participants of a certain traffic encounter, but as such encounters are brief we have developed a mechanism to quickly detect and establish connections. Second, the prototype relies on a peer-to-peer structure, which fits well with transient connections and unpredictable availability of remote peers in such networks. The field trial included 13 unacquainted users driving a five-kilometre route in downtown Stockholm. This constrained, yet realistic,

M. Rauterberg (Ed.): ICEC 2004, LNCS 3166, pp. 541–552, 2004.
© IFIP International Federation for Information Processing 2004

approach gave insights concerning a range of issues, including driver's safety and privacy, and also on the design of the prototype and its performance. The trial demonstrated that the concept was entertaining, but not dangerously distracting. All users agreed that it was fun, however, also suggested improvements, especially on the audio playback. We will summarize the findings together with suggestions for such improvements.

The work presented here is of interest to MANET research. It is a novel application demonstrating where and how ad hoc networking is applicable. It is also of interest to the entertainment computing community as it prototypes a concept designed for a highly mobile situation. Driving could also benefit from safe alternative ways of entertainment.

2   Related Work

Eavesdropping in Sound Pryer relates to a similar effect in Sotto Voce [2]. It is an electronic guidebook application for handheld devices. The aim of this application is to augment museum visits. The idea is that users may select and play audio information. Other users may overhear that information item through their own device. Sotto Voice does not rely on streaming to disseminate the audio. Rather, it mimics eavesdropping by distributing indexes to clips. Consequently, each device is prepared with each sharable piece of audio clip in advance. The evaluation of Sotto Voce [7] is similar to the field trial we outline here. It was evaluated with 47 participants over four days in three museum rooms. First, each participant filled in a questionnaire covering basic questions, such as age and technological experience. They were then given a tutorial on how to use the guidebook. During the tour their conversations were recorded and in two of the three rooms there were video cameras to record their interactions. All events on the PDA were logged. Finally after completed the tour, which took about 15 to 20 minutes the couples were invited to a semi-structured interview. The evaluation showed that eavesdropping was an appreciated addition to electronic guidebooks. Moreover, it also proves that overhearing is interesting and joyful stimuli in socializing. ShoutCar [17] is a prototype to facilitate in-car music listening. It is designed with the mundane car-commuter, especially drivers, in mind. ShoutCar lets the user prepare a play list, which he or she then uploads to a web server. This page is then accessible through a customized browser. The browser reads out the items of the play list and the user may cycle through and select items he or she wants to hear using an input wheel. The design of the ShoutCar was iteratively informed by a group of car-commuters. It was found that many commuters actively entertain and *seek* alternative entertainment while driving. Finally, Sound Pryer relates to the FolkMusic [16] prototype. It is a mobile peer-to-peer application designed for face-to-face interaction that lets user share their play list items with other users close-by. A user may select to listen to any item on any user's play list as long as they remain within certain proximity. When a user selects such item it is streamed over a LAN. The proximity is determined using GPS positioning.

3   Design Rationale

The design of Sound Pryer draws on two broad ides: adding value to traffic encounter using personal technologies, yet honouring driver's safety through careful design.

3.1 Adding Value to Traffic Encounters with Music

The purpose of adding value is to entertain or at least to deepen the experience of a particular situation. Our goal is to add value to *traffic encounters*. It is a highly social situation in a public milieu. Traffic encounters involve people that are co-located on a stretch of road. They may comprise people in vehicles as well as people travelling by other means, such as biking or walking. The most prominent feature of traffic encounters is they are temporally bounded. The participants' high relative speed makes traffic encounters brief; often only enduring a few seconds. Still, some encounters, such as in caravans and inner-city traffic, are more persistent. Traffic encounters are often co-operative. In order to avoid accidents and disturbances, a driver is inclined to adjust their speed to maintain proper relative distance, but also to monitor and take action on other more delicate manoeuvres.

Keeping track of traffic encounters like this is also a pleasant experience. Donald Appleyard and Kevin Lynch argued, already in 1964, that the encounters are central in the road user's experience of driving. They claimed that: "[m]ost impressive of all is the motion of the accompanying traffic, to which he is forced to be attentive, and which even passengers will watch with subconscious concern [3]." We also argue the individual apprehension of a traffic encounters possesses in many cases the same qualities as what appealed to the 19th century flâneur. According to Charles Baudelaire: "He marvels at the eternal beauty and the amazing harmony of life in capital cities...He delights in fine carriages and proud horses, the dazzling smartness of the grooms...the sinuous gait of the women, the beauty of the children... [4]" Similarly, we suggest that from time to time drivers also take such interest in other people and vehicles in encounters. On the other hand, the brief engagements and the enclosing of the drivers in the hull of a vehicle occasionally make everyday life in traffic monotonous and lonesome. In such cases, many drivers are entertained by listening to music. For instance, in a recent study concerning the music listening habits of a group of music enthusiast, it was found that they listened to music 82 % of the time they spent in cars [5].

Our hypothesis is that, hearing what is being played in surrounding cars, even if it only means for a few seconds, would add a new dimension to the apprehension of traffic, beyond the glimpse of the identity of the individual driver and his or her vehicle, and therefore make driving more fun. It combines the experience of listening to music with interest in traffic encounters, which they have to attend to anyway. Thus to add value the Sound Pryer prototype must provide *joint listening* in traffic encounters. This requirement can further be divided into the following aspects:

- Responsiveness: First, the Sound Pryer must reflect well the prevalent traffic encounter and only include peers that seem part of it. This means the networking architecture must swiftly discover node re-configurations. This is most prominent when peers enter wireless range.

- Robustness: Second, when a particular network configuration is established the networking must be able to deliver the MP3 stream at an acceptable quality.

Finally, the prototype must also be able to provide means to help users *identify the source* of music to reflect the interest in the surrounding drivers and vehicles.

3.2   Personal Technologies

Road use is increasingly concerning mobile handheld communication technologies. For instance, more and more people feel it is important to always be reachable and therefore almost always carries a mobile phone. This, in turn, has made the car a popular, yet a controversial, place to make phone calls. It is not far fetched to believe that other handheld and personal computing devices will undergo a similar development. They will increasingly become part of people's everyday life and also accompany the person into the car. Therefore, we believe Sound Pryer staged on personal technology. The experience of Sound Pryer application use is related to the number of co-located users. This in turn is strongly dependant on the spread of it. To increase likelihood of achieving a critical mass of users we believe the importance of assembling Sound Pryer out of standardized (de facto or otherwise settled) and popular personal technologies. However, most currently available applications for PDAs are aimed at supporting work in office-like environments and are not adapted to in-car use. This is evident that most people would probably not bother performing the most fundamental actions such GUIs may require while driving. However, it is possible to design for PDAs to take driving into account, yet allowing *convenient interaction*. In the design of Sound Pryer we have let the following aspects guide us:

- Mounted PDA: First, having security concerns in mind, we do not argue for actually holding the PDA device while driving. On the contrary, in the car a handheld apparatus must likely be mounted at convenient range. As such, it is also easy to hook up the device with capability extending facilities, such as antenna, battery charging, and loud speakers.
- Modest interface: Furthermore, secure and driving-friendly interfaces must be largely audio-based. In this way the in-car interface minimizes the contention for visual attention which driving undoubtedly requires. Furthermore, it should be possible to apprehend the visual parts through quick glances. This means the interface must be uncluttered and "minimalistic".
- Automated operation: Finally, it must be largely automated, working without prompts for input, but letting the user gain control effortlessly whenever he or she finds adequate time.

4   The Sound Pryer Prototype

In order to meet the requirement of the joint listening we have developed an application for PDAs that supports two basic functions. They are *local play* and *remote play*. The local play mode works like a regular MP3 player, that is plays one item at a time from a list of files. The twist is, in local play, the current item is also broadcasted.

Then in remote play, the user may hear the same item as some other player in local play, within a certain range, by capturing this broadcast. These two functions are then combined into *auto mode*, which automatically handles switches from local play to remote play whenever a peer first enters this range.

To meet the responsiveness requirement of joint listening, auto mode is implemented using two important technologies. The first is MANET technology. A MANET is defined as a self-organizing and transient network. Nodes in such networks do not rely on infrastructure, such as, base stations, routers, or DNS servers, to operate. Two nodes may communicate directly, using IP technology, if they are within wireless range, or indirectly via a chain of hops over intermediate nodes. However, such hopping would potentially contradict the responsiveness criteria and include peers not part of a particular encounter. Thus, Sound Pryer does not use multihop ad hoc networking. For similar reasons, in remote play a peer cannot capture via another that captures from a third part. However, any number of peers may capture the stream from a single source in range. Second, as Sound Pryer uses single-hop networking we can use the range of the transmitter to approximate the participants of a particular traffic encounter. That is if two peers are adjacent in the ad hoc network, they must also be close to each other physically. As high relative speed and limited wireless range makes nodes move out of it quickly, the window of opportunity for discovering peers is short. Bandwidth and energy conservation is really secondary to speedy discovery. Also traffic encounters concerns all nodes involved. This seems like a trivial statement, but in the light of previous work on service location this is a novel requirement. In SLP, Jini, and UPnP etc. it is assumed that discovery is one-sided i.e. only one party wants to find a particular resource. In Sound Pryer the discovery procedure must see to that all peers include all other peers. Sound Pryer accomplishes approximation with the Rapid Mutual Peer Discovery algorithm. (See section 4.1 for details.)

To meet the requirement of robustness we use the RTP to exchange MP3 files during encounters. The peer-to-peer model consists of each Sound Pryer being able to receive streams (via RTP client) as well as output streams (via RTP server) on a multicast channel. Auto mode arbitrates auto mode among a group of peers so that one peer will remain in local play and all the others switch over to remote play. The arbitration algorithm is an example of an exponential back-off algorithm, such as the collision detection protocol of Ethernet. (See section 4.2 below for details.)

Fig. 1. The Sound Pryer Interface. A PDA mounted on the dashboard (left). Local play (middle). Remote play (right).

Finally, we have carefully designed the user interface balancing the requirements of identifying the source and on convenient interaction (See figure 1 above). First, as outlined above, auto mode is entirely automatic and thus fulfilling the automated operation requirement. Furthermore, auto mode is accessible to user via two screens, one for each play mode designed in manner suitable for driving, all according to the modest interface principle. The local play screen allows feedback through quick glances and some fundamental control over what the user is listening to. In the white space below the label ribbon Sound Pryer prints the title and artist name of the song if this information is available. The two large buttons (approximately 2 x 1 cm) allows the user to skip forward and backward one item at the time in the play list. The local play interface starts to play the current item on the play list where it was left off, e.g. in the middle of it, as soon it is activated. To stop music the user must exit auto mode, by pressing the 'ok' button in the upper right corner. The second screen is shown in remote play. We found through a series of Wizard of Oz [1] tests with various remote play screen designs, it was more constructive to provide only an impression of identification information than to include what music is being played. On this screen the whereabouts of the source of music is shown i.e. the vehicle colour and vehicle shape, such as sedan, station wagon, or lorry. To stop music from the remote source, a user must exit auto mode by pressing the 'ok' button.

4.1 Implementation

The Sound Pryer application is implemented in C/C++ interfacing the Pocket PC 2002 operating system API. The prototype runs on three sets of devices: the Compaq Ipaq 3760, the Compaq Ipaq 3850 and the HP Ipaq 5450. In the first two cases, Lucent Orinoco Silver WLAN cards running the IEEE 802.11 IBSS mode are used to accomplish single-hop ad hoc networking. In the latter we use the built-in WLAN card in IBSS mode. We achieve decoding of MP3 data by our own port of the publicly available LIBMAD MPEG Audio decoding library [11], to the Pocket PC 2002. We chose to port the LIVE.COM RTP stack [10] to implement the streaming operations performed in local and remote play i.e. the local play includes a RTP server and remote play includes a RTP client. The GUI of the auto mode relies on a Game API [8] for the Pocket PC 2002 handheld devices. It gives direct access to the video memory, which allows us to implement the full-screen landscape design.

Figure 2 below shows an overview of the software components in Sound Pryer. This figure also demonstrates the actions of auto mode in the case of two peers comes within wireless range of each other:

1. First assume local play is running on peer A.
2. The server module selects the current item of the play list. This item corresponds to a MP3 file stored at peer A.
3. The file is streamed to the multicast channel and simultaneously decoded and sent to the audio output module. Music begins to play by peer A.
4. At a later stage Peer A discovers Peer B through the RMPD algorithm and vice versa.
5. The RMPD module dispatches a notification of this event to the auto mode at both peers.

6. Auto mode initiates exponential backoff algorithm. Assume peer A wins the contention. It stops the server. Music playback stops at peer A, however, as Peer B loses the contention it continues local play.
7. The server dispatches a notification to the RMPD module, which then sends a message to peer B informing this decision.
8. The auto mode of Peer A starts remote play.
9. The RTP client dispatches a message to RMPD, which eventually informs peer B.
10. The client of peer A captures the stream of peer B. Music begins to play at peer A.

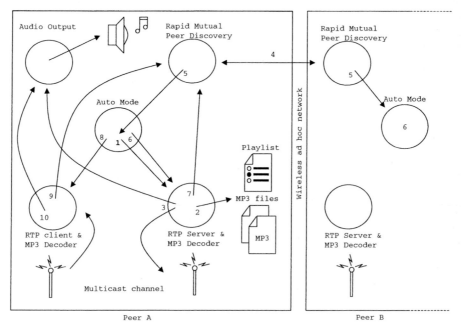

Fig. 2. The Sound Pryer Implementation

In the following sections we will closer examine the Rapid Mutual Peer Discovery and the exponential back-off algorithms of auto mode.

4.2 Rapid Mutual Peer Discovery

The purpose of RMPD is to discover peers in potentially brief traffic encounters. It is similar to AODV HELLO messages [13], but with important addition to accommodate mutual discovery quickly. The RMPD algorithm keeps a list of immediately accessible peers. Each entry in this list contains connectivity information, such as network identifier but also other properties to create an impression of who is providing music in the various user mode interfaces. Each entry is also associated with a timer. The entry is removed from the list when its timer expires. At a regular interval each peer announces its presence by broadcasting a HELLO message, containing the connectivity and auto mode data for that peer. When receiving a hello message from a peer present in the list, the timer of the corresponding timer is reset. Otherwise, an entry is created and appended. However, it would take x seconds before mutual discovery is established with HELLO message rate set to x seconds. To speed up mutual discovery a REPLY message is broadcasted whenever a new entry is inserted in the list. The REPLY message contains the connectivity information of the peer that is about to send it (A) as well as the connectivity information of the peer that was inserted in the list (B). When peers receive this message, they check the following condition: is A unknown and is either B present in the list (or is B this node?)? If so, then the receiving node can safely assume it can reach peer A and appends it to its own list. However, it refrains from sending a REPLY message. Checking this statement reduces the complexity of the total number of message exchanged from $O(n^2)$ to $O(n)$, where n is the number of peers involved.

4.3   The Exponential Back-Off Algorithm

The problem of arbitrating remote play among peers in auto mode, is similar to achieving distributed mutual exclusion [9]. To this problem most solutions are either centralized or distributed [15]. A centralized approach is inappropriate in peer-to-peer networking. Most distributed approaches requires reliable group communication, which is difficult to achieve in wireless ad hoc networking among peers in traffic, due to its extremely transient nature. Exponential back-off algorithms, such as the collision detection protocol of Ethernet, inspire our approach to this issue. The advantage such algorithm is that mutual exclusion can be resolved on each peer without any additional message exchange. This means that Sound Pryer has to keep less state and allows a much simpler architecture. The disadvantage is it may take some time before it is achieved. Basically, the exponential back-off algorithm we have developed for auto mode works as follows: whenever a peer goes into remote play, it waits a random time. If it experiences a failure, that is, there is a peer with a conflicting interest; it waits some more before attempting again. We define conflicting interest to mean the situation when two peers attempt to go into remote play simultaneously. The round-trip time, is the maximum time it takes for a single peer to detect a conflict, which we approximate by the sum of time it takes to stop local play and have RMPD disseminate that to other peers; followed by starting the remote play and having RMPD disseminate that too. Therefore when a peer wants to capture a stream it randomly picks a time slot. The first slot incurs no wait, the second means waiting one round-trip unit of time etc. In the first iteration a peer selects one slot out of two, in the second iteration, one slot out of four etc. For each iteration, when this time expires it checks whether there are any streams available. If this is the case, it stops local play and switches over to remote. If the peer is successfully able to capture, the other will fail and thus continue to stream through local play. There is still a possibility that the conflict will occur but it quickly grows improbable and hence the users are increasingly unlikely to experience interruptions.

5   Field Trial

To test the prototype and better understand the concept we organized a *field trial*. As we designed Sound Pryer to be used on roads among unacquainted drivers, most use situations will be brief and could take place anywhere along the vast road network. The likeliness for an encounter among a small set of unconstrained users is low. These factors constitute a methodological challenge when acquiring realistic feed back on user experience. Thus, we decided to conduct a field trial where the subjects use the prototype during a limited period of time in on a limited route. We conducted three separate trials, which engaged thirteen test subjects in all. We set up rendezvous locations along a circular route at suitable parking lots. The participants should stay unacquainted during the trial, and only meet during traffic encounters to best represent realistic situations. They drove about four laps at the same time, where each lap takes about ten minutes at the speed limit (50 km/h). This created a large number of events where the Sound Pryer concept could be experienced. The cars were equipped with a HP Ipaq 5450 handheld device and two loose speakers mounted on the dashboard. The device was prepared with their personal favourite music. All drivers were video recorded under the trial by a researcher sitting in the front right seat. The recordings were collected in order to pursue a careful analysis of their visible behaviour and increased our ability to understand their reactions as they take place. The drivers were also interviewed directly following the trial. The interviews were structured and all participants had to answer a list of questions.

Results: The field trial allowed us draw conclusions on two levels: the Sound Pryer concept and its prototype implementation. On the conceptual level we have found that joint listening among cars moving in traffic is clearly doable. First, wireless ad hoc networking is a promising technology for streaming MP3 music files with such intent. Second, we have good support in that users understood and appreciated hearing music from others. In line with this, we have found that giving an impression of the source of music through vehicle shape and colour gives is satisfying. Many users did understand and use the hints in their attempts to identify the source. Also, many users enjoyed this aspect. Although entertaining Sound Pryer does not seem dangerously distracting. The video analysis showed that drivers could attend it whenever the context allowed. For instance, sometime users seemed neglected it altogether because they where engaging in relative demanding manoeuvres, e.g. turning or co-ordinating with intense traffic. In the interviews a majority backed this by stating Sound Pryer did not interfere in their driving. Finally concerning the concept, it does not seem that Sound Pryer invades privacy. No users found it particularly intimidating to reveal the shape and the colour of the car. Furthermore, a majority of the users claimed they were willing to distribute music in the manner Sound Pryer demonstrated. The prototype we used in the test needs some improvements in order to better implement the Sound Pryer concept. First and foremost its audio reproduction must be improved, as no users were indecisively impressed with the quality. This concerns both streaming performance, such as removing any disturbances in the audio output, and concealing the back-off negotiation. Although the shape and colour hints of auto mode GUI were adequate in determine the source of music, some users also wanted some sort of help when looking out. This was obvious in situations when there were many similar cars around or very dark. Many users also asked for a control to go back to local play from remote play, when the music of the remote source was unsatisfying. Finally, in some events the range of the wireless ad hoc network did not really reflect users being in the immediate proximity. This happened for instance when it was dark or the source being obscured for some other reason.

6 The Robustness of the Prototype

As the quality of the sound reproduction in the field trial was somewhat disappointing we investigated the performance of the prototype in a lab study. In order to measure the robustness we decided to evaluate the impact of the bandwidth contention for the audio output at a single node. We measured the inter-arrival time of MP3 frames as they are delivered by RTP stack to the application. This is an important metric in streaming media performance, as late frames gives rise to audible gaps in the output and early frames waste bandwidth. However, late frames are not the cause for all disturbances in the output signal. The decoder may skip frames for other reasons, such as when encountering errors. In this particular case, we set up the test as follows. In the lab we placed six HP 5450 Pocket PC PDAs running Sound Pryer in manual mode. In the first test run we had one PDA stream a MP3 file and another capture it. We collected about a minute of data and noted our subjective impressions of the output quality. In the second run we activated the streaming at two PDAs and then activated capturing at the third. Both PDAs were streaming a copy of the file used in the first run. In total we performed five test runs in a similar fashion. In the file used each frame corresponded to about 100 ms of decoded music. On average, the frames are delivered with 30 to 20 ms margin, however occasionally late (or lost) postpones the arrival time. Consequently the standard deviation is about 35 to 50 ms.

Figure 3 shows the histogram of the inter-arrival times. There are two "spikes," the first at the (40, 80) ms interval, and the other at (100,120). Perhaps the first interval is caused due to RTP to compensate for very late frames. The second spike is a consequence of frame size. In the ideal case a frame should be delivered every 100 ms. The result of Figure 3 displays two, somewhat contradictory results. First, it seems that the average frame is delivered in time for play back independent of network load, which is desirable. Yet, there are also some exceptionally long delays occurring independent of load. The frame buffer may conceal occasional short delays for a while. In the case of too many delays, play back will consume the buffer before it is filled up and then disruptions become inevitable. Naturally, long delays will accelerate this process.

7 Conclusion and Future Work

The field trial showed that Sound Pryer was fun and safe on a conceptual level. The user's feedback and the lab test showed the prototype needs various improvements to better reflect the concept. First, in the current design, a user would hear his or her music come on and off at least one time before settling in either local or remote play. To improve the audio performance, the prototype needs to separate the switching of local and remote play in the auto mode from any actual audio playback. This concerns concealing the back-off negotiation and only interrupt local play when the outcome has been decided. Second, the prototype also needs work on the RTP streaming. The inadequate performance may be levitated somewhat with future, more powerful networking and PDA technology, such as quality of service guarantees and real-time

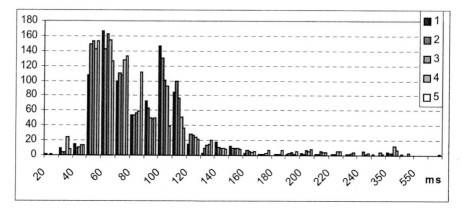

Fig. 3. Histogram of inter-arrival times for each run. To save space buckets left of 250 ms span 10 ms and to the right they span 100 ms.

operating systems. In the mean time we may somewhat approach the problem by increasing buffer lengths. However, this means actually hampering joint listening, as one party will be delayed a few seconds. Third, in terms of user interface, the prototype needs two obvious improvements. The firsts lies in the identification support. Users appreciated being able to receive hints on the source of music, but in some cases it was hard to determine it. Moreover, the opposite was it was also desirable, i.e. to know which users did receive music. To address this, a future design of Sound Pryer may include a lamp that light up the inside of the car, for instance, with a pale blue light. This would help users looking out to locate receivers and it would help user looking for sources. Third, user wanted some control to skip hearing a remote source. For instance, the remote player screen could include two controls, similar to the skip controls of local player screen, which lets user toggle all the remote sources including its own. Fourth, the prototype may also need work on the traffic encounter approximation i.e. using wireless range to determine the parties of a particular encounter. This may be accentuated by future wireless ad hoc networking technologies as they may provide very large range. Using positioning technology, such as GPS, we may calculate an appropriate range to better reflect the boundaries of a traffic encounters.

Acknowledgements. We would like to thank Oskar Juhlin for your support and input to the project and particularly your contributions to the sections on adding value to traffic encounters. Thanks also to the members of the Mobility Studio for your efforts in the field trial and thank you Fredrik Axelsson for your contributions to the Wizard of Oz experiments. We would also like to thank Barry Brown, Lars-Erik Holmquist, and anonymous reviewers for valuable comments on prior versions of this text. The Swedish Research Institute for Information Technology and the Swedish Foundation for Strategic Research through the Mobile Life project funded this research.

References

1. Andersson, G. Höök, K. Mourão, D. Paiva, A. & Costa, M. (2002). Using Wizard of Oz study to inform the design of SenToy, Proc. of DIS, London, UK.
2. Aoiki, P. Grinter, R. Hurst, A. Szymanski M. Thornton, J. & Woodruff, A. (2002). Sotto Voce: Exploring the Interplay of Conversation and Mobile Audio Spaces, Proc. of CHI, Minneapolis, Minnesota, USA.
3. Appleyard, D., Lynch, K. & Myer, J. R. (1964), The View from the Road, M.I.T. Press, Cambridge, Massachusetts, USA.
4. Baudelaire, Charles, The Painter of Modern Life, written 1859, Quoted from Mazlish, Bruce, "The Flâneur: from spectator to representation", in Tester, K. (ed.) The Flâneur, Routledge, London, 1994.
5. Brown, B., Geelhoed, E. & Sellen, A. (2001), The Use of Conventional and New Music Media: Implications for Future Technologies, Proc. of INTERACT'01, Tokyo, Japan.
6. Esbjörnsson, M. & Juhlin, O. (2003). Combining Mobile Phone Conversations and Driving - Studying a Mundane Activity in its Naturalistic Setting, Proc. of ITS, Madrid, Spain.
7. Grinter, R. Aoiki, P. Hurst, A. Szymanski, M. Thornton, J. & Woodruff A. (2002). Revisiting the Visit: Understanding How Technology Can Shape the Museum Visit. Proc. of CSCW'02, New Orleans, Louisiana, USA.
8. Here Comes GAPI! (2003). http://msdn.microsoft.com/library/default.asp? url=/library/en-us/dnppc2k/html/ppc_gapi.asp? frame=true.
9. Lamport, L. (1978). Time, clocks, and the ordering of events in distributed systems, Communications of the ACM, Vol. 21, No. 7.
10. LIVE.COM Streaming Media. (2003). http://www.live.com/liveMedia/.
11. MAD (MPEG Audio Decoder). (2003). http://www.underbit.com/products/mad/.
12. Mobile Ad Hoc Networks (manet) Charter. (2003). http://www.ietf.org/html.charters/manet-charter.html
13. Perkins, C. Belding-Royer, E. & Das, S. Ad Hoc On Demand Distance Vector (AODV) Routing. RFC 3561.
14. Schulzrinne, H. Casner, S. Fredrick, R. & Jacobson V. (1996). RTP: A Transport Protocol for Real-Time Applications. RFC 1889.
15. Singhal, M. (1993). Taxonomy of Distributed Mutual Exclusion Algorithms, Parallel and Distributed Computing, Vol. 18, No. 1.
16. Wiberg, M. (2004). FolkMusic: A Mobile Peer-to-Peer Entertainment System, In Proc. of 37th HICSS, Hawaii, USA.
17. Åkesson, K.P. & Nilsson A. (2002), Designing Leisure Applications for the Mundane Car-Commute, Personal and Ubiquitous Computing, Vol. 6, No. 3, Springer-Verlag, London

Harmonics Table: Audiovisual Expression of Group Interaction on a Sensing Table

Sangwoong Hwang, Hyunchul Park, Chansuk Yang, and Manjai Lee

Digital Media Laboratory, Information and Communications University,
Dogok-dong 517-10, Gangnam-gu, Seoul, Korea
{hwangdang, phc, huewy, manjai}@icu.ac.kr

Abstract. Motion graphics in general is played on a screen. The technology of a sensing table brings this on a table. Mouse pointing on a monitor is changed to cup-shaped pointing devices on a table and the table detects the positions of the cups. According to the movements of the cups, particle animations and sounds are generated on the table. The Harmonics Table is a system which a group of users can experience a harmonized audiovisual expression. This paper introduces an application of interactive motion graphics on the Harmonics Table and describes how a group of users enjoy it in a real life situation.

1 Introduction

We perform a variety of activities on a table such as meeting, having food or talking together. A table is a meaningful piece of furniture that enables several people's getting together. The advent of personal computers reinforces the working capability of an individual. The development of this sort of computing environment resulted in breaking off face-to-face relationships among people even though it improved individual communication ability. People now spend more time in front of their computers than with their family or friends. They even intend to keep their relationships with other people only in cyberspace. A computer has been recognized as a private device by people. Harmonics Table, however, suggests a computing environment with which people can interact while they are looking at one another.

We tried to express the concept of this group interaction by using motion graphics. Motion graphics is a communication method that uses moving graphic images and synchronized sounds. It is mostly used for movie titles, game intros, web sites because it is useful to transmit information effectively. The development of digital media technology made interaction a new element of motion graphics, therefore it is possible that people interact with motion graphics. The interaction with motion graphics is mainly performed on a screen so far. Users could interact with motion graphics only with specific interfaces such as a mouse or a joy stick.

This paper introduces the system that makes people experience the harmonization of graphics, sounds, and movements of cups. The paper also describes the system and function of the Harmonics Table, and how it derives group interactions from the users by using motion graphics.

M. Rauterberg (Ed.): ICEC 2004, LNCS 3166, pp. 553–558, 2004.
© IFIP International Federation for Information Processing 2004

2   Related Work

There are several similar projects technically related to the Harmonics Table. The metaDESK[1] suggests models and prototypes for tangible interfaces. It presents the tangible user interface paradigm and describes its implementation. Sensetable[2] of the MIT Medialab is based on the system which electromagnetically senses multiple objects on a table. Smartskin[3] is a new sensor structure that responds to the gestures of human hands and fingers on an interactive surface. This sensor recognizes the positions of several hands and computes the distance between hands and surface using a net-shaped antenna.

Some projects present how sensing tables and tangible user interfaces are applied to specific situations. Habitat[4] is a project of the Medialab Europe which conducted a research by projecting images of objects on a table to identify other person's behavior in a remote place. Tangible viewpoints[5] is a multimedia storytelling system which explores how physical objects and augmented surfaces can be used in a narrative system. We also referenced Audiopad[6] for graphics and sound implementation. Audiopad is a composition and performance instrument for electronic music which tracks the positions of objects on a tabletop surface and converts their motions into music.

3   Implementation

The basic function of the Harmonics table is to detect the positions of multiple cups and generates particle animations and sounds to these positions on the table. A digitizer is used to detect the position of the cups on the table. Cups are used as tangible user interfaces to generate particle animations and sounds. When the table detects the positions of the cups, it transfers the positioning data to a PC. The PC then projects particle animations on the table by using a beam projector. The sound volume mapped with each graphic image is changed according to the position of the cup. Multiple channel speakers are installed for 3D sound rendering. Movements of cups, particle animations, and sounds can be harmonized on the table.

3.1   Tangible Interface

Cups are tangible interfaces that make users interact with the Harmonics Table. When users put their cups on the table, particle animations and sounds begin to be played on the position of the cups. Users can control particle animations and sounds on the table simply by moving their cups.

Four cups are used for the Harmonics Table operation. Each cup includes small hardware logic and RF receiver. Since a digitizer accepts one device at a time, it can only track a single cup without modification. RF ID is used to resolve this identification problem. This problem is also related with the hardware system.

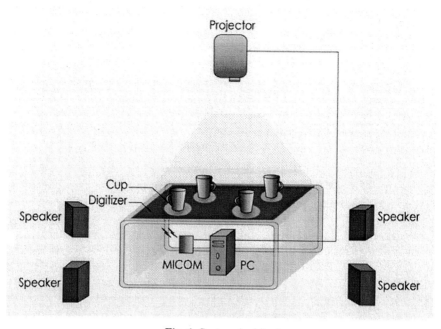

Fig. 1. System Architecture

3.2 Hardware System

A commercial digitizer is used for the base of the Harmonics Table. Being able to support only one object, it is not suitable for group operations, therefore, we modified the digitizer by adding time division multiplexing for multiple objects.

The hardware system manages this problem step by step. A PC transmits an ID number of a cup to the micro controller that is connected to the PC through RS-232C. The micro controller sends RF signal to activate a cup with the partial ID. When the RF receiver in the cup receives the signal from the micro controller, the cup with that ID is turned on and the table detects the position of that specific cup. The response time of each cup is 300ms, so each cup operates only within that time frame. To minimize the delay, the number of objects on the table is limited to four cups. Finally, the position data is transmitted to the PC, and the PC generates graphic images and sounds through a beam projector and multiple channel speakers. The hardware system repeats this process continuously to make all cups work together.

3.3 Software Architecture

Software architecture of the Harmonics Table consists of I/O manager, positioning manager, and graphic and sound manager. The I/O manager manages input and output data that are transmitted between the digitizer and the PC. When positioning data is received from the table, the positioning manager classifies each data according to the ID number of cups and distributes data to the graphic and sound managers.

The graphic and sound managers create particle animations and sounds on the position of each cup in accordance with the position and the ID number of each cup. If the position of any cup is not detected, it is assumed that no cup is on the table and thus no action is taken. Hence, it does not create any object on the table.

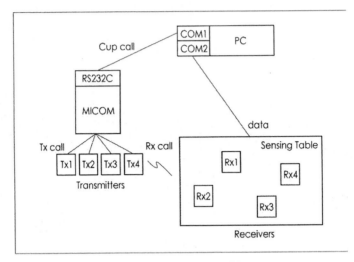

Fig. 2. Hardware System Plan

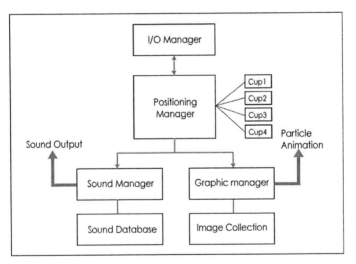

Fig. 3. Software Architecture

4   Content Design

The content design of the Harmonics Table can be divided into two parts, a graphic design and a sound design. Basically, graphic images are presented by particle animations. All images are symmetric patterns such as stars, snowflakes, flowers and water drops. Users can change the shape of each particle image by pointing a specific graphic icon with a cup.

Each cup makes different sound according to their ID number. Different instrument such as piano, violin, cello, and flute is assigned to each cup to make a harmonic sound. The genre of sounds is changed by choosing a graphic icon which represents the pattern of particles at each corner. Each graphical icon is mapped with different musical genre. For example, techno music is played when a star image is selected or waltz is played when a flower image is selected. The migration of sounds is expressed by 3D sound rendering, therefore, users can feel the movements of the cups.

Fig. 4. A group of people enjoy on the Harmonics Table with their cups. They experience an audiovisual harmonization mediated by interactive motion graphics

The most interesting part of the Harmonic Table is the interaction with motion graphics through cups. The users can control motion graphics for themselves. They can experience a harmonization between their actions and motion graphics through the synchronization of particle animations, sounds and movement of the cups. Actually, the Harmonic Table was exhibited at HCI 2004 conference in Korea in February 2004. About 1000 people experienced the Harmonics Table.

5 Conclusion and Future Work

In this paper, we presented the Harmonics Table that detects the positions of cups and generates particle animations and sounds to the positions. With this table, a group of users could experience the harmonization of audiovisual expression and their movements. The use of RF IDs through time division multiplexing made it possible that a group of users interact with several cups on the table together. Motion graphics is turned out to be a good method for appealing emotionally to the users and stimulating group interactions. The combination of graphic images and sounds excited them with audiovisual amusements and lead them to play together. Consequently, the Harmonics Table performed a successful role as an entertainment tool with which a group of users can enjoy together through tangible cups and motion graphics.

Nevertheless, there are some hardware limitations with the Harmonics Table. The number of objects on the table is limited to four cups, and the delayed response time issue of the cups still remains. Up until now, direction has not been an issue since the cup has symmetric shape, but it would be another problem when the direction of a cup needs to be detected.

We are currently improving the system to be able to respond to the physical environment more effectively by adding other attributes of a cup such as direction, weight, temperature and so on. There will be a lot of applications such as multimedia board games by using this system in the future.

Acknowledgement. Many researchers at the Digital Media Laboratory have collaborated on this project. We really appreciate Taehwa Lee, Youngmi Kim, Hyemin Jung, Youngjae Kim and Seongyoon Cho for their help with the hardware construction and the comments on the system design.

References

1. Ullmer, B., Ishii, H.: The metaDESK: models and prototypes for tangible user interfaces. In Proceedings of UIST'97 (1997) 223-232
2. Patten, J., Ishii, H., Hines, J., Pangaro, G.: Sensetable: A wireless Object Tracking Platform for Tangible user Interfaces. In Proceedings of CHI'01, ACM Press (2001) 253-260
3. Rekimoto, J.: SmartSkin: An Infrastructure for Freehand Manipulation on Interactive Surfaces. In Proceedings of CHI'02, ACM Press (2002) 113-120
4. Patel, D., Agamanolis, S.: Habitat: awareness of life rhythms over a distance using networked furniture. In Proceedings of UbiComp2003 (2003) 163-164
5. Mazalek, A., Davenport, G., Ishii, H.: Tangible Viewpoints: A Physical Interface for Exploring Character-Driven Narratives. In Proceedings of SIGGRAPH'02, ACM Press (2002) 153-160
6. Patten, J., Recht, B., Ishii, H.: Audiopad: A Tag-Based Interface for Musical Performance. In Proceedings of NIME'02 (2002)

Hello-Fish: Interacting with Pet Fishes Through Animated Digital Wallpaper on a Screen

Sunyean Jang and Manjai Lee

Digital Media Laboratory, Information and Communications University,
Dogok-dong 517-10, Gangnam-Gu, Seoul, Korea
{yoursun74, manjai }@icu.ac.kr

Abstract. Real life forms have not been seriously considered to be an essential part in ubiquitous computing. Hello-Fish is an Internet-based application that monitors and feeds our fishes which are part of lovely pets. This system allows people to feel the mood interpreted by the movements of the fishes from anywhere. We propose a new interactive system for getting in touch with the living creatures around us in a ubiquitous computing environment.

1 Introduction

In the future ubiquitous computing environment, humans will communicate with smart devices and lot of research has been done on such environment. However not much consideration has been given to the pets which human live with. In this paper, we transformed the pets into more familiar objects on the Internet so that they can be felt to be near your side even though they are actually far way from us. This research is about how to interact with our pets efficiently in the cyberspace.

Fishes are considered to be less active than dogs or cats [1], but they let their owner feel enough affection as an element of adornment in our living environment. What they provide as a decorative element could not be felt unless we are adjacent to them. During our absence, it is almost impossible that we feed them and watch them so that we feel pleasure by their presence as a decorative element. Therefore, we changed real fishes into cyber ones. Furthermore, the cyber fishes coming into existence on the Internet can become diversified as a decorative motif. We can access Internet from everywhere, a real world environment can be moved into a computer-screen connected by network and is transformed into other type of decorative object. Additionally, the movement of fish is interpreted into music. This is a kind of ambient system which provides the same feeling as real fishes swimming in a fish tank mediated through Internet anytime, anywhere.

We can visualize the swimming fishes in our home by making digitally animated wallpaper on a screen. Such movements of fishes on the wallpaper are mapped onto specific music so that it would be easy to feel them even without paying serious attention to it. Hello-Fish is the system with which the real fishes in a fish tank are synchronically mapped with the animated fishes that constitute a wallpaper on a monitor screen.

M. Rauterberg (Ed.): ICEC 2004, LNCS 3166, pp. 559–564, 2004.
© IFIP International Federation for Information Processing 2004

2   System Concept

The Hello-Fish system has multiple components. A camera capturing the image of the fishes in a fish tank sends video signals to a control PC. The control PC computes the speed and location of each fish, uses the information to generate music, and then transmits it to any client which keeps on requesting it from the control PC. Hello-Fish works on the Web. The animated fishes, Flash MX^{TM} objects, on the Web act like real fishes by means of the information made from the control PC. Hello-Fish simultaneously plays music according to the information related to the music generation.

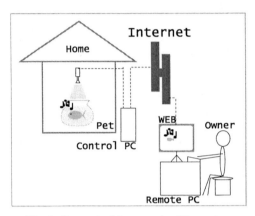

Fig. 1. Conceptual framework of the system

3   System Overview

The Hello-Fish system uses a webcam to capture real-time images of fishes. Each fish identified by the corresponding color is represented on a 2-dimensional coordinate system. The webcam captures 30 image frames every one of which has 640x480 pixels of resolution and sends the frames to the control PC. The color information of the transferred images is changed from RGB to HIS color space. The color of a fish is extracted from HIS. The control PC computes the center point at each color area extracted. Image-threshold methodology for tracing objects is used. Because Local Scale Selection [2], which uses template matching, would need more time for computing, just using simple thresholding is more efficient for reducing the computing time. Four corner points of the area that covers the detected fish are transferred to a client via Internet. The transferred information on the coordinates representing the location of the fish extracted from the control PC is exploited to draw the corresponding animated fish on the screen. Using Hello-Fish system, we can provide food to the fishes via Internet. When one wants to feed fishes, just clicking a proper button on the wallpaper controls the feeding-device attached to the real fish tank. Hello-Fish generates music based on the MIDI specification. The harmonics of the music are composed of 128 different kinds of musical instruments, 16 categorized rhythms, 7 codes, and 4 beat sounds corresponding to the speed, location, and the accelerating rates of the fishes.

4 Tracking System

Even though an inexpensive webcam is used for this subsystem, Dragonfly ^{TM} camera is used because it has its own grabber and is able to send images directly to the control PC without overloading the PC receiving images. The transferred image is in RGB domain. However, the control PC translates RGB domain to HIS domain in order to identify each fish by using Hue value of HIS domain [3]. Two windows are used for the efficient tracking of the fishes. One is 'threshold window' whose location can be assumed to be at the same position of the fish if the threshold window contains a specific color of a fish above some level of a threshold value of the color of the fish. This window moves across an entire image and checks if any fish is included in the window. Once the detection completes, the detected positions of the fishes are memorized. After the execution of 'threshold window', another window, called 'tracking window', is used from next image.

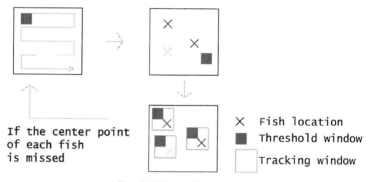

Fig. 2. Fish tracking process

The tracking window, a larger than the threshold window, is located in the center position of the threshold window which is previously memorized. After this process, it doesn't need to check the entire region of every image to find the location of the fishes. The detection of the fishes using a threshold window is accomplished only in the tracking window. Since then, in every transferred image the center position of a tracking window keeps up with the respective threshold window. Only if a threshold window can not detect the position of the fish in the tracking window, this system will check and find the positions using the threshold window across the entire region of the transferred image again. Fig 2 describes the whole process of the detecting fishes. This methodology would prevent the time complexity in computing. However, there is not any method for identifying each fish. In case a school of fishes are in a fish tank, Hello-Fish can not identify each fish in the school, but just captures each fish without any identification. And, a fish that does not move frequently might lead to a confusion on the screen regarding whether the fish died or not. In this system, only 3 fishes of which each color is red, yellow and blue are used as the subjects because the differences among these colors make threshold-method simple.

5 Network System

This system follows the Client-Server model. A client implemented with Flash MX^{TM} continues to send requests to the server in a predefined time-interval. The server responds to the requests sent from a client through TCP/IP. The data is used to draw each fish on the screen to plot location, direction and moving speed. The accurate positions of the fishes are not critical to this approach because the main purpose of this system is to representing the mood of the fish movements than the subtle actions of each fish. If the data is lost during its transfer, the system uses previous data again so that the client can maintain the continuity of the fish movements.

6 Music Generator

MIDI Specification [4] provides the method with which the system is able to produce a variety of sounds and to play various musical instruments. Since a MIDI device is supported by Windows^{TM}, any extra device for supporting MIDI is not required. There are three fundamental principles to make music. These are melody, harmony, and rhythm. The system satisfies these three elements and simultaneously matches the music with the movements of fishes. Each note is chosen based on the location of a fish, and the movement of the fish decides whether or not the system should play the selected notes. A chord for harmony is selected randomly from the five basic chords and the five basic chords are predefined in the system. The pattern of rhythm also is predefined as well because the subtle motions are hardly captured by the system. A base sound is played as background music. This can make the overall mood of a music much richer.

Fig. 3. Difference of Notes

The system can play maximum sixteen notes in a measure. A measure has sixteen notes to be played but all notes are not always generating sound. Only when the movements of a fish are detected at a specific time, then the corresponding note should be played, otherwise, the note is skipped and the system moves to the next note. The system makes a high tone for each note based on the difference between the previous vertical position of a fish and the current one. Fig 3 shows that when the current vertical position of a fish is relatively higher than before, the high tone of the note is played; when it is lower, the low tone would be played. The maximum difference of the tone is limited to two octaves.

In this system, triads as a chord are used for harmony. The main triads as the priming chord are used and are predefined patterns. They are played one by one out of the chosen patterns because a randomly chosen piece of music might not be heard comfortably to human ears. Each fish represents a musical instrument, whenever it moves, the corresponding musical instruments will be played. There are only two types of low tones as background music. When there is no detected movement of fishes, the system just plays a silent low tone music as background music. When the fish moves fast, it plays more dynamic low tone music.

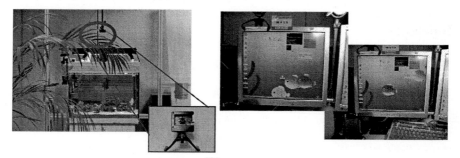

(a) Real fish tank equipped with Dragonfly ™   (b) On-screen animated fishes

Fig. 4. The overall system is composed of a real fish tank and an on-screen wallpaper that reflects the movements of the fishes

7 Conclusion

We have presented the Hello-Fish system that monitors the real-time movements of pet fishes. Color-threshold method is used for motion detection. This method is very simple and needs little time for computing. Music is exploited so that we can feel the movements of the fishes even without seeing them. Since the wallpaper containing animated cyber fishes on a screen has a small footprint, it is hard to overload the computer used to realize the system. Hello-Fish supports the way of interacting with fishes via network. This is done by controlling the feeding-device to feed the fishes. Each cyber fish has the similar size as its real world partner relative to the size of the fish tank so that the sense of reality triggered by the wallpaper can be enhanced. Hello-Fish is an exciting step towards a more natural setting based on the concept of co-existing with living objects in a ubiquitous computing environment. Hello-Fish explores how to obtain the same feeling and mood that we experience with our live pets and fishes even in a remote place.

8 Future Work

The current wallpaper on a screen consists of pre-designed fishes, therefore it is not flexible in terms of the system extension. When more fishes are added in the fish tank, the installed wallpaper would not be able to show the added fishes until it is modified and reinstalled on a client PC. If the wallpaper has a programmed fish library that includes a variety of fish shapes, it can be extended to show any rendered fish on the screen. Moreover, the exact mapping table between the movements of fishes and music is needed because it can make more natural moods which allow us to feel the dynamic movements of fishes simply by listening to the music.

References

1. Mikesell, Dan.: Networking Pets and People .Adjunct proceedings, In Ubicomp 2003 proceeding, ACM Press (2003) 88–89
2. Oliver Chormat.: Recognizing Goldfish? Or Local Scale Selection For Recognition Techniques, SIRS99, University of Coimbra, Portugal (1999) 20-23
3. Rafael C, Gonzalez.: Digital Image Processing. 2nd edn. Prentice Hall, Upper Saddle River, New Jersey 07458 (2002) 295-302

Background Music Generation Using Music Texture Synthesis

Min-Joon Yoo [1], In-Kwon Lee [1], and Jung-Ju Choi [2]

[1] Department of Computer Science, Yonsei University, Seoul 120-749, South Korea.
debussy@cs.yonsei.ac.kr, iklee@yonsei.ac.kr
[2] Division of Media, Ajou University, Suwon 443-749, South Korea.
jungju@ajou.ac.kr

Abstract. This paper suggests a method to synthesize a long background music sequence from a given short music clip in real-time. The copies of input clip are placed with overlapped region, the length of which is computed by random or clip matching method. Based on pitch, rhythm and chord cut criteria, the cutting point of the two clips is computed within the overlapped region. As a result, the two clips are concatenated at the cutting point. Generating some variations such as mirroring, retrograding and transposing of the given music clip makes the synthesized result much more dynamic. Suggested method is especially useful for interactive and real-time applications such as games and web contents.

1 Introduction

Background music along with various sound effects helps audiences to be immersed in various multimedia applications such as animations, games, web contents, and digital movies [4, 9, 11, 14]. Because of various limitations such as memory space and transmission cost, the length of background music is usually limited to be very short and played repeatedly in many applications. However, such a simple repetition of the same music clip would be tedious even if the clip is a masterpiece.

In this paper, we suggest a method to synthesize a long (possibly infinite) music sequence from a given short music clip. Audiences can realize that the resulting synthesized music is similar to the original music clip, but is not a simple repetition of the original clip. The copies of original music clip are placed randomly or using clip matching with some overlaps. Each overlapped region between two clips is analyzed to determine a cutting point, where two clips are cut and concatenated (see Fig. 1(a)). In this sense, our method, called **"music texture synthesis,"** is similar to the patch based texture synthesis techniques [2, 6, 8, 16] that are used for generating a large size texture image from a small input.

Recently, there have been some trials to synthesize a new audio signal from given audio sources [1, 5, 12]. However, most of those work concentrated on synthesizing sound effects but not background music. For the music synthesis we need to consider more about the musical relationships among the musical elements in the input music clip. We also present some extensions of the music synthesis in this paper:

M. Rauterberg (Ed.): ICEC 2004, LNCS 3166, pp. 565–570, 2004.

synthesizing output music from several input music clip variations obtained by mirroring, retrograding, and transposing the source music clip.

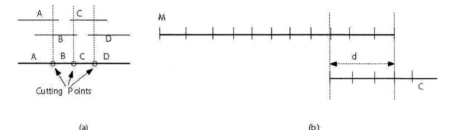

(a)   (b)

Fig. 1. (a) The output music is synthesized by placing the copies of an input clip and concatenating them at some cutting points; (b) Placement is always aligned with measures (M: current output music, C: a copy of input music clip, and d: the number of measures in the overlapped region).

2 Placement

The copies of an input music clip can be placed with various granularities in terms of the musical elements such as beat and measure. Let C be a given input music clip with n measures, and assume that we want to place C near the end of the currently synthesized output music M with some overlapped regions of d measures, where $1 \le d \le n$ (see Fig. 1(b)).

We use one of the two methods to determine the value d: random selection and clip matching methods. In random selection method, d can be randomly selected from the possible range of the value. In clip matching method, the acceptance of a randomly selected value d is determined by computing the cost c of matching in the overlapped region as follow:

$$c = \frac{\sum_{t \in d} (M(t) - C(t))^2}{r},$$ (1)

where r denotes the number of musical events in the overlapped region d. In the above formula, $M(t)$ and $C(t)$ are two musical events that happen at the same time t (or at least matching pair for comparison - see Section 3) in the region d. The difference between the two musical events, $(M(t) - C(t))$, can be measured with various criteria, for example, difference of pitches or durations of two notes. We will present the detailed difference computation schemes later in Section 3. If the cost is less than a given limit, the random value d is accepted as the next translation for the synthesis.

To control the randomness in the selection of d value, we can exploit the probabilistic determination scheme. When a matching cost c for a d is computed, we accept the d value only when the probability:

$$P(c) = e^{-\frac{c}{k}} \qquad (2)$$

is larger than a given limit probability value (we took 0.5 as the limit probability for most of experiments). The predefined constant value k is determined by considering the average cost of matching, which can be used to control the randomness in the placement. The larger the value of k is given, the larger the randomness in selection of d.

3 Cutting Point

After determining the overlapping region d between the current output music M and the input music clip C, we need to decide the exact cutting point in d, where M and C are cut and concatenated. For determining the cutting point, we can exploit various music analysis and synthesis techniques such as melody generation, rhythm analysis, and chord analysis [15]. First, for each note $M(t)$ in the current output music, a matching note in the input clip C is found. If there is a note $C(t)$ in C played at the same time t, $(M(t), C(t))$ can be a matching pair. If not, we pick a nearest note $C(t_*)$ from t, where $t_* < t$, as the matching note of $M(t)$ (see Fig. 2). Similarly, the matching note for each note $C(t)$ can be found in M.

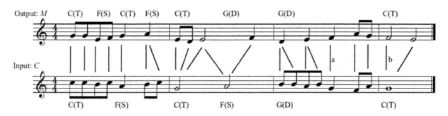

Fig. 2. Determining cutting point: The vertical line segments between the notes of M and C represent the matching pairs. Each chord name is denoted with the class of the chord: one of T (Tonic), S (Subdominant), and D (Dominant). Using pitch cut, two pairs, a and b, are the candidates of the cutting point, which have smallest difference between pitches. With the rhythm cut method, the first measure pair among the four measure pairs is selected as cutting measure pair that has most similar rhythm patterns. With chord cutting method, we can select the third or fourth measure pair, each of which consists of two measures having the same chord.

Pitch Cut: In the melody of typical music, the pitch difference between two adjacent notes is not usually too big [13]. Using this fact, we can design the process to select the cutting point in terms of the pitch variations in the overlapped region. We select the position of a matching note pair with minimum pitch difference as the cutting point. If two or more tied candidates are found, we can randomly select one of the candidates (see Fig. 2).

Rhythm Cut: For determining the cutting measure in terms of rhythm variation, we find a pair of two corresponding measures (the two measures from M and

C overlapped in d) having the most similar rhythm pattern. The number of matching note pairs (denoted as m) having different note durations is counted for each pair of measures. The pair of measures with smallest m can be selected as the cutting measure. Fig. 2 shows an example of finding a cutting measure.

Chord Cut: If the chord sequence for the input music clip is given or analyzed [15], there can be many possibilities to find different cutting points in terms of various chord progression schemes in popular or jazz music [10]. For the convenience in chord analysis, we classified the given chords into the three basic categories as follows (the chord names are given assuming C major key):

- Tonic family: C, Em, and Am
- Subdominant family: F and Dm
- Dominant family: G and Bm^{-5}

In the above classification, we enumerated only the diatonic triads, however, more complex chords used in jazz or popular music can be classified into the above three classes [10]. We also considered various chord substitution rules used in reharmonizing jazz music [10] for the classification. The cutting pair of measures is determined as the pair of measures where two measures have most similar chord progression (see Fig. 2).

Hybrid Method: After deciding the cutting measure by rhythm or chord cut method, we can additionally apply the pitch cut method for the melody in the cutting measure. Using this hybrid method, the exact cutting note is determined in the cutting measure, thus, the melody in the output music can be smoothly connected without any abrupt change.

4   Variations and Results

We can apply the following variations to the given original music clip to generate slightly varied input sources:

- **Mirroring** : The pitch of each note in the original clip is mirrored with respect to the average pitch. For example, in Fig. 3(b), the notes in the original music clip are mirrored with respect to the center pitch 'F'.
- **Retrograding**: The order of notes in the original melody is reversed from end to start (see Fig. 3(c)).

- **Transposing**: The original melody is transposed to some other meter (see Fig. 3(d)).

From the given input music clip, the varied input clips using above operations can be automatically generated and used for creating synthesized music (see Fig. 3(e)), which is usually more dynamic than the music synthesized from a single input clip. We used pitch-cut for determining the cutting points, and clip matching for the placements of source clips in the example in Fig. 3(e).

Fig. 3. Melody synthesis example: (a) 4 measure input music clip, (b) mirrored input (center = F), (c) retrograde input, (d) transposed input (by major 2nd interval), and (e) synthesized output from (a)-(d).

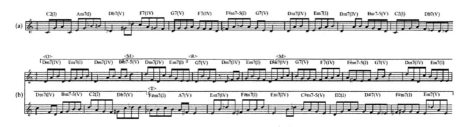

Fig. 4. An example including chords: (a) original input; (b) synthesized output from the original <O>, retrograde <R>, mirrored <M>, and transposed <T> inputs. We used hybrid method combining chord-cut and pitch-cut to generate the output.

Fig. 4 shows a practical example including the chord progression. In this example, we applied the variations such as transposing, mirroring, and retrograding to generate various input sources from the given original clip with 8 measures. When we generate the variations of an input music clip (with chords), the generated melody is possibly not compatible with the chords. In this case, the pitches of some notes in the varied melody are slightly modified by considering the available notes of various modes in jazz theory [3]. The modification process can be automated by the systematic rules defining available and avoided notes in seven possible modes such as Ionian, Lydian, Aeolian, etc. This modification makes the resulting melody become more suitable with the chords. Readers can access more results of this research by internet [17] including some examples with melody and accompaniment.

5 Conclusion

In this paper, we suggested a method to synthesize a long music sequence from a given short input music clip. Our method is inherently greedy-type, thus, they can be tuned for interactive and real-time applications. Instead of packaging a long music sequence within a single multimedia content, the background music can be synthesized from a short input music clip in real-time. We are investigating better methods by exploiting more musical criteria for cutting and placing the music clip. For example, a more intelligent chord-cut method can be used by considering non-diatonic scale chords such as secondary dominants [10]. For the placement, we can exploit more sophisticated algorithm using MRF (Markov Random Field) that is often used in texture synthesis [6, 16]. Although we tested our methods for the music of MIDI format, we believe the methods can also be applicable to the audio signal with the aids of music perception techniques [7].

References

1. Cardle, M., Brooks, S., Bar-Joseph, Z., and Robinson, P.: Sound-by-Numbers: Motion-Driven Sound Synthesis. Proceedings of ACM SIGGRAPH/Eurographics Symposium on Computer Animation (2003)
2. Cohen, M., Shade, J., Hiller, S., and Deussen, O.:Wang Tiles for Image and Texture Generation. Proceedings of ACM SIGGRAPH 2003 (2003) 287-294
3. Coker, J.: Improvising Jazz. Fireside publisher (1986)
4. Cook, P.: Real Sound Synthesis for Interactive Applications. AK Peters (2002)
5. Dubnov, S., Bar-Joseph, Z., El-Yaniv, R., Lischinski, D., and Werman, M.: Synthesis of Audio sound Textures by Learning and Resampling of Wavelet Trees. IEEE Computer Graphics and Applications, 22(4) (2002) 38-48
6. Efros, A., and Freeman, W.: Image Quilting for Texture Synthesis and Transfer. Proceedings of ACM SIGGRAPH 2001 (2001) 341-346
7. Gold, B., and Morgan, N.: Speech and Audio Signal Processing: Processing and Perception of Speech and Music. Wiley Text Books (1999)
8. Kwatra, V., Schödl, A., Essa, I., Turk, G., and Bobick, A.: Graphcut Textures: Image and Video Texture Synthesis Using Graph Cuts. Proceedings of ACM SIGGRAPH (2003)
9. Laybourne, K.: The Animation Book. Three Rivers Press (1998)
10. Levine, M.: The Jazz Theory Book. Sher Music Co. (1996)
11. Marks, A.: The Complete Guide to Game Audio. CMP Books (2001)
12. Parker, J., and Chan, S.: Sound Synthesis for theWeb, Games, and Virtual Reality. Paper Sketch at SIGGRAPH 2003 (2003)
13. Perricone, J.: Melody in Songwriting. Hal Leonard Publisher (2000)
14. Rose, J.: Producing Great Sound for Digital Video. CMP Books (1999)
15. Rowe, R.: Machine Musicianship. MIT Press (2004)
16. Wei, L., and Levoy, M., Fast Texture Synthesis Using Tree Structured Vector Quantization. Proceedings of ACM SIGGRAPH (2000) 479-488
17. Music Texture Synthesis Research Page: http://visualcomputing.yonsei.ac.kr/research/musictexture.html

A Progressive Sounding Object Model in Virtual Environment

Qiong Zhang and Taiyi Chen

College of Computer Science and Technology, Zhejiang University, P. R. China
madisonzhang@yahoo.com

Abstract. Realistic audio is a requisite part of an immersive VR system. Previous research primarily focused on sound transmission modeling, e.g. room acoustics modeling. A progressive sounding object model based on modal synthesis is proposed in this article to integrate sound source modeling with sound transmission simulation. It is characterized by direct construction from geometry data plus a handful of material properties of the virtual object, progressive representation in multiple levels and natural binaural modeling.

1 Introduction

Sound has long been acknowledged as an effective channel in human-computer interaction [1]. Strictly speaking, there're two primary steps involved in rendering realistic sound, i.e., sound generation (sound source modeling) and sound rendering (sound transmission modeling from sound source to the eardrums of the user) [2,3]. We notice that the first step is conspicuously avoided in most situations and prerecorded or pre synthesized sounds are used instead. Actually, it is important to perform sound source modeling in rendering contact sounds for interactive simulations [4]. van den Doel et al [4] developed a system for automatic generation sounds based on a physically motivated model called modal synthesis. It models a vibrating object by a bank of damped harmonic oscillators that are excited by an external stimulus. The synthesis equation is $q(t) = \sum_{i=1}^{n} A_i e^{-d_i t} \sin \omega_i^d t$, where A_i is the mode gain, d_i is the decay rate and ω_i^d is the mode frequency. The effectiveness of this model is further demonstrated by Avanzini et al [5] and O'Brian et al [6].

The progressive sounding object model proposed in this paper extends the modal synthesis method in several aspects. After calculating all the model parameters given the geometry and material properties of the virtual object, all the modes are ordered based on perceptual criteria so that the sound could be synthesized in a progressive way. 3D filtering is integrated into the synthesis process in a very natural way that makes this originally computation-intensive process a trivial task.

M. Rauterberg (Ed.): ICEC 2004, LNCS 3166, pp. 571–576, 2004.

2   A Progressive Sounding Object Model

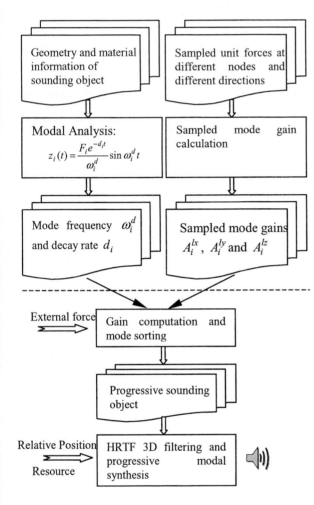

The sound produced by a solid object and then heard by the end user in virtual environments depends on quite a few of factors. Those factors can be roughly classified into two groups, namely static and dynamic group. The static group is independent of interaction, which includes geometry and material properties of the object. By contrast, the dynamic one is dependent on interaction and simulation context, which primarily include external force to produce sound on the object, the relative position between sounding object and the user, room acoustical properties and so on. As illustrated in Fig 1, the whole process to derive progressive sounding object could be divided into two parts. Though it is a dynamic model, large part of the computation as shown in the top half part of Fig 1 could be done offline. Only the bottom half should be run in real time.

Fig. 1. Derivation of progressive sounding object

2.1   A Sounding Object Model Based on Modal Synthesis

The free vibration problem of a multi-degree of freedom (DOF) system can be described by following generalized eigenvalue problem [7]:

$$(K - \lambda M)\phi = 0 \tag{1}$$

Where K and M are known as stiffness and mass matrix, λ is the eigenvalue (square of undamped natural frequency, i.e. ω^2) and ϕ is the corresponding mode shape.

Accordingly, the discretized structural dynamics problem can be expressed as follows:

$$M\ddot{y}(t) + C\dot{y}(t) + Ky(t) = f(t) \tag{2}$$

Where C is the system's damping matrix, $y(t)$, $\dot{y}(t)$ and $\ddot{y}(t)$ are the vectors of node displacement, velocity and acceleration respectively, $f(t)$ is the external force.

Premultiplying Φ^T and substituting $y(t) = \sum_{i=1}^{n} z_i(t)\phi_i$ and $C = \alpha M + \beta K$ into (2), we eventually can get mode equations in a set of single degree oscillators:

$$\ddot{z}_i(t) + 2\xi_i\omega_i\dot{z}_i(t) + \omega_i^2 z_i(t) = F_i \tag{3}$$

Where $\omega_i = \sqrt{K_i/M_i}$ ($M_i = \phi_i^T M\phi_i$, $K_i = \phi_i^T K\phi_i$) are the undamped natural frequencies and damping ratio is $\xi_i = \alpha/2\omega_i + \beta\omega_i/2$ and $F_i = \phi_i^T f(t)/M_i$.

Without loss of generality, we assume that $f(t)$ is a very short-time impulsive force applied at time 0 and zero initial conditions. The analytic solutions for (3) are:

$$z_i(t) = (F_i e^{-d_i t}/\omega_i^d) * \sin \omega_i^d t \tag{4}$$

Where damped mode frequency $\omega_i^d = \omega_i\sqrt{1-\xi_i^2}$, $d_i = \xi_i\omega_i$ is the decay rate.

Assuming the discretized sounding object has L nodes in total on the surface and $3l-2$, $3l-1$, $3l$ are three corresponding DOFs at node l. The deviation from equilibrium of the surface at this node could be described by:

$$q_l(t) = (y_{3l-2}(t) + y_{3l-1}(t) + y_{3l}(t)).n_l \tag{5}$$

$$= \sum_{i=1}^{n} (a_{i(3l-2)}n_x.n_l + a_{i(3l-1)}n_y.n_l + a_{i(3l)}n_z.n_l)e^{-d_i t}\sin \omega_i^d t$$

Where n_l is the normal vector at node l and n_x, n_y and n_z is the unit vector in X, Y and Z direction respectively.

Considering each node on the surface could be seen as an individual sound source, the sound actually emitted from the vibrating solid object is very complicated and could be roughly expressed as the summation of the surface deviation of all the surface nodes:

$$Q(t) = \sum_{l=1}^{L} q_l(t) = \sum_{i=1}^{n} A_i e^{-d_i t}\sin \omega_i^d t \tag{6}$$

Where $A_i = \sum_{l=1}^{L}(a_{i(3l-2)}n_x.n_l + a_{i(3l-1)}n_y.n_l + a_{i(3l)}n_z.n_l)$.

The continuous contact force can be thought of infinite series of short duration impulse. Because the modes behave linearly, the output of the vibrating sounding object driven by this force can be written as a sum of contributions from each of these impulses.

2.2 Sounding Object in Multiple Levels of Details

Sounding objects derived from finite element method usually have a large number of modes. For real time applications such as immersive virtual environments, it should be very beneficial if we can sort those modes based on perceptual criteria so that final sound can be synthesized progressively. However, unlike progressive geometry models that we could build it in advance, part of modal models (i.e. the mode gain A_i) is dependent on the simulation context and always changing. Therefore, it makes the progressive representation of sounding objects more challenging.

van den Doel et al [8] proposed a scheme to order modes. However, it only works for predefined position and direction of the contact force since the mode gain are predetermined rather than calculated in real time. Obviously, mode gain plays a very important role in determining the perceptual significance of a mode. It's desirable to have modes ordered in real time based on perceptual criteria. Here we adopt a procedure in two steps, i.e. offline preprocessing and subsequent real time calculation. The preprocessing process could be described as follows:

<u>Step 1</u> Given object's material and geometry properties, stiffness and mass matrix K and M are derived through finite element method. Damping matrix C is further calculated. The materials properties involved are Young's modulus E, Poisson's ratio v, and density ρ. Two constants α and β [7] are used to determine damping ratio.

<u>Step 2</u> Base on equation (1), the relevant characteristic frequencies ω_i and corresponding mode shapes ϕ_i for the object are pre-computed.

<u>Step 3</u> After calculating damping ratio ξ_i, we can solve damped mode frequency ω_i^d and decay rate d_i. Only the modes falling in human audible frequency range are retained and those mode frequencies are transformed into Bark scale $BARK_i$.

<u>Step 4</u> Assuming a unit impulse force is applied at node l at time 0 in X direction, calculate mode gain A_i^{lx}. Similar, we could calculate A_i^{ly} and A_i^{lz} respectively if the force is in Y and Z direction. By applying the unit impulse force at different nodes and in different directions, the mode gains are sampled $3L$ times in total. Due to the linearity of modal synthesis, mode gain under any n dimensional impulse force could be expressed in linear combination of those sampled mode gains.

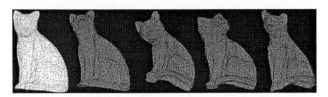

Fig. 2. An example of original models and their first four modes

Figure 2 shows a cat model in original form and their first four modes. This model uses following materials parameters: E= $2\times10^{10} pa$, v=0.3, ρ =2500(kg/m3), α =0 and β =1×10^{-7}. The number of nodes and elements (tetrahedron) are 2637 and 9568 respectively. In the real time simulation, mode gain A_i is calculated as the linear combination of sampled mode gains based on the location and direction of contact force. Fig 3 shows part of the modes calculated from the cat example in Fig 2. The horizontal axes of left and right figures are in frequency and Bark respectively.

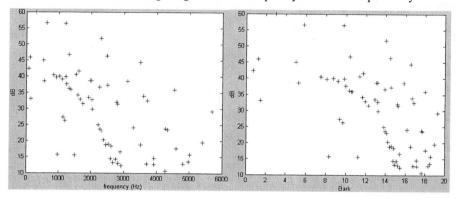

Fig. 3. Part of modes calculated from the model in Fig 1, the number of modes shown up is 70

Similar with van den Doel's method [10], inter-modes masking effects is approximated by considering masking of narrowband noises at $BARK_i$ with power A_i^2 / d_i. However, all the modes in a same critical band are summed together to obtain a single noise masker for each critical band like MPEG psychoacoustic model 1 [9].

At first, any mode whose power is below the absolute threshold is discarded. Then, an approximately triangular spreading function is used to estimate the effects of masking across critical bands [9]. Finally, all the modes are ordered by the difference between the mode power and masking threshold at this frequency. By that way, the progressive sounding object can be constructed dynamically in real time simulation. The number of modes eventually used in audio synthesis is dependent on the availability of system resources. Preliminary experimental results show that generally we can get good enough synthesized sound with first 50 or less modes.

3   Sounding Object with Position Information

After obtaining sounding object in multiple levels of details, the next step is to model the sound transmission process from sound source to the eardrums of the end user. In virtual environment, the convolution of mono sound signal with appropriate *Head-Related Impulse Response* (HRIR) is typically featured as the key component of realistic sound generation [2]. However, it's usually desirable to use *Head-Related Transfer Function* (HRTF) multiplication in frequency domain instead due to the fact that the computation of convolving sound signal from a particular point is quite huge.

Since each mode can be seen as a narrowband noise or pure tone when decay is very weak, it could be further thought as the spectral representation of an audio signal. As a result, HRTF filtering process could be integrated into modal synthesis directly. That is, for each mode, we can only consider HRTF frequency response at this specific frequency. We argue that the simplification for general applications is worthwhile considering large computation involved if we perform similar filtering after modal synthesis. Furthermore, the directional information of the virtual sound source (which includes azimuth and elevation) can be thought as part of the intrinsic parameters of modal models, just like mode frequency/decay rate. By that means, the HRTF representing different directions can be easily integrated to synthesize sound from a moving source. Currently, no room acoustical simulation is considered in our implementation.

4   Conclusion

A progressive sounding object model is developed with five parameters, two of them, i.e. mode frequency and decay rate, could be derived from object geometry and material properties. The other three are dependent on real time interaction. Among them, mode gain is dependent on the contact location/direction, azimuth and elevation is dependent on the relative position between sounding object and user.

By precomputing the mode gains at sampling locations/directions, the mode gains under any forces can be easily obtained using linear combination of those sampling values. This enables us to build up progressive sounding object in real time. Furthermore, binaural filtering is integrated into modal synthesis in a natural way. Further research will be focusing on better binaural model and room acoustic simulation integration.

References

1. W.Buxton, Introduction to this special issue on nonspeech audio. *Human Computer Interaction*, 4(1):1–9, 1989.
2. Q. Zhang Q, Z. Pan and J. Shi, ARE: An audio reality engine in virtual environment, *Int. Journal of Virtual Reality*, 4(3): 37-43, 1999.
3. Tsingos I, Funkhouser T et al. Modeling acoustics in virtual environments using the uniform theory of diffraction, In *Proc of SIGGRAPH 2001*, 545–552, Los Angeles, USA, 2001.
4. van den Doel K, Kry P G, and Pai D K, FoleyAutomatic: Physically-based Sound Effects for Interactive Simulation and Animation, In *Proc of SIGGRAPH 2001*, 537-544, Los Angeles, USA, 2001.
5. F. Avanzini, et al, Physically-based Audio Rendering of Contact. In *Proc of IEEE Int. Conf. on Multimedia and Expo 2002*, Lausanne, Switzerland, vol. 2, 445-448, 2002.
6. J. O'Brien, C. Shen, and C. M. Gatchalian, Synthesizing Sounds from Rigid-Body Simulations, In *Proc of 2002 ACM SIGGRAPH Symposium on Computer Animation*, 175-182, San Antonio , USA, 2002.
7. A. Shabana, *Theory of Vibration*, Springer-Verlag, New York, USA, 1991.
8. K. van den Doel. et al, Measurements of Perceptual Quality of Contact Sound Models, In *Proc of the 2002 Int. Conf. on Auditory Display*, 345-350, Kyoto, Japan, 2002.
9. T. Painter and A. Spanias, Perceptual Coding of Digital Audio, *Proceedings of the IEEE*, 88(4):451-513, 2000.

Visual Media Engineering

Automatic Visual Data Management System

Jae-Ho Lee, Sung-Hoon Park, Young-Jin Choi, and Whoi-Yul Kim

Image Engineering Laboratory, Division of Electrical and Computer Engineering,
Hanyang University, Seoul, Republic of Korea
(jhlee, shpark, yjchoi@vision.hanyang.ac.kr,
wykim@hanyang.ac.kr)
http://vision.hanyang.ac.kr

Abstract. In this paper, we introduce an automatic video management system for personal video recorder. With the system, visual data can be summarized and indexed based on the face recognition techniques. The developed system also supplies basic summarizing, indexing, and retrieving functionalities for visual data. Several conventional algorithms are adapted for cut detection and video summarizing. And MPEG-7 visual descriptors are utilized to retrieve similar scene. For face detection in real-time, the Haar-like feature method is applied and PCA/LDA method is selected for face recognition. The resulting index generates not only a preview of a movie, but also allows non-linear access with thumbnails. Moreover, implemented face recognition techniques makes character based video summarization and indexing possible in stored video data.

1 Introduction

As the digital broadcasting has been popular, a number of homes are purchasing the PVR (Personal Video Recorder). And individual visual data is getting massive as the price of digital storage is getting lower. These popularizations of digital visual data make the needs of management of data for individual system. By the way, the current system includes only the basic functions such as receiving, recording, and playing. And the management functionality is only for the huge systems like broadcasting and digital library. Therefore, we introduce the automatic visual data management system for personal video recorder in this paper. The developed system can summarize and index the visual data based on face recognition techniques. And also the system supplies the retrieval functionality to search the visual data. The resulting index generates not only a preview of a movie, but also allows non-linear access and efficient editing.

To develop the system, some sorts of techniques are combined. It can be mainly divides as scene change detection, video summarizing, and content-based retrieval. In scene change detection step, the adaptive threshold and gradual transition detection methods are applied [1][2]. And to make a representative frame, key frame extraction method is applied [3]. To perform a semantic summarization, the segmented shots are clustered to compose story units. The algorithm proposed by Yeung is used in this step [4]. To obtain content-based summarization, clustering is applied while

M. Rauterberg (Ed.): ICEC 2004, LNCS 3166, pp. 579–585, 2004.

considering the duration of each shot segment. And MPEG-7 visual descriptor is utilized as the feature for content-based retrieval. In practice, the most useful source of video management is the face information. To make a face-based video summarization, face detection and recognition have to be adapted as preprocessing. In this development, the Harr-like feature method is utilized for face detection algorithm [5]. And, the PCA/LDA based face recognition is selected to recognize the actor in video data [6].

In this paper, we introduce a video summarizing system that generates summarized video efficiently. The summary information generated by the presented tool provides users an overview of video content, and guides them visually to move to a desired position quickly in a video. Also, the tool makes it possible to find shots similar to a queried one or face, which is useful for editing different video streams into a new one.

2   Implementation of Functionalities

The functions of a developed system consist of mainly four parts:
1. Generation of an overview of video contents; to find a desired position in video data.
2. Query by example or face; to find similar shots to a queried one in a large amount of video data.
3. Nonlinear editing; to support simple editing based on the summarized video.
4. Actor based indexing; to find scenes which contains queried person in a video
Each image in the summary index becomes a representative frame of the cluster which is composed of a number of shot segments. Users can find similar shots to his or her favorite shot by querying with an example in the index. Also, a new video stream can be easily generated by moving shot segments from the summary index. All of these operations have been designed simply, so they can be executed with a home electronics interface.

2.1   Scene Change Detection

To make a video summarization, a video stream is segmented into a set of shots as a preprocessing step by detecting scene changes. The adaptive threshold and gradual transition detection methods are applied in this step [1][2]. In this stage, three MPEG-7 color descriptors: color layout, dominant color, and color structure are computed and saved as the features to be utilized in the summarization and retrieval process. In addition the visual rhythm method is added to get more confidential results [7].

Abrupt scene change detection is done simply by computing the distance between two sets of features extracted from adjacent frames. Since the number of abrupt scene changes is highly dependent upon the threshold value, an adaptive method can be used using the average and deviation of the local duration [1]. To detect a gradual change, the distance value between the current frame and the ones at the k frame is computed by Bescos's plateau method [2]. To detect the exact location of the plateau form, metrics such as symmetry, slope fail (distance decreasing on rising phase, or vice versa), maximum of distance and distance difference when scene change occurs are used. Values of 10, 20, 30, and 40 were chosen as k for the various durations of gradual changes. The Color Layout Descriptor (CLD) was used as the feature of distance to detect these abrupt and gradual scene changes.

For key-frame extraction of the segmented video shots, some approaches have been proposed recently. In this paper, the oldest attempt to automate the key-frame extraction was adapted [3], because it chooses as a key frame the frame appearing after each detected shot boundary, and this method is appropriate for a PVR which receives video data via a broadcasting system.

2.2 Video Summarization

With our tool, a video summary is generated in three ways: semantic-based, content-based, and face-based summarization. Semantic summarization is for videos that have stories such as dramas or sitcoms, while content-based summarization is for videos that do not contain stories such as sports videos. After the scene change detection step, a video summarization process follows. To perform a semantic summarization, the segmented shots are clustered to compose story units. To obtain content-based summarization, clustering is applied while considering the duration of each shot segment. In both, the distance between shots is measured using a MPEG-7 color layout descriptor and a color structure descriptor.

By comparing key frames from the scene change detection step, the process of shot clustering is followed by a modified time-constrained method. Time-constrained clustering is based on the observation that similar shot segments separated in time have a high probability to be located in other story units. As a result, remote shots are not in the same story unit using a time windowing method, even though the shots have similar features. A hierarchical clustering method merges shot segments that have similar features and neighbor each other in the time domain into the identical cluster. The time window comparing regions is fixed as 3000 seconds. Yeung proposed a Scene Transition Graph (STG) to generate story units from clustering results [4]. In this system, we assumed that the story is the top layer of the structure, and each story is organized by clusters. These clusters also have some key frames of the scene.

Content-based summarization focuses on the coincidence of content without temporal information. This method can be applied especially in sports videos. For example, in a soccer video, player scenes, goal scenes, and audience scenes can all be classified separately.

2.3 Face Based Video Indexing

Face recognition and detection techniques can also be utilized in summarization in video data. The PCA/LDA face recognition method was adapted in recognition process [6]. And the Haar-like feature utilized in face detection stage to the pseudo real-time process [5]. This summarization scheme can be utilized efficiently for user in accessing or retrieving specially in drama.

2.4 Video Segment Editing

Video editing, which is based on a summarized index, is also supported with the developed system. In the editing procedure, the segmented shots can be removed or merged into a new video stream by the user. Users can generate a video stream that consists of their favorite shots using this editing tool. Each of these functions is designed to be used easily with the use of a remote control. The user chooses the shot segment, cluster, or story in the video indexes using a remote control. This only requires pushing the insert and move button on a remote control to edit. With this simple process, a user can make his or her favorite scenes easily.

2.5 Video Retrieval

A query of similar scenes can be achieved with the developed system. The MPEG-7 descriptors are used to find similar scenes in query by example methods [8]. This function plays an important role by providing user convenience with quick searching of favorite scenes for editing or direct access. If a user orders a retrieval function by clicking the query image in one index, the similar key frames are retrieved along with all saved summary indexes.

3 Experimental Results

The developed system can generate key frame based indexing information automatically. Figure 1 shows the result of face detection and scene change detection. With the extracted key frames, retrieval and editing can be achieved easily.

Fig. 1. The results of face detection and scene change detection in a video stream.

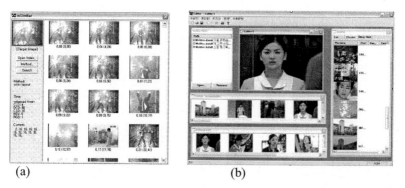

Fig. 2. Video editing and retrieval results, (a) The retrieval results in key frames, (b) The results of new video segment with three different video clips

Figure 2(a) shows the retrieval results of the queried scene by user. And Figure 2(b) presented the editing results with three different video clips. One of the most useful functions of the developed system is supporting the face-based video summarization. Accessing to the specific point of scene and editing of specific person can be achieved easily with this function. The face based video summarization is displayed in Figure 3.

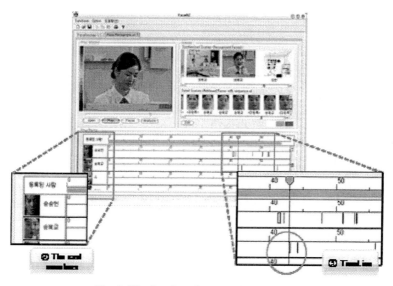

Fig. 3. The face based summarizing results.

The cast member and timelines of individual actor were shown to user can access to the desired position with this information. Also, editing and retrieval in the visual data can be built. The developed system also supports the content-based and time-based summarization. Semantic summarization is useful to quick-view for drama or movie, while content-based summarization is for searching the similar scene especially in sport video.

Fig. 4. The results of content-based summarization and semantic-based summarization.

4 Conclusions

In this paper, we have introduced our video summarizing tool. The resulting tool enables users to access a video easily through a generated summarization index. In addition, the summarization index also supports other operations that can be helpful and interesting for users: querying a scene and editing a video stream. The MPEG-7 descriptors are used to obtain video summarization and to retrieve a queried scene. The proposed tool was devised to be operated inexpensively with a simple interface; therefore, it can be embedded in a PVR. Furthermore, the system can be extended for a video search engine with internet connectivity of PVR using the MPEG-7 technique.

References

1. Y. Yusoff, W. Christmas, and J. Kittler: Video shot cut detection using adaptive thresholding, British Machine Vision Conference (2000)
2. J. Bescos, J.M. Menendez, G. Cisneros, J Cabrera, and J.M. Martinez: A unified approach to gradual shot transition detection, IEEE Proc. of International Conference on Image Processing, vol. 3, (2000) 949 -952
3. B. Shahraray, and D. Gibbon: Automatic generation of pictorial transcripts of video programs, SPIE proc. of Multimedia Computing and Networking (1995) 512-518

4. M. Yeung, and B.L. Yeo: Segmentation of video by clustering and graph analysis, Computer Vision and Image Understanding Journal, vol. 71, no. 1 (1998) 97-109
5. P. Viola and M.J. Jones: Robust real-time object detection, Technical Report Series, Compaq Cambridge research Laboratory, CRL 2001/01 (2001)
6. W.Y. Kim, J.H. Lee, H.S. Park, and H.J. Lee: PCA/LDA Face Recognition Descriptor using Pose Transformation, ISO/IEC JTC1/SC29/WG11 MPEG2002/M8934 (2002)
7. A method for cut detection based on visual rhythm, Guimar, S.J.F.; Couprie, M.; Leite, N.J.; De Albuquerque Araujo;Computer Graphics and Image Processing, 2001 Proceedings of XIV Brazilian Symposium on , 15-18 Oct. (2001) 297 – 304
8. B. S. Manjunath et al.: Introduction to MPEG-7, John Wiley & Sons Ltd., West Sussex, England (2002).

Development of Extemporaneous Performance by Synthetic Actors in the Rehearsal Process

Tony Meyer and Chris Messom

IIMS, Massey University, Auckland, New Zealand
T.A.Meyer@massey.ac.nz

Abstract. Autonomous synthetic actors must invent variations of known material in order to perform given only a limited script, and to assist the director with development of the performance. In addition, the synthetic actors need to learn through the rehearsal process, as their human counterparts do, via feedback from the director. Through the production of two performances, involving both human and synthetic actors, a variety of methods of creating extemporaneous performance and utilising feedback to select the most effective performance variations will be examined. One method of varying the performance is the manner in which lines of dialogue are delivered. The paper outlines use of a statistical technique to create three variations of a performance; each variation was then ranked, and these rankings used to weight the variances in individual lines to create a superior variation. This allowed quick evaluation of many lines, without having to score each individual line.

1 Synthetic Actors

1.1 Synthetic Actors and Computer Theatre

Computer theatre "is about providing means to enhance the artistic possibilities and experiences of professional and amateur actors" [1]; we are concerned with live, real-time, theatrical performances that use computers in the artistic process. Historically, these characters are typically (especially the most well-known examples) only electronic puppets, whose behaviour is directly simulated by a puppeteer, although recently 'extra' characters in films have been autonomous synthetic actors (for example, in *Lord of the Rings: Return of the King*, controlled by the MASSIVE software [2]).

It is the category of autonomous synthetic actors that is the authors' focus. To interact with the human actors, the synthetic actors must possess a variety of actuators and sensors, such as audio and visual recognition and generation [3]. The project currently includes speech synthesis and recognition, a graphics generator, and a vision system. The speech systems use the Microsoft™ Speech SDK; the graphics generator uses the 3D engine from *Unreal Tournament 2003*, via the Gamebots [4] module (see Figure 1). The design of the project allows other sensors and actuators to be added as necessary; for example, for a brief scene requiring physical interaction between

M. Rauterberg (Ed.): ICEC 2004, LNCS 3166, pp. 586–591, 2004.

human and synthetic actors in *The Porcelain Salamander* (described below) a very simple robotic actuator will be utilised.

Fig. 1. Synthetic actors as generated images

2 Aims

2.1 Improvisation

The aim of an improvised theatrical performance (whether part of a rehearsal, or otherwise) is to appear to play extemporaneously by "inventing variations…with whatever materials are at hand" [5], rather than to perform "with little or no preparation" [5]. Anderson and Evens define improvisation as "creating minor to extensive variations on a routine in a satisficing manner in real time" [6]. While autonomously creating a believable and dramatically valid theatrical performance with no preparation may be beyond synthetic actors, the equally valid task of creating interesting variations of known behaviour is certainly not.

Improvisation plays an important role in theatrical performances, even those comprised of scripted dialogue. Improvisation fills the gaps left by the script (most movement and how dialogue should be expressed); essentially, the playwright provides a task, but it is up to the actor to decide how to execute that task to maximise the enjoyment of the performance by the audience. In addition, although the playwright and director both begin the rehearsal process with a particular expression of the performance in mind, this is refined during the rehearsal process, typically through minor alterations of dialogue or of the actor's perception of their character. The way in which the actor decides to improvise their performance contributes to this process, by expanding the range of possibilities visible to the director.

2.2 Learning

The other key role of the rehearsal process is practice: sections of the play are performed, feedback is gained from the director (and possibly other actors), and, using that feedback to alter the performance, the section is performed again, until an optimum performance is achieved. Typically each section will be rehearsed several times per rehearsal, then a break is taken (during which the actor is expected to consider methods of further improving their performance), and then the section is again rehearsed at the next rehearsal.

Current synthetic actors tend to learn outside of this process – a director will review the performance by the synthetic actor, usually after the human actors' performances are finalised, and alter it until it fits with the performance. This typically involves manually altering parameters of the performance or introducing random elements into the performance (as the human component of the performance is unable to be changed). A more balanced development, and more truly autonomous synthetic actors, would result from human and synthetic actors together modifying their performances to suit each other, as the rehearsal process progresses. A major difficulty that arises is that the feedback given to each actor during the rehearsal process is very limited – in particular, only a few attempts at each scene can be made; actors are expected to extrapolate an understanding of what is required from this and use that to evaluate possible performance improvisations (outside the rehearsal arena).

3   Methodology

To test various methods of generating improvisational performances and learning through the rehearsal process, two live stage performances featuring synthetic actors will be produced. Each production will include a small number of human actors acting alongside a small number of synthetic actors, who will play roles that a human actor would have difficult portraying (typically as a result of physical constraints). Throughout the production, data will be collected and analysed, through quantitative methods and phenomenological analysis of qualitative data.

The first of these productions, scheduled to be performed in late June 2004, will be an adaptation of the short story *The Porcelain Salamander* (by Orson Scott Card), featuring four human actors and one leading and three minor synthetic parts. The story is dramatic (essentially a fable), rather than comedic; the fantasy setting of the story is well suited to experimental theatre, and will assist the traditional theatrical 'suspension of disbelief'. The magical and slightly unreal nature of the character and story also provides some leeway with the level to which the speech and graphics must appear realistic.

The salamander character is well suited to a synthetic actor, as it is "not alive, but has been given the gift of movement and speech" [7], much like synthetic characters themselves. The character is relatively simple, but is a lead, so still requires a level of performance above that of simple scripting. The character behaves differently depending on which other (human) characters are currently on stage, and moves through various emotional states (particularly happiness, fear and sadness). For a successful performance, the audience must understand how one of the other (human) characters could come to love the salamander character, and the salamander's final sacrifice must draw an emotional response from the audience.

4 Preliminary Results

4.1 Dynamic Selection of Affect for Generated Speech

The synthetic actors have the same script available as the human actors, which includes all the words to be spoken, but almost no information about *how* the lines should be delivered. A human actor uses a variety of techniques to decide on the appropriate delivery of each line [8], including analysis of the context of the line, the words in the line itself, and their perception of the character they are playing and the state of the other characters. The synthetic actor begins without a model of the character (but may have generic knowledge from a prior performance), so must initially rely solely on the lines of dialogue.

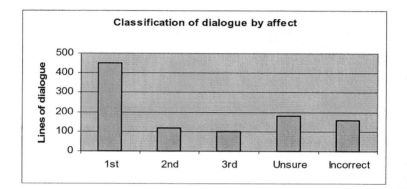

Fig. 2. Cross-validation results from classifying lines of dialogue into affect categories.

Seven basic methods of dialogue delivery were implemented, mimicking the basic emotions of happiness, sadness, anger, disgust, and fear [9], along with surprised and 'neutral' unaltered speech. For each line of dialogue a score for each emotion was determined using a statistical technique [10]; the strongest scores were combined to determine the desired delivery. To vary the performance, the synthetic actor was able to alter the combination of scores (e.g. use just the strongest score, or combine the two strongest scores). To learn from the performance, the synthetic actor trains on each line of dialogue, indicating that it matches one or more of the delivery methods. Even without any training on the current performance, results are satisfactory, with around 45% of lines correctly delivered and only around 16% of lines unable to be delivered correctly given three attempts (see Figure 2).

4.2 Application of Director Feedback

In one rehearsal, four attempts at each scene involving the salamander character, using a different delivery method for each line (generated as above), were carried out. With each of the first three attempts, each of the five scenes (each comprised of between five and eighteen lines by the synthetic actor) was rated by the director with a simple score, with ten corresponding to a performance where all lines were well delivered, and zero corresponding to a performance where every line should have been delivered differently. These three attempts were independent (i.e. no training was done between these attempts), with the first attempt ranking highest and the second attempt lowest. The fourth attempt used these scores to combine the affect tags for each of the three performances to deliver a final performance superior to all three prior performances (see Figure 3).

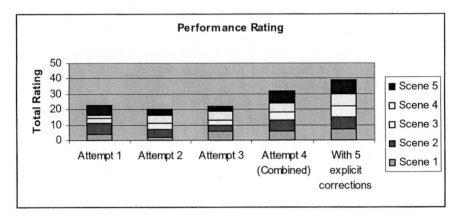

Fig. 3. Performance ratings (by the director) of three generated attempts and two attempts utilising feedback.

To combine the affect tags, the system weighted the score of the tag for each attempt with the rank given to that scene and selected the tag with the highest weighted result. This meant that where the system was much more certain that it was correct, the choice of tag would not necessarily be simply the one from the attempt with the highest rank. The fourth (combined) attempt therefore combined the strengths of each of the three previous attempts line-by-line, rather than simply scene-by-scene, as it was ranked. This did not allow for the fourth attempt to use any tags not used in any of the three previous attempts, however, and so around 10% of lines (scattered throughout the scenes) still failed to be delivered as effectively as possible.

This technique allows quick evaluation of many lines, without the director having to score each individual line; when combined with the ability to explicitly instruct the actor that a particular line (delivered poorly compared to the others in the scene, or delivered poorly in all previous attempts) should be delivered in a particular emotion, successive performances rapidly improved (see Figure 3). In the future, more sophisticated methods of combining this data to select more effective improvisation choices will be evaluated.

5   Conclusion

Dramatically effective extemporaneous performance within a scripted performance is an achievable goal for autonomous synthetic actors. Although the rehearsal process only offers a limited amount of feedback, the synthetic actors are, like their human counterparts, able to extract sufficient training data from this feedback to learn which forms of improvisation are particularly effective for each component of the performance. Through the production of two live stage performances with a cast including both human and synthetic actors, various techniques of extracting this data, and applying it to the development of a character model, will be fully evaluated.

References

1. C. Pinhanez, "Computer Theatre," M.I.T. Media Lab, Perceptual Computing Section Technical Report 378, 1996.
2. "MASSIVE", [online] 2004, http://www.massivesoftware.com/index.html (Accessed: 11 March 2004)
3. T. A. Meyer and C. H. Messom, "Development of Computer-Actors Using the Interval Script Paradigm," presented at 9th Annual New Zealand Engineering & Technology Post Graduate Conference, Auckland, New Zealand, 2002.
4. R. Adobbati, A. N. Marshall, A. Scholer, S. Tejada, G. A. Kaminka, S. Schaffer, and C. Sollitto, "Gamebots: A 3D Virtual World Test-Bed for Multi-Agent Research," presented at Second International Workshop on Infrastructure for Agents, MAS, and Scalable MAS, Montreal, Canada, 2001.
5. Houghton Mifflin Company, The American Heritage® Dictionary of the English Language, 4th Ed. ed: Houghton Mifflin Company, 2000.
6. J. Anderson and M. Evens, "Constraint-Directed Improvisation," presented at Eleventh Biennial Canadian Society for Computational Studies of Intelligence Conference, Canada, 1996.
7. O. S. Card, "The Porcelain Salamander," in Unaccompanied Sonata and Other Stories: Dial Press, 1981.
8. G. Colson, Voice Production and Speech. London: Museum Press Limited, 1963.
9. A. Ortony and T. J. Turner, "What's Basic About Basic Emotions?," Psychological Review, vol. 97, pp. 315-331, 1990.
10. T. A. Meyer, "Dynamically Determining Affect during Scripted Dialogue", [online] 2004, http://www.massey.ac.nz/~tameyer/research/computertheatre/docs/tameyer-pricai.pdf (Accessed: March 8 2004)

An Efficient CLOD Method for Large-Scale Terrain Visualization

Byeong-Seok Shin and Ei-Kyu Choi

Inha University, Department of Computer Science and Engineering
253 Yonghyeon-Dong, Nam-Gu, Inchon, 402-751, Republic of Korea
bsshin@inha.ac.kr, g2021356@inhavision.inha.ac.kr

Abstract. Terrain visualization requires a lot of processing time and storage since terrain information contains huge amount of height-field data. One of the optimization methods is quadtree-based continuous level-of-detail (CLOD). Although it can produce moderate quality of images in real-time, flickering may occur in consecutive frames due to inadequate feedback. We propose a method to maintain constant frame rate without flickering by controlling the number of triangles in view frustum. It avoids abrupt change of the amount of triangles using temporal coherence.

1 Introduction

In some applications such as interactive computer games, GIS, and flight simulation, terrain visualization becomes the most important component. Since terrain information inherently contains huge amount of data, real-time terrain visualization is difficult even though throughput of graphics hardware has been improved. Therefore several optimization methods using a variety of data structures and simplification algorithm have been proposed [1-3].

Two types of data structures are mainly used for representing simplified terrain data, binary-tree structure called ROAM [4] and quadtree structure [5-7]. Quadtree is more common since it is adequate for implementing view frustum culling and continuous level-of-detail. It can generate terrain images in real-time by adjusting accuracy level according to viewing condition. However, when the number of triangles exceeds upper-bound of hardware capacity, it is impossible to display the triangles in real time and frame rate decreases. So previous methods may cause flickering, which is oscillation of the number of triangles in consecutive frames since these methods excessively increase or decrease the number of polygons on the way to converge optimal value.

We propose a method to mitigate the flickering of quadtree-based CLOD. While the previous methods adjust target resolution by considering only the difference of the number of triangles, our method exploits weighted average of the global resolution of previous frames as well as the difference of the number of triangles. This avoids abrupt changes in consecutive frames and guarantees constant update rate.

In section 2, we briefly review the quadtree-based CLOD. In section 3 and 4, we explain our method in detail and show some results. Lastly, we conclude our work.

M. Rauterberg (Ed.): ICEC 2004, LNCS 3166, pp. 592–597, 2004.

2 Quadtree-Based Continuous Level-of-Detail

Lindstrom presented a method that uses a dynamically changing quadtree and a bottom up strategy to determine whether a node has to be subdivided or should be merged with adjacent nodes [5]. The main disadvantage of this bottom up strategy is that the pixel error function has to be evaluated for all points of the height field. If modifications of the triangulation are necessary, all affected nodes should be updated.

Rottger *et.al* [7] proposed an algorithm that uses a top-down strategy to create a triangulation and exploits geo-morphing. Vertex removal is performed depending on its distance to the view point as well as local surface roughness. Using a top-down approach we only need to visit a fraction of the whole data set in each frame, which allows for high frame rates even with large height fields. Since the number of triangles downloaded into graphics pipeline is determined by global image resolution, it can control the image quality so as to accommodate hardware capacity.

Most important task in quadtree-based CLOD is to determine whether current node can have child nodes or not by applying accuracy level determination function to each node using a set of error metric. At first, we have to consider the distance to a specific point on a terrain. As shown in figure 1, node size (d) should be enlarged as the distance (l) increases to satisfy $l / d < C$. Here, C is the minimal desired resolution of image. The number of triangles is determined by the value of C. When we set a large value, more triangles will be produced from quadtree.

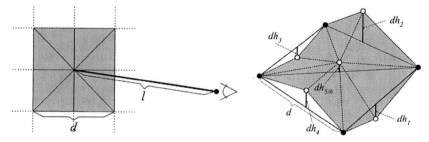

Fig. 1. Global resolution criteria: distance versus size of quadtree nodes (left), and surface roughness estimated from the elevation difference (right).

With the second criterion we want to increase the resolution for regions of high surface roughness. When dropping one level of the hierarchy, new error is introduced at exactly five points: at the center of the quadtree node and the four midpoints of its edges. An upper bound to the approximation error can be given by taking the maximum of the absolute values of the elevation difference dh_i computed along four edges and two diagonals of the nodes (see figure 1 right), which is called $d2$.

$$f = \frac{l}{d \cdot C \cdot \max(c \cdot d2, 1)} \qquad \text{subdivide if } f < 1. \tag{1}$$

Consequently, the subdivision criterion which includes the $d2$-values for handling surface roughness can now be given in terms of a decision variable f. The newly introduced constant c specifies the desired global resolution. It directly influences the number of polygons to be rendered per frame.

3   An Efficient CLOD Method

During dynamically adjusting the number of triangles, it might exceed upper bound of hardware capability. So we cannot maintain the constant frame rate. In previous method, decision variable f is used for limiting the number of polygons. Here the most significant parameter that determines whether a quadtree cell should be subdivided is C. When the viewer moves forward terrain surface, the number of polygons in current frame increases in comparison to that of the previous frame. This implies that the possibility of exceeding upper bound of hardware capacity becomes higher. So we have to reduce the value of C with respect to the amount of increase. On the contrary, when a viewer is distant from terrain surface, the value of C should be increased to make the best use of hardware capability. The value of C in i-th frame can be defined as follows:

$$C_i = C_{i-1} - \Delta n_{i-1} / a \quad \text{where } \Delta n_i = (N_i - N_{i-1}).$$ (2)

Where N_i is the number of polygons in i-th frame, and a is a constant used to normalize n_i into valid range of C. In general, this can control the number of polygons fairly well when n_i is small. However, if the number of polygons stiffly increase or decrease due to abrupt change of viewing condition, the value of C can be fluctuated in consecutive frames.

In this paper, we propose an efficient method to make the number of triangles rapidly converge to appropriate value as well as to eliminate flicker. When controlling the minimal global resolution C in current frame (C_i), we exploits a trend of changes of C's in several previous frames. Another parameter c also influences on maintaining frame rate. Using small c (less than 1.0), smooth transition of the number of polygons can be possible. However, it takes a long time to converge to the desired resolution. So it cannot make the best use of hardware capability for some time. On the other hand, larger c allows the overall resolution rapidly converge to the desired value. However it may also produce flicker. The optimal value of c cannot be uniquely determined since it varies according to several rendering situation. So we need a method to produce flickering-free animation irrespective of the value of c.

Flickering is originated from repetition of increase and decrease of triangle number. In that case, if the number of polygons increases (decreases) in current frame, it is possible to expect that the number of polygons in the next frame will decrease (increase). This implies that the sign of n_i for current frame is almost opposite to that of the next frame. Based on this property, we exploits the weighted average value of C's used to determine the number of triangles in previous frames as follows.

$$C_i = \sum_{k=0}^{r-1} C_{i-k-1} w_k \quad \text{where } \sum_{k=0}^{r-1} w_k = 1 \quad .$$ (3)

Where r is the number of frames of which the C values are considered. In order to exploit temporal coherence, discrete linear weight function that returns larger value for more recently produced frame is used as follows.

$$w(k) = -\frac{2}{r^2}k + \frac{2}{r} \quad . \tag{4}$$

Experimental results show that there is no significant difference when using linear and other higher-order functions. Equation (3) can be rewritten by assigning equation (2).

$$C_i = \sum_{k=0}^{r-1}(C_{i-k-2} - \Delta n_{i-k-2})w_k \quad = \sum_{k=0}^{r-1}C_{i-k-2}w_k - \sum_{k=0}^{r-1}\Delta n_{i-k-2}w_k$$
$$\cong C_{i-1} - \sum_{k=0}^{r-1}\Delta n_{i-k-2}w_k \quad . \tag{5}$$

The second term of equation (5) is weighted average of n_i in consecutive frames by considering temporal coherence. So we should store the value of n_i for some frames.

We categorize states of frames in an animation sequence into stable states and flickering states. When a frame is in a stable state, signs of n_i's are almost the same. Therefore convergence speed may slightly decrease when applying our new method. Even though it requires additional memory for storing the value of C's, the size of additional storage can be negligible. When a frame is in a flickering state, sign of n_i is opposite to that of n_{i-1}. So our method can reduce abrupt change of the number of polygons. It guarantees to produce the maximum number of polygons within upper bound of throughput of graphics hardware.

4   Experimental Results

In order to shown how efficient our method, we compare the n_i's of previous method and our new algorithm. Both methods are implemented on a PC equipped with Pentium IV 2.2GHz CPU, 1GB main memory, and NVIDIA GeForce4 graphics accelerator. We use height-field dataset of which the resolution is 2049×2049.

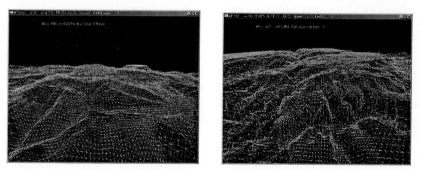

Fig. 2. Visualization of terrain data used for experiment.

Figure 3 depicts how to changes of n_i according to the value of desired global resolution (that is c). As mentioned before, using smaller c value (0.1~1.0), smooth transition of the number of polygons can be possible until it reaches the desired resolution. However, it takes a long time to converge to the desired value. On the other hand, larger c value (more than 3) results in severe oscillation. In order to show the efficiency of our method we set the value of c as 5.0.

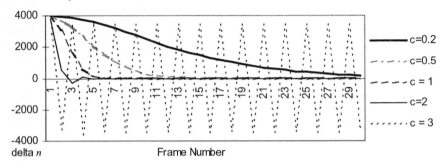

Fig. 3. Changes of the number of triangles according to the desired global resolution c.

Figure 4 shows the changes of n_i according to the value of r. When r is small ($r=2$), a little fluctuation is observed. On the contrary, using larger r (r 6), convergence time becomes longer. However, the influence of r is trivial in comparison to the other parameters.

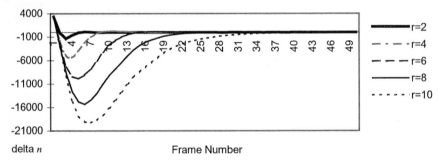

Fig. 4. Changes of the number of triangles according to the value of r.

Figure 5 shows the changes of n_i's when applying previous method and our method to test data. In case of using the previous method based only on the difference of the number of triangles in current frame, flickering occurs in several ranges of the animation. However, applying our method can reduce the flickering in all of the ranges for the same camera path. This means that our method guarantees constant frame rate without flickering even in severe condition.

5   Conclusion

Terrain visualization is important technology in large-scale virtual environment rendering especially for interactive games. Although quadtree-based CLOD method can produce moderate quality of images, flickering may occur in consecutive frames due to inadequate feedback. We propose a method to guarantee constant frame rate without flickering by adjusting the number of triangles in view frustum. It avoids abrupt change of the amount of triangles using temporal coherence of consecutive frames. Experimental results show that our method produces flickering-free animation in large-scale terrain visualization even in severe condition.

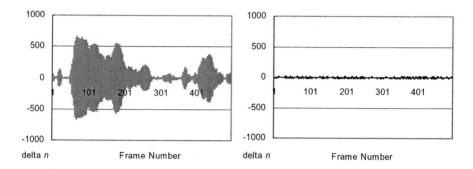

Fig. 5. Changes of the number of triangles when applying previous method (top) and our method (bottom) with c=5, while moving forward camera along the same predefined path.

Acknowlegdement. This research was supported by University IT Research Center Project.

References

1. Hoppe, H. : Smooth View-Dependent Level-of-Detail Control and Its Application to Terrain Rendering, Proceedings of IEEE Visualization 98, (1998) 35-42
2. Lindstrom, P., Pascucci, V. : Terrain Simplification Simplified : A General Framework for View-Dependent Out-of-Core Visualization, IEEE Transactions on Visualization and Computer Graphics, Vol. 8 (2002) 239-254
3. Lindstrom, P. : Out-of-Core Simplification of Large Polygonal Models, ACM SIGGRAPH (2000) 259-262
4. Duchaineau, M., Wolinsky, M., Segeti, D., Miller, M., Aldrich, C., Mineev-Weisstein, M. : ROAMing Terrain: Real-time Optimally Adaptive Meshes, ACM SIGGRAPH (1997) 81-88
5. Lindstrom, P., Koller, D., Ribarsky, W., Hodges, L., Faust, M., Turner, G. : Real-Time Continuous Level of Detail Rendering of Height Fields, ACM SIGGRAPH (1996) 109-118
6. Rottger, S., Heidrich, W., Slasallek, P., Seidel, H. : Real-time Generation of Continuous Level of Detail for Height Fields, Proc. of 6th International Conference in Central Europe on Computer Graphics and Visualization, (1998) 315–322
7. Pajarola, R., Zurich, E. : Large Scale Terrain Visualization Using the Restricted Quadtree Triangulation, Proceedings of IEEE Visualization 98, (1998) 19

Integrating Ideas About Invisible Playgrounds from Play Theory into Online Educational Digital Games

Darryl Charles and Moira McAlister

Computing and Information Engineering, University of Ulster, BT52 1SA. Northern Ireland
{dk.charles,m.mcalister}@ulster.ac.uk;

Abstract. This paper explores novel ideas about the use of modern digital games for educational purposes, and especially online games. We propose a framework that utilises an approach related to invisible playgrounds, so that a game is not only played within the virtual space provided by individual computers but is distributed across both digital and non-digital formats. We argue that educational games constructed on this sort of multi-modal, distributed framework can be extremely effective at engaging and immersing students in an educational process.

1 Introduction

While many individual aspects of the use of digital games in education have been explored before, this paper discusses a different angle; the merging together of many of the strands of research to provide a framework for educational games in which there are multi-modes of access, both digital and non-digital. Our work centres on utilising the multi-player aspects of online role play games (RPGs) to develop an environment where student co-operation may form the basis for a range of learning activities. We believe that this genre is ideal for educational gameplay because it provides an opportunity to place a strong emphasis on building communities, supporting collaboration and encouraging communication towards active and explorative learning. Online game environments may be constructed to not only to address learning objectives of a curriculum but also to address softer aspects of studentship relating to participation, sharing, community, belonging, responsibility, access to information, communication, and debate.

2 Background

While the concept of an educational computer game has existed for some time, only recently has the real potential of digital games as educational tools been recognized and more fully understood. Indeed, recent research has shown that when correctly designed computer game software may be utilized within education to increase the rate of learning, improve retention, and avoid stagnation in learning [1]. Furthermore, the structure of online digital games in particular lend these type of games to

M. Rauterberg (Ed.): ICEC 2004, LNCS 3166, pp. 598–601, 2004.

supporting modern educational goals [6] and student centric approaches such as co-operative learning, communities of practice, inquiry and problem-based learning, as well as peer-based assessment. The format of modern digital games may be harnessed to enable students to self-pace their learning and control the construction of their own knowledge. Additionally, much of the learning within an effective digital game environment can be considered to be largely subconscious so that we may think of this type of education experience as "learning by stealth" [3]. Digital games have been recognized by academics as being very good at structuring learning and actively engaging participants. In fact it has been argued that the playing of a modern digital game is inherently educational because of the active and critical learning process involved and, for example, the building of an appreciation of design and semiotic principles [2] through the interpretation and response to gameplay challenges.

There are two key reasons [3] that explain our interest in developing digital games for education: The desire to harness the motivational power of games, especially aspects that may make learning fun and a belief that learning by doing is a very effective way to learn. However, most educational games have not been particularly effective [3] at realising these because games tend to be too simplistic in comparison with mainstream computer and videogames and the tasks are often too competitive. Tasks are poorly designed and the range of activities is severely limited within the game, and the student often becomes aware that they are being coerced into learning. These are very real dangers in any educational digital game, particularly with products for older children because their expectations are so high. However, this should not put us off trying to harness the power of digital games for education.

Two research topics from play theory research of particular interest for our research are the notions of the magic circle and invisible playgrounds [4]. A magic circle is defined as the boundary to the space in which a game takes place, and with formal games this boundary is quite explicit through the games rules and peoples understanding of the rules – the rules creating a special set of meanings to guide the play of the game. Games with formal rules may be thought of as a closed system, whereas play in a general culture format is more of an open system. For traditional non-digital games and most digital computer and videogames games it may be considered that the majority of play occurs within a closed system, that players enter the magic circle to play the game and withdraw entirely from the bounds of the game world and it's rules when they are finished. The idea of an invisible playground frames the concept that play may continue away from the situational norm, for example in the school playground, at work, or on the high street. In this way the boundaries that normally restrict the gameplay for digital games may be broken.

3   Providing Learning Within a Digital Game

Learning by stealth by definition reflects the nuances of teaching and learning. Effective teaching has to utilize techniques to ensure that knowledge is communicated to the learner. The issues addressed include analyzing the level of understanding of the learner, evaluating the level of understanding by examining the knowledge and adjusting the delivery to reflect the needs of the learner.

This analysis and evaluation happens "in situ" and can be assessed using tests to quantify understanding. There are a number of techniques which can be used to perform this task: requiring the learner to perform a specified set of tasks in order to attain achievement at a certain level, and requiring the learner to answer questions at specified stages of a study programme in order to determine the level of abstraction appropriate to progression. The provision of a distributed learning environment in the form of a digital game introduces a number of issues which influence how monitoring, marking and feedback can be provided.   The issues include [5]: Portability – a distributed game environment demands that the software must be available to the user when required, Adaptability – the game must be able to maintain a profile of attainment and adjust delivery and assessment to fit with the learner's new skill set, Persistency – the learner's personal accumulation of resources and knowledge must be immediately available despite changes in technology, intuitiveness – the environment must be able to be used by people who have no previous experience of the technology.

Digital games retain the user's attention by the fact that users are able to progress to new levels of difficulty. Thus the users are able to explore and extend their own mental boundaries through interaction with the game. The boundaries on progression are generally limited to their ability to learn new sequences of interaction.   Such learning curves are usually rapid.

In education software learners must attain set goals before proceeding. If this method of operation was directly transferred to an educational digital game then the level of frustration could have a detrimental effect on the learner's interaction with the game. The timeframe to achieve goals will differ from one person to another and the learning curve will be much longer. Therefore, the boundaries which are applied to the learner in an educational digital game must be acceptable to the learner. To do this the learner must be able to understand the reasons and agree to the benefits that could be achieved if goals are attained before progression.

4   Integrating the Game into the Learning Environment

There are two basic forms of curriculum content that interest us because of the contrast between them: Traditional subject matter that may be taught quite easily in the classroom situation, e.g. science, maths or computing, and more modern or non-traditional subject matter where the students learn more easily by experience, exploration and experiment, e.g. citizenship, entrepreneurship.

Consider the creation of a persistent game world based on Role Play Game (RPG) concepts with citizenship learning outcomes mapped into progress throughout the game. Exploiting the pervasive nature of modern computing and communication technologies, student access to the game world and communication with other game participants may be either through the game web site portal, by logging on to the game world via a PC, or by use of a mobile phone. Citizenship can be considered to address three themes: Environment – how decisions made by individuals can effect the local environment and relationships within society, Government – how an individual can influence decision making through interacting effectively with the body politic locally, nationally and even globally, Inter-connectivity – the interdependence of local, national, European and global societies in terms of environment, politics, trade, cooperation and responsibility. It may be argued that goals of citizenship education in relation to these themes may be most fruitfully pursued through activities and meaningful experiences. Providing a persistent virtual environment for actively exploring real-world citizenship can make the learning experience for this area of the curriculum much more enjoyable and rewarding.

Commercial digital role play games already have a strong emphasis on community, social hierarchies, political systems, civilization, rules and participation. Take a current example such as the very popular massively online RPG "Star Wars Galaxies" and we may argue that this game already explores issues of citizenship. In this game players choose a role for their avatar from a choice of professions such musician, engineer, politician, and soldier. Players may decide to build cities, form social hierarchies, create their own laws, establish industries, employ other characters and engage in many other activities that mirror real-world living – albeit in a fantasy realm. They may choose not to participate fully within the online community but more often than not, if they do not contribute positively to the collective then their experience is often much less rewarding and they will not become positively integrated into the virtual society. This is at the core of online gaming citizenship – does a participant contribute positively to the game and to their fellow participants?

5   Conclusion

Within this paper we discussed the application of ideas about the invisible playground to educational digital games. We have shown that this concept may be used to construct a distributed game framework over digital and non-digital modes that can be more effective and immersive than standard educational computer games – particularly with aspects of the curriculum that have been traditionally difficult to teach.

References

1. Druckman D. & Bjork R. A. "In the Mind's Eye: Enhancing Human Performance". 1991.
2. Gee J P. "What Video Games have to Teach us About Learning and Literacy", Palgrave Macmillan, 2003.
3. Kirriemuir J & McFarlane A. "Literature Review in Games and Learning", A Report for NESTA Futurelab, 2003. http://www.nestafuturelab.org/.
4. Salen K. & Zimmerman E., "Rules of play: Game Design Fundamentals", MIT Press 2004, p 92 & 578-579.
5. Sharples M, "The Design of Personal Mobile Technologies for Lifelong Learning", Computer & Education, Number 34, 2000, p 177-193.
6. Squire K, "Video Games in Education", International Journal of Intelligent Games & Simulation, pp 49-62. 2003.

EffecTV: A Real-Time Software Video Effect Processor for Entertainment

Kentaro Fukuchi[1], Sam Mertens[2], and Ed Tannenbaum[3]

[1]The University of Electro-Communications, 1-5-1 Chofugaoka, Chofu-shi Tokyo, Japan
fukuchi@megaUI.net
[2]Vecna Technologies, Inc., 5004 Lehigh Ave / College Park, MD 20740, USA
smartens@vecna.com
[3]Crockett, CA 94525, USA
et@et-arts.com

Abstract. EffecTV is a real-time software video effect processor based on motion detection and image processing techniques. EffecTV was released in 2001 as an open source software, and has been growing the number of features and effects through contributions from the open source community. EffecTV has been used for various purpose - desktop toy applications, by visual jockeys (VJs), in theatrical plays and other stage performances. In this paper, we describe the implementation of EffecTV and some case studies.

1 Introduction

EffecTV[1] is a real-time effect processor runs on a usual PC with a video capturing device. It has more than 40 amazing effects based on various image processing and motion recognition techniques and employs some estimation algorithms (also known as "DEMO" code) to achieve real-time processing.

EffecTV processes a video input from a video camera connected to the PC in real-time, and the users can experience themselves on a display with various visual effects. Most effects are designed to reflect motion in a captured image, therefore, the users move their bodies to get more exciting visuals.

By default, EffecTV accepts 320§240 pixels digitized video input in 30 frames per second (FPS), the same as standard (NTSC) video input, and outputs images in the same screen size and FPS with a low latency. The latency depends on the hardware and has not been measured precisely yet, but we estimate it at less than 1/15 second, because both digitizing process and visual effect process costs at most 1/30 second.

EffecTV detects the motion of the participants in front of the camera and it is used to process a visual effect. Normally, the participant interacts with EffecTV only via the camera to enjoy visuals. EffecTV requires an additional device, however, such as a keyboard or a joypad, to change the effect. In some cases, the effect can be changed periodically with a timer.

---

[1] The first version was released in 2001 with only 8 effects, and increased the number of effects under continuing open source development.

M. Rauterberg (Ed.): ICEC 2004, LNCS 3166, pp. 602–605, 2004.

2 Visual Effect

We introduce a few of the visual effects for EffecTV. These effects were very popular for various situations and have high interactivity.

Fig. 1. Screenshots of QuarkTV, RadioacTV and OpTV.

- QuarkTV

QuarkTV makes a dissolve effect: a moving object is broken up into dots. Fig. 1 shows only the moving hands were affected, while the other part of the body and the background were not.

- RadioacTV

RadioacTV creates a spreading light effect surrounds moving objects (fig. 1). To detect the motion in input images, the last frame is used as a background frame against the current input frame and the difference of luminosity between those two frames is recognized as the motion.

- NervousTV

NervousTV is similar to QuarkTV, but makes a comical motion effect. NervousTV has 32 frames ring buffer and stores the last 32 input frames. For every output frame, it selects a frame from the buffer randomly. As a result, a sequential action is broken up and instead resembles a very quick or "nervous" action.

- OpTV

OpTV is a combination of the real-time visual effect and an optical art (fig. 1). OpTV generates an animated black and white optical pattern (e.g. swirl, stripes, circles), and applies an exclusive OR operation to the image and a binarized input image.

3 Case Studies

Since 2001 we have had a number of installations and demonstrations. We found there were different problems and achievements for different situations. We categorized those situations to some cases described in this section.

3.1 Interactive Toy

In this case, a camera aims to participants and the participants see themselves with a visual effect on a screen. Because the effect reflected their motion, they were encouraged to move their bodies to get more exciting results. We installed this style of EffecTV configuration in various settings. Here we describe three typical locations.

3.1.1 Open-Air Musical Event

We had two installations at open-air musical events near Mt. Fuji in August and September 2003. We installed a video projector with a 4x4 meter screen, and an infrared camera to capture the image during the all-night dance event. An operator sat behind the screen and occasionally changed effects.

In this situation, the visitors tended to interact with their friends to show actions that had particular visual effect results to each other. Often they found new actions to achieve more funny results. For example, a visitor began juggling some balls in front of the screen, while other visitors performed a mock kung-fu fight like in some video games or TV animations.

3.1.2 Museum

We had a 4 days exhibition of EffecTV at Aoyama, Tokyo. EffecTV was installed in a small room and we used a video projector with a 2 meters height screen, showing a full-sized image of the visitors. The difference from the previous open-air situation is that the visitors were not as active in interacting with the installation. But, when an individual found a trick to achieve an interesting visual, he or she tended to show the trick to his or her friends.

This experience showed us that EffecTV serves not only as interaction between a human and computer, but also as interaction between humans. Sometimes the audience was not interested in EffecTV, but in their friends or a complete stranger to them; in those situations, the attention was on the impromptu performer, not on EffecTV. We believe this is one of the important characteristics of a good entertainment system.

3.2 Stage Performance

We installed screens on stages and video cameras aimed at performers on the stages. EffecTV was used to enhance the visual of performers and the operator controlled it along the progression on the stage. We describe 3 typical cases of this setting.

3.2.1 Visual Jockey

Visual Jockey (VJ) is a term used to represent a person who create live visuals based on a music, like a DJ (Disc Jockey) does to create live sound. Basically VJs perform pre-recorded visuals to display onstage. Recently some VJs have started to use real-time effect to enhance the visuals of musicians on the stages. Whether a musician was playing the guitar, drumming, or scratching the turntable, every motion was useful to create visuals synchronized to the music.

3.2.2 Dance Performance

We used EffecTV to enhance a dance performance on a stage in "Hatena 5th" party at Shinjuku Loft, March 12, 2004. A dancer in front of a screen performed on the music and EffecTV created visuals from the performance and was displayed on the screen. We mainly used OpTV for the visual.

We introduced a new visual effect called the "mirroring effect" which displays the mirror image of the dancer with the optical effect as seen in most fight of fig. 1, and it created the illusion that there was another dancer of the optical graphics on the screen, and both dancers interacted with each other.

3.2.3 Theatrical Play

EffecTV was used to add some special effects to a play on the stage in "Shitsuon (Room temperature)"(Kera, 2001) at Aoyama Round Theatre. The play was a kind of horror story, and the special effects were intended to frighten the audiences. Three screens were installed around a round stage and a video camera was set beside the stage. EffecTV used to add some visuals to the actors' motion.

Conventional visual effects for a play do not reflect the action of the actors, but put a pre-recorded video clip on the stage. The visual is synchronized to the action on the stage by the operator's control, and sometimes that synchronization is lost by an unexpected motion or poor timing. By contrast, our visual effects are created from the action of the actors directly; therefore there is no synchronization problem. Furthermore, there is no requirement to put any additional sensing devices such as an RF emitter on the actors to capture his position or pose.

4 Related Work

Ed Tannenbaum's "Recollections"[1] series traces the participant's silhouette and creates an animation based on the recorded motion of the silhouette. He noted "[this artwork] is completed by the viewer; it is a collaboration. Even the most inhibited people seem to rise to the occasion and create beautiful images." We observed that the same thing happened during installations of EfecTV. "plk53l"[2] is an open platform to provide interoperability between real-time video processing software. We plan to port EffecTV's effects to the platform.

Acknowledgement. We thank all EffecTV developers and users for their active contributions.

References

1. Recollections. http://et-arts.com/reco.htm.
2. plk53l http://www.piksel.no/

Web-Based Tool for Analyzing Emotions Through Images and Generating a Music Therapy System

Taesik Kim[1] and Hyeyoung Kim[2]

[1] Dept. of Computer Engineering, Keimyung University, Daegu, Korea
tskim@kmu.ac.kr
[2] Dept. of Nursing, Catholic Sangji College, Andong, Korea
hye3268@mail.csangji.ac.kr

Abstract. A web-based tool that can be used to generate music therapy system is proposed. The tool can generate a psychological testing system and users can select images that represent best their psychological state. After completing some stages, the user can listen the most adequate music for their current psychological situation. This tool makes it possible for a developer to input and arrange questions using images and stages. It is possible to offer various skills to a developer through this tool for developing desired types during all processes. This tool consists of five database tables that store information about hierarchical structure, image, music and has seven modules written with ASP. The tool has an especially considerable merit in cases of enlargement or functional substitution, because a developer who designs a system can change the imaging of questions and it is possible to register, modify and delete new image and music easily.

1 Introduction

In a day a person's feeling may change many times. Sometimes people get happy, sometimes very angry and sad. In the latter cases, music might help people to loose their stress [1],[2]. People must know what kind of music to listen to. Moreover not all people can control their emotions all the time. Therefore the therapy system generated by the tool proposed in this research may help people to decide what kind of music to listen and how to loose stress. The tool consists of a hierarchical structure, database tables that store information about images, music, and has seven software modules written with ASP. The tool has a considerable merit in case of enlargement because a developer who designs a test and therapy system can change imaging of questions and it is possible to register, modify and delete new images and music easily. Nowadays, a lot of people want to develop their web pages. However, it is not easy for everybody and sometimes it takes long time to make a simple web page. Furthermore, if the developer's profession is not web-programming, it's not easy for them to collect ideas and start new systems [3]. Considering all of these things, we need a system which can help people to make their web pages even if they don't have knowledge about designing a web page. Using the proposed tool, a developer chooses images, music, sounds and backgrounds, then the tool should make everything automatically. At anytime, a developer can change the structure of the therapy system.

M. Rauterberg (Ed.): ICEC 2004, LNCS 3166, pp. 606–609, 2004.

2   Structure of Tool

The architecture of the tool is divided into three parts. They are database, software tool for analyzing emotion and music therapy through images, and a web page for final usage. The database consists of five tables: a table of images for psycho analysis, a music decision table, a music files information table, a background image table, and a guide information table.

2.1 Program Module

1) imagemanage.asp
This module is for managing images (such as adding new images, showing sub-images, editing image information, and deleting images).
2) add.asp
This module saves image file names, guide content, background music, and background images to a database.
3) delete.asp
This module removes information about images from the database.
4) modify.asp
This module is used for editing information of added images.
5) create.htm
This module is used for installing links between images.
6) showchild.asp
This module shows hierarchical structure of the images.
7) addmusic.asp
This module manages information of finally played music after psycho analysis.

3   Making Music Therapy System Using the Tool

3.1 Structure of Music Therapy System

Psychology of people may be divided into angriness, sadness and happiness, and each class consists of three sub-classes [4],[5]. Furthermore, sub-classes can be divided into several secondary sub-classes. For example, the result of the happiness division may be being delighted, being safe, or being happy and from these sub classes come other actions like smiling, laughing, etc.

3.2 Database

Generally, data is divided into three parts: images for analyzing, the music for its user, and background images to be shown when music is played. According to the structure, we will need a total of 63 images for psycho-analyzing and 135 music files suitable for psychics of people.

1) Images used for analyzing

Images were drawn according to research on high school students' feelings and changes of their feeling during a day spent outside with family. Actually, images were drawn by students' themselves. They expressed their feeling with images, when they get angry, when they felt good and when they got upset.

2) Music therapy

Regarding the music, the emotion and atmosphere might be different. Actually it is very difficult to decide which music is good for a certain emotion. In this research, we applied the research result that shows the effectiveness of classical music on changing peoples' emotional states [1],[6]. Taking from the result, we collected different types of classical music

3) Background images

The background image is as much important as the music to be played. It must be the most suitable for emotions and feelings of people. Therefore, many types of background images were collected making detailed researches.

3.3 Execution of Music Therapy System

The user chooses one of the shown images, which he thinks that is suitable for their feelings. This is used for defining top class. [See the example shown below (Fig. 1).]

Fig. 1. Psychological Test   **Fig. 2.** Middle Class

After selecting one of three images to define the middle class, anoher three images will be shown and user must select one of them (Fig. 2). In this window, as we said above, the user will choose one image which is most suitable for his current situation. After selecting this, the process will go to final step (Fig. 3). After finishing third test, the window (Fig. 4) will appear with a list of music.

4   Conclusions

This research might be very useful for educational purposes. Testing the emotion of students through images is not a simple thing. If someone wants to develop such a music therapy system in a web environment, he should have knowledge about web system design. However, the proposed tool provides people with a very simple way. He can add a list of music, images, and design a hierarchical structure for psychological testing quite easily. Actually, this system may be used not only for psychological testing through images, but also for other purposes like testing the character of people and let them listen to music suitable for their character. We believe this tool will help teachers and professors, especially those working in the field of medical science, to get more information about current feelings of student.

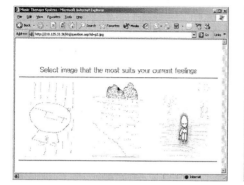

Fig. 3. Bottom Class

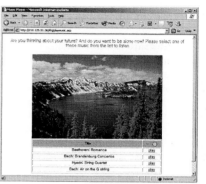

Fig. 4. Listening Music

References

1. Im Yeon,: Introduction to Music Therapy. Music&Life, Seoul (1999) 13-24
2. Student Life Center,: Analyzing Emotion. Daegu Education University Press, Daegu (2002)
3. Kim, Dong: Web based Creativity Developing System. Master Thesis, Seoul Education University (2001) 5-20
4. Im Ho.: Consideration of Analyzing Emotion for .Nasarat University Press(1999) 1-4
5. Park Young,: The World of Psychology Analysis. Music&Life, Seoul (1998) 31-35
6. Hankuk Art Therapy Association :Introduction to Art Therapy. Donga Munwhasa, Seoul (2001) 117-133

Turning Photo Annotating Tasks into Instant Messaging Fun: Prototyping, User Trials, and Roadmapping

Yuechen Qian and Loe M.G. Feijs

Eindhoven University of Technology, 5600 MB Eindhoven, Netherlands
{y.qian, l.m.g.feijs}@tue.nl

Abstract. In this article we report on our research that integrates photo annotation tasks into online chatting. Users of our system can share and annotate digital photos online while chatting. There are two major innovations: first, users can add annotations and comments to photos in a collaborative manner and secondly, the software itself extracts information from conversations to generate extra annotations. The boring and tedious task of annotating photos is turned into an essential part of an attractive fun activity, viz. online chatting. This article also provides a roadmap towards a systematic analysis of linguistic aspects of automated interpretation of message conversations.

1 Introduction

Many systems have been prototyped to facilitate the easy and attractive use of digital photos. Zoomable user interfaces are used in PhotoMesa Image Browser for users to search and browse photos [1]. Advanced systems support similarity-based image browsing [2], automatic image clustering [3], and photo concept browsing [4]. Unfortunately, the lack of meaningful metadata that describe the place, time, and event in which photos were taken remains one of the problems that hinder the easy use of photos. MSN Messenger and Yahoo Messenger provide various technical solutions for social communication. Picasa's Hello system even allows online users to browse photos simultaneously while chatting. The information passing by instant messaging systems can be used in the quest for meaningful metadata of digital photos. We have developed an innovative chatting system that not only allows online users to share and annotate photos together, but also can automatically extract meaningful data from messages. We developed a roadmap towards automated interpretation of messages.

2 Talkim: Sharing and Annotating Photos Online

As shown in Fig. 1, the user interface of our system consists of the message area on the left, the photo sharing area in the middle, and the photo search area on the right. Participants of a chatting session have the same view on the message and photo

M. Rauterberg (Ed.): ICEC 2004, LNCS 3166, pp. 610–613, 2004.
© IFIP International Federation for Information Processing 2004

sharing areas. When a user drag-n-drops an image onto his photo sharing area, the others will see the same image in their photo sharing areas, as in Picasa's Hello system.

Fig. 1. A snapshot of Talkim's user interface.

Different from the Hello system, Talkim's photo sharing area also functions as a whiteboard. Users can simultaneously put text annotations to anywhere in the photo sharing area and move them freely. This direct annotation function [5] is essential here: it helps to raise attention and create a focus of discussion. A user would otherwise have to type lengthy sentences to explain interesting elements in a photo. In our system users can easily pinpoint interesting elements such as a building, a person, or a pet in photos. To the best of our knowledge, it is for the first time that the photo annotating task is achieved by using the online whiteboard concept.

Talkim also extract annotations from messages. Four annotation types were worked out in our system. They are *location of taking*, *time/date of taking*, *event of taken*, and *persons in photo*. First, Talkim parses messages that are complete fact sentences. For example, "This photo was taken in Finland". Once recognized, such a message is directly added to the photo sharing area as an annotation. Secondly, Talkim recognizes messages that are complete questions, such as "where was it taken?" Such messages provide contexts for processing subsequent messages. Thirdly, Talkim handles ellipsis sentences such as "in a restaurant". A message "in a restaurant", as a reply to a message "where was it taken", can be treated as a location-related annotation. We defined several schemas to recognize and categorize different types of messages.

3   User Trials

We conducted several user trials on our system. Four pairs of people were invited. Persons in a pair know each other well. Each pair used our system for 30 minutes. We recorded all messages that were sent by users. We identified occurrences of question-and-answer dialogues. As shown in Fig. 2, our system managed to identify "at home" as an annotation of the type *location of taking*.

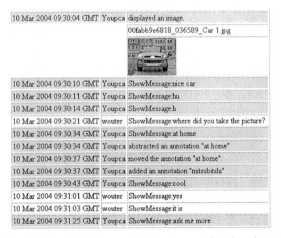

Fig. 2. Part of the log file that recorded the conversation done by two users.

Participants all liked the integration of photo sharing and chatting. One pair continued to use our system for a while after their session was finished. All participants liked the functionality that they can put annotations onto the photos and move annotations around. Our analysis shows that large amount of metadata were added to photos. Two participants found even played a "grabbing" game: one moves an annotation while the other tries to grab it and move it to another place. They thought it was fun and they played this game many times throughout the user trial. They often used the on-screen annotating functionality to chat, not only for annotating photos.

4   Roadmap

Linguistic analysis is crucial to improve the automated analysis and understanding of message conversation. Meaning can be derived by following the syntactic structure of the text [6]. We distinguish three levels: words, sentences and dialogues.

At the level of words, words have to be assigned a grammatical category and if possible aspects of their meaning have to be retrieved. Errors deserve special attention. If the conversation language is known, a minimization of the Levenshtein edit distance to the closest dictionary word should suffice for the errors like "picuter". For long un-recognizable words, such as "girlfriendshouse", we propose a separate dictionary-based splitter. In categorization, two important categories are pronouns and prepositions. Personal pronouns are easy to recognize. They indicate persons and will be a rich source of annotations. The "wh" pronouns indicate questions and they can be used to determine the annotation type of the subsequent answer. Prepositions can help to determine the annotation type ("in" is either place or time). Dis-ambiguation is doable by name if the following word indicates a place, time, or event.

At the level of sentences, sentences have to be assigned a sentence type, the phrase structure has to be parsed, and if possible aspects of their meaning have to be retrieved. Though messages are short and simple, semantic analysis still is challenging because of frequent ellipsis and linguistic pointers. For syntax we propose to use a straightforward phrase structure grammar. Any bottom-up parsing technique or backtracking top-down technique will suffice. Prepositional phrases are particularly important because they contain many clues. For semantic analysis it is necessary to develop underlying models, e.g. for personal preferences and for relations between people.

At this level of dialogues, dialogues are used to determine whether recognized sentences should be treated as annotations or not. Such dialogic analysis is necessary to categorize ellipsis and ambiguous sentences. Asynchrony is yet another challenge in dialogic analysis. When chatting online, participants can talk about things in an interleaving manner, having parallel threads of topics. This makes it difficult to extract annotations. We expected that formal dialogue theory will help to solve these issues.

5 Concluding Remarks

Whereas taking photos, editing them and sharing them with others is considered a creative and highly rewarding process by many people, the difficulty of classifying and grouping them has always been difficult and tedious. Most of the propositions that promise to automate these tasks rely on the assumption that photos are annotated, which in fact they are not, thus shifting the problem from one tedious task to another even more tedious task. Precisely the latter task is turned into fun by the type of application investigated here. The result of the user trials of our system shows the enthusiasm that the participants had on our system. The integration of photo browsing and chatting facilitates online photo sharing and discussing activities. Putting this annotating task in a social context makes the photo annotating task fun and appealing. Allowing users to freely annotate photos on the photo itself produce a large amount of annotations without many computational difficulties. Such information can be directly used in photo search even without further processing. Finally, the roadmap represented here shows the way ahead to improve automated annotation extraction.

References

1. Bederson, B.B.: PhotoMesa: a zoomable image browser using quantum treemaps and bubblemaps. In Proceedings of ACM UIST 2001. 71-80
2. Rodden, K., Basalaj, W., Sinclair, D., Wood, K.: Does organisation by similarity assist image browsing? In Proc. SIGCHI CHI 2001. 190-197
3. Platt, J.C., Czerwinski, M., Field, B.A.: PhotoTOC: Automatic clustering for browsing personal photographs. MSR-TR-2002-17, Microsoft Research, 2002.
4. Qian, Y., Feijs, L.M.G: Stepwise Concept Navigation. In de Moor, A., Ganter, B. (Eds.): Using Conceptual Structures of ICCS 2003. Germany. 2003. 255-268
5. Shneiderman, B., Kang. H.: Direct Annotation: A Drag-and-Drop Strategy for Labeling Photos. Proc. International Conf. on Information Visualisation, 2000.
6. Rosetta, M.T.: Compositional Translation. Kluwer International Series in Engineering and computer science: Volume 273. (1994).

Author Index

Lecture Notes in Computer Science

For information about Vols. 1–3063

please contact your bookseller or Springer